edexcel

EDEXCEL

# GCSE SCIENCE

## Additional Science Teacher Book



Series Editor: Mark Levesley
Aaron Bridges
Ann Fullick
Richard Grime
Miles Hudson
Penny Johnson
Sue Kearsey
Jim Newall
Sue Robilliard
Maggie Rumble
Nigel Saunders
James de Winter

A PEARSON COMPANY

Published by Pearson Education Limited, a company incorporated in England and Wales, having its registered office at Edinburgh Gate, Harlow, Essex, CM20 2JE.
Registered company number: 872828



First published 2011
10 9 8 7 6 5 4 3 2 1

**British Library Cataloguing in Publication Data**
A catalogue record for this book is available from the British Library
ISBN 978 184690 901 6



Typeset by Juice Creative Ltd
Printed in the UK by Scotprint

**Acknowledgements**
The publisher would like to thank all the teachers and students who helped in the development and trialling of this course, including: Alex Dawes; Ben Lovick; David Liebeschuetz; Garry Robinson; Gaynor Kendall; Peter Bowen-Walker; Steven Rowe; Sandra Fox; Stephen Winrow-Campbell.

Every effort has been made to contact copyright holders of material reproduced in this book. Any omissions will be rectified in subsequent printings if notice is given to the publishers.

# Contents

# How to use this book

Our handy teacher books contain all the lesson activities from the Teacher and Technician Planning Packs in an easy-to-use, easy-to-transport format. The slim, full-colour volumes can be slipped into a bag or briefcase to be taken home for marking or short-term planning.

Literacy activities support students who find literacy a barrier to understanding science.

Consolidated lesson plans to assist in the quick planning of lessons.

Quick identification of specification points covered in the lesson.

How Science Works points from the specification indicated.

Definition of the key terms can be found in the glossary in the Student Book and on the ActiveTeach.

Worksheet thumbnails for easy recognition.

Stretch and Support activities are clearly indicated.

H icon identifies specification points and content aimed at Higher Tier students.

B2: Topic 1 The building blocks of cells

## B2.8 Clones

16

This lesson extends the work on asexual reproduction to describe clones and explore some of the problems and advantages of cloning. The process of cell nuclear transfer for cloning of mammals is described in more detail for more able students.

### Specification coverage

**1.17** Recall that cloning is an example of asexual reproduction that produces genetically identical copies

**1.18** H Demonstrate an understanding of the stages in the production of cloned mammals, including: a) removal of diploid nucleus from a body cell b) enucleation of egg cell c) insertion of diploid nucleus into enucleated egg cell d) stimulation of the diploid nucleus to divide by mitosis e) implantation into surrogate mammals

**1.19** Demonstrate an understanding of the advantages, disadvantages and risks of cloning mammals

HSW *12* The use of contemporary science and technological developments and their benefits, drawbacks and risks

There are also opportunities to cover HSW *3* and HSW *13*.

### Key terms

clone
H enucleate
implant
surrogate mother
uterus

**Reproduction confidence**
**Starter 1** A/L
As students come into class, give each one a sticky note. Ask them to write down three things they learned about asexual and sexual reproduction from the last lesson, give a confidence rating to their understanding of each of their statements. Pick five statements that have low confidence ratings and throw a related question to the whole class. These points can be picked up on in this lesson.

**What is a clone?**
**Starter 2** Lit
Write the word 'clone' in the middle of the board, and ask students to suggest related words and how they should be linked to make a concept map. It is possible at this point that they can only offer information they have learnt from films and the media, but this can be revisited in *Plenary 2* at the end of the lesson to explore misconceptions from these sources.

**The pros and cons of cloning**
**Exploring 1**
**Worksheet B2.8a** provides a set of statements that present some of the advantages and disadvantages of cloning animals.

Stretch Students further research the advantages and disadvantages of cloning, including finding examples other than Dolly, to evaluate whether the problems encountered in Dolly's case are universal or just chance.
Support Students sort the statements and canvass other students as to whether they are for or against animal cloning.

**Growing plant clones**
**Exploring 2** Prac
**Worksheet B2.8b** is a practical on taking plant cuttings that introduces the idea of clones. Full details can be found on the Teacher and technician practical sheet B2.8.

Stretch Ask students to explain fully how this investigation clarifies which characteristics are genetically determined and which are partly or wholly controlled by the environment.
Support Ask students to describe the method for producing plant clones as a series of bullet points.

**Student Book spread B2.8 (AT)**
**Explaining 1**
Students suggest which characteristics the puppies may have that are identical to the parent and which characteristics may vary.
Stretch Ask students to consider what a cloned human might feel, and to write a diary entry for a cloned human who has just found out how he/she was made.
Support Give students the questions in the **AT** document *Cloning questions* to complete to help them see various sides of the cloning argument.

**H Sequencing the cloning method (AT)**
**Explaining 2**
A series of statements are provided on the **AT** document *Cloning*. Present these on the board and ask students to sequence them in the correct order to describe the process of cloning by the method used to produce Copycat and Dolly.
Stretch Ask students to write two paragraphs about the difference between 'natural breeding' and cloning. They should include the terms 'haploid', 'diploid' and 'fertilisation'.

**Cloning brainstorm**
**Plenary 1** A/L
Ask pupils to jot down as many facts about cloning as they can and then organise their ideas in a more systematic way (e.g. benefits, drawbacks and risks). A spokesperson for each group should then share with the class how their group has organised the information and what information they know.

**What is a clone? – revisited**
**Plenary 2** A/L Lit
Revisit the concept map produced in *Starter 1* and ask students to amend anything that they got wrong then, and to add anything new that they have learnt in this lesson. If appropriate to your students, consider comparing the media view of cloning with the scientific view to identify differences and suggest reasons why these differences may occur.

**Questions of cloning (AT)**
**Homework 1**
**Worksheet B2.8c** presents a series of questions that test learning of the Foundation tier material in this lesson.

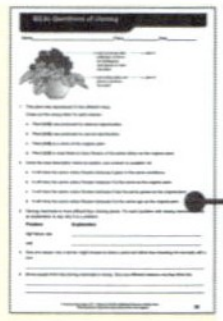

Support Provide the **AT** document *Some cloning answers*. Students should select from these to help them answer questions **3–5**.

**Cloning Snuppy**
**Homework 2**
Worksheet B2.8d provides a series of questions to test learning on all aspects of this lesson, including Higher Tier questions.

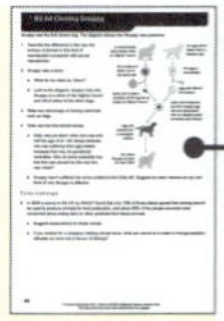

Stretch Ask students to do the 'extra challenge' question.

Student Book pages for easy reference.

Answers to Student Book questions for easy marking.

ActiveTeach resources highlighted to help with planning. There are also extra ActiveTeach assets for each lesson, these include the Key Points and summary exercises.

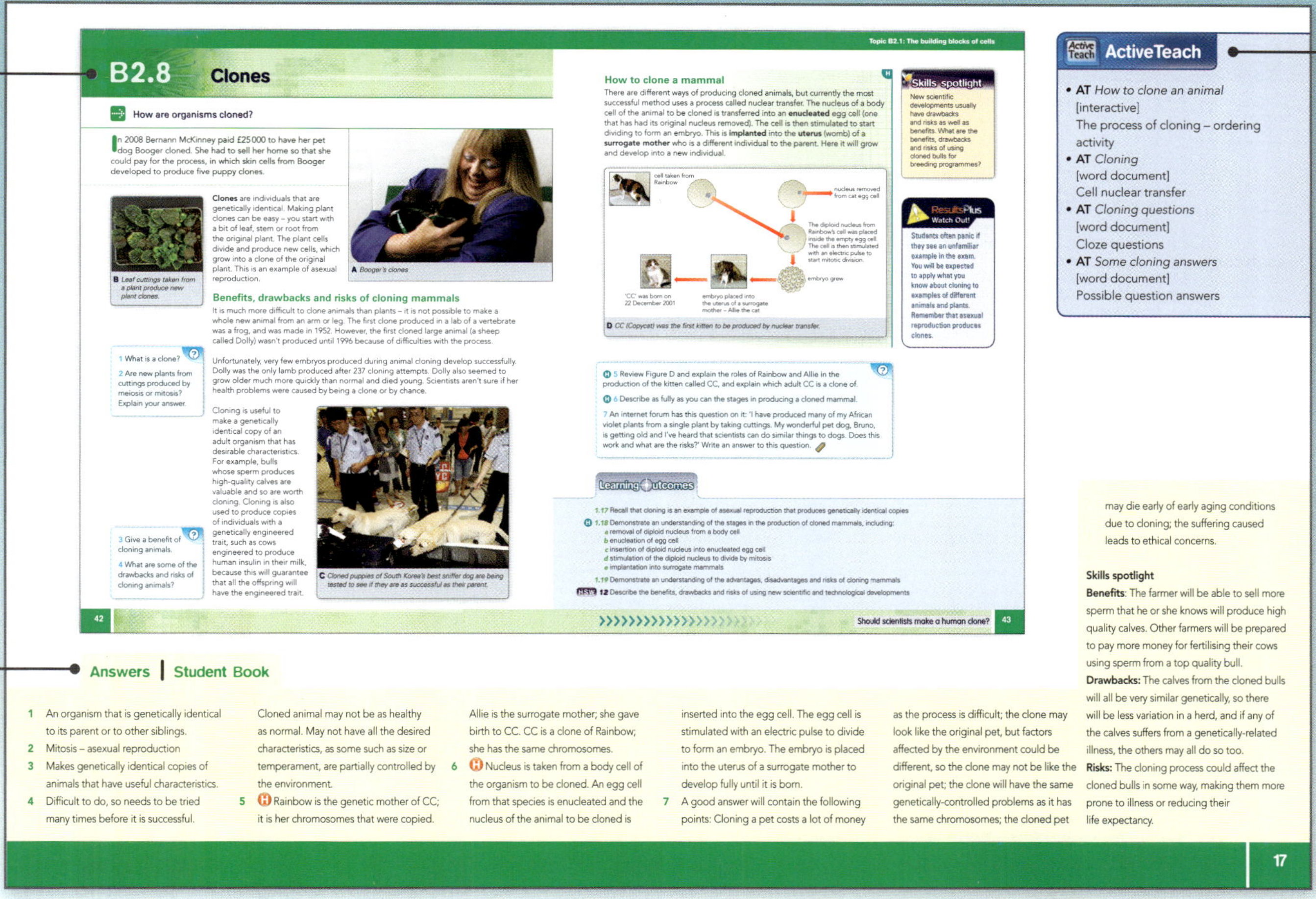

Topic B2.1: The building blocks of cells

# B2.8 Clones

How are organisms cloned?

In 2008 Bernann McKinney paid £25 000 to have her pet dog Booger cloned. She had to sell her home so that she could pay for the process, in which skin cells from Booger developed to produce five puppy clones.

A Booger's clones

**Clones** are individuals that are genetically identical. Making plant clones can be easy – you start with a bit of leaf, stem or root from the original plant. The plant cells divide and produce new cells, which grow into a clone of the original plant. This is an example of asexual reproduction.

B Leaf cuttings taken from a plant produce new plant clones.

## Benefits, drawbacks and risks of cloning mammals

It is much more difficult to clone animals than plants – it is not possible to make a whole new animal from an arm or leg. The first clone produced in a lab of a vertebrate was a frog, and was made in 1952. However, the first cloned large animal (a sheep called Dolly) wasn't produced until 1996 because of difficulties with the process.

Unfortunately, very few embryos produced during animal cloning develop successfully. Dolly was the only lamb produced after 237 cloning attempts. Dolly also seemed to grow older much more quickly than normal and died young. Scientists aren't sure if her health problems were caused by being a clone or by chance.

1 What is a clone?

2 Are new plants from cuttings produced by meiosis or mitosis? Explain your answer.

Cloning is useful to make a genetically identical copy of an adult organism that has desirable characteristics. For example, bulls whose sperm produces high-quality calves are valuable and so are worth cloning. Cloning is also used to produce copies of individuals with a genetically engineered trait, such as cows engineered to produce human insulin in their milk, because this will guarantee that all the offspring will have the engineered trait.

C Cloned puppies of South Korea's best sniffer dog are being tested to see if they are as successful as their parent.

3 Give a benefit of cloning animals.

4 What are some of the drawbacks and risks of cloning animals?

## How to clone a mammal

There are different ways of producing cloned animals, but currently the most successful method uses a process called nuclear transfer. The nucleus of a body cell of the animal to be cloned is transferred into an **enucleated** egg cell (one that has had its original nucleus removed). The cell is then stimulated to start dividing to form an embryo. This is **implanted** into the **uterus** (womb) of a **surrogate mother** who is a different individual to the parent. Here it will grow and develop into a new individual.

cell taken from Rainbow

nucleus removed from cat egg cell

The diploid nucleus from Rainbow's cell was placed inside the empty egg cell. The cell is then stimulated with an electric pulse to start mitotic division.

embryo grew

embryo placed into the uterus of a surrogate mother – Allie the cat

'CC' was born on 22 December 2001

D CC (Copycat) was the first kitten to be produced by nuclear transfer.

**Skills spotlight**

New scientific developments usually have drawbacks and risks as well as benefits. What are the benefits, drawbacks and risks of using cloned bulls for breeding programmes?

**ResultsPlus Watch Out!**

Students often panic if they see an unfamiliar example in the exam. You will be expected to apply what you know about cloning to examples of different animals and plants. Remember that asexual reproduction produces clones.

H 5 Review Figure D and explain the roles of Rainbow and Allie in the production of the kitten called CC, and explain which adult CC is a clone of.

H 6 Describe as fully as you can the stages in producing a cloned mammal.

7 An internet forum has this question on it: 'I have produced many of my African violet plants from a single plant by taking cuttings. My wonderful pet dog, Bruno, is getting old and I've heard that scientists can do similar things to dogs. Does this work and what are the risks?' Write an answer to this question.

**Learning Outcomes**

1.17 Recall that cloning is an example of asexual reproduction that produces genetically identical copies

H 1.18 Demonstrate an understanding of the stages in the production of cloned mammals, including:
a removal of diploid nucleus from a body cell
b enucleation of egg cell
c insertion of diploid nucleus into enucleated egg cell
d stimulation of the diploid nucleus to divide by mitosis
e implantation into surrogate mammals

1.19 Demonstrate an understanding of the advantages, disadvantages and risks of cloning mammals

HSW 12 Describe the benefits, drawbacks and risks of using new scientific and technological developments

42 | Should scientists make a human clone? | 43

**ActiveTeach**

- **AT** *How to clone an animal* [interactive]
  The process of cloning – ordering activity
- **AT** *Cloning* [word document]
  Cell nuclear transfer
- **AT** *Cloning questions* [word document]
  Cloze questions
- **AT** *Some cloning answers* [word document]
  Possible question answers

## Answers | Student Book

1 An organism that is genetically identical to its parent or to other siblings.
2 Mitosis – asexual reproduction
3 Makes genetically identical copies of animals that have useful characteristics.
4 Difficult to do, so needs to be tried many times before it is successful. Cloned animal may not be as healthy as normal. May not have all the desired characteristics, as some such as size or temperament, are partially controlled by the environment.
5 H Rainbow is the genetic mother of CC; it is her chromosomes that were copied. Allie is the surrogate mother; she gave birth to CC. CC is a clone of Rainbow; she has the same chromosomes.
6 H Nucleus is taken from a body cell of the organism to be cloned. An egg cell from that species is enucleated and the nucleus of the animal to be cloned is inserted into the egg cell. The egg cell is stimulated with an electric pulse to divide to form an embryo. The embryo is placed into the uterus of a surrogate mother to develop fully until it is born.
7 A good answer will contain the following points: Cloning a pet costs a lot of money as the process is difficult; the clone may look like the original pet, but factors affected by the environment could be different, so the clone may not be like the original pet; the clone will have the same genetically-controlled problems as it has the same chromosomes; the cloned pet may die early of early aging conditions due to cloning; the suffering caused leads to ethical concerns.

Skills spotlight

**Benefits:** The farmer will be able to sell more sperm that he or she knows will produce high quality calves. Other farmers will be prepared to pay more money for fertilising their cows using sperm from a top quality bull.
**Drawbacks:** The calves from the cloned bulls will all be very similar genetically, so there will be less variation in a herd, and if any of the calves suffers from a genetically-related illness, the others may all do so too.
**Risks:** The cloning process could affect the cloned bulls in some way, making them more prone to illness or reducing their life expectancy.

17

Quick identification of specification points covered in the Practice Controlled Assessment.

Consolidated lesson plan to assist in the quick planning of a straight-forward class practical.

Practice Controlled Assessment

C2: Topic 2 Ionic compounds and analysis

# C2.9 Precipitation

86

This lesson challenges students to investigate the effect of changing the volume of one reactant in a precipitation reaction. The activity may be run as a practice controlled assessment task or as a straight-forward class practical. The preparation of one sample of magnesium carbonate should take about 30 minutes but this does not include drying time.

## Specification coverage

***2.11*** Demonstrate an understanding of the method needed to prepare a pure, dry sample of an insoluble salt

***2.12*** Prepare an insoluble salt by precipitation

***0.2*** Represent chemical reactions by word equations and simple balanced equations

***0.3*** Write balanced chemical equations including the use of state symbols (s), (l), (g) and (aq)

This lesson provides opportunities to cover HSW *1*, HSW *5*, HSW *6*, HSW *7*, HSW *8*, HSW *10* and HSW *11*.

### Before the lesson

If you intend to use this activity as a practice controlled assessment task, you should ensure that students are familiar with any equipment they may be expected to use so that they can plan their own investigation. In the week or two before the task show them this equipment and, if appropriate, allow them to practice using it. Students should be familiar with the use of a balance to measure and record masses. They should also be familiar with the use of measuring cylinders, filter paper and filter funnels. It may be good preparation to show students one or more of Skills sheets 19 to 26 to show what is expected of them in their actual controlled assessment task.

### Starter

Show the names of some ionic compounds. Students work in pairs to decide which compounds are soluble in water, and which are insoluble. Suitable soluble compounds are sodium chloride, sodium carbonate, ammonium carbonate, magnesium sulfate, magnesium nitrate, silver nitrate. Suitable insoluble compounds are magnesium carbonate, silver chloride, calcium sulfate, magnesium hydroxide. Lead on to the idea that certain combinations of soluble compounds will produce a precipitate, and that this is a useful way to make insoluble compounds.
Follow this by reading the additional information below the opening section of page 134 of the Student Book. They may then read the brief description of the activity provided by the 'Your task' box.

### Option 1: Straight-forward class practical

Students follow the instructions on **Worksheet C2.9b**. The worksheet lists the apparatus needed and gives instructions for investigating what happens to the yield of magnesium carbonate when the mass of magnesium sulfate is changed. Students must record their observations, and use mass measurements to determine the mass of magnesium carbonate in their sample. The range of data that students need to collect is given on **Worksheet C2.9c**.

You could ask students to come up with one or two further hypotheses, based on their observations in this practical.

### Plenary

On page 135 of the Student Book you will find two examples of the sort of work that students may produce for this task. The examples focus on the overall plan. You could share these with students after they have completed their own work. This will help them to understand the assessment criteria and so make it easier for them to evaluate their work and to see how they can improve it. Moderator comments on each of the Student Book extracts can be found at the end of the assessment guidance for this investigation on the CD-ROM. The examples can also be found on the **AT** document *Student examples*.

### Option 2: Running the activity as a practice controlled assessment task (PCA)

We have provided a full range of support resources to allow the running of this practical as a practice controlled assessment task. A recommended structure is outlined below (to be used over a number of sessions). Marking guidance for all three parts of the practice task can be found on the CD-ROM that accompanies the TTPP. To save time when using these practice controlled assessment tasks, you may wish to focus on a particular aspect or skill rather than working through all three parts of the task.

#### Part A Planning

1. Students should be given the Student brief on **Worksheet C2.9a**. They can use Part A of the Workbook that is provided to help pupils with their practice controlled assessments. They should be given about 1 hour to do this planning.

#### Part B Observations

2. Students should be asked to carry out the practical task to collect evidence using the method they have planned in Part A. They should refer to the Student brief on **Worksheet C2.9a**. They can use Part B of the Workbook that is provided to help pupils with their practice controlled assessments. They should be given about 30 minutes to collect their primary evidence.
3. If there is a problem with their own planned method, students may be asked to follow the method set out on **Worksheet C2.9b**. This will still enable students to access the full range of marks for Part B and Part C of the practice controlled assessment task.
4. In Part B, students are required to gather some secondary evidence. The evidence can be quantitative or qualitative. It can be from a variety of sources but students must note where they found their evidence and evaluate the quality of the source as part of this task. Skills sheet 22 provides students with further guidance on researching for and evaluating secondary evidence. This part of the task could be done outside of the lesson but must be supervised.

#### Part C Conclusions

5. Students follow the instructions set out on the Part C section of the Student brief on **Worksheet C2.9a**. They should use their data from Part B and the secondary evidence they have collected when doing this. They can use Part C of the Workbook that is provided to help pupils with their practice controlled assessments. They should be given about 1 hour to work on their conclusions.

The **AT** includes video clips showing a group of students working through elements of this investigation with teacher support.

Two ways of running the lesson clearly marked, either as an ordinary class practical or as a Practice Controlled Assessment lesson.

Clear structure for running a Practice Controlled Assessment divided into the different areas that students will be marked on.

Student Book pages for easy reference.

Focus on specific assessment criteria for the relevant Practice Controlled Assessment skill.

ActiveTeach resources highlighted to help with supporting students through the Practice Controlled Assessment.

Practice Controlled Assessment

## C2.9 Precipitation

How can we make magnesium carbonate using a precipitation reaction?

Rock climbing can be scary, putting you under stress and making you sweat. You do not want sweaty, slippery hands when you are climbing a rock face several hundred metres above the ground. Rock climbers rub 'chalk' into their hands to keep them dry. This is not the sedimentary rock made from calcium carbonate. Instead, it is magnesium carbonate, $MgCO_3$, which is able to absorb water really well. Without it, rock climbing would be even scarier.

**A** *This climber is on a sheer rock face. Magnesium carbonate is 'hygroscopic', which means that it absorbs moisture. This property helps to keep the climber's hands dry, providing more friction between them and the rock.*

Some salts are soluble in water but others are not. For example, all sodium salts are soluble and most sulfates are soluble. Some combinations of soluble salts will react together to form an insoluble salt, the precipitate. For example, silver nitrate and sodium chloride are soluble. Their solutions react together, when mixed, to form a precipitate of silver chloride:

silver nitrate + sodium chloride → silver chloride + sodium nitrate

$AgNO_3(aq) + NaCl(aq) \rightarrow AgCl(s) + NaNO_3(aq)$

Notice how the ions involved appear to have 'swapped places' in this precipitation reaction. Silver ions from the silver nitrate solution combine with chloride ions from the sodium chloride solution to form insoluble silver chloride. This precipitate can then be separated from the unreacted ions in solution by **filtration**, washed on the filter paper, then dried in a warm oven.

**Your task**

You are going to plan an investigation to test how the amount of magnesium carbonate formed in a precipitation reaction changes when one of the substrates is varied. Your teacher will provide you with some materials to help you organise this task.

**Learning Outcomes**

2.11 *Demonstrate an understanding of the method needed to prepare a pure, dry sample of an insoluble salt*

2.12 *Prepare an insoluble salt by precipitation*

134

### ResultsPlus Build Better Answers

When planning an investigation like this, you will be assessed on your *overall plan*. There are 4 marks available for this skill. Here are two extracts that focus on this skill. Other skills that you need for the assessment are dealt with in other lessons.

**Student extract 1** A basic response for this skill

*I am going to add 25 cm³ of sodium carbonate solution to a beaker and then add 10 cm³ of magnesium sulfate solution. This will form magnesium carbonate, which is insoluble. I will record the mass of a piece of filter paper and then use the filter paper to filter the magnesium carbonate out of the solution. I will wash the paper and residue with water and then dry it in a warm oven. I will then measure the mass of the filter paper and the dry magnesium carbonate. I will then do this experiment again with different volumes of magnesium nitrate solution.*

This is a good start because the student has given clear instructions on how they are planning to carry out the practical.

However, they will not be able to access all the marks because they do not explain the range of other volumes they are planning to test.

**Student extract 2** A good response for this skill

*... I will try it again with 10 cm³, 15 cm³, 20 cm³ and 25 cm³ of the magnesium sulfate solution. I have chosen this range because it will allow me to work out if less or the same amount of each solution is needed to get the maximum amount of precipitate. I think that by carrying out this investigation I will be able to test my hypothesis that the amount of magnesium carbonate formed depends on the volume of magnesium sulfate used.*

Here, the student continues from the end of the extract above.

The method explains how the hypothesis will be tested.

The student has stated the range of tests they are going to carry out.

The student has also explained why this range has been chosen.

**ResultsPlus**

**To access 2 marks**
- Provide a logically ordered method that will produce results
- Choose a range of data or observations that will test the hypothesis

**To access 4 marks**

You also need to:
- Explain how your method will test the hypothesis
- Explain why you have chosen your range of data or observations

How did people make copies of engineering drawings before the photocopier was invented? 135

### ActiveTeach

- **AT** *C2.9 Precipitation [interactive]* *Investigating precipitation*
- **AT** *C2.9 Assessment criteria* [presentation] Understanding the CA marking criteria
- **AT** *C2.9 Specification points* [word document] Edexcel specification points
- **AT** *C2.9 Student examples* [word document] Examples for students to assess

### Key terms

filtration

### Assessment criteria

**Overall plan**

0 No relevant method given.

1-2 **a)** Produces a method that is ordered in a logical way and would produce results that can later be analysed. The method covers all the main points needed, such as: measure 25 cm³ of sodium carbonate and 10 cm³ of magnesium sulfate plus 15 cm³ of water; mix these together and stir; filter to separate the precipitate; wash the precipitate on the filter paper; dry the precipitate in a warm oven; determine the mass of magnesium carbonate obtained. Repeat with other volumes of magnesium sulfate.

**b)** Range of data/observations chosen that would test the hypothesis, e.g. gives three or four different volumes of magnesium sulfate.

3-4 **a)** The method also includes an explanation as to why it would test the hypothesis, e.g. 'I think that by carrying out this investigation I will be able to test my hypothesis that the mass of magnesium carbonate formed is dependent on the volume of magnesium sulfate solution used.'

**b)** Range of data/observations chosen that would test the hypothesis and an explanation of why the range was chosen, e.g. 'I will then do this experiment again with 10 cm³, 15 cm³, 20 cm³ and 25 cm³ of the magnesium sulfate solution. I have chosen this range because using this range of volumes will allow me to work out if less or the same amount of each solution is needed to get the maximum mass of precipitate.'

87

# B2.1 Plant and animal cells



This lesson looks at the main structures in cells and explains to students how an understanding of cells was made possible by the development of the light microscope.

## Specification coverage

***1.2*** Describe the function of the components of a plant cell including chloroplast, large vacuole, cell wall, cell membrane, mitochondria, cytoplasm and nucleus

***1.3*** Describe the function of the components of an animal cell including cell membrane, mitochondria, cytoplasm and nucleus

***1.4*** Describe how plant and animal cells can be studied in greater detail with a light microscope

HSW ***2*** The interpretation of data, using creative thought, to provide evidence for testing ideas and developing theories

There are also opportunities to cover HSW ***7***, HSW ***11*** and HSW ***14***.

## Key terms

cell
cell membrane
cell wall
cellulose
chlorophyll
chloroplast
cytoplasm
DNA
light microscope
mitochondria
nucleus
organelle
vacuole

### Cells

**Starter 1** Lit

Ask students to write a simple definition of a cell. Ask for a volunteer to read out their definition and see if others agree with it or can add to it. Work towards a common definition and write it on the board.

### Looking at animal cells (AT)

**Exploring 1** Prac

Students use **Worksheet B2.1a**. Full details are given on the Teacher and technician practical sheet B2.1 (1). The **AT** document *Making a slide 1* may help.

Stretch Students measure the diameter of the field of view and estimate sizes of structures they can see.

Support Have a micrograph of human cheek cells projected on the board to help students identify the cells under the microscope and label them appropriately.

### Ideas about the cell

**Exploring 3**

Ask students to read the introductory paragraph on page 28 of the Student Book, if they have not already done so. Have a micrograph of cells under relatively low magnification projected behind you. Ask students to work through **Worksheet B2.1c**, considering how ideas about the cell nucleus developed.

Stretch Students answer question **3**.

Support Supply a grid with about half the table completed, so students have to fill in a few gaps only.

### What have you learnt?

**Plenary 1** Lit

Read out, or display, a number of sentences about this lesson and ask the students if they are true or false – if false, ask students to correct the statement. For example: The nucleus controls all the activities of the cell (T). Chloroplasts contain the green pigment chlorophyll needed for photosynthesis (T). All plant cells contain chloroplasts (F). Animal cells are smaller than plant cells (T). All cells have a cell membrane (T). Only animal cells have a cellulose cell wall (F).

### Cell structures

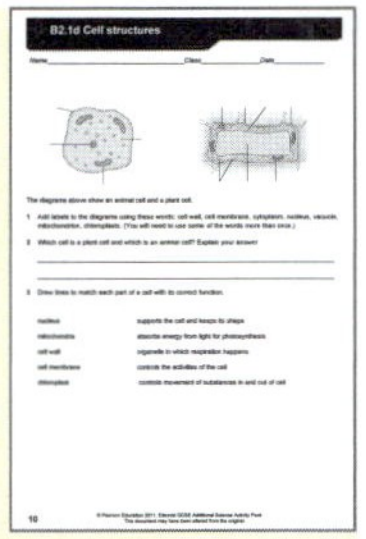

**Homework 1**

**Worksheet B2.1d** is designed for students needing support and contains simple questions.

Support For question **1** the words could be supplied for cutting and pasting on to the diagrams.

### Microscopes

**Starter 2**

Have a microscope in front of you. Ask students what a microscope is, how they work and why they are important. Explain that the study of cells would not be possible without the invention of the microscope and ask students to suggest why.

### Looking at plant cells

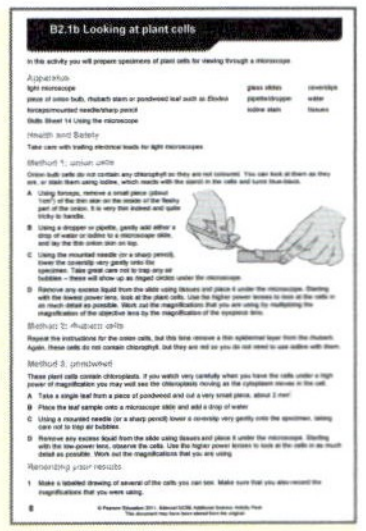

**Exploring 2** Prac

Students follow the instructions in **Worksheet B2.1b**. Full details are given on the Teacher and technician practical sheet B2.1 (2).

Stretch Students measure the diameter of the field of view and estimate sizes of structures they can see.

Support Have a micrograph of onion cells/rhubarb cells/*Elodea* cells (whichever you are using) projected on the board to help students identify the cells they are seeing under the microscope and label them appropriately.

### Student Book spread B2.1

**Explaining 1**

Introduce the structures found in all cells and then the additional structures found in plant cells. Ask students to list the differences and then ask them to read though the Student Book text.

Stretch Students complete the work, label the diagrams and answer questions to a high standard, including question **6**.

Support Students complete the work and label the diagrams. They attempt the questions but not question **6**.

### Concept map

**Plenary 2** AfL

Ask students to make a table or concept map summarising the structures they would expect to see in an animal cell and in a plant cell, and their function. Make sure they are clear that structures such as the nucleus, cell membrane, cytoplasm and mitochondria are common to all cells.

### Cell structures

**Homework 2**

**Worksheet B2.1e** is designed for more able students.

Stretch

Ask students to do the 'extra challenge' question on the sheet.

# B2.1 Plant and animal cells

What are the differences between plant cells and animal cells?

For centuries people thought disease was caused by bad air or being cursed. Now we can use light microscopes to see some of the microorganisms that make us ill.

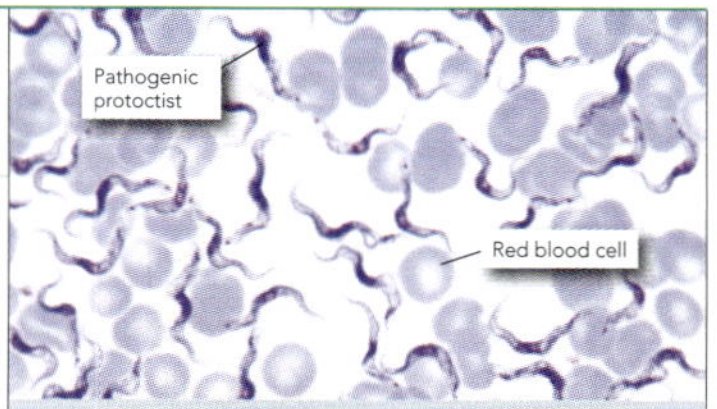


**A** *A tiny protoctist that causes sleeping sickness. (Magnification × 400)*

In **light microscopes**, light passes through a specimen and then through magnifying lenses so you see the object much bigger than it really is.

Microscopes are used to learn about the structure and the function of **cells**, of which organisms are made.

1 Why are microscopes so useful?

2 What is the purpose of a lens in a microscope?

Plant and animal cells have some features in common:

- **Cell membrane** – separates the contents of the cell and its surroundings. It controls the movement of substances like oxygen, glucose and carbon dioxide into and out of the cell.
- **Cytoplasm** – where many of the chemical reactions needed to carry out life processes take place. It also contains **organelles** (tiny structures that carry out specific jobs).
- **Nucleus** – an organelle that contains **DNA**, which is the genetic material. The nucleus also controls all the activities of the cell.
- **Mitochondria** – organelles in which respiration occurs (oxygen and glucose react to release energy needed by the cell). They are very tiny and cannot be seen easily through a light microscope at low magnification.

3 What is the function of the cell membrane?

4 Why can't you see mitochondria in the light micrograph of a cell?

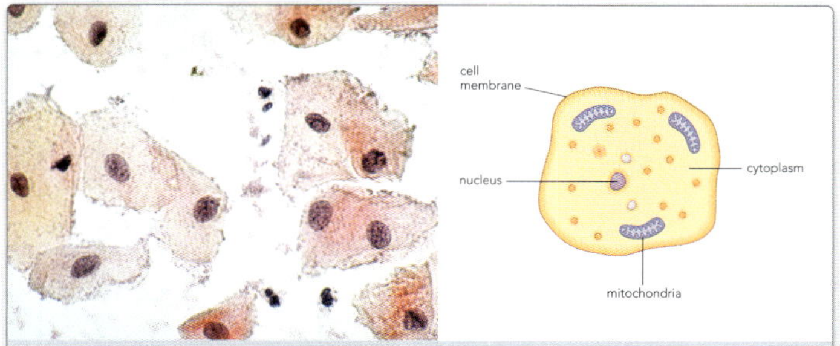


**B** *A light micrograph (magnification × 2900) and a diagram of a simple animal cell.*



## Plant cells

Plant cells also have some other structures:

- **Cell wall** – made of tough **cellulose** to support the cell and allow it to keep its shape.
- Large **vacuole** – a space in the cytoplasm that is filled with cell sap and helps to support the plant by keeping the cells rigid.
- **Chloroplasts** – organelles that contain **chlorophyll**, a green substance that absorbs light energy used in photosynthesis.

**ResultsPlus Watch Out!**

Make sure you don't confuse cell membranes and cell walls. All cells have cell membranes on the outside of the cytoplasm. Only plant cells have cell walls.

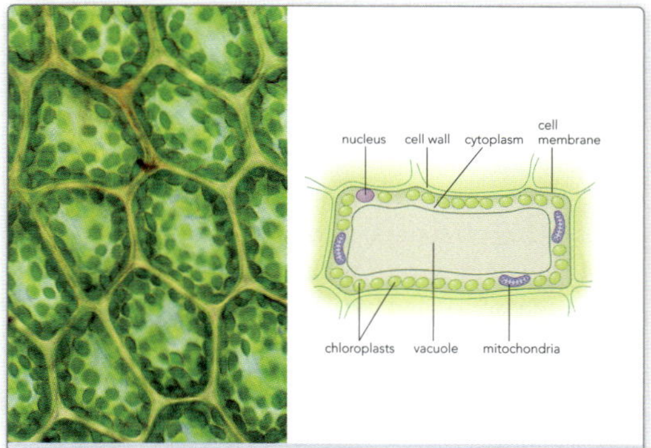


**C** *A light micrograph (magnification × 836) and a diagram of a simple plant cell.*

**Skills spotlight**

Sometimes scientists get their inspiration from the work of other scientists. In 1831 Robert Brown (1773–1858) wrote a paper showing that he had found organelles, which he called nuclei, inside the cells of an orchid plant. Suggest what hypothesis Matthias Schleiden (1804–1881) then tested, having read Brown's paper.

5 Why did our knowledge of the structures inside cells only develop after microscopes were invented?

6 a What are the similarities and differences in structure between a typical animal cell and a plant cell?
b Why are some of these features only found in plant cells?

7 List the structures visible in an animal cell and a plant cell using a light microscope, then make a table to show the functions of all the structures.

**Learning Outcomes**

1.2 Describe the function of the components of a plant cell including chloroplast, large vacuole, cell wall, cell membrane, mitochondria, cytoplasm and nucleus

1.3 Describe the function of the components of an animal cell including cell membrane, mitochondria, cytoplasm and nucleus

1.4 Describe how plant and animal cells can be studied in greater detail with a light microscope

HSW 2 Interpret data, using creative thought, to provide evidence for testing ideas and developing theories

Is the stuff you scrape off your teeth living?



## ActiveTeach

- **AT** *Microscopes and cells* [BBC video]
  How models of the cell have changed
- **AT** *Animal cells* [interactive]
  Parts of an animal cell – labelling activity
- **AT** *Plant cells* [interactive]
  Functions of cell parts – matching activity
- **AT** *Making a slide 1* [word document]
  Making a cheek cell slide
- **AT** *Animal cell structure* [diagram]
  Figure B – diagram labelling activity
- **AT** *Plant cell structure* [diagram]
  Figure C – diagram labelling activity

## Answers | Student Book

1 Because they enable us to see things that are too small to see with the naked eye.

2 To magnify the object so you see it much bigger than it really is.

3 To separate the cell contents and the environment; to control the movement of substances between the cytoplasm and the environment.

4 Because they are too small to be seen at the level of magnification at which you are looking at the cell.

5 Because most cells are too small to see with our eyes alone and the parts inside them are even smaller, so we couldn't see them or understand what went on inside them until microscopes were developed to magnify the cells.

6 a Similarities – cell membrane, nucleus, cytoplasm, mitochondria
Differences – plant cells have cell walls, large vacuoles and sometimes chloroplasts
b Because plants need more support (the function of the cell wall and vacuole), and they carry out photosynthesis – hence the chloroplasts.

7 Animal cell: cell membrane, cytoplasm, nucleus, mitochondria
Plant cell: cell membrane, cytoplasm, nucleus, mitochondria, cell wall, large vacuole, chloroplasts
For a full answer see the table in the Answers section in the TTPP.

**Skills spotlight**

Having learnt from Brown's paper that the cells of an orchid plant had nuclei, Schleiden went on to study the cells of many other species of plant in order to test the hypothesis that all plant cells had nuclei.

# B2.2 Inside bacteria



This lesson looks at the influence of electron microscopes on our knowledge and understanding of cell structures and introduces students to the components of bacterial cells.

## Specification coverage

***1.1*** Describe the function of the components of a bacterial cell including chromosomal DNA, plasmid DNA, flagella and cell wall

***1.5*** Demonstrate an understanding of how changes in microscope technology have enabled us to see cells with more clarity and detail than in the past, including simple magnification calculations

HSW ***14*** How uncertainties in scientific knowledge and scientific ideas change over time and the role of the scientific community in validating these changes

There are also opportunities to cover HSW ***10*** and HSW ***12***.

## Key terms

chromosomal DNA
electron microscope
flagella
plasmid DNA

### What's inside bacteria?

**Starter 1** Lit

Write the word 'bacteria' on the board. Discuss with students the components that they would expect to find in bacterial cells. Write up each component suggested around the central word. Leave this up until the end of the lesson.

### Comparing images of cells

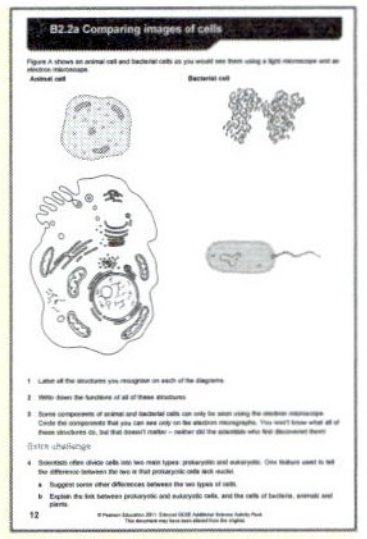

**Exploring 1**

**Worksheet B2.2a** gives students drawings of animal and bacterial cells under light and electron microscopes so they can appreciate the difference in the detail seen.

**Stretch** Students could investigate the functions of some of the additional components of the animal cells visible with the electron microscope.

**Support** Work through the labelling of the diagrams with the students. Do not expect them to answer question **4**.

### Student Book spread B2.2

**Explaining 1**

Student should work their way through the questions on the spread.

**Stretch** Ask students to summarise the differences between bacterial DNA and the DNA in, human cheek cells, for example. They should suggest: i) DNA in bacteria is not contained within a nucleus; ii) a bacterial cell also contains short sections of DNA called plasmids that carry extra information.

**Support** Work through questions with students before they attempt to answer them.

### Checking up ideas

**Plenary 1** Lit

Return to the word 'bacteria' from *Starter 1* and build up a collaborative mind map around the word. Compare the map developed to the original points on the board and discuss how many of their original ideas were right and how many were wrong.

### Looking at cell contents

**Homework 1**

**Worksheet B2.2c** is designed for students needing support.

The word list at the bottom of the sheet should be removed before copying for the majority of students.

**Support** Supply the word list from the lower half of the sheet.

### The limits of light microscopes

**Starter 2** AfL

Have a quick question and answer session about the components of plant and animal cells. Then introduce the idea that light microscopes are limited in their magnification and that a different technology allows us to investigate deeper into cells and to discover what goes on inside smaller organisms, such as bacteria.

### Development of microscope technology

**Exploring 2**

For **Worksheet B2.2b** students should have access to the Internet to research and develop a timeline which tells the story of the development of the microscope and the importance to our understanding of the cell.

**Stretch** Students develop a full timeline with explanations of the importance of the developments in microscopy to our understanding of the cell.

**Support** Each group of students can work on one part of the timeline and then put everything together to produce the finished result.

### Magnifications (AT)

**Explaining 2**

Practise working out microscope magnifications. The **AT** presentation *Magnification* includes questions on magnification.

**Stretch** Students should answer questions that involve rearranging equations and calculations involving standard form and decimals.

**Support** Students should answer questions using whole numbers only and are not required to use standard form. Only the first part of the **AT** presentation *Magnification* is needed.

### Designing mark schemes

**Plenary 2** AfL

Ask students to use Figure B on page 30 of the Student Book to write a question about it and to design a mark scheme for the answer. Encourage students to think up questions that are worth more than 1 or 2 marks, and require extended answers. If time allows, students could try out their questions on one another.

### Cells and the electron microscope

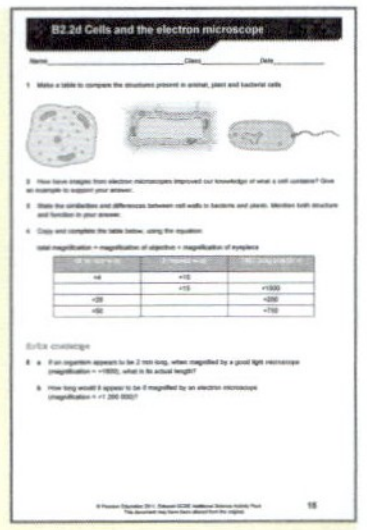

**Homework 2**

**Worksheet B2.2d** is designed for more able students.

**Stretch** Ask students to do the 'extra challenge' question on the sheet.

# B2.2 Inside bacteria

What are bacterial cells like?

Antoni van Leeuwenhoek (1632–1723) used a microscope he had made to look at plaque he scraped off his teeth. He discovered it contained what he called *tiny animalcules*. They were what we now call bacteria.

Microscopes have improved greatly in the last 350 years. The best modern light microscopes can magnify specimens more than 1500 times. An average person magnified this much would be over 2.5 km tall! With a magnification like this, we can observe very small structures inside cells. For example, we can see inside bacterial cells. Bacteria are single-celled organisms that are much smaller than plant or animal cells.

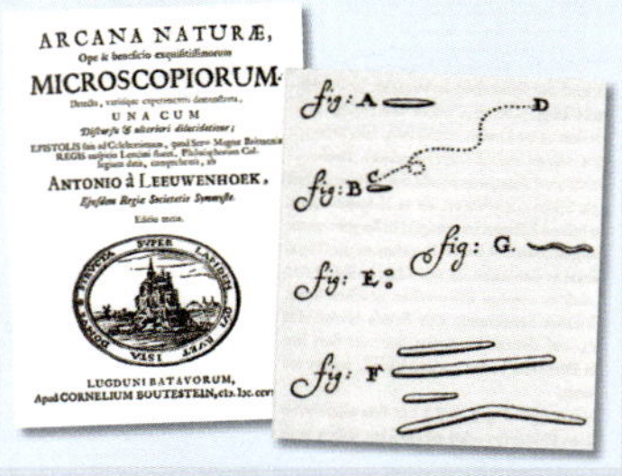


**A** *Bacteria as Leeuwenhoek drew them in 1683, in a letter to the Royal Society.*

1 What are the parts labelled A, B, C and D on the electron micrograph of a bacterium in Figure B?

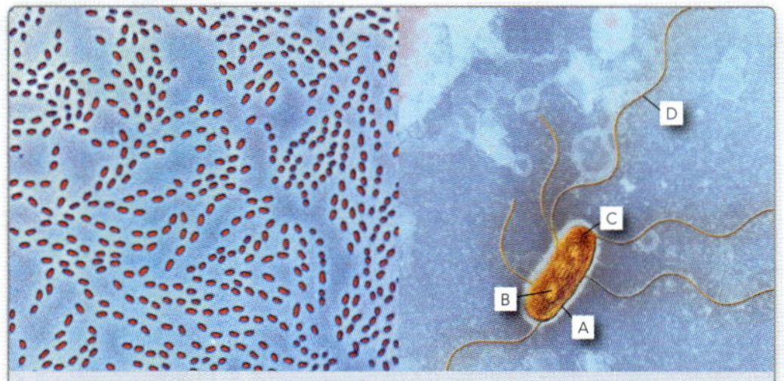


**B** *A light micrograph (left, magnification x 1758) and an electron micrograph (right, magnification x 2626) of bacteria. The difference in both magnification and clarity is easy to see.*

2 What are the differences between the two types of DNA found in bacterial cells?

In the 1930s the **electron microscope** was invented. This uses a beam of electrons to magnify specimens up to about 2000000 times. This would make an average person 3333 km tall! Electron microscopes also produce very clear images and have helped us to discover much more about the detailed structure of cells. For example, light microscopes show us that bacteria do not have nuclei. Electron microscopes show us that bacterial cells contain two types of DNA. **Chromosomal DNA** is a giant loop of DNA containing most of the genetic material. It is not neatly packaged like plant or human chromosomes. **Plasmid DNA** comes in small loops and carries extra information.

## Bacterial cells

Using information from the electron microscope we know that bacterial cells have a cell wall that is different to the cell wall of plants. It does a similar job but it is more flexible and not made of cellulose.

Some bacteria also have **flagella** on the outside of the cell. These are long, whip-like structures that bacteria can use to move themselves along.

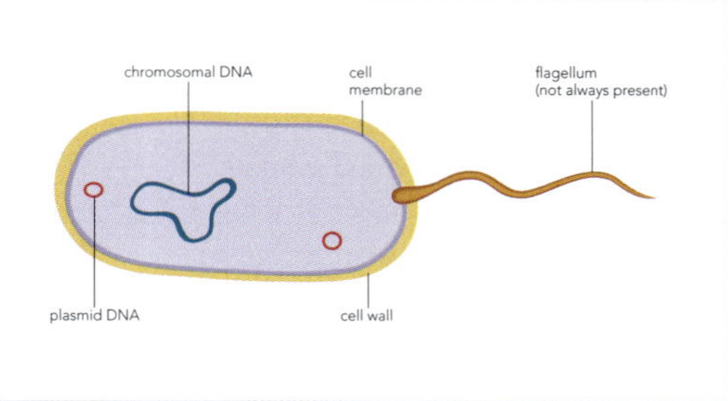


**C** *The structure of a bacterial cell.*

3 What are the advantages of the electron microscope compared to the light microscope?

4 **a** What are the magnifications of a good light microscope and an electron microscope?
**b** How much more powerful is the electron microscope?

5 **a** A specimen appears 1 mm in length under the light microscope at a magnification of × 1500. What is its actual length?
**b** What length would the specimen in part **a** appear under the maximum magnification of an electron microscope?

6 Draw and label a diagram to show the structure of a bacterial cell and the functions of each part.

7 Explain the importance of the development of light and electron microscopes.

**ResultsPlus Watch Out!**

Remember that bacterial cells have a cell wall, only one circular chromosome but no nucleus.

**Maths skills**

The length of the magnified object = the length of the object × the **magnification**

And by rearranging this formula we know that:

$$\text{the length of the object} = \frac{\text{the length of the magnified object}}{\text{the magnification}}$$

The first paragraph of page 30 tells us that an average person magnified 1500 times would be 2500 m tall. From this we can work out the size of an average person:

$$\text{height of an average person} = \frac{2500}{1500} = 1.666\text{ m} = 1.7\text{ m (to 1d.p.)}$$

We can say that the length of the magnified object and the length of the object are in **direct proportion** as they increase and decrease in the same ratio.

**Skills spotlight**

What did Van Leeuwenhoek think bacteria were? How have his ideas been tested and changed since 1683?

**Learning Outcomes**

1.1 Describe the function of the components of a bacterial cell including chromosomal DNA, plasmid DNA, flagella and cell wall

1.5 Demonstrate an understanding of how changes in microscope technology have enabled us to see cells with more clarity and detail than in the past, including simple magnification calculations

HSW 14 Explain how uncertainties in scientific knowledge and scientific ideas change over time and the role of the scientific community in validating these changes.





## ActiveTeach

- **AT** *Inside bacteria* [interactive]
  Structure of bacterium – scene investigation
- **AT** *Magnification* [presentation]
  Questions on magnification
- **AT** *Bacterial cell structure* [diagram]
  Figure C – diagram labelling activity

## Answers | Student Book

1 A – cell wall, B – chromosomal DNA, C – plasmid DNA, D – flagellum

2 Chromosomal DNA is a long loop and contains most of the genetic information for the bacterium. Plasmid DNA is a small loop that carries extra bits of information.

3 Electron microscope has greater magnification and clarity.

4 **a** light – more than 1500×, electron – about 2 000 000×
**b** 1000× more powerful

5 **a** 0.0007 mm **b** 1400 mm

6 Drawn diagram of bacterium as on p31, main parts labelled with function: bacterial cell wall – very flexible, gives cell shape and support; flagellum – long, whip-like structure that beats to move the bacterium about; chromosomal DNA – main loop of DNA that carries most of the genetic information; plasmid DNA – small loop of DNA that contains extra bits of information; cell membrane – controls which substances enter and leave the bacterial cell.

7 A good answer will contain the following points: bacterial cells are much smaller than plant and animal cells; light microscopes allowed some cell detail of plant and animal cells to be seen, but bacteria were tiny shapes; the best light microscopes give limited clarity and magnification, so could tell that there was no nucleus in a bacterial cell but couldn't see any detail; light microscopes give fairly detailed images of organelles of plant and animal cells; electron micrographs give detail of bacterial cells organelles.

**Skills spotlight**

Leeuwenhoek called bacteria 'little animals'. With the improvement of light microscopes and with the development of electron microscopes, which give an even greater magnification, we can see that the internal structure of bacteria and animal cells is different. We no longer consider bacteria as animals.

# B2.3 DNA



This lesson looks at the structure and role of DNA and some of the ethical issues associated with the question of a national DNA database.

## Specification coverage

**1.6** Recall that a gene is a section of a molecule of DNA and that it codes for a specific protein

**1.7** Describe a DNA molecule as: a) two strands coiled to form a double helix b) strands linked by a series of complementary base pairs joined together by weak hydrogen bonds: i) adenine (A) with thymine (T) ii) cytosine (C) with guanine (G)

HSW **13** How and why decisions about science and technology are made, including those that raise ethical issues, *and about the social, economic and environmental effects* of such decisions.

## Key terms

adenine
base chromosomes
complementary base pair
cytosine
double helix
DNA
gene
guanine
hydrogen bond
thymine

### DNA evidence

**Starter 1** AfL

Show a clip from a detective/crime programme with SOCOs at work. Ask students what is going on and what sort of evidence is being looked for. Write 'DNA' on the board and ask students where it is found in the body and why it can be used to convict criminals. Discuss their answers and ask them to keep those initial answers until the end of the lesson.

### Making a DNA model

**Exploring 1**

Students use **Worksheet B2.3a** to make a 3D model of the DNA double helix.

**Stretch** Students could investigate how the DNA code is translated and produce complementary RNA strands to the DNA model they have made.

**Support** Students need support to colour the complementary bases the same each time and to recognise that only certain pairs can be formed.

### Using DNA to catch a killer

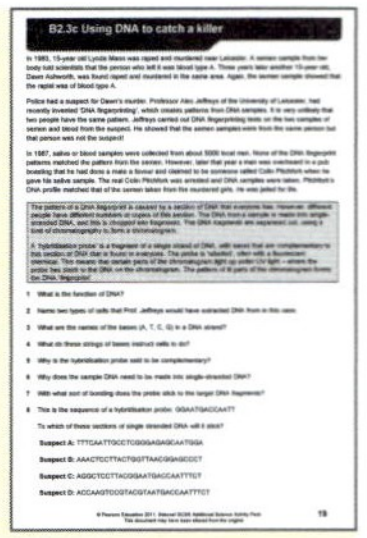


**Exploring 3**

**Worksheet B2.3c** explains how the use of DNA has changed crime detection through the case of Colin Pitchfork, the first person convicted using DNA evidence.

**Stretch** Students carry out research into the way improvements in technology have allowed cold cases to be investigated and produce a newspaper report.

**Support** Read through the story and think about the questions together before students answer the questions themselves

### Return to DNA

**Plenary 1** AfL Lit

Students write the first part of two statements about DNA, one beginning with an A and the other with a G (e.g. A molecule of DNA …, Guanine is …). They hand their sentence starters onto each other and then have to complete them according to base pairing rules – so the sentence that starts with an A must be completed with a T. Get students to read out some of their answers – both the straightforward and the contrived!

### The DNA molecule

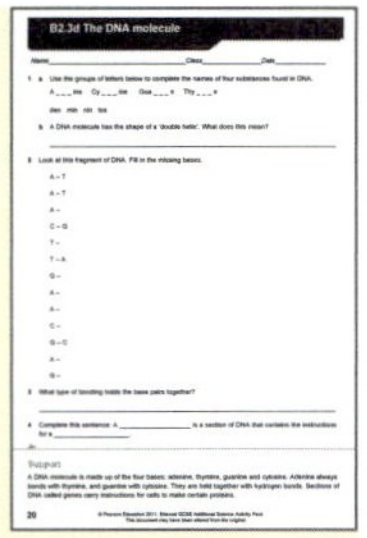


**Homework 1**

Remove the paragraph at the bottom of the **Worksheet B2.3d** before copying for the majority of students.

**Support** Supply the 'help' paragraph from the lower half of the worksheet.

### DNA 'fingerprints'

**Starter 2**

Describe the case of Anna Anderson and then ask students how they think the issue could be resolved using today's technology. Elicit the idea that we all have different DNA and this can be used to identify people, like a sophisticated fingerprint. But it is more useful than fingerprints because your DNA is more similar to people you are related to than to strangers.

### DNA and ethics

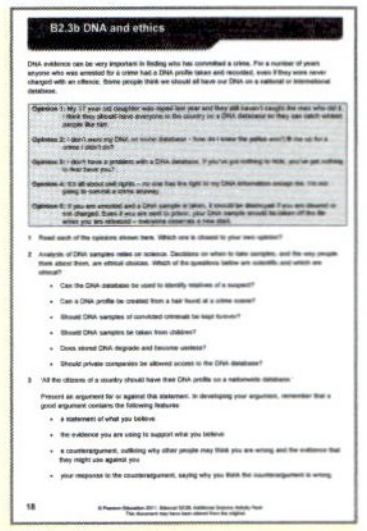


**Exploring 2**

**Worksheet B2.3b** introduces students to the idea that DNA can be held on a database to help identify criminals and gives them a number of different opinions on the idea.

**Stretch** Students can demonstrate that they have developed a clear understanding and recognise the ethical issues which surround such science.

**Support** Students work through the opinions and questions. Ask them to make a list of all the opinions expressed about the issues of a national database.

### Student Book spread B2.3

**Explaining 1**

Talk to students about the story of the false Anastasia and the role of DNA in revealing the truth.

**Stretch** Students work in pairs to produce an explanation of what happens in a genetic disease like cystic fibrosis and come up with ideas for how these diseases might be treated.

**Support** Work with students to make a simple flowchart to explain how the instructions in the DNA result in a protein that is used in the cell or the whole organism.

### Summarising DNA

**Plenary 2** AfL

Ask students to work in pairs. Each student thinks of five quick questions to test their partner's understanding of the structure of DNA, including base pairing. Give students a few minutes to write down their questions – then they take it in turn to ask each other a question until they have used up all their ideas.

### Proteins in DNA

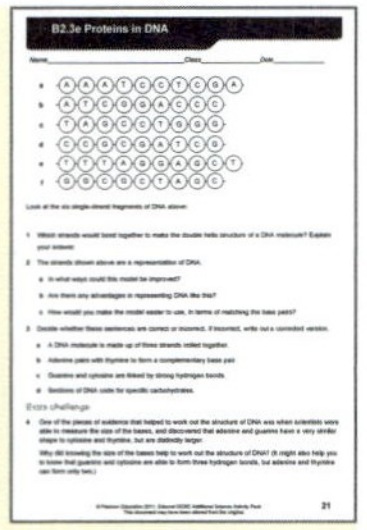


**Homework 2**

**Worksheet B2.3e** is designed for more able students.

**Stretch** Students answer the 'extra challenge' question.

# B2.3 DNA

## What is DNA?

On the 17th of July 1918, the Russian secret police shot the Russian royal family, including the Tsar's youngest daughter, Grand Duchess Anastasia. A woman, called Anna Anderson, later claimed that she was Anastasia and had escaped. Anderson died in 1984. In 1994 DNA testing on some of her tissue showed that she was not Anastasia. Another body was later found and shown to be Anastasia's from DNA testing completed in 2009.

**A** *DNA analysis showed Anna Anderson was really a Polish woman called Franziska Schanzkowska.*

The **chromosomes** in the nuclei of your cells contain your genetic information. They are made of a chemical called **DNA**. Sections of the DNA molecule called **genes** contain instructions for specific proteins that are used in your body.

1 What is a gene?

One gene contains the instructions for one protein. Often several genes work together to produce what is needed for a single feature. For example, your eye colour is the result of proteins made by several different genes. So is the size and shape of your nose, and many other features of your body. Some genes also carry the instructions for the proteins that control the chemical processes in your body.

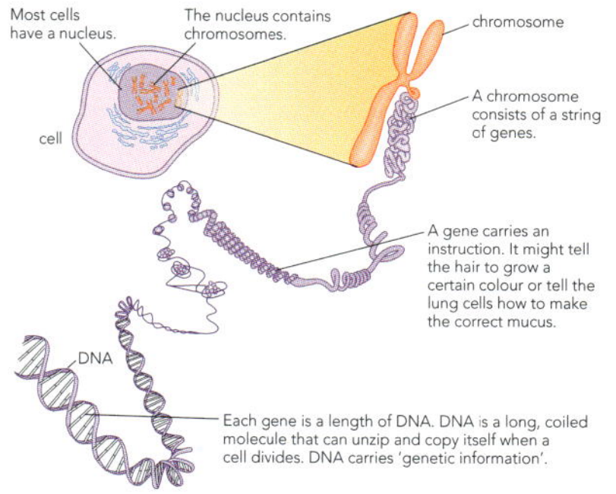


**B** *DNA, genes and chromosomes.*

## The structure of DNA

There are two strands in a molecule of DNA that are coiled together to form a spiral known as a **double helix**. The two strands are linked together at regular intervals by chemicals called **bases**.

The bases always pair up in the same way because of the complementary (matching) shape of the molecules. **Adenine** (A) pairs with **thymine** (T) and **cytosine** (C) pairs with **guanine** (G). The matching bases are known as **complementary base pairs**. They are joined together by weak **hydrogen bonds**. The order of the bases in DNA contains the information needed to form the proteins for body cells. We each have a slightly different order of bases in our genes and this makes us all slightly different.

2 Suggest why a different order of bases in a gene for hair colour in two people may make them have different coloured hair.

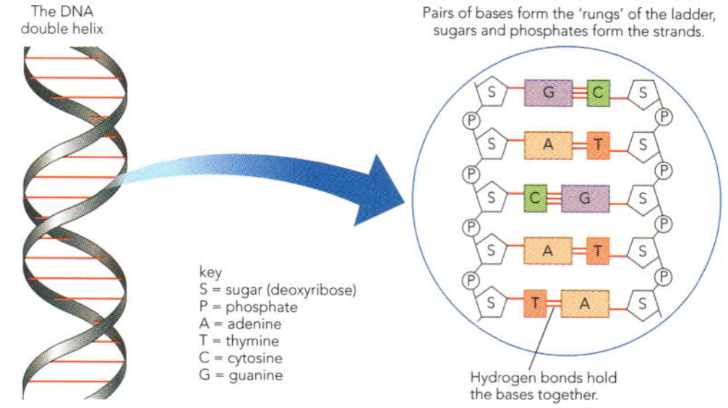


**C** *The structure of DNA.*

3 **a** What shape is the DNA molecule?
**b** What are the four bases found in DNA?
**c** A DNA molecule is made up of two strands. How are they joined together?

4 Why does adenine always bond with thymine and never with cytosine?

5 Why is DNA so important?

6 The actor Clint Eastwood, who is now in his seventies, publicly thanked his mother 'for her genes'. Explain what a gene is and what he meant.

### Skills spotlight

If you commit a crime, your DNA is kept on a database. Some people argue that there should be a national DNA database with all of us on it. Who do you think should be consulted about a decision like this?

### Learning Outcomes

**1.6** Recall that a gene is a section of a molecule of DNA and that it codes for a specific protein

**1.7** Describe a DNA molecule as:
*a* two strands coiled to form a double helix
*b* strands linked by a series of complementary base pairs joined together by weak hydrogen bonds:
*i* adenine (A) with thymine (T) *ii* cytosine (C) with guanine (G)

HSW **13** Explain how and why decisions that raise ethical issues about uses of science and technology are made





## ActiveTeach

- **AT** *DNA supersleuth 1* [video] Structure of DNA
- **AT** *DNA supersleuth 2* [video] How DNA fingerprinting works
- **AT** *What makes up a DNA molecule?* [interactive] Key terms: DNA molecule – matching activity

## Answers | Student Book

1 A section of DNA on a chromosome that codes for a protein.

2 The different proteins produced by the different order of bases are different colours.

3 **a** Two strands coiled/twisted to form a double helix.
**b** Adenine, thymine, cytosine and guanine
**c** By hydrogen bonds between particular pairs – A-T and C-G

4 Due to the shape of the molecules, hydrogen bonds can form between A and T but not between A and C within a DNA molecule.

5 DNA is important because it contains the information to develop a new cell or a new individual. The instructions are used to produce proteins.

6 A gene is a short piece of DNA that codes for a characteristic. Genes are passed from parent to offspring during reproduction, and this explains why you have some characteristics like those of your mother and some that are like those of your father. The genes that Clint Eastwood inherited from his mother may have helped him remain fit and healthy for over seven decades.

**Skills spotlight**

The police, human rights groups, the court system, the government.

# B2.4 Extracting DNA

This lesson challenges students to investigate the best conditions needed to extract DNA from plant cells.
The activity may be run as a practice controlled assessment task. The practical work can be completed in a one hour lesson.

## Specification coverage

***1.8*** Investigate how to extract DNA from cells

This activity provides opportunities to cover HSW *1*, HSW *5*, HSW *6*, HSW *7*, HSW *8*, HSW *10* and HSW *11*.

### Before the lesson

Ensure that students are familiar with any equipment they may be expected to use so that they can plan their own investigation. In the week or two before the task show them this equipment and, if appropriate, allow them to practice using it. Students will need to be able to use a water bath at a fairly precisely controlled temperature, use a blender and manipulate very cold ethanol. It may be good preparation to show students one or more of Skills Sheets 19 to 26 to show what is expected of them in their actual controlled assessment task.

### Starter

**Ways of extracting DNA**

Ask students how they think they might get DNA out of cells and what difficulties might be faced. Note down ideas on the board to see if they are answered as they do the practical.

Alternatively, give pupils a list of the stages of the practical and ask them to put it in the right order. You can use this as an opportunity to discuss changing conditions as well.

Follow this by reading the additional information below the opening section of page 34 of the Student Book. They may then read the brief description of the activity provided by the 'Your task' box.

### Option 1: Straight-forward class practical

You may wish to run the activity as a straight-forward class practical. Students follow the instructions on **Worksheet B2.4b**. The range of data that students need to collect is given on **Worksheet B2.4c** which students will also need. This sheet guides students through recording, considering their results, and evaluating their investigation.

You could ask students to come up with one or two further hypotheses, based on their observations in this practical.

### Plenary

On page 35 of the Student Book you will find two examples of the sort of work that students may produce for this task. The examples focus on planning a practical. You could share these with students after they have completed their own work. This will help them to understand the assessment criteria and so make it easier for them to evaluate their work and to see how they can improve it. Moderator comments on each of the Student Book extracts can be found at the end of the assessment guidance for this investigation on the CD-ROM. The examples can also be found on the **AT** document *Student examples*.

### Option 2: Running the activity as a practice controlled assessment task (PCAT)

We have provided a full range of support resources to allow the running of this practical as a practice controlled assessment task. A recommended structure is outlined below (to be used over a number of sessions). Marking guidance for all three parts of the practice task can be found on the CD-ROM that accompanies the TTPP. To save time when using these practice controlled assessment tasks, you may wish to focus on a particular aspect or skill rather than working through all three parts of the task.

#### Part A Planning

1. Students should be given the Student Brief on Worksheet B2.4a. They can use Part A of the Workbook that is provided to help pupils with their practice controlled assessments. They should be given about 1 hour to do this planning.
2. The method for this practical is complicated and students would not be expected to work this out for themselves. Students should be given either a modified copy of **Worksheet B2.4b** or a set of instructions could be displayed on a whiteboard. This can then be used to help students discuss what the variables are in the practical and what they could choose to investigate.

#### Part B Observations

3. Students carry out the practical task to collect evidence using the method they have planned in Part A. Once again, they should refer to the Student Brief on Worksheet B2.4a. They can use Part B of the Workbook that is provided to help pupils with their practice controlled assessments. They should be given about 1 hour to collect their primary evidence.
4. If there is a problem with their own planned method, students may be asked to follow the method set out on **Worksheet B2.4b**. This will still enable students to access the full range of marks for Part B and Part C of the practice controlled assessment task.
5. In Part B, students are required to gather some secondary evidence. The evidence can be quantitative or qualitative. It can be from a variety of sources but students must note where they found their evidence and evaluate the quality of the source as part of this task. Skills Sheet 22 provides students with further guidance on researching for and evaluating secondary evidence. This part of the task could be done outside of the lesson but must be supervised.

#### Part C Conclusions

6. Students follow the instructions set out on the Part C section of the Student Brief on Worksheet B2.4a. They should use their data from Part B and the secondary evidence they have collected when doing this. They can use Part C of the Workbook that is provided to help pupils with their practice controlled assessments. They should be given about 1 hour to work on their conclusions.

The **AT** includes video clips showing a group of students working through elements of this investigation with teacher support.

Practice Controlled Assessment

# B2.4 Extracting DNA

Can you extract DNA from common foods?

In 2009 an American man was imprisoned for selling cheap, frozen catfish as expensive fresh grouper, red snapper and flounder. The scam was discovered by extracting the DNA from the fish, testing it and comparing it to the DNA from known species.

The genetic information carried in DNA is different for each species. This means DNA can be used to identify different organisms. For example, scientists have shown that some chicken meat is contaminated with beef because they have discovered cow DNA in the chicken breasts! To do this the first step is to extract DNA from the cells. Some cells contain more DNA than others.

**A** *The label can claim this fish is anything from catfish to cod – but the DNA doesn't lie!*

**Your task**

You are going to plan an investigation that will allow you to find out whether changing the method of DNA extraction improves the DNA yield. Your teacher will provide you with some materials to help you organise this task.

**Learning Outcomes**

*1.8 Investigate how to extract DNA from cells*

## ResultsPlus Build Better Answers

When planning an investigation like this, you will be assessed on your *overall plan*. There are 4 marks available for this skill. Here are two extracts focusing on this skill. Other skills that you need for the assessment are dealt with in other lessons.

**Student extract 1** — A basic response for this skill

*I will put the mixture in a hot water bath for a while and then cool it down again. To make the mixture I am going to mix detergent with salty water and then mix this with some peas that have been mashed up. I will then put the mixture in a blender, blend it, filter it and add an enzyme. I will then pour cold liquid down the side of the test tube and the DNA will float on the top. I am going to test lots of different vegetables like this.*

Give detailed instructions because ideally someone else should be able to carry out the practical in the same way and get the same results.

Your instructions should be in a logical order so that they are easy to follow.

It would be better to explain what sort of vegetables and how many.

**Student extract 2** — A good response for this skill

*I am going to measure out 50 g of thawed frozen peas and mash them up. I will then mix them with salty water which includes 3 g of salt dissolved in 90 cm³ of water with 10 cm³ of detergent added. The mixture will then be left in a water bath at 60 °C for 15 minutes and then cooled in an ice bath for 5 minutes. I will then filter the mixture and add 2 drops of a protease enzyme. Finally I will pour 10 cm³ of iced ethanol down the side of the tube and DNA will float to the surface of the tube. I will measure the DNA layer with a ruler to see what thickness it is. I will do this experiment again for soya beans, sweetcorn and cress.*

This student has missed part of the plan out – they should have explained how this method will allow them to test their hypothesis.

Stating the quantities makes it easy for someone else to follow the method.

This time the student has clearly explained the range of vegetables to be tested.

**ResultsPlus**

**To access 2 marks**

- Provide a logically ordered method that will produce results
- Choose a range of data or observations that will test the hypothesis

**To access 4 marks**

You also need to:

- Explain how your method will test the hypothesis
- Explain why you have chosen your range of data or observations





## ActiveTeach

- **AT** *B2.4 Extracting DNA* [video]
  Students work through the investigation
- **AT** *B2.4 Moderator comments* [word document]
  Moderator comments on the video
- **AT** *B2.4 Assessment criteria* [presentation]
  Understanding the CA marking criteria
- **AT** *B2.4 Student task sheet* [word document]
  CA video checklist
- **AT** *B2.4 Specification points* [word document]
  Edexcel specification points
- **AT** *B2.4 Student examples* [word document]
  Examples for students to assess

## Assessment criteria

### Quality of evidence

**0** No relevant method given.

**1-2 a)** Produces a method that is ordered in a logical way and would produce results that can later be analysed. The method covers all the main points needed, such as: mixing peas with detergent and salt; leaving in a water bath for 15 minutes; cooling the reaction in an ice bath; blending and filtering the mixture; adding a protease and then cold ethanol to precipitate the DNA; repeating with different temperatures of water bath.

**b)** Range of data/observations chosen that would test the hypothesis, e.g. 40°C, 60°C and 80°C.

**3-4 a)** The method also includes an explanation as to why it would test the hypothesis, e.g. 'I am trying to find out if changing the technique in this practical affects the amount of DNA extracted. I am going to change the temperature of the water bath to see if this increases or decreases the yield of DNA.'

**b)** Range of data/observations chosen that would test the hypothesis and an explanation of why the range was chosen, e.g. 'I think that trying 20°C above and below the suggested temperature will give a wide enough range of temperatures to assess the impact on the amount of DNA extracted'.

# B2.5 DNA discovery



This lesson looks at how the structure of DNA was discovered and at the sequencing of the human genome.

## Specification coverage

**1.9** Explain how the structure of DNA was discovered, including the roles of Watson, Crick, Franklin and Wilkins

**1.10** H Demonstrate an understanding of the implications of sequencing the human genome (Human Genome Project) *and of the collaboration that took place within the project*

HSW *1* The collection and analysis of scientific data

There are also opportunities to cover HSW *2*, HSW *3*, HSW *12* and HSW *13*.

## Key terms

genome
Human Genome Project (HGP)

### DNA

**Starter 1**

Discuss the reaction that Watson and Crick got when Watson announced that they had discovered the 'secret of life' on 28th February 1953 at the Eagle pub in Cambridge after he'd helped build a model of DNA.

### Chargaff's rules (AT)

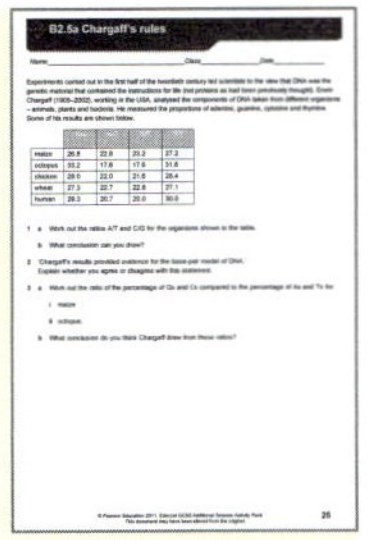

**Exploring 1**

Students work through **Worksheet B2.5a**, answering the questions.

**Stretch** Ask students to write a question of their own about Chargaff. If time allows, they could swap questions with a partner, and then attempt to answer each other's.

**Support** Go through one of the ratio calculations from the **AT** presentation *Chargaff's rules* as an example. Students could also miss out question **2**.

### The double helix

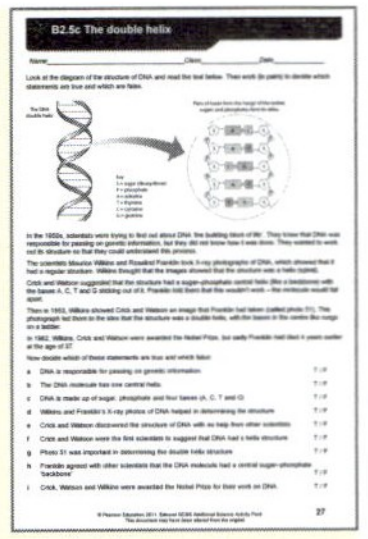

**Exploring 3**

Students work through **Worksheet B2.5c**, either individually or in small groups.

**Stretch** Students write three or four more true/false statements based on the passage to test their partner.

**Support** Give out copies of the worksheet, one between two, and highlighter pens. Read through the passage as a class, and suggest which statements should be highlighted as an aid to answering the questions.

### Who did what?

**Plenary 1**

Ask students for the names of the four people who are best known for their work on the double helix structure of DNA. Then ask students to rank the people in order of how deserving they were of the Nobel Prize, starting with the person they feel most deserved to get it. Invite students to give reasons why the choices were made.

### DNA discovery

**Homework 1**

Ask students to draw a storyboard or cartoon strip about the discovery of the structure of DNA.

**Support** Supply the text (not the questions) from **Worksheet B2.5c** as a crib sheet.

### The DNA story

**Starter 2** Lit

Display the image of Watson and Crick and their DNA model. Ask students to produce and annotate a flowchart to show how they think scientists such as Watson and Crick develop a structural model for a molecule like DNA. This will lead into the following tasks on how the double helix model of DNA actually came about.

### Watson and Crick

**Exploring 2**

Students use question **1** from **Worksheet B2.5b** to sort out the evidence that Watson and Crick used, and how they used it in their model.

**Stretch** Students answer both questions. Following question **2**, ask students to justify the use of secondary data in the HGP.

**Support** Go through one example from question **1**, writing it up on the board and then ask students to complete the rest of the examples.

### Student Book spread B2.5

**Explaining 1**

Students read the text and answer the questions.

Ask students to work in groups of four. Each of them takes the role of one of the discoverers of the structure of DNA and explains to the rest of the group why their role was so important and why they deserved to win the Nobel prize.

**Stretch** Higher Tier students answer questions 3 to **6**.

**Support** Provide the answers to question **7** as an aid for the role play task.

### H Judging the genome

**Plenary 2** AfL

Ask students to work in pairs to write down two lists, one giving benefits which might come from the sequencing of the human genome and the other listing some of the ethical implications of our knowledge of the human genome. Ask students to compare their lists with other pairs until all points are covered.

### H HGP ethics

**Homework 2**

Ask students to write a response to this statement: 'The work of Watson, Crick, Franklin and Wilkins has created a monster, by which all of us will be judged by our genes.'

**Stretch** Guide students towards using their understanding of the sequencing of the human genome in completing this homework.

# B2.5 DNA discovery

What is the human genome project?

Each year scientific Nobel Prizes are awarded for chemistry, physics and medicine. Each prize-winner gets a solid gold medal and about £1 000 000 (although because scientists collaborate this is often shared).

**A** In 1962 James Watson and Francis Crick, along with Maurice Wilkins, were awarded a Nobel Prize for discovering the structure of DNA.

**B** This X-ray photograph of DNA, taken by Franklin, shows that DNA is a double helix. However you need to be an expert to interpret the image.

In London in the 1950s, Maurice Wilkins (1916–2004) and Rosalind Franklin (1920–1958) were studying the structure of DNA using X-rays. Franklin directed beams of X-rays at purified DNA and used photos to record how the molecule scattered the X-rays. From the patterns (see Figure B) she could work out how the groups of atoms in the DNA molecule were arranged.

In Cambridge, James Watson (1928– ) and Francis Crick (1916–2004) were trying to build a 3D molecular model of DNA using the data from a number of other scientists. They used X-ray results from the London team including some of Franklin's best X-ray images that Wilkins had shown them without Franklin's permission. It was the detail in her images that gave Watson and Crick the clues they needed to build their double helix model.

However, when Watson and Crick published their paper in 1953, their only reference to the London team was a footnote. Eventually the contribution made by Franklin and Wilkins became clear. In 1962 James Watson, Francis Crick and Maurice Wilkins won a Nobel Prize for discovering the structure of DNA. Sadly, Rosalind Franklin died aged just 37, 4 years before the Nobel Prize was awarded.

1 Who discovered the structure of DNA?

2 How did the London team and the Cambridge team differ in the way that they tried to work out the structure of DNA?

## Understanding the human genome

H

The **Human Genome Project** (**HGP**) was an international effort that involved scientists working in 18 different countries and sharing the data they collected using the latest developments in IT to help them.

In 2003, after 13 years of work, the HGP was complete. Scientists had worked out the sequence (order) of the 3 billion base pairs that make up the human **genome**. Although each human being has a unique DNA sequence, the project shows that everyone has at least 99.9% of their DNA in common!

H 3 What is the difference between a gene and a genome?

Knowing the sequence of the human genome has many implications for science and medicine. It is being used to develop:

- improved testing for genetic disorders, to discover if people are carrying a faulty allele
- new ways of finding genes that may increase the risk of certain diseases, e.g. Alzheimer's, heart disease
- new treatments and cures for disorders, e.g. gene therapy, where scientists try to replace or mend faulty genes that cause the disorder (see Figure C)
- new ways of looking at changes in the genome over time – this shows us how humans have evolved and the evolutionary relationships between different species
- personalised medicines – these are medicines that work with a particular genotype and target diseases more effectively, with fewer side effects.

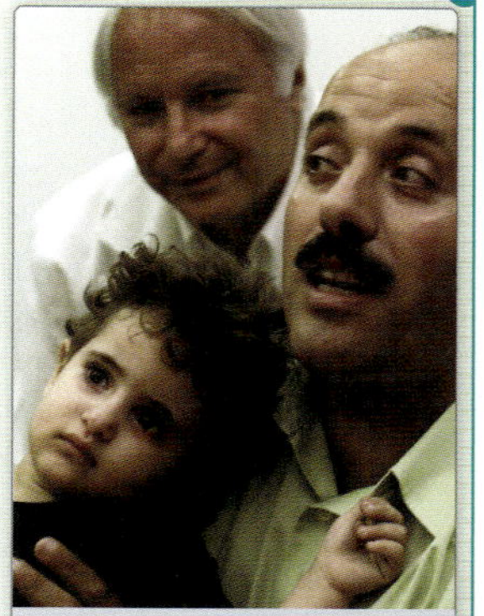

**C** This boy, Salsabil Abu Said, used to suffer from a disease called SCID. His immune system was not working and he had to be shielded from contact with people. In 2002, he was cured using gene therapy. However, things are not always so successful. In 1999, Jesse Gelsinger died while taking part in a gene therapy experiment.

**ResultsPlus Watch Out!**

A genome is all the genes in an individual. Do not confuse genes and alleles. A gene is part of a chromosome and alleles are varieties of one gene.

**Skills spotlight**

The HGP involved a huge amount of data that had to be collected and analysed. Explain how this was achieved in a short period of time and justify this approach.

H 4 a What was the human genome project?
b How did the attitude of the scientists involved in the HGP differ from those who worked on the structure of DNA?

H 5 The HGP analysed the DNA from five different individuals. Why might this limit the knowledge we have and how could we solve this problem?

H 6 What ethical issues does the HGP raise? You could divide your answer into the following areas: testing for genetic disease, gene therapy and personalised medicine.

7 Describe the roles played by the different scientists in the discovery of the structure of DNA.

**Learning Outcomes**

1.9 Explain how the structure of DNA was discovered, including the roles of the scientists Watson, Crick, Franklin and Wilkins

H 1.10 Demonstrate an understanding of the implications of sequencing the human genome (Human Genome Project) and of the collaboration that took place within this project

HSW 1 Describe the collection and analysis of scientific data





## ActiveTeach

- **AT** *DNA databases* [BBC video] Report on police DNA database
- **AT** *Louise Smith: a DNA case study* [BBC video] How DNA data helped catch killer
- **AT** *The discovery of DNA* [BBC video] Wilkins, Franklin, Crick, & Watson
- **AT** *Who discovered the structure of DNA?* [interactive] Timeline: DNA discoveries – ordering activity
- **AT** *Chargaff's rules* [presentation] Ratio calculations

## Answers | Student Book

1 James Watson and Francis Crick, using data obtained by Maurice Wilkins and Rosalind Franklin.

2 Watson and Crick worked on theoretical models and used evidence from other scientists. Wilkins and Franklin carried out practical investigations using X-rays.

3 H A gene is a short section of DNA that carries the instructions for making a protein, while a genome is the entire DNA sequence of an individual.

4 H a The HGP was a project to sequence the human genome – all of the DNA on all of the chromosomes.

H b Scientists working on the structure of DNA competed with other groups working on the same thing. By contrast, the scientists worked together on the HGP and shared the data they collected.

5 H Not all the alleles in the human population will be present. You would need to use DNA from more individuals.

6 H See full answer in the TTPP for ethical issues raised by the HGP.

7 A good answer will contain the following points: Watson and Crick used data obtained by other people; they built a model based on the data and worked in a theoretical way; Franklin used X-rays to look at the structure of DNA; Wilkins showed her photos to Crick and Watson without permission; the data from the photos allowed Watson and Crick to confirm the correct hypotheses.

**Skills spotlight**

The HGP was a project shared by scientists in 18 different countries. This made it much easier to share ideas and break down the work into smaller bits, so that different research groups didn't duplicate work. Sharing the work speeded up the rate of generating results. IT speeded up the analysis of the huge amounts of data. The results of the project may help people in the future, so speeding up the project may well save lives.

# B2.6 Genetic engineering



This lesson looks at the basic technique of genetic engineering with benefits and drawbacks related to specific examples.

## Specification coverage

**1.11** Demonstrate an understanding of the process of genetic engineering including the removal of a gene from the DNA of one organism and the insertion of that gene into the DNA of another organism

**1.12** Discuss the advantages and disadvantages of genetic engineering to produce GM organisms, including: a) beta carotene in golden rice to reduce vitamin A deficiency in humans b) the production of human insulin by genetically modified bacteria c) the production of herbicide-resistant crop plants

HSW *12* The use of contemporary science and technological developments and their benefits, drawbacks and risks

There are also opportunities to cover HSW *13*.

## Key terms

beta–carotene
biodiversity
genetic engineering
genetically modified organisms (GMOs)
golden rice
herbicide

### Genetic engineering

**Starter 1** AfL

Ask students five questions to test their background knowledge of genetic engineering. They should keep their answers until the end of the lesson when they will look at them again.

### Modelling a process

**Exploring 1**

Tell students that genetic engineering involves inserting new genes into the DNA of an organism. Then give students a long length of paper and a short length and some scissors and sticky tape. Ask them to create a model of genetic engineering using these items and to explain how their model works and what each item represents.

**Stretch** Students generate ideas about the process, i.e. how in practice can chromosomes be 'cut'?

**Support** Remind students of the definitions of genes and chromosomes and suggest what each length of paper represents.

### Student Book spread B2.6

**Exploring 1**

Students use the text and Figure B on page 38 to discover what goes on in genetic engineering.

**Stretch** Tell students about the attempts by scientists to produce genetically engineered plants which will contain a vaccine to human diseases such as hepatitis B. Ask them to write down what they think would be the possible advantages and disadvantages of this biotechnology.

**Support** For question 5, provide students with an incomplete flowchart to show the process of genetic engineering and ask them to fill in the gaps.

### Summing up genetic engineering

**Plenary 1** AfL

Return to the questions used in *Starter 1* and ask students to think how their answers might have changed now. Discuss the questions again as a class and then ask students to rewrite their answers.

### Genetic engineering reverse word

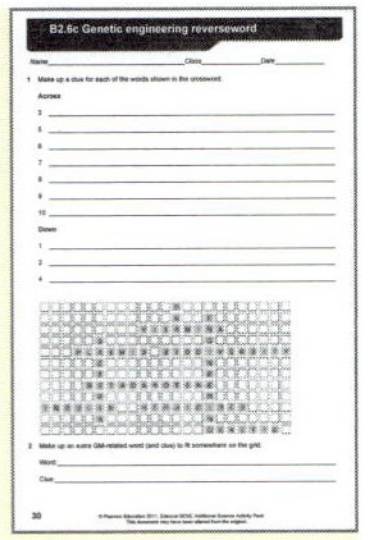

**Homework 1** Lit

**Worksheet B2.6c** requires students to make up clues for key words in a crossword.

**Support** Provide an example, e.g. a clue for Vitamin A might be 'Helps the immune system to work properly.'

### Really useful

**Starter 2**

Ask students to design a bacterium, plant or animal that is capable of doing something useful that similar organisms cannot do. Challenge students to say how they might go about making such an organism and introduce the idea that genes from some organisms can be added to others in a process called genetic engineering (also called genetic modification).

### Attitudes to GMOs

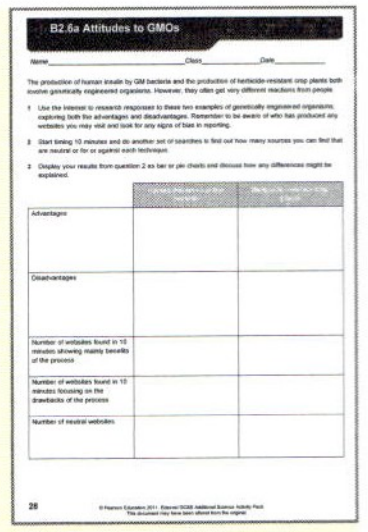

**Exploring 2**

Using **Worksheet B2.6a** students carry out a research exercise looking at different attitudes to the use of genetically engineered bacteria for the production of human insulin and the production of genetically engineered herbicide resistant plants.

**Stretch** Ask students to try to explain why different people/websites have the different opinions that they have identified.

**Support** Provide some examples of bias in reporting GMOs, so that students know what to look out for.

### Debating GM foods

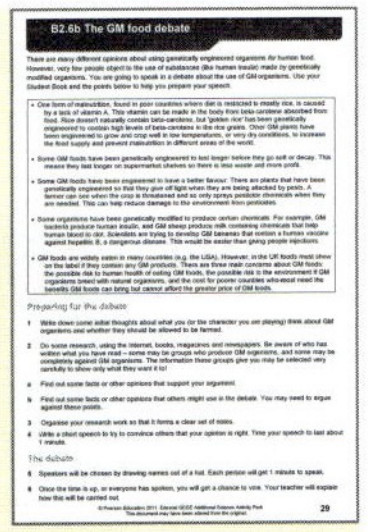

**Explaining 1**

Students use the textbook and the information on **Worksheet B2.6b** to put together a one-minute speech either supporting or disagreeing with the use of genetically engineered organisms.

**Stretch** Students should include further examples to support their arguments.

**Support** Students develop arguments for or against genetic engineering of organisms – Skill Sheet **6** may be useful. They could produce a poster with the pros and cons shown.

### Checking definitions

**Plenary 2** Lit

Students should write a short dictionary definition of 'genetic engineering'. If time allows they could check their definition against the glossary and the definitions given in other dictionaries.

### GMOs: a summary

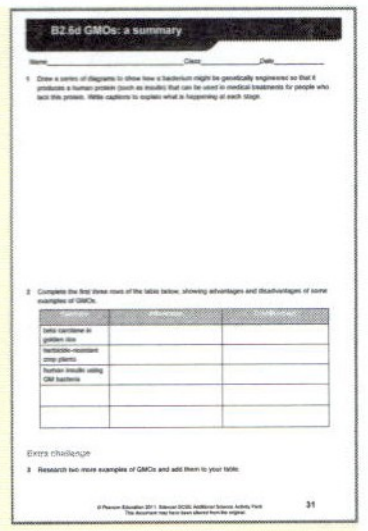

**Homework 2**

**Worksheet B2.6d** covers the process of genetic engineering as well as the advantages and disadvantages of the examples of GMOs in the specification.

**Stretch** Students answer the 'extra challenge' question.

# B2.6 Genetic engineering

How can we best use genetic engineering?

To show that a genetically engineered characteristic can be passed on from parents to their offspring, the pigs in Figure A were genetically engineered so their trotters glowed green in UV light. When they bred naturally, piglets with green-glowing trotters was born.

1 What is genetic engineering?

2 Why are enzymes important in genetic engineering?

Scientists can remove a gene from one organism and insert it into the DNA of another organism. This process is called **genetic engineering**. For example, scientists have inserted the gene for human insulin into bacterial plasmid DNA. The genetically modified (GM) bacteria can then make human insulin, which is used by people with diabetes. Organisms like these bacteria are known as **genetically modified organisms (GMOs)**.

A *Genetically engineered pigs – their trotters glow in UV light (top).*

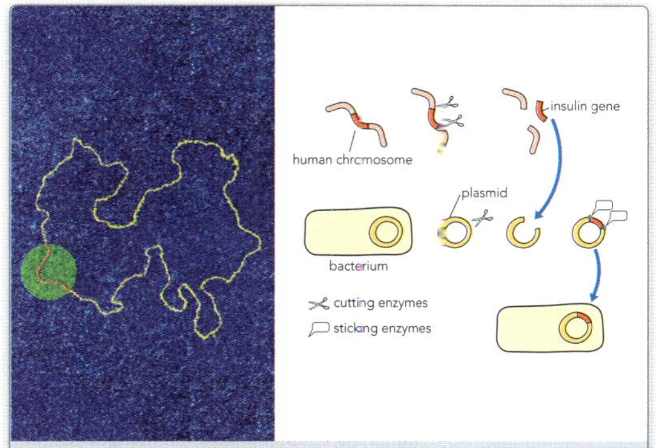


B *Genetic engineering – the green circle in the photo on the left shows the extra bit of DNA that has been added to this bacterial plasmid; the diagram shows the process of adding a human insulin gene to a bacterial plasmid.*

The production of human insulin by genetically modified (GM) bacteria has many advantages. Insulin used to be extracted from dead cattle and pigs but insulin from GM bacteria can now be used by vegans. It also means that the supply of insulin is not affected by animal diseases or the numbers of animals slaughtered for meat. Using bacteria in fermenters, insulin can be made in vast quantities and can be made more cheaply. The one slight disadvantage is that as bacteria produce the insulin slightly differently there are minute differences and it does not suit everyone.

Plants and animals can also be genetically engineered. For example, **golden rice** plants are normal rice plants that have had two extra genes inserted so that they make **beta-carotene** in the grains. Beta-carotene is needed by humans to produce vitamin A. A lack of vitamin A can cause death because the immune system does not work properly. It can also cause blindness.

However, some people are concerned that the GM rice will crossbreed with wild rice plants and contaminate the wild rice DNA. Others worry that eating GM organisms might harm people (although there is no evidence of this). Some people say the levels of beta-carotene in golden rice are not high enough to make much difference to children's health. GMOs can also be expensive to buy and some are made so that they do not produce fertile seed (meaning farmers have to buy new seed each year).

C *Beta-carotene makes wild rice (left) yellow (right).*

Scientists have added genes to some plants to make them **herbicide** resistant. This can reduce the amount of crop spraying needed because the farmer can use one much heavier spray of herbicide rather than several smaller doses. There may be drawbacks, including the development of herbicide-resistant weeds as cross-pollination with wild plants takes place. There may also be a loss of **biodiversity** as fewer weeds survive, meaning loss of food and shelter for animals.

3 What is golden rice?

4 How would eating golden rice solve the problems caused by lack of vitamin A?

5 Make a flowchart to show the steps in the process of genetic engineering.

6 Make a table to show the advantages and disadvantages of GM golden rice.

**Skills spotlight**

Draw up a table to compare the benefits of GM human insulin compared to insulin taken from cattle and pigs slaughtered for meat.

7 a Explain the potential benefits of bacteria engineered to produce human insulin and of herbicide-resistant plants.

b Using the same examples as in part a, discuss some of the drawbacks of genetic engineering.

8 Write a piece for a campaign website, either *for* or *against* genetic engineering. You must explain the process and why it is done, and then give your own opinion.

**Learning Outcomes**

*1.11* Demonstrate an understanding of the process of genetic engineering, including the removal of a gene from the DNA of one organism and the insertion of that gene into the DNA of another organism

*1.12* Discuss the advantages and disadvantages of genetic engineering to produce GM organisms, including:
- *a* beta-carotene in golden rice to reduce vitamin A deficiency in humans
- *b* the production of human insulin by genetically modified bacteria
- *c* the production of herbicide-resistant crop plants

HSW *12* Describe the use of contemporary science and technological developments and their benefits, drawbacks and risks



Why do cancers form lumps? 39

## ActiveTeach

- **AT** *Genetically modified crops* [interactive]
  GM crops in the UK – debating activity

## Answers | Student Book

1 Scientists can remove a gene from one organism and insert it into the DNA of another organism.

2 Used to cut out the desired gene, cut open the host DNA, and join the new gene with the host DNA.

3 Genetically engineered rice that makes beta-carotene in the grains. Beta carotene makes the rice yellow in colour.

4 Golden rice contains high levels of beta carotene. The body uses beta carotene to make vitamin A. Plenty of beta carotene in the diet means plenty of vitamin A in the body.

5 Flowchart should include the transfer of a small amount of DNA from a cell of one organism to the DNA in a cell of a different species.

6 See full answer table in TTPP.

7 (H) a Bacteria producing human insulin: the substance is vital to the people who use it; it is pure; it is the human version of insulin rather than the animal version; no need to rely on animal products, which were variable in supply; cheap; any other sensible points. Herbicide-resistant crop plants: apply one strong herbicide to get rid of all the weeds; no need to spray so often, reducing herbicide costs and lowering the environmental impact of farming.
**b** Bacteria producing human insulin: any point based on ethical problems with genetic engineering.
Herbicide-resistant crop plants could: crossbreed with wild plants and produce herbicide-resistant weeds; reduce biodiversity; lead to the need for more spraying; any other sensible point.

8 A good answer will contain the following points: DNA removed from donor cell; plasmid DNA opened out; gene from donor added to plasmid DNA; DNA joined together again; done so that a useful protein from a donor can be made by the bacterial DNA; students should give an opinion.

**Skills spotlight**

**Advantages**: DNA is less likely to be rejected; there is no need to kill animals to obtain it; the supply is more reliable; it is cheaper and cleaner. **Disadvantages**: it cannot be used by everyone.

# B2.7 Mitosis and meiosis



This lesson introduces students to mitosis and meiosis and the roles that the different types of cell division play in growth and reproduction.

## Specification coverage

***1.13*** Describe the division of a cell by mitosis as the production of two daughter cells, each with identical sets of chromosomes in the nucleus to the parent cell, and that this results in the formation of two genetically identical diploid body cells

***1.14*** Recall that mitosis occurs during growth, repair and asexual reproduction

***1.15*** Recall that, at fertilisation, haploid gametes combine to form a diploid zygote

***1.16*** Describe the division of a cell by meiosis as the production of four daughter cells, each with half the number of chromosomes, and that this results in the formation of genetically different haploid gametes

**HSW** ***11*** Presenting information, developing an argument *and drawing a conclusion*, using scientific, *technical and mathematical* language, conventions and *symbols, and ICT tools*

There are also opportunities to cover **HSW** *3*.

### Life cycles

**Starter 1**

Ask students to roughly sketch a human life cycle, showing stages such as adult, baby, egg and sperm. Ask them to add labels to show processes such as birth, growth and fertilisation. Take suggestions from around the class for the meaning of each process and discuss any differences in definitions. The life cycle drawings could be revisited in *Plenary 1*.

### Mitosis and meiosis diagrams

**Exploring 1**

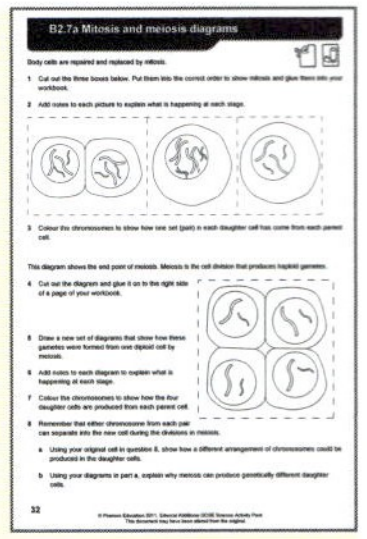
B2.7a Mitosis and meiosis diagrams

The diagrams in **Worksheet B2.7a** will help students prepare their own flowcharts for the processes of mitosis and meiosis.

**Stretch** Ask students to include a reference to different alleles for the same gene on a chromosome pair in order to explain as fully as they can at this stage how meiosis produces genetically different daughter cells.

**Support** Students could use Figures B and D to help them prepare their flowcharts. For meiosis, copy the image of the parent cell from mitosis as a starting point.

### Sexual and asexual reproduction

**Exploring 3**

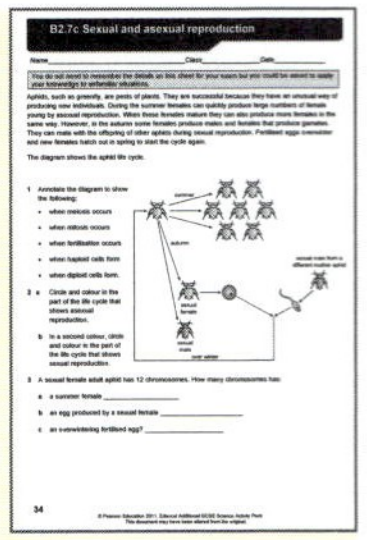
B2.7c Sexual and asexual reproduction

**Worksheet B2.7c** provides a diagram of an aphid life cycle, which students annotate to show when different types of reproduction occur.

**Stretch** Remove the diagram from the sheet and ask students to draw their own diagram of the life cycle using the information given at the top of the sheet.

**Support** Remind students of the differences between meiosis and mitosis before they start the sheets, by having the glossary to refer to.

### Life cycles revisited

**Plenary 1** **AfL**

Ask students to add anything that they have learnt to the diagram of a human life cycle that they drew for *Starter 1*. Take examples of additions from around the class to make sure that all the key points from the lesson have been covered.

### Reproduction crossword

**Homework 1**

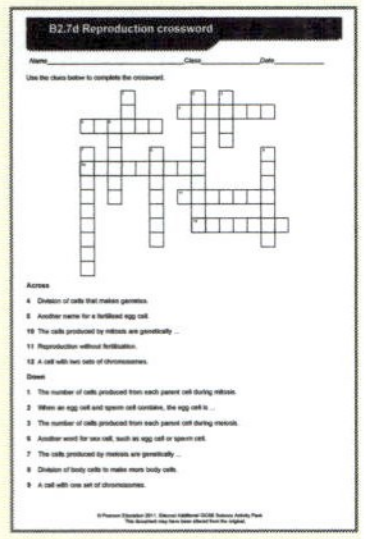
B2.7d Reproduction crossword

**Worksheet B2.7d** contains a crossword that will help them revise many of the key words learnt in this lesson.

**Support** Provide students with a list of the answer words to help complete the crossword.

### What's the difference?

**Starter 2** **Lit**

Ask students to discuss and write down the key difference between the following pairs of words: gene, allele; chromosome, DNA; reproduction, growth. Take examples from around the class for discussion.

### Root tip squash

**Exploring 2** **Prac**

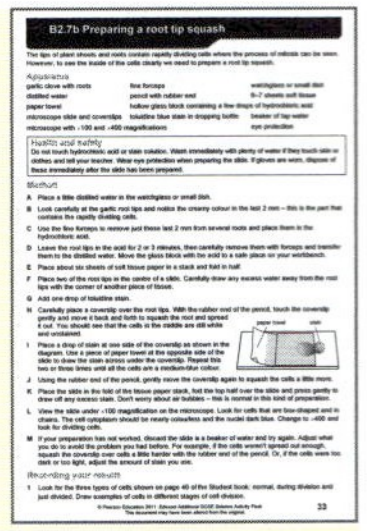
B2.7b Preparing a root tip squash

In **Worksheet B2.7b** students examine a microscope slide of a root tip squash to view cells during mitotic division. Full details are given on the Teacher and technician practical sheet B2.7.

**Stretch** Students calculate the field of view under different lenses and estimate the size of cells.

**Support** Use a digital microscope to identify cells at different stages of division.

### Student Book spread B2.7

**Explaining 1** **Lit**

Discuss with students the differences between 'haploid' and 'diploid'.

**Stretch** Students could try to answer the question 'Why do animals generally reproduce sexually?' through research and/or class discussion.

**Support** To help describe duplication of chromosomes during cell division, show students a clothes peg from which the spring has been removed. From one side it will look like a 'one-chromatid chromosome', but turned to the wider side it will look like two chromatids, which can then be divided into two separate chromosomes.

### Which kind of division? (AT)

**Plenary 2** **AfL**

Ask students to write the words 'mitosis' and 'meiosis' on separate scraps of paper. The **AT** document *Cell division* contains a list of statements about cell division. Read each statement out in turn and ask students to hold up the name of the correct process.

### Mitosis and meiosis questions

**Homework 2**

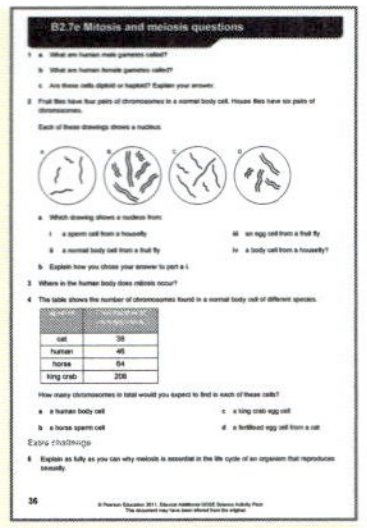
B2.7e Mitosis and meiosis questions

**Worksheet B2.7e** contains a set of questions that will test students' understanding of this lesson.

**Stretch** Ask students to do the 'extra challenge' question.

# B2.7 Mitosis and meiosis

What are mitosis and meiosis?

Cells usually send signals to each other to stop dividing when there are enough of them. Cancer cells don't respond – they just keep dividing. Scientists are investigating the use of GM bacteria to transport proteins into cancer cells to kill the cancer cells.

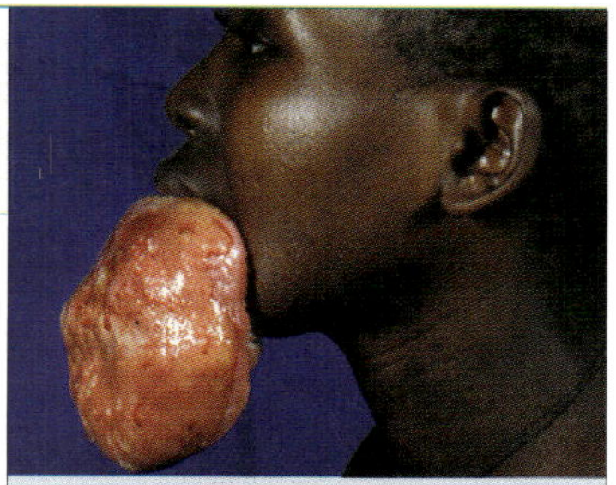

A A cancer is caused by uncontrolled cell division.

## Mitosis

Most of the cells in your body contain a nucleus, and most nuclei contain two copies of each chromosome. This makes them **diploid** cells. Human diploid cells contain two sets of 23 chromosomes. Body cells (all cells except sperm and egg cells) are diploid.

1 Explain what is meant by a diploid cell.

2 Using Figure B, describe as fully as you can what happens during mitosis.

To make more body cells, during **growth** or to replace damaged cells, body cells divide using a process called **mitosis**. This process begins with the chromosomes making copies of themselves in a process called **DNA replication**. The copies of the chromosomes separate and the cell then divides. This produces two **daughter cells**, which are genetically identical to each other and to the **parent cell**.

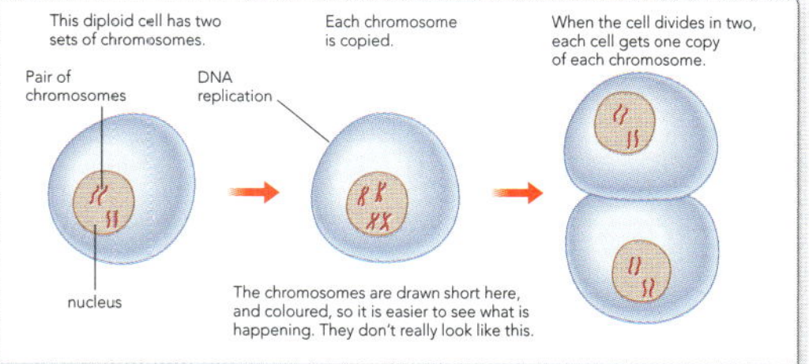


B During mitosis, one cell divides to form two identical daughter cells.

3 How many parents does an individual have in organisms that reproduce by:
a asexual reproduction
b sexual reproduction?

## Different kinds of reproduction

Mitosis can produce new, complete individuals in a process called **asexual reproduction**. Bacteria cells often do this by splitting in half. Some plants reproduce asexually by making new plantlets attached to the parent plant, which then split off to grow on their own.

In many organisms a different process called **sexual reproduction** produces new individuals. This requires two sex cells or **gametes**. These are different to body cells in that they only contain one set of chromosomes, so these are **haploid** cells. The two gametes fuse during **fertilisation** and produce a diploid cell called a **zygote**. The zygote develops into a ball of cells (an **embryo**).

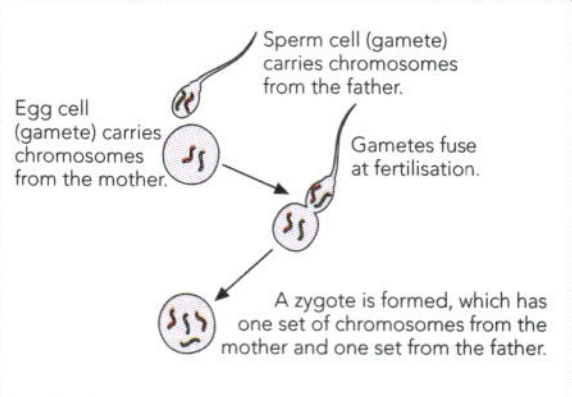


C A diploid zygote cell is formed during fertilisation.

4 What is the process in which a zygote develops into an embryo?

**ResultsPlus Watch Out!**

Students often confuse the spelling of mitosis and meiosis. The words look similar but they describe very different processes. Remember: Mi2osis for *two* sets of chromosomes, Me1osis for *one* set of chromosomes.

## Gamete formation

A different kind of cell division called **meiosis** is needed to produce haploid gametes. Meiosis also starts with DNA replication, but this is then followed by *two* cell divisions. The first separates the two sets of chromosomes and the second separates the copies of each chromosome. This produces four haploid daughter cells, each containing one set of chromosomes.

In a diploid cell, each chromosome in a pair contains the same genes but may have different versions of those genes (**alleles**). So the chromosomes in a pair are slightly different. In meiosis, these slightly different chromosomes are split between the daughter cells in a random way to produce gametes that are genetically different from each other.

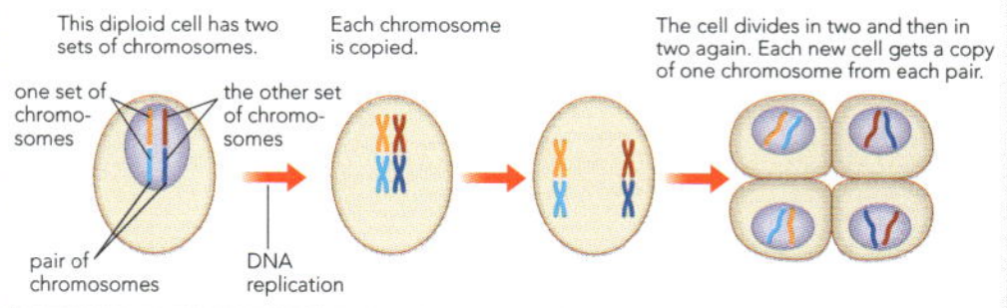


D During meiosis, one diploid cell forms four haploid cells.

**Skills spotlight**

Scientists present information in diagrams to help explain the relationship between processes. Draw a flowchart of a human life cycle and mark the presence of diploid and haploid cells in the cycle. Identify when mitosis and meiosis occur to produce these cells.

5 Draw up a table to summarise the similarities and differences between mitosis and meiosis.

6 Are all the body's cells genetically identical or not? Explain your answer.

**Learning Outcomes**

1.13 Describe the division of a cell by mitosis as the production of two daughter cells, each with identical sets of chromosomes in the nucleus as the parent cell, and that this results in the formation of two genetically identical diploid body cells

1.14 Recall that mitosis occurs during growth, repair, and asexual reproduction

1.15 Recall that, at fertilisation, haploid gametes combine to form a diploid zygote

1.16 Describe the division of a cell by meiosis as the production of four daughter cells, each with half the number of chromosomes, and that this results in the formation of genetically different haploid gametes

HSW 11 Present information using scientific conventions and symbols



Would it be a good idea to make copies of your favourite pet?



## ActiveTeach

- **AT** *Mitosis and meiosis* [interactive]
  Key stages mitosis/meiosis – sorting activity
- **AT** *Cell mitosis* [diagram]
  Figure B – diagram labelling activity
- **AT** *Cell meiosis* [diagram]
  Figure D – diagram labelling activity
- **AT** *Cell division* [word document]
  Match statements to processes

## Key terms

allele
asexual reproduction
daughter cell
diploid
DNA replication
embryo
fertilisation
gamete
growth
haploid
meiosis
mitosis
parent cell
sexual reproduction
zygote

## Answers | Student Book

1 A cell that contains two sets of chromosomes.

2 In a body cell before mitosis, all the chromosomes are copied. During division the copies of each chromosome move to opposite sides of the cell, and the cell divides in two to produce two identical cells.

3 **a** One **b** Two

4 Mitosis

5

| | Mitosis | Meiosis |
|---|---|---|
| Number of cells formed from one cell | 2 | 4 |
| Number of sets of chromosomes in daughter cells | 2 | 1 |
| Processes division is needed for | Growth, repair, asexual reproduction | Producing gametes |
| Are daughter cells identical or not? | Yes | No |

6 A good answer will contain the following points: all the diploid cells in the body should be genetically identical; this is because they have been produced by mitosis from the single cell of the zygote; however, haploid cells contain only half the genetic information that is found in a diploid body cell; it would also be reasonable to mention that mutation during cell division may mean body cells are not completely identical, but this answer is not expected.

**Skills spotlight**

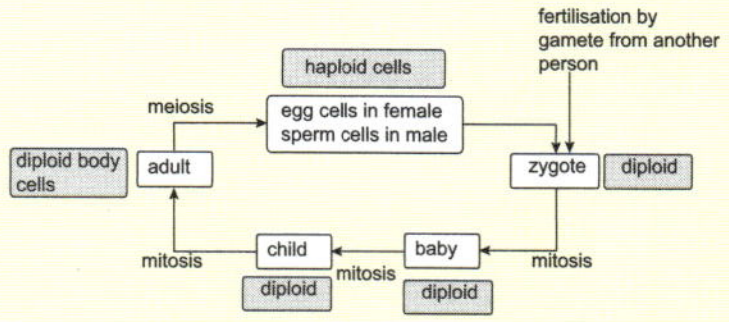

# B2.8 Clones



This lesson extends the work on asexual reproduction to describe clones and explore some of the problems and advantages of cloning. The process of cell nuclear transfer for cloning of mammals is described in more detail for more able students.

## Specification coverage

***1.17*** Recall that cloning is an example of asexual reproduction that produces genetically identical copies

***1.18*** H Demonstrate an understanding of the stages in the production of cloned mammals, including: a) removal of diploid nucleus from a body cell b) enucleation of egg cell c) insertion of diploid nucleus into enucleated egg cell d) stimulation of the diploid nucleus to divide by mitosis e) implantation into surrogate mammals

***1.19*** Demonstrate an understanding of the advantages, disadvantages and risks of cloning mammals

HSW ***12*** The use of contemporary science and technological developments and their benefits, drawbacks and risks

There are also opportunities to cover HSW *3* and HSW *13*.

## Key terms

clone
H enucleate
implant
surrogate mother
uterus

### Reproduction confidence

**Starter 1** AfL

As students come into class, give each one a sticky note. Ask them to write down three things they learned about asexual and sexual reproduction from the last lesson, give a confidence rating to their understanding of each of their statements. Pick five statements that have low confidence ratings and throw a related question to the whole class. These points can be picked up on in this lesson.

### The pros and cons of cloning

**Exploring 1**

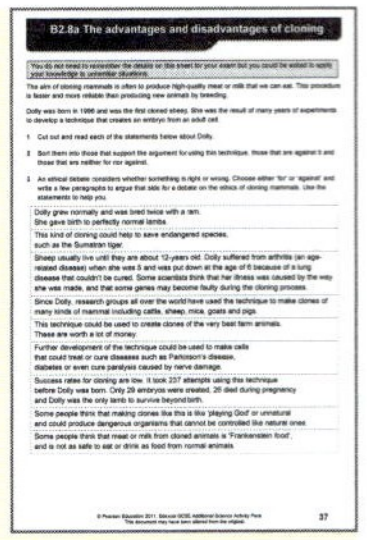

**Worksheet B2.8a** provides a set of statements that present some of the advantages and disadvantages of cloning animals.

Stretch Students further research the advantages and disadvantages of cloning, including finding examples other than Dolly, to evaluate whether the problems encountered in Dolly's case are universal or just chance.

Support Students sort the statements and canvass other students as to whether they are for or against animal cloning.

### Student Book spread B2.8 (AT)

**Explaining 1**

Students suggest which characteristics the puppies may have that are identical to the parent and which characteristics may vary.

Stretch Ask students to consider what a cloned human might feel, and to write a diary entry for a cloned human who has just found out how he/she was made.

Support Give students the questions in the **AT** document *Cloning questions* to complete to help them see various sides of the cloning argument.

### Cloning brainstorm

**Plenary 1** AfL

Ask pupils to jot down as many facts about cloning as they can and then organise their ideas in a more systematic way (e.g. benefits, drawbacks and risks). A spokesperson for each group should then share with the class how their group has organised the information and what information they know.

### Questions of cloning (AT)

**Homework 1**

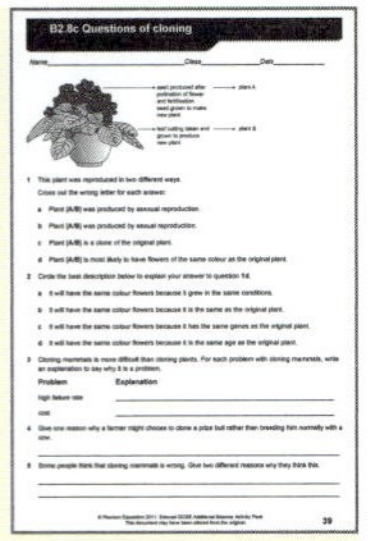

**Worksheet B2.8c** presents a series of questions that test learning of the Foundation tier material in this lesson.

Support Provide the **AT** document *Some cloning answers*. Students should select from these to help them answer questions **3–5**.

### What is a clone?

**Starter 2** Lit

Write the word 'clone' in the middle of the board, and ask students to suggest related words and how they should be linked to make a concept map. It is possible at this point that they can only offer information they have learnt from films and the media, but this can be revisited in *Plenary 2* at the end of the lesson to explore misconceptions from these sources.

### Growing plant clones

**Exploring 2** Prac

**Worksheet B2.8b** is a practical on taking plant cuttings that introduces the idea of clones. Full details can be found on the Teacher and technician practical sheet B2.8.

Stretch Ask students to explain fully how this investigation clarifies which characteristics are genetically determined and which are partly or wholly controlled by the environment.

Support Ask students to describe the method for producing plant clones as a series of bullet points.

### H Sequencing the cloning method (AT)

**Explaining 2**

A series of statements are provided on the **AT** document *Cloning*. Present these on the board and ask students to sequence them in the correct order to describe the process of cloning by the method used to produce Copycat and Dolly.

Stretch Ask students to write two paragraphs about the difference between 'natural breeding' and cloning. They should include the terms 'haploid', 'diploid' and 'fertilisation'.

### What is a clone? – revisited

**Plenary 2** AfL Lit

Revisit the concept map produced in *Starter 1* and ask students to amend anything that they got wrong then, and to add anything new that they have learnt in this lesson. If appropriate to your students, consider comparing the media view of cloning with the scientific view to identify differences and suggest reasons why these differences may occur.

### Cloning Snuppy

**Homework 2**

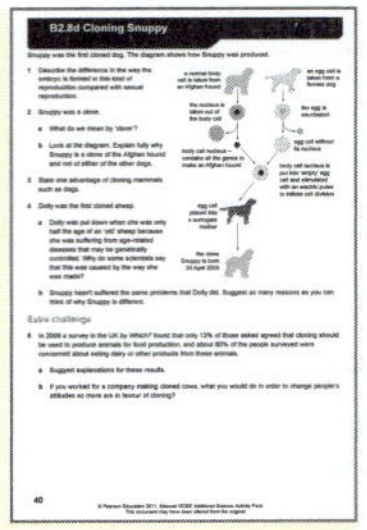

Worksheet B2.8d provides a series of questions to test learning on all aspects of this lesson, including Higher Tier questions.

Stretch Ask students to do the 'extra challenge' question.

# B2.8 Clones

How are organisms cloned?

In 2008 Bernann McKinney paid £25 000 to have her pet dog Booger cloned. She had to sell her home so that she could pay for the process, in which skin cells from Booger developed to produce five puppy clones.

A *Booger's clones*

B *Leaf cuttings taken from a plant produce new plant clones.*

**Clones** are individuals that are genetically identical. Making plant clones can be easy – you start with a bit of leaf, stem or root from the original plant. The plant cells divide and produce new cells, which grow into a clone of the original plant. This is an example of asexual reproduction.

1 What is a clone?

2 Are new plants from cuttings produced by meiosis or mitosis? Explain your answer.

## Benefits, drawbacks and risks of cloning mammals

It is much more difficult to clone animals than plants – it is not possible to make a whole new animal from an arm or leg. The first clone produced in a lab of a vertebrate was a frog, and was made in 1952. However, the first cloned large animal (a sheep called Dolly) wasn't produced until 1996 because of difficulties with the process.

Unfortunately, very few embryos produced during animal cloning develop successfully. Dolly was the only lamb produced after 237 cloning attempts. Dolly also seemed to grow older much more quickly than normal and died young. Scientists aren't sure if her health problems were caused by being a clone or by chance.

Cloning is useful to make a genetically identical copy of an adult organism that has desirable characteristics. For example, bulls whose sperm produces high-quality calves are valuable and so are worth cloning. Cloning is also used to produce copies of individuals with a genetically engineered trait, such as cows engineered to produce human insulin in their milk, because this will guarantee that all the offspring will have the engineered trait.

C *Cloned puppies of South Korea's best sniffer dog are being tested to see if they are as successful as their parent.*

3 Give a benefit of cloning animals.

4 What are some of the drawbacks and risks of cloning animals?

## How to clone a mammal

There are different ways of producing cloned animals, but currently the most successful method uses a process called nuclear transfer. The nucleus of a body cell of the animal to be cloned is transferred into an **enucleated** egg cell (one that has had its original nucleus removed). The cell is then stimulated to start dividing to form an embryo. This is **implanted** into the **uterus** (womb) of a **surrogate mother** who is a different individual to the parent. Here it will grow and develop into a new individual.

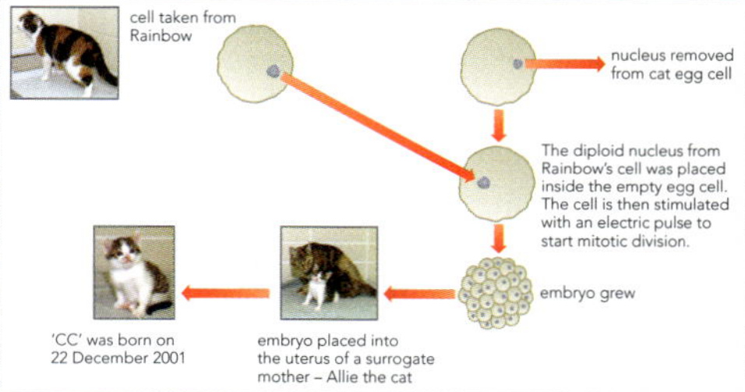


D *CC (Copycat) was the first kitten to be produced by nuclear transfer.*

**Skills spotlight**

New scientific developments usually have drawbacks and risks as well as benefits. What are the benefits, drawbacks and risks of using cloned bulls for breeding programmes?

**ResultsPlus Watch Out!**

Students often panic if they see an unfamiliar example in the exam. You will be expected to apply what you know about cloning to examples of different animals and plants. Remember that asexual reproduction produces clones.

H 5 Review Figure D and explain the roles of Rainbow and Allie in the production of the kitten called CC, and explain which adult CC is a clone of.

H 6 Describe as fully as you can the stages in producing a cloned mammal.

7 An internet forum has this question on it: 'I have produced many of my African violet plants from a single plant by taking cuttings. My wonderful pet dog, Bruno, is getting old and I've heard that scientists can do similar things to dogs. Does this work and what are the risks?' Write an answer to this question.

**Learning Outcomes**

1.17 Recall that cloning is an example of asexual reproduction that produces genetically identical copies

H 1.18 Demonstrate an understanding of the stages in the production of cloned mammals, including:
- a removal of diploid nucleus from a body cell
- b enucleation of egg cell
- c insertion of diploid nucleus into enucleated egg cell
- d stimulation of the diploid nucleus to divide by mitosis
- e implantation into surrogate mammals

1.19 Demonstrate an understanding of the advantages, disadvantages and risks of cloning mammals

HSW 12 Describe the benefits, drawbacks and risks of using new scientific and technological developments





## ActiveTeach

- **AT** *How to clone an animal* [interactive]
  The process of cloning – ordering activity
- **AT** *Cloning* [word document]
  Cell nuclear transfer
- **AT** *Cloning questions* [word document]
  Cloze questions
- **AT** *Some cloning answers* [word document]
  Possible question answers

## Answers | Student Book

1 An organism that is genetically identical to its parent or to other siblings.

2 Mitosis – asexual reproduction

3 Makes genetically identical copies of animals that have useful characteristics.

4 Difficult to do, so needs to be tried many times before it is successful. Cloned animal may not be as healthy as normal. May not have all the desired characteristics, as some such as size or temperament, are partially controlled by the environment.

5 H Rainbow is the genetic mother of CC; it is her chromosomes that were copied. Allie is the surrogate mother; she gave birth to CC. CC is a clone of Rainbow; she has the same chromosomes.

6 H Nucleus is taken from a body cell of the organism to be cloned. An egg cell from that species is enucleated and the nucleus of the animal to be cloned is inserted into the egg cell. The egg cell is stimulated with an electric pulse to divide to form an embryo. The embryo is placed into the uterus of a surrogate mother to develop fully until it is born.

7 A good answer will contain the following points: Cloning a pet costs a lot of money as the process is difficult; the clone may look like the original pet, but factors affected by the environment could be different, so the clone may not be like the original pet; the clone will have the same genetically-controlled problems as it has the same chromosomes; the cloned pet may die early of early aging conditions due to cloning; the suffering caused leads to ethical concerns.

**Skills spotlight**

**Benefits**: The farmer will be able to sell more sperm that he or she knows will produce high quality calves. Other farmers will be prepared to pay more money for fertilising their cows using sperm from a top quality bull.
**Drawbacks:** The calves from the cloned bulls will all be very similar genetically, so there will be less variation in a herd, and if any of the calves suffers from a genetically-related illness, the others may all do so too.
**Risks:** The cloning process could affect the cloned bulls in some way, making them more prone to illness or reducing their life expectancy.

# B2.9 Stem cells



This lesson covers the sources of stem cells, their potential uses and some of the problems that their use creates both from a scientific aspect and an ethical standpoint.

## Specification coverage

***1.19*** Demonstrate an understanding of the advantages, disadvantages and risks of cloning mammals

***1.20*** Recall that stem cells in the embryo can differentiate into all other types of cells, but that cells lose this ability as the animal matures

***1.21*** Demonstrate an understanding of the advantages, disadvantages and risks arising from adult and embryonic stem cell research

**HSW** *13* How and why decisions about science and technology are made, including those that raise ethical issues, and about the social, *economic and environmental* effects of such decisions

There are also opportunities to cover **HSW** *12*.

## Key terms

adult stem cell
differentiated
embryonic stem cell
stem cell

### Different kinds of cells

**Starter 1** AfL

Give students two minutes to jot down as many different kinds of cell in their body as they can think of. Take a selection from around the class and then ask how those cells came to be. Try to elicit the idea that they all came originally from the division and subsequent specialisation of cells that look alike in the embryo.

### The use of embryos for stem cell research (AT)

**Exploring 1** Lit

**Worksheet B2.9a** presents a set of different viewpoints on the use of human embryos for stem cell research.

**Stretch** Students choose three different viewpoints and prepare arguments based on each.

**Support** A series of statements is provided on the **AT** document *Points of view* for this activity. Students match the statements to the points of view given in the worksheet, giving reasons for each match.

### Student Book spread B2.9

**Explaining 1**

Explain the differences between embryonic stem cells and adult stem cells, both in their source and their potential. Follow this with a discussion of the advantages, disadvantages and risks of using each kind of stem cell in research for treatment of diseases.

**Stretch** Ask students to consider the difficulties for the law and for ethical debate in areas of rapidly developing science research such as stem cells.

**Support** Prepare a table with the headings 'Advantages' 'Disadvantages' 'Risks' and work with students to complete it using the information in the Student Book.

### How useful are stem cells?

**Plenary 1** AfL

Ask students to produce three different answers to the question 'How useful are stem cells?' Allow three minutes and then take examples from around the class. For each answer, ask students to categorise it as a benefit or a drawback or risk of using the technique.

### Using stem cells

**Homework 1**

**Worksheet B2.9c** contains questions that cover the key points of this lesson.

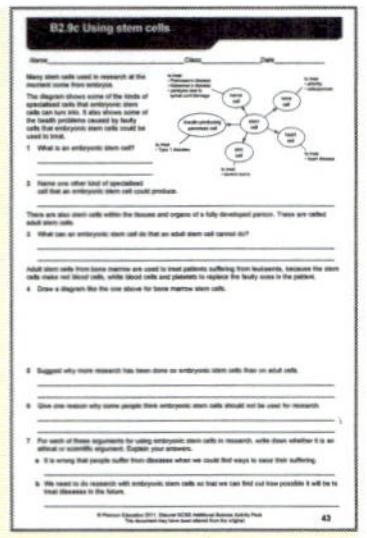


**Support** Tell students that they need not attempt question **5**.

### Human cloning

**Starter 2** AfL

Remind students about what they learnt in the last lesson about cloning mammals. Ask them to consider how this technique could be applied to humans. Give them three minutes to jot down three questions that they would like answered or concerns that they might have over producing human clones like this. Take examples from around the class.

### Researching treatments with stem cells

**Exploring 2**

**Worksheet B2.9b** describes four sources of stem cells and asks students to carry out research that extends their knowledge of the advantages, disadvantages and risks of using stem cells from each source.

**Stretch** Students do the research without reference to the sheet, identifying sources of stem cells on their own.

**Support** Ask students to only consider two of the stem cell sources.

### Stem cell videos (AT)

**Explaining 2**

Find a video on the Internet (e.g. *YouTube*) that explains what stem cells are. Or use the three videos on the **AT**. The **AT** document *Stem cell video questions* provides questions for students to use with the videos.

**Stretch** Ask students to explain how the extension of the technique for producing cloned mammals discussed in the last lesson has made possible the production of embryonic stem cells for use in treatments.

**Support** Students could use the alternative set of supported questions in the **AT** document *Stem cell questions*.

### Concept map

**Plenary 2** AfL Lit

Write the terms 'adult stem cell' and 'embryonic stem cell' on the board and ask students to suggest related words and how they should link to produce a concept map for the lesson.

### New ways and new problems

**Homework 2**

**Worksheet B2.9d** introduces new areas of research into techniques and problems caused by the use of stem cells.

**Stretch** Ask students to do the 'extra challenge' question.

# B2.9 Stem cells

How are stem cells useful?

The girl in Figure A is Cady, who was killed in a car crash in 2002. After her death, Dr Panayiotis Zavos took some of her cells and stored them. He wants to use them to create a cloned embryo and bring to life a person who is genetically identical to Cady.

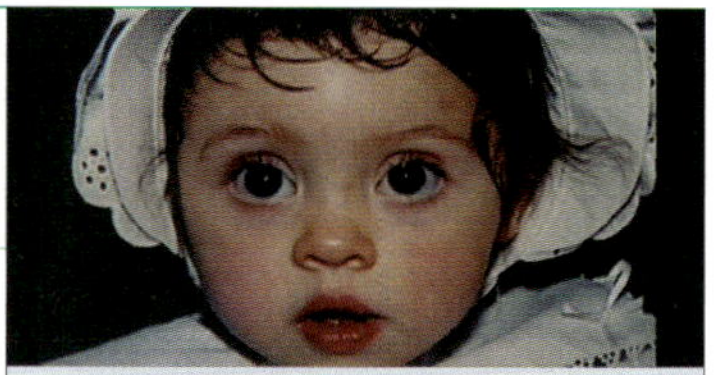

**A** *Cady – a girl that Dr Panayiotis Zavos wants to bring back to life.*

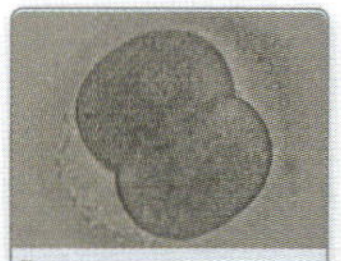

**B** *A human embryo produced from a cloned adult cell.*

In most countries trying to produce cloned humans is illegal. However, in the UK scientists can produce cloned human embryos for research but these embryos must be killed after 14 days.

There is a lot of interest in human embryos because when they are a few days old the cells in them are **embryonic stem cells**.

When a **stem cell** divides it can produce more stem cells or it can produce other types of cells that are specialised or **differentiated** (e.g. neurones, muscle cells, skin cells). Once a cell has differentiated it cannot turn into another type of cell. Stem cells in differentiated body tissues (**adult stem cells**) can only differentiate into a few types of cell. However, embryonic stem cells can develop into almost every type of human cell.

One way of collecting embryonic stem cells is to use leftover embryos created for couples having fertility treatment. However, when the embryonic stem cells are extracted, the embryo is killed, so this procedure is controversial. That's why scientists are interested in using adult cells to make cloned embryos.

1 Explain the meanings of these terms:
a differentiate
b stem cell.

2 Name four different kinds of differentiated cell in the body.

3 Describe two sources of stem cells.

**C** *Some people think that because human embryos are potential people, destroying them is murder.*

## Stem cell treatments

Since the 1960s, adult stem cells from bone marrow have been used to treat leukaemia (a cancer of certain white blood cells). The patient's white blood cells are destroyed and adult stem cells from someone else are put into the patient. These cells then multiply and produce new, healthy white blood cells. This is known as a bone marrow transplant. The treatment does not always work because the body destroys cells from other people if they are too different.

This problem may be solved using cloning. If a cloned embryo is created using a skin cell from a person with leukaemia, the embryonic stem cells can be taken and used to produce the cells that make white blood cells. These will survive inside the patient because their body will recognise them as their own cells.

Since embryonic stem cells can turn into nearly every type of human cell, these cells could be used to treat many more problems than adult stem cells could. However, this technique could also be used illegally by people like Dr Zavos to produce human clones.

Scientists have started to investigate ways of turning differentiated body cells into stem cells by reprogramming them. If this works, it will help avoid the ethical problem of using embryos. But further research is still needed to make any treatment with stem cells safe because if they are injected into a body they may produce the wrong kind of cell or even create cancer cells.

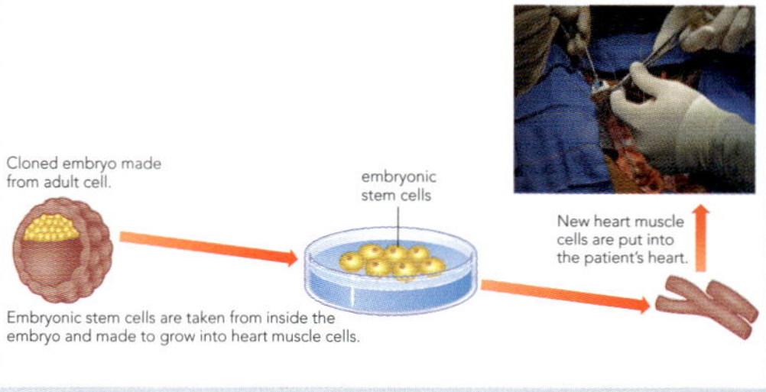


**D** *Embryonic stem cells could be used to treat many medical problems.*

**ResultsPlus Watch Out!**

Students often confuse adult and embryonic stem cells. Make sure you learn the difference and are clear in your answers which sort of stem cell you are writing about. Embryonic stem cells can develop into almost any type of cell.

**Skills spotlight**

Science alone does not provide a method for making decisions about ethical issues. Even though scientists can use adult cells to make cloned embryos to get stem cells, is it right to use these embryos and destroy them?

4 Draw up a table to show the benefits, drawbacks and risks of using embryonic stem cells and adult stem cells to treat human disorders.

5 Compare and contrast the benefits and drawbacks of using embryonic stem cells and adult stem cells in research and treatment.

**Learning Outcomes**

1.19 Demonstrate an understanding of the advantages, disadvantages and risks of cloning mammals

1.20 Recall that stem cells in the embryo can differentiate into all other types of cells, but that cells lose this ability as the animal matures

1.21 Demonstrate an understanding of the advantages, disadvantages and risks arising from adult and embryonic stem cell research

HSW 13 Explain how and why decisions that raise ethical issues about uses of science and technology are made





## ActiveTeach

- **AT** *A tail of cell division* [video] Stem cell research: brittle stars
- **AT** *What we've found out about stem cells 1* [video] Information on stem cells Part 1
- **AT** *What we've found out about stem cells 2* [video] Information on stem cells Part 2
- **AT** *What we've found out about stem cells 3* [video] Information on stem cells Part 3
- **AT** *Embryonic stem cell use* [interactive] For or against? – debating activity
- **AT** *Stem cell video questions* [word document] Questions to answer
- **AT** *Points of view* [word document] Matching statements
- **AT** *Stem cell questions* [word document] Support questions

## Answers | Student Book

1 **a** To become different, as in different kinds of cell.
**b** A kind of cell that can produce other kinds of cell through division.

2 Heart cell, bone cell, nerve cell, blood cell, muscle cell, skin cell (many others possible).

3 Any two of: early embryo, umbilical cord of baby, adult stem cells from differentiated tissue, reprogrammed body cells, created from cloned embryos.

4 See the full answer in the TTPP.

5 A good answer will contain the following points: adult stem cells are not as easy to extract from tissue; research using embryonic stem cells is usually easier practically; embryonic stem cells can be obtained from embryos not used in IVF treatment, although this creates an ethical issue as the embryo is destroyed; many countries won't allow this, so research cannot be carried out legally; in other countries there are very strict laws about what research can and cannot be done with embryonic stem cells; embryonic stem cells can turn into nearly every type of human cell; adult stem cells can only produce a limited range of specialised cells.

**Skills spotlight**

The answer should reflect an understanding that different people have different views about right and wrong. For example, some people believe that a human embryo is equivalent to a living person. They will say that destroying an embryo is the same as killing a person, and therefore wrong. Many people think that a ball of a few cells don't have the same rights as a living person, and can see the potential benefits of treatments to cure diseases. They think this research is acceptable, even if embryos are destroyed.

# B2.10 Protein manufacture



This lesson explains how the DNA code is linked to the formation of proteins.
The processes of transcription and translation are described for Higher Tier students.

## Specification coverage

***1.22*** Describe how the order of bases in a section of DNA decides the order of amino acids in the protein

***1.23*** H Demonstrate an understanding of the stages of protein synthesis, including transcription and translation: a) the production of complementary mRNA strand in the nucleus b) the attachment of the mRNA to the ribosome c) the coding by triplets of bases (codons) in the mRNA for specific amino acids d) the transfer of amino acids to the ribosome by tRNA e) the linking of amino acids to form polypeptides

HSW ***3*** Many phenomena can be explained by developing and using scientific theories, *models* and ideas.

## Key terms

| | |
|---|---|
| amino acid | protein synthesis |
| base triplet | ribosome |
| codon | RNA |
| cytoplasm | transcription |
| genetic code | transfer RNA (tRNA) |
| messenger RNA (mRNA) | translation |
| polypeptide | uracil |

### Making sentences

**Starter 1** AfL

Ask students to create sentences that include three key words, e.g. gene, chromosome, protein; DNA, base, pair; structure, helix, strand. Take examples from around the class to assess what students remember from work on DNA structure earlier in this topic.

### Decoding messages

**Starter 2**

Write the letters EJTQOQUQOG on the board and ask students if they can work out what it means. Lead them to the idea that it is a code for something, which can be decoded. Similarly, the genetic code in DNA is decoded to form the string of amino acids in a protein.

### Modelling protein formation (AT)

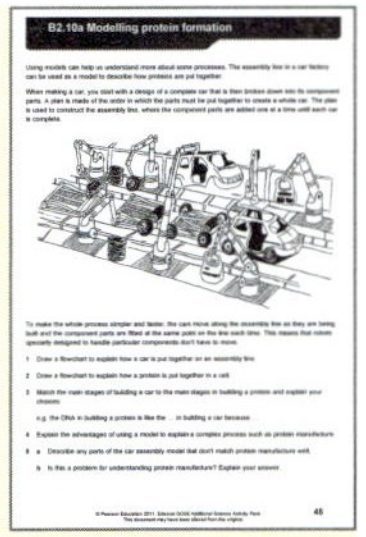


**Exploring 1**

**Worksheet B2.10a** links with the Skills spotlight for this lesson to explore the usefulness of the car factory model in explaining protein formation.

Stretch Students could extend the assembly model to show how it could explain the formation of different proteins on the same ribosome.

Support Give students copies of the cards in the **AT** document *Protein formation* to help them answer questions **1–3** on the worksheet.

### H Building proteins

**Exploring 2**

**Worksheet B2.10b** gives students the opportunity to transcribe a sequence of DNA bases and then translate them in order to build an amino acid chain.

Stretch Ask students to suggest why there are many checks made during transcription and translation to make sure the copying is accurate.

### H Looking at protein synthesis

**Exploring 3**

Ask students to storyboard an animation that helps explain the processes of DNA transcription and translation. Provide students with colour copies of Figure C in the Student Book to help with this. Students could then compare their storyboards with an animation on the Internet, and identify any weaknesses in their own storyboards that they could improve. Suitable animations can be found on the *Learn Genetics* website and *Wisc online*.

Stretch Students should compare several Internet animations to evaluate their effectiveness in presenting the key facts clearly.

### Student Book spread B2.10

**Explaining 1** Lit

Remind students that proteins are built from amino acids and that a gene is a piece of DNA that codes for a protein. Ask students to suggest how these two pieces of information link.

Stretch Ask students to find out about how mRNA may be modified after transcription but before translation, to remove exons, so that different proteins may be made from the same gene after translation.

Support Give students the set of cards from the **AT** document *Protein flowchart* to use as a basis for their own flowchart.

### Sure, unsure, know more

**Plenary 1** AfL

Ask students to write down one thing about protein synthesis that they are sure about, one thing they are unsure about and one thing that they want to know more about. Take examples from around the class and revise the things that students are having difficulty with.

### H Transcription and translation

**Plenary 2** AfL Lit

Ask students to write the words 'transcription' and 'translation' on separate scraps of paper. The **AT** document *Cell division* contains a list of statements about transcription and translation.

### Making a protein

**Homework 1**

**Worksheet B2.10c** presents questions about a simple model to explain how proteins are made using the DNA code.

Support Add the words DNA, gene, chromosome, amino acid, protein, genetic code to the sheet before printing to help with questions **1–3**.

### H Codes for proteins

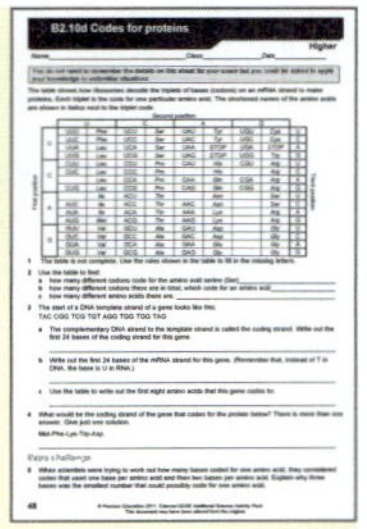


**Homework 2**

**Worksheet B2.10d** gives more able students further opportunity to explore the link between DNA codons and the amino acids in a polypeptide chain.

Stretch Ask students to do the 'extra challenge' question.

# B2.10 Protein manufacture

How are proteins made?

Haemophilia is a disease in which blood does not clot properly. This can be caused by a lack of a blood protein called Factor VIII. In the 1980s scientists examined the structure of Factor VIII. A protein's structure is produced by a code in the order of bases in the gene. Knowing the structure of the protein allowed the scientists to work back to what the gene must look like. They found the gene in 1984.

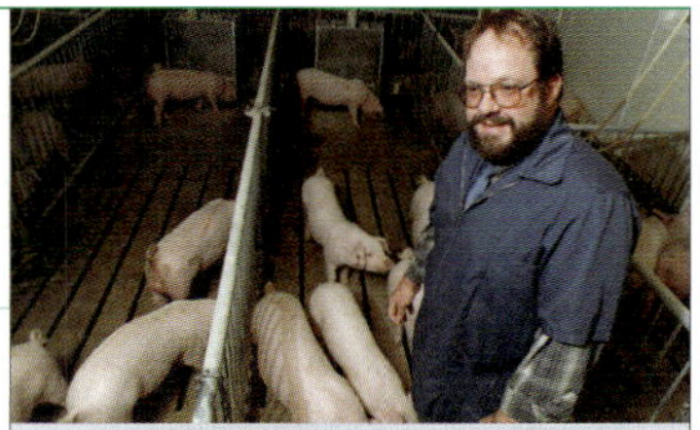

**A** *Today, the gene for Factor VIII can be produced in the milk of these genetically engineered pigs.*

The order of bases on a DNA strand forms the **genetic code**. There are only four bases (adenine, A; cytosine, C; guanine, G; thymine, T) but they can be arranged in any sequence, for example ATTAGCG.

There are 20 different **amino acids** in human proteins. A cell uses the sequence of bases in DNA to synthesise (build) chains of these amino acids. These chains then form proteins. This process is called **protein synthesis**.

Each amino acid is identified by a different group of bases. A specific order of bases in DNA produces a specific order of amino acids in the chain and so produces a particular protein.

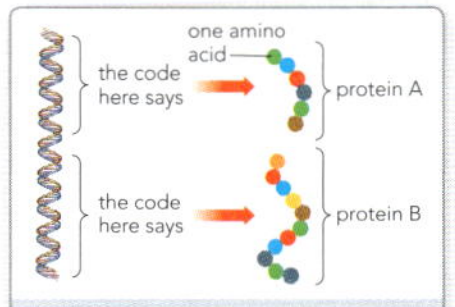


**B** *Translating the DNA code into proteins.*

1 What are proteins made of?

2 What controls the sequence of amino acids that are joined together to make a specific protein?

3 Why do different parts of DNA produce different proteins?

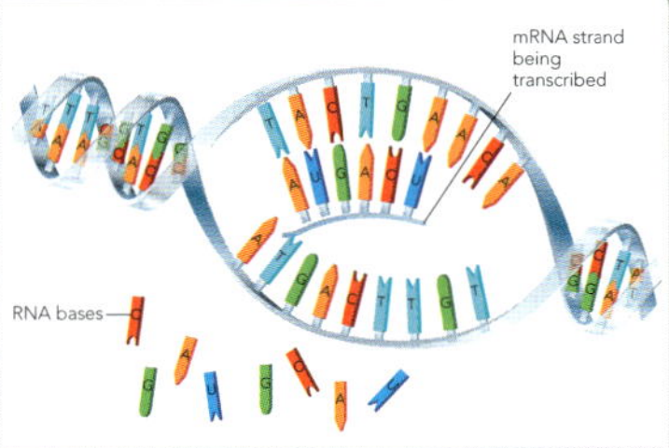


**C** *Transcription of DNA to produce mRNA.*

## Transcription

H

The process of making a protein takes place in two stages. The first is **transcription**, which takes place inside the nucleus. Here, the DNA in a gene unzips by breaking the weak hydrogen bonds between bases in the double helix. One strand of the gene is used as a template. Bases that are complementary to this strand link together opposite it, forming a molecule of **messenger RNA (mRNA)**.

RNA is very similar to DNA but only has one strand (not two) and has a base called **uracil (U)** instead of thymine. mRNA is small enough to move out of the nucleus into the cell's **cytoplasm**.

## Translation

H

In the cytoplasm, the mRNA attaches to a small structure called a **ribosome**. The ribosome moves from one end of the mRNA strand to the other, decoding the bases in groups of three, known as **base triplets** or **codons**. Each amino acid is attached to a **transfer RNA (tRNA)** molecule, and each tRNA molecule has a triplet of bases. The triplet of bases controls which amino acid is attached.

As the ribosome moves to the next codon on the mRNA, the tRNA with complementary bases lines up with the codon. The tRNA releases the amino acid that it was carrying which joins on to the growing amino acid chain. The tRNA is released as the ribosome moves on to the next codon, where the next tRNA with its amino acid lines up. This continues until the mRNA strand is completely decoded. The chain of amino acids is called a **polypeptide**. The polypeptide then twists and folds and may link up with other polypeptides, to become a protein.

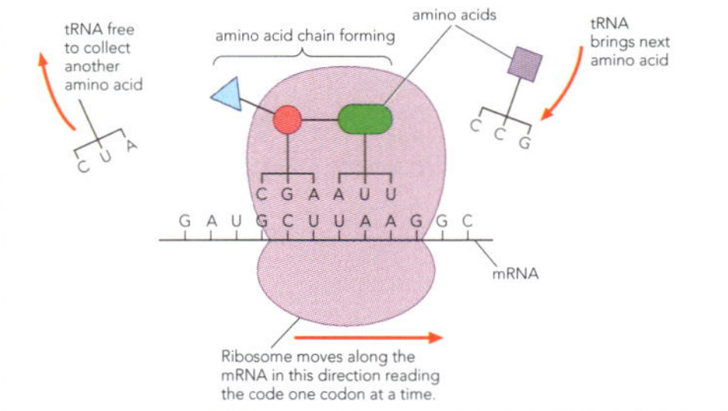


**D** *During translation, the ribosome moves along the mRNA strand lining up tRNA molecules so their amino acids can be joined to the growing amino acid chain.*

5 Describe as fully as you can how different proteins are made from the genetic code. Include bases, amino acids and proteins in your answer.

**ResultsPlus Watch Out!**

To avoid muddling the words *transcription* (in the nucleus) and *translation* (in the cytoplasm). Remember transcribing is the copying of something exactly and translating is changing it into something different (like another language), in this case changing from base codes into amino acid sequence in a protein.

H 4 Describe the differences between translation and transcription.

**Skills spotlight**

Scientists use models to help understand and explain what they see. A car factory, where a whole car is put together in a sequence from pieces using a plan, could be used as a model for protein synthesis. What are the strengths and weaknesses of this model?

**Learning Outcomes**

1.22 Describe how the order of bases in a section of DNA decides the order of amino acids in the protein

H 1.23 Demonstrate an understanding of the stages of protein synthesis, including transcription and translation:
- a the production of complementary mRNA strand in the nucleus
- b the attachment of the mRNA to the ribosome
- c the coding by triplets of bases (codons) in the mRNA for specific amino acids
- d the transfer of amino acids to the ribosome by tRNA
- e the linking of amino acids to form polypeptides

HSW 3 Describe how phenomena are explained using scientific models





## ActiveTeach

- **AT** *Protein synthesis* [interactive]
  Ordering the steps in protein synthesis
- **AT** *Protein formation* [word document]
  Modelling protein formation
- **AT** *Protein flowchart* [word document]
  Support cards for flowchart
- **AT** *Cell division* [word document]
  Transcription and translation
- **AT** *Ribosome translation* [diagram]
  Figure D – diagram labelling activity

## Answers | Student Book

1 Amino acids

2 The genetic code in DNA controls the order of amino acids in the chain, which defines the protein produced.

3 The code in each gene is different, so make different amino acid sequences.

4 (H) Transcription is the copying of one DNA strand to produce a strand of complementary mRNA. Translation is the use of the mRNA code to make the amino acid chain. Transcription is done in the nucleus where the DNA is protected, and translation is done in the cytoplasm of the cell where the ribosomes are.

5 A good answer will contain the following points: each gene has a unique sequence of bases; the sequence of bases is used to make a unique sequence of amino acids in a chain; the order of amino acids in the chain decides which protein is formed; so each gene makes a different protein; (H) the roles of transcription in transferring the code from DNA to mRNA, and translation where the code from the mRNA is used to produce the amino acid chain, should be included.

**Skills spotlight**

**Strengths**: An initial plan is translated into a product. Existing pieces are put together in a sequence to give the finished product. Different plans could be used with different components on the same assembly line to produce different cars. This models the way different genes control the sequence of different amino acids put together on the same ribosome.

**Weaknesses:** The amino acid chain made by the code then folds up into a 3D shape, while a car is made from pieces which are already 3D; (H) copies of the same component part are stationed at a particular point of a car assembly line where they are added, while in protein manufacture the amino acids are brought one at a time.

# B2.11 Mutations



In this lesson students learn how the shape and function of protein molecules depends on the unique sequence of amino acids from which they are formed, and how mutations may change this.

## Specification coverage

***1.24*** Describe each protein as having its own specific number and sequence of amino acids, resulting in different-shaped molecules that have different functions, including enzymes

***1.25*** Demonstrate an understanding of how gene mutations change the DNA base sequence and that mutations can be harmful, beneficial or neither

**HSW** ***3*** Many phenomena can be explained by developing and using scientific theories, *models* and ideas

## Key terms

mutation

### Protein revisit

**Starter 1** AfL

Ask each student to write down three things that they think the person sitting next to them should have learnt in the last lesson. Then ask students to ask each other in pairs whether they agree on the things they should have learnt. Ask them to agree a final list of the three most important points.

### Modelling protein shapes (AT)

**Exploring 1** Prac

**Worksheet B2.11a** explores some ideas about the 3D shapes of proteins, and how this is affected by the amino acid sequence in the protein. Full details can be found on the Teacher and technician practical sheet B2.11.

**Stretch** Ask students to evaluate how well the model can explain protein shapes, and to develop criteria to evaluate the strengths and weaknesses of this particular model.

**Support** The **AT** document *Modelling proteins* will support students in answering the questions.

### Different kinds of proteins

**Exploring 3**

Ask students to research a range of proteins that they may have come across previously, and a few key ones that link to what they already know, e.g. keratin in hair, collagen in the cartilage of the outer ear, actin strands in muscle, or the enzyme amylase. Ask them to find out their function in the body and how the shape of the molecule makes it useful.

**Stretch** Students could research images of the 3D shapes of different proteins.

**Support** Students research just one or two proteins from the selection.

### Mutation concept cobweb

**Plenary 1** AfL Lit

Write the word 'mutation' in the middle of the board and ask students to suggest related words and how they should be placed, giving a reason for their placement. Encourage discussion to find as many useful links between words as possible.

### Proteins and mutation

**Homework 1**

**Worksheet B2.11c** presents questions that cover the learning of this lesson.

**Support** To support question **1**, add the following word box to the sheet before copying.

| | | | |
|---|---|---|---|
| hair | dissolve | oxygen | fibrous |
| blood | globular | strong | |

### Mutant heroes

**Starter 2**

Give students one or two minutes to jot down the names of mutant heroes from films or books. In pairs, ask them to identify what it is that makes them 'mutant'. Take examples from around the class, asking students to clarify how the character became mutant. Draw out the idea that a mutant is a change from what is normal or usual.

### H The effect of mutations

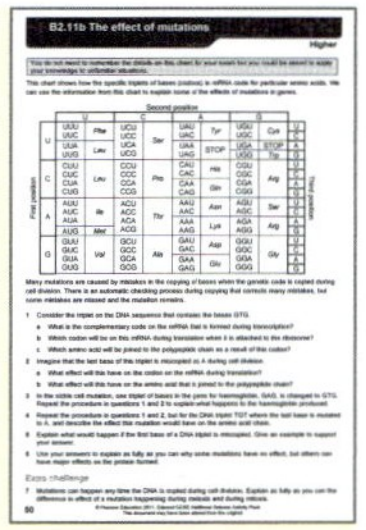

**Exploring 2**

**Worksheet B2.11b** is suitable for students who have covered the Higher material in lesson B2.10. It uses the DNA triplet code table to help explain the effects of different gene mutations.

**Stretch** Ask students to do the 'extra challenge' question.

### Student Book spread B2.11 (AT)

**Explaining 1** Lit

Provide an animation that explains the effect of the haemoglobin mutation on sickle cell disease. A good example can be found online at the *Dolan DNA Learning Centre*.

**Stretch** Students work independently using a photocopy of the text with colour highlighter pens to indicate the text they have chosen.

**Support** The **AT** document *Mutation theory* will help students prepare their answer.

### Protein and mutation quiz

**Plenary 2** AfL

Ask pupils to design a quiz sheet about this topic and the last and swap their sheets with other students for them to answer. These could be done as multiple choice, which will make any marking of correct/incorrect answers easier.

### Catching flu

**Homework 2**

**Worksheet B2.11d** uses the context of the proteins that act as cell surface markers to look at how some mutations can be harmful due to the change in protein shape.

**Stretch** Ask students to do the 'extra challenge' question.

# B2.11 Mutations

How do mutations happen?

**S**tumpy the duck has a rare condition called polymelia. This means that the genes in his body made four legs, not the usual two.

**A** Stumpy

The number and order of the amino acids in the chain is specific for each protein. For example the protein insulin, which helps cells take in glucose, has a small chain of 51 amino acids in an order that no other protein has. Haemoglobin is a much larger, complex protein found in red blood cells. It carries oxygen and is made of four linked chains, two of which have 141 amino acids and two have 146 amino acids.

1 Find the names of three proteins on this page.

2 What is the link between the type of protein that keratin is and where it is found in the body?

3 Explain why the shapes formed by the amino acid chains in haemoglobin are important.

The order of the amino acids causes the chain to fold up in a particular way and gives the protein a specific 3D shape. Some proteins such as keratin found in human hair and nails, form long, strong fibrous molecules. Other proteins such as insulin, haemoglobin and enzymes, have a round 'globular' (blobby) shape. This helps them move around inside cells and the rest of the body easily. The shape of enzymes is particularly important in the way they work. Each enzyme has a unique shape caused by its amino acid sequence. An enzyme can only work in one kind of reaction because of its shape. We say that each enzyme is specific to the reaction.

**B** Keratin is the main protein in stags' antlers.

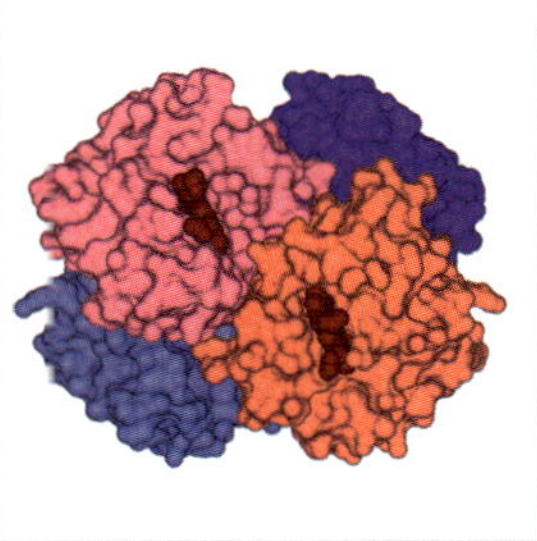

**C** The 3D shapes formed by the different chains of amino acids in haemoglobin means it can carry oxygen.

## The effect of mutations

A **mutation** is a change in the sequence of bases in the genetic code. Some changes in the code have no effect on the amino acid sequence produced, so the protein shape is not affected. Others, such as the sickle-cell mutation in the gene that produces haemoglobin, replace one amino acid in the chain with another. This can cause the protein to fold up in a different way and have a different shape, which will affect the way it works.

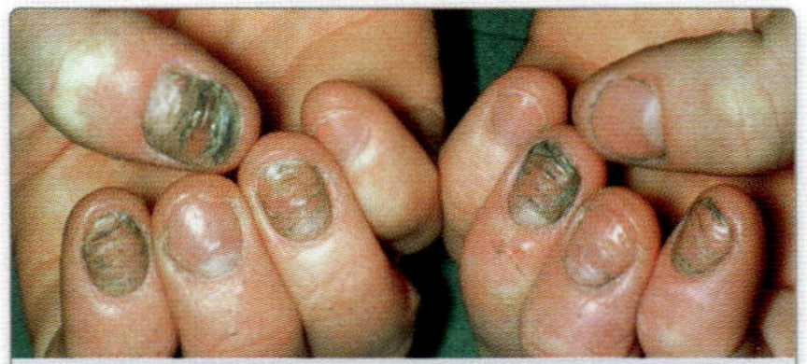

**D** A mutation in a keratin gene can cause misshapen nails.

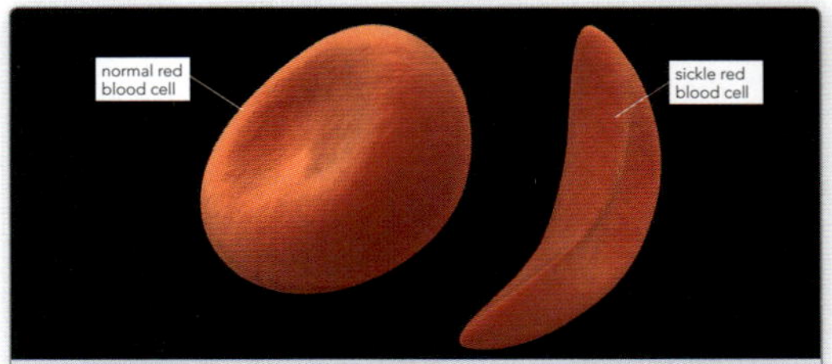


**E** When sickle cell haemoglobin is not carrying oxygen, the molecules can stick together in long fibres, making the red blood cells pointy and sickle-shaped. These cells easily get stuck in small blood vessels.

**ResultsPlus Watch Out!**

Do not forget that a mutation in a gene can produce a new allele. The normal allele for the haemoglobin gene can mutate to become the sickle-cell allele.

Mutations may be harmful or may have no effect, and some can be beneficial to the organism. For example, some mutations in bacteria make them resistant to the effects of antibiotics. Bacteria that have the mutation survive when that antibiotic is used, but bacteria without the mutation die.

4 Describe the effect of the sickle-cell mutation on cell shape.

5 Explain why the sickle-cell mutation is a problem.

6 A mutation in the gene for keratin causes brittle hair. Explain as fully as you can why it does this. Include DNA, amino acids and proteins in your answer.

**Skills spotlight**

Theories can help us explain what we see. Explain how the theory that a protein is coded for by the order of bases in DNA can help explain the effect of the sickle-cell mutation.

**Learning outcomes**

1.24 Describe each protein as having its own specific number and sequence of amino acids, resulting in different shaped molecules that have different functions, including enzymes

1.25 Demonstrate an understanding of how gene mutations change the DNA base sequence and that mutations can be harmful, beneficial or neither

HSW 3 Describe how phenomena are explained using scientific theories and ideas



How can an enzyme change the colour of your skin?



## ActiveTeach

- **AT** *Tales of the mutant leopard 1* [video]
  DNA mutations
- **AT** *Tales of the mutant leopard 2* [video]
  Colour variations in animals
- **AT** *What is a mutation?* [interactive]
  Proteins and mutations – true-or-false quiz
- **AT** *Modelling proteins* [word document]
  Writing frame
- **AT** *Mutation theory* [word document]
  Writing frame

## Answers | Student Book

1 Haemoglobin, keratin, insulin

2 It forms long, fibrous strong molecules that can protect the ends of the fingers and toes, or join together to give long hair molecules.

3 They need to be the right shape to hold the oxygen molecules in place while the red blood cells move around the body.

4 It changes the round, disc shape of a normal red blood cell into a sickle shape with points at opposite sides of the cell.

5 Sickle cells get stuck in small blood vessels, so they stop carrying oxygen to where the body needs it and block the blood from getting through to the parts of the body beyond the blockage, so they don't get enough oxygen.

6 A good answer will contain the following points: each gene has a unique sequence of bases; the mutation changes the base code in the gene; the amino acid chain that is produced from that gene is different; the order of amino acids in the chain decides which protein is formed, and its shape; the 'new' amino acid chain doesn't form the same shape of protein; the hair formed from that protein is weaker and breaks more easily, causing brittle hair.

**Skills spotlight**

The sickle-cell mutation is a change to one base in the haemoglobin gene. The amino acid sequence is thought to be put together from the order of bases in the gene so if the order of bases in the gene changes, then the amino acid sequence may be different and the protein formed may behave differently from usual.

# B2.12 Enzymes



This lesson introduces enzymes as proteins and explains their role in catalysing chemical reactions, both inside and outside cells. Note that the role of enzymes in digestion is covered in more detail in Lesson B2.31.

## Specification coverage

***1.26*** Describe enzymes as biological catalysts

***1.27*** Demonstrate an understanding that enzymes catalyse chemical reactions occurring inside and outside living cells, including: a) DNA replication b) protein synthesis c) digestion

HSW ***13*** How and why decisions about science and technology are made, *including those that raise ethical issues, and about the social*, economic and environmental effects of such decisions

## Key terms

catalyst
digestion
enzyme

### Soft rot

**Starter 1**

Show students a piece of fruit that has started to go soft due to decay by a mould fungus. Explain that the fungus is growing through the fruit with microscopic fungal threads and 'eating' it. Try to link the idea of the softness to digestion in order to absorb food molecules, as in the human gut.

### Enzymes in washing

**Exploring 1** Prac

**Worksheet B2.12a** investigates the effect of enzymes in cleaning 'biological' stains from fabric. Full details can be found on the Teacher and technician practical sheet B2.12 (1).

Stretch Students develop criteria to use in their evaluation of the effectiveness of the different detergents.

Support Students could use their results to produce an advert for the best detergent.

### Student Book spread B2.12

**Explaining 1** Lit

Ask students to consider what would happen if cells didn't contain enzymes. Focus on the facts that enzymes are not reactants – they are left unchanged at the end, which means they are ready to catalyse the reaction of other reactant molecules.

Stretch Students carry out research to add to their tables, including the names of other enzymes. It should become clear to them that enzyme names end in –ase.

Support Give students a frame for the table.

### Enzyme clues

**Plenary 1** AfL

Give students the words listed below from this lesson and ask them to write crossword clues for each word. After three minutes, ask them to exchange their clues with a neighbour to test them. Where a clue is not effective, ask the neighbour to identify why it needs improving. Words: catalyst, enzyme, protein, catalase, digestion, synthesis.

### Enzyme wordsearch

**Homework 1**

**Worksheet B2.12c** is designed for students needing support.

Support Add the following word box to the sheet before copying.

| | | |
|---|---|---|
| enzyme | protein | catalyst |
| inside | biological | digestion |
| synthesis | reaction | replication |

### Different kinds of enzymes

**Starter 2** AfL

Show some examples of products that contain enzymes, such as bio-washing detergents and meat tenderiser, either from a collection of objects or from photos downloaded from the Internet. Ask students why enzymes are used in these products.

### Do all cells contain catalase? (AT)

**Exploring 2** Prac

**Worksheet B2.12b** provides guidance for students to plan their own investigation. Full details can be found on the Teacher and technician practical sheet on B2.12 (2).

Stretch Tell students that an assay is a test that measures the amount of a chemical.

Support Ask students to sequence the statements on the **AT** document *Catalase investigation* to produce a plan for the investigation.

### Demonstration of a catalyst (AT)

**Explaining 2** Demo

This demonstration aims to show students the effect of the enzyme catalase on the rate of breakdown of hydrogen peroxide. Full details can be found on the Teacher and technician practical sheet B2.12 (3).

Stretch Present the three parts of the demonstration without questioning. Ask students to note the results then draw their own conclusions.

Support A writing frame is provided on the **AT** document Catalyst demo *writing frame* to help students record the results.

### What do enzymes do?

**Plenary 2** AfL

Ask students to produce three different answers to the question '*What do enzymes do?*' Allow three minutes and then take examples from around the class. For each answer, ask students to explain the importance of the enzyme in what it is doing.

### Blocking enzyme action

**Homework 2**

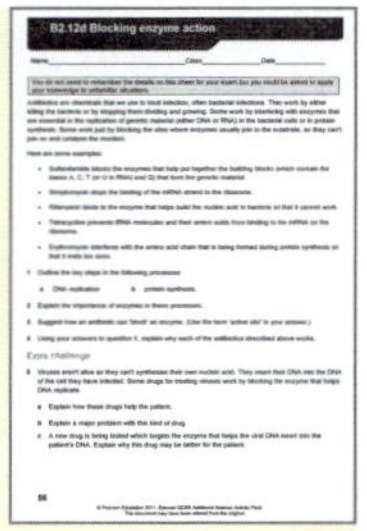

**Worksheet B2.12d** uses the context of how antibiotics limit bacterial growth to review the role of enzymes in DNA replication and protein synthesis.

Stretch Ask students to do the 'extra challenge' question.

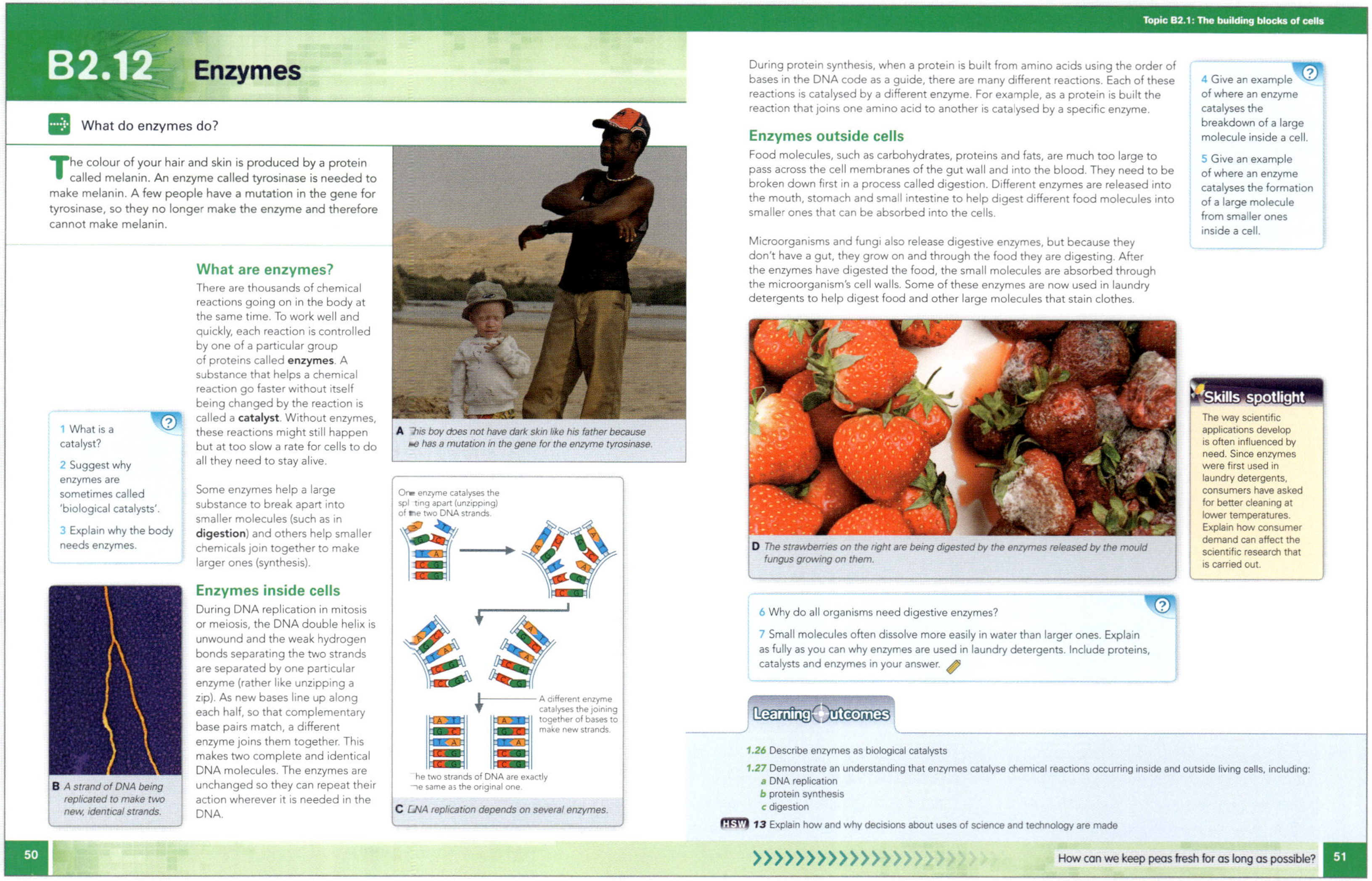



# B2.12 Enzymes

What do enzymes do?

The colour of your hair and skin is produced by a protein called melanin. An enzyme called tyrosinase is needed to make melanin. A few people have a mutation in the gene for tyrosinase, so they no longer make the enzyme and therefore cannot make melanin.

**A** This boy does not have dark skin like his father because he has a mutation in the gene for the enzyme tyrosinase.

## What are enzymes?

There are thousands of chemical reactions going on in the body at the same time. To work well and quickly, each reaction is controlled by one of a particular group of proteins called **enzymes**. A substance that helps a chemical reaction go faster without itself being changed by the reaction is called a **catalyst**. Without enzymes, these reactions might still happen but at too slow a rate for cells to do all they need to stay alive.

Some enzymes help a large substance to break apart into smaller molecules (such as in **digestion**) and others help smaller chemicals join together to make larger ones (synthesis).

1 What is a catalyst?

2 Suggest why enzymes are sometimes called 'biological catalysts'.

3 Explain why the body needs enzymes.

## Enzymes inside cells

During DNA replication in mitosis or meiosis, the DNA double helix is unwound and the weak hydrogen bonds separating the two strands are separated by one particular enzyme (rather like unzipping a zip). As new bases line up along each half, so that complementary base pairs match, a different enzyme joins them together. This makes two complete and identical DNA molecules. The enzymes are unchanged so they can repeat their action wherever it is needed in the DNA.

**B** A strand of DNA being replicated to make two new, identical strands.



**C** DNA replication depends on several enzymes.

During protein synthesis, when a protein is built from amino acids using the order of bases in the DNA code as a guide, there are many different reactions. Each of these reactions is catalysed by a different enzyme. For example, as a protein is built the reaction that joins one amino acid to another is catalysed by a specific enzyme.

4 Give an example of where an enzyme catalyses the breakdown of a large molecule inside a cell.

5 Give an example of where an enzyme catalyses the formation of a large molecule from smaller ones inside a cell.

## Enzymes outside cells

Food molecules, such as carbohydrates, proteins and fats, are much too large to pass across the cell membranes of the gut wall and into the blood. They need to be broken down first in a process called digestion. Different enzymes are released into the mouth, stomach and small intestine to help digest different food molecules into smaller ones that can be absorbed into the cells.

Microorganisms and fungi also release digestive enzymes, but because they don't have a gut, they grow on and through the food they are digesting. After the enzymes have digested the food, the small molecules are absorbed through the microorganism's cell walls. Some of these enzymes are now used in laundry detergents to help digest food and other large molecules that stain clothes.

**D** The strawberries on the right are being digested by the enzymes released by the mould fungus growing on them.

**Skills spotlight**

The way scientific applications develop is often influenced by need. Since enzymes were first used in laundry detergents, consumers have asked for better cleaning at lower temperatures. Explain how consumer demand can affect the scientific research that is carried out.

6 Why do all organisms need digestive enzymes?

7 Small molecules often dissolve more easily in water than larger ones. Explain as fully as you can why enzymes are used in laundry detergents. Include proteins, catalysts and enzymes in your answer.

**Learning Outcomes**

1.26 Describe enzymes as biological catalysts

1.27 Demonstrate an understanding that enzymes catalyse chemical reactions occurring inside and outside living cells, including:
a DNA replication
b protein synthesis
c digestion

HSW 13 Explain how and why decisions about uses of science and technology are made





## ActiveTeach

- **AT** *Catalase investigation* [word document] Sequencing statements
- **AT** *Catalyst demo* [word document] Writing frame

## Answers | Student Book

1 A substance that helps a reaction to go faster but does not get used up in the reaction.

2 They are catalysts that are only made in living cells.

3 To speed up reactions in our cells so that they happen fast enough for the cells to stay alive.

4 DNA replication

5 Protein synthesis or formation of new DNA strands from bases

6 Because they need to break large food molecules down until they are small enough to pass into the blood through cell membranes.

7 A good answer will contain the following points: stains on clothes are often caused by foods or by biological material such as sweat; some enzymes break down these molecules inside the body – they are biological catalysts. these enzymes can catalyse the breakdown of the molecules in stains into smaller molecules in laundry detergents; for example, as egg stain contains protein, protease enzymes in laundry detergents catalyse the breakdown of the stain into smaller chains of amino acids; the smaller molecules dissolve more easily in water and so can be washed away; all enzymes are themselves protein molecules, but are unchanged by the reaction and are ready to catalyse more breakdowns.

**Skills spotlight**

Consumers want clean clothes, but now they also want to do wash at lower temperatures. Scientific research is expensive. It is easier to find funding if the results of the research help the company funding it to make a profit. Research that finds enzymes that work best at lower temperatures in new laundry detergents will give the detergent manufacturer a big advantage over their competitors, so they can sell more of their product.

# B2.13 Enzymes and temperature

This lesson challenges students to investigate the effect of temperature on the enzyme amylase. The activity may be run as a practice controlled assessment task or as a straight-forward class practical. The practical work will take approximately 1 hour.

## Specification coverage

***1.32*** Investigate the factors that affect enzyme activity

This activity provides opportunities to cover HSW *1*, HSW *5*, HSW *6*, HSW *7*, HSW *8*, HSW *10* and HSW *11*.

### Before the lesson

Ensure that students are familiar with any equipment they may be expected to use so that they can plan their own investigation. In the week or two before the task show them this equipment and, if appropriate, allow them to practice using it. The use of a spotting tile for mixing drops of iodine solution and liquidised foods, to show the presence of starch, would be helpful.

It may be good preparation to show students one or more of Skills Sheets 19 to 26 to show what is expected of them in their actual controlled assessment task.

### Starter

**Washing at different temperatures**

Show students a biological washing detergent and point out the recommended washing temperature on the packaging. Ask them to suggest why there is a particular temperature recommendation and what effect using a higher or lower temperature than this may have on the effectiveness of the enzymes in the detergent.

Follow this by reading the additional information below the opening section of page 52 of the Student Book. They may then read the brief description of the activity provided by the 'Your task' box.

### Option 1: Straight-forward class practical

Students follow the instructions on **Worksheet B2.13b**. The worksheet suggests only three temperatures for testing, but students could choose their own range of temperatures for the water baths: from around 4°C in an ice/salt bath to about 70°C. Students could prepare repeat tubes at each temperature, or compare results from different groups to provide repeats for analysis. The range of data that students could collect is given on **Worksheet B2.13c**. Different animals use different forms of amylase to digest carbohydrates in their diet. Ask them to use their results to predict the optimum temperature for amylase from species, such as a fish, a bird, a reptile and a mammal.

### Plenary

On page 53 of the Student Book you will find two examples of the sort of work that students may produce for this task. The examples focus on writing a hypothesis. You could share these with students after they have completed their own work. This will help them to understand the assessment criteria and so make it easier for them to evaluate their work and to see how they can improve it. Moderator comments on each of the Student Book extracts can be found at the end of the assessment guidance for this investigation on the CD-ROM. The examples can also be found on the **AT** document *Student examples*.

### Option 2: Running the activity as a practice controlled assessment task (PCAT)

We have provided a full range of support resources to allow the running of this practical as a practice controlled assessment task. A recommended structure is outlined below (to be used over a number of sessions). Marking guidance for all three parts of the practice task can be found on the CD-ROM that accompanies the TTPP. To save time when using these practice controlled assessment tasks, you may wish to focus on a particular aspect or skill rather than working through all three parts of the task.

#### Part A Planning

1. Students should be given the Student Brief on Worksheet B2.13a. They can use Part A of the Workbook that is provided to help pupils with their practice controlled assessments. They should be given about 1 hour to do this planning.
2. Students should be reminded that iodine solution is used to test for the presence of starch.

#### Part B Observations

3. Students carry out the practical task to collect evidence using the method they have planned in Part A. Once again, they should refer to the Student Brief on Worksheet B2.13a. They can use Part B of the Workbook that is provided to help pupils with their practice controlled assessments. They should be given about 1 hour to collect their primary evidence.
4. If there is a problem with their own planned method, students may be asked to follow the method set out on **Worksheet B2.13b**. This will still enable students to access the full range of marks for Part B and Part C of the practice controlled assessment task.
5. In Part B, students are required to gather some secondary evidence. The evidence can be quantitative or qualitative. It can be from a variety of sources but students must note where they found their evidence and evaluate the quality of the source as part of this task. Skills Sheet 22 provides students with further guidance on researching for and evaluating secondary evidence. This part of the task could be done outside of the lesson but must be supervised.

#### Part C Conclusions

6. Students follow the instructions set out on the Part C section of the Student Brief on Worksheet B2.4a. They should use their data from Part B and the secondary evidence they have collected when doing this. They can use Part C of the Workbook that is provided to help pupils with their practice controlled assessments. They should be given about 1 hour to work on their conclusions.

The **AT** includes video clips showing a group of students working through elements of this investigation with teacher support.

Practice Controlled Assessment

# B2.13 Enzymes and temperature

How does temperature affect enzymes?

Frozen peas can contain higher levels of nutrients, such as vitamins, than fresh peas sold in shops. This is because cell processes in the peas start breaking down the nutrients as soon as the peas are picked. Freezing the peas slows these processes down to a very slow rate.

The processes in pea cells that break down nutrients are like many processes in cells – they are controlled by **enzymes**. Enzymes help to speed up the rate of reactions. If the enzymes are affected in any way, the rate of reaction usually slows down. We can use this idea to test how different factors can affect enzymes.

**A** *Within 2 hours of being picked, these peas will be frozen and ready for packaging.*

**Your task**

You are going to plan an investigation that will allow you to find out how the rate of an enzyme-controlled reaction is affected by temperature. Your teacher will provide you with some materials to help you organise this task.

**Learning Outcomes**

*1.32 Investigate the factors that affect enzyme activity*

## ResultsPlus Build Better Answers

When planning an investigation like this, one of the skills you will be assessed on is your ability to *write a hypothesis*. There are 4 marks available for this skill. Here are two extracts focusing on this skill. Other skills that you need for the assessment are dealt with in other lessons.

**Student extract 1** A basic response for this skill

I think that if you make a reaction hotter then it will go faster and I think that reactions which contain enzymes probably work like this just like any other reaction so I am going to get some amylase and put it in a test tube and test what happens when I heat it up.

- Use your scientific knowledge to say why you think your hypothesis is correct.
- You just need one sentence which says what you think will happen in your investigation.
- You don't need to give any practical detail in this section.

**Student extract 2** A good response for this skill

I think that changing the temperature of a reaction which is controlled by an enzyme will change the rate of the reaction up to a certain point. After this point I think that the rate of reaction will slow down. I think this because I know that when the temperature of any reaction increases the molecules have more energy and are more likely to collide and react. I also know that enzymes are damaged if they get too hot so I think that if you heat the reaction up too much the enzyme will be damaged, it will not work and the reaction will slow down.

- This is a clear hypothesis which will be easy to test.
- This student has done a good job of using their own relevant scientific knowledge to justify their hypothesis.
- It would be better to use the scientific word 'denatured' here.

**ResultsPlus**

**To access 2 marks**

- Provide a hypothesis that is appropriate for most of the task
- Try to justify your hypothesis

**To access 4 marks**

- Provide a hypothesis that is appropriate for the full scope of the task
- Justify your hypothesis using relevant scientific ideas

52 Does washing your clothes in cold water work? 53

## ActiveTeach

- **AT** *B2.13 Enzymes and temperature* [interactive]
  Enzymes and temperature
- **AT** *B2.13 Assessment criteria* [presentation] PowerPoint
  Understanding the CA marking criteria
- **AT** *B2.13 Specification points* [word document]
  Edexcel specification points [SB Page 53]
- **AT** *B2.13 Student examples* [word document]
  Examples for students to assess
- **AT** *Action of enzymes* [interactive]
  Effect of temperature

## Assessment criteria

### Hypothesis

**0** No relevant hypothesis provided.

**1-2 a)** Provides a hypothesis that is appropriate for most of the task, e.g. explains that increasing the temperature will make the reaction happen faster.
**b)** Partially justifies the hypothesis, e.g. may explain that adding energy to a reaction makes molecules move faster so they react more quickly.

**3-4 a)** Provides a hypothesis that is appropriate for the full scope of the task based on relevant scientific ideas, e.g. students may suggest that amylase has an optimum temperature when it digests starch fastest. [Students may not actually use the term optimum temperature but if the point is described correctly they will be able to access the mark.]
**b)** Justifies the hypothesis fully using relevant scientific ideas, e.g. suggests that amylase has an optimum temperature when it digests starch fastest because below that temperature the molecules have less energy for reaction, and above that temperature the enzyme starts to denature and so cannot hold the substrate molecule in its active site correctly.

# B2.14 Enzyme action



This lesson uses evidence from observations of enzyme action to evaluate the lock-and-key hypothesis

## Specification coverage

**1.28** Describe the factors affecting enzyme action, including: a) temperature b) substrate concentration c) pH

**1.29** Recall that enzymes are highly specific for their substrate

**1.30** Demonstrate an understanding of the action of enzymes in terms of the 'lock-and-key' hypothesis

**1.31** Describe how enzymes can be denatured due to changes in the shape of the active site

HSW *2* The interpretation of data, *using creative thought*, to provide evidence for testing ideas and developing theories

There are also opportunities to cover HSW *3*, HSW *10* and HSW *11*.

## Key terms

active site
denature
lock-and-key hypothesis
specific
substrate

### Boiled egg white

**Starter 1**

Remind students that enzymes are proteins such as the mixture of proteins in egg white (albumen). Show students uncooked egg white and heated egg white. Ask students to consider how enzymes might be changed by heat.

### Stopping fruit going brown

**Starter 2**

Cut an apple or pear in half and sprinkle lemon juice over the cut surface of one half. Explain that cutting the fruit breaks open cells and releases the enzymes that were inside them. Ask them to describe the changes they see happening, and to suggest a reason for any differences they see between the two halves.

### Enzyme action

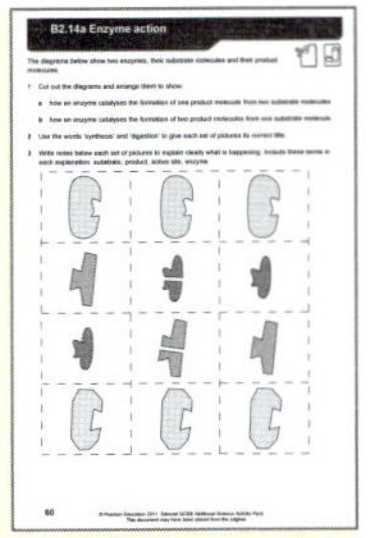


**Exploring 1**

In **Worksheet B2.14a** students cut out and arrange diagrams to show how the lock-and-key hypothesis explains the synthesis and digestion of molecules.

**Stretch** Students could use the diagrams to storyboard an animation that explains synthesis and digestion, including providing script for a voice-over.

**Support** Provide Figure E in page 55 of the Student Book to guide students in producing their diagrams using the worksheet pieces.

### Optimum pH

**Exploring 2** **Prac**

**Worksheet B2.14b** gives the method for an investigation into the effect of pH on enzyme activity. See Teacher and technician practical sheet B2.14 for full details.

**Stretch** Ask students to identify the limitations of the method they have used and consider how best to overcome these given the restrictions of time and equipment available.

**Support** Restrict the pHs tested by the students to 4, 6 and 8. This should simplify interpretation and produce a peak at pH 6.

### Student Book spread B2.14

**Explaining 1** **Lit**

Help students identify each of the observations that need to be explained by the lock-and-key hypothesis by highlighting the appropriate sentences on the whiteboard. Then ask groups of students to take a different observation and construct a few sentences to show how the hypothesis explains the observation.

**Stretch** Students should work individually to explain each observation.

**Support** Tackle the explaining observations part of the activity as a group, asking students to suggest a sentence to construct each explanation.

### Action of enzymes (AT)

**Explaining 2**

The **AT** interactive *Action of enzymes* from Lesson B2.13 could be used with this lesson. The interactive shows an investigation into the effect of temperature and pH on an enzyme-catalysed reaction.

**Stretch** Students could write their own explanations for the results shown.

**Support** Pause the interactive frequently to make sure students understand what is happening and why it happens.

### Enzymes mark scheme

**Plenary 1** **AfL**

Ask students to look at Figure E of the lock-and-key hypothesis in the Student Book. They should write a question about it and design a mark scheme for the answer. Encourage students to think up questions that are worth more than 1 or 2 marks. If time allows, students could try out their questions on one another.

### Key facts

**Plenary 2** **AfL** **Lit**

Ask each student to write down three facts learnt during the lesson. Then ask the students to share their facts in groups and to compile a master list, including the most-common fact learnt and the least-common fact. A spokesperson for each group could then share their ideas with the class to see if other groups had the same most-common fact.

### Enzyme questions (AT)

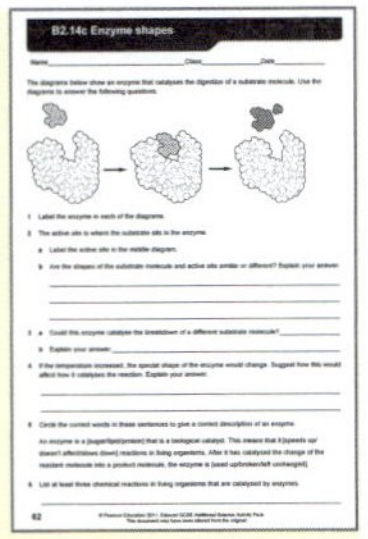


**Homework 1**

**Worksheet B2.14c** presents questions that cover the learning of this lesson.

**Support** A sheet of enzyme and substrate shapes is provided in **AT** document *Enzyme shapes*. Students should match the enzyme to the substrate and explain their choice.

### Enzyme shapes

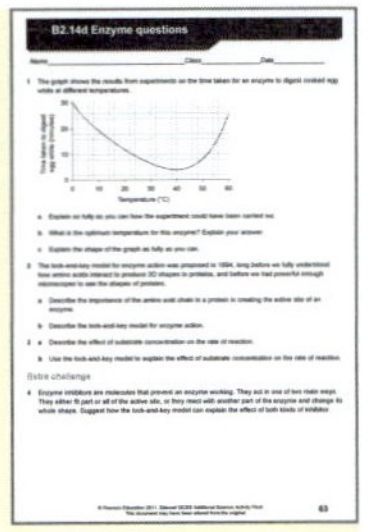


**Homework 2**

**Worksheet B2.14d** presents questions that cover the learning of this lesson.

**Stretch** Ask students to do the 'extra challenge' question.

# B2.14 Enzyme action

How do enzymes work?

Bacteria that grow inside giant columns of ikaite (a kind of rock) in deep water near Greenland contain enzymes that work well at very low temperatures. Using enzymes like these in laundry detergents could mean washing in cold water still gets clothes clean.

A An ikaite column in deep water near Greenland

1 What is the normal temperature of the main human organs?

2 What is meant by optimum temperature?

The molecules that enzymes work on are called **substrate** molecules. Enzymes catalyse the change of substrate molecules into product molecules better at some temperatures than others, so the rate of reaction is faster.

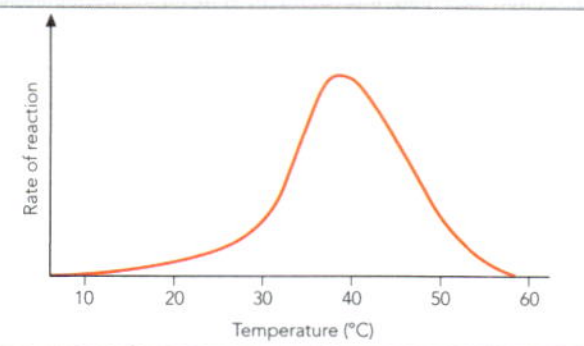


B *Many human enzymes have an optimum temperature that is close to the normal temperature of the main organs.*

At temperatures much above or below an optimum (best) value, enzymes don't work as well. This is partly why the processes in your body don't work as well when you have a fever.

Enzymes also often work best at an optimum pH. Most enzymes in cells work best at about pH7, but enzymes in the digestive system have to work well at much higher or lower pHs.

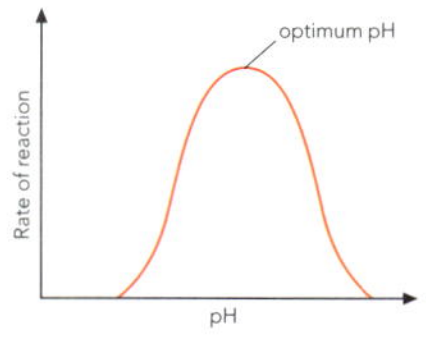


C *The pH can affect how well an enzyme works.*

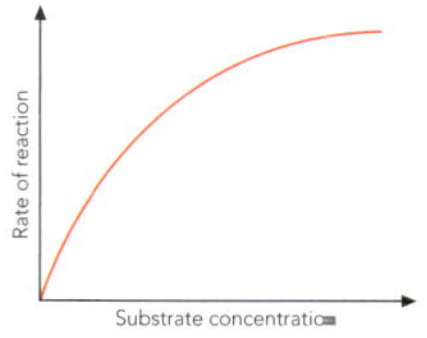


D *The concentration of the substrate affects the rate of reaction.*

The rate of a reaction catalysed by an enzyme will also increase as the concentration of substrate increases but only up to a point. Beyond that concentration, there is no further change in reaction rate. This is because the enzyme cannot work on the substrate any faster than at this rate. So adding more substrate molecules will make no difference to the rate.

## Specific enzymes

Another key feature of enzymes is that each enzyme will only work with a particular substrate, or small group of similar substrates. We say they are highly **specific** for the substrate. This feature is used to name enzymes, for example:

- carbohydrases catalyse the breakdown of carbohydrates
- proteases catalyse the breakdown of proteins.

## Explaining the observations

All the substrate molecules for one particular enzyme have the same 3D shape in some part of their molecules. This suggests that shape is important in enzyme action.

Looking at the 3D shapes of enzymes and their substrates shows that the substrate fits neatly into an **active site** in the enzyme. The active site has a different shape in different enzymes. Since the shape of the substrate fits tightly into the hole of the active site, this model of how enzymes work is called the '**lock-and-key**' **hypothesis**.

Changing the pH or temperature a little changes the shape of the active site so the substrate does not fit as well. Too much change will break the bonds within the enzyme. This can change the shape so much that it **denatures** the enzyme and destroys the active site.

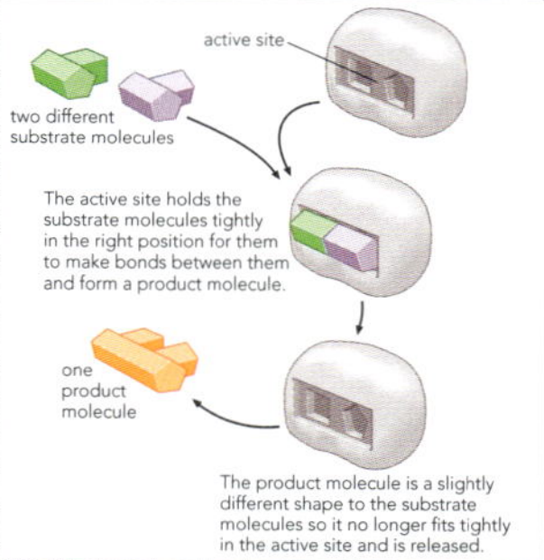


E *When two substrate molecules sit in the active site of this enzyme, they easily form new bonds to produce one new product molecule.*

3 Stomach contents have a pH of about 2. Sketch a graph to show the rate of reaction against pH for an enzyme that digests food in the stomach.

4 State three factors that can affect how well enzymes work.

**ResultsPlus Watch Out!**

Students often use the phrase 'enzymes are denatured' without explaining that the high temperature changes the shape of the active site and the substrate cannot bind to it.

5 How does the 'lock-and-key' hypothesis explain the specificity of enzymes for their substrates?

6 Describe how the 'lock-and-key' hypothesis explains the synthesis of one molecule from two substrates. Include the active site in your answer.

**Skills spotlight**

Scientists interpret data to provide evidence for testing ideas. Explain how the results from the effect of temperature on enzyme activity support the idea of an active site in enzymes.

**Learning Outcomes**

1.28 Describe the factors affecting enzyme action, including:
*a* temperature *b* substrate concentration *c* pH

1.29 Recall that enzymes are highly specific for their substrate

1.30 Demonstrate an understanding of the action of enzymes in terms of the 'lock-and- key' hypothesis

1.31 Descrbe how enzymes can be denatured due to changes in the shape of the active site

HSW 2 Describe how data is used by scientists to provide evidence that increases our scientific understanding

3 Describe how phenomena are explained using scientific theories, models and ideas





## ActiveTeach

- **AT** *Proteins and enzymes* [interactive]
  Proteins: structure and function – quiz
- **AT** *Enzyme shapes* [word document]
  Enzyme and substrate shapes

## Answers | Student Book

1 Just below 40 °C (37 °C), i.e. the highest point on the graph in Figure B.

2 The temperature at which an enzyme works best.

3 Graph similar to that in Figure C, but with the peak shown to occur at a pH of 2.

4 Temperature, pH, substrate concentration

5 The shape of the active site of the enzyme must match the shape of the substrate molecule. As substrate molecules are different shapes, an enzyme can only work with one type of substrate.

6 A good answer will contain the following points: the two substrate molecules fit into the active site of the enzyme molecule, side by side; this brings them close enough together to react and join to make one product molecule; then they are released from the active site.

**Skills spotlight**

The results from testing enzyme activity at different temperatures show that there is a temperature at which the enzyme works best. This is the temperature at which the substrate molecules have enough energy to move into the active site quickly and also fit well into the active site, so the reaction takes place as quickly as possible. At higher temperatures the substrate molecules still have plenty of energy but the shape of the enzyme's active site changes, so the rate of reaction slows down. Eventually the active site will be destroyed altogether as the enzyme denatures and the reaction will stop completely.

# B2.15 Aerobic respiration

This lesson looks at the link between aerobic respiration in cells and gas exchange in the lungs, and introduces the process of diffusion along concentration gradients.

## Specification coverage

**2.1** Recall that respiration is a process used by all living organisms that releases the energy needed for life processes

**2.2** Explain how the human circulatory system facilitates respiration, including: a) glucose and oxygen diffuses from capillaries into respiring cells b) carbon dioxide diffuses from respiring cells into capillaries

**2.3** Define diffusion as the movement of particles from an area of high concentration to an area of lower concentration

**2.4** Demonstrate an understanding of how aerobic respiration uses oxygen to release energy from glucose and how this process can be modelled using the word equation for aerobic respiration

HSW **3** Many phenomena can be explained by developing and using scientific theories, models and ideas

There are also opportunities to cover HSW *1*, HSW *6*, HSW *7* and HSW *8*.

### A breath of fresh air

**Starter 1** AfL

Ask students to write down an explanation of what would happen if they stopped breathing, and why they think this is and agree on a group explanation. Add any important words from the group explanations on the board. Make sure that any misconceptions are identified, clarified and addressed as they appear.

### Energy and life

**Starter 2**

Find a good video clip of some bioluminescent fish (e.g. via *YouTube*, or use BBC's *Blue Planet* 'The Deep' episode). Ask students to watch the clip, and then to brainstorm as many ways as possible in which they think animals use energy. Once this has been done, ask students to identify which uses involve detection of energy, and which involve the organism generating the energy.

### Observing blood vessels

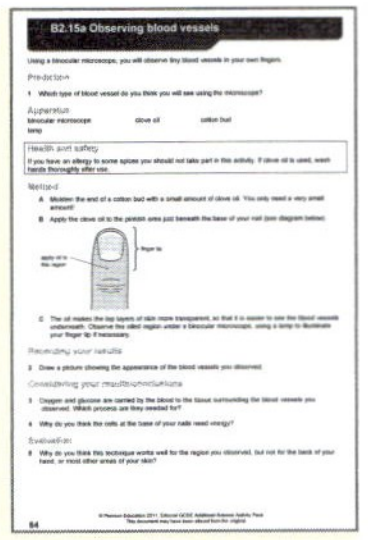

**Exploring 1** Prac

**Worksheet B2.15a** will provide a context for the explanation of diffusion later on in the lesson. Full details can be found on the Teacher and technician practical sheet B2.15 (1).

**Stretch** Students could try to work out a way in which they could measure the actual size of the blood vessels they observe.

**Support** Students work together in groups, performing each step of the procedure at exactly the same time, including the drawing of the results.

### Diffusion in pink gel blocks

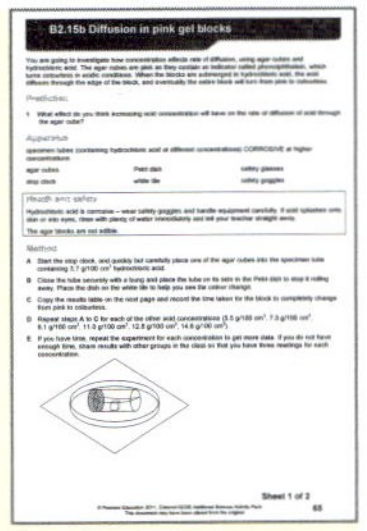

**Exploring 1** Prac

**Worksheet B2.15b** looks at the effect of concentration on rate of diffusion. Full details can be found on the Teacher and technician practical sheet B2.15 (2).

**Stretch** Challenge students to relate breathing and blood flow to this practical.

**Support** Help students to devise a way to model the experiment using trays and balls/marbles of two different colours.

### Measuring rates of respiration

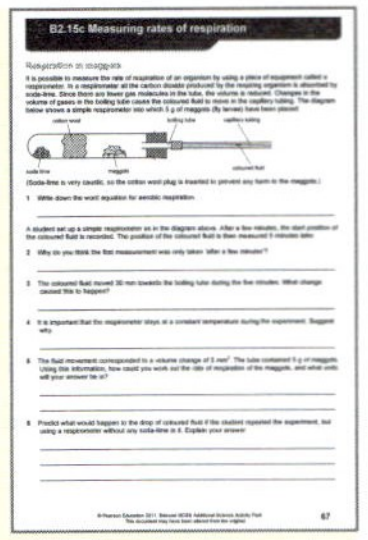

**Exploring 3**

**Worksheet B2.15c** provides an opportunity for students to explore how changes in gas volume allow respiration rate to be measured in terms of oxygen consumption.

**Stretch** Ask students to consider how respiration rates in humans could be measured.

**Support** Ask students to annotate the word equation for aerobic respiration to explain where each of the reactants comes from, and where the products end up.

### Student Book spread B2.15 (AT)

**Explaining 1**

The **AT** presentation *Visualising cells* shows the relative sizes of cells, mitochondria and glucose molecules.

**Stretch** Ask students to suggest some of the limiting factors on the amount of oxygen that an athlete can get into the blood.

**Support** Challenge students to come up with a flowchart showing how oxygen in the air ends up being used in respiration in a muscle cell.

### Definitions

**Plenary 1** AfL Lit

Each student should write down a definition of aerobic respiration and diffusion. Then they write down one sentence to explain how diffusion relates to respiration

### Key facts

**Plenary 2** AfL

Demonstrate the action of changing a Bunsen flame from yellow to blue and explain why this happens, then ask students to use this idea as an analogy for what happens in aerobic respiration. They should try to associate different aspects of the two processes and identify any limitations in using this model.

### Poster summary

**Homework 1**

Give students needing support a list of key words from the lesson and ask them to produce an illustrated poster that explains each word.

**Support** Provide students with definitions of the words for them to use, and ask them to use these to produce their own definitions.

### Diffusion and respiration

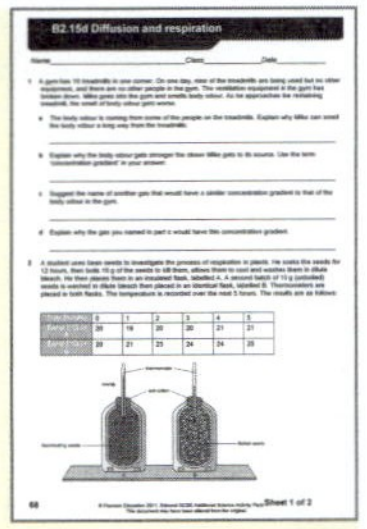

**Homework 2**

**Worksheet B2.15d** includes questions on diffusion of gases, investigating the respiration of seeds and the difference between breathing and respiration.

**Stretch** Ask students to do the 'extra challenge' question on the sheet.

# B2.15 Aerobic respiration

How do cells get what they need for aerobic respiration?

Eero Mäntyranta has unusual blood. As a result of an inherited mutation his blood contains higher than normal numbers of red blood cells. This gave him a competitive advantage over other athletes.

**A** *Eero Mäntyranta, from Finland, won seven Olympic cross-country skiing medals in the 1960s.*

All organisms are made of cells and energy is needed to power the many processes a cell carries out. This energy is released in a series of enzyme-catalysed reactions known collectively as **respiration**. Put simply, respiration is the release of energy from food molecules that acts as fuel for the cell.

1 Suggest why farm animals that are not allowed to move around need less food than farm animals that can wander around freely.

Cells that are more active have higher energy requirements. During exercise the muscles contract to cause movement, and this requires a great deal of energy from respiration. Growing and dividing cells also need lots of energy to power the building of new cell materials.

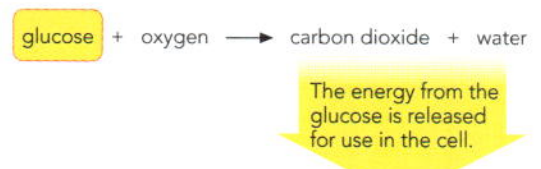


**B** *Aerobic respiration is a complex series of reactions but what happens can be modelled using a word equation.*

In **aerobic respiration** oxygen is used to release energy from molecules such as **glucose**. The glucose and oxygen are converted into carbon dioxide and water and energy is released for use in the cell.

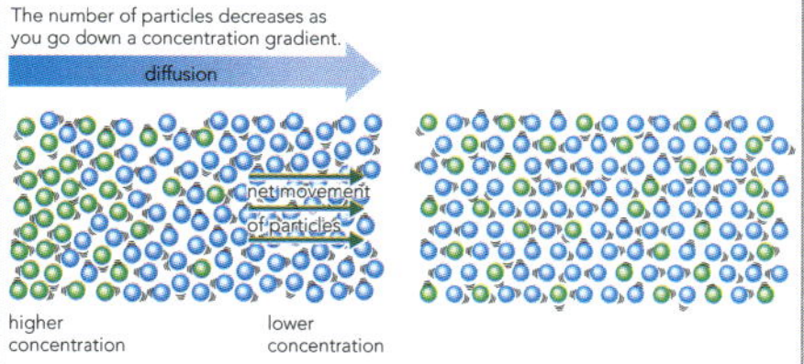


**C** *The green particles are diffusing along a concentration gradient.*

## Delivering glucose and oxygen

In humans, the glucose and oxygen needed for respiration are carried around the body and into tissues by blood. As well as carrying glucose and oxygen, blood must also carry waste carbon dioxide away from respiring cells. All these substances move between respiring cells and tiny blood vessels called **capillaries** by a process called **diffusion**. Diffusion occurs when particles of a substance spread out, moving from an area where they are in higher concentration to an area where they are in lower concentration. The particles diffuse down a **concentration gradient**.

In respiring cells, oxygen and glucose levels fall as they are used up in aerobic respiration. At the same time, carbon dioxide levels in the cells rise.

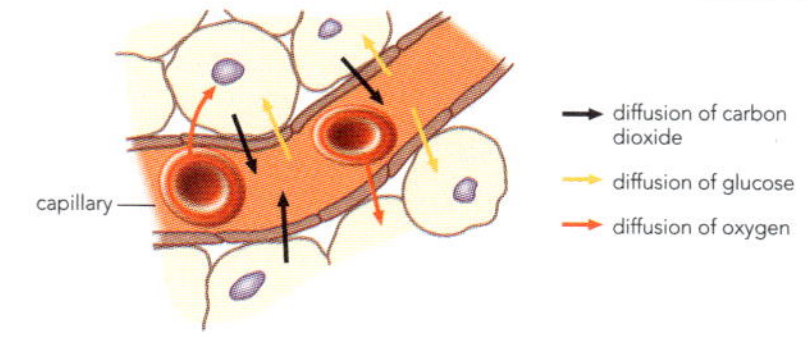


**D** *Movement of substances between capillaries and cells by diffusion*

2 Explain why oxygen diffuses into respiring cells but carbon dioxide diffuses out of them.

3 Capillaries have very thin walls. Why do you think this is important?

## Gas exchange

Lung tissue is spongy and full of tiny air sacs (alveoli). These sacs are surrounded by capillaries, and oxygen that enters the body through the lungs moves into the blood by diffusion. Carbon dioxide also leaves the blood by diffusion into the air spaces. As one gas is entering the bloodstream another one is leaving it; this is called **gas exchange**.

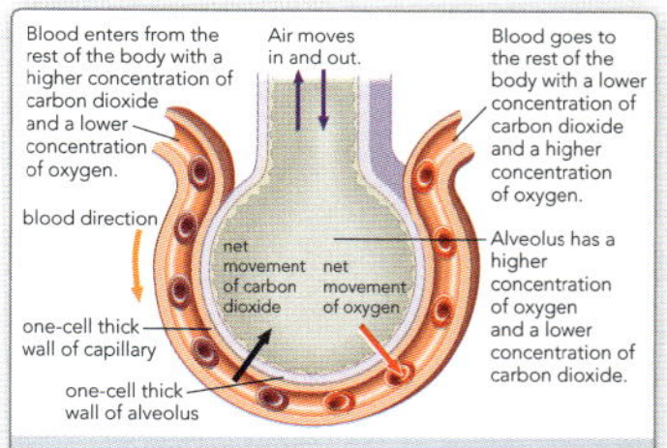


**E** *Gas exchange in the lungs*

4 Describe how oxygen enters the blood in the lungs.

5 Glucose and oxygen are needed for aerobic respiration to occur. Which of these two molecules contains the energy that is released in respiration?

6 Describe two processes inside cells that require energy to occur.

7 Suggest why Eero Mäntyranta had a competitive advantage over most other athletes.

### Skills spotlight

Models can help us to understand how processes happen at a molecular level.

**a** Explain how a word equation is a model for what happens to a molecule of glucose in aerobic respiration.

**b** Breaking bonds between atoms releases energy and making bonds between atoms requires energy input. Use the word equation model and your knowledge of bonds to describe simply how energy is released in aerobic respiration.

### ResultsPlus Watch Out!

Students often lose marks because they think that respiration is the same as breathing and gas exchange. Remember that breathing is to do with lungs, gas exchange occurs at the cell surface and respiration happens inside the cell.

### Learning Outcomes

2.1 Recall that respiration is a process used by all living organisms that releases the energy in organic molecules

2.2 Explain how the human circulatory system facilitates respiration including: a glucose and oxygen diffuses from capillaries into respiring cells b carbon dioxide diffuses from respiring cells into capillaries

2.3 Define diffusion as the movement of particles from an area of high concentration to an area of lower concentration

2.4 Demonstrate an understanding of how aerobic respiration uses oxygen to release energy from glucose and how this process can be modelled using the word equation for aerobic respiration

HSW 3 Describe how phenomena are explained using scientific models



Why do climbers use oxygen when they try to conquer the highest peaks in the world?



## ActiveTeach

- **AT** *Take a deep breath* [video]
  Aerobic respiration, breathing
- **AT** *Gas exchange by diffusion* [interactive]
  Diffusion in alveolus – labelling activity
- **AT** *Aerobic respiration* [interactive]
  Key terms in aerobic respiration – quiz
- **AT** *Visualising cells* [presentation]
  Cells, mitochondria and molecules

## Key terms

| | |
|---|---|
| aerobic respiration | diffusion |
| capillaries | gas exchange |
| concentration gradient | glucose |
| | respiration |

## Answers | Student Book

1 Movement is achieved through muscle contraction, which requires energy from respiration. This energy comes from the breakdown of food molecules (i.e. glucose), so less movement means less food required.

2 Oxygen concentrations are higher in blood than in respiring cells, so oxygen diffuses from blood to respiring cells. Carbon dioxide concentration is higher in respiring cells than in blood, so carbon dioxide diffuses from respiring cells to blood.

3 Less distance for substances (such as $CO_2$, $O_2$, glucose etc.) to diffuse, so diffusion will be faster.

4 Oxygen enters the body when air is breathed into the lungs, via the alveoli. Blood circulating through the lungs has a lower concentration of oxygen than the air in the alveoli does, so oxygen moves into the blood.

5 Glucose

6 Muscle contraction uses energy to shorten muscle. Cell growth/division uses energy to build new components of the cell, e.g. proteins/enzymes/lipids etc.

7 A good answer will include the following points: red blood cells carry oxygen; oxygen is needed for respiration; respiration releases energy; the more oxygen supplied to a cell, the more energy it can release using respiration; Eero has more red blood cells than usual; more oxygen will reach his muscle tissues in a given time; the increased rate of respiration in his muscle cells allows them to contract faster without tiring.

**Skills spotlight**

**a** A word equation shows that atoms in a molecule of glucose are rearranged to form new products from the same atoms. The products are molecules of water and carbon dioxide. It is a simple model because it does not: name or give the numbers of each type of atom; show the intermediary steps: show the role of enzymes in the reaction; give any information about the energy changes.

**b** The formation of new bonds between atoms in the molecules of carbon dioxide and water releases more energy than is needed to break the bonds in the glucose molecule. Overall energy is released.

# B2.16 Investigating the effects of exercise

This lesson challenges students to investigate the effect of exercise on breathing and heart rates. The activity may be run as a practice controlled assessment task or as a straight-forward class practical. The practical work can be completed in one hour but this will not allow time for repeat experiments. If a full investigation with repeats is carried out this may take up to two hours.

## Specification coverage

***2.5*** Investigate the effect of exercise on breathing rate and heart rate

This activity provides opportunities to cover HSW *1*, HSW *5*, HSW *6*, HSW *7*, HSW *8*, HSW *10* and HSW *11*.

### Before the lesson

Ensure that students are familiar with any equipment they may be expected to use so that they can plan their own investigation. In the week or two before the task show them this equipment and, if appropriate, allow them to practice using it. Students should be able to find their own pulse.

It may be good preparation to show students one or more of Skills Sheets 19 to 26 to show what is expected of them in their actual controlled assessment task.

### Starter

**Breathing and heart rates**

Ask everyone in the class to record their breathing rate for one minute while you control the stopwatch, record your own at the same time. Then collect and jot down all the breathing rates and work out the class average. Ask students what might affect the different breathing rates and what this tells them about the problems of making generalisations about breathing rates. Repeat the process for the heart rate, using the pulse in the wrist to take the measurements.

Ask students to look up average resting breathing rates and heart rates on the Internet and compare the results from several different sources with the class spread, the class averages and their own personal figures.

### Option 1: Straight-forward class practical

Students follow the instructions on **Worksheet B2.16b**. This gives students clear instructions about how to measure their own resting breathing and heart rate, the rates after different periods and levels of exercise and how to make decisions about how to display their data. The range of data that students need to collect is given on **Worksheet B2.16c**.

You could ask students to come up with one or two further hypotheses, based on their observations in this practical.

### Plenary

On page 59 of the Student Book you will find two examples of the type of work which students may produce for this task. The extracts focus on using secondary evidence. You could share these with students after they have completed their own work. This will help them to understand the assessment criteria and so make it easier for them to evaluate their work and to see how they can improve it. Moderator comments on each of the Student Book extracts can be found at the end of the assessment guidance for this investigation on the CD-ROM. The examples can also be found on the **AT** document *Student examples*.

### Option 2: Running the activity as a practice controlled assessment task (PCAT)

We have provided a full range of support resources to allow the running of this practical as a practice controlled assessment task. A recommended structure is outlined below (to be used over a number of sessions). Marking guidance for all three parts of the practice task can be found on the CD-ROM that accompanies the TTPP. To save time when using these practice controlled assessment tasks, you may wish to focus on a particular aspect or skill rather than working through all three parts of the task.

#### Part A Planning

1. Students should be given the Student Brief on Worksheet B2.16a. They can use Part A of the Workbook that is provided to help pupils with their practice controlled assessments. They should be given about 1 hour to do this planning.

#### Part B Observations

2. Students carry out the practical task to collect evidence using the method they have planned in Part A. Once again, they should refer to the Student Brief on Worksheet B2.16a. They can use Part B of the Workbook that is provided to help pupils with their practice controlled assessments. They should be given about 1 hour to collect their primary evidence.
3. If there is a problem with their own planned method, students may be asked to follow the method set out on **Worksheet B2.16b**. This will still enable students to access the full range of marks for Part B and Part C of the practice controlled assessment task.
4. In Part B, students are required to gather some secondary evidence. The evidence can be quantitative or qualitative. It can be from a variety of sources but students must note where they found their evidence and evaluate the quality of the source as part of this task. Skills Sheet 22 provides students with further guidance on researching for and evaluating secondary evidence. This part of the task could be done outside of the lesson but must be supervised.

#### Part C Conclusions

5. Students follow the instructions set out on the Part C section of the Student Brief on **Worksheet B2.16a**. They should use their data from Part B and the secondary evidence they have collected when doing this. They can use Part C of the Workbook that is provided to help pupils with their practice controlled assessments. They should be given about 1 hour to work on their conclusions.

Practice Controlled Assessment

# B2.16 Investigating the effects of exercise

What effect does exercise have on your breathing rate and your heart rate?

At very high altitude the air pressure and the oxygen concentration of the air is lower than at sea level. This makes it hard for the cells of your body to get enough oxygen. Even the simplest activity is very hard work. You puff and pant, and your heart races, just with the effort of walking.

**A** *Climbers often use oxygen to help their bodies cope with the conditions high up on a mountain.*

Climbers and athletes often wear heart beat monitors to show their heart rates when they are climbing mountains or training. You can also monitor your heart rate by taking your pulse. Your pulse is the surge of blood in your arteries as your heart pumps blood around your body, so by counting your pulse you can measure the number of times your heart beats.

When you exercise your muscles need lots of energy. The energy comes from aerobic respiration which needs oxygen (as well as glucose) and produces carbon dioxide. The oxygen and carbon dioxide enter and leave our bodies when we breathe and they are carried in the blood. This means that exercise can cause a change in heart rates and breathing rates.

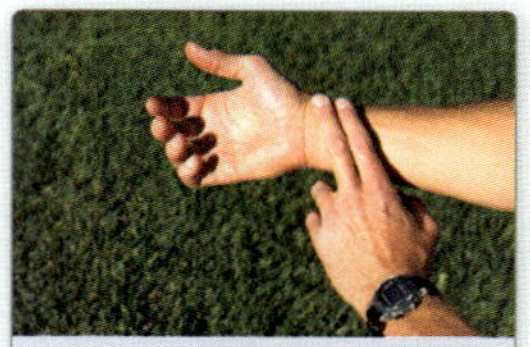

**B** *You can take your pulse in your wrist. Don't use your thumb because it has a pulse too.*

**Your task**

You are going to plan an investigation that will allow you to find out more about the effect of exercise on your breathing and heart rate. Your teacher will provide you with some materials to help you organise this task.

**Learning Outcomes**

*2.5 Investigate the effect of exercise on breathing rate and heart rate*

## ResultsPlus Build Better Answers

When planning an investigation like this, one of the skills you will be assessed on is your ability to collect and use *secondary evidence*. There are 2 marks available for this skill. Here are two extracts that focus on this skill. Other skills that you need for the assessment are dealt with in other lessons.

**Student extract 1** **A basic response for this skill**

*I found a website and I have written the web address below. It has a table which looked at the effect of caffeine on heart rate. It seems that caffeine speeds up the heart rate. I also found a graph in a book which shows me what resting heart rate should be for people of different ages.*

This evidence is not relevant to the investigation which is being carried out.

Provide a full web address so that someone else could look up the same information.

It is a good idea to give more than one example if you can – although this one does not give us a clear reference so it would be difficult for someone else to find this secondary evidence.

**Student extract 2** **A good response for this skill**

*I found a website and I have written the web address below. It has a table of results from a practical which looked at the effect of exercise on heart rate. The web site is run by a university (detailed below) and the results are properly referenced to the work of another scientist so I think that this is a trustworthy web site. I also found a graph in a book which shows me what happens to breathing rates during exercise but there was no detail about how the experiment was carried out, when it was done or who conducted it so I don't think that this source is quite as valuable.*

This practical is relevant to the investigation so is more useful.

The student has evaluated how trustworthy the website is.

The student has also evaluated the information from the book.

**ResultsPlus**

**To access 1 mark**

- Collect secondary evidence that is relevant to your hypothesis
- Record your secondary evidence in an appropriate way

**To access 2 marks**

You also need to comment on the quality of the sources of your secondary evidence.





## ActiveTeach

- **AT** *B2.16 Effects of exercise* [video]
  Students work through the investigation
- **AT** *B2.16 Moderator comments* [word document]
  Moderator comments on the video
- **AT** *B2.16 Assessment criteria* [presentation]
  Understanding the CA marking criteria
- **AT** *B2.16 Student task sheet* [word document]
  CA video checklist
- **AT** *B2.16 Specification points* [word document]
  Edexcel specification points
- **AT** *B2.16 Student examples* [word document]
  Examples for students to assess

## Assessment criteria

**Secondary evidence**

**0** No secondary evidence collected.

**1** Records secondary evidence from different sources, such as at least two different websites or a website and a textbook. The evidence is presented clearly, with the sources referenced.

**2** The quality of the sources of secondary evidence is commented upon, e.g. comments that a website is particularly reliable because it comes from a recognisable source or unreliable because there is no information about the way the practical was conducted.

# B2.17 Anaerobic respiration



This lesson looks at the effects of exercise on the body and how this can lead to anaerobic respiration and post-exercise oxygen consumption.

## Specification coverage

**2.6** Explain why heart rate and breathing rate increase with exercise

**2.7** Calculate heart rate, stroke volume and cardiac output, using the equation cardiac output = stroke volume × heart rate

**2.8** Demonstrate an understanding of why, during vigorous exercise, muscle cells may not receive sufficient oxygen for their energy requirements and so start to respire anaerobically

**2.9** Demonstrate an understanding of how anaerobic respiration releases energy from glucose and how this process can be modelled using the word equation for anaerobic respiration

**2.10** Recall that the process of anaerobic respiration releases less energy than aerobic respiration

**2.11** Describe how a build-up of lactic acid requires extra oxygen to break it down. This is called excess post-exercise oxygen consumption or EPOC (formerly known as oxygen debt)

**2.12** Explain why heart rate and breathing rate remain high after exercise

HSW *11* Presenting information, developing an argument and drawing a conclusion, using scientific, technical and mathematical language, conventions and symbols, and ICT tools

There are also opportunities to cover HSW *3* and HSW *10*.

### Heartbeat

**Starter 1**

Find a sound clip of a normal heartbeat. Ask students to listen to it, and then see what they can tell you about the person they are listening to. Is it an adult or a child? Someone relaxing or exercising? How can they tell? Use this to get students thinking about the fact that heart rate can vary for several reasons.

### EPOC and exercise

**Exploring 1**

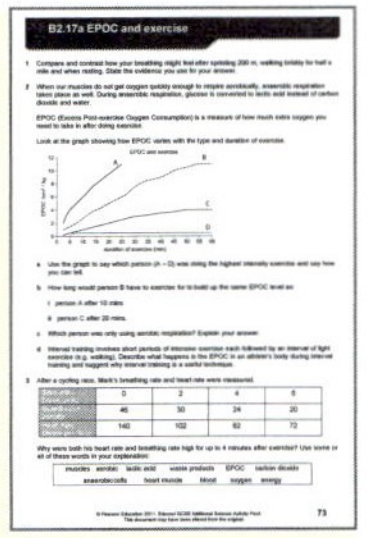
B2.17a EPOC and exercise

In **Worksheet B2.17a** students interpret secondary data, concentrating on breathing rate and heart rate for different intensities of exercise and what happens to the body.

Stretch Ask students to predict how EPOC values would vary for people of different body mass.

Support In question **2**, talk through how increased intensity and duration of exercise both give higher EPOC values.

### Where is the energy? (AT)

**Explaining 1**

Glucose stores lots of chemical energy, lactic acid stores a reasonable amount and carbon dioxide stores little. By considering this students should be able to see why anaerobic respiration releases less energy than aerobic; the difference in energy between the reactants and the products is greater for aerobic.

Stretch Students could model the reaction using molecular models (see diagrams on the **AT** presentation *Glucose and lactic acid molecules*).

Support Use simple energy level diagrams to help students see the differences between the energy released in aerobic and anaerobic respiration.

### Respiration sentences

**Plenary 1** AfL Lit

Write the words 'heart rate', 'cardiac output', 'stroke volume', 'activity', 'aerobic respiration' and 'anaerobic respiration' on the board. Ask students to write down the beginnings of three sentences using some of these words, and then to swap these to see if a partner can complete them.

### Respiration roundup

**Homework 1**

B2.17c Respiration roundup

**Worksheet B2.17c** provides summary questions that cover the key ideas covered in the last two lessons.

Support Discuss question **4** with students before they answer it.

### Walk or sprint?

**Starter 2**

Ask students to suggest the effects of hard exercise, i.e. what do they feel like when they have been exercising hard? A video clip could also support this, showing athletes finishing an 800m race. Then get them to suggest why their muscles ache and why they continue to breathe heavily after finishing the exercise.

### Investigating EPOC

**Exploring 1** Prac

B2.17b Investigating EPOC

Students investigate the level of exercise at which EPOC starts to occur. See **Worksheet B2.17b**. Full details can be found on the Teacher and technician notes B2.17.

Stretch Ask students to suggest reasons for the variation in oxygen consumption for different students doing the same exercise.

Support Help students work out the oxygen consumption by writing calculations on the board.

### Student Book spread B2.17

**Explaining 2**

Students read the section on EPOC. See how well they have understood the idea by asking why they continue to breathe rapidly even when intense exercise has been stopped.

Ask students to complete the cardiac output values in the table in the **AT** presentation *Cardiac output*.

Stretch Challenge students to suggest a further reason why extra oxygen is needed after exercise.

Support Construct a sequence on the board to organise the events that occur in anaerobic respiration, and what happens to the lactic acid generated.

### Cardiac output and exercise

**Plenary 2** AfL Lit

Write the phrase cardiac output in the middle of the board, and ask students to suggest related words and how they should be linked to make a concept map, giving a reason for their placement.

### Diffusion and respiration

**Homework 2**

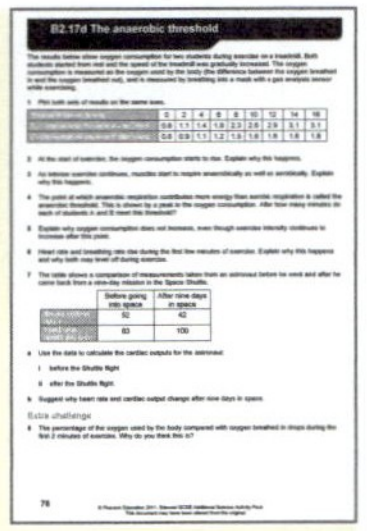
B2.17d The anaerobic threshold

**Worksheet B2.17d** provides secondary data on oxygen consumption for students to interpret and link to aerobic and anaerobic respiration.

Stretch Students answer the 'extra challenge' question.

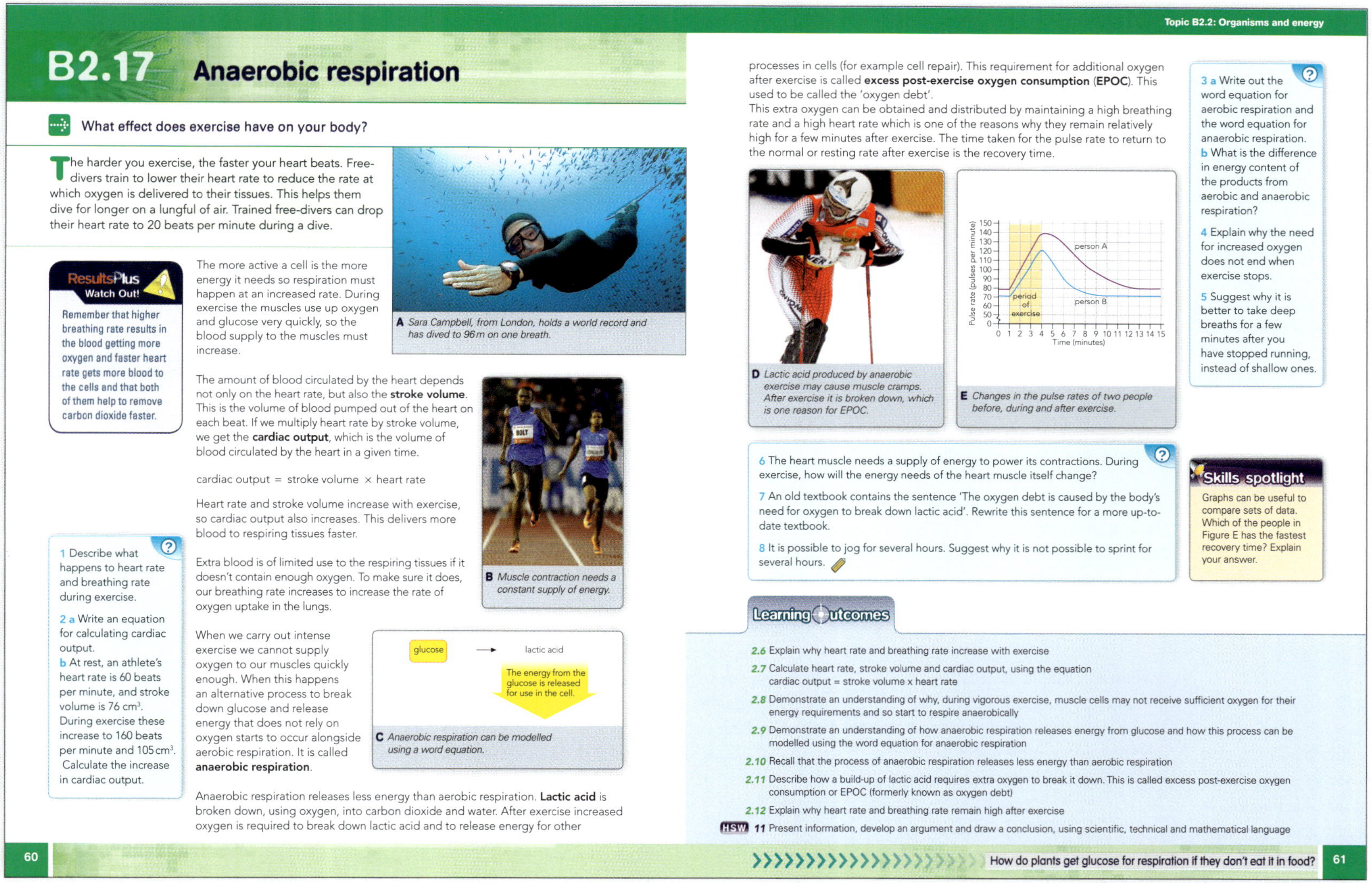



# B2.17 Anaerobic respiration

What effect does exercise have on your body?

The harder you exercise, the faster your heart beats. Free-divers train to lower their heart rate to reduce the rate at which oxygen is delivered to their tissues. This helps them dive for longer on a lungful of air. Trained free-divers can drop their heart rate to 20 beats per minute during a dive.

**A** *Sara Campbell, from London, holds a world record and has dived to 96 m on one breath.*

**ResultsPlus Watch Out!**

Remember that higher breathing rate results in the blood getting more oxygen and faster heart rate gets more blood to the cells and that both of them help to remove carbon dioxide faster.

The more active a cell is the more energy it needs so respiration must happen at an increased rate. During exercise the muscles use up oxygen and glucose very quickly, so the blood supply to the muscles must increase.

The amount of blood circulated by the heart depends not only on the heart rate, but also the **stroke volume**. This is the volume of blood pumped out of the heart on each beat. If we multiply heart rate by stroke volume, we get the **cardiac output**, which is the volume of blood circulated by the heart in a given time.

cardiac output = stroke volume × heart rate

Heart rate and stroke volume increase with exercise, so cardiac output also increases. This delivers more blood to respiring tissues faster.

**B** *Muscle contraction needs a constant supply of energy.*

1 Describe what happens to heart rate and breathing rate during exercise.

2 a Write an equation for calculating cardiac output.
b At rest, an athlete's heart rate is 60 beats per minute, and stroke volume is 76 $cm^3$. During exercise these increase to 160 beats per minute and 105 $cm^3$. Calculate the increase in cardiac output.

Extra blood is of limited use to the respiring tissues if it doesn't contain enough oxygen. To make sure it does, our breathing rate increases to increase the rate of oxygen uptake in the lungs.

When we carry out intense exercise we cannot supply oxygen to our muscles quickly enough. When this happens an alternative process to break down glucose and release energy that does not rely on oxygen starts to occur alongside aerobic respiration. It is called **anaerobic respiration**.

glucose → lactic acid

The energy from the glucose is released for use in the cell.

**C** *Anaerobic respiration can be modelled using a word equation.*

Anaerobic respiration releases less energy than aerobic respiration. **Lactic acid** is broken down, using oxygen, into carbon dioxide and water. After exercise increased oxygen is required to break down lactic acid and to release energy for other processes in cells (for example cell repair). This requirement for additional oxygen after exercise is called **excess post-exercise oxygen consumption** (**EPOC**). This used to be called the 'oxygen debt'.
This extra oxygen can be obtained and distributed by maintaining a high breathing rate and a high heart rate which is one of the reasons why they remain relatively high for a few minutes after exercise. The time taken for the pulse rate to return to the normal or resting rate after exercise is the recovery time.

**D** *Lactic acid produced by anaerobic exercise may cause muscle cramps. After exercise it is broken down, which is one reason for EPOC.*

Pulse rate (pulses per minute)
Time (minutes)
person A
person B
period of exercise

**E** *Changes in the pulse rates of two people before, during and after exercise.*

3 a Write out the word equation for aerobic respiration and the word equation for anaerobic respiration.
b What is the difference in energy content of the products from aerobic and anaerobic respiration?

4 Explain why the need for increased oxygen does not end when exercise stops.

5 Suggest why it is better to take deep breaths for a few minutes after you have stopped running, instead of shallow ones.

6 The heart muscle needs a supply of energy to power its contractions. During exercise, how will the energy needs of the heart muscle itself change?

7 An old textbook contains the sentence 'The oxygen debt is caused by the body's need for oxygen to break down lactic acid'. Rewrite this sentence for a more up-to-date textbook.

8 It is possible to jog for several hours. Suggest why it is not possible to sprint for several hours.

**Skills spotlight**

Graphs can be useful to compare sets of data. Which of the people in Figure E has the fastest recovery time? Explain your answer.

**Learning Outcomes**

2.6 Explain why heart rate and breathing rate increase with exercise
2.7 Calculate heart rate, stroke volume and cardiac output, using the equation cardiac output = stroke volume x heart rate
2.8 Demonstrate an understanding of why, during vigorous exercise, muscle cells may not receive sufficient oxygen for their energy requirements and so start to respire anaerobically
2.9 Demonstrate an understanding of how anaerobic respiration releases energy from glucose and how this process can be modelled using the word equation for anaerobic respiration
2.10 Recall that the process of anaerobic respiration releases less energy than aerobic respiration
2.11 Describe how a build-up of lactic acid requires extra oxygen to break it down. This is called excess post-exercise oxygen consumption or EPOC (formerly known as oxygen debt)
2.12 Explain why heart rate and breathing rate remain high after exercise
HSW 11 Present information, develop an argument and draw a conclusion, using scientific, technical and mathematical language



How do plants get glucose for respiration if they don't eat it in food?



## ActiveTeach

- **AT** *Anaerobic respiration* [interactive]
  Key terms in anaerobic respiration – quiz
- **AT** *Cardiac output* [presentation]
  Calculating cardiac output
- **AT** *Glucose and lactic acid* [presentation]
  Molecular models

## Key terms

anaerobic respiration
cardiac output
excess post-exercise oxygen consumption (EPOC)
lactic acid
stroke volume

## Answers | Student Book

1 Heart rate and breathing rate increase

2 **a** Cardiac output = stroke volume × heart rate
**b** Rest - output = 60 × 76 = 4560 $cm^3$/min. Exercise - output = 16 800 $cm^3$/min. Output increase = 16 800 – 4560 = 12 240 $cm^3$/min.

3 **a** Aerobic: glucose + oxygen → carbon dioxide + water; Anaerobic: glucose → lactic acid
**b** More energy stored in lactic acid than in products of aerobic respiration.

4 Lactic acid from anaerobic respiration requires extra oxygen to break it down; increased oxygen is required to release energy for other processes in cells after exercise.

5 More oxygen enters the blood (via the lungs), so the excess post-exercise oxygen consumption (EPOC) need is met more quickly.

6 The heart muscle will need more energy for increased rate of contraction.

7 EPOC is caused by the body's need for extra oxygen to break down lactic acid produced during anaerobic respiration; increased oxygen is required to release energy for other processes (e.g. cell repair) in cells after exercise.

8 A good answer will contain the following points: aerobic respiration can only supply oxygen fast enough for jogging; but not for such a big increase in respiration of the active muscles during sprinting; anaerobic respiration used when sprinting; heart rate and breathing rate can only increase up to a certain point; the body has to get rid of lactic acid that accumulates during anaerobic respiration; it doesn't release enough energy to sprint over long periods.

**Skills spotlight**
Person B's pulse rate returns to their pre-exercise (resting) level at 9 minutes, which is faster than person A at 13 minutes, so person B has a faster recovery time.

# B2.18 Photosynthesis



This lesson introduces the process of photosynthesis and looks at how leaf structure is adapted to carry out this function effectively.

## Specification coverage

***2.13*** Describe how the structure of the leaf is adapted for photosynthesis, including: a) large surface area b) containing chlorophyll in chloroplasts to absorb light c) stomata for gas exchange (carbon dioxide, oxygen and water vapour)

***2.14*** Demonstrate an understanding of how photosynthesis uses light energy to produce glucose and how this process can be modelled using the word equation for photosynthesis

HSW *3* Many phenomena can be explained by developing and using scientific theories, *models and ideas*

There are also opportunities to cover HSW *1*, HSW *3*, HSW *6*, HSW *7*, HSW *8* and HSW *11*.

## Key terms

chlorophyll
chloroplast
photosynthesis starch
stomata (stoma)
surface area to volume ratio

### Common themes

**Starter 1**

Show students a selection of morphologically diverse plants, e.g. pond weed, a cactus, a spider plant, a succulent. Ask students to identify what they all have in common, and what this suggests. Can they also suggest how the differences are useful for each plant?

### What is it? (AT)

**Starter 2**

Show the **AT** image *SEM of leaf*, which is a scanning electron micrograph of a leaf lower epidermis in which stomata are clearly visible. Get students to guess what they are looking at, giving them clues if necessary. Students can then suggest what purpose these pores might have.

### Structure of a leaf

**Exploring 1** Prac

Students look at slides of leaf sections under the microscope. See **Worksheet B2.18a**. Full details can be found on the Teacher and technician practical sheet B2.18 (1).

Stretch Students observe slides from 'unusual' leaves and try to identify the same tissues in each species.

Support Provide students with descriptions only of tissue layers and/or features, related to photosynthesis. Ask them to match descriptions to the structures they observe.

### Chromatography and starch tests for variegated leaves

**Exploring 2** Prac

Students test variegated leaves for chlorophyll. See **Worksheets B2.18b** and **B2.18c**. Full details can be found on the Teacher and technician practical sheet on B2.18 (2).

Stretch Ask students to explain why leaving the plant in a cupboard for a few days leads to destarching.

Support Students could be provided with a model chromatogram, which they could use to calculate Rf values to identify the pigments.

### Student Book spread B2.18

**Explaining 1**

Through questioning, build up the word equation for photosynthesis, and from there annotate it to explain how leaf structure relates to each substance produced.

Stretch Ask students what the limitations of the word equation model are; what does it not tell us about the process of photosynthesis? Students could also try to complete a balanced equation.

Support Students could assemble a word equation using prepared cards with each of the components involved printed onto them. Challenge students to identify products, reactants, energy-rich molecules and so on.

### Where does the mass come from?

**Explaining 2**

Show students a picture of an acorn and an oak tree and ask them to compare the sizes. Ask where the mass comes from? Explain that the (non-water) mass of the oak tree originates from carbon dioxide from the atmosphere, and water absorbed by the roots. These are used to build glucose, which is turned into the molecules that the plant cells are made from.

Stretch Students produce their own explanations of plant growth.

Support Provide a copy of the word equation for photosynthesis during this discussion.

### Adaptations for photosynthesis (AT)

**Plenary 1** AfL

Provide students with the **AT** document *Leaf structure diagram*, which is a large unlabelled diagram of a leaf cross-section. Students should add labels and explanations to the diagram to relate the leaf structure to photosynthesis.

### Sentence starters

**Plenary 2** AfL Lit

Provide a set of sentences for students to complete in their own words, including a connecting word such as 'and', 'because', 'but', 'however', 'is', 'so', 'such as', 'therefore', 'to', 'which'. Examples could be: 'Leaves have pores or stomata…'; 'Chlorophyll absorbs light…'

### Leaf structure and photosynthesis

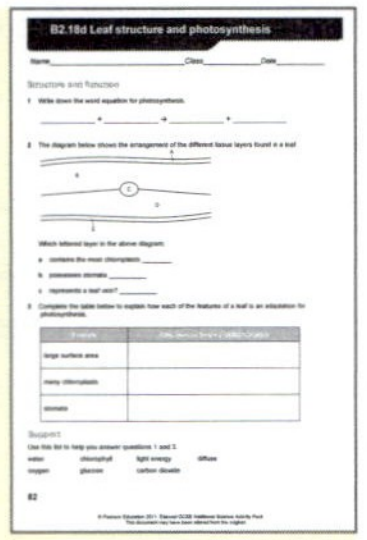


**Homework 1**

**Worksheet B2.18d** provides questions about the content of this lesson.

Support Write 'upper leaf surface', 'lower leaf surface' and 'layer with air spaces' next to the diagram before photocopying and supply the word list from the lower half of the sheet.

### Van Helmont's willow tree

**Homework 2**

**Worksheet B2.18e** provides questions to reinforce the idea of where the mass of a tree comes from, and evaluation questions on Van Helmont's original experiment.

Stretch Students answer the 'extra challenge' question.

# B2.18 Photosynthesis

What is starch, and where does the energy it contains come from?

Marathon runners often change their diet several days before a race, eating large amounts of starchy food like potatoes, rice or pasta. The excess carbohydrate is stored in the form of 'glycogen' and can be broken down when glucose is needed to power their long journey.

**A** *A lot of starch is found in foods like potatoes and pasta. Plants use starch to store energy.*

> 1 State two differences between the reactions of photosynthesis and aerobic respiration.

**Starch** is made by joining together thousands of glucose molecules. When starch is broken down in digestion, glucose is released and can be used for respiration. Plant cells also need to respire and so need a supply of glucose. Plants can actually manufacture their own glucose using the simple raw materials of carbon dioxide and water. This process is called **photosynthesis**. Plants can also store the glucose they make as carbohydrates, like starch.

the energy from sunlight

carbon dioxide + water → glucose + oxygen

**B** *Photosynthesis can be modelled using a word equation.*

Photosynthesis is a complex series of enzyme-catalysed reactions which occurs inside cell organelles called **chloroplasts**.

Light is the energy source for photosynthesis and is absorbed by a green substance inside chloroplasts called **chlorophyll**. Without chlorophyll, photosynthesis cannot occur. Chlorophyll transfers the light energy into the stored chemical energy in glucose.

> 2 a Which parts of the variegated leaf in Figure C lack chlorophyll?
> b Suggest why variegated plants tend to grow more slowly than normal plants.

**C** *The leaves of this variegated plant have some areas without chloroplasts. The leaf on the right has been tested for starch using iodine solution which turns blue-black if starch is present. Only the areas of the leaf that contain chlorophyll contain starch.*

## Leaf adaptations

The leaf is the main plant organ in which photosynthesis occurs. Leaves have several adaptations for photosynthesis, including the presence of chloroplasts containing chlorophyll to absorb light energy. Leaves are broad and flat to provide a very large surface area which helps them absorb as much light energy as possible.

On the underside of a leaf there are microscopic pores called **stomata** (singular = **stoma**). The stomata open in response to light. These pores allow carbon dioxide in the atmosphere to diffuse into the leaf, to be taken up by photosynthesising cells. Oxygen produced by these cells can also diffuse from the inside of the leaf out to the atmosphere. Plant cells produce water in respiration, some of which evaporates from their surfaces and diffuses out of the leaf.

The air spaces inside the leaf give the cells a large **surface area to volume ratio** for efficient gas exchange.

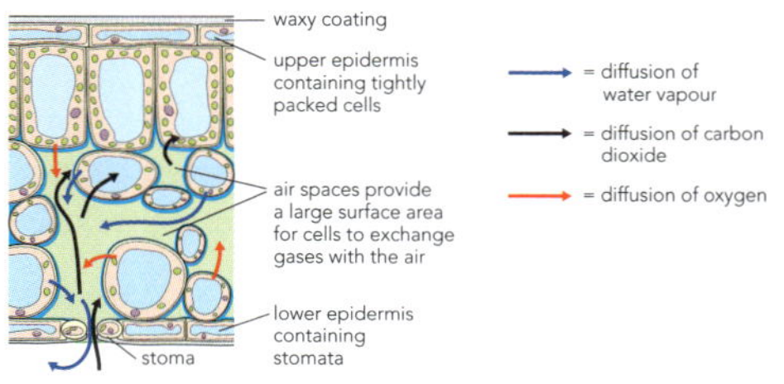


**D** *Cross-section through a leaf, showing gas exchange through a stoma.*

> 5 If the stomata on a leaf become blocked why does this cause the leaf to die?
> 6 Photosynthesis can take place in any plant cells that contain chloroplasts. Explain how leaves are adapted to make them very efficient as sites for photosynthesis.

**Skills spotlight**

Theories are used to explain phenomena. It used to be thought that plants grew by eating soil! Explain the theory that we now use to explain how plants grow and how this theory matches our observations about soil levels in pot plants better.

> 3 Stomata usually close when it is dark and open when it is light. Why do you think they do it this way round and not the other?
> 4 If a potato is left in sunlight it will develop a green colour on its surface. Suggest what is responsible for the green colour and why this might be an advantage for a potato.

**ResultsPlus Watch Out!**

Many students think that plants don't respire. All plant cells respire and they have mitochondria just like animal cells.

**Learning Outcomes**

2.13 Describe how the structure of the leaf is adapted for photosynthesis, including:
a large surface area
b contains chlorophyll in chloroplasts to absorb light
c stomata for gas exchange (carbon dioxide, oxygen and water vapour)

2.14 Demonstrate an understanding of how photosynthesis uses light energy to produce glucose and how this process can be modelled using the word equation for photosynthesis

HSW 3 Describe how phenomena are explained using scientific theories and ideas



Why might an increase in greenhouse gases be good news for plants?



## ActiveTeach

- **AT** *Making glucose* [interactive]
  Photosynthesis – matching game
- **AT** *Increasing the rate of photosynthesis* [interactive]
  $CO_2$ and photosynthesis – multiple choice
- **AT** *Leaf structure diagram* [word document]
  Label cross-section diagram
- **AT** *Gas exchange through a stoma in a leaf* [diagram]
  Figure D – diagram labelling activity
- **AT** *SEM of leaf* [image]
  SEM image of a leaf lower epidermis, showing stomata

## Answers | Student Book

1 Photosynthesis requires an energy input; aerobic respiration releases energy. Photosynthesis uses carbon dioxide and water; aerobic respiration produces them. Photosynthesis produces glucose and oxygen; aerobic respiration uses them.

2 **a** The white/cream-coloured parts
**b** Less chlorophyll in pale portions of leaf means less light absorbed and so less photosynthesis. Less glucose is produced for plant growth.

3 Plants can't photosynthesise without light, so there is no need for carbon dioxide when it is dark. Stomata shut to prevent water loss from leaves.

4 The green colour is chlorophyll. This allows the potato to photosynthesise and make its own food as it starts to grow.

5 Carbon dioxide cannot enter the leaf and so the cells inside will not be able to photosynthesise and make food and oxygen for respiration.

6 A good answer will contain the following points: chloroplasts in leaf cells contain chlorophyll, which absorbs light energy; leaves are broad so a large surface area is exposed to light to maximise light absorption; Leaves are thin, so carbon dioxide and water vapour only have a short distance to diffuse to reach the photosynthesising cells; The lower surface of the leaf has stomata that allow gases to enter and leave by diffusion; Air spaces inside the leaf allow diffusing gases to move easily into and away from cells and gives surrounding cells a large surface area to volume ratio for efficient gas exchange; Leaves have a network of veins, to deliver water for photosynthesis and take away glucose made in photosynthesis.

**Skills spotlight**

The current theory used to explain how plants grow is that they manufacture their own food using carbon dioxide, water and energy from sunlight. This theory is supported by the observation that soil levels do not decrease as a plant grows, since the theory does not require any of the soil mass to be used to manufacture food for the plant.

# B2.19 Factors affecting the rate of photosynthesis



This lesson challenges students to investigate the effect of changing the light intensity on the rate of photosynthesis by varying the distance of a lamp from a water plant. The activity may be run as a practice controlled assessment task or as a straight-forward class practical. The practical work will take about two hours.

## Specification coverage

***2.16*** Investigate how factors, including the effect of light intensity, $CO_2$ concentration or temperature, affect the rate of photosynthesis

This activity provides opportunities to cover HSW *1*, HSW *5*, HSW *6*, HSW *7*, HSW *8*, HSW *10* and HSW *11*.

### Before the lesson

Ensure that students are familiar with any equipment they may be expected to use so that they can plan their own investigation. In the week or two before the task show them this equipment and, if appropriate, allow them to practice using it. In this investigation students may find it useful to practice setting up a similar practical including inverting a test tube full of water over a filter funnel.

If students are to use light meters it may also be a good idea to allow students to familiarise themselves with how they work.

It may be good preparation to show students one or more of Skills Sheets 19 to 26 to show what is expected of them in their actual controlled assessment task.

### Starter

**Greenhouses**

Ask students to investigate hydroponics – or if they don't have access to the Internet, simply to think about conditions in a greenhouse. Ask them to list what sort of conditions plants are given in these very artificial environments and to think about why. Follow this by reading the additional information below the opening section of page 64 of the Student Book. They may then read the brief description of the activity provided by the 'Your task' box.

### Option 1: Straight-forward class practical

You may wish to run the activity as a straight-forward class practical. Students follow the instructions on **Worksheet B2.19b**. They are reminded to allow the system to equilibrate each time before collecting data. The technique given uses distance of the light from the plant to give an indirect measurement of light intensity. You may choose to give students light meters to measure light intensity directly. The range of data that students need to collect is given on **Worksheet B2.19c**. You could ask students to come up other hypotheses, based on their observations in this practical. For example they could consider the effect changing carbon dioxide levels and different temperatures on the rate of photosynthesis, observed in a similar experimental set-up.

### Plenary

On page 65 of the Student Book you will find two examples of the sort of work that students may produce for this task. The examples focus on processing evidence. You could share these with students after they have completed their own work. This will help them to understand the assessment criteria and so make it easier for them to evaluate their work and to see how they can improve it. Moderator comments on each of the Student Book extracts can be found at the end of the assessment guidance for this investigation on the CD-ROM. The examples can also be found on the **AT** document *Student examples*.

## Option 2: Running the activity as a practice controlled assessment task (PCA)

We have provided a full range of support resources to allow the running of this practical as a practice controlled assessment task. A recommended structure is outlined below (to be used over a number of sessions). Marking guidance for all three parts of the practice task can be found on the CD-ROM that accompanies the TTPP. To save time when using these practice controlled assessment tasks, you may wish to focus on a particular aspect or skill rather than working through all three parts of the task.

### Part A Planning

1. Students should be given the Student brief on Worksheet B2.19a. They can use Part A of the Workbook that is provided to help pupils with their practice controlled assessments. They should be given about 1 hour to do this planning.

### Part B Observations

2. Students carry out the practical task to collect evidence using the method they have planned in Part A. Once again, they should refer to the Student brief on **Worksheet B2.19a**. They can use Part B of the Workbook that is provided to help pupils with their practice controlled assessments. They should be given about 2 hours to collect their primary evidence.
3. If there is a problem with their own planned method, students may be asked to follow the method set out on **Worksheet B2.19b**. This will still enable students to access the full range of marks for Part B and Part C of the practice controlled assessment task.
4. In Part B, students are required to gather some secondary evidence. The evidence can be quantitative or qualitative. It can be from a variety of sources but students must note where they found their evidence and evaluate the quality of the source as part of this task. Skills Sheet 22 provides students with further guidance on researching for and evaluating secondary evidence. This part of the task could be done outside of the lesson but must be supervised.

### Part C Conclusions

5. Students follow the instructions set out on the Part C section of the Student brief on **Worksheet B2.19a**. They should use their data from Part B and the secondary evidence they have collected when doing this. They can use Part C of the Workbook that is provided to help pupils with their practice controlled assessments. They should be given about 1 hour to work on their conclusions.

The **AT** includes video clips showing a group of students working through elements of this investigation with teacher support.

Practice Controlled Assessment

# B2.19 Factors affecting the rate of photosynthesis

What factors affect the rate of photosynthesis?

Would you buy a mobile phone, a cooking pot and a car made from plants? More and more of the plastics we use are being made from plant materials instead of chemicals from oil. Fortunately plants produce around 243 billion tonnes of dry plant material every year by photosynthesis. If we are careful there will be plenty of plants to eat as well as all the bioplastics we want and need.

Glucose is made by photosynthesis and it is quickly turned into starch in the plant. The starch is then later broken down into sugars which are used in a variety of ways in the plant.

Oxygen is given off as a waste product during photosynthesis. You can't see this oxygen in land plants, but in water plants such as *Elodea* the oxygen given off is seen as a stream of tiny bubbles.

Factors such as light levels and the temperature of the water will affect the rate at which photosynthesis takes place.

**A** *This car is the first Formula 3 racing car designed and made from sustainable and renewable materials. For example, the wing mirrors contain potato starch.*

**Your task**

You are going to plan an investigation that will allow you to find out how light levels affect the rate of photosynthesis. Your teacher will provide you with some materials to help you organise this task.

**Learning Outcomes**

**2.16** *Investigate how factors, including the effect of light intensity, $CO_2$ concentration or temperature, affect the rate of photosynthesis*

## ResultsPlus Build Better Answers

When planning an investigation like this, one of the skills you will be assessed on is your ability to *process evidence*. There are 4 marks available for this skill. Here are two extracts focusing on this skill. Other skills that you need for the assessment are dealt with in other lessons.

### Student extract 1 — A basic response for this skill

The results I collected from my experiment can be processed like this:
When the lamp was 10 cm away the number of bubbles in a minute were 22, 20 and 19. The middle reading is 20 so I will take this as my mean.
When the lamp was 20 cm away the readings were 18, 10 and 18. I can add these up and divide by 3 to get a mean of 15.3.
I can plot a bar chart to show these results.

This is not the way to work out a mean – check that you are using the correct mathematical skill.

This result looks like an anomaly. It may be best not to include it in the mean calculation.

All of this information would be better in a table.

Plotting a chart or graph can be a good way to show your results clearly – but a bar chart is not necessarily the best way to display these results.

### Student extract 2 — A good response for this skill

| Distance of lamp from plant (cm) | Number of bubbles of oxygen-rich gas produced /min | | | |
|---|---|---|---|---|
| | Reading 1 | Reading 2 | Reading 3 | Average (mean) |
| 10 | 20 | 22 | 19 | 20.6 |
| 20 | 18 | 19 | 18 | 18.3 |
| 30 | 14 | 14 | 14 | 14 |
| 40 | 12 | 10 | 9 | 10.3 |

I then plotted a line graph which shows the results clearly and has all the correct labels and headings. My line graph is shown below.

Calculating a mean average is a good idea here.

The line graph is a good way to show the pattern in the results. This can help when you try to draw a conclusion.

### ResultsPlus

**To access 2 marks**

- Attempt to process all your collected evidence
- Use appropriate maths skills
- Present your processed evidence in an appropriate way

**To access 4 marks**

- Process all your evidence in an appropriate way, using maths skills if appropriate
- Present it in a way that allows you to draw a conclusion

64 ›››››››››››››››››››› Why can't growers keep increasing light levels to increase crop yields? 65

## ActiveTeach

- **AT** *B2.19 Rate of photosynthesis* [interactive]
  Factors on photosynthesis rates
- **AT** *B2.19 Assessment criteria* [presentation]
  Understanding the CA marking criteria
- **AT** *B2.19 Specification points* [word document]
  Edexcel specification points
- **AT** *B2.19 Student examples* [word document]
  Examples for students to assess

## Assessment criteria

**Processing evidence**

**0** Evidence is not processed.

**1-2 a)** An attempt is made to process all collected evidence using mathematical skills if appropriate, e.g. attempts to work out the mean if repeat results have been taken.

**b)** An attempt is made to present the processed evidence in a way that is appropriate for the topic, e.g. attempts a simple line graph.

**3-4 a)** Processes primary data and secondary evidence using appropriate mathematical processes, e.g. successfully calculates means if repeats have been taken.

**b)** Processed evidence is presented in a way that allows conclusions to be drawn, e.g. uses means to plot line graph with appropriate headings and labels.

# B2.20 Limiting factors

40

This lesson covers the effect of limiting factors on the rate of photosynthesis.

## Specification coverage

**2.15** Demonstrate an understanding of how limiting factors affect the rate of photosynthesis, including: a) light intensity b) $CO_2$ concentration c) temperature

HSW *11* Presenting information, developing an argument and drawing a conclusion, using scientific, technical and mathematical language, conventions and symbols, and ICT tools

There are also opportunities to cover HSW *1*, HSW *6*, HSW *7*, HSW *8* and HSW *10*.

## Key terms

limiting factor

### Growing plants

**Starter 1**

Ask students to imagine that they have been given a small strawberry plant. What would they do with it to help a farmer increase the length of the strawberry season? Students should discuss their ideas in groups, and then after a few minutes you can start to pull together ideas for discussion.

### Algal balls and carbon dioxide

**Exploring 1** Prac

**Worksheet B2.20a** details how changing the concentration of sodium hydrogencarbonate solution that you put plants in affects the rate of photosynthesis. Full details can be found on the Teacher and technician practical sheet B2.20 (1).

Stretch If oxygen probes are used, students could use the graphs to calculate the initial rate of oxygen production for each solution.

Support Set up the controls as a class demonstration.

### Student Book spread B2.20

**Explaining 1**

Students read coverage of limiting factors then you quiz them on what they think the limiting factor for photosynthesis is for plants in different conditions. Can the students justify their suggestions scientifically?

Stretch Ask students why increasing temperature doesn't lead to quite the same shape graph as you get when increasing carbon dioxide concentration.

Support Ask students to think up a mnemonic to remember the three main limiting factors for photosynthesis. You could use $CO_2$LT as an example.

### Question time (AT)

**Plenary 1** AfL Lit

The **AT** presentation *Jumbled sentences* has a series of explanations about factors affecting rates. Students comment on the accuracy of each statement. Where there are issues with the statements, students should note what they are and then rewrite the statement.

### Plant design

**Homework 1**

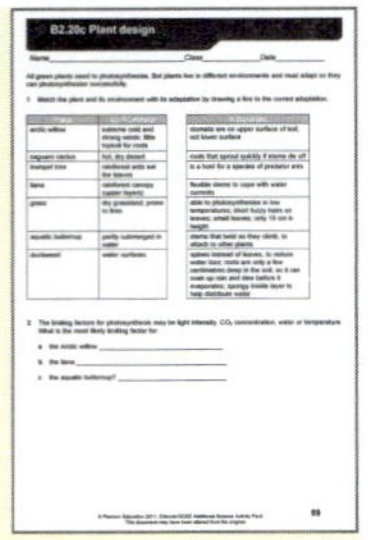

**Worksheet B2.20c** asks students to interpret adaptations of different plants to harsh environments using their knowledge of limiting factors.

Support Ask students to omit question **2**.

### Arctic plants

**Starter 2**

Show students an image of arctic tundra during the summer, and ask them to suggest why the plants are so small. Ask them to consider the difference in rates of photosynthesis between winter and summer and why photosynthesis may be limited even if there is almost 24-hour daylight.

### *Elodea* and temperature

**Exploring 2** Prac

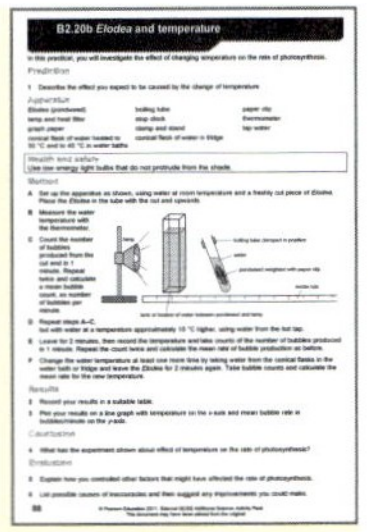

**Worksheet B2.20b** details how varying the temperature affects the rate of photosynthesis, using the 'counting bubbles from *Elodea*' method. Full details can be found on the Teacher and technician practical sheet B2.20 (2).

Stretch Students design an experiment to find the optimum temperature for photosynthesis.

Support Limit the experiment to two temperature conditions.

### Limiting factors in everyday situations

**Explaining 2**

Demonstrate how the principle of limiting factors applies to any process that is dependent on several factors. Ask students to evaluate the strengths and weaknesses of the model for explaining limiting factors in photosynthesis.

Stretch Ask students to think up an entirely different example and sketch a graph to show the possible limiting factors.

Support Use a visual analogy, in which the height of each side of a container represents the abundance of a factor that affects rate of photosynthesis.

### Graphs

**Plenary 2** AfL

Draw the graph from Figure B in page 67 of the Student Book showing how increasing light intensity affects rate of photosynthesis. Students should annotate the graph to explain what the limiting factor is or could be in different regions of the graph.

### Limiting factors

**Homework 2**

**Worksheet B2.20d** provides a quantitative model for how chloroplasts use light energy to convert raw materials to glucose. The questions apply the model to limiting factors.

Stretch Students answer the 'extra challenge' question.

# B2.20 Limiting factors

Is there a limit to how much photosynthesis rates can be increased?

If a plant has too little water, it wilts. This causes its stomata to close and so it will not photosynthesise well. Plants grown in warm greenhouses lose a lot of water and are more likely to wilt. This problem is overcome for some crop plants by growing them in water – a technique called hydroponics.

**A** *In hydroponics, plants are grown in a constant supply of water.*

To maximise plant growth, the rate of photosynthesis must be maximised as the glucose made in photosynthesis is used to make proteins for growth, as well for respiration.

For photosynthesis to take place there must be a supply of carbon dioxide, water, a suitable temperature and light to provide the energy for the reactions to occur.

A plant grown in dim light with ample carbon dioxide and water will photosynthesise slowly. Increasing the amount of carbon dioxide or water will not increase the rate of photosynthesis. Only increasing the amount of light will increase the rate. In this case, light is the **limiting factor**.

In any process that is affected by several factors, the maximum rate at which the process can occur is controlled by the factor that is in shortest supply. That factor is the limiting factor.

1 What factors could limit the rate of photosynthesis in a plant cell?

Figure B shows the effect of light intensity on the rate of photosynthesis in a plant (other variables were kept constant). Initially an increase in light intensity causes an increase in the rate of photosynthesis. The plant can photosynthesise faster if it is given more light and so light intensity is the limiting factor in these conditions. In the flat part of the graph the rate of photosynthesis is constant even though more light energy is available. One possibility is that carbon dioxide concentration is now the limiting factor. Another limiting factor could be temperature. The enzymes involved in photosynthesis are working as fast as they can but raising the temperature would allow the rate to increase further.

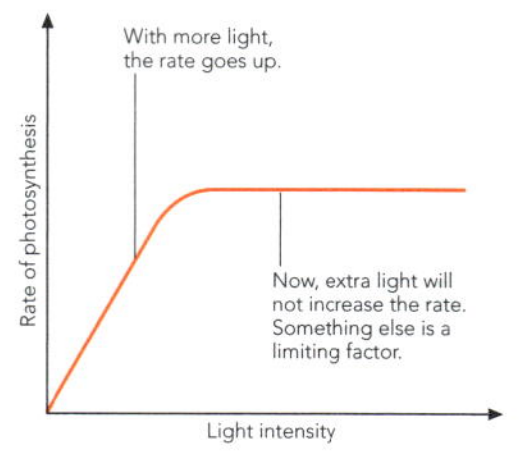


**B** *Increasing the light intensity will increase the rate of photosynthesis until the increase is halted by a limiting factor.*

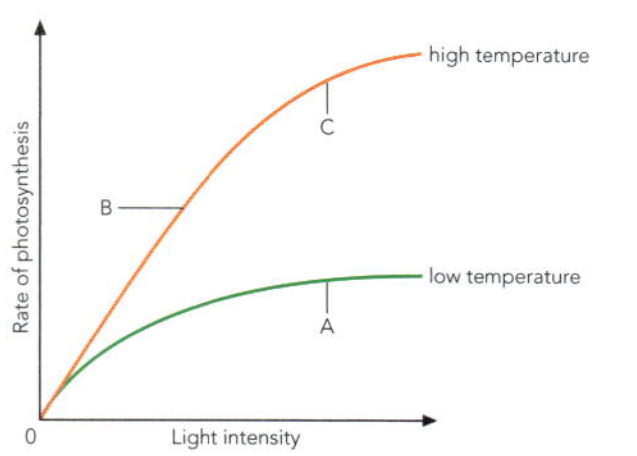


**C** *Temperature can be a limiting factor in photosynthesis.*

2 a Copy the graph in Figure B and draw in another line to suggest what would happen if the experiment were repeated again with a higher concentration of carbon dioxide.
b If the experiment were repeated at a higher carbon dioxide concentration but the results were exactly the same, what does this tell you about the limiting factor in the flat part of the graph?

3 Explain which factors might be limiting at each stage (A–C) shown in Figure C.

4 Name one limiting factor in a well-lit warm greenhouse and explain how its effect could be reduced.

5 In a forest, some plants grow in the shade and have very dark green leaves. Using this information, suggest what the main limiting factor is for these plants and how they are adapted to survive in these conditions.

6 In a commercial greenhouse, a light automatically switches on at 17:00 in winter and a heater is turned on when the inside temperature drops below 21 °C. Explain both these features of the greenhouse.

**Skills spotlight**

Explain what features you would look for to see whether a rate of photosynthesis is constant or changing and why plotting a graph makes these things easier to see.

**ResultsPlus Watch Out!**

Students sometimes think that photosynthesis happens in the light and respiration in the dark. Respiration happens all the time. If a factor is limiting it does not stop photosynthesis, it means that it will not go any faster.

**Learning Outcomes**

2.15 Demonstrate an understanding of how limiting factors affect the rate of photosynthesis, including:
a light intensity
b $CO_2$ concentration
c temperature

HSW 11 Present information using scientific conventions and symbols



How does water get to the top of a tree? 

## ActiveTeach

- **AT** *Growing crops in greenhouses* [BBC video]
  Hydroponic greenhouses in Spain
- **AT** *Factors limiting photosynthesis* [interactive]
  Limits on photosynthesis – true-or-false quiz
- **AT** *Jumbled sentences* [presentation]
  Factors affecting growth

## Answers | Student Book

1 Availability of water, carbon dioxide, and light; presence of chloroplasts; temperature

2 a Graph shows the rate of photosynthesis continuing to increase above the level shown by the first line, before flattening out at a higher level.
b It tells you that carbon dioxide concentration is not a limiting factor, which suggests that temperature probably is.

3 Stage A: temperature is limiting as when the experiment is repeated at a higher temperature (stage B) the rate increases. Stage B: light intensity is limiting at this stage, because as it increases so does the rate.
Stage C: carbon dioxide is probably limiting now, since the temperature is high and light intensity no longer makes a difference.

4 Carbon dioxide concentration; this could be increased by burning wood or a fossil fuel inside the greenhouse.

5 Growing in shade suggests light intensity is the main limiting factor. Adaptation seems to be increased levels of chlorophyll to enable the plants to capture as much light as possible.

6 A good answer will include the following points: when daylight ends, artificial lighting comes on to provide a 24-hour light source; so photosynthesis can happen for 24 hours every day; artificial heating maintains a constant inside temperature of 21 °C so that low temperatures do not limit the rate of photosynthesis; Both features provide optimum conditions to maximise the rate of photosynthesis of plants inside the greenhouse; faster photosynthesis increases crop growth, as the glucose made is used for growth and respiration.

**Skills spotlight**

On a graph of rate of photosynthesis against a variable, such as light intensity, temperature or carbon dioxide concentration, an upwards-sloping line indicates that the rate of photosynthesis is increasing as the independent variable increases. A level line indicates that the rate of photosynthesis is constant. A graph makes it easier to see relationships between variables, compared to a table of data.

# B2.21 Water transport



This lesson covers the movement of water, glucose and mineral salts through a plant, and the processes of osmosis, active transport and transpiration that are involved.

## Specification coverage

***2.17*** Explain how the loss of water vapour from leaves drives transpiration

***2.18*** Explain how water, glucose and mineral salts are transported through a plant, including: a) mineral uptake in roots by active transport b) the role of the xylem and phloem vessels

***2.19*** Describe how root hair cells are adapted to take up water by osmosis

***2.20*** Define osmosis as the movement of water molecules from an area of higher concentration of water to an area of lower concentration of water through a partially permeable membrane

HSW ***2*** The interpretation of data, using creative thought, to provide evidence for testing ideas and developing theories

There are also opportunities to cover HSW ***1***, HSW ***3***, HSW ***6***, HSW ***8***, HSW ***10***, and HSW ***11***.

## Key terms

active transport
osmosis
partially permeable
phloem
potometer
root hair cell
transpiration
xylem

### Flower dye

**Starter 1**

Set up a white carnation with a split stem, half in water containing blue food colouring and half in water containing red food colouring. This will need to be done in advance. Use this as a discussion point to get students asking questions and suggesting what has happened.

### Osmosis in action (AT)

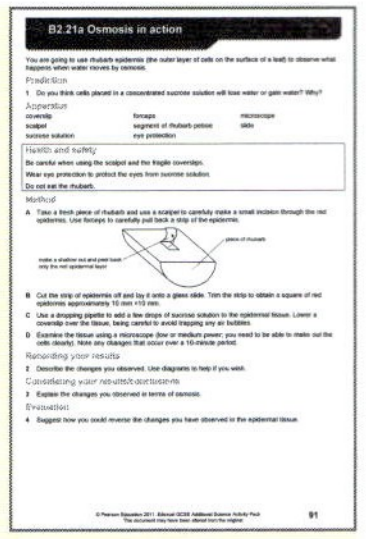

**Exploring 1** Prac

Students observe rhubarb cells placed in a concentrated sucrose solution. See **Worksheet B2.21a**. Full details can be found on the Teacher and technician practical sheet B2.21 (1).

Stretch Ask students to come up with alternative explanations for what is happening.

Support The **AT** document *Osmosis in plant cells* has diagrams of cells at different stages of plasmolysis and jumbled up sentences.

### Student Book spread B2.21 (AT)

**Explaining 1**

Use Figure C in the Student Book (or **AT** document *Osmosis in plant cells*) to explain how water enters cells by osmosis across the cell membrane, and how this relies on the concentration gradient of water molecules.

The **AT** document *Celery and food dye* links to how water enters, moves up through, and exits the plant.

Stretch Ask students to explain why a plant loses more water on a dry, warm and windy day than when it is damp, cool and still.

Support Ensure students understand the difference between diffusion and osmosis.

### Water transport

**Plenary 1** AfL Lit

Write the phrase 'water transport' in the middle of the board and ask students to suggest related words and how they should be linked to make a concept map, giving a reason for their placement.

### Plant roots

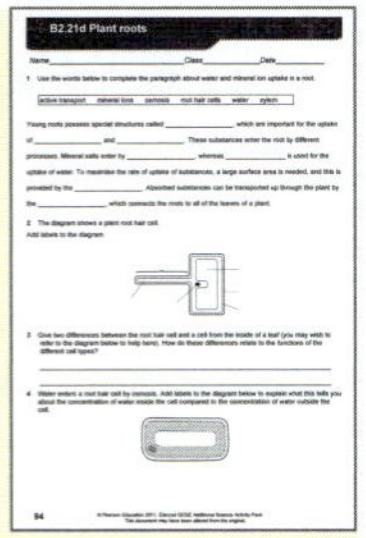

**Homework 1**

Students use **Worksheet B2.21d** to summarise water transport and osmosis.

Support Students can omit question **4**.

### Roots

**Starter 2**

Show students some images of plant roots, including roots in soil and less conventional scenarios e.g. hydroponics and aerial roots. Ask students to work in groups to discuss the functions of roots. Get feedback after a minute or so, and establish that the main functions are anchorage and absorption.

### Water loss from leaves (AT)

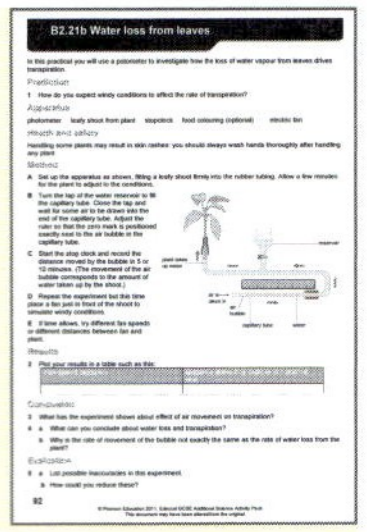

**Exploring 2** Prac

Students use a potometer to measure the rate at which a plant loses water through transpiration. See **Worksheet B2.21b**. Full details can be found on the Teacher and technician practical sheet on page B2.21 (2).

Stretch Ask students to predict what would happen to the rate of transpiration if the stomata are blocked.

Support Run the activity as a demo, providing students with the **AT** document *Potometer writing frame*.

### Active transport in roots

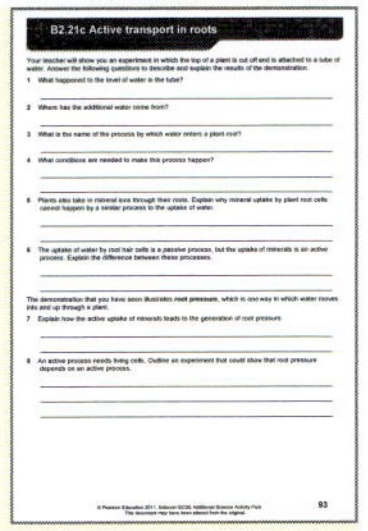

**Explaining 2** Demo

**Worksheet B2.21c** provides a set of questions that can be used with a demonstration of root pressure. Full details for the demonstration can be found on the Teacher and technician practical sheet B2.21 (3).

Stretch Students should watch the demonstration and then write their own description of the role of active transport in root cells in generating movement of water and minerals in plants.

Support Work together with the students.

### Definitions

**Plenary 2** Lit

Ask students to write down definitions of the terms 'osmosis' and 'transpiration', making them as clear and succinct as possible. If there is time, ask some of students to read out their definitions and get the rest of the class to discuss how it can be improved.

### Water cycle

**Homework 2**

Ask students to describe the passage of a water molecule from the ground into the air, via a plant, explaining the processes involved. They should then compare this with the movement of mineral salts into a plant.

Stretch Give examples of plants that live in different conditions and ask students to suggest what particular problems they will experience in relation to water and mineral uptake and how they might get around them.

# B2.21 Water transport

How does water move from the ground up to the leaves of a plant?

Plants normally lose water as water vapour through the stomata in their leaves. If the stomata are all closed, water vapour cannot escape. In some plants water is forced out through special structures in the edges of the leaves. This process is called guttation.

**A** *These droplets were squeezed out of the leaf due to water pressure inside the plant.*

1 How is a root hair cell adapted to its function?

2 In what ways is osmosis similar to diffusion, and in what ways is it different?

3 Why is diffusion of water vapour out of stomata not an example of osmosis?

Roots do more than just anchor a plant in the ground – they take up water and mineral salts from the soil. The surface of roots have specialised **root hair cells** with long thin extensions that reach into the surrounding soil. The root hairs provide a large surface area for substances to enter the root.

**ResultsPlus Watch Out!**

Students often confuse diffusion and osmosis. A variety of substances move by diffusion but osmosis is the movement of only water and needs a partially permeable membrane.

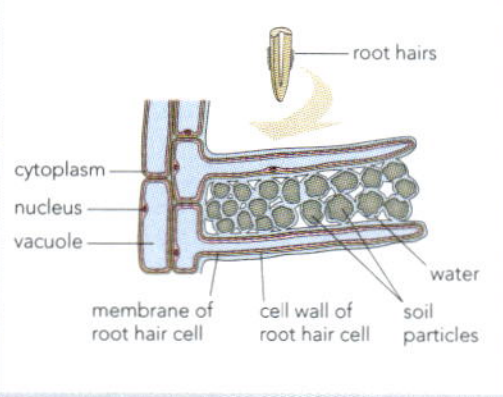


**B** *A root hair cell*

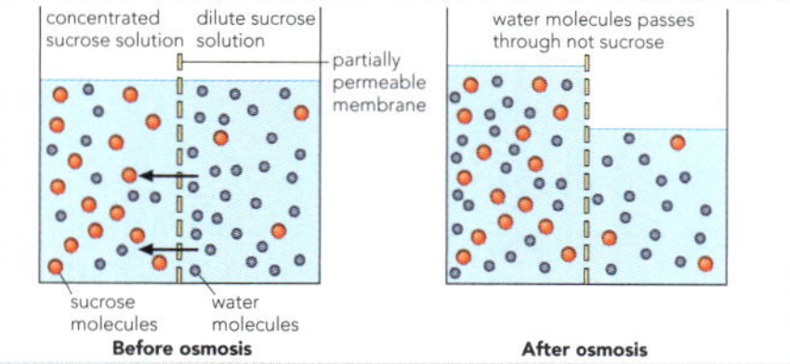


**C** *Diffusion of water molecules from a dilute to a concentrated sucrose solution across a partially permeable cell membrane (osmosis).*

## Osmosis and active transport

Water enters the root hair cells by **osmosis**. In this process, water moves across a **partially permeable membrane** (a membrane that only certain substances can pass through) from a region where water is in higher concentration to a region where it is in lower concentration.

In Figure C water molecules will move from solution B, where they are in higher concentration, to solution A, where they are in lower concentration. The water moves by diffusion. The sucrose molecules cannot move between the solutions because they are too big to fit through the gaps in the partially permeable membrane.

Roots can absorb nitrate and other mineral ions dissolved in soil water even if their concentration is higher in the plant than in the soil water. Absorbing particles *against* a concentration gradient is called **active transport**. The energy needed for this process comes from respiration.

## Plant transport systems

Once water and minerals have entered the root cells, they need to get to all the plant's tissues. Plants possess specialised tissue, called **xylem**, to transport water and dissolved mineral salts. Xylem tissue consists of long cells that die and form hollow tubes. These tubes also give support to the plant.

The glucose made in leaves by photosynthesis is converted to sucrose and transported to other parts of the plant by strands of living **phloem** tissue.

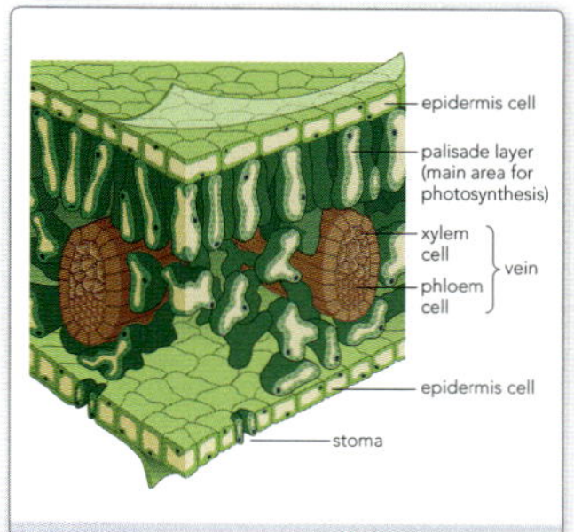


**D** *The veins in a leaf contain xylem and phloem.*

**Skills spotlight**

Look at the potometer in Figure E. When a fan is switched on near the plant, the air bubble moves faster. Explain how this experiment supports the idea that loss of water vapour from leaves pulls water into the plant.

## Moving water against gravity

Water that evaporates from the surface of cells inside a leaf moves out of the leaf by diffusion when the stomata are open. This maintains a concentration gradient, so more water evaporates and diffuses out of the leaf. The loss of water from the leaf pulls water and dissolved mineral salts up through the xylem from the roots. This process is called **transpiration**. Factors that increase evaporation will also increase transpiration.

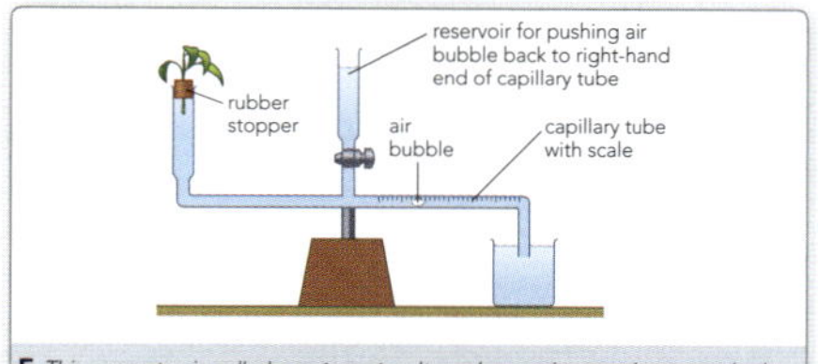


**E** *This apparatus is called a* ***potometer****. It can be used to monitor transpiration. As the stem takes up water, the air bubble moves along the capillary tube.*

4 How do mineral salts get from the soil to the leaves of a plant?

5 Suggest why transpiration rates decrease at lower temperatures.

6 Explain why sunny and warm conditions usually cause the rate of transpiration to increase.

**Learning Outcomes**

**2.17** Explain how the loss of water vapour from leaves drives transpiration

**2.18** Explain how water, glucose and mineral salts are transported through a plant, including: **a** mineral uptake in roots by active transport **b** the role of xylem and phloem vessels

**2.19** Describe how root hair cells are adapted to take up water by osmosis

**2.20** Define osmosis as the movement of water molecules from an area of higher concentration of water to an area of lower concentration of water through a partially permeable membrane

**HSW** **2** Describe how data is used by scientists to provide evidence that increases our scientific understanding



Why won't drinking seawater help shipwrecked sailors to survive?



## ActiveTeach

- **AT** *Fishing for the right balance?* [video]
  Osmosis and water intake
- **AT** *How does water move in plants?* [interactive]
  Key terms: water transport in plants – quiz
- **AT** *Celery and food dye* [word document]
  Diagram of water transport
- **AT** *Osmosis in plant cells* [word document]
  Match diagrams and statements
- **AT** *Potometer writing frame* [word document]
  Prediction and results
- **AT** *Xylem and phloem in leaf veins* [diagram]
  Figure D – diagram labelling activity

## Answers | Student Book

1 The long, thin structure gives the cell a large surface area to volume ratio, which increases the efficiency of water absorption from soil water into the root.

2 Similarity: movement of a substance from an area of higher to an area of lower concentration. Differences: osmosis is movement of water only and is always through a partially permeable membrane.

3 Does not involve water moving through a partially permeable membrane.

4 Mineral salts are moved into the roots from the soil by active transport, which requires energy. They are then transported in solution in xylem tissue from the roots to the leaves.

5 At lower temperatures evaporation of water from inside the leaf is slower, and the diffusion of water vapour out of the leaf is also slower, so transpiration slows down as these processes drive it.

6 A good answer will include the following points: warmth means water evaporates faster from the cells in the leaf; this forms water vapour; concentration of water vapour molecules in the leaf increases; this forms a steeper concentration gradient between the inside and outside of a leaf than on a cooler day; warm, sunny conditions mean stomata are fully open on warm sunny conditions; more water vapour diffuses out of the leaf than on a cooler day.

**Skills spotlight**

The bubble moving faster shows that more water is being taken up by the plant. The fan increases the rate at which water is lost from the leaves because moist air surrounding the plant is blown away, maintaining a steep concentration gradient between the inside and the outside of the leaves. Water only gets into a plant through its roots and so this experiment supports the hypothesis that loss of water from the leaves pulls water into the plant through its roots.

# B2.22 Investigating osmosis

This lesson challenges students to investigate the effect of different concentrations of sucrose solution on potato tissue due to osmosis. The activity may be run as a practice controlled assessment task or as a straight-forward class practical. The practical work will take about 1 hour if no repeats are carried out.

## Specification coverage

***2.21*** Investigate osmosis

This activity provides opportunities to cover **HSW** *1*, **HSW** *5*, **HSW** *6*, **HSW** *7*, **HSW** *8*, **HSW** *10* and **HSW** *11*.

### Before the lesson

Ensure that students are familiar with any equipment they may be expected to use so that they can plan their own investigation. In the week or two before the task show them this equipment and, if appropriate, allow them to practice using it.

It may be good preparation to show students one or more of Skills Sheets 19 to 26 to show what is expected of them in their actual controlled assessment task.

### Starter

**Preparing vegetables**

When we prepare vegetables e.g. potatoes for cooking we put them in water until we can cook them. The water should not contain any salt. Have some potato chips that have been cut and prepared beforehand, some left in plain water and some in salty water. Ask students to come up with ideas about why we do this. This can be a class discussion or students can use secondary sources such as cookery books or the Internet to find the answer.

Follow this by reading the additional information below the opening section of page 70 of the Student Book. They may then read the brief description of the activity provided by the 'Your task' box.

### Option 1: Straight-forward class practical

You may wish to run the activity as a straight-forward class practical. Students follow the instructions on **Worksheet B2.22b**. Students are given detailed instructions on how to carry out an investigation on the effect of different strength sucrose solutions on osmosis in potato tissue. The range of data that students need to collect is given on **Worksheet B2.22c**.

You could ask students to come up with one or two further hypotheses, based on their observations in this practical – for example they could consider the effect of salt rather than sucrose solutions, they could consider a bigger range of concentrations, they could consider the use of different types of vegetables and which would give the clearest results.

### Plenary

On page 71 of the Student Book you will find two examples of the sort of work that students may produce for this task. The examples focus on assessing quality of evidence. You could share these with students after they have completed their own work. This will help them to understand the assessment criteria and so make it easier for them to evaluate their work and to see how they can improve it. Moderator comments on each of the Student Book extracts can be found at the end of the assessment guidance for this investigation on the CD-ROM. The examples can also be found on the **AT** document *Student examples*.

### Option 2: Running the activity as a practice controlled assessment task (PCA)

We have provided a full range of support resources to allow the running of this practical as a practice controlled assessment task. A recommended structure is outlined below (to be used over a number of sessions). Marking guidance for all three parts of the practice task can be found on the CD-ROM that accompanies the TTPP. To save time when using these practice controlled assessment tasks, you may wish to focus on a particular aspect or skill rather than working through all three parts of the task.

#### Part A Planning

1. Students should be given the Student brief on **Worksheet B2.22a**. They can use Part A of the Workbook that is provided to help pupils with their practice controlled assessments. They should be given about 1 hour to do this planning.

#### Part B Observations

2. Students carry out the practical task to collect evidence using the method they have planned in Part A. Once again, they should refer to the Student brief on **Worksheet B2.22a**. They can use Part B of the Workbook that is provided to help pupils with their practice controlled assessments. They should be given about 1 hour to collect their primary evidence.
3. If there is a problem with their own planned method, students may be asked to follow the method set out on **Worksheet B2.22b**. This will still enable students to access the full range of marks for Part B and Part C of the practice controlled assessment task.
4. In Part B, students are required to gather some secondary evidence. The evidence can be quantitative or qualitative. It can be from a variety of sources but students must note where they found their evidence and evaluate the quality of the source as part of this task. Skills Sheet 22 provides students with further guidance on researching for and evaluating secondary evidence. This part of the task could be done outside of the lesson but must be supervised.

#### Part C Conclusions

5. Students follow the instructions set out on the Part C section of the Student brief on **Worksheet B2.22a**. They should use their data from Part B and the secondary evidence they have collected when doing this. They can use Part C of the Workbook that is provided to help pupils with their practice controlled assessments. They should be given about 1 hour to work on their conclusions.

The **AT** includes video clips showing a group of students working through elements of this investigation with teacher support.

# B2.22 Investigating osmosis

How does solute concentration affect plant cells?

Plants and animals, including people, need to drink plenty of water to live, but in very rare cases too much water can kill you. A huge water overload in the body makes your blood very dilute. This causes the brain cells to swell as a result of osmosis. This can lead to seizures and even death. Too much salt water does the opposite – the salt in your blood makes water leave your body cells and they shrivel up.

**A** *Leah Betts took an ecstasy tablet at her 18th birthday party. Ecstasy stops you feeling thirsty. Leah drank large amounts of water to try and avoid dehydration and the excess water killed her.*

Water moves in and out of plant and animal cells by osmosis. Plant cells contain dissolved sugars and other chemicals. If plant cells are surrounded by water or a dilute solution of sugars, water moves into the cells by osmosis. The cells swell up and the stems are firm and support the leaves. If plant cells lose water they become floppy and shrink in size. The plant eventually wilts because the stems get thinner and the leaves cannot be held up any more.

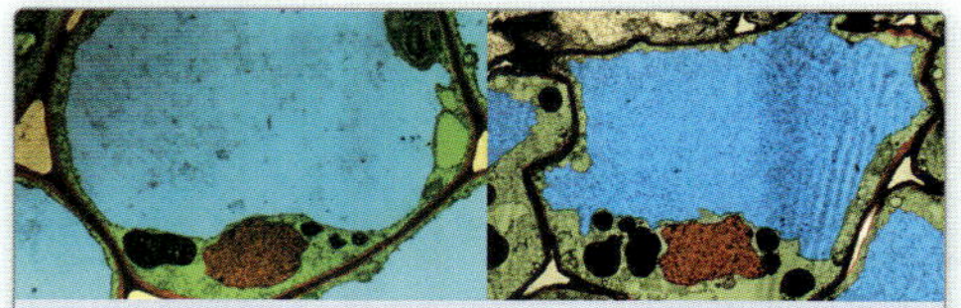

**B** *Plant cells look very different when water moves in or out by osmosis.*

**Your task**

You are going to plan an investigation that will allow you to find out about the effect of different strength sucrose solutions on plant cells. Your teacher will provide you with some materials to help you organise this task.

**Learning Outcomes**

**2.21** *Investigate osmosis*

## ResultsPlus Build Better Answers

When planning an investigation like this, one of the skills you will be assessed on is your ability to assess the *quality of evidence*. There are 4 marks available for this skill.

**Student extract 1** A basic response for this skill

All chips were 30 mm to start with.

| | Final length of potato chip (mm) | | |
|---|---|---|---|
| | Sample 1 | Sample 2 | Sample 3 |
| Concentrated sugar solution | 25 | 26 | 24 |
| Less concentrated sugar solution | 30 | (25) | 31 |
| Water | 33 | 34 | 32 |

This is the table of results I found on the internet and I am using it as my secondary evidence. I think that the figure which has the ring around it does not fit with the pattern of the others and I will leave it out of any calculations I do. My own results had one odd reading where the length of a potato chip placed in water had increased by 6 mm which was more than 5% change. I think that this is also an anomalous result.

The student has identified and dealt with an anomalous reading in the secondary evidence.

The student has also identified where there are anomalies in their own results.

**Student extract 2** A good response for this skill

My table of results taken from the internet is given above. This has one anomalous reading. There is also one anomalous reading from my own results. I am going to use both my own results and the secondary evidence to calculate the mean change in length of my potato chips. I will leave these two anomalous results out of my calculations however because if I included them it could mean that my answer would be shifted away from the true figure. When I draw my graph I will also draw a line of best fit.

The student has explained *why* anomalies should not be included in calculations.

The student has explained that anomalous results will not be included in calculations.

Drawing a line of best fit on a graph also helps to reduce the effect of anomalous results.

### ResultsPlus

**To access 2 marks**

- Comment on the quality of your primary and secondary evidence
- Deal with any anomalies appropriately
- Say if you do not think there are any anomalies in your evidence

**To access 4 marks**

- Take account of any anomalies in your primary and secondary evidence
- Explain any adjustments you need to make to your evidence
- If you do not think there are anomalies, explain this and say that you are using all your evidence



## ActiveTeach

- **AT** *B2.22 Investigating osmosis* [video]
  Students work through the investigation
- **AT** *B2.22 Moderator comments* [word document]
  Moderator comments on the video
- **AT** *B2.22 Assessment criteria* [presentation]
  Understanding the CA marking criteria
- **AT** *B2.22 Student task sheet* [word document]
  CA video checklist
- **AT** *B2.22 Specification points* [word document]
  Edexcel specification points
- **AT** *B2.22 Student examples* [word document]
  Examples for students to assess

## Assessment criteria

### Quality of evidence

**0** No comments made on the quality of the data/observations.

**1-2 a)** Comments on the quality of the primary evidence, dealing with anomalies appropriately (if no anomalies in evidence, candidates need to state this). For example, plots line of best fit.

**b)** Comments on the quality of the secondary evidence, dealing with anomalies appropriately (if no anomalies in evidence, candidates need to state this). For example, does not include anomalies in calculations.

**3-4 a)** Explains any adjustments to the evidence needed, or decision not to exclude evidence. For example, explains that the anomalies have been left out of the mean calculations because they would move the values further away from the true values.

**b)** Takes account of anomalies in primary and secondary evidence when processing evidence (using all evidence if no anomalies). For example, does not include anomalies in calculations of means.

# B2.23 Organisms and their environments

This lesson introduces students to fieldwork techniques for collecting data on organisms in their environment in order to investigate the relationship between them.

## Specification coverage

***2.22*** Investigate the relationship between organisms and their environments using fieldwork techniques

***2.23*** Investigate the distribution of organisms in an ecosystem, using sampling techniques, including:

a) pooters b) sweep nets/pond nets c) pitfall traps d) quadrats; and measure environmental factors, including: e) temperature f) light intensity g) pH

**HSW** ***5*** Planning to test a scientific idea, answer a scientific question, or solve a scientific problem

There are also opportunities to cover **HSW** ***1***, **HSW** ***6***, **HSW** ***7***, **HSW** ***8***, **HSW** ***10*** and **HSW** ***11***.

## Key terms

| | |
|---|---|
| biodiversity | population size |
| distribution | quadrat |
| ecosystem | random sampling |
| environment | representative |
| habitat | systematic sampling |
| pitfall trap | |
| pond net | |
| pooter | |

### Estimating populations

**Starter 1**

Show students images of, e.g. a field containing many flowers of one species, and a densely packed seal colony or such like. Ask them how they would go about estimating the population size of each organism. Lead to the idea of sampling a small area and extrapolating from that.

### Exploring biodiversity

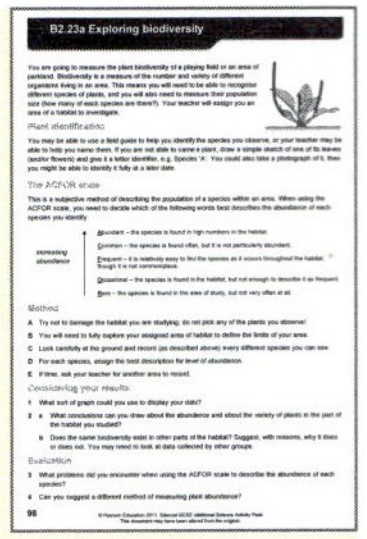

**Exploring 1** **Prac**

Students use a subjective, qualitative measure for the plant biodiversity of a playing field. See **Worksheet B2.23a**. Full details can be found on the Teacher and technician practical sheet B2.23 (1).

**Stretch** Ask students to use the data from different groups to identify a variable that has an effect on abundance and/or distribution.

**Support** Students could use a more simple scale (e.g. Abundant, Frequent, Rare) to facilitate the collection of data.

### Analysing secondary data

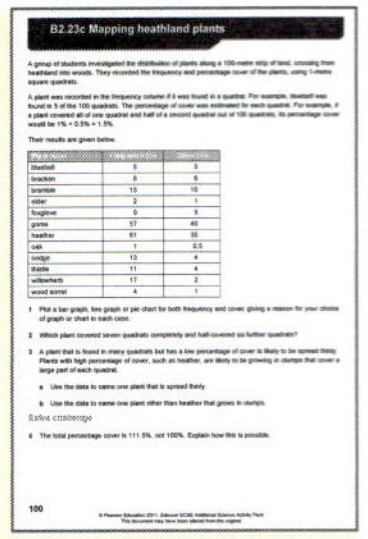

**Exploring 3**

In **Worksheet B2.23c** students analyse data on the frequency and percentage cover of plants along 100 quadrats placed along a 100-metre transect between woodland and heathland.

**Stretch** Ask students to design a survey to investigate if the pH of the soil affects the type and frequency of plants found.

**Support** Omit questions 3 and 4 when copying the sheet for students.

### Fit for purpose

**Plenary 1** **AfL**

Students should draw up a table for the four pieces of sampling equipment, and give an example of a hypothesis about the distribution of organisms that each could be used to test. Extend this to cover the three environmental conditions (temperature, light intensity and pH) and ask how these could be measured.

### Fieldwork plan

**Homework 1**

Ask students to write a plan for an investigation into the differences in the distribution of insects between night and day in a woodland, considering what factors are different at different times of day.

**Support** Give students the list of apparatus they could use in this investigation, and discuss what each item could be used for before they write their plan.

### Deadly plants

**Starter 2**

Use the Venus fly trap footage from the BBC series 'Life' (available on their YouTube channel) as a stimulus to get students thinking about the fact that organisms respond to their environment. You could also ask them why different species of plant are only found in specific areas – what determines distribution?

### Earthworm populations (AT)

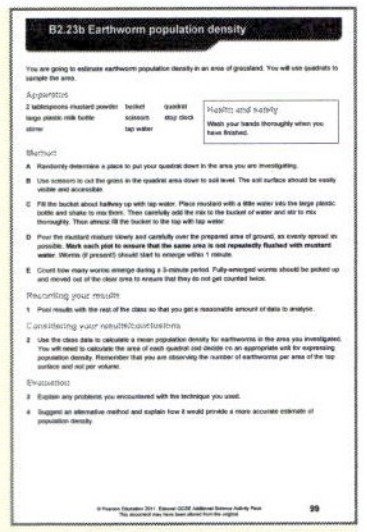

**Exploring 2** **Prac**

Students calculate earthworm population density in an area of grassland using quadrat sampling. See **Worksheet B2.23b**. Full details can be found on the Teacher and technician practical sheet B2.23 (2).

**Stretch** Students could come up with hypotheses to explain why earthworms come to the surface when mustard is added.

**Support** Supply students with sample data to analyse from the **AT** presentation *Example data*.

### Student Book spread B2.27 (AT)

**Explaining 1**

Have a pooter, sweep net, pitfall trap and quadrat to hand or use the Student Book diagrams. Explain how each is used. Show a pH meter, a light meter and a thermometer and discuss how environmental conditions can be measured. Use the **AT** presentation *Random sampling* to discuss random sampling.

**Stretch** Ask students what they could do if the random samples by chance are all clustered in the same area.

**Support** Provide a further explanation of the differences between random and systematic sampling.

### Instructions

**Plenary 2** **Lit**

Ask students to take it in turns to describe to their neighbour how they would get an accurate estimate of the number of thistles on a sand dune on a beach. After listening, each person should feed back any comments they have about the instructions, for example were they clear? Were any procedure steps missed out? Were there any mistakes?

### Quadrat sampling

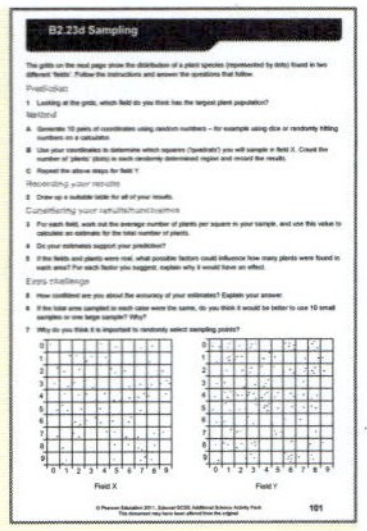

**Homework 2**

**Worksheet B2.23d** has secondary data to analyse and questions about using quadrat sampling to estimate a population size, and also introduces the idea of random sampling.

**Stretch** Students answer the 'extra challenge' questions.

# B2.23 Organisms and their environment

How does the environment affect the organisms living in it?

The sensitive plant *Mimosa pudica* has a trick to prevent its leaves being eaten. When an insect lands on it, the leaves respond rapidly by drawing water out of the cells by osmosis. The leaves fold up and the insect falls off and leaves hungry.

**A** *The leaves of* Mimosa pudica *fold up when touched.*

1 Name some factors that affect the size of a plant population.

**ResultsPlus Watch Out!**

Students find it difficult to describe biodiversity. It is the variety of species of plants and animals in an area, not the variety of individuals.

2 It is important that pitfall traps are not left unchecked for too long. Why do you think this is?

The conditions in an **environment** determine which organisms (plants, animals and microorganisms) can survive in it. The icy conditions of the Arctic and the humid heat of the rainforest each present challenges for living organisms. They must be adapted to their environments and be able to respond to any changes.

Ecologists study the **biodiversity** of life found in an **ecosystem** or **habitat**, where a particular organism is found (its **distribution**), as well as how many individuals there are in a group of the same species (the **population size**). These data are used to monitor changes in population size or distribution or to test hypotheses about what sort of organisms exist in a certain place.

**Sampling** means looking at a small portion of an area or population. In **random sampling** every point within an area has an equal chance of being selected. This means the sample is likely to be **representative** of the whole area.

## Sampling techniques

A **pooter** is used to catch small invertebrates through an inlet tube by sucking sharply on a second tube connected to the container. In areas with long grass a **sweep net** can be used to catch some of the organisms present. Similarly, a **pond net** can be used to sample aquatic habitats.

**B** *A pitfall trap, sweep net and pooter*

**Pitfall traps** are useful for trapping small animals such as spiders, beetles and woodlice. They can be set up and left overnight so it is possible to catch organisms that might not be active during the day.

**Quadrats** are square frames of known size, which are typically used to sample the number and population of different plant species in a habitat. The quadrat is placed at random locations, for example by throwing, and the number of plants of each type that appear within the quadrat are counted. For spreading plants like clover the percentage of the quadrat area that is covered by that plant is estimated.

Random sampling is used to estimate a total population size by scaling up the mean number of one type of plant per quadrat.

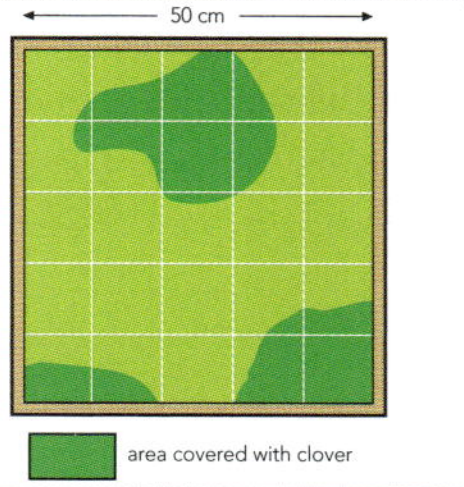


**C** *Sampling clover with a quadrat*

3 Population density is one way to record the abundance of a organism. What do you need to know to calculate this value?

4 How would you expect light intensity to affect plant distribution?

By considering the varying conditions in a habitat, such as at different points in a field, it is possible to understand why the organisms that live there are able to do so. For example, understanding how light intensity varies might help to explain the distribution of different species of plants. Other factors such as temperature, soil or water pH may also have an effect in determining which organisms can survive in any given part of a habitat.

When investigating changes in a habitat caused by one environmental factor it is sometimes useful to carry out **systematic sampling** along a line. For example, quadrats could be placed at regular intervals along a straight line.

5 Light intensity and temperature change not only during the course of a day but also from season to season. Describe how these factors change between winter and summer and suggest how this might affect the organisms that live in a woodland habitat.

6 Suggest why scientists spend time trying to find out which organisms are present in an area before a big building project goes ahead and explain how they get an good estimate of the numbers of each species present.

**Skills spotlight**

It is important that scientists test their ideas. How could you set up a long-term study to test the hypothesis that use of weedkillers on a farm affects insect biodiversity of a nearby hedgerow?

**Learning outcomes**

*2.22 Investigate the relationship between organisms and their environment using fieldwork techniques*

*2.23 Investigate the distribution of organisms in an ecosystem, using sampling techniques, including:*
- *a pooters*
- *b sweep nets/pond nets*
- *c pitfall traps*
- *d quadrats*

*and measure environmental factors, including:*
- *e temperature*
- *f light intensity*
- *g pH*

HSW *5 Plan to test a scientific idea, answer a scientific question, or solve a scientific problem by controlling relevant variables*



How can you count the number of whales in the ocean?



## ActiveTeach

- **AT** *Beetle losses* [BBC video] News report on losses of UK insects
- **AT** *The census consensus* [video] Using quadrats for sampling
- **AT** *Changing environments* [interactive] Environmental conditions – matching
- **AT** *Sampling equipment* [interactive] Equipment in the field – matching
- **AT** *Estimating populations* [presentation] Discussion stimulus
- **AT** *Random sampling* [presentation] Quadrats and random sampling
- **AT** *Example data* [presentation] Random and systematic samples

## Answers | Student Book

1 Light, water, soil, nutrients, space, temperature, disease, grazing animals

2 Predatory animal in the pitfall trap might eat some of the other animals in the trap!

3 Need to know the actual area of the region (e.g. 500 m²) and the population size of the organism (e.g. 1500 individuals). Calculate the number of individuals per unit area (e.g. 1500/500 m² = 3 individuals/m²).

4 Plants need light for photosynthesis. There will be more plants in lighter areas.

5 Suggestions: light intensity increases in summer, so plants grow faster. Herbivores have more food so their populations increase, and so do the populations of animals higher up the food chain. Temperature increases in summer so plant growth will be faster. Mammals don't need as much food to supply the energy needed to maintain their body temperature.

6 A good answer will contain the following points: to monitor whether change due to the site impacts on species diversity and population sizes; to find out if there are rare species that need protection from the building works; to monitor whether habitat creation restoration measures are working; to get an accurate estimate of the numbers of each species present need to use sampling techniques to identify the species present in different habitats on the site; then scale up the population density estimates for their samples to a total population size estimate, using the total areas of each type of habitat; Additional credit should be given for naming or describing an appropriate sampling method.

**Skills spotlight**

Need for controls – so a site that uses weedkiller is compared to a site that doesn't. Large sample size, so several sites of each type. Control other factors that might affect insect biodiversity, e.g. type of crop plant, distance to the hedgerow, types of plants growing in the hedgerow and similar age/height of hedgerow, use of pesticides and fertilisers as well as use of weedkillers. Take samples in each area at the same times of year for a number of years and examine changes in the populations of the different organisms.

# B2.24 Investigating the distribution of organisms in an ecosystem

48

This lesson challenges students to investigate the distribution of organisms between two different habitats within an ecosystem, one of which could show more human impact than the other e.g. mown grass or long grass. The activity may be run as a practice controlled assessment task or as a straight-forward class practical. The practical work will take about two hours.

## Specification coverage

***2.22*** Investigate the relationship between organisms and their environment using fieldwork techniques including: a) pooters b) sweep nets/pond nets c) pitfall traps d) quadrats and measure environmental factors including e) temperature f) light intensity g) pH

This activity provides opportunities to cover HSW *1*, HSW *5*, HSW *6*, HSW *7*, HSW *8* and HSW *11*.

### Before the lesson

Ensure that students are familiar with any equipment they may be expected to use. In this investigation students should be familiar with the concept of random sampling using a quadrat, mapping areas and a grid system. Students should also practise using light meters and soil pH meters before working in the field.

It is important that students understand how they could use pooters, sweep nets and pitfall traps to investigate how conditions affect the distribution of animals. These techniques will have been introduced in lesson B2.23 and students should be given some experience handling all the equipment referred to in specification statement 2.23. It may be good preparation to show students one or more of Skills Sheets 19 to 26 to show what is expected of them in their actual controlled assessment task.

### Starter

**Ecosystems**

Put together a short presentation of several different ecosystems e.g. a seashore, a wildflower meadow, a woodland and a pasture grazed by sheep. Ask students to discuss the type of organisms they might find in each ecosystem and estimate the numbers of each type of organism in the picture. Then discuss the difficulties in doing this and how you might actually attempt to measure the numbers more accurately. Students could look for secondary evidence on how to do this and examples of school field work on the Internet.

Follow this by reading the additional information below the opening section of page 74 of the Student Book. They may then read the brief description of the activity provided by the 'Your task' box.

### Option 1: Straight-forward class practical

You may wish to run the activity as a straight-forward class practical. Students follow the instructions on **Worksheet B2.24b**. Students look at the distribution of plants in two different ecosystems, one more affected by humans than the other. They have to select five random sites in the first ecosystem using mapping, a grid and a random number table. Students measure environmental conditions, such as light intensity, soil pH or temperature in each quadrat. Students repeat the measurements in the second ecosystem and use their results to consider the impact of human activities on the distribution of organisms in the two areas. The range of data that students need to collect is given on **Worksheet B2.24c**.

### Plenary

On page 75 of the Student Book you will find three examples of the sort of work that students may produce for this task. The examples focus on controlling variables. You could share these with students after they have completed their own work. This will help them to understand the assessment criteria and so make it easier for them to evaluate their work and to see how they can improve it. Moderator comments on each of the Student Book extracts can be found at the end of the assessment guidance for this investigation on the CD-ROM. The examples can also be found on the **AT** document *Student examples*.

### Option 2: Running the activity as a practice controlled assessment task (PCA)

We have provided a full range of support resources to allow the running of this practical as a practice controlled assessment task. A recommended structure is outlined below (to be used over a number of sessions). Marking guidance for all three parts of the practice task can be found on the CD-ROM that accompanies the TTPP. To save time when using these practice controlled assessment tasks, you may wish to focus on a particular aspect or skill rather than working through all three parts of the task.

### Part A Planning

1. Students should be given the Student brief on **Worksheet B2.24a**. They can use Part A of the Workbook that is provided to help pupils with their practice controlled assessments. They should be given about 1 hour to do this planning.
2. There are a large number of different practicals available. Choose one appropriate to the resources available to you. Many schools have access to grassy areas such as playing fields and in this case students could investigate the differences between mown and unmown areas. If you do not have access to grassy areas in school it is possible to use a local park. If this is the case it may be easier to compare areas which receive more or less trampling.

### Part B Observations

3. Students carry out the practical task to collect evidence using the method they have planned in Part A. Once again, they should refer to the Student brief on **Worksheet B2.24a**. They can use Part B of the Workbook that is provided to help pupils with their practice controlled assessments. They should be given about 2 hours to collect their primary evidence.
4. If there is a problem with their own planned method, students may be asked to follow the method set out on **Worksheet B2.24b**. This will still enable students to access the full range of marks for Part B and Part C of the practice controlled assessment task.
5. In Part B, students are required to gather some secondary evidence. The evidence can be quantitative or qualitative. It can be from a variety of sources but students must note where they found their evidence and evaluate the quality of the source as part of this task. Skills Sheet 22 provides students with further guidance on researching for and evaluating secondary evidence. This part of the task could be done outside of the lesson but must be supervised.

### Part C Conclusions

6. Students follow the instructions set out on the Part C section of the Student brief on **Worksheet B2.24a**. They should use their data from Part B and the secondary evidence they have collected when doing this. They can use Part C of the Workbook that is provided to help pupils with their practice controlled assessments. They should be given about 1 hour to work on their conclusions.

The **AT** includes video clips showing a group of students working through elements of this investigation with teacher support.

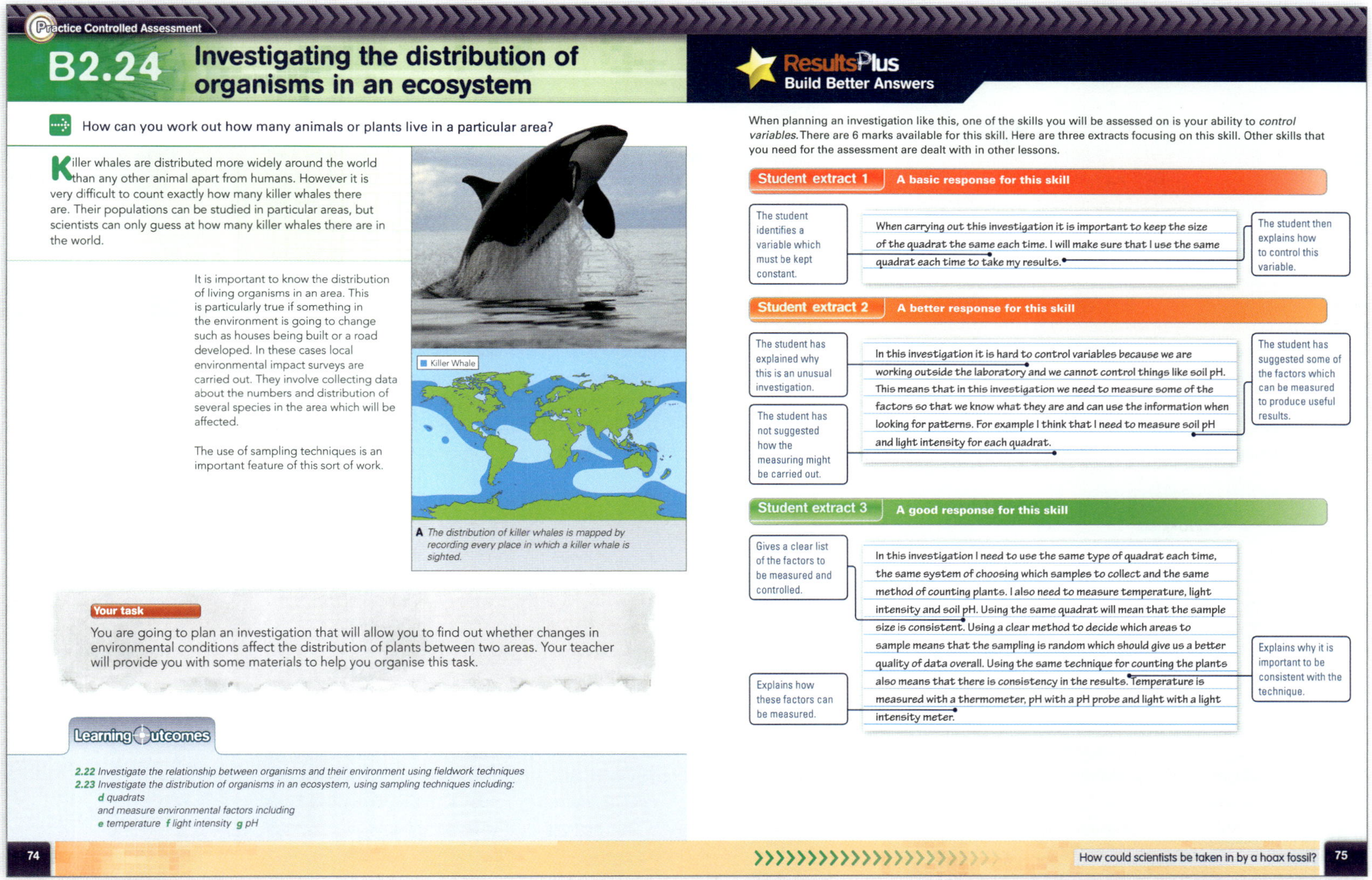
Practice Controlled Assessment

# B2.24 Investigating the distribution of organisms in an ecosystem

How can you work out how many animals or plants live in a particular area?

Killer whales are distributed more widely around the world than any other animal apart from humans. However it is very difficult to count exactly how many killer whales there are. Their populations can be studied in particular areas, but scientists can only guess at how many killer whales there are in the world.

It is important to know the distribution of living organisms in an area. This is particularly true if something in the environment is going to change such as houses being built or a road developed. In these cases local environmental impact surveys are carried out. They involve collecting data about the numbers and distribution of several species in the area which will be affected.

The use of sampling techniques is an important feature of this sort of work.



A The distribution of killer whales is mapped by recording every place in which a killer whale is sighted.

**Your task**

You are going to plan an investigation that will allow you to find out whether changes in environmental conditions affect the distribution of plants between two areas. Your teacher will provide you with some materials to help you organise this task.

**Learning outcomes**

*2.22 Investigate the relationship between organisms and their environment using fieldwork techniques*
*2.23 Investigate the distribution of organisms in an ecosystem, using sampling techniques including:*
*d quadrats*
*and measure environmental factors including*
*e temperature f light intensity g pH*

**ResultsPlus Build Better Answers**

When planning an investigation like this, one of the skills you will be assessed on is your ability to *control variables.* There are 6 marks available for this skill. Here are three extracts focusing on this skill. Other skills that you need for the assessment are dealt with in other lessons.

**Student extract 1** A basic response for this skill

When carrying out this investigation it is important to keep the size of the quadrat the same each time. I will make sure that I use the same quadrat each time to take my results.

- The student identifies a variable which must be kept constant.
- The student then explains how to control this variable.

**Student extract 2** A better response for this skill

In this investigation it is hard to control variables because we are working outside the laboratory and we cannot control things like soil pH. This means that in this investigation we need to measure some of the factors so that we know what they are and can use the information when looking for patterns. For example I think that I need to measure soil pH and light intensity for each quadrat.

- The student has explained why this is an unusual investigation.
- The student has not suggested how the measuring might be carried out.
- The student has suggested some of the factors which can be measured to produce useful results.

**Student extract 3** A good response for this skill

In this investigation I need to use the same type of quadrat each time, the same system of choosing which samples to collect and the same method of counting plants. I also need to measure temperature, light intensity and soil pH. Using the same quadrat will mean that the sample size is consistent. Using a clear method to decide which areas to sample means that the sampling is random which should give us a better quality of data overall. Using the same technique for counting the plants also means that there is consistency in the results. Temperature is measured with a thermometer, pH with a pH probe and light with a light intensity meter.

- Gives a clear list of the factors to be measured and controlled.
- Explains how these factors can be measured.
- Explains why it is important to be consistent with the technique.

74 75 How could scientists be taken in by a hoax fossil?

## ActiveTeach

- **AT** *B2.24 Organisms in ecosystem* [interactive]
  Investigating the distribution
- **AT** *B2.24 Assessment criteria* [presentation]
  Understanding the CA marking criteria
- **AT** *B2.24 Specification points* [word document]
  Edexcel specification points
- **AT** *B2.24 Student examples* [word document]
  Examples for students to assess

## Assessment criteria

### Controls

**0** No relevant controls given.

**1-2 a)** Identifies one appropriate variable that needs to be controlled, e.g. size of quadrat, method of choosing where to sample, method of counting plants. Pupils should also explain that they cannot control soil pH, temperature and light intensity but they can measure them so that they know how these factors vary.

**b)** Describes how this variable is controlled, e.g. use the same quadrat, use a clear method to decide which areas to sample means that the sampling is random, use the same technique for counting the plants.

**3-4 a)** Identifies some relevant variables, e.g. two from the list above.

**b)** Describes how these variables are controlled, e.g. from the list above.

**5-6 a)** Identifies a range of appropriate variables to control, e.g. all of the above.

**b)** An appropriate explanation is given of why these variables are controlled, e.g. same size of quadrat means that the method of sampling is consistent, keeping the method of choosing where to sample and the method of counting plants the same also means that sampling is consistent. Pupils should also explain that they cannot control soil pH, temperature and light intensity but they can measure them so that they know how these factors vary. They should be able to describe how these factors will be measured.

# B2.25 Fossils and evolution



This lesson explains the importance of the fossil record in providing evidence for change in organisms over time, including the reasons for, and problems caused by, gaps in the fossil record.

## Specification coverage

***3.1*** Evaluate the evidence for evolution, based on the fossil record

***3.2*** Explain why there are gaps in the fossil record, including: a) because fossils do not always form b) because soft tissue decays c) because many fossils are yet to be found

H ***3.3*** Explain how the anatomy of the pentadactyl limb provides scientists with evidence for evolution

HSW ***14*** How uncertainties in scientific knowledge and scientific ideas change over time *and the role of the scientific community in validating these changes*

There are also opportunities to cover HSW *2*.

## Key terms

evolution
fossil
fossil record
H pentadactyl

### Evolution mind map

**Starter 1** Lit

Ask each student to write a definition of 'evolution', then to work in pairs and then small groups to refine their definition, using mind mapping. Eventually the groups share with the whole class.

### Evolution

**Starter 2**

Show students an ordered set of shapes that are gradually changing, one to the next. One shape is missing, and students draw that shape and justify why they have drawn it in the way that they have. This helps students to start thinking about the fact that things do change over a period of time (evolution), without worrying about how this process happens (Darwin's theory of evolution).

### Evolution of the horse

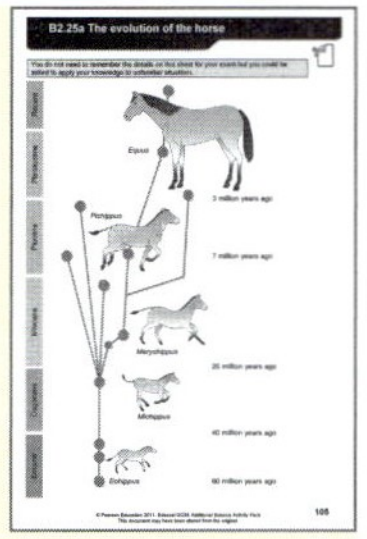
B2.25a The evolution of the horse

**Exploring 1**

Students read the text on **Worksheet B2.25a** and complete the task. Students do not need to recall details of the evolution of the horse.

**Stretch** Ask students to list other features of the horse anatomy that might have changed.

**Support** Supply some of the links, e.g. *Merychippus* with *Merychippus* foot; *Mesohippus* foot with marsh.

### Fossil formation

**Exploring 2**

Ask students what you need to prove a theory. Students spend a short time finding out about how different types of fossils are formed and then write down which types of fossils provide the best evidence, and justifying their answers.

**Stretch** Students investigate several different types of fossil formation and write a report comparing the value of the evidence from rock fossils and ice fossils.

**Support** Ensure students understand that the rocks that form earliest are usually at the base of a rock sequence.

### Student Book spread B2.25

**Explaining 1**

Ask students to read the section on fossilisation, and then see how well they have understood the idea by asking why not all dead organisms form fossils.

**Stretch** Ask students to suggest why there is a history of opposition to the idea that species change over time.

**Support** Supply a word list for students to use in answering question **6**.

### Gaps in the fossil record (AT)

**Explaining 2**

Discuss the gaps in the fossil record. Consider the difficulties of getting and interpreting fossil evidence.

The **AT** presentation *Different fossils* provides images of different fossils.

**Stretch** Ask students to consider and explain how much more difficult it is to compare features such as blood pigments than pentadactyl limbs.

**Support** Provide some fossils for students to look at and handle. Ask them to list what they can determine about the organism and what they can't.

### What have you learnt?

**Plenary 1** AfL

Summarise lesson content through a question and answer session, e.g. What do fossils show us? What are the problems with the fossil record? How can you use the fossil record as evidence of evolution?

### The fossil record

**Plenary 2** Lit

Write the phrase 'fossil record' in the middle of the board, and ask students to suggest related words and how they should be linked to make a concept map, giving a reason for their placement.

### The story of Piltdown man

B2.25b The story of Piltdown man

**Homework 1**

**Worksheet B2.25b** gives students information about the Piltdown man hoax and requires them to use the information given and what they have learnt and understood in the lesson to answer a series of questions.

**Support** Miss out questions **4** and **6**.

### H The pentadactyl limb and evolution

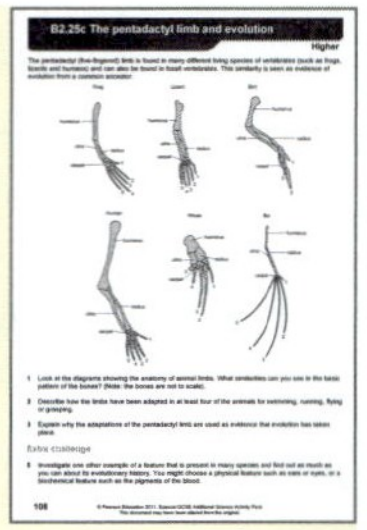
B2.25c The pentadactyl limb and evolution

**Homework 2**

**Worksheet B2.25c** is aimed at more able students and includes Higher Tier questions.

**Stretch** Students answer the 'extra challenge' question.

# B2.25 Fossils and evolution

What can fossils tell us about the history of life on Earth?

In 1912 fragments of a skull and jawbone were found at Piltdown, Sussex. Scientists thought the bones were from an ancestor of modern humans. In 1953 it was proved that the 'Piltdown Man' bones were a hoax (and were actually from modern humans and orang-utans). So ideas about human evolution had to change again.

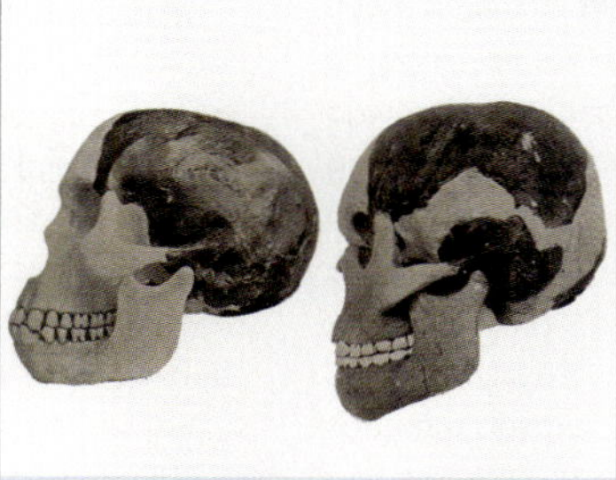

**A** *Different scientists put the 'Piltdown Man' bone fragments together in different ways, as they thought about what our ancestors looked like.*

1 What is a fossil?

2 Why is there no fossil record of the earliest cells?

**Fossils** are the preserved traces or remains of organisms that lived thousands or millions of years ago. We find fossils when the rocks containing them are weathered. The history of life on Earth as shown by the fossils from different periods of time is known as the **fossil record.** This suggests that organisms have changed gradually through time (a process called **evolution**).

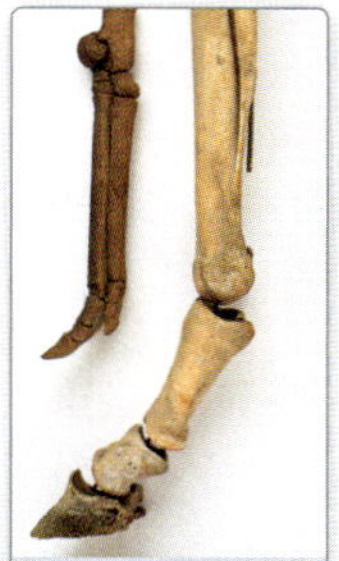

**B** *Differences in the limb bone fossils show how horses have evolved over time.*

The fossil record has many gaps in it. Soft tissues decay and do not usually form fossils, so soft-bodied organisms leave little fossil evidence behind. Other dead organisms did not form fossils because the hard parts were destroyed. Many fossils are buried deep in the earth and have not yet been found.

These gaps mean that scientists must interpret how organisms changed over time from incomplete data. The same sets of fossil data can be interpreted in different ways, often because fossils are frequently damaged or incomplete. The scientists who first found *Megalosaurus* fossils thought it had a huge head and walked on four legs. They hadn't found all the bones. Better fossil evidence shows it was a small-headed dinosaur walking on two legs.

3a Why are there gaps in the fossil record?

b How do these gaps affect explanations of how organisms have changed through time?

**C** *Scientists changed their idea of what Megalosaurus looked like as more fossil remains were found and the evidence became more complete.*

The more fossil evidence we can collect, the better conclusions we can draw. We can date fossils accurately now and use computers to model how the organism might have looked.

## More evidence for evolution

H

Most vertebrates have limbs, and though the limbs may look very different on the outside, the internal bone structure is very similar. This is also true of fossil vertebrates. Even fossil ancestors of limbless living vertebrates have the same basic five-fingered (**pentadactyl**) limb structure. This suggests that all vertebrates evolved from one common ancestor hundreds of millions of years ago. Looking at the fossil record, scientists can explain the evolution of different forms of pentadactyl limb in different vertebrate species as adaptations to different ways of living and moving.

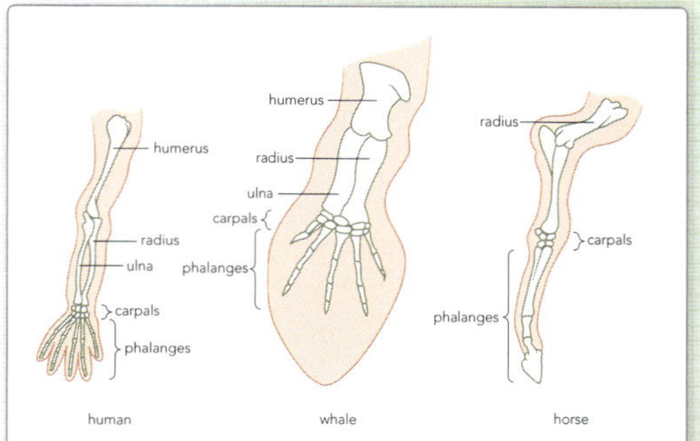


**D** *The similarities in the bone structures of these pentadactyl limbs are evidence of a common ancestor.*

6 Explain the problems that scientists have in interpreting the fossil record.

**ResultsPlus Watch Out!**

Students sometimes give only one reason for the gaps in the fossil record. Remember that soft tissue decays so some fossils do not form and many fossils are yet to be found.

H 4 How is the fossil record used as evidence to support the idea of evolution?

H 5 a What are the similarities between the limbs of the different animals shown in Figure D?

b How does evolution help to explain similar features in very different organisms?

**Skills spotlight**

Uncertainties in scientific knowledge and ideas change over time as we find out more. Explain why modern scientists would be unlikely to be fooled by 'Piltdown Man'.

**Learning Outcomes**

*3.1* Evaluate the evidence for evolution, based on the fossil record

*3.2* Explain why there are gaps in the fossil record, including:
*a* because fossils do not always form
*b* because soft tissue decays
*c* because many fossils are yet to be found

H *3.3* Explain how the anatomy of the pentadactyl limb provides scientists with evidence for evolution

HSW 14 Describe how scientists share data and discuss new ideas, and how over time this process helps to reduce uncertainties and revise scientific theories





## ActiveTeach

- **AT** *Stories in stone* [video] Fossilisation
- **AT** *Different fossils* [presentation] Fossil image information

## Answers | Student Book

1 Preserved remains of organisms that lived long ago.

2 Single-celled organisms are soft with no hard parts, so they decayed and didn't form fossils.

3 **a** Many organisms don't form fossils – conditions are not always right to preserve them, soft-bodied organisms usually decay without leaving fossils. Many fossils may exist but have yet to be found. We only have fossils for some, not all, of the intermediate stages in the fossil record.

**b** The story isn't complete. Scientists can't see back to the earliest soft-bodied organisms. An organism intermediate between two different stages may not have been found. Fossils are not always complete and may have important bits missing etc. Any other sensible points.

4 Evolution suggests that organisms have changed gradually over time. Fossils provide evidence of gradual changes in organisms happening over a long time.

5 **a)** H The limbs all have a radius, a series of carpals (wrist bones) and phalanges (digits).

**b)** Evolution is the change over time of organisms. If organisms are related, they will have evolved from the same ancestor a long time ago. So they will share some of the features which they have inherited from that ancestor.

6 The fossil record contains many gaps, since most living organisms are not preserved as fossils when they die, especialy soft-bodied organisms without any bones or shells, like our earliest ancestors. Some fossils will have been damaged or destroyed since they were formed, and others exist but have not been found. This means scientists have to work from incomplete data that is often open to much interpretation when piecing together the fossil record.

**Skills spotlight**

There are much better ways of dating fossils, so modern scientists would tell very quickly that the bones weren't old. DNA analysis would show that the bones came from different species of modern animals. Computer analysis would show that the bones didn't really fit together and couldn't be modelled. Any other sensible suggestions.

# B2.26 Growth

52

This lesson looks at growth and differentiation in animal and plant cells and revisits the idea of stem cells from Lesson B2.9.

## Specification coverage

***3.4*** Describe growth in terms of increase in size, length and mass

***3.5*** Interpret growth data in terms of percentile charts

***3.6*** Explain how cell division, elongation and differentiation contribute to the growth and development of a plant

***3.7*** Explain how cell division and differentiation contribute to the growth and development of an animal

HSW ***5*** Planning to test a scientific idea, answer a scientific question, or solve a scientific problem

HSW ***7*** Working accurately and safely, individually and with others, when collecting first-hand data

There are also opportunities to cover HSW ***6*** and ***8***.

## Key terms

differentiation
elongation
stem cells
growth
percentile

### What do you know about growth?

**Starter 1** *Lit*

Write the word 'growth' on the board. Ask students to write down three scientific facts about growth. Then go around the class and take one fact from each person until all suggestions from the class have been covered. Write up each fact. Leave this up until the end of the lesson.

### Growth in plant cells

**Exploring 1** Prac

Students use Skills Sheet 14 and **Worksheet B2.26a** to do microscope work on the regions of growth in a plant shoot. Full details can be found on the Teacher and technician practical sheet on B2.26.

Stretch Students also complete steps E–H on the worksheet.

Support Refer students to Figure C on page 79 of the Student Book showing the different regions of growth in a plant stem and talk students through the differences as they draw the cells.

### Student Book spread B2.26

**Explaining 1**

Ask students to consider the differences in animal and plant cells and what this might mean to how they grow. Students then read the Student Book to find out the answers.

Stretch Push able students to work out that plant cells can only get bigger while the cell wall is soft, so they elongate first and then create more cytoplasm. Animal cells can increase in size steadily as they have no restricting cell wall.

Support Explain the charts in the Student Book, including an explanation of percentiles.

### Checking up ideas about growth

**Plenary 1** *AfL*

Return to the word 'growth' from *Starter 1* and ask students to work in pairs to write three facts about growth, using as much knowledge gained in the lesson as possible. Go around the class and add them to the earlier points. Also see if students now recognise any of their earlier points as wrong or over simplified.

### Seedlings and growth

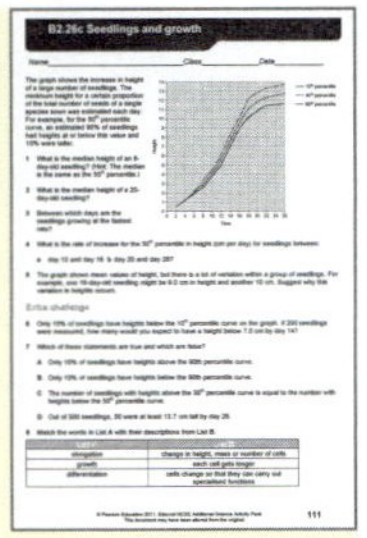

**Homework 1 Worksheet B2.26c** is aimed at students needing support.

Support Remind students of the meaning of the median. Weaker students could miss out questions **5**, **6** and **7**. Questions **6** and **7** involve percentiles – a Higher Tier skill.

### Growing from seed

**Starter 2** *AfL*

Bring a selection of seeds into the classroom. Hold each of them up and ask students to guess how big the plant that will develop from the seed is going to be. (Make sure you label each seed so you know what it is and roughly how big the plant will be.)

### Measuring the height of a tree

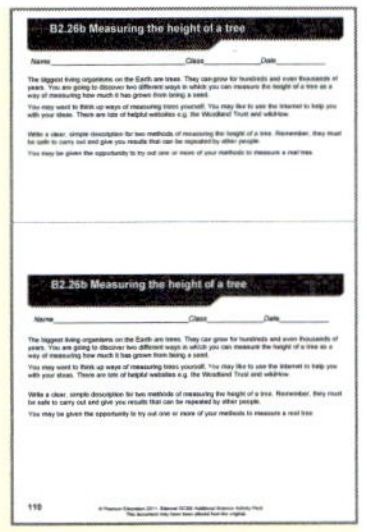

**Exploring 2**

Use the Skills spotlight box on page 79 of the Student Book to introduce this activity. **Worksheet B2.26b** supports students in planning methods.

Stretch Ask students to use the fixed angle of elevation method as one of their ways of measuring the height of the tree.

Support Guide students to the web resource you feel they will be best able to use or print out one of the methods for them from the websites given above and allow them to copy the method.

### What about cell differentiation?

**Explaining 2**

Show students a piece of bamboo and tell them it has an area of meristem cells at each joint along the stem. Ask students to explain why bamboo can grow so quickly and explain the differences between growth in bamboo, an oak tree and a person.

Stretch Ask students a range of questions about cell division in humans – see the TTPP.

Support Students work through the relevant paragraph of the Student Book and answer question 3 on page 78.

### Growth – true or false?

**Plenary 2** *AfL*

Students work in pairs, each formulating a statement (or statements) about growth that may be true or false. They test their partner. Select some examples for the whole class to try.

### Human growth

**Homework 2 Worksheet B2.26d** looks at growth charts for children using ideas about cell division.

Stretch Students answer the 'extra challenge' question, which includes Higher Tier skills on calculation and interpretation of percentiles.

# B2.26 Growth

How do plants and animals grow differently?

A giant redwood tree can be almost 120 m tall and over 2000 years old but it starts life as a tiny seed with a mass of only 3–5 mg.

A

**ResultsPlus Watch Out!**

Describing growth as 'getting bigger' is not as good as saying that there is an increase in cell number and cell size.

When organisms grow they get bigger. The easiest way to observe **growth** is to measure an increase in size, length or mass. For example, health professionals measure the mass and height of babies and children regularly to check that they are growing normally. Each child is compared to a chart to find out which **percentile** of the population they fall into.

**Maths skills**

**Percentiles** are used to compare a certain characteristic (e.g. mass) against the total population.

A large sample of 6-month-old babies is taken and ranked by mass. The sample is then split into 100 equally sized groups. The group with the highest masses is the 100th percentile and the group with the lowest masses is the 1st percentile. A 6-month-old baby can then be allocated a percentile depending on which group their mass falls into.

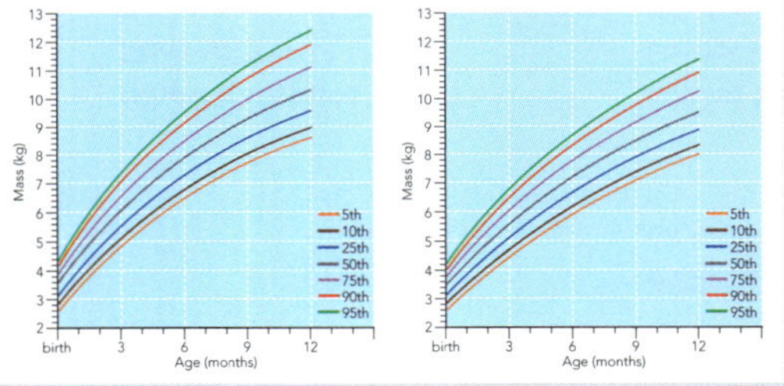

**B** *Mass-for-age percentiles for boys (left) and girls (right), birth to 12 months. Generally babies should be between the 95th and 5th percentiles. Also if their percentile changes by two or more, this may indicate a problem.*

However, you have to be careful when you measure growth. When you blow up a balloon it gets bigger but the amount of balloon material is the same. Growth in a living organism involves two processes. There is an increase in the number of cells in a living organism involves two processes. There is an increase in the number of cells when a cell divides to form two identical cells, and these then get bigger.

1 A balloon gets bigger when you blow it up but this isn't growth. Why not?

2 How does cell division lead to growth?

3 How do meristems help trees grow so tall?

## Growth in plants

Plants grow all through their lives. Plants have special areas called 'meristems' just behind the tip of their roots and shoots where the cells keep dividing. However, growth in plants isn't just about cell division. Once the cells have divided they get longer (**elongation**).

As a plant stem or root continues to grow, the older meristem cells start to become specialised – they **differentiate.** A meristem cell can differentiate into any type of plant cell. For example, a cell in a shoot can become a leaf cell containing chlorophyll or a new cell in a root can differentiate to become a root hair cell.

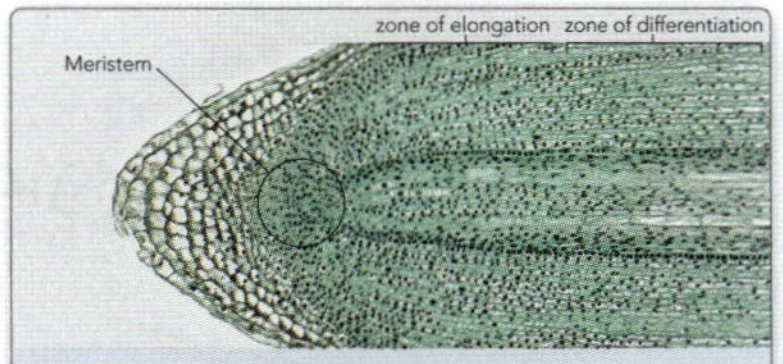

**C** *The tip of a plant shoot has areas where cells divide, elongate and differentiate into many different types of cells.*

## Growth in animals

Growth in animals also involves cell division. But animals differ from plants because they stop growing when they become adults.

In an animal, cells that can differentiate to form a number of different types of specialised cells are called **stem cells**. These cells develop into the specialised tissues and organs of an animal's body. In an embryo, the stem cells can differentiate and form almost every type of cell needed in the body. Adults have relatively few stem cells. Each type of adult stem cell can only form a limited range of cells, such as blood cells or skeletal tissues. This is why most animals cannot re-grow a damaged limb or body part but plants can grow new shoots, roots and leaves.

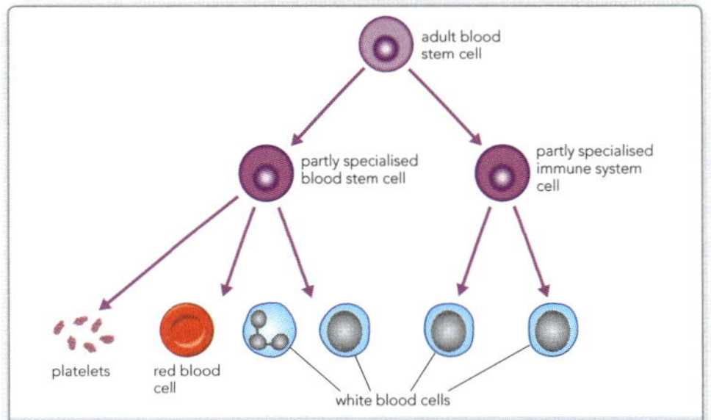

**D** *Adult blood stem cells can only differentiate into different types of blood cells.*

4 a List as many different cell types that you can think of which could differentiate from a human embryonic stem cell.
b How does this differ from the number of cells that can differentiate from an adult stem cell?

5 Why is it relatively easy to grow an entire plant from a single meristem cell but impossible (so far) to grow a new adult animal from a single adult stem cell?

6 Explain the similarities and differences between growth in plants and in animals.

**Skills spotlight**

Giant redwoods are very tall. Plan two ways of measuring the height of a giant redwood and discuss the advantages and disadvantages of each method in terms of risk and quality of data.

**Learning Outcomes**

*3.4* Describe growth in terms of increase in size, length and mass
*3.5* Interpret growth data in terms of percentile charts
*3.6* Explain how cell division, elongation and differentiation contribute to the growth and development of a plant
*3.7* Explain how cell division and differentiation contribute to the growth and development of an animal
HSW 5 Plan to test a scientific idea, answer a scientific question, or solve a scientific problem by choosing appropriate resources


Why is blood red?


**ActiveTeach**

- **AT** *How do plants and animals grow?* [interactive]
  Plant and animal growth – sorting activity
- **AT** *Differentiation of adult blood stream stem cells* [diagram]
  Figure D – diagram labelling activity

## Answers | Student Book

1 Because there is still the same amount of balloon material, or similar. The balloon doesn't have cells so they can't elongate or divide.

2 It increases the number of cells in the organism so it gets bigger.

3 Because they never stop growing

4 **a** Nerve cell (neurone), muscle cell, bone cell, blood cell, skin cell, many other answers possible
**b** Adult stem cells can only differentiate into a few different types of cell, e.g. adult blood stem cells can differentiate into the different types of blood cell but nothing else.

5 Meristem cells can differentiate into any type of plant cell so all the cells and tissues needed for a new individual can be produced. Adult stem cells can only differentiate into a few different types of cells and so it is impossible to produce an entire new organism.

6 A good answer will contain the following points: growth in both plants and animals involves cell division and cell growth; plant cell division is followed by elongation and then differentiation; there are constant regions of cell division (meristems) where cells divide to form undifferentiated cells, so plants grow throughout their lives; in animals cell division is immediately followed by differentiation and there is no elongation; once cells have differentiated they can only form more of the same type of cell; growth stops at adulthood in animals.

**Skills spotlight**

A variety of methods could be chosen. Whichever methods students choose to describe, they should show an awareness of the advantages and limitations of each.

# B2.27 Blood

This lesson looks at the main components of blood and their function.

## Specification coverage

***3.8*** Recall the structure and function of the following parts of the blood including: a) red blood cells b) white blood cells c) plasma d) platelets

**HSW** ***11*** Presenting information, developing an argument and drawing a conclusion, using scientific, technical and mathematical language, conventions and symbols and ICT tools

There are also opportunities to cover **HSW** ***4*** and ***13***.

## Key terms

antibodies
haemoglobin
plasma
platelets
red blood cells
tissue
white blood cells

### Blood as an organ

**Starter 1** **AfL**

Write the following statement on the board: 'Blood is an organ'. Ask students what they know about blood and why it might be described as an organ. Look at the first part of the Student Book page 80 to confirm their answer or explain the situation to them. If necessary, re-ask the same question to confirm that students have grasped the idea of blood as an organ.

### Looking at human blood (AT)

**Exploring 1** **Prac**

Students follow the instructions on **Worksheet B2.27a** using a prepared blood slide. Full details can be found on the Teacher and technician practical sheet B2.27.

**Stretch** Students should try to identify as many different types of white blood cells as possible. Give students a graticule and ask them to produce a more accurate estimate of the ratio of red : white blood cells.

**Support** Work with students to look at a projected image of a prepared slide.

### Blood cells

**Exploring 3**

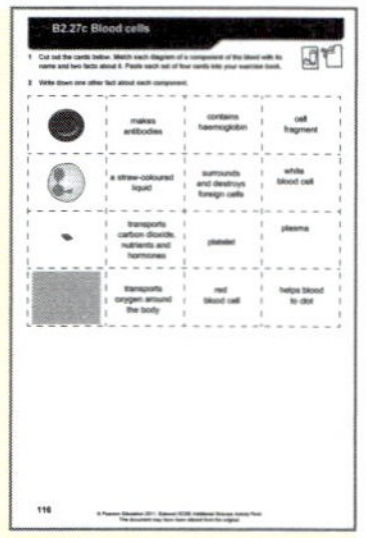

Students complete **Worksheet B2.27c** to match each component of the blood with its function.

**Stretch** Ask students to investigate bone marrow transplants, to find out why they are needed, what affects their success, and the risks involved.

**Support** Supply the diagrams and name labels unseparated, so that students need only match the two functions to each component.

### Revisiting blood

**Plenary 1** **Lit**

Ask students to write down five important facts about blood and rank them in terms of importance. They should then compare their list with that of a partner and decide a joint list. Encourage students to justify their decisions.

### The main components of blood

**Homework 1**

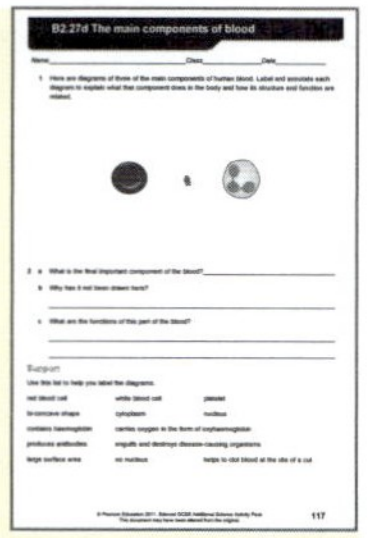

Using **Worksheet B2.27d** students label and annotate diagrams of red blood cells, white blood cells and platelets and then answer questions on the appearance and function of plasma.

**Support** Supply the labels (shown in the bottom half of the sheet).

### Blood questions

**Starter 2**

Ask students to write down the answers to these questions about the blood.

1. Approximately how much blood is in your body?
2. How many main components make up the blood?
3. Why is your blood red?

Ask them to keep their answers and see if they are right and how much they have learnt at the end of the lesson.

### Giving blood

**Exploring 2**

**Worksheet B2.27b** directs students to use the National Blood Service website to find out more about the need for blood donation.

**Stretch** Extend the task to ask students to consider how people could be encouraged to register as blood donors.

**Support** Direct students to use pages 80 and 81 of the Student Book to help produce their poster.

### Student Book spread B2.27

**Explaining 1**

Use Figure C on page 81 to discuss the main components of the blood and their functions in the body. Pick up the theme of blood transfusions and work through with students the ways in which the different components of blood are used in treatment, rather than whole blood transfusions, which are now relatively rare.

**Stretch** Students consider why there are different types of white blood cell.

**Support** Discuss blood loss in terms of lack of oxygen and food reaching the tissues.

### Back to blood questions

**Plenary 2** **AfL**

Ask each student to write one multiple choice question (with four choices). Students work together to test their knowledge, allowing each student to mark his/her own work and challenge questions that are ambiguous, confusing or have incorrect answers.

### Blood cells and their functions

**Homework 2**

**Worksheet B2.27e** is aimed at more able students

**Stretch** Students answer the 'extra challenge' question.

# B2.27 Blood

## Why is blood so important?

If you lose a lot of blood during an operation or in an accident you could die. People donate blood that can be used to help save other people's lives. A bag or unit contains 470 $cm^3$ of blood. About 8000 units are needed every day in hospitals around the UK.

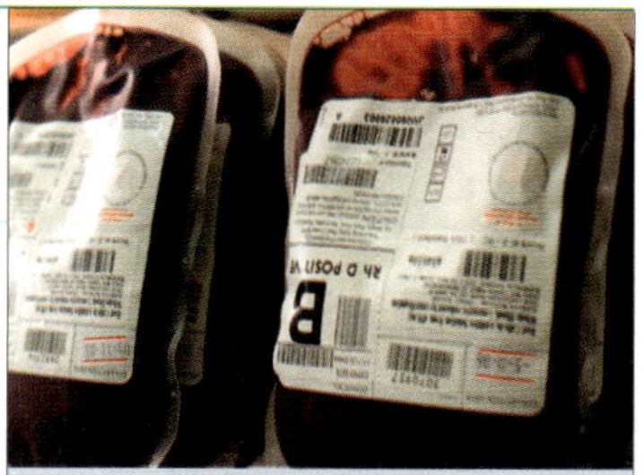

A Donated blood saves lives.

An adult has about 5 litres of blood. Although blood is a liquid, it is also an organ containing many different types of specialised cells that carry out particular functions in your body. These have all differentiated from blood stem cells and become specialised.

> 1 During what process do blood cells become specialised?

### The composition of blood

Blood is made up of four main components: **plasma**, **red blood cells**, **white blood cells** and **platelets**.

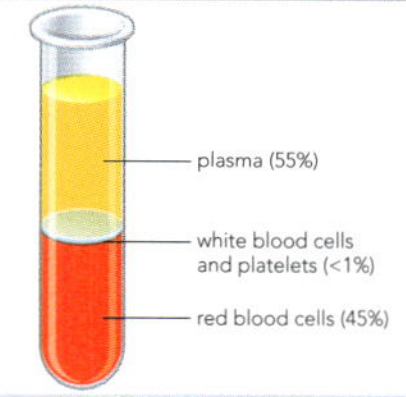


B The proportions of the different components of blood.

Plasma is a yellow liquid. It transports dissolved substances, such as carbon dioxide, food substances and hormones.

> **ResultsPlus Watch Out!**
> Students often remember the role or function of a blood cell but forget that its shape and contents help it to carry out that role. Red blood cells contain haemoglobin, which helps them to carry oxygen to the tissues.

Red blood cells contain the red pigment **haemoglobin**. Haemoglobin can combine reversibly with oxygen to form oxyhaemoglobin:

haemoglobin + oxygen ⇌ oxyhaemoglobin

When blood passes through the lungs the haemoglobin combines with oxygen. Oxyhaemoglobin is transported in red blood cells around the body to the tissues, where the oxygen is then released so that the **tissue** cells have oxygen for aerobic respiration.

> 2 Explain how red blood cells are adapted to carry as much oxygen as possible.

A red blood cell has the shape of a biconcave disc – it has a dimple on both sides (see Figure C). This adaptation gives a large surface area to volume ratio for oxygen to diffuse into and out of the cell. A red blood cell also has no nucleus and this makes room for as much haemoglobin as possible.

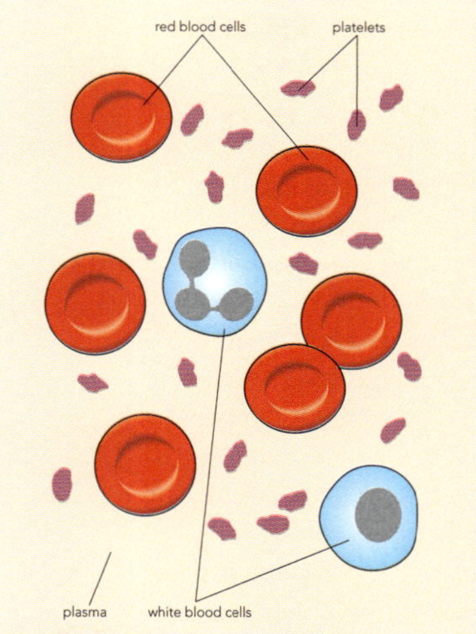


C The main types of cells and cell fragments in the blood.

White blood cells are part of the body's defences against disease. Some white blood cells make **antibodies**. These are proteins that bind to the microorganisms that cause disease and destroy them. Other white blood cells surround and destroy any foreign cells that get into the body. All white blood cells have a nucleus.

Platelets are tiny fragments of cells (and so do not have nuclei). They are important in making blood clot if you cut or damage your blood vessels. The clot dries out and forms a scab which also stops microorganisms getting into the body.

> 3 People with a disorder called thrombocytopenia do not have enough platelets. Suggest one symptom of this disease. Explain your reasoning.

> 4 Draw a table to show the main components of blood and their functions.
> 5 a Why is haemoglobin needed for cellular respiration to take place?
> b Why do you think people who have just given blood may feel a bit tired?
> 6 Explain the following statements:
> • In some diseases the red blood cells are the wrong shape and people affected will die without regular transfusions of normal blood.
> • Drugs given to prevent rejection after an organ transplant can destroy the white blood cells and people affected can suffer many infections.

> **Skills spotlight**
> An argument is a discussion in which evidence is presented for and against an idea, and then used to reach a decision.
> In the UK only 4% of people donate blood and hospitals often get close to running out. Construct an argument against paying people for their donated blood.

**Learning Outcomes**

3.8 Recall the structure and function of the following parts of the blood, including:
a red blood cells
b white blood cells
c plasma
d platelets

HSW 11 Present information, develop an argument and draw a conclusion, using scientific, technical and mathematical language





## ActiveTeach

- **AT** *Blood donors* [BBC video] Facts on blood donation
- **AT** *What is in your blood?* [interactive] The components of blood – game

## Answers | Student Book

1 They differentiate as they form from blood stem cells in the bone marrow.

2 Their biconcave disc shape gives them a big surface area for oxygen diffusion. They have no nucleus, so that as much haemoglobin as possible fits in. Haemoglobin in red blood cells combines reversibly with oxygen, so it can deliver it to where it is needed.

3 Their blood may not clot properly if they cut themselves, leading to excessive blood loss and possibly infection, because they lack platelets which make the blood clot.

4 See the table in Answers in the TTPP.

5 **a** Because aerobic cellular respiration needs oxygen and haemoglobin combines with oxygen in the lungs to form oxyhaemoglobin. When blood is transported around the body to the cells, the oxyhaemoglobin in the red blood cells gives up its oxygen in the tissues where the oxygen levels are low.
**b** They have a smaller volume of blood than normal. They can't transport as much oxygen and glucose around their body at once as normal, which can leave them lacking energy and feeling tired.

6 Red blood cells in the body supply oxygen to cells. If the cells are the wrong shape, they cannot carry oxygen around the body as well as normal. If cells don't get the oxygen they need, then they will die, eventually causing death of the whole body. Regular transfusions add normal red blood cells to the body to avoid the problem. White blood cells help to protect the body from disease. If they are destroyed by drugs, then the body is much more likely to be affected by microorganisms that invade the body, and so suffer more diseases than normal.

**Skills spotlight**

**For:** Any sensible points for, such as: more people might give blood if they were paid for it; you could get more of the rarer blood groups by paying more for them; it would help to make sure hospitals don't run out.
**Against:** It is currently a gift so it costs the health service nothing, whereas paying for blood would be very expensive; people might give blood more often than is healthy to get the money; people might be coerced into giving blood to get money; people who need money to feed drug addictions etc. would be likely to give blood if they were paid, which increases the risk of contamination and disease, especially if they are not honest about any conditions they have.

# B2.28 The heart



This lesson looks at the structure and function of the parts of the heart.

## Specification coverage

***3.9*** Describe the grouping of cells into tissues, tissues into organs, and organs into organ systems

***3.10*** Explain how the structure of the heart is related to its function, including: a) the four major blood vessels associated with the heart (pulmonary artery, pulmonary vein, aorta and vena cava) b) left atrium and ventricle to pump oxygenated blood c) right atrium and ventricle to pump deoxygenated blood d) valves to prevent backflow (names not required) e) left ventricle has a thicker muscle wall than the right ventricle f) the direction of blood flow through the heart

HSW ***14*** How uncertainties in scientific knowledge and scientific ideas change over time and the role of the scientific community in validating these changes

There are also opportunities to cover HSW ***2***, HSW ***3*** and HSW ***7***.

## Key terms

| | |
|---|---|
| aorta | pulmonary vein |
| atrium | septum |
| deoxygenated | valve |
| organ | vena cava |
| oxygenated | ventricle |
| pulmonary artery | |

### Your heart

**Starter 1**

Ask students to work in groups to think up some idioms about the heart (cry your heart out, heart of stone, etc.). Run through these to confirm that the heart is often perceived to be the seat of our emotions and then ask students whether they think this is true, or whether the heart in fact has a more mundane purpose.

### Dissecting a lamb's heart (AT)

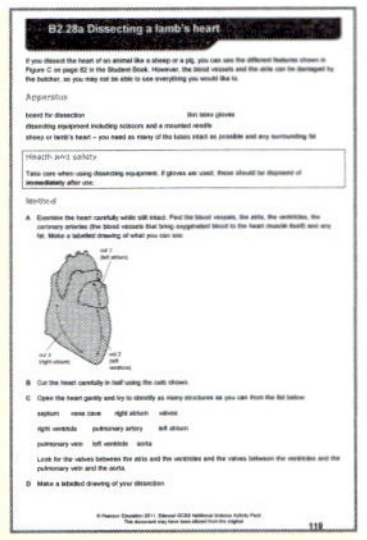

**Exploring 1**

**Demo / Prac**

Students follow the instructions on **Worksheet B2.28a** to carry out a dissection of a lamb's heart. Alternatively use the images on the **AT** presentation *Dissected heart*. Full details can be found on the Teacher and technician practical sheet B2.28.

**Stretch** Ask students how they think the heart they have dissected might differ from a human heart.

**Support** Students arrange the dissected heart in the same manner as in the labelled image.

### Student book spread B2.28

**Explaining 1**

Remind students of the organisation of cells, tissues and organs and ask them to think about why both the blood and the heart are organs. It is useful to describe the features and functions of the heart before students carry out the dissection in *Exploring 1*.

**Stretch** Students write a paragraph explaining why both the blood and the heart are regarded as organs although they are very different.

**Support** Explain the structure of the heart and refer to some of the different tissues found in different parts of the heart.

### Human heart model

**Plenary 1** AfL

Give groups of students different parts of the heart (right atrium, right valve, aorta, etc.) and then challenge them to arrange themselves into the order in which blood will flow through them. Then ask students whose parts contain oxygenated blood to put their hands up. Then repeat for deoxygenated blood.

### How does the heart work?

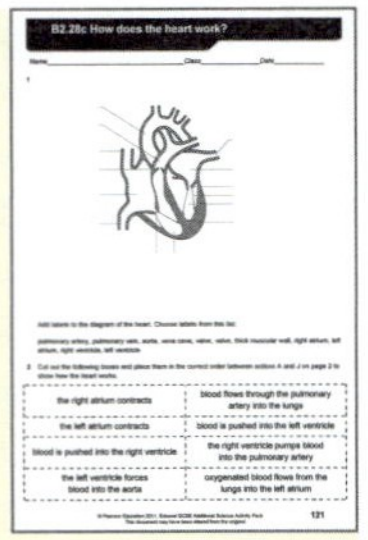

**Homework 1**

**Worksheet B2.28c** reinforces how the structure of the heart is related to its function.

**Support** For question 2, supply two more correct positions, e.g. 'B the right atrium contracts' and 'E blood flows through the pulmonary artery into the lungs'.

### Introducing the heart

**Starter 2** Lit

Use a list of words (vein, artery, muscle, atrium, ventricle, valve, etc.) that students may have heard of at Key Stage 3. Students then need to write a true sentence about the heart using one of the words.

Go around the class asking for the sentences.

### Labelling a diagram of the heart

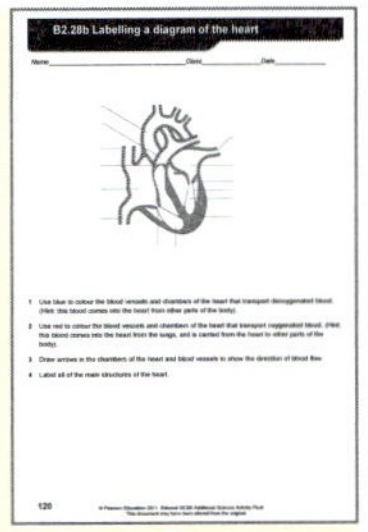

**Exploring 2**

Using **Worksheet B2.28b** students colour in and label the main structures of the heart.

**Stretch** Ask students to annotate the labels to explain the functions of the different structures.

**Support** Students can use Figure C on page 82 to help them with the labelling or **AT** presentation *Diagram of the heart*.

### How the heart works

**Explaining 2**

Explain to students how the heart works to pump the blood. You could also introduce the idea that it is the closing and opening of the valves that makes the heart sounds you hear on a stethoscope. To illustrate this, you can use a microphone connected to a loudspeaker to hear it, or there is an iPhone app.

**Stretch** Discuss, then ask students to write an explanation of why the heart is often called a 'double pump' by biologists.

**Support** Talk though the animation several times as necessary.

### Heart jigsaw

**Plenary 2**

Cut up 4–5 copies of the diagram on **Worksheet B2.28b** into 5–6 pieces. Then muddle these all up and the whole class has to join them back together to make whole diagrams. Then the diagrams are stuck to a piece of paper and the parts are labelled by groups.

### Galen and the heart

**Homework 2**

**Worksheet B2.28d** provides questions to answer based on comprehension of the text about Galen and their knowledge of the heart.

**Stretch** Students answer the 'extra challenge' question.

# B2.28 The heart

How does your heart work?

We often associate the heart with our emotions. Perhaps this is because people can feel their hearts responding when they are angry or stressed. Scientists, however, know that the heart is nothing more than a pump, which is not very romantic!

A What does a heart represent?

1 Why is blood an example of an organ?

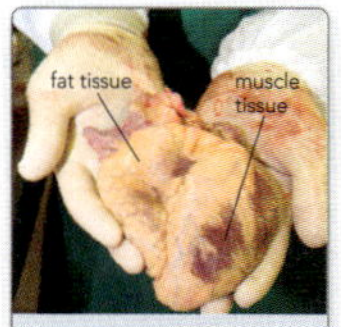


B The heart is composed of different tissues.

## Cells, tissues and organs

A group of the same type of specialised cells forms a tissue (e.g. muscle tissue is made of muscle cells). An **organ** contains several different tissues working together to carry out a particular function in the body. The heart is an organ that pumps blood to the lungs and around the body.

## The structure and function of the heart

Blood coming from the tissues is low in oxygen (**deoxygenated**). It is pumped by the heart to the lungs where the haemoglobin in red blood cells picks up oxygen and the blood becomes **oxygenated**. This oxygenated blood returns to the heart and is pumped around the body to the tissues and cells.

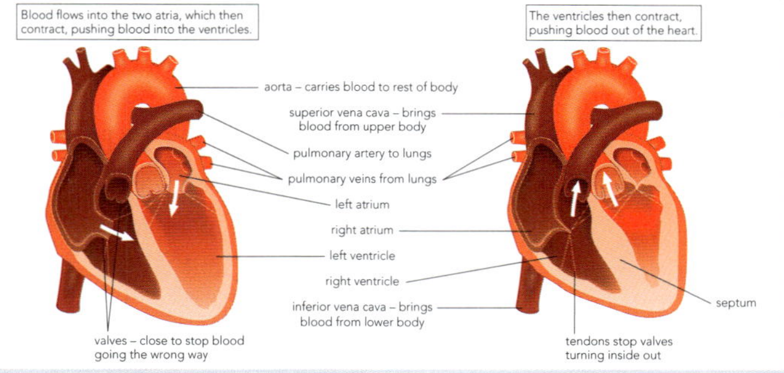


C The structure of the human heart.

The left and right sides of the heart work together, filling and emptying at the same time. However, to explain the different parts of the heart and how they work we often follow the blood right through the heart, looking at each side in turn. The two sides of the heart are completely separated by the muscular **septum**.

A **vena cava** brings blood from the body into the **right atrium**. When the atrium is full, muscles in the wall contract and force the blood through the **valves** into the **right ventricle**. The valves are flaps of tissue that stop the blood flowing backwards.

When the ventricle is full of blood the muscles of the ventricle wall contract, forcing blood out through more valves into the **pulmonary artery**. This carries deoxygenated blood to the lungs where it picks up oxygen.

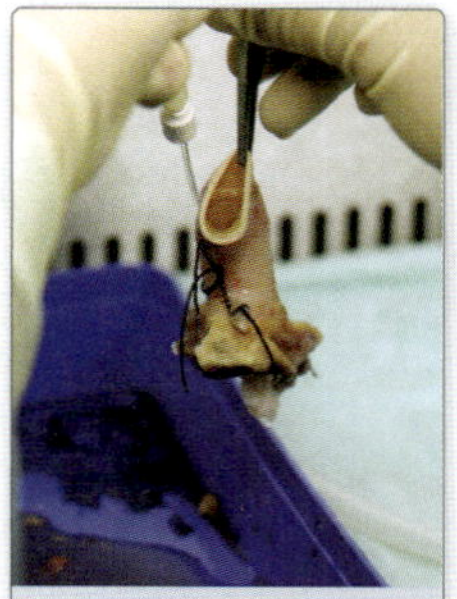

D A dissected part of an aorta, for use in a transplant. The aorta is about the width of a garden hosepipe.

The oxygenated blood returns from the lungs to the **left atrium** of the heart in the **pulmonary vein**. When the atrium is full, it contracts and forces the blood through valves into the **left ventricle**. Once the ventricle is full of oxygenated blood the muscles of the ventricle wall contract. This forces blood out through more valves into the **aorta**. The aorta is the large blood vessel that carries oxygenated blood around the body.

The muscle wall of the left ventricle is thicker than that of the right ventricle because it has to pump blood all around the body rather than just to the lungs.

2 What is:
a oxygenated blood
b deoxygenated blood?

**ResultsPlus Watch Out!**

Students sometimes get confused when asked to describe the route of the blood through the heart. It is a good idea to start with the deoxygenated blood in the right atrium.

3 What is the function of the valves in the heart?

4 a Which side of the heart pumps deoxygenated blood?
b Why is the muscular wall of the left ventricle thicker than that of the right ventricle?
c Why do you think the heart is sometimes called a double pump?

5 Describe what happens to a volume of blood from the time it goes into the heart from a vena cava until it is pumped out through the aorta.

**Skills spotlight**

Ideas about how the heart works have changed over time. The second century Greek doctor Galen was not allowed to dissect human bodies. He thought that blood flowed from one side of the heart to the other through lots of invisible holes in the septum. How does this compare to modern ideas about the heart?

**Learning Outcomes**

3.9 Describe the grouping of cells into tissues and tissues into organs

3.10 Explain how the structure of the heart is related to its function, including:
- a the four major blood vessels associated with the heart (pulmonary artery, pulmonary vein, aorta, vena cava)
- b left atrium and ventricle to pump oxygenated blood
- c right atrium and ventricle to pump deoxygenated blood
- d valves to prevent backflow (names not required)
- e left ventricle has a thicker muscle wall than the right ventricle
- f the direction of blood flow through the heart

HSW 14 Describe how scientists share data and discuss new ideas, and how over time this process helps to reduce uncertainties and revise scientific theories





## ActiveTeach

- **AT** *Structure and function of the heart* [interactive]
  Structures in the heart – matching activity
- **AT** *Cardiac output* [presentation]
  Calculating cardiac output
- **AT** *Dissected heart* [presentation]
  Images of a dissected heart
- **AT** *Diagram of the heart* [presentation]
  Drag and drop diagram
- **AT** *Structure of the human heart* [diagram]
  Figure C – diagram labelling activity

## Answers | Student Book

1 It is a collection of tissues (groups of specialised cells) working together to carry out a particular function in the body.

2 a Blood carrying oxygen (in oxyhaemoglobin molecules attached to the red blood cells)
**b** Blood carrying little or no oxygen in the red blood cells

3 To stop the backflow of blood/ensure blood flows forward through the heart to maintain a circulation

4 a The right
**b** The left ventricle pumps blood all around the body but the right side only pumps blood to the lungs, so the left side needs to be more powerful.
**c** One side collects blood from the body and pumps it to the lungs, while the other side collects blood from the lungs and pumps it to the body. The two sides act as two separate pumps.

5 A good answer will contain the following points: vena cava brings blood from the body into right atrium; right atrium contracts and forces blood through valve into right ventricle; right ventricle contracts and pumps blood through valve into pulmonary artery; blood flows to lungs where it becomes oxygenated; flows back to heart in pulmonary vein and enters left atrium; atrium contracts and forces blood through valve into left ventricle; left ventricle contracts and forces oxygenated blood out of heart through a valve into aorta and so around the body.

**Skills spotlight**

Modern ideas about the heart are based on dissection and surgery on living, beating hearts. We now know that the heart is two separate pumps and that blood does not flow from one side to the other through invisible holes in the septum. Followed by a description of circulation as in question 5 answer.

# B2.29 The circulatory system

This lesson describes organ systems with the circulatory system as an example, with details of the structures of the blood vessels.

## Specification coverage

**3.9** Describe the grouping of cells into tissues, tissues into organs and organs into organ systems

**3.11** Describe how the circulatory system transports substances around the body, including: a) arteries transport blood away from the heart b) veins transport blood to the heart c) capillaries exchange materials with tissues

HSW 3 Many phenomena can be explained by developing and using scientific theories, models and ideas

There are also opportunities to cover HSW 6, HSW 8, HSW 10 and HSW 11.

## Key terms

arteries
blood vessels
capillaries
circulatory system
organ system
veins

### Cells, tissues, organs – what next?

**Starter 1** AfL Lit

Ask students to write down a definition of tissues and organs. Introduce the idea of organ systems – for example the way the blood vessels make a circulatory system when combined with the heart. Note that the blood is not part of the circulatory system. The circulatory system consists of the heart and the blood vessels.

### Finding your pulse rate

**Exploring 1** Prac

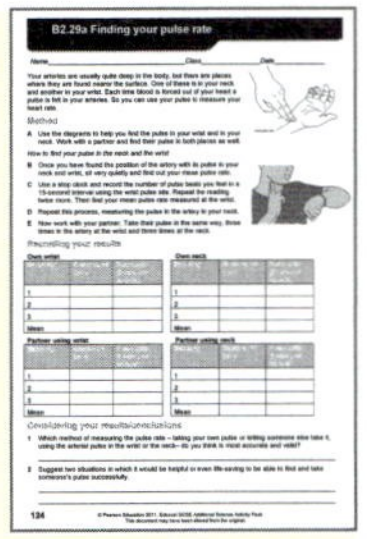


In **Worksheet B2.29a** students learn to find the arterial pulse in their wrist and their neck. Full details can be found on the Teacher and technician practical sheet B2.29 (1).

Stretch Ask students to suggest why it is not good practice to use your thumb to take a pulse.

Support Omit measurement of pulse in the neck and support students in suggesting why measuring your own pulse may not be as valid.

### Student Book spread B2.29

**Explaining 1**

Use the text and images in the Student Book to talk students through the circulatory system as an example of an organ system. Point out functions of the main vessels and explain how the pulmonary artery and pulmonary vein are unusual.

Stretch Students write and sequence additional statements to make a flowchart that includes other organs, e.g. digestive system, kidneys.

Support Tell students the identity of the starting and finishing cards.

### Summing up

**Plenary 1**

Use the Skills spotlight to initiate a discussion about the circulatory system, e.g. why do donors often open and close their fist when giving blood?

### Circulatory system crossword

**Homework 1**

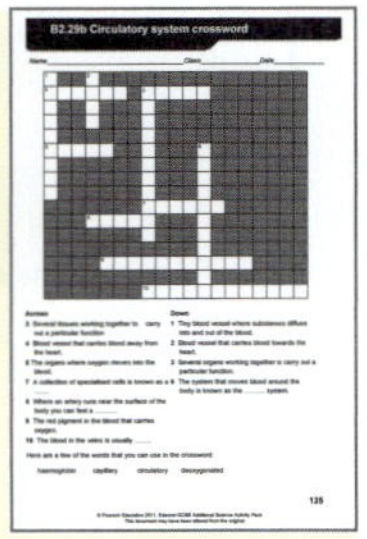


**Worksheet B2.29b** is a crossword of key words from the lesson.

Support Supply some of the more difficult words from the bottom section of the sheet.

### Taking over from the heart

**Starter 2**

Use the image of the heart-lung machine on page 84 of the Student Book to talk through with students the importance of a transport system in the body. Ask students to suggest analogies for the circulatory system (e.g. rail network, central heating system, etc.)

### The blood vessels

**Exploring 2**

Discuss the idea of valves in the veins, to make sure the blood doesn't flow backwards – link this back to work in the previous lesson on the heart.

Stretch Ask students to say some differences between vein valves and heart valves (e.g. heart valves in the left side of the heart regulate the flow of oxygenated blood, higher pressure in heart, different shape).

Support Explain the valves in the veins in the leg as being analogous to a series of lock gates on a canal.

### Looking at blood vessels

**Explaining 2** Prac

Students use prepared slides to look at the structure of arteries, veins and capillaries. Full details can be found on the Teacher and technician practical sheet B2.29 (2). Students draw and label their diagrams.

Stretch Students estimate the diameter of the vessels and explain the relative sizes.

Support Project a slide of the vessels under the microscope or display images of the three types of blood vessel from the **AT** presentation *Blood vessels.*

### Role play

**Plenary 2** AfL

Ask students to work in groups to decide how they would model the circulatory system using the playground, some chalk, some bright red T shirts, some dark red T shirts and themselves.

### Veins in space

**Homework 2**

**Worksheet B2.29c** provides comprehension questions on experiments on astronauts living in microgravity.

Stretch Students answer the 'extra challenge' question.

# B2.29 The circulatory system

What is the circulatory system?

The heart pumps blood around the body all the time. If surgeons have to operate on a person's heart, they need to keep it still. The heart is stopped and a heart–lung machine takes over. It oxygenates the blood and moves it round the body while the operation is being carried out.

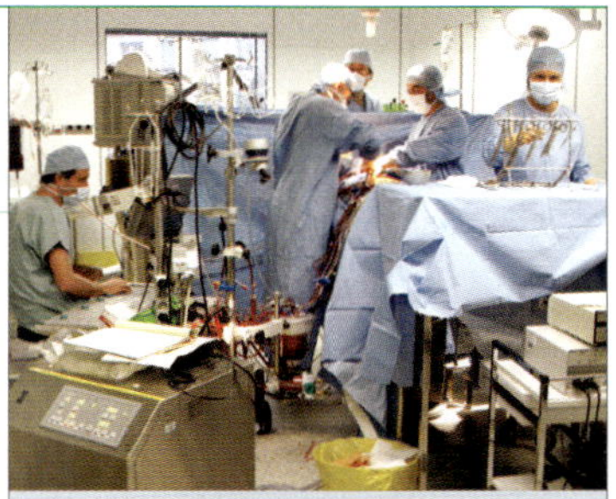

**A** *An artificial heart–lung machine in action.*

The heart pumps blood around the body so that all the cells in the body can get the oxygen and nutrients that they need. However, it is not the only organ that helps to do this. **Blood vessels** are also needed.

Blood vessels are tube-shaped organs that carry blood. There are three types: **arteries**, **capillaries** and **veins**.

**ResultsPlus Watch Out!**

Students often muddle up the directions in which arteries and veins carry blood. Remember that Arteries carry blood Away from the heart.

Arteries carry blood away from the heart. The blood in arteries has to be under high pressure so that it can reach all parts of the body. So arteries have strong, thick walls.

Capillaries allow substances to diffuse into and out of the blood into, the cells in tissues. To help this process capillaries have very thin walls.

Veins have wide passages inside them and carry blood to the heart. They are wide because the blood flows relatively slowly under low pressure.

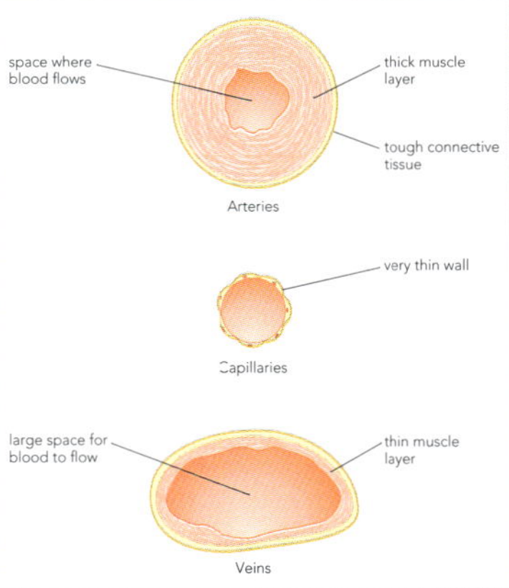


**B** *The structure of arteries, capillaries and veins.*

1 What is the name for all the tubes that carry blood around the body?

2 a What is an artery?
b Explain why an artery is an organ.

3 a What is the function of capillaries?
b How are capillaries adapted to this function?
c Why is this function important?

## Organ systems

Groups of specialised cells working together are called tissues and tissues that work together form organs. Groups of organs that work together are called **organ systems**. The heart and blood vessels form an organ system called the **circulatory system**.

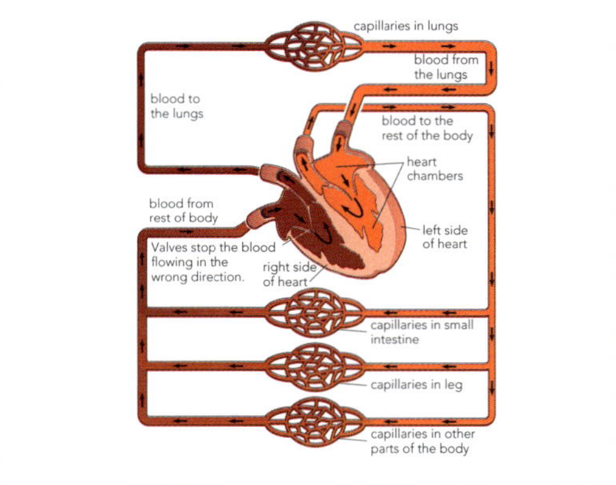


**C** *The circulatory system.*

**Skills spotlight**

When you give blood, a hollow needle is inserted into a vein in your arm. You open and close your hand gently and blood is collected in a bag. When the needle is removed, a cotton wool pad is held to the hole it leaves, and then a plaster is put firmly over it. You are advised to take it easy after giving blood. Explain this process using our modern ideas about the circulatory system.

4 What is an organ system?

5 What is the function of the circulatory system?

6 Which type of blood vessel usually carries deoxygenated blood?

7 Describe the route of a small volume of blood from a capillary in your muscle where it has just given up its oxygen until it returns to the same place loaded with oxygen again. Include in your answer what substances pass into or out of the blood at each stage.

**Learning Outcomes**

*3.9* Describe the grouping of cells into tissues, tissues into organs and organs into organ systems

*3.11* Describe how the circulatory system transports substances around the body, including:
*a* arteries transport blood away from the heart
*b* veins transport blood to the heart
*c* capillaries exchange materials with tissues

HSW *3* Describe how phenomena are explained using scientific theories and ideas





## ActiveTeach

- **AT** *Heart to heart*
  [interactive]
  Journey of the blood – ordering activity
- **AT** *Blood vessels*
  [presentation]
  Microscope views
- **AT** *Structure of arteries, capillaries and veins.*
  [diagram]
  Figure B – diagram labelling activity
- **AT** *Circulatory system*
  [diagram]
  Figure C – diagram labelling activity

## Answers | Student Book

1 Blood vessels

2 **a** A blood vessel that carries blood away from the heart
**b** It contains different tissues (groups of specialised cells) that work together to perform a function.

3 **a** To allow substances to diffuse into and out of the blood
**b** They have very thin walls
**c** This allows substances like oxygen and glucose to be delivered to respiring cells, and waste products to be taken away. It also allows gas exchange in the blood in the lungs.

4 A group of organs working together to carry out a function in the body.

5 To move blood around the body so that the various substances in it can be transported to where they are needed.

6 Veins

7 Oxygen moves into muscle by diffusion; blood moves through network of capillaries into vein; travels back to heart and enters heart through vena cava; moves into right atrium, then right ventricle, and then pulmonary artery; carried to lungs and travels through capillaries in lungs where oxygen moves into red blood cells by diffusion; moves through capillaries into pulmonary vein and taken back to heart; enters left atrium, then left ventricle, and then aorta; moves through arteries into capillaries ready to give up the oxygen by diffusion again.

**Skills spotlight**

Needle into vein not artery, so blood flows out at a steady rate and you don't lose too much. Opening and closing hand uses muscles in the arm, squeezing blood along the veins. Cotton wool pad and plaster seal the wound until clotting takes place. You have a reduced blood volume and fewer red blood cells so less food and oxygen get to your cells and you need time to recover.

# B2.30 The digestive system



This lesson looks at the structure and functions of different parts of the digestive system.

## Specification coverage

***3.12*** Describe the functions of the parts of the digestive system including: a) mouth b) oesophagus c) stomach d) large and small intestines e) pancreas f) liver (H) g) gall bladder

***3.13*** Explain the role of the muscular wall of the alimentary canal in peristalsis

**HSW** ***11*** Presenting information, *developing an argument and drawing a conclusion,* using scientific, technical and mathematical language, conventions and symbols *and ICT tools*

There are also opportunities to cover **HSW** ***3***.

## Key terms

alimentary canal
bile
bolus
digestion
digestive system
enzyme
faeces
(H) gall bladder
oesophagus
pancreas
peristalsis
saliva
villi

### Why do we need a digestive system?

**Starter 1**

Place some foods (e.g. raw egg, some meat, orange juice, tomatoes, a biscuit and some cake) in a blender. Then ask: Who would like to taste some of my fantastic new health drink? Obviously, if there are any volunteers explain that we can't actually try it because we've prepared it in the lab. Then explain that a similar process happens to everything you eat – you have to break it down.

### Sorting the digestive system

**Exploring 1** **AfL**

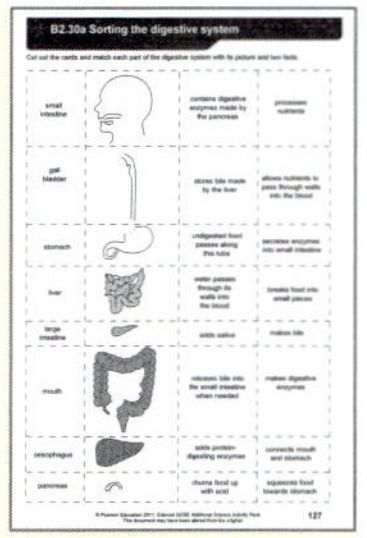

Students use cards from **Worksheet B2.30a**. Students simply match up the cards in fours.

**Stretch** Ask students to put the organs into two groups and to justify their grouping (for instance 'organs that food passes through', 'organs that food does not pass through').

**Support** Use the slightly more simple **Worksheet B2.30b**.

### Modelling peristalsis

**Explaining 2**

Students need to understand the role of the muscular walls of the alimentary tract in moving food through the body. Use the analogy of squeezing a tube of toothpaste to explain what happens. Discuss the effect of slow or rapid peristalsis.

**Stretch** Ask students to plan a simple physical model that could be used to demonstrate peristalsis, showing the effect of the circular muscles.

**Support** Show students the peristalsis animation from the *3D 4 Medical* website to help them understand the process.

### Summing up

**Plenary 1** **Lit**

Set a sequencing task on the order of organs, followed by writing descriptions (e.g. that have to be exactly five words long) for what each organ does. Remind students that enzymes are involved in the breakdown of the food and that they will be learning more about them in the next lesson.

### Modelling peristalsis

**Homework 1**

Students complete a storyboard for an animation/cartoon to illustrate peristalsis.

**Support** Remind students to use terms such as oesophagus, small intestine, circular muscles, etc.

### A tube from mouth to anus

**Starter 2**

Put a blank table up on the board with the names of the organs a–g from the spec. (Note that Foundation students don't need g.) Then ask students to suggest what each of the organs does. Fill in the table. Then come back to this in the plenary and add additional information.

### Student Book spread B2.30 (AT)

**Explaining 1**

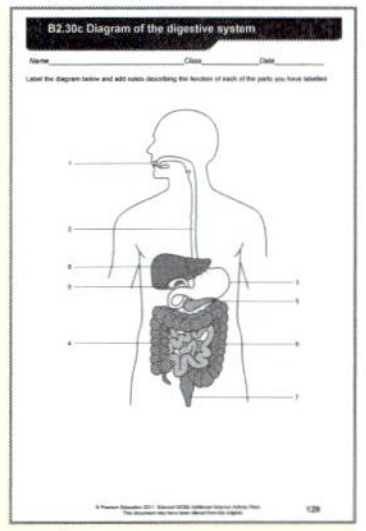

Use Figure B on page 86 and the **AT** presentation *The digestive system*. Students label the diagram on **Worksheet B2.30c** which can then be stuck into their books or files.

**Stretch** Students consider what a gall stone might be and what effect gall stones might have on the body if they block the bile duct.

**Support** Explain to students why the alimentary canal is coiled up.

### Explaining what goes on in the digestive System

**Explaining 3**

Ask students to storyboard an animation that helps explain what happens to food once it is eaten. Provide students with colour copies of Figure B in the Student Book to help with this.

**Stretch** Ask students to compare their storyboards with an animation on the Internet, and identify any weaknesses in their own storyboards that they could improve.

**Support** Students use the information on pages 86 and 87 of the Student Book to help them write their commentary.

### Organs in the digestive system (AT)

**Plenary 2**

The **AT** presentation *The digestive system* provides a drag-and-drop version of Figure B on page 86 for students to complete. There should be functions of the organs as well as names of the organs for students to position correctly.

### Questions on the digestive system

**Homework 2**

More able students complete **Worksheet B2.30d**, which includes a Higher Tier questions on the function of the gall bladder.

**Stretch** Students answer the 'extra challenge' questions.

# B2.30 The digestive system

What is the digestive system?

Around the world snakes, ants, fresh blood mixed with milk and witchetty grubs are just some of the treats people enjoy eating. Whatever we eat, we need to be able to digest it.

**A** *Witchetty grubs (a type of moth caterpillar) are eaten by Aboriginal people living in the deserts of Australia.*

1 What happens in your digestive system?

Food contains a lot of large insoluble molecules that cannot get into the blood. These need to be broken down into small soluble molecules such as glucose, which can pass into the blood and so be used in cells.

2 Explain why the digestive system is an organ system.

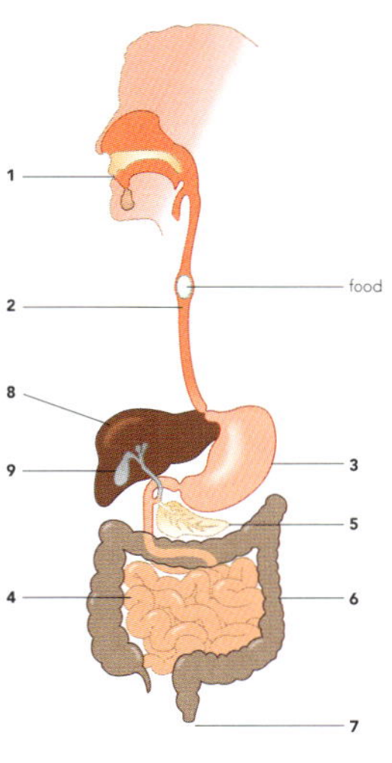


**B** *The human digestive system.*

Food is broken down in a process called **digestion**, which takes place in an organ system called the **digestive system**. The digestive system is made up of the **alimentary canal**, a muscular tube running through the body from mouth to anus, and several other organs that make chemicals needed for digestion (including **enzymes**).

1 **Mouth:** where food is taken into the body. During chewing, teeth break up the food into small pieces. This increases the surface area for digestive enzymes to work on. The tongue helps to form the chewed food into a ball called a **bolus**. The bolus gets coated in **saliva**, which lubricates it and makes it easier to swallow. Saliva also contains an enzyme that starts to break down the starch in food.

2 **Oesophagus:** a muscular tube between the mouth and the stomach. Muscles contract in waves to squeeze the food down towards the stomach. This is called **peristalsis**.

3 **Stomach:** a muscular bag that makes acid and some enzymes (most importantly, enzymes to digest proteins). It churns the food up with these juices by peristalsis to make a thick paste.

4 **Small intestine:** a long, coiled, muscular tube where most of the large insoluble food molecules are broken down into smaller soluble molecules. It contains lots of digestive enzymes made by the pancreas and it makes its own digestive enzymes as well. The molecules of digested food are absorbed into the blood using finger-shaped projections called **villi**, which contain capillaries. Food is moved along by peristalsis.

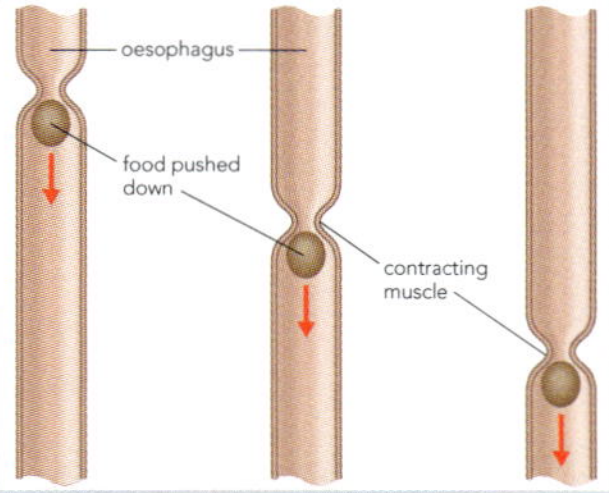


**C** *Peristalsis takes place all through the digestive system, pushing the food along the alimentary canal.*

5 **Pancreas:** this organ makes digestive enzymes and releases them into the first part of the small intestine.

6 **Large intestine:** undigested food passes into this wide, thin-walled tube. Water diffuses back into the blood leaving the waste material (**faeces**) behind.

7 **Anus:** where the undigested food is passed out of the body.

8 **Liver:** digested food is absorbed by the small intestine and dissolves in the blood plasma. Once in the blood, it is taken to the liver to be processed. Some of the molecules are broken down even more. Some are built up into larger molecules again. The liver also makes **bile**, which helps in the digestion of fats.

H 9 **Gall bladder:** a small organ that stores the bile made by the liver and releases it into the small intestine when it is needed.

**ResultsPlus Watch Out!**

Bile is *stored* in the gall bladder but it is *made* in the liver.

3 a Name the parts of the alimentary canal.
b Name the other organs that are part of the digestive system.

4 What is peristalsis and why is it so important in the digestive system?

H 5 Suggest three organs in which you would expect to find bile.

6 Compare the functions of the stomach, the small intestine and the large intestine.

**Skills spotlight**

Some scientists measured the mass of food eaten each day by a group of 14 volunteers. They also measured the mass of faeces the volunteers produced each day. Describe how you would process and present the data produced by this investigation. You may find it helpful to include a sketch.

**Learning Outcomes**

3.12 Describe the functions of the parts of the digestive system, including: a mouth, b oesophagus, c stomach, d small and large intestines, e pancreas, f liver, H g gall bladder

3.13 Explain the role of the muscular wall of the alimentary canal in peristalsis

HSW 11 Present information using scientific conventions and symbols



Why could the contents of your stomach damage your skin?



## ActiveTeach

- **AT** *Digestive enzymes* [interactive]
  Enzyme function – matching activity
- **AT** *The digestive system* [presentation]
  Drag and drop diagram

## Answers | Student Book

1 Large, insoluble food molecules are broken down into smaller, soluble food molecules that can pass out of the digestive system into the blood and be carried around the body to the cells where they are needed.

2 Because it is made up of a number of different organs that are all connected and working together to carry out a particular function in the body.

3 **a** Mouth, oesophagus, stomach, small intestine, large intestine, anus
**b** Pancreas, liver, gall bladder, bile duct

4 Peristalsis is the rhythmic contraction and relaxation of the circular muscles of the gut, which is vital for squeezing food through the digestive system.

5 H Liver, gall bladder, small intestine

6 A good answer will contain the following points: stomach – bag of muscle; contains enzymes to break down protein; contains hydrochloric acid to kill bacteria; little or no absorption of digested food; muscles squeeze in peristalsis to churn up the food; small intestine – long, coiled, muscular tube; contains lots of digestive enzymes to break down the large insoluble food molecules into smaller soluble molecules; makes digestive enzymes; receives digestive enzymes from the pancreas; site where molecules of digested food are absorbed into the blood through villi; food is moved along by peristalsis; large intestine – wide, thin-walled tube; water leaves the undigested food by diffusion; no digestion takes place; no digestive enzymes made.

**Skills spotlight**

Whichever method students use, look for correct terminology and a sketch of a graph or chart that clearly represents the data collected.

# B2.31 Breaking down food



Amend intro This lesson describes the role of enzymes in the chemical digestion of food in the digestive system including proteases, lipase and bile.

## Specification coverage

***3.14*** Explain the role of digestive enzymes, including: a) carbohydrases, including amylase, which digest starch to simple sugars b) proteases, including pepsin, which digest proteins to amino acids c) lipase, which digests fats to fatty acids and glycerol

H ***3.15*** Explain the role of bile in neutralising stomach acid and emulsifying fats

HSW ***3*** Many phenomena can be explained by developing and using scientific theories, models and ideas

There are also opportunities to cover HSW ***1***, HSW ***6***, HSW ***7***, HSW ***8***, HSW ***10*** and HSW ***11***.

## Key terms

amino acids
amylase
carbohydrases
carbohydrate
H emulsify
H emulsion
fat
fatty acid
glycerol
lipase
pepsin
protease
protein
starch
sugar

### Remember enzymes?

**Starter 1** AfL

Brainstorm enzymes and put up a big concept map or spider diagram on the board of everything students can remember about them. Keep that diagram up throughout the lesson and ask students to bear in mind what they know when they are thinking about digestive enzymes.

### Investigating the action of amylase (AT)

B2.31a Investigating the action of amylase

**Exploring 1** Prac

In **Worksheet B2.31a** students have the opportunity to investigate the action of amylase from their own saliva. Full details can be found on the Teacher and technician practical sheet B2.31 (1).

Stretch Ask students how they would modify the investigation to investigate the effects of temperature and/or pH on enzyme action.

Support Students carry out just the iodine test to see that starch disappears.

### Student Book spread B2.31

**Explaining 1**

Ask students for examples of foods that contain lots of starch. Explain the role of carbohydrases in the digestive system for breaking down carbohydrates like starch into simple sugars.

Stretch Show students a model of starch and then ask them to describe how some different sorts of amylase might produce different sugar products.

Support Supply students with a list of all the key words from the spread, and ask them to write down the most important fact about each one.

### Summarising carbohydrate digestion

**Plenary 1** Lit

Students produce a flowchart explaining how starchy food is broken down in the digestive system. An alternative would be to give students the text and ask them to transfer the information on to a flow chart.

### Digestive enzyme wordsearch

B2.31c Digestive enzyme wordsearch

**Homework 1** Lit

**Worksheet B2.31c** asks students to write a short description of words they find in a wordsearch.

Support Write the words hidden in the wordsearch on the sheet before copying.

### Enzyme facts

**Starter 2** Lit

Ask each student to write down the five most important things they can remember about enzymes and try to put everything they have remembered in order of importance. They then get together in groups of four or six and see how much agreement there is. Gather ideas and end up with a list of important facts about enzymes on the board.

### Investigating the activity of pepsin

B2.31b Investigating the activity of pepsin

**Exploring 2** Prac

In **Worksheet B2.31b** students investigate the effect of pepsin at different pHs on solid, cooked egg white. Full details can be found on the Teacher and Technician Practical sheet B2.31 (2).

Stretch Ask students how they would find the pH at which pepsin is the most active.

Support Explain to students that tubes 1, 2 and 3 model the mouth, stomach and small intestine respectively.

### H How do enzymes bring about digestion of your food?

**Explaining 2**

Demonstrate the way that fats/oils and water don't mix by adding cooking oil to water or olive oil to vinegar. Then use an emulsifier to get them to mix, and explain that bile acts as an emulsifier (and a neutraliser).

Stretch Ask why it is important to increase the surface area of nutrients in the intestine.

### Enzymes in action

**Plenary 2**

Refer back to the concept map produced in *Starter 1*. Ask students to reflect on how this fits in with what they have learned about the digestive enzymes – look for understanding of different types of enzymes for different food types.

### Digestion in the body

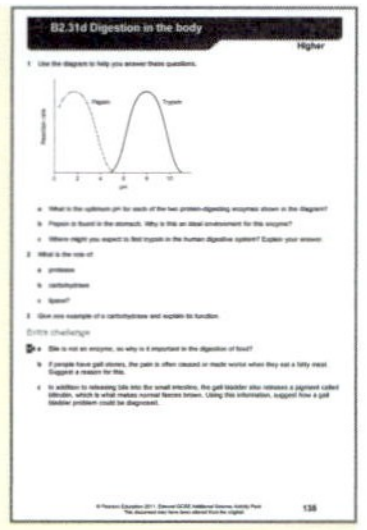
B2.31d Digestion in the body

**Homework 2**

**Worksheet B2.31d** includes Higher Tier questions on the importance of bile.

Stretch Students answer the 'extra challenge' question.

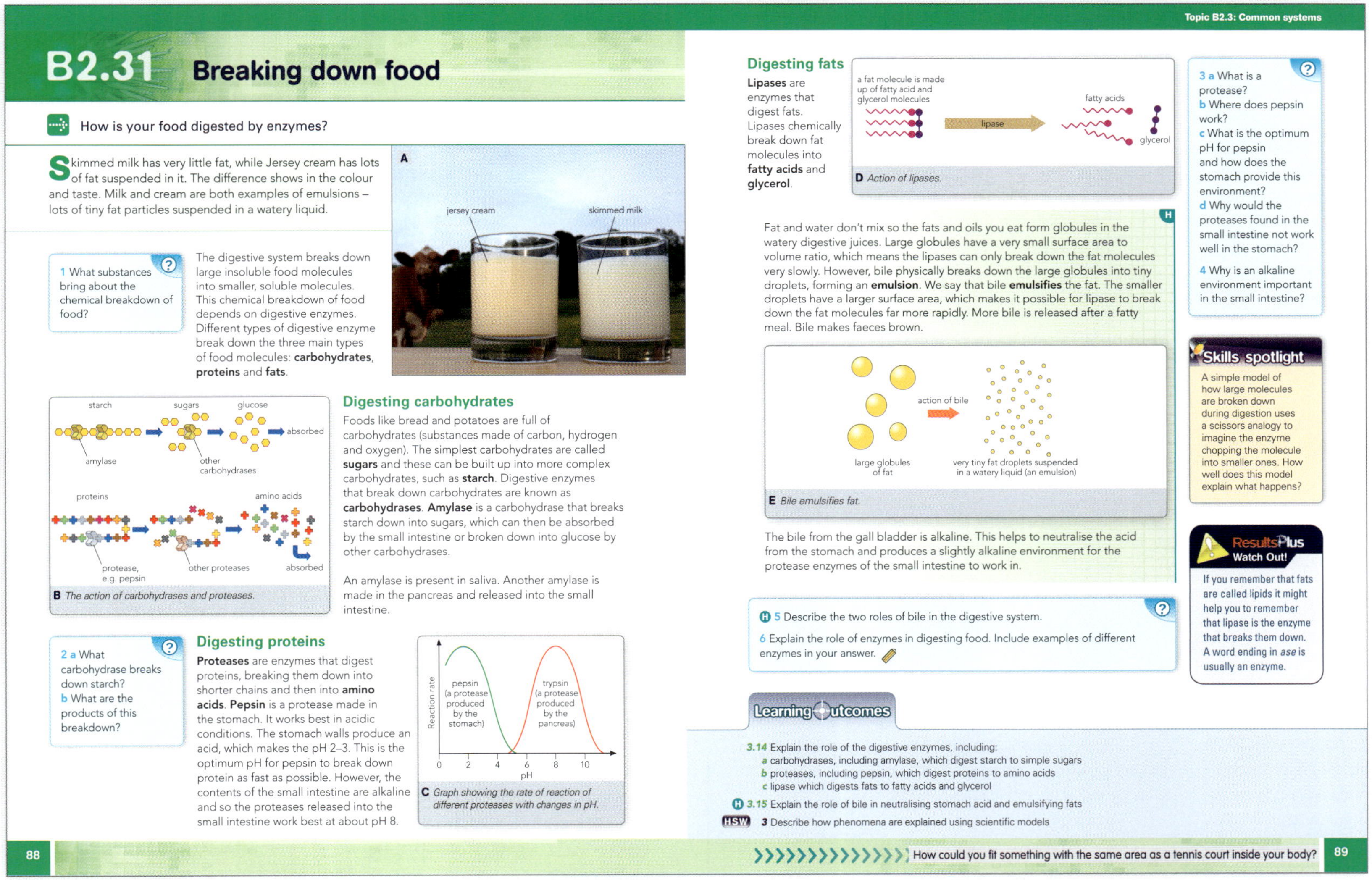



## B2.31 Breaking down food

How is your food digested by enzymes?

Skimmed milk has very little fat, while Jersey cream has lots of fat suspended in it. The difference shows in the colour and taste. Milk and cream are both examples of emulsions – lots of tiny fat particles suspended in a watery liquid.

A

jersey cream

skimmed milk

1 What substances bring about the chemical breakdown of food?

The digestive system breaks down large insoluble food molecules into smaller, soluble molecules. This chemical breakdown of food depends on digestive enzymes. Different types of digestive enzyme break down the three main types of food molecules: **carbohydrates**, **proteins** and **fats**.

starch, sugars, glucose, absorbed, amylase, other carbohydrases, proteins, amino acids, protease, e.g. pepsin, other proteases, absorbed

B *The action of carbohydrases and proteases.*

### Digesting carbohydrates

Foods like bread and potatoes are full of carbohydrates (substances made of carbon, hydrogen and oxygen). The simplest carbohydrates are called **sugars** and these can be built up into more complex carbohydrates, such as **starch**. Digestive enzymes that break down carbohydrates are known as **carbohydrases**. **Amylase** is a carbohydrase that breaks starch down into sugars, which can then be absorbed by the small intestine or broken down into glucose by other carbohydrases.

An amylase is present in saliva. Another amylase is made in the pancreas and released into the small intestine.

2 a What carbohydrase breaks down starch?
b What are the products of this breakdown?

### Digesting proteins

**Proteases** are enzymes that digest proteins, breaking them down into shorter chains and then into **amino acids**. **Pepsin** is a protease made in the stomach. It works best in acidic conditions. The stomach walls produce acid, which makes the pH 2–3. This is the optimum pH for pepsin to break down protein as fast as possible. However, the contents of the small intestine are alkaline and so the proteases released into the small intestine work best at about pH 8.

Reaction rate; pH; 0, 2, 4, 6, 8, 10; pepsin (a protease produced by the stomach); trypsin (a protease produced by the pancreas)

C *Graph showing the rate of reaction of different proteases with changes in pH.*

### Digesting fats

**Lipases** are enzymes that digest fats. Lipases chemically break down fat molecules into **fatty acids** and **glycerol**.

a fat molecule is made up of fatty acid and glycerol molecules; lipase; fatty acids; glycerol

D *Action of lipases.*

3 a What is a protease?
b Where does pepsin work?
c What is the optimum pH for pepsin and how does the stomach provide this environment?
d Why would the proteases found in the small intestine not work well in the stomach?

4 Why is an alkaline environment important in the small intestine?

H

Fat and water don't mix so the fats and oils you eat form globules in the watery digestive juices. Large globules have a very small surface area to volume ratio, which means the lipases can only break down the fat molecules very slowly. However, bile physically breaks down the large globules into tiny droplets, forming an **emulsion**. We say that bile **emulsifies** the fat. The smaller droplets have a larger surface area, which makes it possible for lipase to break down the fat molecules far more rapidly. More bile is released after a fatty meal. Bile makes faeces brown.

large globules of fat; action of bile; very tiny fat droplets suspended in a watery liquid (an emulsion)

E *Bile emulsifies fat.*

The bile from the gall bladder is alkaline. This helps to neutralise the acid from the stomach and produces a slightly alkaline environment for the protease enzymes of the small intestine to work in.

**Skills spotlight**

A simple model of how large molecules are broken down during digestion uses a scissors analogy to imagine the enzyme chopping the molecule into smaller ones. How well does this model explain what happens?

**ResultsPlus Watch Out!**

If you remember that fats are called lipids it might help you to remember that lipase is the enzyme that breaks them down. A word ending in *ase* is usually an enzyme.

H 5 Describe the two roles of bile in the digestive system.

6 Explain the role of enzymes in digesting food. Include examples of different enzymes in your answer.

**Learning Outcomes**

3.14 Explain the role of the digestive enzymes, including:
a carbohydrases, including amylase, which digest starch to simple sugars
b proteases, including pepsin, which digest proteins to amino acids
c lipase which digests fats to fatty acids and glycerol

H 3.15 Explain the role of bile in neutralising stomach acid and emulsifying fats

HSW 3 Describe how phenomena are explained using scientific models

How could you fit something with the same area as a tennis court inside your body?




## ActiveTeach

- **AT** *Where does digestion take place?* [interactive] Digestive processes – matching activity
- **AT** *Food tests* [word document] Iodine and Benedict's tests
- **AT** *The action of carbohydrates and proteases* [diagram] Figure B – diagram labelling activity

## Answers | Student Book

1 Enzymes

2 **a** Amylase **b** Sugars

3 **a** An enzyme that breaks down protein
**b** In the stomach
**c** pH 2–3; the stomach walls produce an acid
**d** Because the proteases that work in the small intestine work at their best in an alkaline environment.

4 Because the proteases in the small intestine work best at about pH 8.

5 (H) Neutralising stomach acid and emulsifying fats

6 A good answer will contain the following points: mouth – slightly alkaline saliva in the mouth suits amylase, which breaks down starch; when amylase gets into stomach it is denatured in the acid and stops working, so there is no more carbohydrate breakdown in the stomach; acid pH of stomach is ideal for pepsin, a protease that breaks down proteins; when food enters the small intestine it is neutralised by alkaline bile, which stops pepsin working (denatures it); slightly alkaline condition, ideal for pancreatic enzymes, including amylase, trypsin (protease) and lipase, so they work at optimum rate to break down carbohydrates, proteins and fats.

**Skills spotlight**

Students should understand the scissors model as useful in showing that a large molecule is chopped up into smaller pieces and that many food molecules are long chains, so it is almost as if individual units are cut off. They should point out the limitations – enzymes to 'cut' use chemical reactions; the small pieces are always specific molecules (so same size); often more than one molecule is produced, e.g. water is often formed.

# B2.32 Villi



This Higher Tier lesson describes the role of the villi and their adaptations to allow efficient absorption of the soluble products of digestion. Note that coeliac disease, used as a context throughout the spread, does not need to be recalled.

## Specification coverage

(H) **3.16** Explain how the structure of the villi (large surface area, single layer of cells and capillary network) allows efficient absorption of the soluble products of digestion

HSW **3** Many phenomena can be explained by developing and using scientific theories, models and ideas

There are also opportunities to cover HSW **6** and HSW **10**.

## Key terms

concentration gradient
(H) villi

### (H) Why, where and how is food absorbed?

**Starter 1** Lit

Students complete the following sentences to show what they know about the absorption of food from the gut.

1. It is it important that the insoluble food you eat is broken down into soluble food molecules in the digestive system…
2. Food needs to be absorbed from the digestive system into the blood...
3. The absorption of food takes place...
4. Diffusion is important in the digestive system…

### (H) Investigating the surface area of the small intestine

**Exploring 1**

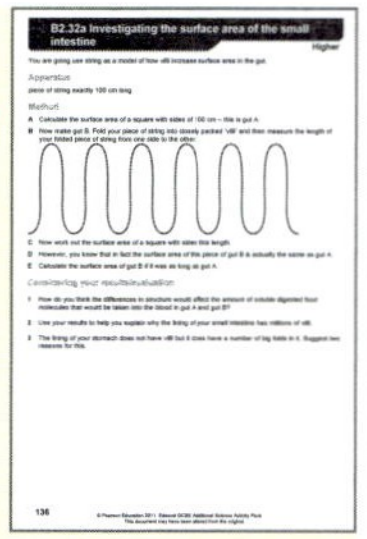
B2.32a Investigating the surface area of the small intestine

In **Worksheet B2.32a** students use string as a model of how villi increase surface area in the gut. Complete the activity and answer questions **1–3** on the worksheet.

Stretch Students estimate the increase of surface available in the villi in their model compared with a smooth gut.

### (H) Student Book spread B2.32

**Explaining 1**

Tell students that the key to the body successfully absorbing the necessary soluble products of digestion that it needs are the villi of the small intestine. Show Figure C in the Student Book and talk about the role of the villi in the small intestine.

Stretch Explain what is meant by concentration gradient.

### (H) Structure of the villus

**Plenary 1** Lit

Look at Figures B and C in the Student Book. Give students a list of characteristics of a villus and ask them to match each to the correct explanation as to why they help maintain efficient absorption of food.

### (H) Explaining coeliac disease

**Homework 1**

B2.32b Explaining coeliac disease

Students use **Worksheet B2.32b** to plan a presentation in any format they choose to inform students in Years 10–11 about the cause of coeliac disease and the importance of diagnosis and treatment.

### (H) Why is gluten-free labelling important?

**Starter 2**

Bring an item of gluten-free food into the class. Show them the gluten-free food with the clear labelling. Ask if any students or members of their family are affected by coeliac disease. Explain that if someone has coeliac disease that is not treated, they may have problems absorbing their food properly.

### (H) Looking at villi

**Exploring 2** Prac

Students use a microscope to look at the anatomy of the villi. They can use Skills Sheet 14. Full details can be found on the Teacher and technician practical sheet B2.32.

Stretch Students work out the magnification of the image and hence the actual size of the villi.

### (H) Coeliac disease and the villi

**Explaining 2**

B2.32b Explaining coeliac disease

**Worksheet B2.32b** provides an explanation of coeliac disease. Describe what coeliac disease does and how it affects the gut.

Stretch Students produce an article explaining the importance of clear labelling of food to show if it does or does not contain gluten, and the negative impact that mistaken intake of gluten can have on the health of someone with coeliac disease in terms of weight and balanced food intake.

### (H) Absorbing digested food

**Plenary 2** AfL

Ask students to work in pairs. One student lists the key characteristics needed for diffusion to take place as quickly as possible. The other lists the main ways in which the villi of the large intestine make diffusion more efficient. Students compare lists to see how they match. Summarise for the whole class.

### (H) The absorption of zinc

**Homework 2**

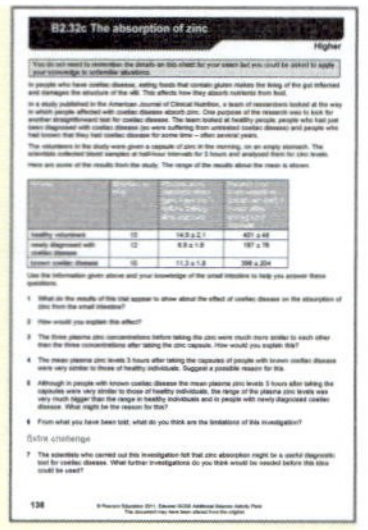
B2.32c The absorption of zinc

Students answer the questions on **Worksheet B2.32c** where they have to analyse and comment on information based on a study of zinc uptake in healthy people and people with coeliac disease.

Stretch Students answer the 'extra challenge' question.

# B2.32 Villi

How do digested food molecules get into the blood?

These breads and cakes look delicious but the food on the right would make people with coeliac disease very ill. Their bodies react to gluten, a protein found in cereals like wheat and barley, and this damages the lining of the small intestine. This is why gluten warnings are important on food labels.

**A** *Some people can't eat food containing gluten. The food on the left is gluten free but the food on the right contains wheat.*

> 1 a We say that digested food is absorbed. What does 'absorbed' mean?
> b Where does absorption occur?

Large insoluble food molecules are broken down into small soluble molecules by digestive enzymes. These products of digestion must be absorbed from the small intestine into the blood, to be delivered to the cells where they are needed.

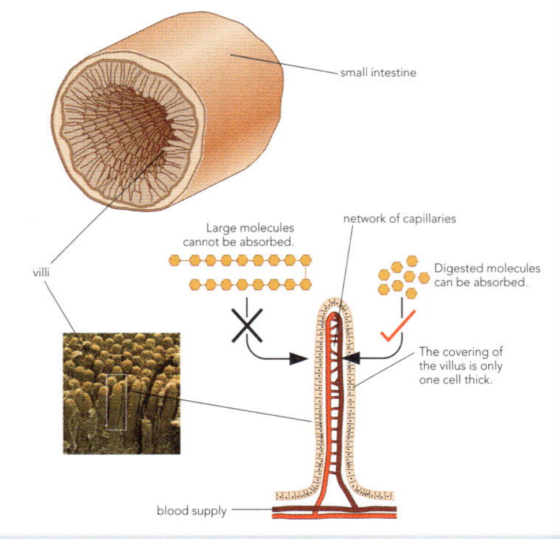


**B** *The structure of a villus.*

## Absorbing food in the small intestine

Digested food passes into the blood by diffusion through the intestine and capillary walls. The bigger the surface area available, the more diffusion can take place.

The small intestine is a tube about 5 m long and 2.5 cm in diameter. If the inside surface was smooth the surface area would only be about 0.5 $m^2$ and very little absorption would take place. However, the lining of the small intestine has millions of finger-like folds called **villi** that make the surface area much bigger. If it were opened out, the surface area would actually be about 200 $m^2$ (tennis-court sized!). This means much more diffusion can take place.

Each villus has a good network of blood capillaries. This means there is always a lower concentration of soluble food molecules in the blood than there is inside the small intestine because soluble food molecules are constantly moved away in the blood. This steep **concentration gradient** between the two areas means diffusion takes place rapidly down it. Finally, there is only a single layer of cells between the contents of the small intestine and the blood vessels in the villi. This means there is only a short distance over which the soluble food molecules need to diffuse. The large surface area, good blood supply and short distances all make the diffusion of dissolved food molecules into the blood as efficient as possible.

> 2 What adaptations does the small intestine have for absorption?
> 3 a Explain what a concentration gradient is.
> b What effect does it have?

## Evidence for the importance of villi

Evidence that the villi are important for increasing the efficiency with which the soluble products of digestion are absorbed into the blood can come from studying coeliac disease. In this disease the villi may be lost. People affected cannot absorb the products of digestion properly. They often become very thin as a result.

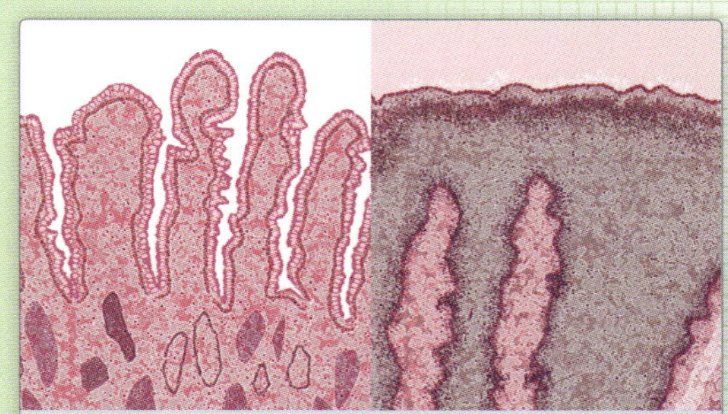

**C** *The effects of coeliac disease on villi in the small intestine can clearly be seen in the picture on the right.*

> 4 a Look at Figure C. What is the difference between the normal lining of the gut and the gut affected by coeliac disease?
> b Use your answer to part a to suggest how coeliac disease can be used as evidence for the importance of a large surface area for the absorption of digested food.
>
> 5 Explain how the presence of villi in the gut makes the absorption of the soluble products of digestion so efficient.

**Skills spotlight**

Some students make a model gut out of a membrane that lets soluble food molecules through. They put starch solution and amylase inside the 'gut,' and show that sugars move out of the gut by diffusion into the surrounding water. Discuss some of the uses and limitations of this simple model of a gut.

**ResultsPlus Watch Out!**

When asked about absorption in the small intestine, students often say that it has a large surface area. They forget to mention that it is very long and has lots of villi and that each villus has a large surface area.

**Learning outcomes**

H 3.16 Explain how the structure of villi (large surface area, single layer of cells and capillary network) allows efficient absorption of the soluble products of digestion

HSW 3 Describe how phenomena are explained using scientific models



How much saliva do you produce every day?



## ActiveTeach

- **AT** *What do villi do?* [interactive]
  Absorption of food – gap-fill activity
- **AT** *Structure of a villus* [diagram]
  Figure B – diagram labelling activity

## Answers | Student Book

1 **a** It means the digested food passes through the intestine and capillary walls and enters the blood by diffusion.
**b** In the small intestine, in the villi

2 The inside surface is covered in villi and it has a good blood supply around it.

3 **a** The difference in concentration between one area and another.
**b** Substances diffuse down a concentration gradient from an area of higher concentration to an area of lower concentration. A steep concentration gradient means the diffusion happens faster.

4 **a** In the gut affected by coeliac disease the villi are no longer sticking out into the small intestine, so there is no longer a large surface area for absorption.
**b** People suffering from coeliac disease have a lot of unpleasant symptoms, including serious weight loss. This shows how important a large surface area for absorption of digested food is, since without it people suffer from these problems.

5 A good answer will contain the following points: The villi provide a very large surface area for the absorption of digested food; There is a single cell layer between the inside of the villus and the contents of the gut, minimising the diffusion distances; There is a capillary network inside each villus so food molecules diffuse almost directly into the blood and are moved away in the circulation, which maintains a good concentration gradient between the contents of the small intestine and the blood.

**Skills spotlight**

Uses – models enzymes breaking down large molecules into small, soluble products; soluble products of digestion passing out of the gut by diffusion; includes a thin membrane so there is a short diffusion distance. Limitations – membrane is smooth so doesn't model effect of villi on surface area; no blood flow so doesn't model the concentration gradient in a living gut; any other sensible points.

# B2.33 Enzyme concentration



This lesson challenges students to investigate the effect of different concentrations of amylase on starch using visking tubing as a model of the alimentary canal. The activity may be run as a practice controlled assessment task or as a straight-forward class practical. The practical work will take at least one full hour session.

## Specification coverage

***3.17*** Investigate the effect of different concentrations of digestive enzymes, using and evaluating models of the alimentary canal

This activity provides opportunities to cover HSW *1*, HSW *3*, HSW *5*, HSW *6*, HSW *7*, HSW *8*, HSW *10* and HSW *11*.

## Key terms

amylase

### Before the lesson

Ensure that students are familiar with any equipment they may be expected to use so that they can plan their own investigation. In the week or two before the task show them this equipment and, if appropriate, allow them to practice using it. In this investigation it will help if students have both made up a model gut using Visking tubing and carried out Benedict's test for simple reducing sugars before the practical.

It may be good preparation to show students one or more of Skills Sheets 19 to 26 to show what is expected of them in their actual controlled assessment task.

### Starter

**Starchy staples**

Students think of staple foods from around the world – most are rich in starch e.g. rice, potatoes, wheat, etc. Amylase is found in human saliva and pancreatic juices almost everywhere. The levels of the enzyme amylase in the saliva are linked to the amount of carbohydrates in the diet. Scientists discovered that people who eat starchy food have more copies of the amylase gene than people who eat high protein diets. Put *http://www.thetech.org/genetics/news.php?id=62* up on the interactive white board to show students some current research on starch and the amylase gene.

Read the information on page 92 of the Student Book and the brief description of the activity provided by the 'Your task' box.

### Option 1: Straight-forward class practical

Students follow the instructions on **Worksheet B2.33b**. This contains the instructions for students to make model guts of visking tubing and place starch suspension inside along with different concentrations of amylase. The range of data that students need to collect is given on Worksheet B2.33c. Students can also plan another way of investigating the effect of different concentrations of amylase on starch without the added complication of the Visking tubing.

### Plenary

On page 93 of the Student Book you will find two examples of the sort of work that students may produce for this task. The examples focus on drawing conclusions. You could share these with students after they have completed their own work. This will help them to understand the assessment criteria and so make it easier for them to evaluate their work and to see how they can improve it. Moderator comments on each of the Student Book extracts can be found at the end of the assessment guidance for this investigation on the CD-ROM. The examples can also be found on the **AT** document *Student examples*.

### Option 2: Running the activity as a practice controlled assessment task (PCA)

We have provided a full range of support resources to allow the running of this practical as a practice controlled assessment task. A recommended structure is outlined below (to be used over a number of sessions). Marking guidance for all three parts of the practice task can be found on the CD-ROM that accompanies the TTPP. To save time when using these practice controlled assessment tasks, you may wish to focus on a particular aspect or skill rather than working through all three parts of the task.

#### Part A Planning

1. Students should be given the Student brief on **Worksheet B2.33a**. They can use Part A of the Workbook that is provided to help pupils with their practice controlled assessments. They should be given about 1 hour to do this planning.

#### Part B Observations

2. Students carry out the practical task to collect evidence using the method they have planned in Part A. Once again, they should refer to the Student brief on **Worksheet B2.33a**. They can use Part B of the Workbook that is provided to help pupils with their practice controlled assessments. They should be given about 1 hour to collect their primary evidence.
3. If there is a problem with their own planned method, students may be asked to follow the method set out on **Worksheet B2.33b**. This will still enable students to access the full range of marks for Part B and Part C of the practice controlled assessment task.
4. In Part B, students are required to gather some secondary evidence. The evidence can be quantitative or qualitative. It can be from a variety of sources but students must note where they found their evidence and evaluate the quality of the source as part of this task. Skills Sheet 22 provides students with further guidance on researching for and evaluating secondary evidence. This part of the task could be done outside of the lesson but must be supervised.

#### Part C Conclusions

5. Students follow the instructions set out on the Part C section of the Student brief on **Worksheet B2.33a**. They should use their data from Part B and the secondary evidence they have collected when doing this. They can use Part C of the Workbook that is provided to help pupils with their practice controlled assessments. They should be given about 1 hour to work on their conclusions.

The **AT** includes video clips showing a group of students working through elements of this investigation with teacher support.

Practice Controlled Assessment

# B2.33 Enzyme concentration

Does the rate of starch digestion depend on the concentration of amylase?

You produce about 1.5 litres of saliva every day. The concentration of carbohydrase enzymes in the saliva varies from person to person.

Saliva contains the enzyme **amylase**, a carbohydrase which starts to break down starch into simple sugars. Starch digestion starts in the mouth and is completed in the small intestine. Once the starch is fully digested, the simple sugars diffuse into your blood through the villi. The simple sugars are carried around your body to be used in the cells.

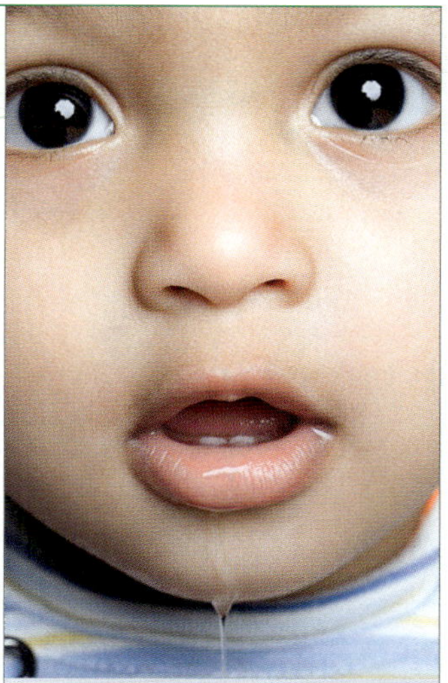

*A Babies often dribble saliva, but as we get older we keep it in our mouths.*

**Your task**

You are going to plan an investigation that will allow you to find out the effect of different concentrations of an enzyme on the breakdown of food. You will need to use a model of the alimentary canal and evaluate how well it represents what really happens. Your teacher will provide you with some materials to help you organise this task.

**Learning Outcomes**

*3.17 Investigate the effect of different concentrations of digestive enzymes, using and evaluating models of the alimentary canal*

## ResultsPlus Build Better Answers

When planning an investigation like this, one of the skills you will be assessed on is your ability to draw *conclusions based on evidence*. There are 6 marks available for this skill. Here are two extracts focusing on this skill. Other skills that you need for the assessment are dealt with in other lessons.

**Student extract 1 — A typical response for this skill**

I think that increasing the concentration of the enzyme speeds up the rate of reaction, but only up to a certain point. I think that this is a proportional relationship because when one factor (the concentration) increases the other (the time) decreases by the same amount each time. I can see this from my graph which shows a steady fall in time taken for a positive result, up to a certain point and then it slows down and flattens off. I can also see this from the graph I found in the text book which shows how the rate of reaction changes with the concentration of the enzyme for another enzyme controlled reaction.

- There is an important point missing here – the student should have said if this conclusion supports their hypothesis or not.
- The student has talked about the relationship between the two variables.
- This is good use of both primary and secondary information.

**Student extract 2 — A good response for this skill**

I think that increasing the concentration of the enzyme speeds up the rate of reaction, but only up to a certain point. I can see this from my graph which shows a steady fall in the time taken for a positive result up to a certain point and then flattens off. This supports my hypothesis that changing the concentration of the enzyme would change the rate of reaction. This is a directly proportional relationship for the first part of the graph. This also fits with my scientific knowledge that enzymes are biological catalysts which speed up reactions. When there are more enzymes there are more catalysts to speed up the rate of the reaction. The rise in the rate of reaction will stop when there are enough enzyme molecules for each molecule of substrate. Adding more enzyme after this point will have no effect on the rate of the reaction – it is going as fast as possible. I can also see this from the graph I found in the text book which shows how the rate of reaction changes with the concentration of the enzyme for another enzyme controlled reaction.

- This is good because it refers to the way that the conclusion supports the hypothesis.
- To access higher marks you need to use your scientific knowledge to explain what you think is happening in the investigation.

**ResultsPlus**

**To access 4 marks**

- Provide a conclusion based on all your collected evidence
- Explain your conclusion
- Describe any relevant mathematical relationships in your conclusion

**To access 6 marks**

You also need to:

- Refer to the original hypothesis in your conclusion
- Refer to other scientific ideas in your conclusion

92

How big a machine is needed to model your large intestine?

93

## ActiveTeach

- **AT** *B2.33 Enzyme concentration* [video]
  Students work through the investigation
- **AT** *B2.33 Moderator comments* [word document]
  Moderator comments on the video
- **AT** *B2.33 Assessment criteria* [presentation]
  Understanding the CA marking criteria
- **AT** *B2.33 Student task sheet* [word document]
  CA video checklist
- **AT** *B2.33 Specification points* [word document]
  Edexcel specification points
- **AT** *B2.33 Student examples* [word document]
  Examples for students to assess

## Assessment criteria

### Conclusions based on evidence

**0** No relevant conclusions are made.

**1-2 a)** Makes a relevant conclusion based on all collected evidence but no link is made to the hypothesis.

**b)** An attempt is made to explain the conclusion using the collected evidence and appropriate mathematical relationships.

**3-4 a)** A conclusion is made that links to the hypothesis and is based on all the collected evidence.

**b)** The conclusion is explained using the collected evidence and appropriate mathematical relationships.

**5-6 a)** A conclusion is made that is linked to the hypothesis and based on the primary data and secondary evidence as well as scientific ideas.

**b)** The conclusions are explained using relevant scientific ideas, all collected evidence and appropriate mathematical relationship. May work out the gradient for the first part of the graph.

# B2.34 Probiotics and prebiotics

This lesson looks at probiotics, prebiotics and plant stanol esters, explaining what they are and presenting ideas and evidence for students to evaluate.

## Specification coverage

***3.18*** Evaluate the evidence for the claimed benefits of the use of functional foods as part of a healthy diet, including a) probiotics containing *Bifidobacteria* and lactic acid bacteria *Lactobacillus* b) prebiotic oligosaccharides c) plant stanol esters

**HSW** ***13*** How and why decisions about science and technology are made, *including those that raise ethical issues*, and about the social, economic *and environmental* effects of such decisions

There are also opportunities to cover **HSW** ***8*** and **HSW** ***11***.

## Key terms

| | |
|---|---|
| *Bifidobacteria* | oligosaccharide |
| cholesterol | plant stanol ester |
| functional food | prebiotic |
| *Lactobacillus* | probiotic |

### What are functional foods?

**Starter 1** Lit

Show student some functional foods – or empty containers, e.g. Flora™ pro.activ margarine Benecol™ drink, and ask them to suggest definitions for the words below. They should NOT open the Student Book at this stage of the lesson. If they have no idea, just put a dash. Keep the table for the plenary session: functional food; probiotic; *Lactobacillus*; prebiotic; oligosaccharide; plant stanol ester; cholesterol.

### How true are these claims?

**Starter 2**

Show students one or more of the adverts for cholesterol-reducing spreads or yoghurts. Ask them how scientific they think the claims are, if they think that particular foods really can improve health and what evidence they would like to see to back up those claims.

### Evaluating probiotics

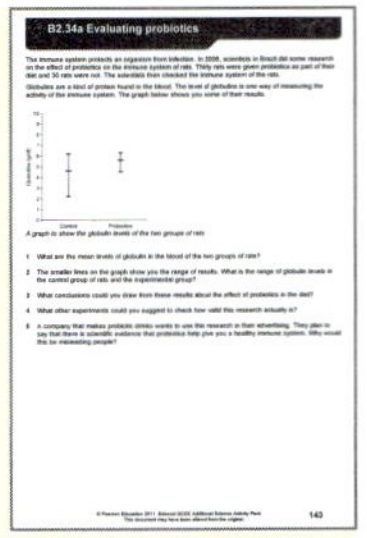

**Exploring 1**

**Worksheet B2.34a** gives information, data and questions to answer on a piece of published Brazilian research looking at the effect of probiotics on the immune system of rats.

**Stretch** Students can visit the *Scielo* website with the original paper.

**Support** Provide students with a clear and simple explanation of why an increase of globulins in the blood could be used as evidence that probiotics support the immune system.

### The case for probiotics

**Exploring 2**

**Worksheet B2.34b** discusses a banned Actimel™ advert. Through the questions, students explore the case for the benefits of these functional foods and evaluate the evidence as it is presented. Students can use Skills Sheet 5 *Evaluating claims*.

**Stretch** Ask students to write a paragraph explaining the decision they made about which type of poster to produce.

**Support** Work with students to produce a list on the board of the main points.

### Reducing cholesterol

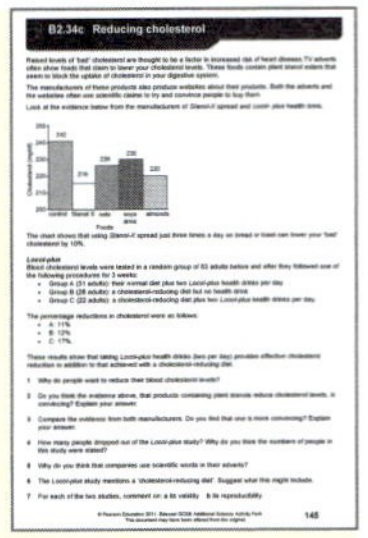

**Exploring 3**

**Worksheet B2.34c** follows on from *Starter 2*, looking at more claims made in adverts for Stanol-X spread and Locol-plus products. Students explore how much real science is present in the claims, and look at the standard of evidence provided.

**Stretch** Students use the official websites from Benecol™ and Flora™ in order to answer the questions.

**Support** Focus mainly on questions **1–5**, looking at the data.

### Student Book spread B2.34

**Explaining 1**

Explain functional foods and discuss how many of them students have come across, which of the claims they know about, etc. Introduce ideas of evidence and how valid it might or might not be.

**Stretch** Emphasise the evidence base or lack of it, the tendency for research to be funded by vested interests, the use of information or names which sound very scientific but which are not really evidence-based.

**Support** Emphasise what the different functional foods do and how popular they have become but that the evidence still isn't clear.

### Defining words

**Plenary 1** AfL Lit

Ask students to return to the list of words in *Starter 1* and to now try again to fill in simple definitions for the words, ideally without referring to the Student Book. Try to get a consensus to fill in definitions on the board.

### Designing packaging

**Plenary 2**

Ask students to design the packaging for a new yoghurt. The yoghurt contains prebiotics, probiotics and plain stanol esters. They then need to come up with some succinct claims to put on the packaging. As an extension they could suggest what sort of evidence might be needed to back up those claims scientifically.

### How useful are functional foods?

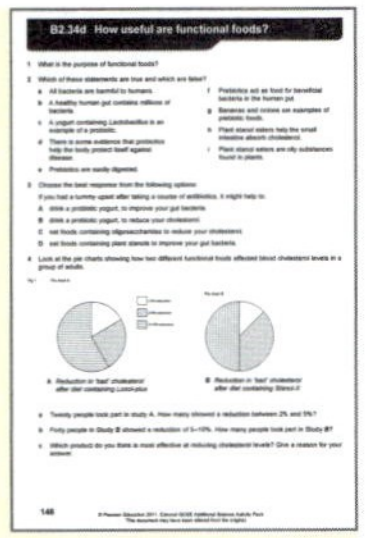

**Homework 1**

**Worksheet B2.34d** is concerned with all functional foods and is the more accessible of the two homework sheets.

**Support** Miss out question **4**.

### Investigating prebiotics

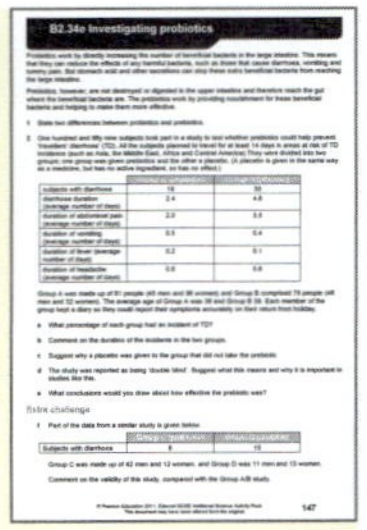

**Homework 2**

**Worksheet B2.34e** focuses on prebiotics and asks students to interpret data from a recently published clinical study.

**Stretch** Students answer the 'extra challenge' question.

# B2.34 Probiotics and prebiotics

Do probiotics and prebiotics improve your health?

People affected by cystic fibrosis make thick sticky mucus that can stop their pancreas releasing enzymes into the small intestine. They have to take replacement enzymes to help them digest their food.

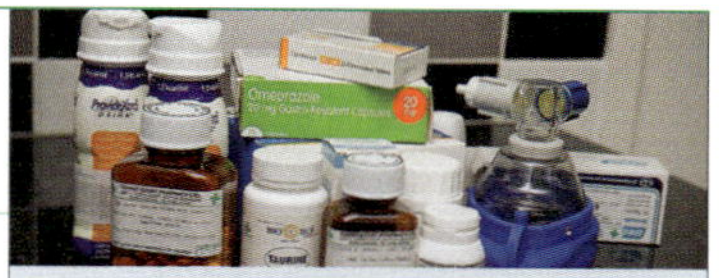

**A** *The enzymes that someone with cystic fibrosis must take every day.*

Many healthy people now eat **functional foods** as well as their normal food. These foods claim to make you healthier.

## Probiotics

The digestive system contains about $10^{13}$ bacteria – that's more bacteria than you have cells in your body! Some of these bacteria can cause problems but most provide health benefits. They help break down food and protect against disease-causing microorganisms.

**Probiotics** contain live bacteria often called 'friendly' or 'beneficial' bacteria. These are usually ***Lactobacillus*** and ***Bifidobacteria***, which produce lactic acid in the gut. The manufacturers of probiotic foods such as yogurts or yogurt drinks claim that these will make you healthier by improving your digestive system, helping your body protect itself against disease and reducing allergies. However, in 2010 scientists at the European Food Safety Agency looked at the evidence for 180 health claims for probiotics. They rejected 10 completely and said there was not enough evidence to support the other 170 claims.

1 Suggest one reason why people might eat functional foods.

2 What do probiotic foods contain?

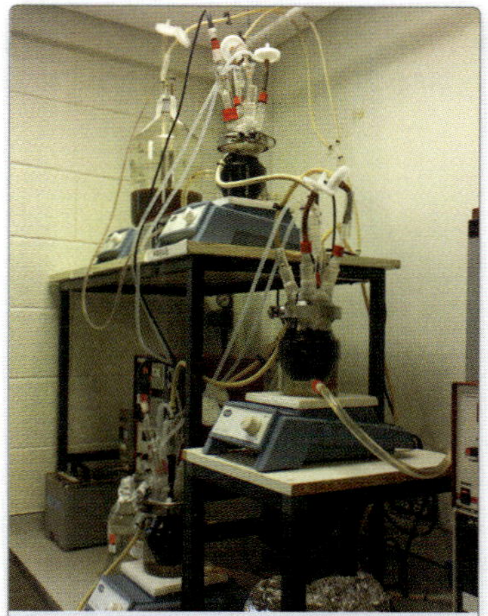

**B** *The model of a large intestine that scientists at Reading University use to investigate the effects of functional foods.*

## Plant stanol esters

**Plant stanol esters** are oily substances found in plants. Scientists have discovered that these can stop the small intestine absorbing **cholesterol**, lowering the levels of cholesterol in the blood. High cholesterol levels are linked to a raised risk of heart disease. Plant stanols are now used in many foods such as yogurt, drinks and spreads. There is clear evidence that they have an effect.

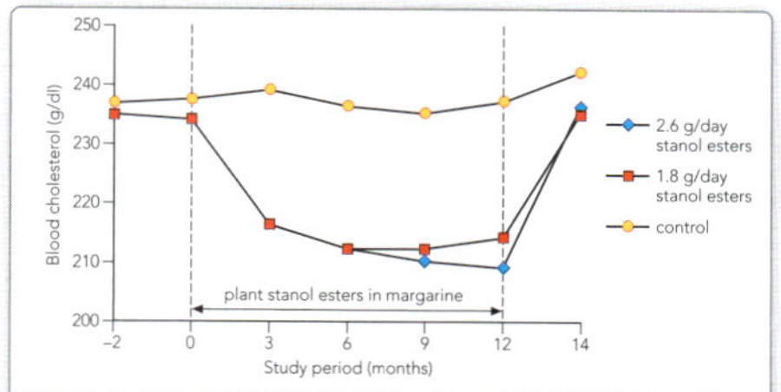


**C** *The effect on blood cholesterol of eating spread with and without plant stanol esters for 12 months.*

## Prebiotics

**Prebiotics** are substances that the body can't digest. They act as food for the 'beneficial' bacteria in the gut and encourage their growth. Tomatoes, bananas, onions and asparagus all contain **oligosaccharides**, a common form of prebiotic. You also find prebiotics in specially made dairy products or sold in capsules. The evidence is growing that prebiotics can increase the beneficial bacteria in your gut and so help maintain good health. The graph in Figure D shows the effect of adding an oligosaccharide to the diet on the recurrence of diarrhoea in a group of 142 patients.

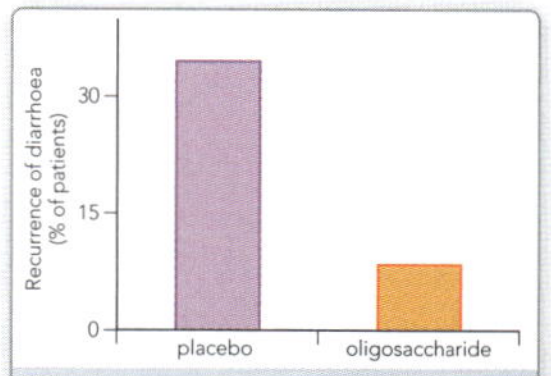


**D** *The effect on diarrhoea of adding an oligosaccharide to the diet, from a study of 142 patients*

3 a What do prebiotic foods contain?
b How are prebiotics claimed to work?

4 What is a plant stanol ester?

### Skills spotlight

People need to be able to rely on the science used in adverts to help them make decisions. In 2009 an advert for a probiotic yogurt drink claiming that it was 'scientifically proven to help support your kids' defences' was banned. Why do you think it was banned?

5 How would you evaluate the data given in Figure D on the impact of oligosaccharides on health?

6 a Explain what is meant by a functional food.
b Looking at Figure C, what do you think the control group ate?
c Explain what other controls would need to be in place in the diet.
d Is it worth taking the higher dose of plant stanols? Explain your answer.

7 A new functional food for toddlers is being advertised on TV, claiming to increase the numbers of 'good bacteria' in the gut. How would you evaluate these claims?

### Learning Outcomes

3.18 Evaluate the evidence for the claimed benefits of the use of functional foods as part of a healthy diet, including:
a probiotics containing *Bifidobacteria* and lactic acid bacteria *Lactobacillus*
b prebiotic oligosaccharides
c plant stanol esters

HSW 13 Explain how and why decisions about uses of science and technology are made





## Answers | Student Book

1 They think they will help them digest food better/make their immune system work better/prevent possible health problems in the future, etc.

2 Live bacteria to increase the numbers of beneficial bacteria in your digestive system.

3 a Oligosaccharides that cannot be digested by humans but provide nutrients for some kinds of bacteria.
b They act as food for beneficial bacteria and so increase the number of beneficial bacteria in your digestive system.

4 Compounds that stop cholesterol being absorbed from inside the small intestine into the blood.

5 Less likely to suffer from diarrhoea than people who are given a placebo; suggests oligosaccharide provides protection against diarrhoea; but study only looked at 142 patients; don't know if those patients were a random sample of the population; cannot extrapolate the results to the wider population without further study.

6 a A food that is claimed to make you healthier when you eat it.
b A diet with no stanol esters included.
c The diets of all groups need to be as similar as possible, apart from the difference in amount of stanol esters.
d Blood cholesterol is lowered; as high blood cholesterol is a risk factor for heart disease, so including stanol esters in the diet should help prevent heart disease. Further studies would be needed.

7 See data that showed: an increase in numbers of beneficial bacteria in the guts of toddlers who ate the food compared with those who didn't; only difference in the test and control groups was the functional food; a large study, so that random differences between toddlers didn't mask the overall effect.

**Skills spotlight**

The scientific evidence was not robust enough. The studies weren't big enough. There is some good evidence that probiotics can benefit adults. However, much of the evidence in children – and there isn't a lot – comes from studies on children who were ill and often children in developing countries. It was ruled that there wasn't enough evidence that the yoghurt would improve the immune response in healthy, well-fed British children.

# C2.1 Mendeleev



This lesson examines the key features of Mendeleev's periodic table, its use to successfully predict the existence and properties of some elements that had yet to be discovered, and the position of metals and non-metals in the periodic table.

## Specification coverage

***1.1*** Explain how Mendeleev: a) arranged the elements, known at that time, in a periodic table by using properties of these elements and their compounds b) used his table to predict the existence and properties of some elements not then discovered

***1.2*** Classify elements as metals and non-metals according to their position in the periodic table

**HSW** ***2*** The interpretation of data, using creative thought, to provide evidence for testing ideas and developing theories.

There are also opportunities to cover **HSW** ***1*** and **HSW** ***14***.

## Key terms

periodic table

### Sorting
**Starter 1**

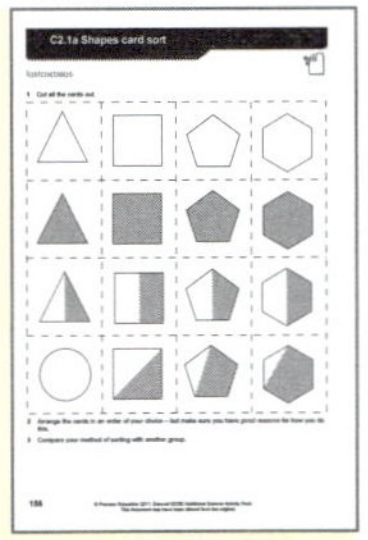

Students sort the cards on **Worksheet C2.1a** into at least two groups. Students should feed their method back to the class for discussion. Is there a general agreement on the best way to sort the cards, or disagreement?

### Elements card sort
**Exploring 1**

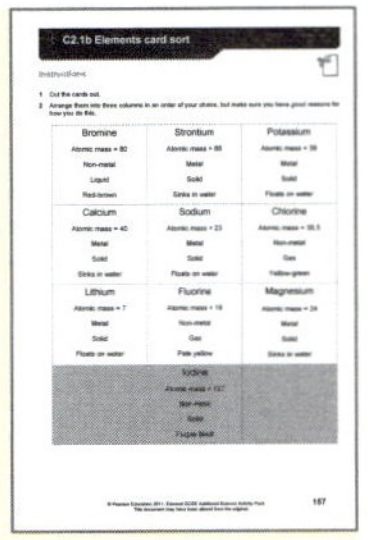

**Worksheet C2.1b** has 12 element cards (2 blanks). Ask the students to arrange the elements themselves (as Mendeleev had done).

**Stretch** Give the students the three shaded cards and omit chlorine or bromine, and either sodium or calcium.

**Support** Only give the students the 9 unshaded cards (which require no gaps).

### Student Book spread C2.1
**Explaining 1**

Point out that Mendeleev arranged elements into seven horizontal 'series' and one of eight vertical 'groups'. Refer to Figures B and C on pages 118 and 119 respectively.

**Stretch** Mendeleev thought the atomic mass for tellurium Te had been measured incorrectly, and that it should have been 125. Ask students to explain why he thought this.

**Support** Refer to 'series' 1, 2 and 3 only because these have a simpler pattern and are closer to the modern periodic table than the others.

### Radio Mendeleev
**Plenary 1**

Radio was not known in Mendeleev's time but what if it were? Students write a short radio piece, aimed at scientists, about Mendeleev's exciting new table. They share their piece with the rest of the class. Instead of a live performance, it could be recorded and played back, as on real radio.

### Mendeleev's periodic table
**Homework 1**

Ask students to produce an illustrated poster or leaflet describing Mendeleev's periodic table, how it was arranged and other important features that made it successful.

**Support** Give students the specific points you want including in the poster.

### The periodic table
**Starter 2** **AfL**

Show the modern periodic table. Ask students to note down one thing they know about it, one thing they are not sure about and one thing they would like to find out about. Students feed their notes back to the rest of the class for discussion.

### Making predictions
**Exploring 2**

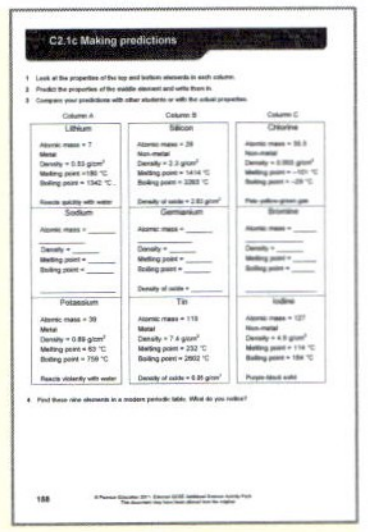

Using **Worksheet C2.1c** students make predictions about the properties of an element in between two others, and compare their predictions with the actual properties of this element.

**Stretch** Germanium is often described as a 'semi-metal' or 'metalloid'. Suggest what this might mean.

**Support** Question **1** is easier than questions **2** and **3**.

### Leaving gaps (AT)
**Explaining 2**

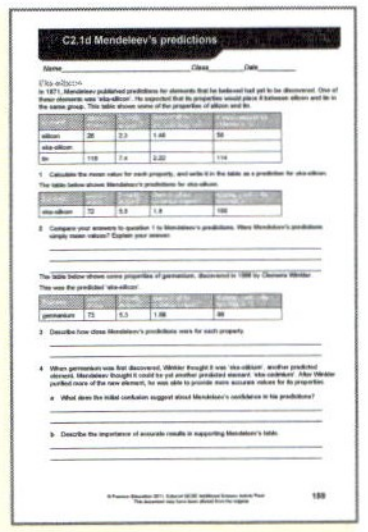

Explain the importance of Mendeleev leaving gaps in his periodic table. The **AT** presentation *Properties of eka-aluminium and gallium* shows Mendeleev's predictions for gallium. **Worksheet C2.1d** examines another of Mendeleev's predicted elements and its properties.

**Stretch** Students discuss differences in measurements of gallium.

**Support** In question **1**, work out the first mean atomic mass with the students.

### Mendeleev's table sentence starters
**Plenary 2** **Lit**

Ask students to complete starter sentences using connecting words. They should be encouraged to complete each sentence in more than one way, using a different connecting word each time. Suitable sentences include 'The elements were arranged …', 'Iodine and tellurium were swapped …', 'Mendeleev left gaps …'.

### Predicting properties
**Homework 2**

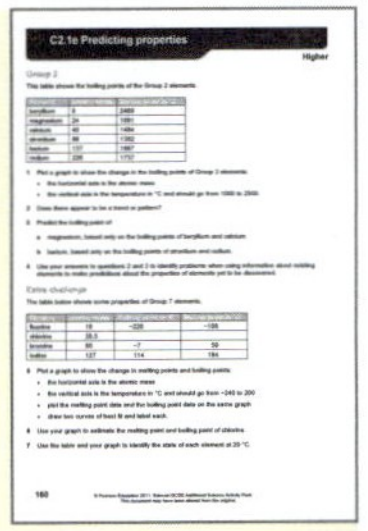

**Worksheet C2.1e**, for more able students, is a data handling exercise using supplied information about the properties of group 2 and 7 elements. Graph paper will be needed.

**Stretch** Students answer the 'extra challenge' questions.

# C2.1 Mendeleev

How did Dmitri Mendeleev make his periodic table of elements?

By the 1860s 63 elements were known. Chemists were keen to make a table that organised the elements in a helpful way, but this proved difficult. In one table of elements, every eighth element had similar properties. Unfortunately, this worked only as far as calcium so it was not a success.

Then in 1869, the Russian chemist Dmitri Mendeleev (1834–1907) was busy writing the second volume of his chemistry textbook. He was having trouble deciding which elements to write about next. Mendeleev's solution was to construct a table.

**A** *A monument to Mendeleev in St Petersburg.*

Mendeleev's table is now called the **periodic table**. To make his original table, Mendeleev used the latest measurements of atomic masses (called 'weights' then) available. He also carefully considered the properties of the different elements.

1 What information about the elements did Mendeleev use to develop his table?

Mendeleev arranged the elements in order of increasing atomic mass. Other chemists had tried this before, but Mendeleev sometimes broke this rule. He did this so that elements with similar properties lined up in his table. For example, iodine should come before tellurium according to its atomic mass. Mendeleev swapped the positions of these two elements so that they lined up with elements with similar properties.

ResultsPlus Watch Out!

Remember that in a periodic table the periods are the rows and the groups are the columns.

## Leaving gaps

Mendeleev put elements with similar properties into horizontal rows in his first table. However, he continued to work on his table. By 1871, he settled on a table in which elements with similar properties were organised into vertical columns, just as in the modern periodic table. Unlike other chemists, Mendeleev thought that there must be elements still to discover, so he left gaps for them.

| Series | Group 1 | Group 2 | Group 3 | Group 4 | Group 5 | Group 6 | Group 7 | Group 8 | |
|---|---|---|---|---|---|---|---|---|---|
| 1 | H1 | | | | | | | | |
| 2 | Li 7 | Be 9 | B 11 | C 12 | N 14 | O 16 | F 19 | | |
| 3 | Na 23 | Mg 24 | Al 27 | Si 28 | P 31 | S 32 | Cl 35.5 | | |
| 4 | K 39 | Ca 40 | ? 44 | Ti 48 | V 51 | Cr 52 | Mn 55 | Fe 56 Ni 59 | Ce 59 Cu 63.5 |
| 5 | (Cu 63.5) | Zn 65 | ? 68 | ? 72 | As 75 | Se 79 | Br 80 | | |
| 6 | Rb 85 | Sr 88 | Y 89 | Zr 91 | Nb 93 | Mo 96 | ? 100 | Ru 101 Pd 106 | Rh 103 Ag 108 |
| 7 | (Ag 108) | Cd 112 | In 115 | Sn 119 | Sb 122 | Te 128 | I 127 | | |

**B** *Mendeleev's 1871 table with modern chemical symbols and atomic masses. The red boxes are gaps left for elements not known at the time.*

2 What, in Mendeleev's table, suggests that he was not sure where to put copper (Cu) and silver (Ag)?



## Making predictions

Mendeleev used the gaps in his table to make predictions about the properties of undiscovered elements. One of these predictions was for an element that he called eka-aluminium. When gallium was discovered shortly afterwards in 1875, its properties closely fitted those he had predicted for eka-aluminium.

| Property | Eka-aluminium (Ea) | Gallium (Ga) |
|---|---|---|
| atomic mass | About 68 | 70 |
| density of solid (g/cm³) | 6.0 | 5.9 |
| melting point | Low | 29.8 °C |
| formula of oxide | $Ea_2O_3$ | $Ga_2O_3$ |
| density of oxide (g/cm³) | 5.5 | 5.88 |
| reacts with acids and alkalis? | Yes | Yes |

**C** *The predicted properties of eka-aluminium and the actual properties of gallium*

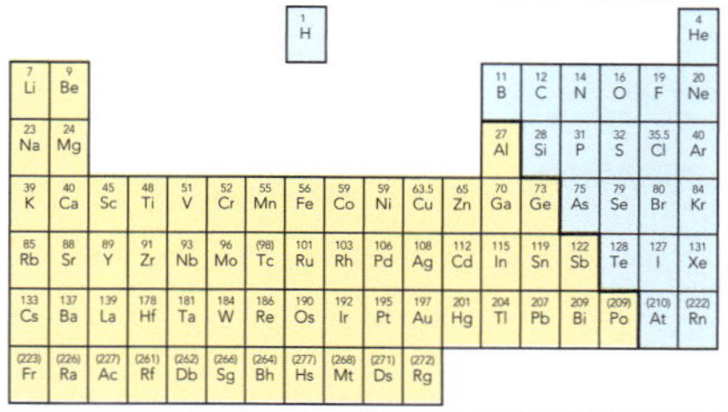

**D** *The main part of the modern periodic table, highlighted to show the locations of **metals** (yellow) and **non-metals** (blue).*

3 Explain why the discovery of gallium was seen as a successful test of Mendeleev's periodic table.

4 a What was the general order in which Mendeleev arranged the elements in his table?
b Explain why Mendeleev put tellurium before iodine in his table, instead of the other way round.

5 Use the periodic table to find out if krypton, Kr, is a metal or non-metal.

### Skills spotlight

Scientists sometimes have ideas (or inspiration) that allow them to make new steps in scientific understanding. Identify two new ideas Mendeleev had to develop his table and how the evidence supported these ideas.

6 Suggest why Mendeleev predicted that eka-aluminium would be a metal and not a non-metal.

7 Describe two ways in which Mendeleev's arrangement of elements was new at the time. For each feature, explain what he did and why it was useful. Include relevant examples.

### Learning Outcomes

1.1 Explain how Mendeleev: a arranged the elements, known at that time, in a periodic table by using properties of these elements and their compounds b used his table to predict the existence and properties of some elements not then discovered

1.2 Classify elements as metals or non-metals according to their position in the periodic table

HSW 2 Describe the importance of creative thought in the development of hypotheses and theories



## ActiveTeach

- **AT** *Mendeleev's Periodic Table 1* [BBC video]
  How Mendeleev had the idea
- **AT** *Mendeleev's Periodic Table 2* [BBC video]
  Importance of periodic table
- **AT** *The periodic table and its development* [interactive]
  All about the periodic table – quiz
- **AT** *Properties of eka-aluminium and gallium* [presentation]
  Comparing properties

## Answers | Student Book

1 He used the latest atomic masses, and the properties of the different elements.

2 Copper and silver appear in two places, Group 8 and Group 1 in brackets.

3 Gallium's properties matched the predicted properties of eka-aluminium, described by Mendeleev several years earlier. This supported the ideas behind Mendeleev's table.

4 **a** Increasing atomic mass.
**b** To put iodine and tellurium in the same groups as elements with similar properties.

5 Non-metal.

6 The elements near it on the table are mostly metals.

7 The following points will be included: he used the most accurate information he could find; he broke the order of increasing atomic weight so that elements with similar properties would go in the same group, e.g. swapping the positions of iodine and tellurium; he left gaps for elements not then discovered, so he was free to put other elements in the positions that best matched their properties; he used his table to make predictions about the properties of elements not then discovered and he used the table as a way of predicting new discoveries. An example is gallium, which matched the properties of an element, eka-aluminium, Mendeleev had predicted.

### Skills spotlight

Mendeleev used the properties of the elements to create his table. He understood that there were elements yet to be discovered and that he should leave gaps for them; he used his table to predict the properties of these elements; he broke the principles behind his table (increasing atomic weight) if that better suited the properties of the elements, e.g. swapping the positions of iodine and tellurium.

# C2.2 Structure of the atom



This lesson examines the basic structure of the atom, the properties of the three main subatomic particles and the relationship between the number of protons and electrons in an atom.

## Specification coverage

**1.3** Describe the structure of an atom as a nucleus containing protons and neutrons, surrounded by electrons in shells (energy levels)

**1.4** Demonstrate an understanding that the nucleus of an atom is very small compared to the overall size of the atom

**1.5** Describe atoms of a given element as having the same number of protons in the nucleus, and that this number is unique to that element

**1.6** Recall the relative charge and relative mass of: a) a proton b) a neutron c) an electron

**1.7** Demonstrate an understanding that atoms contain equal numbers of protons and electrons

HSW *2* The interpretation of data, using creative thought, to provide evidence for testing ideas *and developing theories*

There are also opportunities to cover HSW *3*, HSW *10* and HSW *14*.

### What's an atom?

**Starter 1** AfL

Ask students to write down one or two things they know about atoms, compare with a neighbour to compile a longer list of information and then feed back to the rest of the class. This should help to establish the existing knowledge and understanding of the students, and any misconceptions to be dealt with.

### Atomic structure

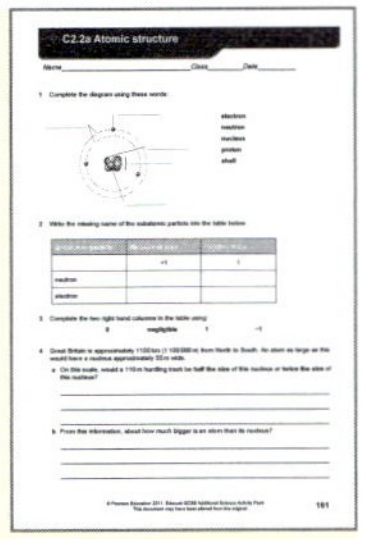

**Exploring 1**

Ask the students to produce a simple labelled model of an atom

Stretch Ask students to consider the relative scale of the nucleus and the atom.

Support **Worksheet C2.2a** includes an unlabelled diagram and an unfilled table for students to complete.

### Student Book spread C2.2 (AT)

**Explaining 1**

The Student Book explains the basic structure of the atom and the properties of the three main subatomic particles.

Stretch Ask the students to suggest why the values are relative to those of a proton, and not one of the other two particles.

Support Show the **AT** presentation *The size of the nucleus.*

### Little lies

**Plenary 1** AfL Lit

Students work in pairs. Each one writes three statements about atoms – two should be true and one should be false. The students take it in turns to uncover each other's false statement and give a reason why it is false. They write down the true and corrected statements to make a permanent record.

### Atomic true or false?

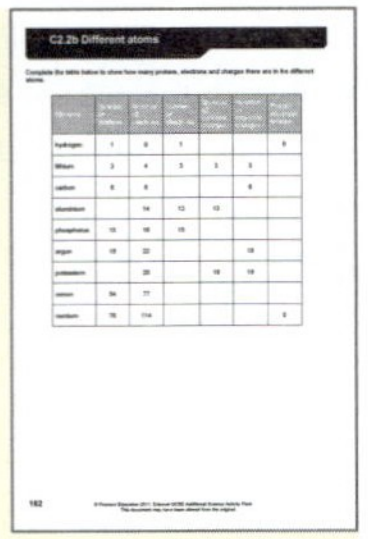

**Homework 1**

**Worksheet C2.2c**, for students needing support, has statements about atoms that are either true or false.

Support Discuss the completed example on the sheet to make sure the students understand what is being asked of them

### What's the question?

**Starter 2**

Show Figure A on page 120 in the Student Book. Ask the students to write down a question based on the image e.g. 'how was the image made?' They share their question with another student or group and feed back to the class.

### Evidence for a nucleus

**Exploring 2**

This activity supports the Skills spotlight in the Student Book. Assign students either positive charges or negative charges. Emphasise the differences in results between the two models.

Stretch Ask students to describe the limitations of the activity in modelling the behaviour of positively charged particles, protons and electrons.

Support Limit the numbers of students involved at any one time so that more can observe the results.

### Different atoms

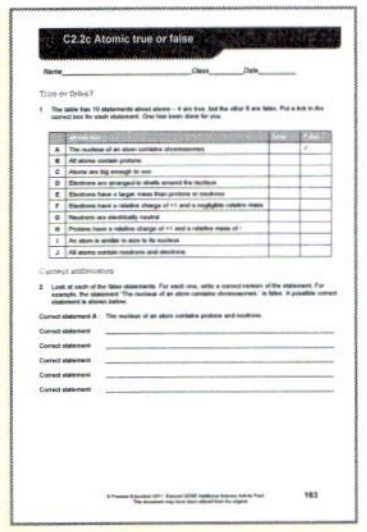

**Explaining 2**

**Worksheet C2.2b** has partial details of several different atoms for students to complete.

Stretch Ask students to calculate more precise relative masses for neutrons and electrons, and to suggest why less precise numbers are suitable for many purposes.

Support Explain how there must be equal numbers of protons and electrons in an atom for there to be no overall charge.

### I have learned …

**Plenary 2** AfL

Working in several small groups, each group writes one new thing they have learned about atoms in the lesson. Each group passes their sheet to the next group, who have to write a different new thing on the sheet. The sheets continue to be passed around until they return to the start. Each group feeds back one example to the rest of the class.

### Atomic structure

**Homework 2** Lit

Ask students to produce flash cards explaining the structure of the atom, and the properties of the three main subatomic particles.

Stretch The students should include named examples of atoms.

# C2.2 Structure of the atom

What is inside an atom?

Atoms are incredibly tiny. It is not possible to see an individual atom, let alone see what is inside one. Figure A is not a photo but a computer image made by a microscope that measures the electrical resistance between an incredibly fine electrode and a surface. The information is used by a computer to make an image of the surface.

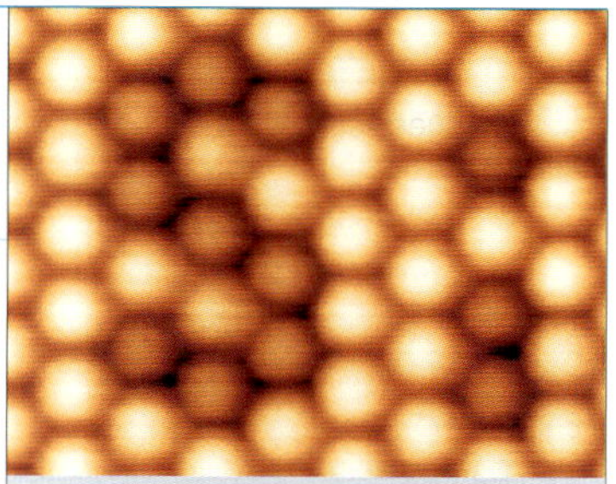

A The chemical symbol for silicon 'written' by individual silicon atoms surrounded by tin atoms. The colours were added by the computer to make the image clearer.

**Atoms** are the smallest particles of an element that can take part in chemical reactions. They are too small to see directly. However from the results of many experiments to understand their structure, scientists have concluded that each atom contains an even smaller object at its centre, called the **nucleus**. This is about 20000 times smaller than the atom itself.

1 Assuming that a nucleus is 20000 times smaller than an atom, calculate the diameter of the nucleus of an atom which is scaled up to 100 m in diameter.

B Most of an atom is empty space. The diameter of the London Eye is 135 m. If an atom could be made the same size, its nucleus would be about the size of a pea.

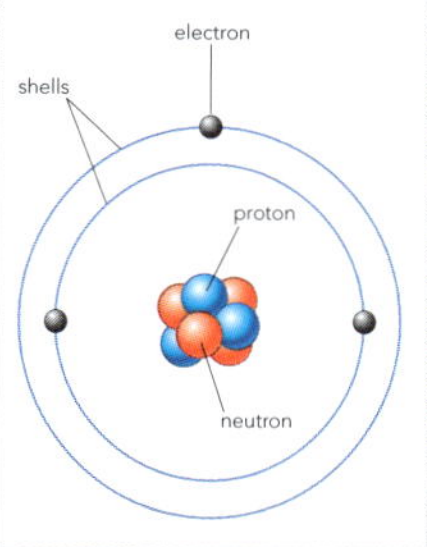


C A diagram of a lithium atom.

2 What can you say about the size of the nucleus shown in Figure C compared to the size of the lithium atom?

## Subatomic particles

Atoms are made from three types of subatomic particle. The nucleus contains **protons** and **neutrons**. It is surrounded by **electrons**. The electrons are arranged in **shells** (or **energy levels**) at different distances from the nucleus.



3 How many protons, neutrons and electrons are there in the lithium atom shown in Figure C?

Subatomic particles have very, very small masses and electrical charges. Rather than give their actual masses and charges, it is more convenient to describe their masses and charges compared to a proton. These are called the particle's **relative mass** and **relative charge**.

| Subatomic particle | Relative mass | Relative charge |
|---|---|---|
| proton | 1 | +1 |
| neutron | 1 | 0 |
| electron | negligible ($\frac{1}{1840}$) | –1 |

D The masses and charges of subatomic particles, compared to the mass and charge of a proton.

**ResultsPlus Watch Out!**

You may be asked to complete a table like the one in D. Make sure that you read the headings to the columns carefully. They could be in a different order.

4 Which subatomic particle has the lowest mass?

5 Where is most of the mass of an atom found?

## Atoms and elements

Every atom of a particular element has the same number of protons. No two elements have the same number of protons in their atoms. For example, all hydrogen atoms contain one proton, and all helium atoms contain two protons. All atoms contain the same number of protons as electrons. This means that they have no overall charge.

6 An aluminium atom has 13 electrons and 14 neutrons.
a How many protons does it have?
b Explain why an aluminium atom is electrically neutral.
c An atom has 14 protons and 14 neutrons. Explain why it cannot be an aluminium atom.

7 Imagine you have to describe the structure of an atom to a friend on the phone without the use of picture or video messaging. Write down what you would say.

**Skills spotlight**

In an experiment in 1909, positively charged particles were fired at gold atoms. Most of them went straight through the atoms, but some were repelled at an angle. This was evidence for a positively charged nucleus at the centre of the atom. Suggest why most of the particles went straight through the gold atoms.

**Learning Outcomes**

1.3 Describe the structure of an atom as a nucleus containing protons and neutrons, surrounded by electrons in shells (energy levels)
1.4 Demonstrate an understanding that the nucleus of an atom is very small compared to the overall size of the atom
1.5 Describe atoms of a given element as having the same number of protons in the nucleus, where this number is unique to that element
1.6 Recall the relative charge and relative mass of: a a proton b a neutron c an electron
1.7 Demonstrate an understanding that atoms contain equal numbers of protons and electrons
HSW 2 Describe how data is used by scientists to provide evidence that increases our scientific understanding

Can you use the periodic table as a table? 

## ActiveTeach

- **AT** *Discovering electrons* [BBC video]
  J J Thomson and Crookes tube
- **AT** *Electron shells* [BBC video]
  Bohr and electron energy levels
- **AT** *What do you know about atomic structure?* [interactive]
  The structure and mass of atoms - game
- **AT** *Label the atom* [interactive]
  Atomic structure – diagram labelling activity
- **AT** *The size of a nucleus* [presentation]
  Visualising nuclei
- **AT** *Diagram of a lithium atom* [diagram]
  Figure C – diagram labelling activity

## Key terms

atom
electron
energy level
neutron
nucleus
proton
relative charge
relative mass
shell

## Answers | Student Book

1 100 ÷ 20000 = 5 × $10^{-3}$ m (5 mm)
2 The nucleus cannot be drawn to the correct scale – it is too large.
3 3 protons, 4 neutrons (7 – 3 = 4), 3 electrons.
4 The electron has the lowest mass.
5 Most an atom's mass is in its nucleus.
6 **a** 13 protons.
**b** There are equal numbers of positive charges (from the protons) and negative charges (from the electrons), and the neutrons are electrically neutral.
**c** Aluminium atoms all have 13 protons but atom A has 14 protons.
7 A good answer will contain the following points.
- the atom has a nucleus at the centre containing positively charged protons and electrically neutral neutrons.
- negatively charged electrons are arranged in shells around the nucleus.
- atoms have equal numbers of protons and electrons.
- suitable examples, e.g. lithium atoms have three protons and electrons, and four neutrons.

**Skills spotlight**

Most of an atom is empty space (the nucleus is very much smaller than the atom as a whole) so most of the particles went straight through the atoms. Note: recall of this experiment is not required by the specification.

# C2.3 The modern periodic table



This lesson examines atomic number, mass number, relative atomic mass and isotopes.
It introduces the arrangement of the elements in the modern periodic table.

## Specification coverage

**1.8** Explain the meaning of the terms: a) atomic number b) mass number c) relative atomic mass

**1.9** Describe the arrangement of elements in the periodic table such that: a) elements are arranged in order of increasing atomic number, in rows called periods b) elements with similar properties are placed in the same vertical column, called groups

**1.10** H Demonstrate an understanding that the existence of isotopes results in some relative atomic masses not being whole numbers

**1.11** H Calculate the relative atomic mass of an element from the relative masses and abundances of its isotopes

HSW *14* How uncertainties in scientific knowledge and scientific ideas change over time and the role of the scientific community in validating these changes

There are also opportunities to cover HSW *3* and HSW *10*.

### Atomic words

**Starter 1** Lit

Show these words on the board: 'atom', 'nucleus', 'proton', 'neutron', 'electron', 'shell'. Ask each student to write two sentences using at least three of these. Ask all the students to save their sentences for the plenary. Leave the words on the board during the lesson.

### Atomic wordsearch

C2.3a Atomic Wordsearch

**Starter 2**

**Worksheet C2.3a** is a wordsearch for nine words connected with atoms and the periodic table. There are clues to help students complete the words first.

### How many subatomic particles?

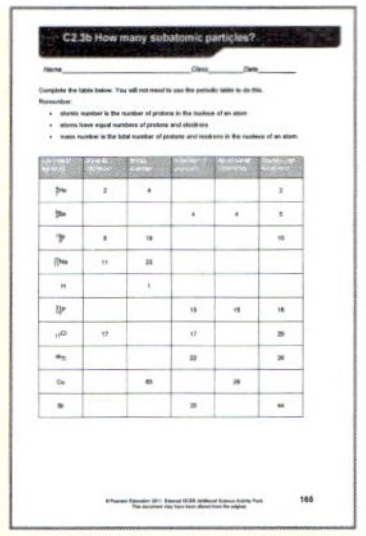

C2.3b How many subatomic particles?

**Exploring 1**

**Worksheet C2.3b** asks students to determine the number of protons, neutrons and electrons in given atoms.

Stretch Students should be able to complete the last four rows in the sheet.

Support The first four rows of the sheet are the most straightforward to complete.

### H Calculating relative atomic mass (AT)

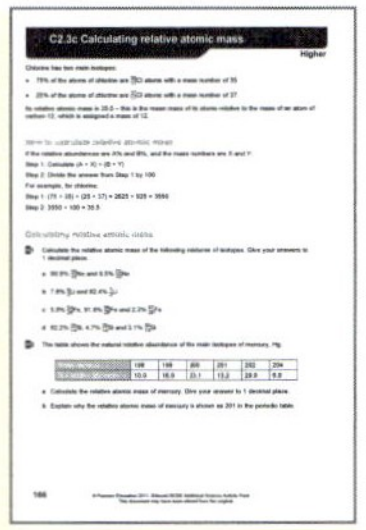

C2.3c Calculating relative atomic mass

**Exploring 2**

**Worksheet C2.3c** allows students to practise calculating relative atomic masses from relative abundances and the mass numbers of isotopes.

Stretch Students write a simple instruction sheet to explain how to calculate relative atomic mass. They could also use the data on the **AT** spreadsheet *Isotope data* to write a spreadsheet formula to calculate this and round it to one decimal place.

### Student Book spread C2.3

**Explaining 1**

Point out that the periodic table has relative atomic masses in it, not mass numbers and that it is arranged in order of increasing atomic number, with groups and periods.

Stretch See page 123. Ask what the relative atomic mass of chlorine would have been if the abundances were the other way round, or if they had both been 50 percent.

Support Students find two elements with the same atomic number, and two elements with the same relative atomic mass.

### Some properties of group 2 elements

**Explaining 2** Demo

Demonstrate the reactions of calcium and magnesium with water and with dilute hydrochloric acid. See the Teacher and technician practical sheet C2.3.

Stretch Ask students to identify the products of the reactions and to write balanced equations.

Support Ask students to write word equations for the reactions.

### Atomic words

**Plenary 1** AfL

Referring back to *Starter 1*, point out the atom words on the board. Ask students to write down what additional things they can now say and then swap with a partner. Each assesses their partner's sentences and feeds their assessment back.

### Group and periods

**Plenary 2** AfL

Give each pupil a sticky note and ask them to write a definition for one of the key terms. The notes are then placed in different areas of the lab – one area for each key term. Read out the best, or those that have problems and ask the students to improve them.

### The modern periodic table

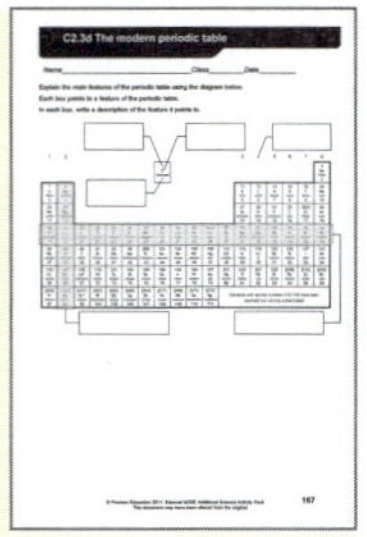

C2.3d The modern periodic table

**Homework 1**

**Worksheet C2.3d**, for students needing support, provides a framework to explain the features of the modern periodic table.

Support Complete some of the boxes with the students to check that they understand what is being asked of them.

### H Isotopes and relative atomic mass

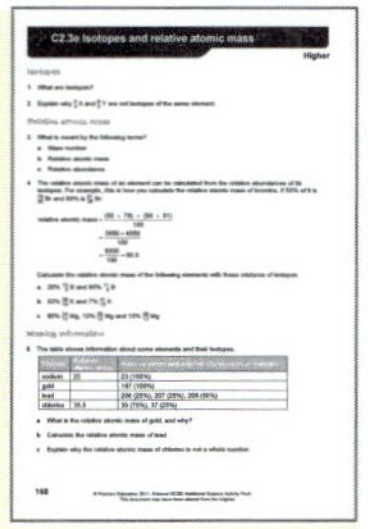

C2.3e Isotopes and relative atomic mass

**Homework 2**

Students make a leaflet or webpage explaining isotopes. It should include the Higher Tier material on abundance and relative atomic mass, with examples for at least two isotopes. Students can work through **Worksheet C2.3e.**

Stretch Ask students to research the meaning of the word 'isotope' and who thought of it.

# C2.3 The modern periodic table

**How are the elements arranged in the modern periodic table?**

Mendeleev's periodic table gradually became accepted by scientists. With a few adjustments as new discoveries were made, it led directly to the modern periodic table. This is now so familiar that you see it on t-shirts and mugs. You can even sit down for a meal at one (see Figure A).

A

1 What are the atomic number and mass number of an element?

For many years, an element's atomic number was just its position on the periodic table. Then, in 1913, scientists worked out that an element's **atomic number** was the number of protons in its atoms.

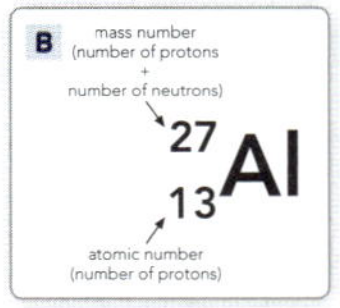


The total number of protons and neutrons in the nucleus of an atom is called its **mass number**. In full chemical symbols like $^{27}_{13}Al$ the top number is the mass number and the bottom one is the atomic number.

This information can be used to calculate the number of protons, neutrons and electrons in an atom. For example, in $^{27}_{13}Al$, there are:

- 13 protons (because the atomic number is 13)
- 27 – 13 = 14 neutrons (mass number minus atomic number)
- 13 electrons (the same as the number of protons).

2 Work out the number of protons, neutrons and electrons in an atom of $^{23}_{11}Na$.

## Relative atomic mass

The mass of an atom is incredibly small, so we use **relative atomic mass** instead of its actual mass in kilograms. The symbol for relative atomic mass is $A_r$. Carbon is used as the standard atom. A carbon-12 atom contains 6 protons, 6 neutrons and 6 electrons. Its relative atomic mass is defined as exactly 12. The masses of all other atoms are compared to this. For example, the mass of a helium-4 atom is one-third that of a carbon-12 atom. So its relative atomic mass is 4.

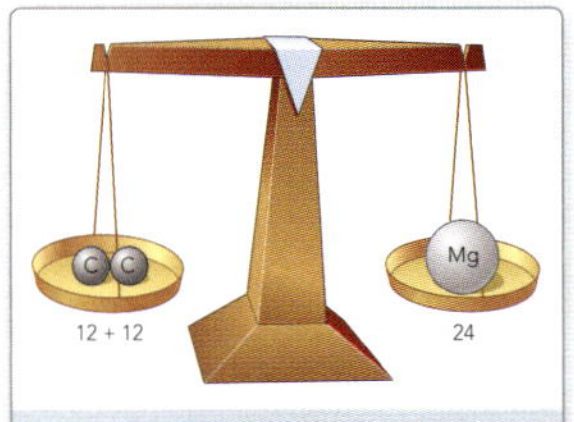


**C** *Most magnesium atoms have the same mass as two carbon-12 atoms, so their relative atomic mass is (12 + 12) = 24.*

**Maths skills**

To find the relative atomic mass of chlorine you need to calculate the average (**mean**) mass of its atoms, where

$$\text{mean} = \frac{\text{sum of values}}{\text{number of values}}$$

3 How are the elements arranged in the modern periodic table?

4 Describe what groups and periods in the periodic table are.

## The modern periodic table

The elements in the modern periodic table are arranged in order of increasing atomic number rather than in order of atomic mass as Mendeleev did. The horizontal rows are called **periods**; the vertical columns are called **groups**. Each group contains elements with similar properties. The main groups are numbered 1 to 7 from left to right. The group on the far right is group 0.



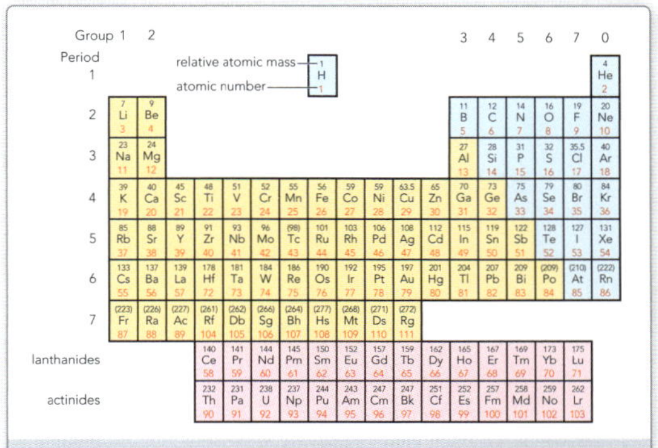


**D** *The modern periodic table shows the element's symbol, relative atomic mass and atomic number.*

**Skills spotlight**

Scientific knowledge and ideas change over time as new evidence becomes available. Explain how the discovery that the atomic number was the number of protons in an atom led to a change in the periodic table.

**ResultsPlus Watch Out!**

In exams, many students get the mass number and atomic number mixed up. Remember that the top number is the *mass* number and is always *more* than the atomic number.

## Isotopes

H

**Isotopes** are different atoms of an element with the same number of protons and electrons but different numbers of neutrons. For example, chlorine atoms always have 17 protons, but some can have 18 neutrons and others have 20 neutrons. These are different isotopes – $^{35}_{17}Cl$ and $^{37}_{17}Cl$.

The presence of isotopes means that some relative atomic masses are not whole numbers. For example, the **relative abundance** (proportion) of $^{35}_{17}Cl$ is 75% of all chlorine atoms, and the relative abundance of $^{37}_{17}Cl$ is 25%. This is why the relative atomic mass of chlorine is 35.5 rather than a whole number:

$$\text{relative atomic mass} = \frac{(75 \times 35) + (25 \times 37)}{(75 + 25)} = \frac{2625 + 925}{100} = \frac{3550}{100} = 35.5$$

H 5 **a** What are isotopes? **b** There are two isotopes of copper: 69% is $^{63}_{29}Cu$ and 31% is $^{65}_{29}Cu$. Calculate the relative atomic mass of copper. Give your answer to one decimal place.

6 The relative atomic mass of titanium is 48. Explain as fully as you can what this means.

**Learning Outcomes**

1.2 Classify elements as metals and non-metals according to their position in the periodic table

1.8 Explain the meaning of the terms: **a** atomic number **b** mass number **c** relative atomic mass

1.9 Describe the arrangement of elements in the periodic table such that: **a** elements are arranged in order of increasing atomic number, arranged in rows called periods **b** elements with similar properties are placed in the same vertical column, called groups

H 1.10 Demonstrate an understanding that the existence of isotopes results in some relative atomic masses not being whole numbers

H 1.11 Calculate the relative atomic mass of an element from the relative masses and abundances of its isotopes

HSW 14 Describe how scientists share data and discuss new ideas, and how over time this process helps to reduce uncertainties and revise scientific theories

How are electron shells filled with electrons? 

## ActiveTeach

- **AT** *Isotope data* [spreadsheet]
  Calculating RAM
- **AT** *Periodic table* [interactive]
  Periodic table groups - scene investigation
- **AT** *The modern periodic table* [diagram]
  Figure D – diagram labelling activity

## Key terms

atomic number
group
H isotopes
mass number
period
relative atomic mass
H relative abundance

## Answers | Student Book

1 Atomic number is the number of protons in the nucleus of an atom, the mass number is the total number of protons and neutrons in the nucleus.

2 11 protons, (23 – 11) = 12 neutrons, 11 electrons.

3 In order of increasing atomic number.

4 Groups are vertical columns containing elements with similar properties. Periods are horizontal rows in the periodic table.

5 H **a** Atoms of an element with the same number of protons and electrons, but different numbers of neutrons.

H **b**

$$\frac{(69 \times 63)+(31 \times 65)}{100} = \frac{4347+2015}{100} = \frac{6362}{100} = 63.6$$

6 The mean mass of its atoms is 48 compared to the mass of an atom of carbon-12, which is assigned a mass of 12.

**Skills spotlight**

Experiments allowed atomic number to be measured. As a result, the elements became ordered in terms of increasing atomic number, rather than increasing atomic mass.

# C2.4 Electron shells



This lesson examines the electronic structures of the first 20 elements, two different methods of representing them and the connections to each element's position in the periodic table.

## Specification coverage

***1.12*** Apply rules about the filling of electron shells (energy levels) to predict the electronic configurations of the first 20 elements in the periodic table as diagrams and in the form 2.8.1

***1.13*** Describe the connection between the number of outer electrons and the position of an element in the periodic table

HSW ***11*** Presenting information, developing an argument and drawing a conclusion, using scientific, technical and mathematical language, conventions and symbols and ICT tools

There are also opportunities to cover HSW ***3***.

## Key terms

electronic configuration

### Atom practice

**Starter 1**

Show the periodic table. Ask students how many protons or electrons there are in the atoms of various elements. Ensure that students recall that the bottom number in each box of the Edexcel periodic table is the atomic number, and that this is the number of protons (and so electrons) in atoms of that element.

### Electron configurations

**Exploring 1**

**Worksheet C2.4a** allows students to practise working out electronic configurations and drawing electron diagrams.

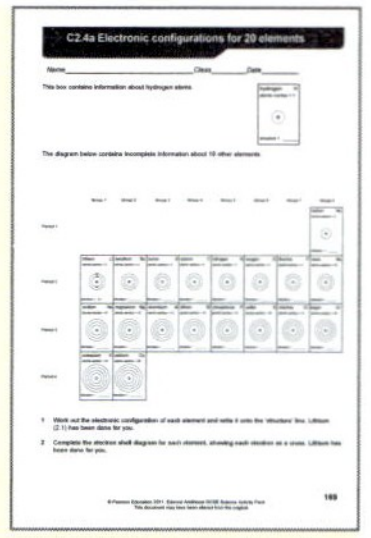

**Stretch** Student to write a simple instruction sheet to explain how to work out electronic configurations using just an atomic number.

**Support** Figure C on page 124 of the Student Book can act as a prompt.

### Student Book spread C2.4 (AT)

**Explaining 1**

Show how the electron shell diagram and electronic configuration for sodium is produced. See **AT** presentation *Electronic configurations*.

**Stretch** More able students are often curious as to why they have to consider only the first 20 elements.

**Support** Show the students how to write electronic configurations and draw simple diagrams, such as those for hydrogen and neon.

### Who am I? (AT)

**Plenary 1** AfL Lit

Students work in pairs. One has the diagram of an atom. The other student has to ask questions about what it contains so that they can draw it themselves. Suitable diagrams can be found on the **AT** document *Electronic configuration cards*.

### Electronic structures

**Homework 1**

**Worksheet C2.4c** for students needing support, allows them to demonstrate their knowledge and understanding of electronic configurations and the periodic table.

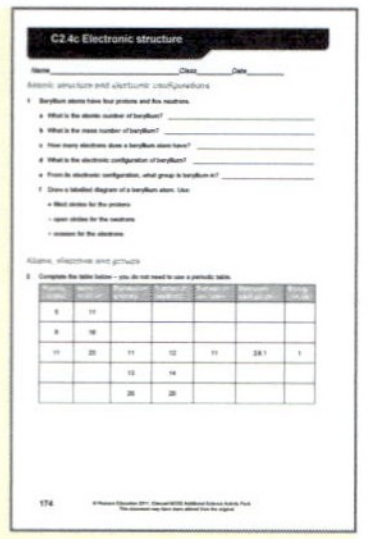

**Support** Go through a similar problem to question 1 with the students.

### Symbols

**Starter 2** Lit

Ask the students to suggest some shorthand ways of showing things that scientists use – such as the number of subatomic particles in an atom. They feed their answers back to the class for discussion.

### Atomic bingo

**Exploring 2**

**Worksheet C2.4b** allows students to practise using the connections between the position of an element on the periodic table and its electronic configuration. There are 20 question slips to call out at random, and 30 different 4 × 4 bingo cards. Students will need access to the periodic table.

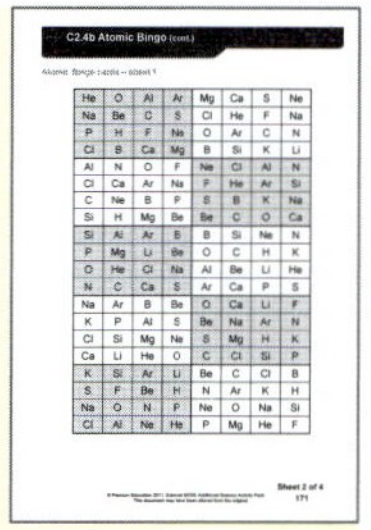

### Connections

**Explaining 2**

Students write the electronic configuration of one element from atomic number 1 to 20 and arrange them into the correct order as in the periodic table. What connections between the electronic configuration and the periodic table are used to achieve this?

**Stretch** Ask the students to discuss whether or not these connections are coincidences.

**Support** Check that students understand that all the elements in a group have the same number of outer electrons, and all the elements in a period have the same number of shells occupied by electrons.

### Quick configurations

**Plenary 2** Lit

Students work in pairs or small groups to devise instructions for writing electronic configurations. The aim is to use as few words as possible. They feed their instructions back to the class for discussion. Whose instructions are the shortest, and do they work?

### Atoms on TV

**Homework 2**

Ask the students to write a storyboard for a television science programme that explains electron shells and how they are filled.

**Stretch** Ask students to explain why shells are filled from the inside out, and why shells are also known as energy levels.

# C2.4 Electron shells

How are the electrons arranged in atoms?

The system of chemical symbols used today was first developed in 1819 by Jöns Jacob Berzelius (1779–1848), a Swedish chemist. Before then several different systems existed. This made it difficult for scientists to understand each other's work. It is important that scientists develop and use systems to communicate their ideas clearly, including for showing the arrangement of electrons in atoms.

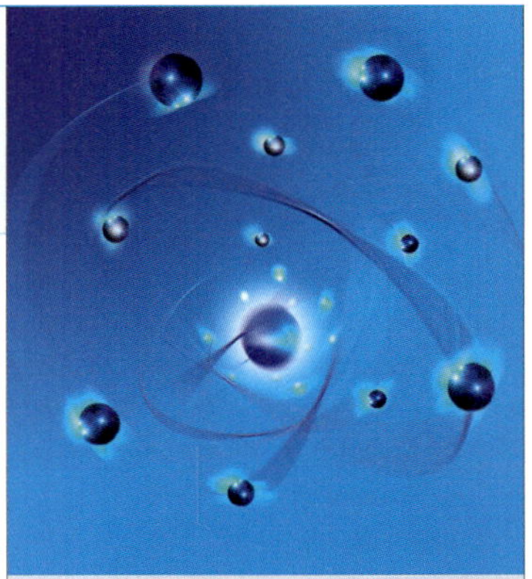

A It is difficult to imagine how electrons are arranged in shells, so a simple way to represent them is needed.

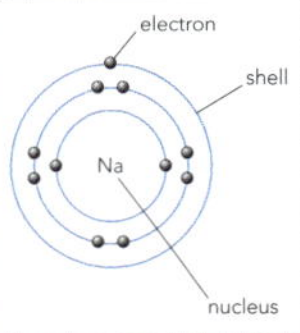


B The electronic configuration for sodium. The protons and neutrons that form the nucleus are replaced by Na, the chemical symbol for sodium.

Electrons are arranged in shells around the nucleus of the atom. Each shell is shown as a circle drawn around the chemical symbol for the atom.

The way in which the electrons are arranged in an atom is called its **electronic configuration**. Figure B shows the electronic configuration for sodium.

Figure C shows the electronic configurations for the first 20 elements in the periodic table (hydrogen to calcium).

1 What is an electronic configuration?

2 How many electrons are there in the outermost shells of lithium (Li) and sulfur (S)?

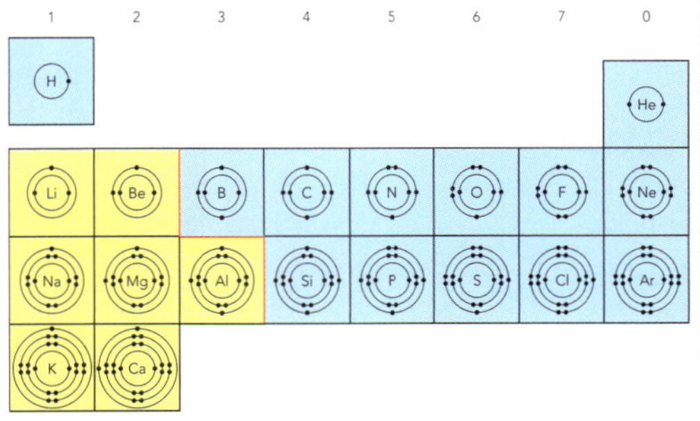


C Electronic configurations of the first 20 elements.

## Finding configurations

Different shells can contain different numbers of electrons. For the first 20 elements:

- the first shell can contain up to two electrons
- the second and third shells both hold up to eight electrons (although the third shell can hold more than this).

Electronic configurations can be worked out using atomic numbers. For example, the atomic number of sodium is 11. This means that there are 11 protons and also 11 electrons. So to fill the shells:

- two electrons fit in the first shell, leaving nine
- eight electrons fit in the second shell, leaving one
- one electron fits into the third shell, leaving none.

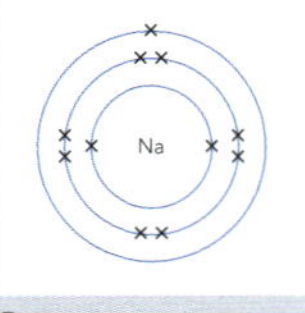


D Electronic configuration diagrams use either dots or crosses to represent the electrons.

3 How can you tell, from the periodic table, the number of electrons in the atoms of an element?

4 What is the maximum number of electrons allowed in each of the first two shells?

Diagrams are not the only way to show electronic configuration. They can be written out instead. For sodium this is 2.8.1 – each number shows how many electrons there are in a shell. The dots separate one shell from the next. This method of showing electronic configurations is easy to write and to understand.

## Spotting connections

There are several connections between an element's electronic configuration and where it is found in the periodic table. For example, the number of occupied shells is the same as the period number. Apart from the elements in group 0, which all have full outer shells, the number of outer electrons is the same as the group number. For example, the electronic configuration of sodium (2.8.1) shows that sodium is in the third period and in group 1.

5 Describe the connection between the electronic configuration of an element and its place in the periodic table.

6 Draw and write the electronic configuration for atoms with the following atomic numbers: a 6 b 17.

7 Two different elements have five outer electrons in their atoms. To which group do they belong and why?

8 The electronic configuration of an element is 2.8.7. What information does this give about the element and its atoms?

### Skills spotlight

Scientists often use conventions and symbols to present information. Describe the advantages of writing electronic configurations rather than drawing them.

### Learning Outcomes

1.12 Apply rules about the filling of electron shells (energy levels) to predict the electronic configurations of the first 20 elements in the periodic table, given the atomic numbers, as diagrams and in the form 2.8.1

1.13 Describe the connection between the number of outer electrons and the position of an element in the periodic table

HSW 11 Present information using scientific conventions and symbols



Where might you find a building made of salt? 

## ActiveTeach

- **AT** *Which elements have these electronic structures?* [interactive]
  Electronic structures – matching activity
- **AT** *Name that element* [interactive]
  Describing elements – matching game
- **AT** *Electronic configurations* [presentation]
  Electron distribution
- **AT** *Electronic configuration cards* [word document]
  Electron distribution cards

## Answers | Student Book

1 An electronic configuration shows the arrangement of electrons in the shells around the nucleus of an atom.

2 A lithium atom has 1 electron in its outer shell. A sulfur atom has 6 electrons in its outer shell.

3 The box for the element in the periodic table shows the atomic number, which is also the number of electrons in the element's atoms.

4 First 2; second 8; (third 8 but not required).

5 The number of occupied shells or numbers in the electronic configuration is the same as the period number for the element. The number of outer electrons is the same as the group number for the element. The total number of electrons is the same as the atomic number, and the elements are arranged in order of increasing atomic number in the periodic table.

6 **a** 2.4 and correct diagram
**b** 2.8.7 and correct diagram

7 Group 5, because the number of outer electrons is the same as the group number.

8 The electronic configuration 2.8.7 shows that the atom contains two electrons in its first shell, eight electrons in its second and seven electrons in its third, outer shell. The atom is in group 7, period 3, of the periodic table.

**Skills spotlight**
Electronic configurations are easily written and typed but drawings are more difficult to do.

# C2.5 Ionic bonds



This lesson examines the formation of ions by the loss or gain of electrons, and the formation of ionic bonds by the transfer of electrons.

## Specification coverage

***2.1*** Demonstrate an understanding that atoms of different elements can combine to form compounds by the formation of new chemical bonds

***2.2*** Describe how ionic bonds are formed by the transfer of electrons to produce cations and anions

***2.3*** Describe an ion as an atom or group of atoms with a positive or negative charge

***2.4*** Describe the formation of sodium ions, Na+, and chloride ions, Cl–, and hence the formation of ions in other ionic compounds from their atoms, limited to compounds of elements in groups 1, 2, 6 and 7

HSW ***11*** Presenting information, *developing an argument and drawing a conclusion*, using scientific, *technical and mathematical language*, conventions and symbols *and ICT tools*.

## Key terms

| | |
|---|---|
| anion | ion |
| bond | Ionic bond |
| cation | |

### Electrons and shells

**Starter 1**

Show the periodic table. Ask students how many electrons there are in the outer shells of atoms of various elements. Ensure that students recall that the number of electrons in the outer shell is the same as the group number (for H to Ca). Ensure that any misconceptions are corrected.

### Atoms and ions

**Exploring 1**

C2.5a Atoms and ions

Using **Worksheet C2.5a** students complete questions and a table showing the loss or gain of electrons by atoms and the formulae of the ions formed.

**Stretch** Ask students to predict the formulae of the ions formed by Rb, Be, Br and I.

**Support** Complete some of the rows in the table for the students. Ask students to complete the table column by column, rather than row by row.

### Student Book spread C2.5

**Explaining 1**

The Student Book describes the formation of cations and anions, and how electrons are transferred from one atom to another.

**Stretch** Ask students to suggest why sodium atoms do not gain seven electrons to form $Na^{7-}$ ions and chlorine atoms do not lose seven electrons to form $Cl^{7+}$ ions.

**Support** Make sure that students understand that only the outer shells are involved.

### Summing it up

**Plenary 1** AfL

Ask students to make revision cards or a summary based on the new ideas in the lesson. Each student should come up with four bullet points, then work with a partner to come up with an agreed list of five bullet points.

### Ions

**Homework 1**

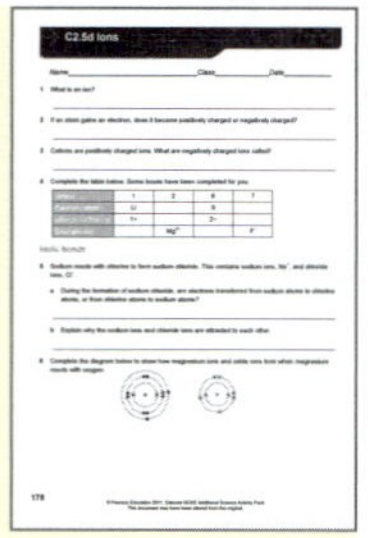
C2.5d Ions

**Worksheet C2.5d** is intended for Foundation tier students.

**Support** Complete one more column in the worksheet before photocopying it.

### Salt

**Starter 2**

Show the photograph of the Salt Palace from page 126 of the Student Book. Ask the students why salt could be strong enough to build a hotel with, yet be able to dissolve in rain. Aim to elicit the idea that the properties of salt are due to its particles and their bonding.

### The formation of ions

**Exploring 2**

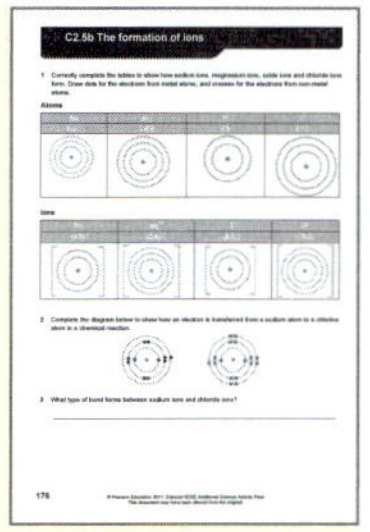
C2.5b The formation of ions

Using **Worksheet C2.5b** students complete electron shell diagrams to show how ions, and sodium chloride, form.

**Stretch** Ask students to draw electron shell diagrams to show the formation of MgO, $MgCl_2$ and/or $Na_2O$

**Support** Complete some of the diagrams for the students.

### The formation of sodium chloride

**Explaining 2**

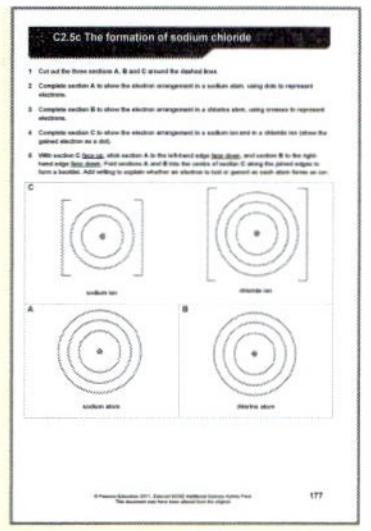
C2.5c The formation of sodium chloride

**Worksheet C2.5c** allows students to produce a small quarter-folded booklet to explain the formation of sodium chloride from sodium and chlorine.

**Stretch** Ask students to make a similar booklet for a more complex compound – e.g. MgO, $MgCl_2$ or $Na_2O$.

**Support** Allow the students to access the diagrams in the Student Book when completing this task.

### All about ions (AT)

**Plenary 2**

The **AT** interactive *All about ions* is a true or false activity which covers the new concepts from the lesson.

### H Ions and ionic bonds

**Homework 2**

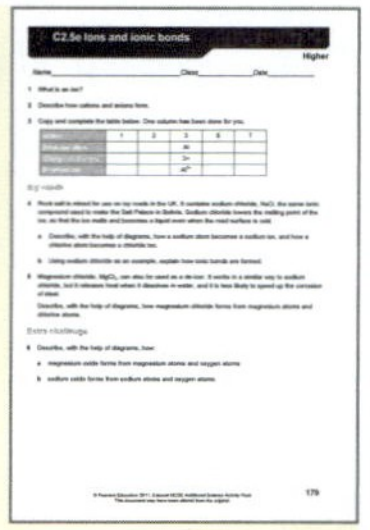
C2.5e Ions and ionic bonds

**Worksheet C2.5e** is intended for Higher Tier students.

**Stretch** Ask the students to complete the 'extra challenge' question.

# C2.5 Ionic bonds

How do ionic bonds form?

A very unusual hotel in the middle of a salt lake in Bolivia, South America, has walls made entirely from blocks of common salt. Luckily there is little rain. Common salt dissolves easily in water because of its type of bonding.

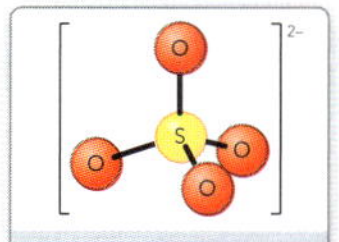


**B** *The sulfate ion $SO_4^{2-}$ consists of a group of atoms with an overall negative charge.*

**A** *Visitors are warned not to lick the walls at the Salt Palace.*

An **ion** is an atom or group of atoms with a positive or negative charge. The atoms of most elements have incomplete outer shells of electrons. This means they can lose or gain electrons during chemical reactions. When this happens, the atoms become ions. Groups of atoms may also become ions if they lose or gain electrons.

1 What is an ion?

### Cations

Metal atoms lose electrons to form positively charged ions called **cations**. For example, sodium atoms Na become sodium ions $Na^+$. The + sign shows that a sodium ion carries a single positive charge.

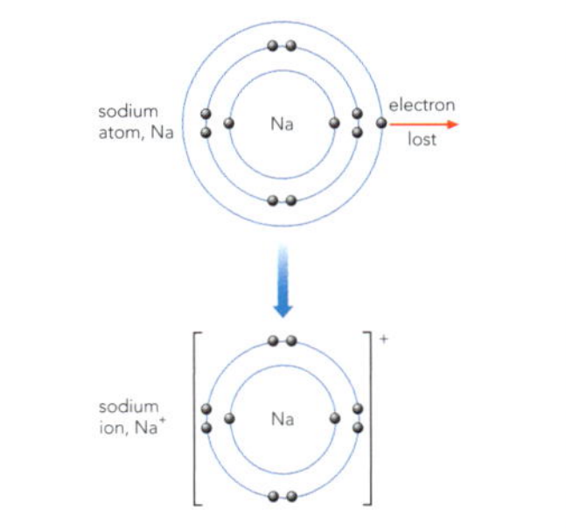


**C** *A sodium atom loses its outermost electron to become a sodium ion. The brackets show that the positive charge belongs to the whole ion.*

| Group number | 1 | 2 |
|---|---|---|
| Number of outer electrons | 1 | 2 |
| Number of electrons lost | 1 | 2 |
| Charge on cation | 1+ | 2+ |
| Example | $Na^+$ | $Mg^{2+}$ |

**D** *In groups 1 and 2 the charge on the ion is linked to the group number.*

Metal atoms lose outermost electrons when they form ions. For elements in groups 1 and 2, the number of outer electrons lost is the same as the group number.

### Anions

Non-metal atoms gain electrons to form negatively charged ions called **anions**. For example, chlorine atoms Cl become chloride ions $Cl^-$. The – sign shows that a chloride ion carries a single negative charge.

Notice that the end of the name changes to –ide when non-metal atoms form ions.

Non-metal atoms gain electrons to complete their outermost shell when they form ions. The number of electrons that atoms in groups 6 and 7 can gain is eight minus the group number. Chlorine is in group 7, so chlorine atoms have seven outermost electrons. The outermost shell can contain eight electrons, so a chlorine atom can gain one electron to complete its outermost shell.

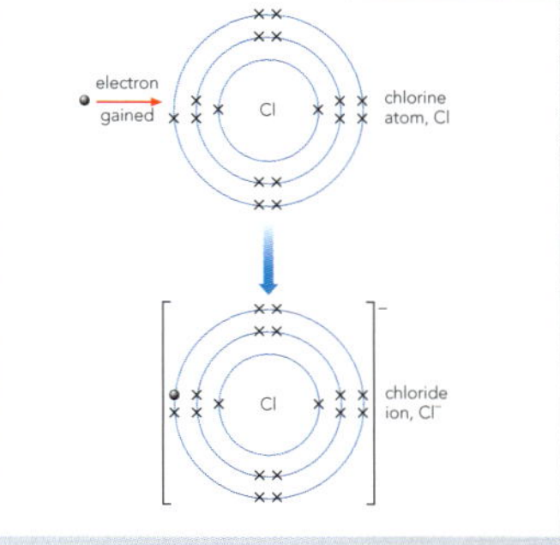


**E** *A chlorine atom gains an electron to become a chloride ion.*

2 Predict the symbols of the ions formed by the following metals:
a lithium (Li) found in group 1 b calcium (Ca) found in group 2.

3 There are three outermost electrons in an aluminium atom.
a Write down the symbol for an aluminium ion.
b Is this a cation or an anion?

4 Draw a diagram involving electron shells and electrons to show how a fluorine atom becomes a fluoride ion.

## Transferring electrons

When atoms of different elements combine to form compounds, new chemical bonds form. For example, when sodium chloride forms, electrons are transferred from sodium atoms to chlorine atoms, forming $Na^+$ ions and $Cl^-$ ions.

These oppositely charged ions attract each other strongly. New chemical **bonds** form, called **ionic bonds**.

| Group number | 6 | 7 |
|---|---|---|
| Number of outer electrons | 6 | 7 |
| Number of electrons gained | 2 | 1 |
| Charge on anion | 2– | 1– |
| Example | $O^{2-}$ | $Cl^-$ |

**F** *The charges on non-metal ions in groups 6 and 7*

**ResultsPlus Watch Out!**

Students are often confused about atoms and ions. Remember that an electron is negative. Non-metal atoms gain electrons and become negative ions. Metal atoms lose electrons and become positive ions.

5 Predict the symbols of the ions formed by the following non-metals:
a sulfur (S) found in group 6 b iodine (I) found in group 7.

6 Explain, in terms of electrons and chemical bonds, what happens when sodium reacts with chlorine to form sodium chloride.

**Skills spotlight**

Scientists use chemical symbols for substances including ions. Describe the information contained in the symbols $Mg^{2+}$ and $O^{2-}$.

**Learning Outcomes**

*2.1* Demonstrate an understanding that atoms of different elements can combine to form compounds by the formation of new chemical bonds

*2.2* Describe how ionic bonds are formed by the transfer of electrons to produce cations and anions

*2.3* Describe an ion as an atom or group of atoms with a positive or negative charge

*2.4* Describe the formation of sodium ions, $Na^+$, and chloride ions, $Cl^-$, and hence the formation of ions in other ionic compounds from their atoms, limited to compounds of elements in groups 1, 2, 6 and 7

HSW *11* Present information using scientific conventions and symbols



What do *sal culinaris, natrum muriaticum* and table salt all have in common?



## ActiveTeach

- **AT** *Brine electrolysis: properties of ions*
  [video]
  Ionic compounds: properties
- **AT** *All about ions*
  [interactive]
  Ionic bonding – true-or-false quiz
- **AT** *How a sodium atom becomes a sodium ion*
  [diagram]
  Figure C – diagram labelling activity
- **AT** *How a chlorine atom becomes a chloride ion*
  [diagram]
  Figure E – diagram labelling activity

## Answers | Student Book

1 Atoms or groups of atoms with a positive or negative charge.

2 **a** $Li^+$ **b** $Ca^{2+}$

3 **a** $Al^{3+}$ **b** cation

4 Diagram showing 7 electrons in outer shell recieving an extra electron forming a complete shell of 8 electrons and with a negative charge.

5 **a** $S^{2-}$ **b** $I^-$

6 A good answer should include the following points.
- sodium atoms transfer their outer electrons to chlorine atoms.
- sodium atoms become positively charged sodium ions.
- chlorine atoms become negatively charged chloride ions.
- these oppositely charged ions attract each other, forming new chemical bonds.

**Skills spotlight**

The symbol $Mg^{2+}$ shows that the particle is an ion, formed from a magnesium atom, and having two positive charges.

The symbol $O^{2-}$ shows that the particle is an ion, formed from an oxygen atom, and having two negative charges.

# C2.6 Ionic compounds

This lesson examines how to work out the formulae of ionic compounds and the importance of correctly naming them. It introduces the concept of an ionic lattice.

## Specification coverage

***2.5*** Demonstrate an understanding of the use of the endings –ide and –ate in the names of compounds

***2.6*** Deduce the formulae of ionic compounds (including oxides, hydroxides, halides, nitrates, carbonates and sulfates) given the formulae of the constituent ions

***2.7*** H Describe the structure of ionic compounds as a lattice structure: a) consisting of a regular arrangement of ions b) held together by strong electrostatic forces (ionic bonds) between oppositely-charged ions

HSW ***11*** Presenting information, *developing an argument and drawing a conclusion*, using scientific, *technical and mathematical language*, conventions and symbols *and* ICT tools.

## Key terms

compound ion
formula
ionic compound
lattice structure

### Ionic lies

**Starter 1**

Students play a game, giving correct and incorrect definitions of anion and cation.

### Formulae of ionic compounds

**Exploring 1**

Using **Worksheet C2.6a** students use the formulae of ions to work out the formulae of ionic compounds.

**Stretch** Omit the table of common ions. Students complete the sheet without the help of their book.

**Support** Check students have correctly completed the table at the top before starting the questions. Fill in some of the formulae for them.

### Student Book spread C2.6

**Explaining 1**

The Student Book explains the use of the –ide and –ate conventions in naming ionic compounds.

**Stretch** Ask students to work out some 'difficult' formulae – e.g. ammonium carbonate, iron(III) sulfate.

**Support** Make sure that students understand why they need to look at the top numbers in the formulae of ions when working out formulae of compounds.

### Formulae

**Plenary 1**

Write a grid of positive and negative ions on the board in the style of **Worksheet C2.6a**. Ask students to work out the formulae of the compounds produced. This could be extended to include the number and names of the different elements present in each compound.

### Names and formulae of ionic compounds

**Homework 1**

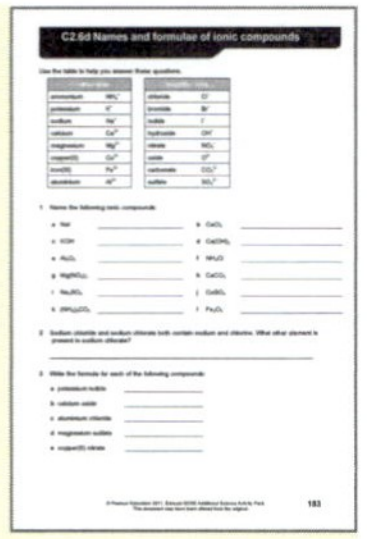

**Worksheet C2.6d** for Foundation tier students uses a table of common ions to help students write the names and formulae of various ionic compounds.

**Support** Complete some of the answers before photocopying the sheet.

### Formulae

**Starter 2**

Show some common formulae on the board – e.g. NaCl, $CO_2$, $H_2O$ and $O_2$. What information do these formulae give? Students feed their ideas back to the class for discussion.

### Elements in ionic compounds

**Exploring 2**

Using **Worksheet C2.6b** students determine the number of elements present in various ionic compounds, and name elements present. Question 3 involves elements not commonly met and requires some searching through the periodic table.

**Stretch** Ask students to answer all the questions.

**Support** Consider removing question 3 from the worksheet before photocopying it for the students.

### H Giant ionic lattice

**Explaining 2**

Demonstrate the regular lattice structure of an ionic compound using a model. Commercial models are available, but marbles constrained in a cardboard or plastic container can also be used to show lattice structures.

**Stretch** Ask students to suggest why, in terms of ions, different crystals have different shapes.

### Loopy names

**Plenary 2**

Lit

Cut up **Worksheet C2.6c.** Each student is given a strip with a formula and a name (these do not match). Start with one student, who reads out the name on their strip. The student with the matching formula calls out their formula: if it is correct, they read out the name on their strip. This continues around the room (there are 32 strips on the sheet).

### H Ionic compounds

**Homework 2**

**Worksheet C2.6e** for Higher Tier students, uses a table of common ions to write the names and formulae of various ionic compounds, and also describe the structure and bonding present.

**Stretch** Ask the students to complete the 'extra challenge' question.

# C2.6 Ionic compounds

How are the formulae of ionic compounds worked out?

The white crystals we put on chips have had many names in the past, including *natrum muriaticum*, muriate of soda, *sal culinaris* and just salt. Scientists have agreed on a name that everyone should use, sodium chloride.

**A** *The name on the label of this homeopathic remedy just means sodium chloride.*

1 Give the formulae for:
a sodium oxide
b magnesium chloride.

**ResultsPlus Watch Out!**

Brackets must be used when more than one of the compound ions is needed to balance the charge on the other ion in a compound. For example, NaOH and $Mg(OH)_2$ are correct, but Na(OH) and $MgOH_2$ are not.

## Working out a formula

**Ionic compounds** contain ions. You can work out the **formula** of an ionic compound if you know which ions are in it. Ionic compounds are electrically neutral because they contain equal numbers of positive and negative charges. In sodium chloride, one $Na^+$ ion is needed for every $Cl^-$ ion, so its formula is NaCl.

Many ionic compounds have ions with different numbers of charges. For example, aluminium oxide contains $Al^{3+}$ ions and $O^{2-}$ ions. Two $Al^{3+}$ ions give a total of six positive charges, and three $O^{2-}$ ions give a total of six negative charges. The formula of aluminium oxide is $Al_2O_3$.

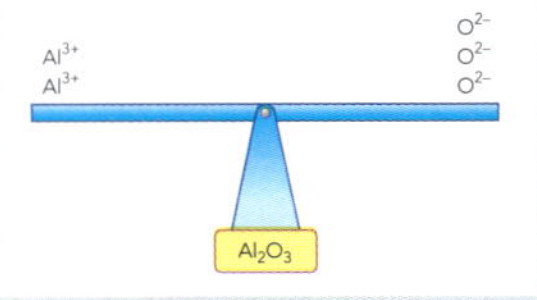

**B** *When working out formulae, it may help to imagine balancing the charges on a see-saw.*

| Positive ions | | Charge | Negative ions | | Charge |
|---|---|---|---|---|---|
| ammonium | $NH_4^+$ | 1+ | chloride | $Cl^-$ | 1– |
| potassium | $K^+$ | 1+ | bromide | $Br^-$ | 1– |
| sodium | $Na^+$ | 1+ | iodide | $I^-$ | 1– |
| calcium | $Ca^{2+}$ | 2+ | hydroxide | $OH^-$ | 1– |
| magnesium | $Mg^{2+}$ | 2+ | nitrate | $NO_3^-$ | 1– |
| copper | $Cu^{2+}$ | 2+ | oxide | $O^{2-}$ | 2– |
| iron (II) | $Fe^{3+}$ | 3+ | carbonate | $CO_3^{2-}$ | 2– |
| aluminium | $Al^{3+}$ | 3+ | sulfate | $SO_4^{2-}$ | 2– |

**C** *Some common ions and their formulae*

## Compound ions

**Compound ions** contain more than one element. For example, the nitrate ion $NO_3^-$ contains one nitrogen atom joined to three oxygen atoms and an extra electron. If two or more compound ions of the same type are needed in a formula, the ion must be written inside brackets. For example, the formula of magnesium nitrate is $Mg(NO_3)_2$. This shows that the two positive charges in one $Mg^{2+}$ ion are balanced by two negative charges from two $NO_3^-$ ions.



## Names of ionic compounds

You may have noticed that the names of some compounds end in –ide and some end in –ate. The –ate ending shows that oxygen atoms are present.

| –ide compounds | | –ate compounds | |
|---|---|---|---|
| potassium bromide | KBr | potassium bromate | $KBrO_3$ |
| iron (II) sulfide | FeS | iron sulfate | $FeSO_4$ |
| calcium carbide | $CaC_2$ | calcium carbonate | $CaCO_3$ |

**D** *Some examples of –ide and –ate compounds*

2 Give the formulae for:
a copper(II) sulfate
b ammonium nitrate.

## The structure of ionic compounds

The ions in an ionic compound are arranged in a regular way, called a **lattice structure**. The ions in sodium chloride pack together in a box-like arrangement, which is why it forms cube-shaped crystals. There are strong electrostatic forces of attraction between the oppositely charged ions. These are the ionic bonds.

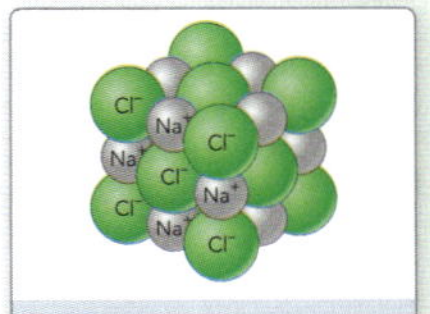

**E** *The lattice structure of sodium chloride*

**F** *Tiny sodium chloride crystals viewed using an electron microscope (magnification x 252).*

3 For each of the following compounds, give the symbols of the ions it contains and its formula:
a potassium chloride
b magnesium oxide
c aluminium hydroxide
d calcium nitrate
e potassium sulfate
f ammonium carbonate.

4 Phosphide ions are $P^{3-}$. Name the elements contained in aluminium phosphide and aluminium phosphate.

(H) 5 Explain, with the help of a diagram, what is meant by lattice structure.

6 Iodised table salt contains an iodine compound to provide extra iodine, which is needed to keep us healthy. This is usually potassium iodide or potassium iodate, which contains the iodate ion $IO_3^-$. Describe the similarities and differences between these two compounds and give their formulae.

**Skills spotlight**

Chemical names provide information about what the named substance contains. Table salt may contain potassium iodide or potassium iodate to avoid iodine deficiency. Explain the difference in the names of these two compounds.

**Learning Outcomes**

**2.5** Demonstrate an understanding of the use of the endings '–ide' and '–ate' in the names of compounds

**2.6** Deduce the formulae of ionic compounds (including oxides, hydroxides, halides, nitrates, carbonates and sulfates) given the formulae of the constituent ions

(H) **2.7** Describe the structure of ionic compounds as a lattice structure: **a** consisting of a regular arrangement of ions **b** held together by strong electrostatic forces (ionic bonds) between oppositely charged ions

HSW **11** Present information using scientific conventions and symbols

Does sodium chloride melt?



## ActiveTeach

- **AT** *Name that compound?* [interactive] Compound names and formulae – noughts and crosses

## Answers | Student Book

1 a $Na_2O$ b $MgCl_2$

2 a $CuSO_4$ b $NH_4NO_3$

3 a $K^+$ and $Cl^-$; KCl b $Mg^{2+}$ and $O^{2-}$; MgO c $Al^{3+}$ and $OH^-$; $Al(OH)_3$ d $Ca^{2+}$ and $NO_3^-$; $Ca(NO_3)_2$ e $K^+$ and $SO_4^{2-}$; $K_2SO_4$ f $NH_4^+$ and $CO_3^{2-}$; $(NH_4)_2CO_3$

4 Aluminium phosphide contains aluminium and phosphorus. Aluminium phosphate contains aluminium, phosphorus and oxygen.

5 (H) A good answer should include the following points.
- lattice structure is the regular arrangement of ions in an ionic compound.
- suitable diagram to illustrate this, e.g. alternating + and – in rows.

6 Both contain potassium and iodine. Potassium iodate contains oxygen but potassium iodide does not. Potassium iodide is KI and potassium iodate is $KIO_3$.

**Skills spotlight**

The ending 'ate' shows that potassium iodate contains oxygen, whereas potassium iodide does not.

# C2.7 Properties of ionic compounds



This lesson investigates the conditions in which ionic compounds will conduct electricity, and their high melting points and boiling points.

## Specification coverage

(H) **2.7** Describe the structure of ionic compounds as a lattice structure: a) *consisting of a regular arrangement of ions* b) held together by strong electrostatic forces (ionic bonds) between oppositely-charged ions

**2.8** Describe (H) **and explain** the properties of ionic substances including sodium chloride and magnesium oxide, limited to: a) melting points and boiling points b) whether they conduct electricity as solids, when molten and in aqueous solution

HSW **12** The use of contemporary science and technological developments and their benefits, drawbacks and risks

## Key terms

aqueous solution
boiling point
electrolysis
melting point
molten

### Testing formulae

**Starter 1**

Write a grid of positive and negative ions on the board in the style of **Worksheets C2.6a** and **C2.6b**. Ask students to work out the formulae of the compounds produced. Check their answers to identify misunderstandings.

### Testing substances

**Exploring 1** Prac

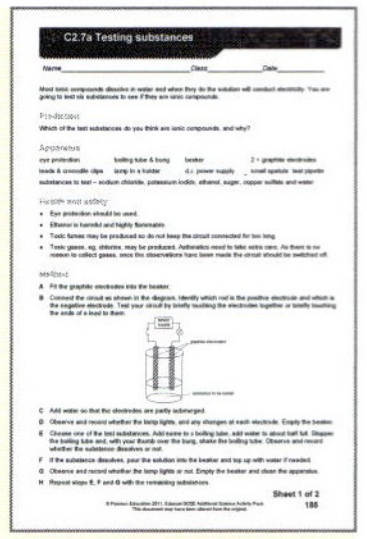

Students carry out a practical to determine whether or not various substances conduct electricity in solution. See **Worksheet C2.7a** and the Teacher and technician practical sheet C2.7 (1) for full details.

**Stretch** Ask students to record their observations at each electrode.

**Support** Consider providing labelled solutions, instead of substances to dissolve, for students with weaker practical abilities.

### Student Book spread C2.7

**Explaining 1**

The Student Book states that ionic compounds conduct electricity when molten or in aqueous solution, but not when solid. Emphasise that this is different from metals, which will also conduct when solid.

**Stretch** Higher Tier students must be able to explain the conduction of electricity by ionic compounds when molten or in aqueous solution.

**Support** Remind students that an electric current will flow only if the circuit is complete, so a substance that cannot conduct electricity will act as a break in the circuit.

### Ionic flow chart

**Plenary 1** AfL

Students work together to devise a flow chart, based on their knowledge and information gained in the lesson, to determine if an unknown solid is an ionic compound or not. They feed their ideas back to the rest of the class, who test the flow chart against the substances used in *Exploring 1* to see if it works.

### Properties of ionic compounds

**Homework 1**

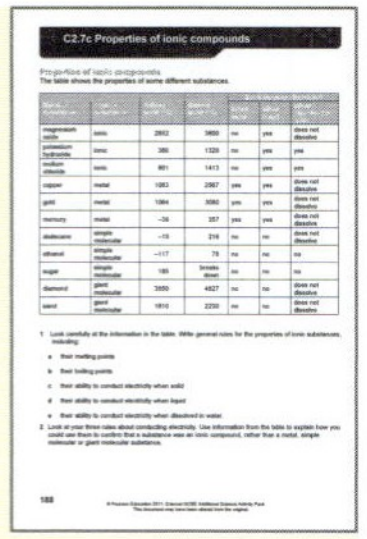

**Worksheet C2.7c** for Foundation tier students covers the physical properties of ionic compounds.

**Support** Cover up question 2 before photocopying the sheet, or ask students to do question 1 only.

### Conducting electricity

**Starter 2**

Ask students to consider how they could test a substance to see if it conducts electricity. What equipment would they need, how would they set it up, and what would they expect to observe? Draw a table on the board of materials that do conduct electricity. Ask students to vote for each one (whether it conducts or not). Keep the results of the vote to revisit in *Plenary 2*.

### Properties of ionic compounds

**Exploring 2**

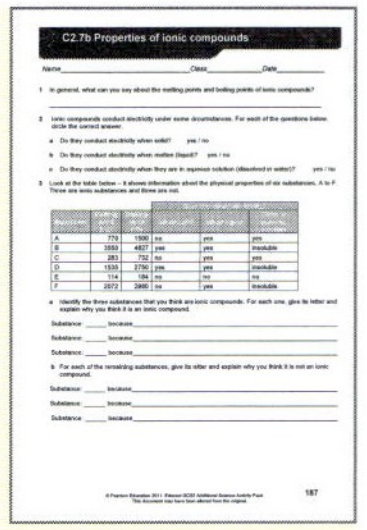

**Worksheet C2.7b** provides questions about identifying ionic compounds from their ability to conduct electricity, and their melting points and boiling points.

**Stretch** Students identify which test on its own allows you to decide whether a substance is ionic or not.

**Support** Ask students to colour in the boxes in the table for substances that conduct when solid, because these cannot be ionic compounds.

### Melting solids

**Explaining 2** Demo

Demonstrate the effect of Bunsen burner heat on different substances. See the Teacher and technician practical sheet C2.7 (2) for full details.

**Stretch** Ask the students to plot a bar chart to illustrate the melting points and boiling points of sodium chloride and magnesium oxide.

**Support** Remind students that the boiling point of a substance will always be higher than its melting point.

### Conducting electricity

**Plenary 2**

Revisit the votes from *Starter 2*. Have any of the students' views changed? If so, in what way and why?

### (H) Ionic compounds

**Homework 2**

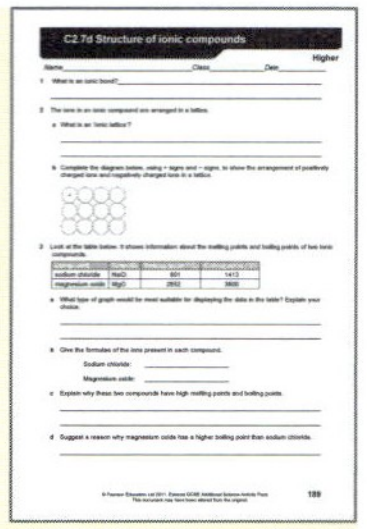

**Worksheet C2.7d** for Higher Tier students covers the ionic lattice and ionic bonding, and explaining the physical properties of ionic compounds.

**Stretch** Ask the students to complete the 'extra challenge' question.

# C2.7 Properties of ionic compounds

What are ionic compounds like?

Some modern bathroom scales do not just show your mass, they also show how much body fat you have. They pass a small electric current through your body. This flows through fat with difficulty but more easily through body fluids containing dissolved salts, so the proportion of body fat can be estimated.

**A** *Body-fat scales measure how easily electricity flows through the body.*

1 What is an aqueous solution?

2 Sodium chloride is soluble in water, but magnesium oxide is insoluble in water. Under what conditions will:
a sodium chloride conduct electricity
b magnesium oxide conduct electricity?

Sodium chloride, magnesium oxide and other ionic substances do not conduct electricity when they are solid. However, they do conduct electricity when they are **molten** (heated until they turn into a liquid). This is why aluminium can be extracted from molten aluminium oxide by **electrolysis**. Ionic substances also conduct electricity when they are in **aqueous solution** (dissolved in water) – this is why sea water will conduct electricity.

**ResultsPlus Watch Out!**

Many students lose marks in exams by simply stating that ionic compounds can conduct electricity. You need to remember the conditions under which they will conduct electricity and that the ions will have to move.

H

Two conditions must be met for a substance to conduct electricity. It must contain charged particles *and* these particles must be free to move. Ionic substances contain charged particles (ions) but these are only free to move from place to place when the ionic compound is molten or in aqueous solution. In the solid form the ions are held in fixed positions, forming a lattice structure in which they can only vibrate.

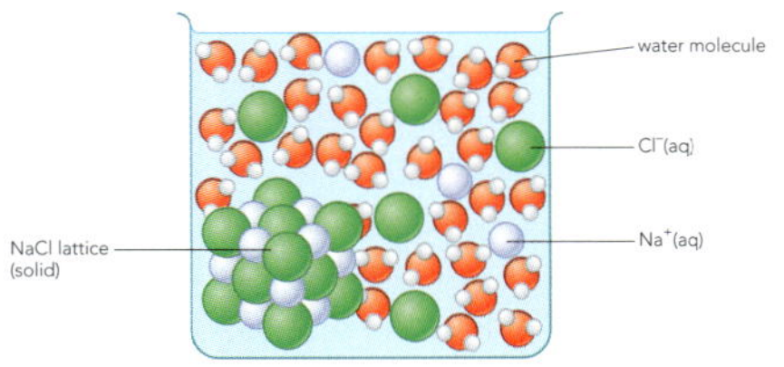


**B** *Ions are free to move in aqueous ionic substances.*

3 Explain the ability of ionic compounds to conduct electricity when:
a molten
b in aqueous solution.

## Melting points and boiling points

The **melting point** of a substance is the temperature at which it changes from a solid to a liquid. Its **boiling point** is the temperature at which it changes from a liquid to gas at its fastest possible rate. Ionic substances have high melting points. They also have high boiling points. This means that they are usually solids at room temperature.

| Ionic substance | Melting point in °C | Boiling point in °C |
|---|---|---|
| sodium chloride, NaCl | 801 | 1413 |
| magnesium oxide, MgO | 2852 | 3600 |

**C** *Sodium chloride and magnesium oxide have high melting and boiling points.*

4 Suggest why magnesium oxide blocks are used to line the inside of blast furnaces, which produce molten iron.

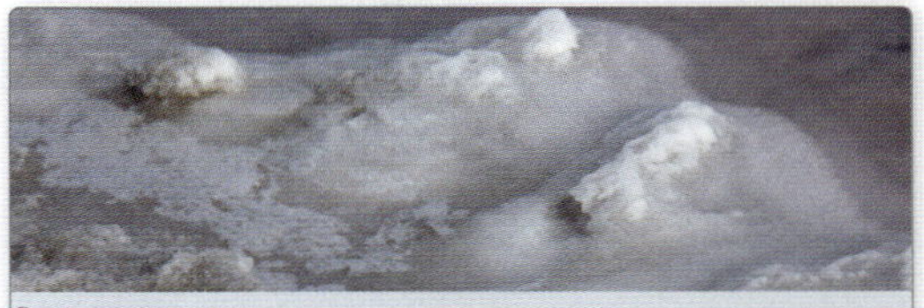

**D** *Molten sodium chloride*

H

Ionic bonds are strong. Energy is needed to break an ionic bond, and there are very many of them in an ionic compound. This is why ionic compounds have high melting points and boiling points.

5 Substance X melts at 1530 °C and conducts electricity when solid. Explain why it is not an ionic compound.

6 Substance Y melts at 373 °C. Describe a simple test you could do to see if it is an ionic compound.

H 7 a Explain why ionic compounds are usually solid at room temperature.
b Using the data on this page, suggest which compound – sodium chloride or magnesium oxide – is likely to have the stronger ionic bonds. Explain your answer.

8 Write bullet-pointed revision notes for the properties of ionic compounds. Include melting points, boiling points and conduction of electricity.

**Skills spotlight**

The use of science and technology can lead to significant benefits. One type of industrial electrical cable, called MICC, contains several copper wires inside a protective copper tube. Magnesium oxide powder, an electrical insulator, is packed between the wires.

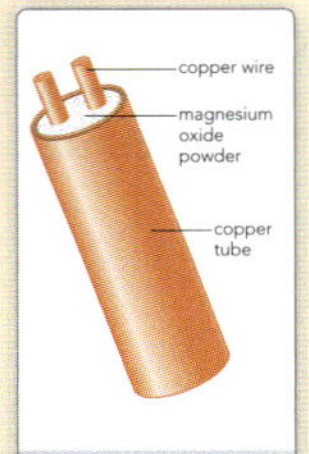


**E** *Cross-section through a MICC cable*

Suggest an advantage of this type of industrial cable over ordinary plastic-coated cable in the event of a fire.

**Learning Outcomes**

2.8 Describe H and explain the properties of ionic substances including sodium chloride and magnesium oxide, limited to:
a melting points and boiling points b their ability to conduct electricity as solids, when molten and in aqueous solution

HSW 12 Describe the benefits, drawbacks and risks of using new scientific and technological developments



Is aspirin soluble? 

## ActiveTeach

- **AT** *All about ionic compounds* [interactive]
  Ionic compounds/bonding – matching activity

## Answers | Student Book

1 A substance dissolved in water.

2 a When molten or in aqueous solution.
b When molten.

3 a The structure changes from a lattice to separate ions, which are free to move.
b Dissolving in water enables the ions to break away from their fixed positions in a lattice and move around.

4 MgO has a very high melting point.

5 It is not an ionic compound as it conducts electricity when solid and ionic compounds only conduct electricity when molten or, if soluble, in aqueous solution.

6 See if it conducts electricity when solid (it should not), then melt or dissolve it and see if it conducts electricity (it should).

7 H a Answer should include the idea that they have high melting points and boiling points because their ions are attracted to each other by strong ionic bonds.

H b A good answer should include the following points.
- magnesium oxide is likely to have stronger ionic bonds.
- this is because magnesium oxide has a higher melting point than sodium chloride.
- magnesium and oxide ions each have two charges, sodium and chloride ions each only have one charge.

8 They conduct electricity when molten or in aqueous solution but not when solid. They have high melting points and boiling points.

**Skills spotlight**

It is acting as an electrical insulator, because it is an ionic compound and these do not conduct electricity when they are solid. Magnesium oxide has a very high melting point, so it is less likely to melt in a fire, keeping the wires inside apart.

# C2.8 Solubility



This lesson introduces some simple rules about the solubility of ionic compounds, and introduces precipitation reactions.

## Specification coverage

***2.9*** Recall the general rules which describe the solubility of common types of substances in water: a) all common sodium, potassium and ammonium salts are soluble b) all nitrates are soluble c) common chlorides are soluble except those of silver and lead d) common sulfates are soluble except those of lead, barium and calcium e) common carbonates and hydroxides are insoluble except those of sodium, potassium and ammonium

***2.10*** Demonstrate an understanding that insoluble salts can be formed as precipitates by the reaction of suitable reagents in solution

HSW ***10*** Using both qualitative and quantitative approaches.

## Key terms

balanced equation
dissolves
insoluble
precipitate
precipitation reaction
salt
solubility
soluble
state symbol

### S words

**Starter 1** Lit

Divide the class into four groups. Give each group a sheet of paper headed with one of the words 'soluble', 'solution', 'solute' or 'solvent'. Each group writes their definition for that word, and then passes the sheet to the next group. Each group feeds back to the rest of the class for any remaining misunderstandings to be identified and dealt with.

### A solubility experiment

**Exploring 1** Prac

Students investigate the relative solubility of lead halides. See **Worksheet C2.8a** and the Teacher and technician practical sheet C2.8 (1) for full details.

**Stretch** Ask students to consider reasons why an ionic substance may be soluble rather than insoluble.

**Support** Consider pairing less practically able students with more practically able ones.

### Student Book spread C2.8

**Explaining 1**

The Student Book describes the use of the solubility rules to explain why precipitation reactions happen in the context of the formation of a precipitate of lead iodide.

**Stretch** Higher Tier students must be able to use state symbols.

**Support** Explain the ways in which the word 'precipitate' can be used.

### Solubility map

**Plenary 1** Lit

Ask students to draw a concept map of the ideas from the lesson, with the word 'solubility' at the centre.

### Solubility problems

**Homework 1**

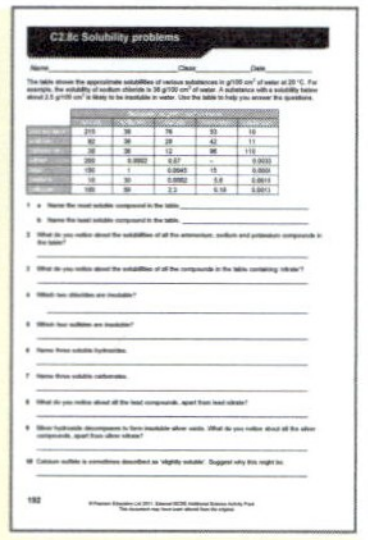

**Worksheet C2.8c**, for Foundation tier students, involves some simple data handling related to the solubility rules.

**Support** Students needing further support may leave out questions **8**, **9** and **10**.

### Solubility

**Starter 2**

Ask students to outline an experiment to find out whether a substance is soluble or insoluble. What apparatus would they need, and how could they tell if a substance had dissolved? Give a couple of minutes to think about this, and then ask selected students to draw a flow chart on the board, with each student adding a further step.

### Soluble or insoluble

**Exploring 2**

**Worksheet C2.8b** provides questions that require the use of simple solubility rules.

**Stretch** Ask the students to explain why school chemistry investigations often use sodium or potassium salts, or nitrates.

**Support** Ask students to identify all the substances that contain sodium, potassium, ammonium or nitrate in their name.

### Precipitates from acids

**Explaining 2** Demo

Demonstrate the formation of silver chloride from hydrochloric acid and barium sulfate from sulfuric acid. See the Teacher and technician practical sheet C2.8 (2) for full details.

**Stretch** Ask students to write balanced symbol equations, including state symbols, for the reactions seen.

**Support** Ask students to explain how they know that silver chloride, silver sulfate and barium sulfate are insoluble in water.

### Testing rules

**Plenary 2** AfL

Students take it in turns to ask each other whether a substance should be soluble or not. Each uses the solubility rules to devise a question for the other to answer. Afterwards, they feed their experience of this back to the class. How easy was it to devise questions? How easy was it to answer them? Did they need to use the table in the Student Book?

### H More solubility problems

**Homework 2**

**Worksheet C2.8d** for Higher Tier students, involves data handling related to the solubility rules.

**Stretch** Ask students to complete the 'extra challenge' question.

# C2.8 Solubility

Is it possible to predict whether a salt will be soluble or insoluble?

Aspirin, acetylsalicylic acid, is a household medicine used to ease pain. Aspirin tablets are not very soluble. They have to be swallowed with a glass of water and it takes time to be absorbed by the stomach. To get around these problems, medicine manufacturers have made aspirin into various soluble substances. These are absorbed much faster, providing quicker relief from pain.

**A** *Some aspirin medicines dissolve better than others.*

1 What is the difference between a substance that is soluble in water and one that is insoluble?

If a substance **dissolves** well in a particular liquid, we say that it is **soluble**. If a substance does not dissolve at all in a particular liquid, we say that it is **insoluble**. A **salt** is a substance that can be made by reacting an acid with an alkali. Figure C shows some rules for identifying which salts are soluble in water and which are not.

**B** *Fertilisers contain soluble salts that plants can absorb through their roots.*

| Soluble in water | Insoluble in water |
|---|---|
| all common sodium, potassium and ammonium salts | |
| all nitrates | |
| most chlorides | silver chloride, lead chloride |
| most sulfates | lead sulfate, barium sulfate, calcium sulfate |
| sodium carbonate, potassium carbonate, ammonium carbonate | most carbonates |
| sodium hydroxide, potassium hydroxide, ammonium hydroxide | most hydroxides |

**C** *Some soluble and insoluble salts*

2 Which substances in this list are soluble in water and which are insoluble in water? Sodium chloride, lead nitrate, calcium sulfate, potassium hydroxide, silver chloride, calcium carbonate, ammonium carbonate.

## Precipitates

Lead nitrate and potassium iodide are salts that are soluble in water. Their solutions react together to produce lead iodide and potassium nitrate. Lead iodide is insoluble in water. It appears as a yellow **precipitate**, made up of particles of lead iodide suspended in the liquid. Here are the equations for the reaction:

lead nitrate + potassium iodide → lead iodide + potassium nitrate

$Pb(NO_3)_2(aq) + 2KI(aq) \rightarrow PbI_2(s) + 2KNO_3(aq)$

Notice how the equation is correctly balanced using numbers in front of KI and $KNO_3$. The **state symbols** show that all the substances are dissolved in water, apart from lead iodide, which is insoluble and so is present as a solid.

A reaction in which an insoluble solid is produced from two soluble substances is called a **precipitation reaction**. It happens if the reactants are soluble and at least one of the products is insoluble but not if all the products are soluble.

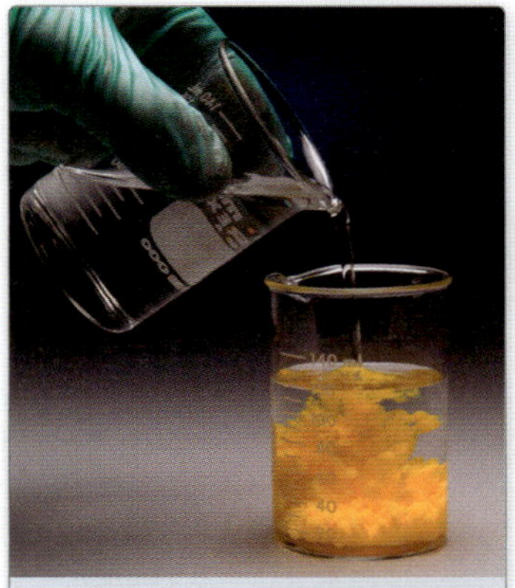

**D** *Lead iodide forms a yellow precipitate.*

**ResultsPlus Watch Out!**

The word precipitate can be used to describe a chemical formed in a precipitation reaction as well as what it does. It can precipitate to the bottom of the beaker. As in 'The yellow precipitate of lead iodide forms and precipitates to the bottom of the beaker.'

3 What is a precipitate?

4 How can you tell from the equation on page 132 that lead iodide forms a precipitate?

5 Explain why lead chloride could form a precipitate but potassium chloride could not.

6 Potassium sulfate $K_2SO_4$ and barium nitrate $Ba(NO_3)_2$ are soluble in water. They react to form potassium nitrate $KNO_3$ solution and insoluble barium sulfate $BaSO_4$.
a Write a word equation for the reaction.
b Write a balanced equation for the reaction and include the state symbols.

7 A school laboratory technician has been asked to make solutions containing a chloride, a nitrate, a carbonate, a sulfate, a hydroxide and a silver salt. Suggest, with reasons, suitable substances that the technician could use.

**Skills spotlight**

Scientists may communicate their work in a quantitative way – which involves numbers. They may also communicate their work in a qualitative way – which involves giving observations without the use of numbers. Give one example from this spread of a quantitative description and one example of a qualitative description.

**Learning Outcomes**

**2.9** Recall the general rules which describe the solubility of common types of substances in water: *a* all common sodium, potassium and ammonium salts are soluble *b* all nitrates are soluble *c* common chlorides are soluble except those of silver and lead *d* common sulfates are soluble except those of lead, barium and calcium *e* common carbonates and hydroxides are insoluble except those of sodium, potassium and ammonium

**2.10** Demonstrate an understanding that insoluble salts can be formed as precipitates by the reaction of suitable reagents in solution

HSW **10** Use qualitative and quantitative approaches when presenting scientific ideas and arguments, and recording observations



How do rock climbers stop their hands getting sweaty on a cliff face? 

## ActiveTeach

- **AT** *Soluble or insoluble?* [interactive]
  Solubility of salts in water – true-or-false quiz

## Answers | Student Book

1 A soluble substance will dissolve in water but an insoluble one will not.

2 Soluble: sodium chloride, lead nitrate, potassium hydroxide, ammonium carbonate.
Insoluble: calcium sulfate, silver chloride, calcium carbonate.

3 The insoluble solid formed in a precipitation reaction.

4 The letter (s) following the formula

5 Lead chloride is insoluble in water but potassium chloride is soluble.

6 **a** potassium sulfate + barium nitrate → potassium nitrate + barium sulfate

**b** $K_2SO_4(aq) + Ba(NO_3)_2(aq) \rightarrow 2KNO_3(aq) + BaSO_4(s)$

7 Any suitable soluble substances (use Table C to check) with the explanation that these substances have been chosen because they are soluble in water.

**Skills spotlight**

The solubility values for aspirin and its calcium salt (and the balanced equations) are quantitative descriptions. The description of the formation of lead iodide (and the word equations) are qualitative descriptions.

# C2.9 Precipitation



This lesson challenges students to investigate the effect of changing the volume of one reactant in a precipitation reaction. The activity may be run as a practice controlled assessment task or as a straight-forward class practical. The preparation of one sample of magnesium carbonate should take about 30 minutes but this does not include drying time.

## Specification coverage

***2.11*** Demonstrate an understanding of the method needed to prepare a pure, dry sample of an insoluble salt

***2.12*** Prepare an insoluble salt by precipitation

***0.2*** Represent chemical reactions by word equations and simple balanced equations

***0.3*** Write balanced chemical equations including the use of state symbols (s), (l), (g) and (aq)

This lesson provides opportunities to cover HSW *1*, HSW *5*, HSW *6*, HSW *7*, HSW *8*, HSW *10* and HSW *11*.

## Before the lesson

If you intend to use this activity as a practice controlled assessment task, you should ensure that students are familiar with any equipment they may be expected to use so that they can plan their own investigation. In the week or two before the task show them this equipment and, if appropriate, allow them to practice using it. Students should be familiar with the use of a balance to measure and record masses. They should also be familiar with the use of measuring cylinders, filter paper and filter funnels. It may be good preparation to show students one or more of Skills sheets 19 to 26 to show what is expected of them in their actual controlled assessment task.

## Starter

Show the names of some ionic compounds. Students work in pairs to decide which compounds are soluble in water, and which are insoluble. Suitable soluble compounds are sodium chloride, sodium carbonate, ammonium carbonate, magnesium sulfate, magnesium nitrate, silver nitrate. Suitable insoluble compounds are magnesium carbonate, silver chloride, calcium sulfate, magnesium hydroxide. Lead on to the idea that certain combinations of soluble compounds will produce a precipitate, and that this is a useful way to make insoluble compounds.

Follow this by reading the additional information below the opening section of page 134 of the Student Book. They may then read the brief description of the activity provided by the 'Your task' box.

## Option 1: Straight-forward class practical

Students follow the instructions on **Worksheet C2.9b**. The worksheet lists the apparatus needed and gives instructions for investigating what happens to the yield of magnesium carbonate when the mass of magnesium sulfate is changed. Students must record their observations, and use mass measurements to determine the mass of magnesium carbonate in their sample. The range of data that students need to collect is given on **Worksheet C2.9c**.

You could ask students to come up with one or two further hypotheses, based on their observations in this practical.

## Plenary

On page 135 of the Student Book you will find two examples of the sort of work that students may produce for this task. The examples focus on the overall plan. You could share these with students after they have completed their own work. This will help them to understand the assessment criteria and so make it easier for them to evaluate their work and to see how they can improve it. Moderator comments on each of the Student Book extracts can be found at the end of the assessment guidance for this investigation on the CD-ROM. The examples can also be found on the **AT** document *Student examples*.

## Option 2: Running the activity as a practice controlled assessment task (PCA)

We have provided a full range of support resources to allow the running of this practical as a practice controlled assessment task. A recommended structure is outlined below (to be used over a number of sessions). Marking guidance for all three parts of the practice task can be found on the CD-ROM that accompanies the TTPP. To save time when using these practice controlled assessment tasks, you may wish to focus on a particular aspect or skill rather than working through all three parts of the task.

### Part A Planning

1. Students should be given the Student brief on **Worksheet C2.9a**. They can use Part A of the Workbook that is provided to help pupils with their practice controlled assessments. They should be given about 1 hour to do this planning.

### Part B Observations

2. Students should be asked to carry out the practical task to collect evidence using the method they have planned in Part A. They should refer to the Student brief on **Worksheet C2.9a**. They can use Part B of the Workbook that is provided to help pupils with their practice controlled assessments. They should be given about 30 minutes to collect their primary evidence.
3. If there is a problem with their own planned method, students may be asked to follow the method set out on **Worksheet C2.9b**. This will still enable students to access the full range of marks for Part B and Part C of the practice controlled assessment task.
4. In Part B, students are required to gather some secondary evidence. The evidence can be quantitative or qualitative. It can be from a variety of sources but students must note where they found their evidence and evaluate the quality of the source as part of this task. Skills sheet 22 provides students with further guidance on researching for and evaluating secondary evidence. This part of the task could be done outside of the lesson but must be supervised.

### Part C Conclusions

5. Students follow the instructions set out on the Part C section of the Student brief on **Worksheet C2.9a**. They should use their data from Part B and the secondary evidence they have collected when doing this. They can use Part C of the Workbook that is provided to help pupils with their practice controlled assessments. They should be given about 1 hour to work on their conclusions.

The **AT** includes video clips showing a group of students working through elements of this investigation with teacher support.

# C2.9 Precipitation

How can we make magnesium carbonate using a precipitation reaction?

Rock climbing can be scary, putting you under stress and making you sweat. You do not want sweaty, slippery hands when you are climbing a rock face several hundred metres above the ground. Rock climbers rub 'chalk' into their hands to keep them dry. This is not the sedimentary rock made from calcium carbonate. Instead, it is magnesium carbonate, $MgCO_3$, which is able to absorb water really well. Without it, rock climbing would be even scarier.

**A** *This climber is on a sheer rock face. Magnesium carbonate is 'hygroscopic', which means that it absorbs moisture. This property helps to keep the climber's hands dry, providing more friction between them and the rock.*

Some salts are soluble in water but others are not. For example, all sodium salts are soluble and most sulfates are soluble. Some combinations of soluble salts will react together to form an insoluble salt, the precipitate. For example, silver nitrate and sodium chloride are soluble. Their solutions react together, when mixed, to form a precipitate of silver chloride:

silver nitrate + sodium chloride → silver chloride + sodium nitrate

$AgNO_3(aq) + NaCl(aq) \rightarrow AgCl(s) + NaNO_3(aq)$

Notice how the ions involved appear to have 'swapped places' in this precipitation reaction. Silver ions from the silver nitrate solution combine with chloride ions from the sodium chloride solution to form insoluble silver chloride. This precipitate can then be separated from the unreacted ions in solution by **filtration**, washed on the filter paper, then dried in a warm oven.

**Your task**

You are going to plan an investigation to test how the amount of magnesium carbonate formed in a precipitation reaction changes when one of the substrates is varied. Your teacher will provide you with some materials to help you organise this task.

**Learning Outcomes**

*2.11 Demonstrate an understanding of the method needed to prepare a pure, dry sample of an insoluble salt*

*2.12 Prepare an insoluble salt by precipitation*

## ResultsPlus Build Better Answers

When planning an investigation like this, you will be assessed on your *overall plan*. There are 4 marks available for this skill. Here are two extracts that focus on this skill. Other skills that you need for the assessment are dealt with in other lessons.

**Student extract 1 — A basic response for this skill**

*I am going to add 25 cm³ of sodium carbonate solution to a beaker and then add 10 cm³ of magnesium sulfate solution. This will form magnesium carbonate, which is insoluble. I will record the mass of a piece of filter paper and then use the filter paper to filter the magnesium carbonate out of the solution. I will wash the paper and residue with water and then dry it in a warm oven. I will then measure the mass of the filter paper and the dry magnesium carbonate. I will then do this experiment again with different volumes of magnesium nitrate solution.*

This is a good start because the student has given clear instructions on how they are planning to carry out the practical.

However, they will not be able to access all the marks because they do not explain the range of other volumes they are planning to test.

**Student extract 2 — A good response for this skill**

*… I will try it again with 10 cm³, 15 cm³, 20 cm³ and 25 cm³ of the magnesium sulfate solution. I have chosen this range because it will allow me to work out if less or the same amount of each solution is needed to get the maximum amount of precipitate. I think that by carrying out this investigation I will be able to test my hypothesis that the amount of magnesium carbonate formed depends on the volume of magnesium sulfate used.*

Here, the student continues from the end of the extract above.

The method explains how the hypothesis will be tested.

The student has stated the range of tests they are going to carry out.

The student has also explained why this range has been chosen.

**ResultsPlus**

**To access 2 marks**

- Provide a logically ordered method that will produce results
- Choose a range of data or observations that will test the hypothesis

**To access 4 marks**

You also need to:

- Explain how your method will test the hypothesis
- Explain why you have chosen your range of data or observations



How did people make copies of engineering drawings before the photocopier was invented?



## ActiveTeach

- **AT** *C2.9 Precipitation [interactive]*
  *Investigating precipitation*
- **AT** *C2.9 Assessment criteria* [presentation]
  Understanding the CA marking criteria
- **AT** *C2.9 Specification points* [word document]
  Edexcel specification points
- **AT** *C2.9 Student examples* [word document]
  Examples for students to assess

## Key terms

filtration

## Assessment criteria

### Overall plan

**0** No relevant method given.

**1-2 a)** Produces a method that is ordered in a logical way and would produce results that can later be analysed. The method covers all the main points needed, such as: measure 25 cm³ of sodium carbonate and 10 cm³ of magnesium sulfate plus 15 cm³ of water; mix these together and stir; filter to separate the precipitate; wash the precipitate on the filter paper; dry the precipitate in a warm oven; determine the mass of magnesium carbonate obtained. Repeat with other volumes of magnesium sulfate.

**b)** Range of data/observations chosen that would test the hypothesis, e.g. gives three or four different volumes of magnesium sulfate.

**3-4 a)** The method also includes an explanation as to why it would test the hypothesis, e.g. 'I think that by carrying out this investigation I will be able to test my hypothesis that the mass of magnesium carbonate formed is dependent on the volume of magnesium sulfate solution used.'

**b)** Range of data/observations chosen that would test the hypothesis and an explanation of why the range was chosen, e.g. 'I will then do this experiment again with 10 cm³, 15 cm³, 20 cm³ and 25 cm³ of the magnesium sulfate solution. I have chosen this range because using this range of volumes will allow me to work out if less or the same amount of each solution is needed to get the maximum mass of precipitate.'

# C2.10 Precipitates



This lesson investigates the formation of precipitates in more detail, with barium sulfate as an example of a precipitate with a medical application.

## Specification coverage

***2.13*** Use solubility rules to predict whether a precipitate is formed when named solutions are mixed together and to name the precipitate

***2.14*** Recall that the insoluble salt, barium sulfate, is given as a 'barium meal' to X-ray patients because: a) it is opaque to X-rays b) it is safe to use as, although barium salts are toxic, its insolubility prevents it entering the blood

***0.2*** Represent chemical reactions by word equations and simple balanced equations

***0.3*** Write balanced equations including the use of state symbols (s), (l), (g) and (aq) for a wide range of reactions in this unit

**HSW** ***10*** Using both qualitative and quantitative approaches.

## Key terms

barium meal
toxic

### Solubility rules

**Starter 1**

Ask students to work in pairs and write down the solubility rules they can remember. They share these in groups to add and amend the rules as necessary. Groups feed one of their rules back, passing if they have already been used. Build the list on the board, amending or discarding any incorrect rules.

### Making an insoluble salt

**Exploring 1** **Prac**

Students prepare silver chloride from silver nitrate and sodium chloride. See **Worksheet C2.10a** and the Teacher and technician practical sheet C2.10 (1) for full details.

**Stretch** Ask students to write the balanced symbol equation for the precipitation reaction.

**Support** Consider pairing less practically able students with more practically able ones.

### Student Book spread C2.10

**Explaining 1**

The Student Book describes the formation of precipitates from suitable mixtures of soluble salts. Two examples are given – lead iodide (the subject of the practical) and copper(II) hydroxide.

**Stretch** Ask students to predict the precipitate formed by some mixtures.

**Support** Show how the ions from each soluble salt 'swap' to form two products, one of which is insoluble and so forms a precipitate.

### Naming precipitates

**Plenary 1**

Give students the names of some soluble compounds – e.g. sodium chloride, potassium sulfate, lead nitrate, silver nitrate. Ask students to identify pairs of solutions that could produce precipitates, and to name the precipitates formed.

### Predicting precipitates

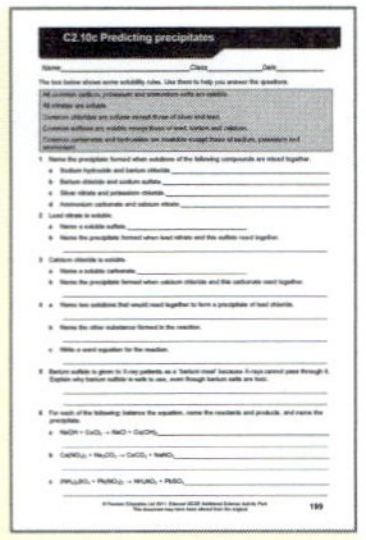

**Homework 1**

**Worksheet C2.10c**, for Foundation tier students, covers the key features of solubility and forming precipitates.

### Soluble or not?

**Starter 2**

Show the students the solubility rules from the Student Book spread C2.8. Provide a range of names for the students to decide if the substance is soluble or not – e.g. sodium chloride, lead chloride, calcium carbonate etc.

### Precipitation reactions

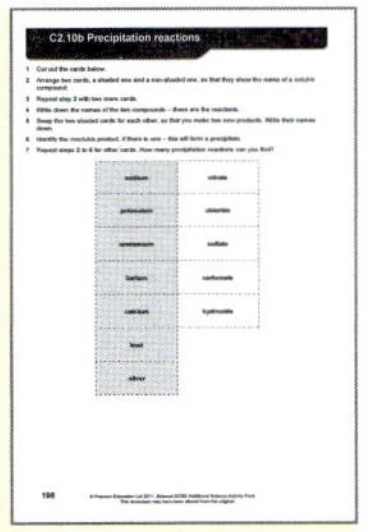

**Exploring 2**

Students use the cards from **Worksheet C2.10b** to identify pairs of solutions that would produce a precipitate.

**Stretch** Ask students to write balanced symbol equations for the precipitation reactions they devise.

**Support** Reduce the number of cards used – e.g. remove 'potassium' and 'ammonium'.

### Barium meals

**Explaining 2** **Demo**

Demonstrate how barium ions in solution can pass through Visking tubing, as a model for why an insoluble barium salt is needed for barium meals. See the Teacher and technician practical sheet C2.10 (2) for full details.

**Stretch** Ask students to work out another mixture that would produce barium sulfate.

**Support** Emphasise that it is the barium ions that are toxic, not the sulfate ions or chloride ions.

### A barium meal

**Plenary 2** **Lit**

Ask students to produce a concept map for the barium meal. It should include the reasons for giving one to a patient, the reasons why barium is important, and for choosing barium sulfate rather than another barium salt, and how barium sulfate can be made.

### H Predicting precipitates

**Homework 2**

**Worksheet C2.10d** for Higher Tier students, covers the key features of solubility and forming precipitates.

**Stretch** Ask the students to complete the 'extra challenge' question.

# C2.10 Precipitates

Can we predict if a precipitate will form in a chemical reaction?

Before the photocopier was invented in the 1930s, diagrams were copied by blueprinting. Paper was treated with a mixture of two soluble iron salts. The original diagram, on tracing paper, was laid on top and left in sunlight. A blue precipitate formed in the lit areas, leaving white lines on a blue background.

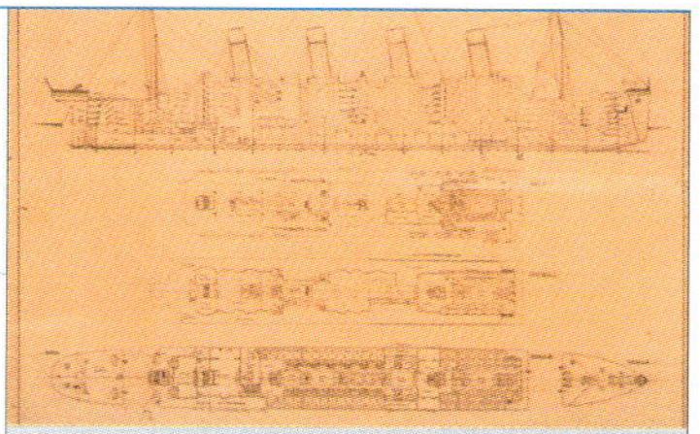

**A** *Blueprint of the RMS Titanic.*

**B** *Copper hydroxide forms a pale blue precipitate.*

It is possible to work out which substances are needed to make a particular precipitate, and also to work out what precipitate will form when two solutions are mixed together.

Consider the precipitation reaction studied on the previous page:

| lead nitrate | + | potassium iodide | → | lead iodide | + | potassium nitrate |
|---|---|---|---|---|---|---|
| (soluble) | + | (soluble) | → | (insoluble) | + | (soluble) |

The ions from the soluble salts have swapped:
- lead iodide forms when lead ions and iodide ions meet
- potassium nitrate forms when potassium ions and nitrate ions meet.

All nitrates are soluble, so potassium nitrate does not form a precipitate. However, most lead salts are insoluble, so lead iodide forms a precipitate. Figure C on page 132 helps you to predict the formation of a precipitate when two named solutions are mixed together – for example, when solutions of copper chloride and potassium hydroxide are mixed:

| copper chloride | + | potassium hydroxide | → | copper hydroxide | + | potassium chloride |
|---|---|---|---|---|---|---|
| $CuCl_2$ | + | 2KOH | → | $Cu(OH)_2$ | + | 2KCl (soluble) |

All common potassium salts and most chlorides are soluble. So potassium chloride does not form a precipitate. Most hydroxides are insoluble according to Figure C on page 132, so copper hydroxide is likely to form a precipitate.

1 Copy the balanced equation and add the correct state symbols.

2 A precipitation reaction occurs when calcium chloride solution and potassium sulfate solution are mixed together.
a Write a word equation for the reaction.
b Using Figure C on page 132, predict which of the two products will form a precipitate.

## Barium meals

Barium sulfate is given to patients to help in diagnosing problems with their intestines. Like bone, barium sulfate is opaque to X-rays, which means that X-rays do not pass through it and are absorbed. The patient swallows a drink, called a **barium meal**, which contains barium sulfate. X-ray photographs are then taken as the barium sulfate passes through the patient's digestive system. The barium sulfate shows up as white on X-ray photographs.

Barium sulfate is used for barium meals but most barium salts are **toxic**. However, barium sulfate is insoluble and this prevents it from entering the blood. This makes it safe to swallow.

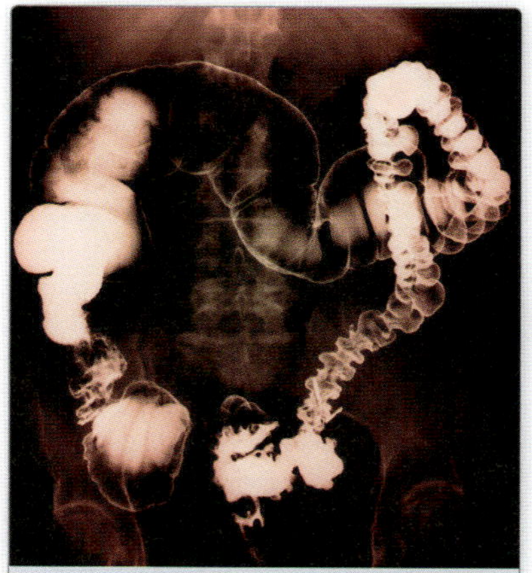

**C** *Barium sulfate shows up as white on X-ray photographs of the digestive system.*

3 Barium chloride $BaCl_2$ and ammonium sulfate $(NH_4)_2SO_4$ react together in a precipitation reaction, forming barium sulfate $BaSO_4$ and ammonium chloride $NH_4Cl$.
a Write a word equation for this reaction.
b Write a balanced equation for the reaction and include state symbols.

**ResultsPlus Watch Out!**

It is useful to remember that to make an insoluble salt XY, mixing X nitrate solution and sodium Y solution will always work.

4 A precipitation reaction occurs when silver nitrate solution and sodium chloride solution are mixed together.
a Write a word equation for the reaction.
b Using Figure C on page 132, predict which of the two products will form a precipitate.

5 Lead carbonate is insoluble. Identify two pairs of solutions that would each make lead carbonate, giving reasons for your choices. Write a word equation for each reaction.

**Skills spotlight**

It is important that scientists test their ideas. Explain how it is possible to predict whether or not a precipitate will form when two solutions are mixed, and describe how you would test this hypothesis.

**Learning Outcomes**

2.13 Use solubility rules to predict whether a precipitate is formed when named solutions are mixed together and to name the precipitate.

2.14 Recall that the insoluble salt, barium sulfate, is given as a 'barium meal' to X-ray patients because
a it is opaque to X-rays b it is safe to use as, although barium salts are toxic, its insolubility prevents it entering the blood

HSW 5 Plan to test a scientific idea, answer a scientific question or solve a scientific problem



What produces a blue-green flame when it is burned?



## Answers | Student Book

1 $CuCl_2$ (aq) + 2KOH (aq) → $Cu(OH)_2$ (s) + 2KCl (aq)

2 a calcium chloride + potassium sulfate → calcium sulfate + potassium chloride
b Calcium sulfate

3 a barium chloride + ammonium sulfate → barium sulfate + ammonium chloride
b $BaCl_2(aq) + (NH_4)_2SO_4(aq) \rightarrow BaSO_4(s) + 2NH_4Cl(aq)$

4 a silver nitrate + sodium chloride → silver chloride + sodium nitrate
b Silver chloride

5 Suitable soluble lead salt, e.g. lead nitrate. Suitable soluble carbonate, e.g. sodium, potassium or ammonium. Suitable word equation to match, e.g. lead nitrate + sodium carbonate → lead carbonate + sodium nitrate.

**Skills spotlight**

Each solution consists of metal ions and non-metal ions dissolved in water. When the two solutions are mixed the ions mix with each other and they can form different combinations. Write down all the different combinations of the metals and non-metals in the salts. Two of these will be the solutions you originally mix, the other two will be possible combinations that will form in the mixture. Use the solubility rules to determine if either of these new combinations is insoluble. If so, a precipitate will form. The prediction can be tested by mixing the solutions and seeing whether or not a precipitate does form.

# C2.11 Ion tests

This lesson introduces the use of flame tests to identify metal ions, and precipitation reactions to identify anions. The role of spectroscopy in the discovery of new elements is examined.

## Specification coverage

***2.15*** Describe tests to show the following ions are present in solids or solutions: a) $Na^+$, $K^+$, $Ca^{2+}$, $Cu^{2+}$ using flame tests b) $CO_3^{2-}$ using dilute acid and identifying the carbon dioxide evolved c) $SO_4^{2-}$ using dilute hydrochloric acid and barium chloride solution d) $Cl^-$ using dilute nitric acid and silver nitrate solution

***2.16*** Recall that chemists use spectroscopy (a type of flame test) to detect the presence of very small amounts of elements and that this led to the discovery of new elements, including rubidium and caesium

**HSW** *2* The interpretation of data, using creative thought, to provide evidence for testing ideas *and developing theories.*

## Key terms

flame test
spectroscopy

### Using precipitates

**Starter 1**

Remind students that silver nitrate and barium nitrate are soluble, but silver chloride and barium sulfate are insoluble. What sort of substances would produce precipitates with silver nitrate and barium nitrate? How could these reactions be useful? Elicit the idea that they could be used to test for chloride and sulfate ions.

### Flame tests

C2.11a Flame tests

**Exploring 1** **Prac**

Students carry out flame tests and identify the metal ions present in 'unknown' test solutions. See **Worksheet C2.11a** and the Teacher and technician practical sheet C2.11 (1) for full details.

**Stretch** Provide additional 'unknown' solutions for students to test, chosen from the known solutions but labelled as 'unknown R' etc.

**Support** Restrict the number of solutions tested to the known ones.

### Student Book spread C2.11

**Explaining 1**

The Student Book describes the use of flame tests to identify metal ions, and also the use of spectroscopy to discover new elements. It also describes the tests for chloride, sulfate and carbonate ions.

**Stretch** Ask students to suggest why flame test colours might be difficult to interpret.

**Support** Explain that there is no pattern to the colours produced by different metals, so they need not try to look for one.

### Ion tests

**Plenary 1** **AfL** **Lit**

Ask each student to devise a multiple-choice question, based on one or more of the chemical tests, with four choices. In groups, each student reads out their question with the four answers, and the other students write down the answer they think is correct. Each student then reads out their correct answer, and the others mark their answers.

### Finding new elements

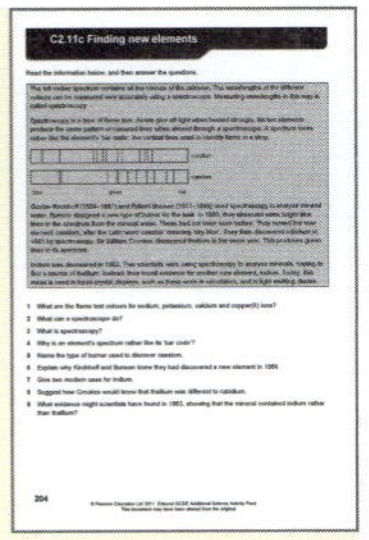
C2.11c Finding new elements

**Homework 1**

**Worksheet C2.11c**, for Foundation tier students, includes a comprehension exercise in which students answer questions about the use of spectroscopy.

**Support** Cover questions **8** and **9** before photocopying.

### Fireworks

**Starter 2**

Show a video clip of fireworks. Ask students why fireworks have different coloured flames. What substances might they contain that produce these?

### Anion tests

C2.11b Anion tests

**Exploring 2** **Prac**

See **Worksheet C2.11b** and the Teacher and technician practical sheet C2.11 (2) for full details.

**Stretch** Provide additional 'unknown' solutions for students to test, chosen from the known solutions but labelled as 'unknown R' etc.

**Support** Consider pairing less practically able students with more practically able ones.

### Making a spectrum

**Explaining 2** **Demo**

Demonstrate how a prism splits the colours present in white light into a spectrum to help illustrate what a spectroscope does. See the Teacher and technician practical sheet C2.11 (3) for full details.

**Stretch** Ask students to suggest why a simple spectroscope might include a low-power microscope to view the spectrum.

**Support** Explain that a flame test only produces light of certain wavelengths.

### Fireworks

**Plenary 2** **Lit**

Ask students to write down a colour sequence for a firework – e.g. green, red, orange, lilac. Their partner has to identify the metals needed in the correct order – e.g. copper, calcium, sodium, potassium. The game can be simplified using fewer colours or made more difficult using a longer sequence.

### Testing crystals

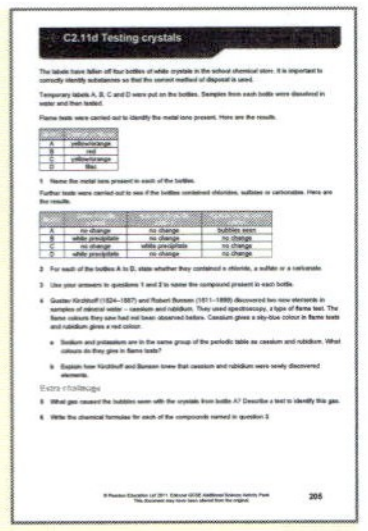
C2.11d Testing crystals

**Homework 2**

**Worksheet C2.11d**, for Higher Tier students, tests understanding of the tests used in the lesson, and the use of spectroscopy in discovering new elements.

**Stretch** Ask the students to complete the 'extra challenge' questions.

# C2.11 Ion tests

How do scientists identify the ions in a substance?

Different metals produce different colours when they are put in a hot flame (see Figure A). This is the basis of atomic absorption spectroscopy, used to identify the elements in samples of water.

A

1 Describe how to test a substance for the presence of sodium ions.

2 Explain why Bunsen and Kirchhoff concluded from their experiments that caesium and rubidium were two different elements.

**Flame tests** are carried out on samples of ionic substances. The most intense colours are obtained from solids, but flame tests also work when the solids are dissolved in water.

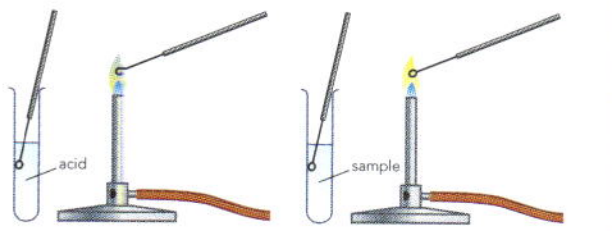


Step 1: Dip the flame test loop in acid, then hold the loop at the edge of the Bunsen burner flame.

Step 2: If the flame changes colour, repeat Step 1 until the loop is clean.

Step 3: Dip the clean flame test loop in the sample, then hold the loop at the edge of the Bunsen burner flame. Observe and record the flame colour.

Step 4: Repeat Steps 1–3 with each sample.

**B** *How to carry out a flame test.*

| Metal ion | | Flame test colour |
|---|---|---|
| sodium | $Na^+$ | yellow |
| potassium | $K^+$ | lilac |
| calcium | $Ca^{2+}$ | red |
| copper(II) | $Cu^{2+}$ | green-blue |

**C** *Flame test colours produced by four different metal ions.*

**D** *The flame test for caesium*

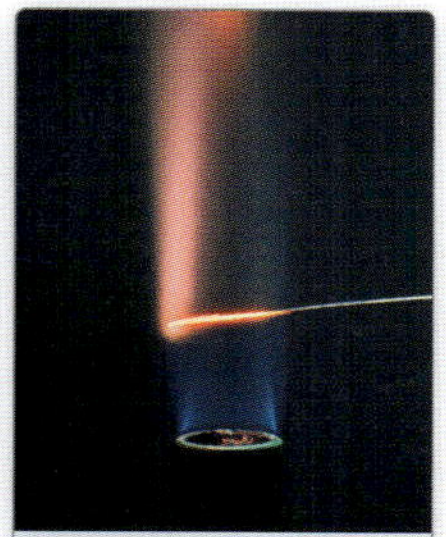
**E** *The flame test for rubidium*

Flame tests have led to the discovery of new elements. In 1860, Robert Bunsen (1811–1899) and Gustav Kirchhoff (1824–1887) used simple **spectroscopy** to study the light given off in flame tests by some samples of mineral water. They used a prism to separate the colours in the light into a spectrum and saw a grey-blue colour that had not been seen before. They realised that they had discovered a new element, which they called caesium, after the Latin word for sky-blue. A year later using the same technique they discovered another new element. They named it rubidium, after the Latin word for dark red.

## Precipitation tests

Certain anions can be identified by precipitation tests. To identify aqueous chloride ions, $Cl^-(aq)$, a few drops of dilute nitric acid are added to the sample solution, which is then shaken. A few drops of silver nitrate solution are then added. A white precipitate of silver chloride forms if the sample contains chloride ions.

To identify aqueous sulfate ions, $SO_4^{2-}(aq)$, a few drops of dilute hydrochloric acid are added to the sample solution, which is then shaken. A few drops of barium chloride solution are then added. A white precipitate of barium sulfate forms if the sample contains sulfate ions.

## Test for carbonate ions

Carbon dioxide is given off when an acid is added to a substance containing carbonate ions, $CO_3^{2-}$. Limewater is used to confirm the identity of the gas. Limewater turns milky when carbon dioxide is bubbled through it.

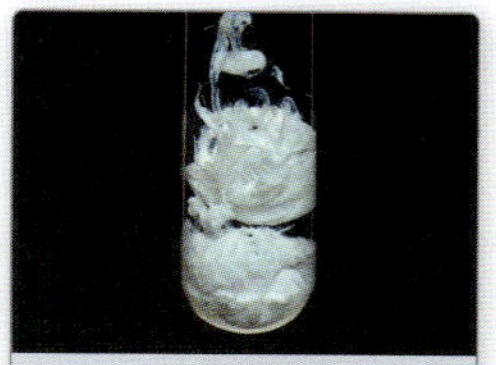
**F** *Silver chloride precipitates in the test for $Cl^-$.*

**G** *Barium sulfate forms a white precipitate in the test for $SO_4^{2-}$*

### Skills spotlight

In 1861, Sir William Crookes examined some factory waste material using the method devised by Bunsen and Kirchhoff. He observed a green colour that had not been recorded before. Crookes named the newly discovered element thallium. Thallium was isolated by Claude-Auguste Lamy in 1862. Suggest why Crookes thought he had discovered a new element and why Lamy's work was important to him.

3 Hydrochloric acid contains chloride ions. Explain why hydrochloric acid cannot be used instead of nitric acid in the silver nitrate test.

4 Sulfuric acid contains sulfate ions. Explain why sulfuric acid cannot be used instead of hydrochloric acid in the barium chloride test.

5 A white solid produces a lilac flame in a flame test. It also produces a white precipitate when tested with barium chloride solution but not when tested with silver nitrate solution.
a Name the metal cation present.
b Name the anion present.
c Give the name of the white solid.

6 A light green solid produces a green-blue flame in a flame test. It also produces a white precipitate when tested with silver nitrate solution but not when tested with barium chloride solution. Give the name and formula of the light green solid.

7 Describe how the laboratory tests described here could be used to distinguish between sodium chloride, potassium chloride, calcium sulfate and sodium carbonate.

### ResultsPlus Watch Out!

Take care not to confuse the acids needed for precipitation tests. *Nitric* acid goes with silver *nitrate*, and hydro*chloric* acid goes with barium *chloride*.

### Learning Outcomes

2.15 Describe tests to show the following ions are present in solids or solutions: **a** $Na^+$, $K^+$, $Ca^{2+}$, $Cu^{2+}$ using flame tests **b** $CO_3^{2-}$ using dilute acid and identifying the carbon dioxide evolved **c** $SO_4^{2-}$ using dilute hydrochloric acid and barium chloride solution **d** $Cl^-$ using dilute nitric acid and silver nitrate solution

2.16 Recall that chemists use spectroscopy to detect the presence of very small amounts of elements and that this led to the discovery of new elements, including rubidium and caesium.

HSW 2 Describe how data is used by scientists to provide evidence that increases our scientific understanding





## ActiveTeach

- **AT** *Making fireworks* [BBC video] Inside a fireworks factory
- **AT** *Flame tests for metal ions* [interactive] Flame tests – matching activity

## Answers | Student Book

1 Carry out a flame test and look to see if the flame turned yellow/orange.

2 Flame tests gave two different colours.

3 Hydrochloric acid would also produce a white precipitate of silver chloride, so you could not tell if the sample really contained chloride ions.

4 Sulfuric acid would also produce a white precipitate of barium sulfate, so you could not tell if the sample really contained sulfate ions.

5 **a** potassium **b** sulfate **c** potassium sulfate

6 Copper(II) chloride, $CuCl_2$

7 A good answer will include the following points.
- Carry out flame tests on all the substances. The substance that produces: a yellow flame will be sodium chloride or sodium carbonate; a lilac flame will be potassium chloride; a red flame will be calcium sulfate.
- Test the two sodium compounds by adding an acid. If a gas is given off, bubble it through limewater. If it turns milky the gas is carbon dioxide and the salt was a carbonate. This will be sodium carbonate.
- Add a few drops of dilute nitric acid to the other sodium compound and shake and a few drops of silver nitrate solution. If this sodium compound is a chloride, a white precipitate of silver chloride will form.

**Skills spotlight**

Crookes knew that different metals produced different coloured flames in flame tests. The green lines in the spectrum had not been seen before. They must have been produced by an unknown element. Lamy's isolation of thallium a year later showed that Crookes was correct.

# C2.12 Covalent bonds



This lesson introduces the idea of covalent bonding as the sharing of electron pairs.

## Specification coverage

***3.1*** Describe a covalent bond as a pair of electrons shared between two atoms

***3.2*** Recall that covalent bonding results in the formation of molecules

***3.3*** Explain the formation of simple molecular, covalent substances using dot and cross diagrams, including:

a) hydrogen b) hydrogen chloride c) water d) methane H e) oxygen f) carbon dioxide

**HSW** ***11*** Presenting information, developing an argument and drawing a conclusion, using scientific, technical and mathematical language, conventions and symbols and ICT tools

There are also opportunities to cover **HSW** ***3***.

## Key terms

atom
covalent bond
dot and cross diagram
double bond
molecule

### Electronic configuration recall

**Starter 1**

Give students a list of elements and their atomic numbers, and ask them to sketch the electron configuration of each atom. The atoms most relevant for this lesson are hydrogen, carbon, oxygen and chlorine.

### Ionic bonding recall (AT)

**Starter 2**

Show students drawings of electronic configurations of pairs of atoms, and ask them how the two atoms would react to form a compound. Start with metal/non-metal combinations and progress to two non-metals. The **AT** presentation *Electronic configurations* can be used for this.

### Working out the formulae (AT)

**Exploring 1**

Using pairs of non-metal elements and their atomic numbers, students work out how the two elements would share electrons to form a covalent molecule. The **AT** presentation *Covalent molecules* can be used to lead a class discussion at the end.

H **Stretch** Remind students of the formulae of ethene and propene and ask them to work out their dot and cross diagrams.

**Support** Students use the **AT** presentation *Covalent molecules* to help them to work out their molecules.

### Modelling molecules

**Exploring 2**

Students use molecular modelling kits to build models of the covalent molecules required by the specification and compare these to dot and cross diagrams.

H **Stretch** Challenge students to work out how electrons are shared and make models using the kit.

**Support** Explain that the 'bonds' in the modelling kit represent pairs of shared electrons.

### Covalent and ionic bonding

**Exploring 3**

**Worksheet C2.12a** provides a set of statements describing covalent and ionic bonding. Students will find this easier if they have done *Starter 2*.

**Stretch** Students write their own list of similarities and differences between ionic and covalent bonding before giving them the cards to sort.

**Support** Remind students what happens in ionic bonding if *Starter 2* has not been used.

### Student Book spread C2.12

**Explaining 1**

Illustrate the idea of a covalent bond by asking students to imagine two toddlers who both want the same toy and will not let go of it – they will be 'bonded' together because they are both holding onto the toy.

**Stretch** Ask students to explain why helium, neon and argon do not exist as molecules.

**Support** Build up dot and cross diagrams on the board, showing the separate atoms.

### Sentence starters

**Plenary 1** AfL Lit

Give students a set of sentences for them to complete in their own words. Suitable starters include: 'Hydrogen atoms join up to form molecules …', 'A covalent bond forms …', 'The formula for methane is $CH_4$ …',

H 'Oxygen and carbon dioxide molecules …'.

### Writing questions

**Plenary 2** AfL Lit

Give students sets of answers to which they have to write the questions. The answers can be the key words from this lesson, formulae of molecules or some simple dot and cross diagrams.

### Covalent molecules

**Homework 1**

**Worksheet C2.12b**, for students working at a lower level, provides questions about the content of this lesson.

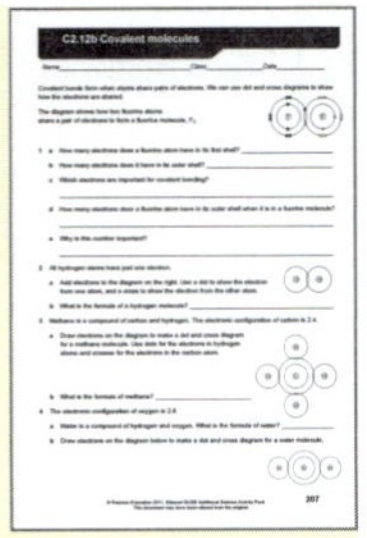

**Support** Look at a dot and cross diagram with students, and ensure they understand that a blank diagram shows the nucleus of the atom and circles for the electron shells.

### Covalent bonding

**Homework 2**

**Worksheet C2.12c**, for students working at a higher level, provides questions about the content of this lesson. This sheet contains some questions from Higher Tier material.

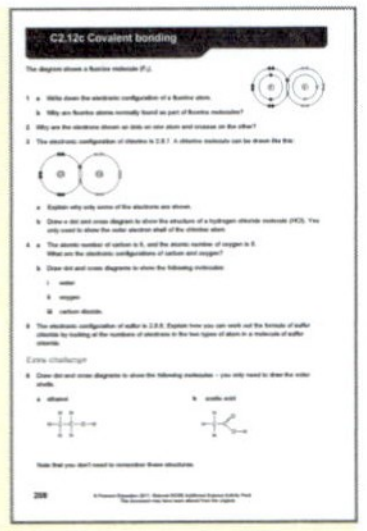

**Stretch** Students answer the 'extra challenge' question.

# C2.12 Covalent bonds

How are atoms of non-metals held together?

Theobromine is one of the molecules in chocolate that makes it taste good. Now you can buy necklaces that show a model of a theobromine molecule. The straight parts of the model show the links between atoms.

A Jewellery inspired by chocolate.

There are many different kinds of molecule in your body, and most of the atoms making up these molecules are non-metal atoms. Most non-metal compounds are held together by pairs of electrons, which form **covalent bonds**. The electrons used in these bonds come from the outermost electron shells of the atoms.

Covalent bonds can form between atoms of the same element. For example, in hydrogen gas two hydrogen **atoms** form one hydrogen **molecule**. Each atom contributes one electron to the covalent bond, allowing both atoms to have full outermost electron shells (remember that the first shell can only have two electrons in it – see page 125).

Figure B is a **dot and cross diagram** showing a hydrogen molecule. Dots and crosses are used to represent the electrons so that you can see which atom each electron is from. There is no difference between the electrons from different atoms.

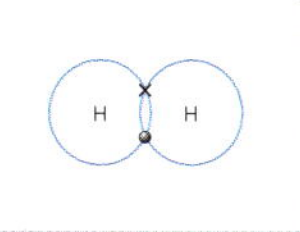

B A dot and cross diagram of a hydrogen molecule ($H_2$)

Covalent bonds also form between atoms of different non-metal elements because all these elements are short of having a full outermost shell of electrons. Figure C shows three other covalent molecules.

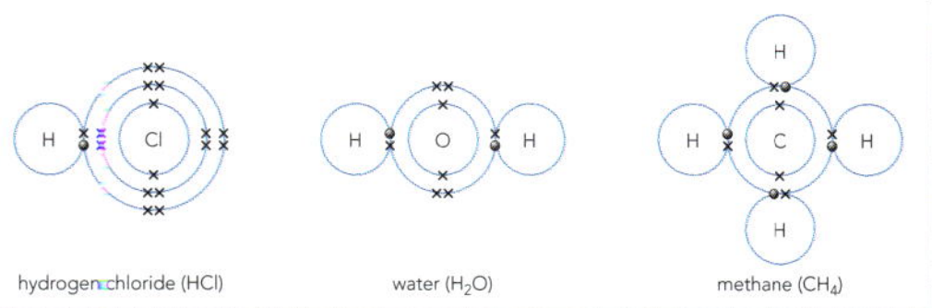


C Dot and cross diagrams of HCl, $H_2O$ and $CH_4$ molecules

**ResultsPlus Watch Out!**

Many students lose marks in an exam by just writing about bonds. Remember when your answer is bond it should always be two words: ionic bond or covalent bond.

1 a How many electrons does a hydrogen atom have?
b How many electrons does hydrogen need to have a full outermost shell?

2 a What is a covalent bond?
b Why do non-metal atoms form covalent bonds?

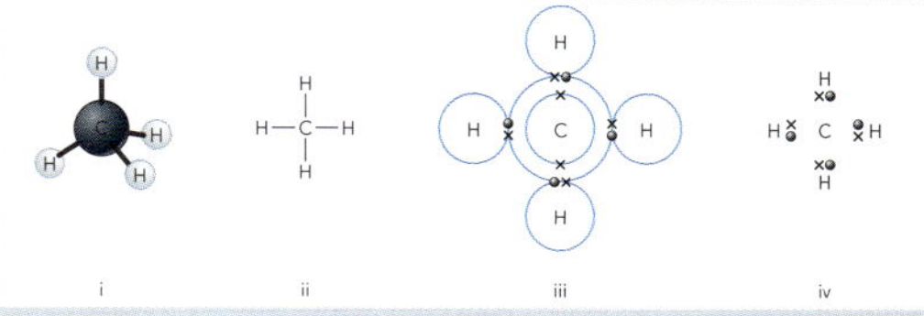

D Different ways of representing the covalent bonds in methane ($CH_4$)

**Skills spotlight**

Scientists use different conventions to represent molecules. Figure D shows some different ways of representing the bonds in a molecule of methane. What are the advantages and disadvantages of each type of drawing?

Atoms can share more than one pair of electrons if this is needed for each atom to have a full outermost shell. Two pairs of shared electrons form a **double bond**.

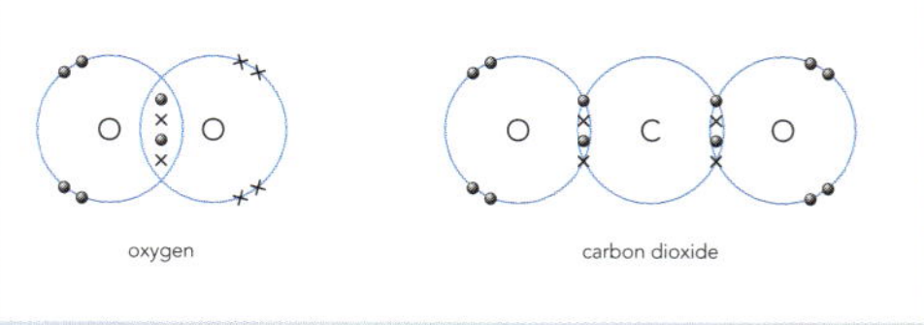


E Oxygen and carbon dioxide molecules contain double bonds.

3 Look at Figure F and compare it to part iii of Figure D. Suggest why the diagram does not need to show the first electron shell in the carbon atom.

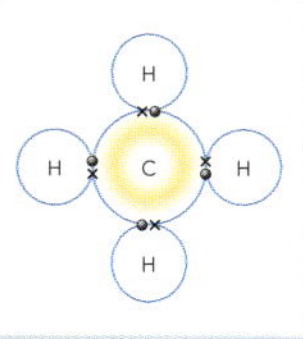

F Dot and cross diagram of methane without the innermost electron shell of the carbon atom.

4 The electronic configuration of carbon is 2.4. How does this tell you that carbon atoms need to share four electrons with other atoms to get a full outermost shell?

5 The electronic configuration of oxygen is 2.6. Draw a diagram to help you to explain why one oxygen atom forms covalent bonds with two hydrogen atoms to form a water molecule.

6 Describe what a covalent bond is and why carbon forms covalent bonds with four hydrogen atoms to form a methane molecule.

**Learning Outcomes**

3.1 Describe a covalent bond as a pair of electrons shared between two atoms
3.2 Recall that covalent bonding results in the formation of molecules
3.3 Explain the formation of simple molecular, covalent substances using dot and cross diagrams, including: a hydrogen b hydrogen chloride c water d methane (H) e oxygen f carbon dioxide
HSW 1 Present information using scientific conventions and symbols



Sand and oxygen both contain covalent bonds. Why is one a solid and one a gas?



## ActiveTeach

- **AT** *How many bonds do these atoms make?* [interactive] Covalent bonding – quiz
- **AT** *Electronic configurations* [presentation] How atoms react
- **AT** *Covalent molecules* [presentation] How atoms react

## Answers | Student Book

1 **a** 1 **b** 2
2 **a** When two atoms share a pair of electrons **b** Non-metal atoms all have outer shells that are nearly full.
3 It is only the electrons in the outer shell that are shared in covalent bonds.
4 The second shell is full when it has 8 electrons, so each carbon atom requires 4 more electrons to fill its outer shell.
5 Suitable diagram with explanation, e.g. oxygen needs two more electrons to fill its outer shell. Each hydrogen atom has only one electron, so oxygen needs to share electrons with two separate hydrogen atoms.
6 A good answer will include the following points: a covalent bond forms when atoms share electrons in their outer shells; one pair of shared electrons is a covalent bond; hydrogen atoms need one more electron to have a full outer shell; each hydrogen atom can only form one covalent bond; carbon atoms need four more electrons to have a full outer shell; each carbon atom can therefore form four covalent bonds; one carbon atom is joined to four hydrogen atoms to form a methane molecule, all the atoms involved can have full outer shells by sharing.

**Skills spotlight**

**i Advantages:** shows how the atoms are arranged in space. **Disadvantages:** doesn't tell us anything about the electrons
**ii Advantages:** simple, and shows how the atoms are joined to each other. **Disadvantages:** doesn't tell us anything about the electrons or the real shape of the molecule
**iii Advantages:** shows how the electrons are shared between different atoms, and how the atoms are joined to each other. **Disadvantages:** doesn't tell us how the atoms are arranged in space, and is fiddly to draw
**iv Advantages:** shows how the electrons are shared between different atoms, and how the atoms are joined to each other, is simple to draw. **Disadvantages:** doesn't tell us about the electrons in the inner shells or how the atoms are arranged in space.

# C2.13 Properties of covalent substances



This lesson looks at the differences between simple and giant molecular covalent compounds.

## Specification coverage

***3.5*** Describe the properties of typical simple molecular, covalent compounds, limited to: a) low melting points and boiling points, in terms of weak forces between molecules b) poor conduction of electricity

***3.6*** Demonstrate an understanding of the differences between the properties of simple molecular, covalent substances and those of giant molecular, covalent substances, including diamond and graphite

***3.7*** (H) Explain why, although they are both forms of carbon and giant molecular substances, graphite is used to make electrodes and as a lubricant, whereas diamond is used in cutting tools

HSW *3* Many phenomena can be explained by developing and using scientific theories, models and ideas.

## Key terms

diamond
giant molecular covalent substances
graphite
lubricant
simple molecular covalent substances

### Changes of state (AT)

**Starter 1**

**Worksheet C2.13a** and the **AT** document *More changes of state* provides a set of cards with the names of various substances and their melting and boiling points. Ask students to put up their hands if their substance is a gas at that temperature, and ask them to explain their decision. Continue by asking for solids or liquids at various temperatures.

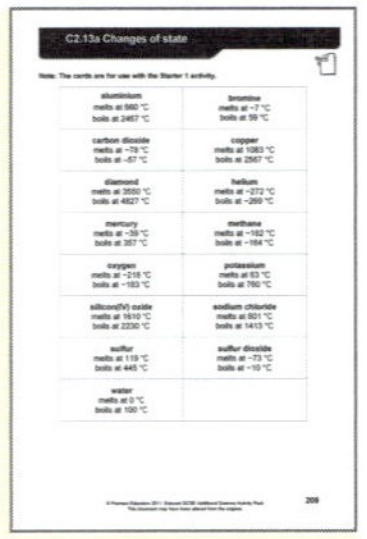

### Models and explanations (AT)

**Exploring 1** Prac

Students build models of giant molecular structures and some simple molecules, and use these to help to explain the different properties. See the Teacher and technician practical sheet C2.13 (1) for full details.

**Stretch** Ask students to build a model of silicon(IV) oxide (see simplified diagram on the **AT** presentation *Silicon(IV) oxide*).

**Support** Have a small part of each model ready-built for students to add to.

### Properties of covalent substances

**Exploring 3** Prac

Students sort the cards on **Worksheet C2.13c.** The cards marked * apply to Higher Tier only. See the Teacher and technician practical sheet C2.13 (2) for full details.

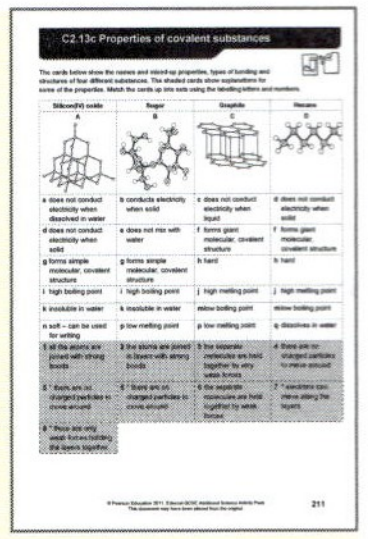

**Stretch** Remove the shaded cards, and ask students to write their own explanations of the properties of the different substances.

**Support** Remind students of the type of bonding in each substance.

### Sentence starters

**Plenary 1** AfL Lit

Ask students to write down the beginnings of three sentences about the content of this lesson, and then to swap these to see if a partner can complete them. Once this has been done, ask some students to read out their completed sentences and ask the rest of the class to say whether or not they are correct, or if they could be improved.

### Properties of carbon and its compounds

**Homework 1**

**Worksheet C2.13d** for students working at a lower level looks at the properties of methane, diamond and graphite.

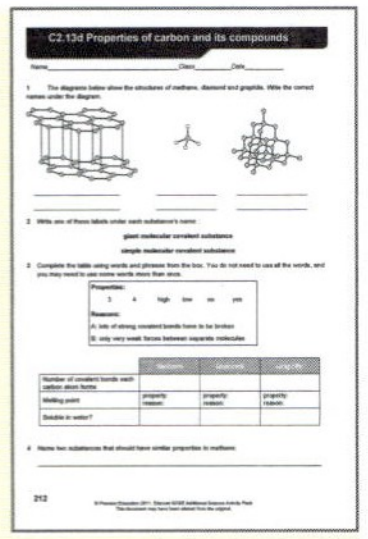

**Support** Remind students of the differences in the properties of diamond, graphite and molecular substances.

### Describing materials

**Starter 2** Lit

Show the students a range of different materials with descriptions of their properties, using the words 'hard', 'soft', 'tough', 'brittle' and 'stiff'. Then ask students to write dictionary definitions for the property words.

### Sand all around

**Exploring 2**

**Worksheet C2.13b** looks at some of the properties of quartz, and asks students to relate the prevalence and uses of sand to the properties of silicon(IV) oxide.

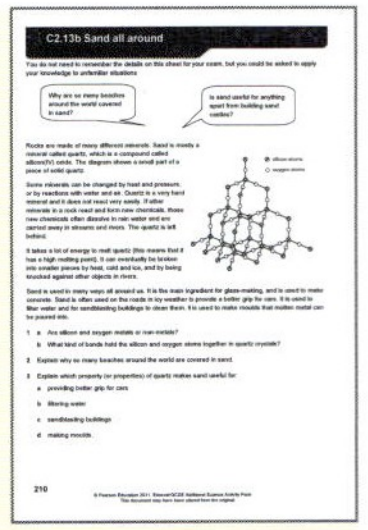

**Stretch** Students produce a short brochure aimed at encouraging people to invest in a new company to mine and sell sand.

**Support** Talk through the questions on the sheet rather than requiring written answers.

### Student Book spread C2.13

**Explaining 1**

For Higher Tier students, note that the delocalised electrons in graphite move mainly along the layers. A lump of graphite will conduct electricity in any direction because it consists of many tiny graphite crystals in different orientations.

**Stretch** Diamond and graphite have slightly different melting points. Ask students to suggest why they both have the same boiling point.

**Support** Make sure that students appreciate the distinction between covalent bonds, and the weak forces between molecules in simple molecular covalent substances.

### Concept maps

**Plenary 2** AfL Lit

Ask students to draw concept maps showing what they know about covalent bonding and the structures and properties of covalently bonded substances.

### Carbon and its compounds

**Homework 2**

**Worksheet C2.13e**, for students working at a higher level, asks students to compare and explain the properties of methane, diamond and graphite. This sheet contains some questions from Higher Tier material.

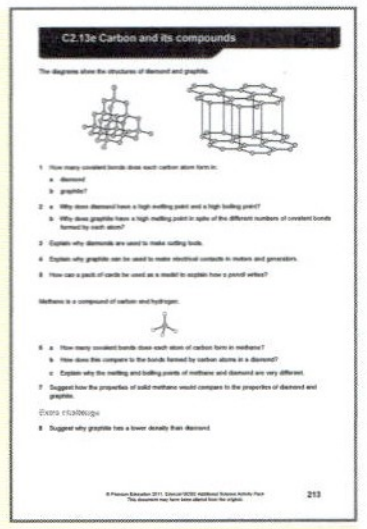

**Stretch** Students answer the 'extra challenge' question.

# C2.13 Properties of covalent substances

What are the properties of covalent substances?

This skull was created by artist Damien Hirst – it is decorated with 221 g of diamonds worth £15 000 000. Diamonds are a form of carbon but the same mass of normal, black-powdered carbon is worth only about £1.

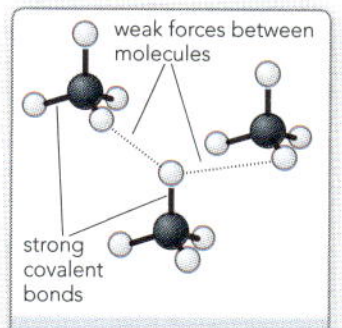


**B** *There are only weak forces between neighbouring molecules of methane.*

1 List three compounds that are simple molecular covalent substances.

2 a Why do most simple molecular covalent substances have low melting and boiling points?
b Why don't they conduct electricity?

3 a Name three giant molecular covalent substances.
b Compare the melting points of these substances to those you named in question 1.
c Explain why the melting points are different.

## Simple molecular covalent substances

**Simple molecular covalent substances** include gases such as hydrogen, methane, oxygen and carbon dioxide, and liquids such as water. These substances have low melting and boiling points because there are only weak forces between neighbouring molecules.

An electric current is a flow of charged particles. The atoms in simple molecular covalent molecules have not lost or gained electrons, so there are no charged particles that can move around. These substances are poor conductors of electricity.

**A** *Damien Hirst created this diamond encrusted skull.*

## Giant molecular covalent substances

Some covalent compounds form **giant molecular covalent substances**. These consist of billions of atoms all joined together by covalent bonds. Most giant molecular substances have high melting and boiling points. This is because all the atoms are joined to other atoms by strong covalent bonds, and a lot of heat energy is needed to break these bonds.

**C** *Diamond will scratch most other substances, and it is used to cut patterns into glass.*

Sand is made of silicon and oxygen atoms joined together in a giant molecular structure. Sand grains are very hard. Carbon can form two different types of giant molecular structure: **diamond** which is very hard and **graphite** which is very soft.



Diamond and graphite have very different properties because of the different ways in which the carbon atoms are arranged. Both have very high melting and boiling points because of the strong covalent bonds between the carbon atoms.

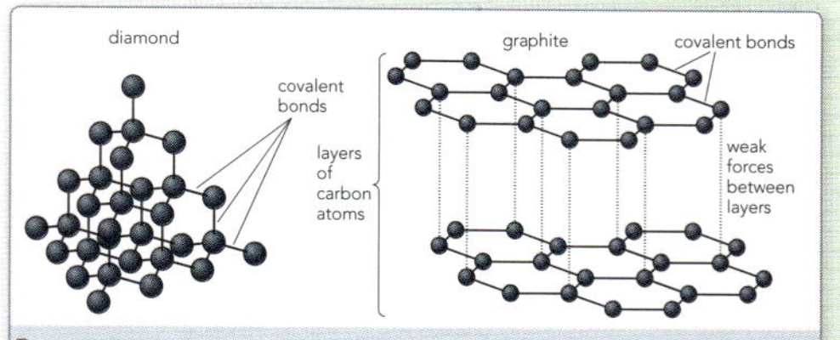


**D** *The structures of diamond and graphite*

There are also differences in the properties.

Diamond:
- is very hard because all the atoms are joined with strong covalent bonds. Diamonds are used to make cutting tools.
- does not conduct electricity because there are no free electrons or charged particles to move around.

Graphite:
- easily rubs away in layers because although the covalent bonds within the layers are very strong, there are only weak forces *between* the layers. It is soft enough to be used as a **lubricant**.
- conducts electricity because there is one electron from each carbon atom that can move along the layers. This means that graphite can be used to make electrodes.

**ResultsPlus Watch Out!**

Simple molecular, covalent substances melt and boil at lower temperatures than giant molecular, covalent ones. Remember that this is because the weak forces *between* the molecules are overcome, not the strong covalent bonds *in* the molecule.

H 4 Why are the substances you named in question 3a usually very hard?

**Skills spotlight**

Scientists often explain observations using models. How does the model for covalent bonding explain why liquid methane will not conduct electricity?

H 5 What property of graphite makes it an unusual giant molecular covalent compound?

H 6 a Explain why diamond is typical of giant molecular covalent substances.
b Explain why graphite is not a typical example.

7 Describe the differences between methane and diamond and H explain the differences in terms of their structures.

**Learning Outcomes**

3.5 Describe the properties of typical simple molecular, covalent compounds, limited to: a low melting points and boiling points, in terms of weak forces between molecules b poor conduction of electricity

3.6 Demonstrate an understanding of the differences between the properties of simple molecular, covalent substances and those of giant molecular, covalent substances, including diamond and graphite

H 3.7 Explain why, although they are both forms of carbon and giant molecular substances, graphite is used to make electrodes and as a lubricant, whereas diamond is used in making cutting tools

HSW 3 Describe how phenomena are explained using scientific models



## ActiveTeach

- **AT** *The diamond makers 1*
  [BBC video]
  A diamond made from peanut butter
- **AT** *The diamond makers 2*
  [BBC video]
  Synthetic diamonds vs natural ones
- **AT** *Forms of carbon*
  [BBC video]
  How diamond and graphite differ
- **AT** *Carbon*
  [video]
  Properties and uses of carbon
- **AT** *All about covalent substances*
  [interactive]
  Covalent substances – matching activity
- **AT** *More changes of state*
  [presentation]
  Melting and boiling points
- **AT** *Silicon(IV) oxide*
  [presentation]
  Diagram of silicon(IV) oxide
- **AT** *The structure of diamond and graphite*
  [diagram]
  Figure D – diagram labelling activity

## Answers | Student Book

1 Any three from hydrogen, methane, oxygen, carbon dioxide, water

2 **a** Weak forces attract the molecules to each other.
**b** No charged particles to move around.

3 **a** sand, diamond, graphite
**b** They are much higher
**c** Giant - all the atoms are joined to each other with strong covalent bonds. Simple - atoms are joined to each other with strong bonds, but there are only weak forces between neighbouring molecules.

4 H Atoms are joined to each other with strong covalent bonds.

5 H It is soft and it conducts electricity.

6 H **a** Diamond is hard, with high melting and boiling points, and does not conduct electricity.w
**b** Graphite is soft and conducts electricity.

7 A good answer will include the following points: methane is a gas at room temperature, whereas diamond is a hard solid with high melting and boiling points; methane consists of individual molecules in which the atoms are joined with strong covalent bonds, but with only weak forces between neighbouring molecules; in simple molecules such as methane, there are only weak attractive forces between neighbouring simple molecules, so the m.p./b.p. are low as not much energy is needed to overcome these forces; H all the atoms in a piece of diamond are joined in one giant 'lattice' with strong covalent bonds. It takes a lot of energy to break the covalent bonds, so diamond has higher melting and boiling points.

**Skills spotlight**

Our model of electricity is of a movement of charged particles. Our model of a covalent substance shows that there are no charged particles which can move, and so liquid methane cannot conduct electricity.

# C2.14 Classifying substances



This lesson challenges students to investigate the properties of several different compounds and from those properties work out what the bonding in the compounds is. The activity may be run as a practice controlled assessment task or as a straight-forward class practical. The practical work can be completed within an hour.

## Specification coverage

**3.4** Classify different types of elements and compounds by investigating their melting points and boiling points, solubility in water and electrical conductivity (as solids and in solution) including sodium chloride, magnesium sulphate, hexane, liquid paraffin, silicon(IV) oxide, copper sulphate, and sucrose (sugar)

This lesson provides opportunities to cover HSW 1, HSW 2, HSW 5, HSW 6, HSW 7, HSW 8, HSW 10 and HSW 11.

### Before the lesson

If you intend to use this activity as a practice controlled assessment task, you should ensure that students are familiar with any equipment they may be expected to use so that they can plan their own investigation. In the week or two before the task show them this equipment and, if appropriate, allow them to practice using it. You may wish to remind students how to set up a series circuit with a bulb or ammeter and a pair of electrodes, and how to use this to determine whether or not a liquid conducts electricity. It may be good preparation to show students one or more of Skills sheets 19 to 26 to show what is expected of them in their actual controlled assessment task.

### Starter

Show students four different piles of white powder and ask them how they would work out which one is flour, sugar, talcum powder and washing powder. Prompt students to suggest the kinds of test they could carry out on the powders (without tasting them) to work out which one is which. Ask them to suggest other substances that can be identified or separated using their properties. Follow this by reading the additional information below the opening section of page 144 of the Student Book. They may then read the brief description of the activity provided by the 'Your task' box.

### Option 1: Straight-forward class practical

Students follow the instructions on **Worksheet C2.14b**. Students are expected to look up some information using secondary sources of information, and to work out for themselves how to test substances for solubility and how to test solutions for conductivity. The range of data that students need to collect is given on **Worksheet C2.14c**, which students will also need. This sheet guides students through recording, considering their results, and evaluating their investigation.

### Plenary

On page 145 of the Student Book you will find two examples of the sort of work that students may produce for this task. The examples focus on evaluating a conclusion. You could share these with students after they have completed their own work. This will help them to understand the assessment criteria and so make it easier for them to evaluate their work and to see how they can improve it. Moderator comments on each of the Student Book extracts can be found at the end of the assessment guidance for this investigation on the CD-ROM. The examples can also be found on the **AT** document *Student examples*.

### Option 2: Running the activity as a practice controlled assessment task (PCA)

We have provided a full range of support resources to allow the running of this practical as a practice controlled assessment task. A recommended structure is outlined below (to be used over a number of sessions). Marking guidance for all three parts of the practice task can be found on the CD-ROM that accompanies the TTPP. To save time when using these practice controlled assessment tasks, you may wish to focus on a particular aspect or skill rather than working through all three parts of the task.

#### Part A Planning

1. Students should be given the Student brief on **Worksheet C2.14a**. This sets out what they need to do and the 'How to attempt the task' section gives further information. They can use Part A of the Workbook that is provided to help pupils with their practice controlled assessments. They should be given about 1 hour to do this planning.

#### Part B Observations

2. Students should be asked to carry out the practical task to collect evidence using the method they have planned in Part A. Once again, they should refer to the Student brief on **Worksheet C2.14a**. They can use Part B of the Workbook that is provided to help pupils with their practice controlled assessments. They should be given about 1 hour to collect their primary evidence.
3. If there is a problem with their own planned method, students may be asked to follow the method set out on **Worksheet C2.14b**. This will still enable students to access the full range of marks for Part B and Part C of the practice controlled assessment task.
4. In Part B, students are required to gather some secondary evidence. The evidence can be quantitative or qualitative. It can be from a variety of sources but students must note where they found their evidence and evaluate the quality of the source as part of this task. Skills sheet 22 provides students with further guidance on researching for and evaluating secondary evidence. This part of the task could be done outside of the lesson but must be supervised.

#### Part C Conclusions

5. Students follow the instructions set out on the Part C section of the Student brief on **Worksheet C2.14a**. They should use their data from Part B and the secondary evidence they have collected when doing this. They can use Part C of the Workbook that is provided to help pupils with their practice controlled assessments. They should be given about 1 hour to work on their conclusions.

The **AT** includes video clips showing a group of students working through elements of this investigation with teacher support.

Practice Controlled Assessment

# C2.14 Classifying substances

How can you use the properties of a substance to work out what kind of bonding it has?

Industrial accidents and spillages can lead to unknown substances escaping into the environment. This can lead to serious problems. Scientists need to test these substances to identify them. Once they know what the substance is, a plan can be made to safely deal with the situation.

Almost all the substances around you consist of atoms joined together by chemical bonds. Substances containing only non-metal elements, or those containing both non-metal and metal atoms, can be joined by ionic or covalent bonds. These different types of bonding give substances different properties.

This also means that you can use the properties of a substance to help you to work out what kind of bonding holds the atoms in the substance together.

**A** *A scientist testing a sample of water.*

**Your task**

You are going to plan an investigation that will allow you to classify different types of compounds by investigating some of their properties. You will be given the following substances: sodium chloride, magnesium sulfate, hexane, liquid paraffin, silicon dioxide, copper sulfate, and sucrose (sugar). Your teacher will provide you with some other materials to help you organise this task.

**Learning Outcomes**

*3.4 Classify different types of elements and compounds by investigating their melting points and boiling points, solubility in water and electrical conductivity (as solids and in solution) including sodium chloride, magnesium sulfate, hexane, liquid paraffin, silicon dioxide, copper sulfate, and sucrose (sugar)*

**ResultsPlus**
**Build Better Answers**

When planning an investigation like this, one of the skills you will be assessed on is your ability to *evaluate your conclusion*. There are 4 marks available for this skill. Here are two extracts focusing on this skill. Other skills that you need for the assessment are dealt with in other lessons.

**Student extract 1** — **A basic response for this skill**

My conclusion is good because it is correct for the few substances I tested. I could make my conclusion better by testing some more substances.

- The small number of substances tested is a weakness, not a strength.
- The student needs to say *why* they think the conclusion is correct.
- The student comments on how the conclusion could be strengthened.

**Student extract 2** — **A good response for this skill**

The 'rules' I worked out for identifying the type of bonding work for all the substances I tested. However there may be other substances that do not fit these 'rules', so my conclusion may not be true for all substances. The results I gathered did fit with the scientific knowledge I have about how the bonding in a molecule affects it's properties. I should test a greater range of substances, and I could find out if there are any other physical properties I could use to help me to work out the type of bonding.

- The student has pointed out a limitation in their conclusion.
- They have suggested how to extend the investigation.
- For higher marks it is important to evaluate your conclusion using scientific knowledge as well as other evidence.

**ResultsPlus**

**To access 2 marks**
- Evaluate how well all your evidence supports your conclusion
- Suggest how your evidence can be improved to strengthen your conclusion

**To access 4 marks**
You also need to:
- Evaluate how well other scientific ideas support your conclusion
- Suggest how the investigation could be extended to support your conclusion

144 ›››››››››››››››››››››› What happens to the oil when there is an oil spill at sea? 145

## ActiveTeach

**AT** *C2.14 Classifying substances* [video]
Students work through the investigation
- **AT** *C2.14 PCA Moderator comments* [word document]
Moderator comments on the video
- **AT** *C2.14 Assessment criteria* [presentation]
Understanding the CA marking criteria
- **AT** *C2.14 PCA Student task sheet* [word document]
CA video checklist
- **AT** *C2.14 Specification points* [word document]
Edexcel specification points
- **AT** *C2.14 Student examples* [word document]
Examples for students to assess

## Assessment criteria

### Evaluation of conclusion

**0** No relevant evaluation is made.

**1-2** **a)** Notes strengths or weaknesses in the conclusion based on both the primary data and secondary evidence, such as 'My conclusion is only based on the substances I tested, so it may not be true for all substances'.

**b)** Makes suggestions about how the conclusion could be supported more by the primary data and the secondary evidence, such as 'My conclusion would have been supported more if I had tested a wider range of substances'.

**3-4** **a)** Conclusion is evaluated based on all collected evidence and relevant scientific ideas, e.g. 'I think that my conclusion is valid for the substances I tested, but it may not be valid for other substances as there may be exceptions to the "rules" I have found'.

**b)** Suggests how all collected evidence can be improved and extended to provide stronger support for the conclusion. Suggests testing a wider range of substances, and finding out if there are any other physical properties that can be measured to help identify the type of bonding in a substance.

# C2.15 Miscible or immiscible?



This lesson covers the differences between miscible and immiscible liquids. The lesson also includes techniques for separating miscible liquids using fractional distillation, and immiscible liquids using a separating funnel.

## Specification coverage

**3.8** Describe the separation of two immiscible liquids using a separating funnel

**3.9** Describe the separation of mixtures of miscible liquids by fractional distillation, by referring to the fractional distillation of liquid air to produce nitrogen and oxygen

HSW **5** Planning to test a *scientific idea, answer a scientific question* or solve a scientific problem.

## Key terms

dissolve
fraction
fractionating column
fractional distillation
immiscible
liquefy
miscible
separating funnel
solution

### Miscible or immiscible?

**Starter 1**

Place some ethanol and water in one bottle and some oil (any type, for example vegetable oil) and water in another. Shake the bottles and ask the students to suggest any differences between the two mixtures. Also ask which they think is easier to separate.

### Fractional distillation of air

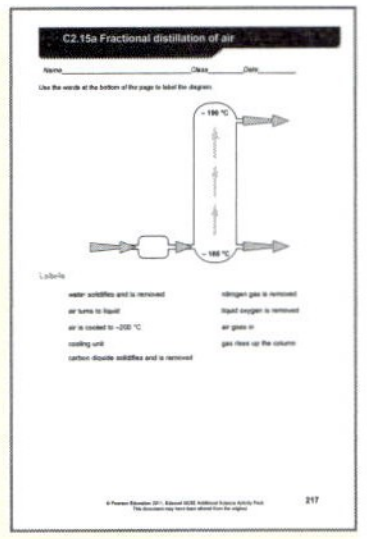

**Exploring 1**

**Worksheet C2.15a** reinforces understanding about how fractional distillation is used to separate the gases in air.

**Stretch** Just give the students the diagram and ask them to add their own explanatory labels.

**Support** Project a copy of the diagram and ask the students to complete the labels on their copy of the diagram.

### Fractional distillation

**Explaining 2** Demo

See the Teacher and technician practical sheet C2.15 (2) for full details.

**Stretch** Explain that due to the temperature gradient in the fractionating column, both the ethanol and the water boil, but the vapour gets richer in the more volatile component (ethanol) as it rises up the column. Water has the higher boiling temperature so it condenses as it moves up the column.

**Support** Remind students about the differences between simple distillation and fractional distillation methods.

### Dealing with an oil spill

**Plenary 1**

Ask students to come up with a series of action points for dealing with a spill of oil at sea. They need to separate the oil from the water and to collect the oil. They also need to clean any birds covered in oil. Tell them that a team of scientific experts will assess their plans, so they need to use scientific language.

### Separating mixtures

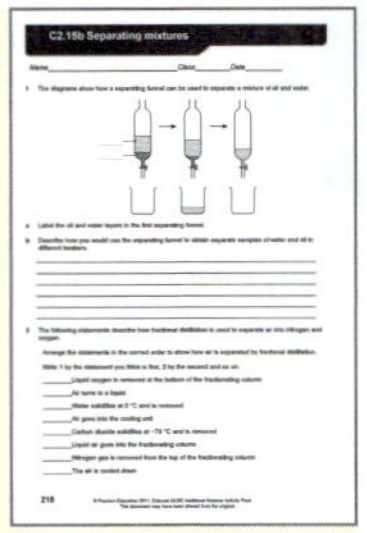

**Homework 1**

**Worksheet C2.15b**, for students needing support, details how a separating funnel works and sequencing phrases to explain how air is separated by fractional distillation.

**Support** Photocopy the worksheet giving students the first two statements in question **2**.

### Oil spills at sea

**Starter 2**

Discuss the problems of oil leaks and show a video clip of an oil leak. Alternatively use newspaper cuttings of an oil disaster or the photograph of the oiled sea bird in the Student Book page 146.

Explain that oil floats on water because it is less dense and because the liquids are immiscible.

### Miscible and immiscible liquids

**Explaining 1** Demo

See the Teacher and technician practical sheet C2.15 (1) for full details. Show the students how water and ethanol mix completely to form a solution, but water and vegetable oil are immiscible.

**Stretch** Use the idea of intermolecular forces to explain why some things are miscible and some are not.

**Support** Students could separate their own mixtures of vegetable oil and water.

### Student Book spread C2.15 (AT)

**Explaining 3**

Explain how air can be separated into oxygen and nitrogen using fractional distillation. Refer to Figure E in the Student Book.

**Stretch** Explain that one way of cooling the air is to allow it to expand from high pressure to low pressure, when heat will be absorbed.

**Support** The **AT** presentation *Boiling points of gases* shows a temperature scale with temperatures from zero downwards and marks the highest and lowest temperature.

### Key facts

**Plenary 2** AfL Lit

Ask students to share three facts learnt in the lesson in groups and to compile a master list, including the most common fact learnt and the least common fact. Select a spokesperson for one group at random to share their ideas with the class. Then ask if other groups had the same most common fact.

### Separating liquids

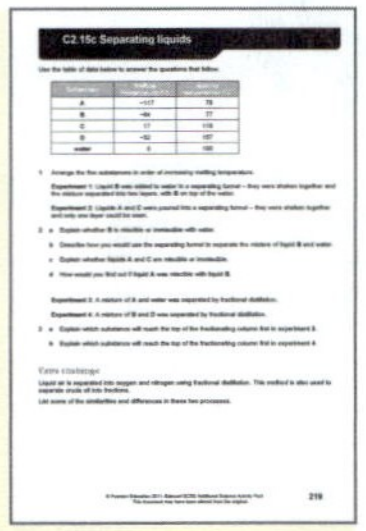

**Homework 2**

**Worksheet C2.15c**, for more able students, involves interpreting data about separating mixtures of liquids.

**Stretch** Ask students to do the 'extra challenge' question on the sheet.

# C2.15 Miscible or immiscible?

How do you separate mixtures of liquids?

This bird has been covered in oil from an oil spill. The oil won't dissolve in water and it stops the bird from flying. The oil needs to be removed from the feathers to save the bird's life.

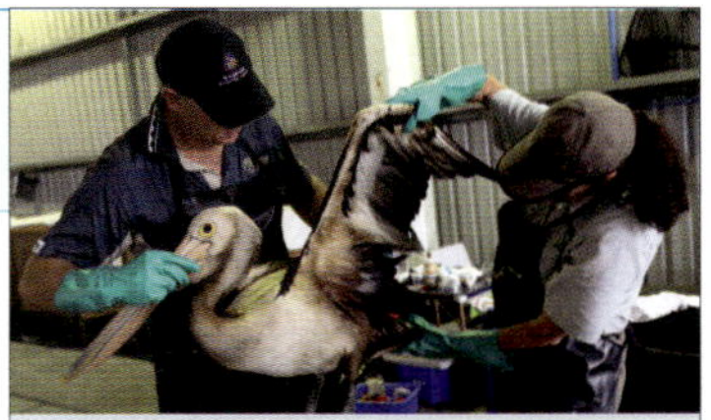

**A** *One of hundreds of oiled birds being cleaned following the Deepwater Horizon oil rig explosion in 2010.*

## Immiscible liquids

Oils do not dissolve in water but form a separate layer floating on top. Liquids that do not mix completely with each other are **immiscible**. When you shake up immiscible liquids they seem to mix but soon separate out again.

Immiscible liquids can be separated using a **separating funnel**. When you open the tap, the lower liquid runs out of the funnel and can be collected in a beaker. You then close the tap before the other liquid starts to run out. Put another beaker under the funnel then open the tap to allow the upper liquid to be collected.

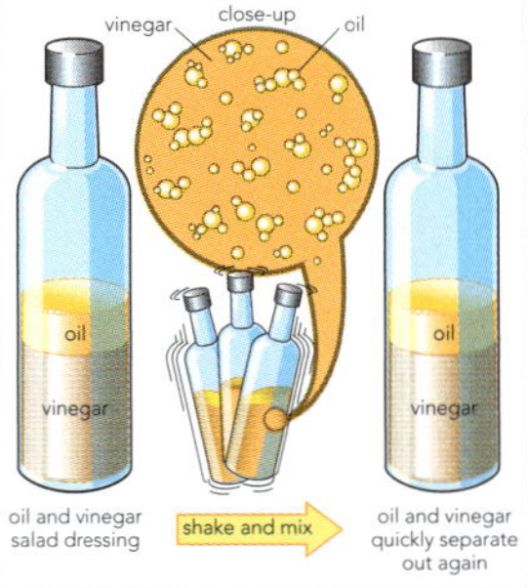


**B** *Oil and vinegar in salad dressing are immiscible.*

**C** *A separating funnel*

1 Why do oil slicks float on the sea?

2 Describe how you would use a separating funnel to separate oil and water.

## Miscible liquids

If two liquids **dissolve** in each other, their particles mix completely to make a **solution**. Liquids like this are **miscible**. They do not separate out once mixed and can only be separated by **fractional distillation**. Fractional distillation can be used to separate mixtures of miscible liquids because they have different boiling points.

The mixture of liquids is heated and the liquids evaporate. The vapours condense in a **fractionating column**. The **fraction** with the highest boiling point condenses near the bottom of the column, and the fraction with the lowest boiling point reaches the top of the column.

This process is used to separate the gases in air. However, first the air has to be turned into a mixture of liquids. This is done by cooling the air so that the water can freeze and be removed. Then the remaining air is cooled to –200 °C when it is **liquefied**.

| | |
|---|---|
| Water | freezes at 0 °C |
| Carbon dioxide | freezes at –79 °C |
| Oxygen | boils at –183 °C |
| Nitrogen | boils at –196 °C |

**D** *Freezing and boiling points of the gases in air*

In the fractionating column, liquid air is warmed up to –185 °C. This causes all the nitrogen to evaporate and rise up the column. Most of the oxygen stays as a liquid and is piped out of the bottom of the column. The oxygen that does evaporate condenses again at the top of the column and runs back down to the bottom.

3 When air is cooled, which substance will solidify first?

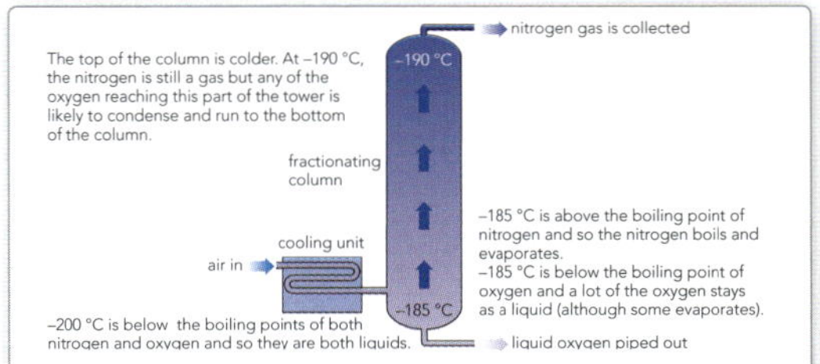


**E** *The distillation of air*

**Skills spotlight**

The oxygen collected from the fractionating column contains some argon. The boiling point of argon is –186 °C. How could you separate oxygen from argon in a second fractionating column?

4 The top of the fractionating column is at about –190 °C. Is that above or below the boiling temperature of oxygen?

5 Hexane boils at 69 °C and octane boils at 126 °C.
a Suggest what temperatures would be needed at the top and bottom of a fractionating column to separate a mixture of hexane and octane.
b Which substance would be collected from the top of the fractionating column?

6 Explain how we can separate oil from vinegar and oxygen from air. Make sure that you include the words fractional distillation, immiscible, miscible and separating funnel in your answer.

**ResultsPlus Watch Out!**

Many students lose marks by getting confused with negative temperatures. A liquid with a boiling temperature of –100 °C boils at a *lower* temperature than one with a boiling temperature of –50 °C.

**Learning Outcomes**

*3.8* Describe the separation of two immiscible liquids using a separating funnel

*3.9* Describe the separation of mixtures of miscible liquids by fractional distillation, by referring to the fractional distillation of liquid air to produce nitrogen and oxygen

HSW 5 Plan to test a scientific idea, answer a scientific question or solve a scientific problem



>>>> In 2005 £100m was spent destroying food containing a banned substance. How was the substance found?



## ActiveTeach

- **AT** *Nitrogen* [video]
  Properties and uses of nitrogen
- **AT** *Boiling point of gases* [presentation]
  Diagram of boiling points
- **AT** *Distillation of air* [diagram]
  Figure E – diagram labelling activity

## Answers | Student Book

1 Oil does not dissolve in water.

2 Place the oil and water in a separating funnel, allow the layers to separate, open the tap and collect the lower water layer in a beaker, close the tap, place a clean beaker under the funnel, open the tap and allow the top oil layer to run out.

3 Water (or ice)

4 Below the boiling temperature of oxygen

5 **a** Temperature at bottom a little below 126 °C, for example 100 °C, temperature at top slightly above 69 °C, for example 75 °C
**b** Hexane

6 A good answer will contain the following points:

- Oil from vinegar: oil and vinegar are immiscible; place them in a separating funnel, allow the layers to separate, open the tap and collect the lower water layer in a beaker, close the tap, place a clean beaker under the funnel, open the tap and allow the top oil layer to run out.
- Oxygen from air: oxygen and air are miscible; air is first cooled down; water and carbon dioxide solidify and can be removed; at -200 °C the air has liquefied; fractional distillation can be carried out; this depends on oxygen and nitrogen having different boiling temperatures; the fractionating column is warmer at the bottom than the top or there is a temperature gradient (specified which way); nitrogen has the lower boiling temperature so boils off; leaving pure oxygen at the bottom.

**Skills spotlight**

A good answer will contain the following points: cool the mixture of argon and oxygen to -200 °C when they will liquefy; pump them into a fractionating column; temperature at the bottom of the column is -184 °C; argon collects as a liquid at the bottom of the column; temperature at the top of the column is -185 °C; oxygen is removed from the top of the column as a gas.

# C2.16 Chromatography



This lesson covers the use of paper chromatography to identify coloured substances, and the applications of chromatography in the food industry and forensic science.

## Specification coverage

**3.10** Describe how paper chromatography can be used to separate and identify components of mixtures, including colouring agents in foodstuffs

**3.11** Evaluate the information provided by paper chromatograms, including the calculation of $R_f$ values, in a variety of contexts, such as the food industry and forensic science

HSW **4** There are some questions that science cannot currently answer and some that science cannot address

There are also opportunities to cover HSW **1**, HSW **6**, HSW **7**, HSW **10**, HSW **11** and HSW **12**.

## Key terms

chromatogram
chromatography
$R_f$ value
solubility
solvent

### Crime scene
**Starter 1**

Show the students a short video clip about the use of chromatography in identifying a forgery – for example, on *YouTube* search for 'CSI chromatography' If this is not available for the lesson, tell the students the story behind the clip and ask what they would have done to test the inks.

### Solubility
**Starter 2** AfL Lit

Ask students to write down the meanings of the following words: soluble, insoluble, solute, solution, solvent, chromatography. Ask the students to indicate how confident they are of each answer by using traffic light colours. They can then feed back to the rest of the class.

### Chromatography of food dyes
**Exploring 1**

In **Worksheet C2.16a** students find the composition of a mixture (a food dye) from chromatograms and evaluate the technique. See the Teacher and technician practical sheet C2.16 for full details.

Stretch Ask students to run the chromatograms for different times.

Support Demonstrate how to prepare the chromatography paper and apply spots of the food dyes.

### Solve the mystery
**Exploring 2**

Ask students to draw a chromatogram, showing the spots for a coloured ink used to write a ransom note and some samples of inks from pens belonging to three suspects. They can then swap chromatograms, calculate the $R_f$ values and identify the ink used to write the note.

Stretch Ask the students to think about the ways that a forensic scientist would make sure that this is evidence suitable to present in court.

Support Provide the students with a blank chromatogram as a template.

### Student Book spread C2.16
**Explaining 1**

Explain how to carry out a paper chromatography experiment to separate a mixture of colours, marking the solvent front when the paper is removed.

Stretch Ask students how chromatography could be used to separate and identify colourless substances – for example, amino acids.

Support Explain that if the level of solvent is above the spots, the food dyes will wash out into the solvent and not move up the paper.

### Using chromatography to identify a substance (AT)
**Explaining 2**

Explain that chromatography is not just used to see if a coloured dye or ink is a single substance or a mixture but can also be used to identify substances. Use the **AT** presentation *Chromatograms* to explain how to calculate the $R_f$ value for each coloured spot for better identification.

Stretch Ask students how they could identify two compounds with similar $R_f$ values. Explain how two-way chromatography works, using a second solvent.

Support Show some simplified chromatograms to make the identification simpler.

### True or false
**Plenary 1** Lit

Read out a number of sentences about this topic and ask the students if they are true or false – if false, ask students to correct the statement. For example: A substance that dissolves in water is soluble (T). A solvent is a solid that dissolves in water (F). Water is the only solvent (F). Chromatography can be used to identify colours in foodstuffs (T). Chromatography can only be used to identify coloured substances (F). Chromatography can be used to solve a crime (T).

### In the hot seat
**Plenary 2** AfL

Ask the students to write one question, using material from this topic. Pull a student name 'out of a hat' to select a student to put in 'the hot seat'. Start a stop clock to count down to 1 minute. Draw further names 'out of the hat' and ask the students to ask their question and to say at the end whether it has been answered correctly or incorrectly. Select further students to sit in the hot seat, if there is time.

### Chromatography
**Homework 1**

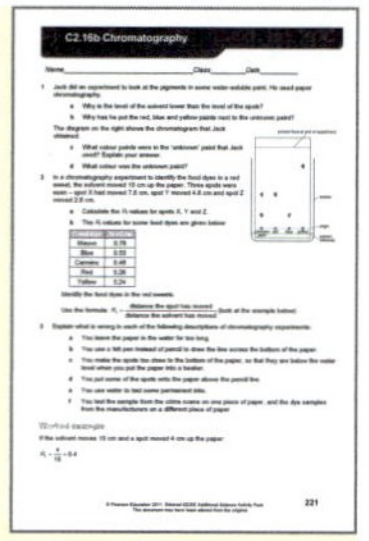


**Worksheet C2.16b**, for students needing support, offers structured questions on interpreting paper chromatograms.

Support Photocopy the worksheet with the worked example given at the bottom.

### Who forged the cheque?
**Homework 2**

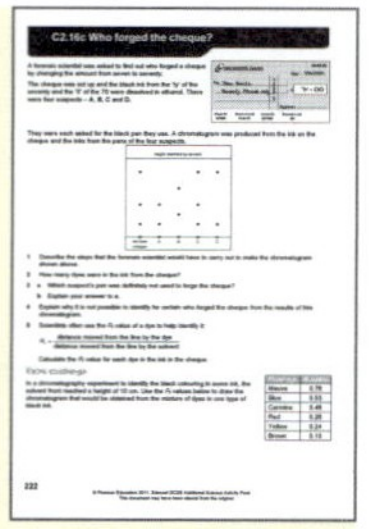


**Worksheet C2.16c**, for more able students, asks them to investigate a forged cheque.

Stretch Students answer the 'extra challenge' question.

# C2.16 Chromatography

What is chromatography and when is it useful?

In 1983, the Sunday Times newspaper paid over £500 000 (in today's money) to publish diaries written by Adolf Hilter. However, scientists analysed the inks in the diaries and discovered that the inks were not available during Hitler's life – the diaries were forgeries.

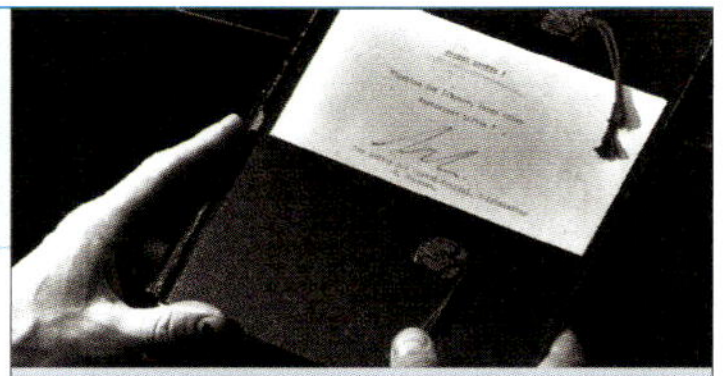

A *One of the fake diaries*

1 How many different compounds are in the colour of substance X in Figure B?

Inks, paints and foods often contain mixtures of coloured compounds. **Chromatography** can be used to find out which colourings are in those substances.

**ResultsPlus Watch Out!**

A compound never rises as fast as the solvent, so $R_f$ values are always less than 1. If you calculated an $R_f$ value bigger than 1, you've made a mistake.

Some coloured compounds dissolve better in a **solvent** than others. They have different **solubilities**. This difference is used to separate different components of mixtures in chromatography.

In paper chromatography, samples are placed near the bottom of a sheet of special paper. Solvent then soaks up the paper. The different components of a mixture are carried by the solvent at different speeds so they are separated. The paper with the separated components on it is called a **chromatogram**.

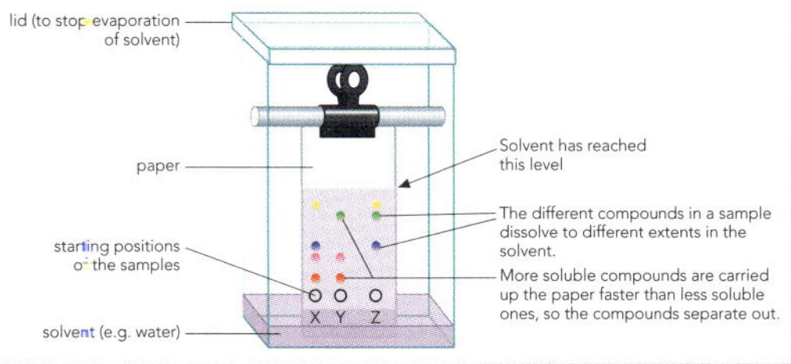


B *Three mixtures separated by paper chromatography*

2 Look at Figure B.
a How many coloured compounds are in mixture X?
b For mixture Y, explain why the green spot is higher than the red spot.
c The solvent has moved 10 cm and the pink compound in Y has moved 2.5 cm. What is the $R_f$ value of this compound?
d State one variable that might change a compound's $R_f$ value.

The $R_f$ **value** is the distance the compound has risen divided by the distance the solvent has risen.

$$R_f = \frac{\text{distance moved by compound}}{\text{distance moved by solvent}}$$

The $R_f$ value of a particular compound does not change if the chromatography conditions are the same. $R_f$ values can be used to identify compounds.

## Uses of chromatography

Scientists at the Food Standards Agency use chromatography to separate and identify food colourings. This helps to keep our food safe.

The police use chromatography to analyse DNA samples to work out if suspects have been at a crime scene. Chromatography can also be used to analyse paints and dyes. This helps museum staff to mix exact copies of old-fashioned paints, to restore old paintings or to identify forgeries.

C *Sudan-1 is a banned food colouring. In 2005, it was discovered in some chilli powder. Foods made using this chilli powder were all destroyed.*

3 In Figure D, the chromatogram on the left shows some common colouring agents found in sweets. The chromatogram on the right shows results for some sweets.

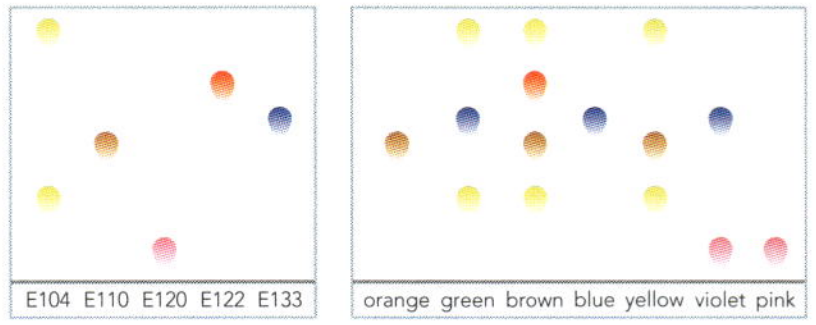


D *Chromatograms showing an analysis of colourings in sweets*

a Which sweets contain one colouring agent?
b Which colouring agents are in the yellow sweet?
c Which colouring agents are in the green sweet?
d The solvent reached a height of 15 cm and the blue spot reached a height of 3 cm. What is the $R_f$ value of the blue colouring agent?
e Why must both chromatograms be done in identical conditions?
f What is the colour of the most soluble substance in these chromatograms?

4 Describe how chromatography can help keep our food safe.

5 Police have taken four orange lipsticks from suspects. Explain the steps needed to show that one of the lipsticks made a mark at a crime scene.

**Skills spotlight**

There are some questions that science cannot tackle. Think up a question about a painting that can be answered by science and one that science cannot address.

**ResultsPlus Watch Out!**

If you draw the apparatus for chromatography, make sure that the line for the solvent is above the bottom edge of the paper but below the samples. This means the solvent will rise to the samples. If you draw it above the samples they will just wash into the solvent.

**Learning Outcomes**

3.10 Describe how paper chromatography can be used to separate and identify components of mixtures, including colouring agents in foodstuffs

3.11 Evaluate the information provided by paper chromatograms, including the calculation of $R_f$ values, in a variety of contexts, such as the food industry and forensic science

HSW 4 Identify questions that science cannot address and explain why these questions cannot be addressed.





## ActiveTeach

- **AT** *How do you separate these mixtures?* [interactive] Ways to separate mixtures – sorting activity
- **AT** *Chromatograms* [presentation] Identifying substances

## Answers | Student Book

1 4

2 a 4
b Green dye travels faster than the red dye
c 0.25
d Any from: temperature, type of solvent, type of paper, thickness of paper

3 a Orange, blue and pink
b E104, E´10
c E104, E133
d 0.2
e Need identical conditions otherwise $R_f$ values can change
f Yellow

4 Chromatography can identify the colourings in the food and, if any are harmful, the food will stop being sold.

5 A good answer will contain the following points:
- details of experiment – samples of lipsticks on a piece of chromatography paper, samples of known orange dyes, add solvent, diagram of set up
- analysis – compare dyes from lipsticks with known samples of dyes, calculate the $R_f$ values, if the $R_f$ values are the same they contain the same dye

**Skills spotlight**
Example of questions that can be answered by science: Which paints were used? Are the paints made from one dye or more? Examples of questions that cannot be answered by science: How good is the artist? Do you like the painting? How valuable is the painting?

# C2.17 Chemical classification



This lesson revises the properties of substances with ionic and covalent bonding and introduces the properties of metals.

## Specification coverage

**4.5** Demonstrate an understanding that elements and compounds can be classified as: a) ionic b) simple molecular covalent c) giant molecular covalent d) metallic, and that each type of substance has different physical properties, including relative melting point and boiling point, relative solubility in water, and ability to conduct electricity (as solids and in solution)

HSW *3* Many phenomena can be explained by developing and using scientific theories, models and ideas

There are also opportunities to cover HSW *10*.

## Key terms

atom
bond
compound
covalent bond
element
giant molecular covalent
ion
ionic bond
malleable
metallic bond
molecule
simple molecular covalent

### Periodic table quiz (AT)

**Starter 1** AfL

Help students to revise earlier learning about the periodic table and electronic configurations using the quiz provided on the **AT** presentation *Periodic table quiz*.

### What type of bonding?

**Exploring 1** Prac

See **Worksheets C2.17a**, **C2.17b** and the Teacher and technician practical sheet C2.17 for full details.

**Stretch** Students use their knowledge of the different types of bonding, and of the properties of metals, to work out their own set of tests to identify types of substance.

**Support** **Worksheet C2.17b** provides a key to help students to work out the type of bonding involved.

### Exceptions to the 'rules'

**Exploring 3**

Give students cards from **Worksheet C2.17c**, and tell them the names of the substances and the types of bonding. Ask students to say which properties are exceptions to the general ones associated with the different types of bonding.

**Stretch** Ask students to find out about the fullerenes as a class of substances, and the origin of the name.

**Support** Give students the cards for graphite, ethanol and mercury only.

### Bonding and properties

**Plenary 1** AfL

The **AT** presentation *Bonding and properties* provides a set of images of different substances with some information about either their properties or their type of bonding, with questions for students to answer. Answers are provided as part of the presentation. If students are entered for the Higher Tier paper, they should be encouraged to include the explanations for the different properties.

### Properties of substances

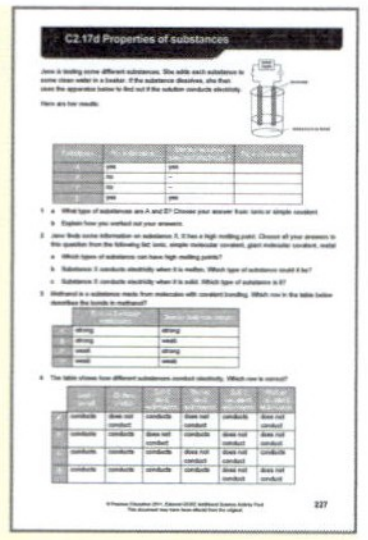

**Homework 1**

**Worksheet C2.17d**, for students working at a lower level, provides questions on the properties of different types of substances.

**Support** Remind students of the properties of the different types of substance and the reasons for them.

### Bonding concept map

**Starter 2** AfL Lit

Ask students to draw a concept map to show what they know about ionic and covalent bonding, and the properties of substances with these types of bonding. You might need to provide word prompts. *Plenary 2* in Lesson C2.13 asked students to draw concept maps for covalent bonding; students could build on these.

### Bonding card sort

**Exploring 2**

**Worksheet C2.17c** provides a set of cards with information about the properties of different substances. Students are asked to sort them according to the type of bonding, or to say if there is insufficient information to classify the substance.

**Stretch** Students could use the melting and boiling point data to try to identify some of the substances described.

**Support** Omit cards F, M, N, P, Q and R.

### Student Book spread C2.17 (AT)

**Explaining 1**

Summary of the properties of substances with ionic and covalent bonding and introduction to the general properties of metals.

**Stretch** Students create a key to identify the type of bonding present in a given substance.

**Support** C2.13 Figure B on page 142 reminds students of the strong and weak forces that give simple covalent molecular substances their properties. This diagram is also available in the **AT** presentation *Simple molecular covalent substances*.

### Sure, unsure, know more

**Plenary 2** AfL

Ask students to individually write down one thing about the classification of substances that they are sure about, one thing they are unsure about and one thing that they want to know more about. Then ask them to work in groups of about five to come up with group lists, and to share these to form a class consensus. Revise the things that students are having difficulty with.

### Classifying substances

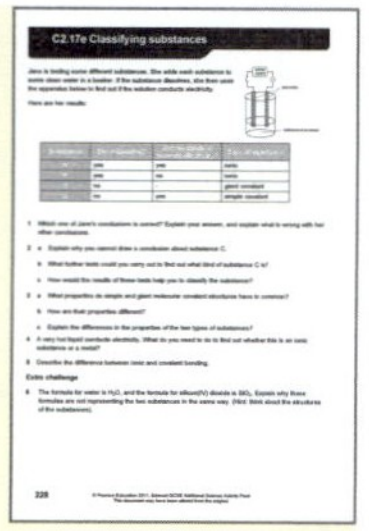

**Homework 2**

**Worksheet C2.17e**, for students working at a higher level, provides questions on this topic and on ionic and covalent bonding.

**Stretch** Students answer the 'extra challenge' question, which goes beyond what is required by the specification.

# C2.17 Chemical classification

What are the different types of chemical bonds?

The photo shows part of an artwork called *Another Place* by Antony Gormley. It consists of 100 human figures made of iron, spread out along two miles of beach. Most of them are underwater when the tide is in. The substances in the air, water, sand and iron contain different types of bonding between their atoms.

The atoms of **elements** in a **compound** are held together with chemical **bonds**. The type of bonding affects the properties of the material.

**A** *Another Place*

| Type of bonding | Ionic | Simple molecular covalent | Giant molecular covalent |
|---|---|---|---|
| How the bonds form | metal atoms lose one or more electrons to form positive **ions** – non-metal atoms gain electrons to form negative ions | atoms share electrons to get a full outer shell – covalent bonds hold atoms together in molecules | atoms share electrons to get a full outer shell – covalent bonds hold billions of atoms together in giant structures |
| Examples | sodium chloride (the main salt in sea water) 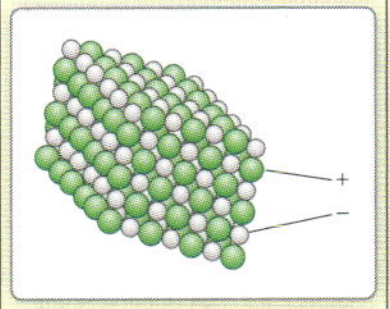 | water, oxygen 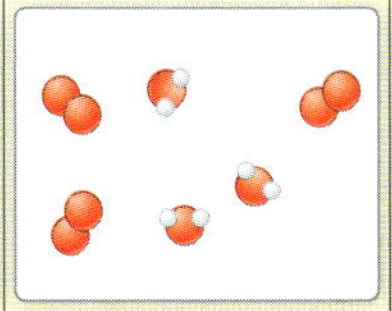 | quartz (the main mineral in sand) 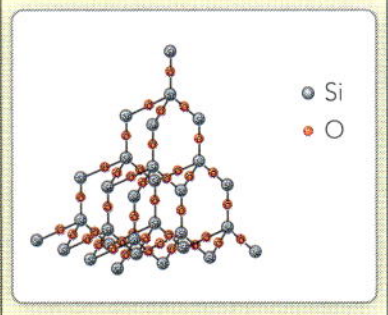 |
| Strength of bonds | strong | strong bonds between atoms in each molecule – weak forces holding the separate molecules together | strong bonds extending across all the atoms in a structure |
| Melting and boiling points | high – ionic substances are solids at room temperature | low – most simple molecular covalent substances are liquids or gases at room temperature | high – giant molecular covalent substances are solids at room temperature |
| Solubility | many dissolve in water | some dissolve in water | insoluble in water |
| Do they conduct electricity? | conduct electricity when molten or in a solution – do not conduct when solid | do not conduct electricity | do not conduct electricity – except graphite, which is a conductor |

**B** *Different types of bonding*

## Properties of ionic and covalently bonded substances

**Ionic bonds** form when a metal reacts with a non-metal. **Covalent bonds** form between atoms of non-metal elements. Figure B summarises how the different types of bonds form, and the properties of substances with the different types of bonding. Materials can be classified according to the type of bonding holding the atoms together. Another type of bonding is found in metals.

1 Methane is a compound of carbon and hydrogen. It is a gas at room temperature.
a What type of bonding holds the atoms together?
b Does methane exist as separate molecules or as a giant molecular covalent substance? Explain your answer.

2 a Which temperature do you think is nearest to the melting point of sand?
A –50 °C B 50 °C C 150 °C D 1500 °C
b Explain your answer.

**ResultsPlus Watch Out!**

Many students make the mistake of referring to molecules of ionic substances. An ionic substance consists of ions, *not* individual molecules.

## Properties of metallic substances

The statues in Figure A are made of iron, which is a metal. Metals are good conductors of heat and electricity and are solids at room temperature. The one exception is mercury, which is a liquid at room temperature. Metals do not dissolve in water and they all conduct electricity. Metals are also **malleable** (can be hammered into shape). The atoms in metals are held together by **metallic bonds**. This gives metals different properties from other types of substance.

**C** *This metal is being hammered to make it into a bowl shape.*

3 A silvery solid conducts electricity. What kind of material is it likely to be?

4 A white powder does not dissolve in water. Explain why this observation does not allow you to say whether the substance has ionic or covalent bonds.

5 Describe a set of tests on physical properties that you could carry out to determine the type of bonding in a substance.

**Skills spotlight**

Scientists use models to help them to explain observations.

**D** *A solution*

Figure D shows a model of a dissolved ionic substance. Use this model to help you explain why ionic substances conduct electricity when they are in solution.

**Learning outcomes**

4.5 Demonstrate an understanding that elements and compounds can be classified as: a ionic b simple molecular covalent c giant molecular covalent d metallic; and that each type of substance has different physical properties, including relative melting point and boiling point, relative solubility in water and ability to conduct electricity (as solids and in solution)

HSW 3 Describe how phenomena are explained using scientific models





## ActiveTeach

- **AT** *Periodic table quiz* [presentation]
  Properties of elements
- **AT** *Simple molecular covalent* [presentation]
  Diagram showing their forces
- **AT** *Bonding and properties* [presentation]
  Comprehension questions

## Answers | Student Book

1 a Covalent
b Separate molecules – it has a low melting/boiling point because it is a gas at room temperature, and this is a characteristic of simple molecular covalent substances. This is because there are only very weak attractive forces between individual molecules.

2 a D
b Sand is a giant molecular covalent substance. These usually have very high melting and boiling points. This is because all the atoms are covalently bonded to each other, covalent bonds are very strong and so high temperatures are needed to break them.

3 Metal

4 Most covalent molecules do not dissolve in water, but also many ionic substances do not dissolve either.

5 A good answer will include the following points:
- use a solid material as part of a circuit
- if the substance conducts electricity, it is a metal
- try dissolving the substance in water
- find out if the solution conducts electricity
- if it does, the substance is an ionic compound
- find the melting or boiling points as substances with low melting or boiling points are usually simple covalent compounds

**Skills spotlight**

The model shows that an ionic substance consists of particles with positive and negative charges that mix with water when the substance is in a solution. These charged particles can carry an electric current.

# C2.18 Metallic bonding and transition metals



This lesson introduces the transition metals, and explains metallic bonding.

## Specification coverage

**4.1** Classify elements as *alkali metals (group 1), halogens (group 7), noble gases (group 0) and* transition metals based on their position in the periodic table

**4.2** Describe the structure of metals as a regular arrangement of positive ions surrounded by a sea of delocalised electrons

**4.3** Describe and explain the properties of metals, limited to malleability and the ability to conduct electricity

**4.4** Recall that most metals are transition metals and that their typical properties include: a) high melting point b) the formation of coloured compounds

HSW *13* How and why decisions about science and technology are made, including those that raise ethical issues, and about the social, economic and environmental effects of such decisions

There are also opportunities to cover HSW *3* and HSW *10*.

## Key terms

delocalised electrons
transition metals

### Key word hangman

**Starter 1** Lit

Ensure that students recall the key vocabulary for this topic by playing a game of hangman using key words from the last lesson. Ask the winners of each round to define the word, and ask the rest of the class to say if their definition is correct.

### Uses of transition metals

**Exploring 1**

Ask students to find out about one or more transition metals – how they are obtained, their uses and any specific properties that make them useful for the purposes described, such as melting point, conductivity or relative reactivity.

**Stretch** Ask students to find out why iron is essential for humans.

**Support** Give students common metals to research – such as iron, copper and gold.

### Models of metals

**Explaining 2** Demo

Model the packing of atoms in a metal using a bubble raft or a tray of polystyrene spheres, and use this to show why metals are malleable. See the Teacher and technician practical sheet C2.18 (1) for full details.

**Stretch** Ask students to suggest why ionic compounds are not malleable.

**Support** Explain the difference to students in step 6

### Writing questions

**Plenary 1** AfL Lit

Give students a set of answers to which they have to write questions. More able students should be able to write more than one question for each answer. The words can be chosen to revise the previous lesson as well as this one, and could just be the key words from the two lessons, or key phrases such as 'coloured compounds', 'rows of atoms slide over one another' etc.

### Metals and bonding

**Homework 1**

**Worksheet C2.18a**, for students working at a lower level, provides questions on the content of the lesson.

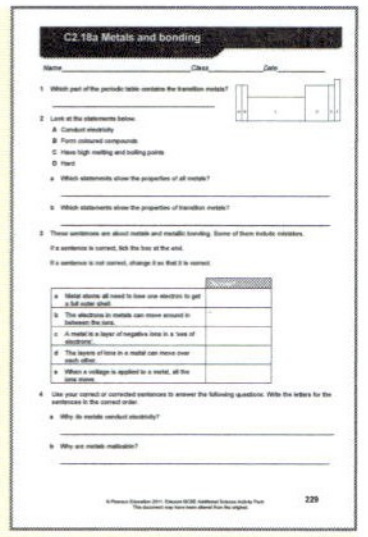

**Support** Students will find this easier if they have completed the summary activity.

### Metals brainstorm

**Starter 2**

Give students 5 minutes working in small groups to come up with the names of as many metals as they can, and to match uses to properties. Ask students to say which property of each metal makes it suitable for the named use.

### Student Book spread C2.18

**Explaining 1**

Help students to remember what 'malleable' means by explaining that the word comes from the Latin 'malleus' meaning hammer.

**Stretch** Ask students to extend the final question on the page to include a comparison with covalent bonding.

**Support** Explain that the 'free' electrons in a metal are still part of the metal – they are not so 'free' that they fall out of the ends of wires.

### Coloured compounds (AT)

**Explaining 3** Demo

Make some compounds of transition metals to show that many of them form coloured compounds. See the Teacher and technician practical sheet on C2.18 (2) for full details.

**Stretch** Ask students to also find out which pigments are named after ores or compounds of transition metals.

**Support** Show students the **AT** presentation *Transition metals*.

### Metals word search (AT)

**Plenary 2** AfL

The **AT** document *Metals wordsearch* is about words relevant to this lesson. Ask students to find the words, and then to write sentences or a coherent paragraph including all the words. It may help some students to give them the words – 'coloured compounds', 'conduct', 'delocalised electrons', 'malleable', 'melting point', 'metallic bonds', 'periodic table', 'positive ions', 'transition'.

### Metallic bonding

**Homework 2**

**Worksheet C2.18b**,for students working at a higher level, provides questions on metallic bonding. Students are also asked to compare metallic and covalent bonding. Students will need a copy of the periodic table to answer question **2**.

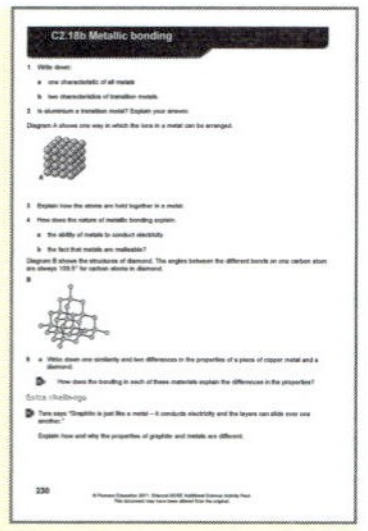

**Stretch** Students answer the 'extra challenge' question.

# C2.18 Metallic bonding and transition metals

How can we explain the properties of metals?

Many oil paints used by artists have names, for example chrome yellow or cobalt blue. These names include the name of a transition metal and it is the metal ion that helps to give the pigment its colour.

A *Colourful chemistry*

## Metallic bonding

Metals are very useful materials. We use them for making cars, sculptures, buildings and tools, and even in colouring materials. The useful properties of metals include malleability and the ability to conduct electricity.

1 Which property of metals is useful in making:
a a car body
b the metal parts of an electrical plug?

All metals have only a few electrons in the outer shells of their atoms. In a solid metal, the atoms are close together and the outer electron shells overlap. The outer electrons are free to move through the structure in a 'sea of electrons'. The electrons are not located in specific atoms, so they are called **delocalised electrons**. The metal atoms form positive ions, which are held together in a regular arrangement.

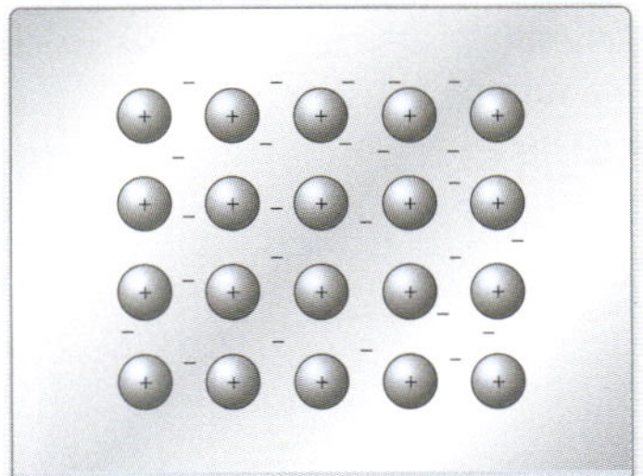

B *The metal ions are held together by a sea of electrons.*

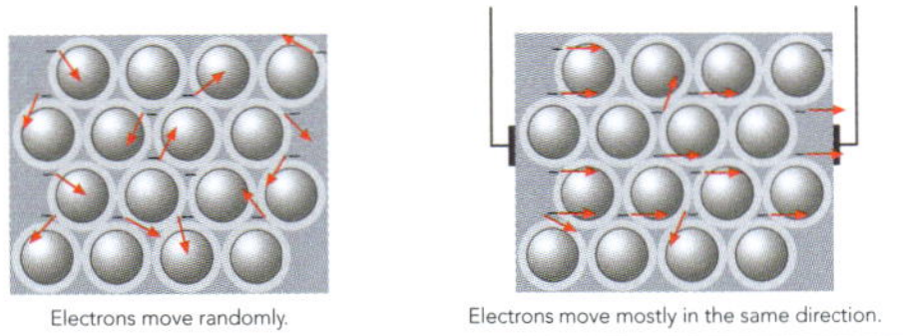


C *Metals conduct electricity because the delocalised electrons can move.*

The delocalised electrons move around randomly between the positive ions in all directions. If a potential difference is applied across a piece of metal, the electrons start to drift in one direction. This movement of electrons is an electric current.

The layers of positive ions in a metal can slide over each other if a large force is applied to a piece of metal. The ions are still held together by the sea of electrons, so the metal spreads out instead of breaking. It is malleable.

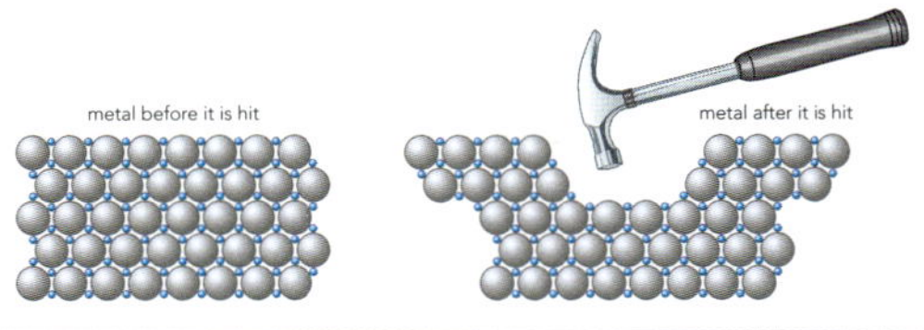


D *Metals are malleable because the layers can slip over each other.*

**ResultsPlus Watch Out!**
Transition metals form coloured compounds. Be careful not to say that they 'form colours' or that they 'are coloured'.

## Transition metals

Most metals are **transition metals**. These are in the central block of the periodic table. Most transition metals have high melting points and form coloured compounds.

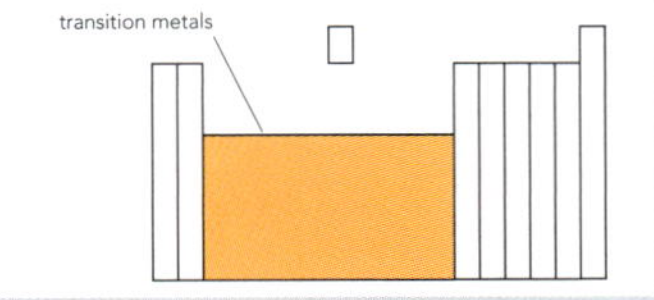


E *The position of the transition metals in the periodic table.*

2 Name four different transition metals. (You may need to look at the periodic table on page 119).
3 Write down two typical properties of transition metals.
4 Why do all metals conduct electricity?
5 Explain why metals are malleable.
6 Describe the properties of metals and how these properties are related to their uses.

**Skills spotlight**
Many decisions about science are made for environmental reasons. Compounds of cobalt, nickel and many other transition metals are toxic. Some of these compounds are used in artists' oil paints to give them colour. Government regulations prohibit manufacturers from using these compounds in household paint. Suggest why these compounds are still allowed in artists' paints even though they are toxic to humans. Do you think this should be allowed?

**Learning Outcomes**
4.1 Classify elements as ... transition metals based on their position in the periodic table
4.2 Describe the structure of metals as a regular arrangement of positive ions surrounded by a sea of delocalised electrons
4.3 Describe and explain the properties of metals, limited to malleability and the ability to conduct electricity
4.4 Recall that most metals are transition metals and that their typical properties include:
a high melting point b the formation of coloured compounds
HSW 13 Explain how and why decisions about uses of science and technology are made

152

Can you make a piece of metal explode? 153

## ActiveTeach

- **AT** *How are properties related to bonding?*
  [interactive] Chemical bonding and properties – quiz
- **AT** *Transition elements*
  [interactive]
  Properties and uses – quiz
- **AT** *Metals wordsearch*
  [word document]
  Find and use important words
- **AT** *Transition metals*
  [presentation]
  Paint and transition metals

## Answers | Student Book

1 **a** Malleability (or strength)
**b** Ability to conduct electricity
2 Any four transition metals named.
3 They have high melting points, and form coloured compounds.
4 The (delocalised) electrons that move around between the ions can move.
5 The layers of ions can slip over each other.
6 A good answer will contain the following points:
- metals are malleable
- which means they can be hammered into different shapes
- because the layers of ions can slide over one another
- this makes them useful for making objects such as cars
- metals conduct electricity
- because they contain delocalised electrons
- that can move between atoms when a potential difference is applied
- this makes them useful for making wires and electrical components.

**Skills spotlight**
Children may come into contact with paints used in houses, or dust from paint that is wearing away. This is unlikely to happen with paint used only on paintings, so there is a much smaller chance of harm. Most students should conclude that transition metal compounds should still be allowed in artists' paints.

# C2.19 Alkali metals



This lesson introduces the alkali metals and looks at their reactions with water and the trend in reactivity.

## Specification coverage

**4.1** Classify elements as alkali metals (group 1), *halogens (group 7), noble gases (group 0) and transition metals* based on their position in the periodic table

**4.6** Describe alkali metals as: a) soft metals b) metals with comparatively low melting points

**4.7** Describe the reactions of lithium, sodium and potassium with water to form hydroxides which are alkaline, and hydrogen gas

**4.8** Describe the pattern in reactivity of the alkali metals lithium, sodium and potassium with water and use this pattern to predict the reactivity of other alkali metals H and explain the pattern

HSW *2* The interpretation of data, using creative thought, to provide evidence for testing ideas and developing theories

There are also opportunities to cover HSW *10* and HSW *11*.

## Key terms

alkali metals
reactivity

### Alkali metals

**Starter 1**

Show students bottles containing lithium, sodium and potassium, and pieces of copper, aluminium and iron. Ask them to say what properties all metals have, and also to say what will happen to the iron if it is left in contact with moist air for too long. Then ask them to say how they could test the elements in the bottles to show that they were metals, and to suggest why they are stored in oil.

### Trends in the alkali metals (AT)

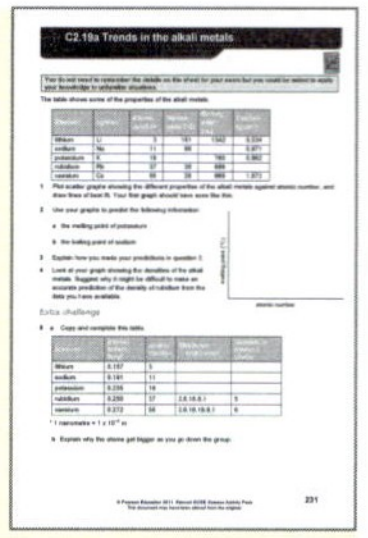

**Exploring 1**

**Worksheet C2.19a** provides some information about the properties of the alkali metals, and asks students to plot the data and to predict the missing quantities.

Stretch Students answer the 'extra challenge' question on the worksheet.

Support The **AT** *Alkali metal trends* provides the data in the table.

### Student Book spread C2.19

**Explaining 1**

The Skills spotlight box asks students to predict how fast rubidium and caesium will react with water.

Stretch Ask students to look at the positions of beryllium and calcium in the periodic table and to predict which will be the most reactive.

Support Demonstrate how to balance the equations shown, and make sure that students realise that the balanced equations are similar for all the alkali metals.

### Sentence starters (AT)

**Plenary 1** AfL Lit

The **AT** document *Sentence starters* provides a set of statements about alkali metals and their reactions for students to complete. The obvious continuations to most starters involve using 'because' as a connective, but students should be encouraged to use other connectives if they can.

### The alkali metals

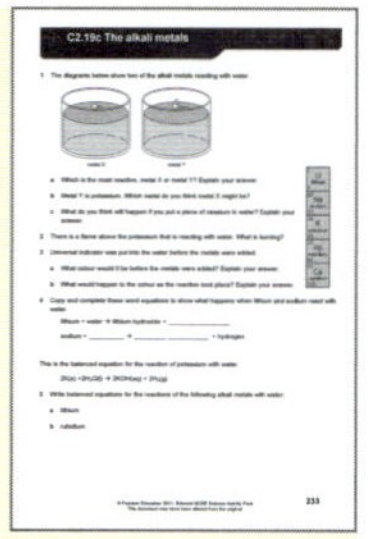

**Homework 1**

**Worksheet C2.19c**, for students needing support, provides questions to reinforce the learning in this topic.

Support Remind students of the trend in reactivity, and that the equations for the reactions of the alkali metals are all similar.

### Electronic configurations

**Starter 2**

Tell students, for example, that beryllium, magnesium and calcium have similar reactions to each other. Ask the students with those elements to compare their electronic structures and to suggest why they have similar chemical properties. Ask them to suggest which other groups of elements have similar reactions to each other, concentrating on groups 1, 7 and 8.

### H Alkali metal trends

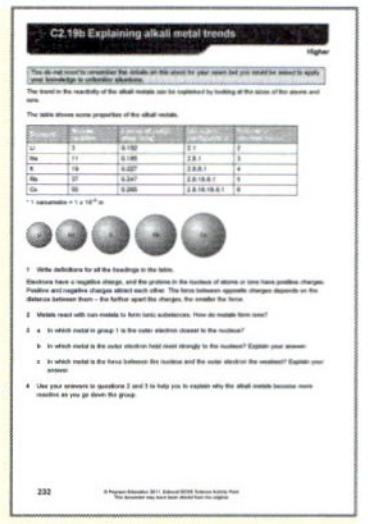

**Exploring 2**

**Worksheet C2.19b** explains the trend in reactivity of the elements in group 1 in simple terms.

Stretch Ask students to suggest why the metals in group 2 are less reactive than the corresponding metals in group 1. Tell them that the atomic radii of the group 2 metals are smaller than the corresponding group 1 metals.

### Reactions with water

**Explaining 2** Demo

Demonstrate the reactions of lithium, sodium and potassium with water. See the Teacher and technician practical sheet C2.19 for full details.

Stretch Tell students that the alkali metals react with an acid to form a salt and hydrogen. Ask them to predict how fast the three metals will react compared to one another.

Support Remind students how the colours of universal indicator relate to the classification of substances as acids or alkalis.

### Key facts

**Plenary 2** AfL

Write the names of the alkali metals and some transition metals on labels, and stick one on the back of each student. Give students 5 minutes to ask other students questions about 'their' metal to help them to work out what is stuck to their back. When all students know what their metal is, they can be asked to group themselves into alkali metals and transition metals.

### Reactions of the alkali metals

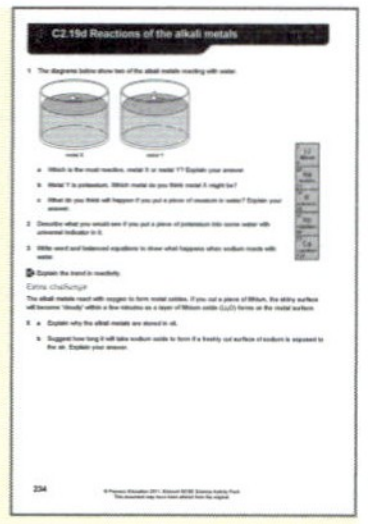

**Homework 2**

**Worksheet C2.19d**, for more able students, provides questions to reinforce the learning in this topic. This sheet includes some Higher Tier material.

Stretch Students answer the 'extra challenge' question.

# C2.19 Alkali metals

What are the properties of the alkali metals?

Many streetlamps provide a yellowish light because they contain sodium. Sodium vapour gives out yellow light when electricity passes through it, in a similar way to its yellow flame test.

**A** *The yellow glow from sodium lights can be seen above many cities at night.*

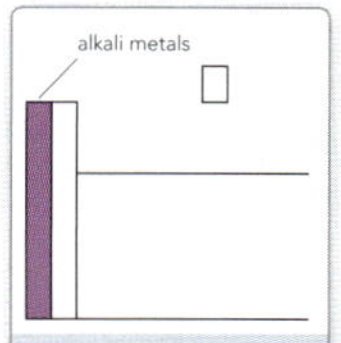


**B** *The position of the alkali metals in the periodic table*

The **alkali metals** are found in group 1 in the periodic table. They are solids at room temperature but they have low melting points compared to other metals (sodium melts at only 97 °C). They are all soft metals and can all be cut with a knife. The atoms in the alkali metals are held together by metallic bonding.

**ResultsPlus Watch Out!**

Be careful that you do not say that the metals in group 1 are alkalis. They *produce* alkalis when they react with water.

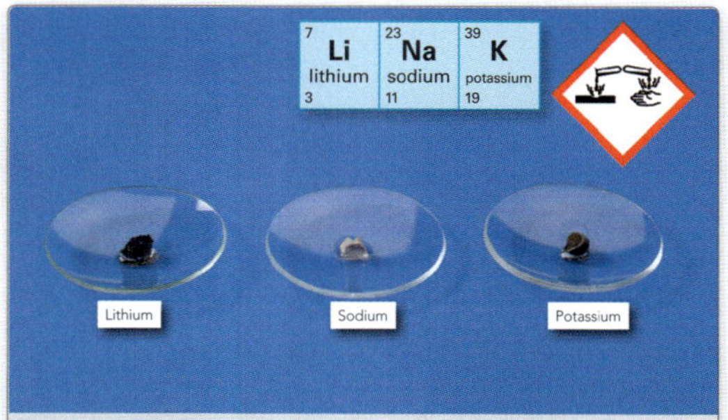


**C** *The first three alkali metals*
*Hazard symbol reproduced with the kind permission of the secretariat of the United Nations Commission for Europe.*

1 Write down two physical properties of the alkali metals.

2 a Write a word equation to show the reaction of sodium with water.

b Write a balanced equation for the reaction.

The alkali metals are in the same group of the periodic table, so they all have similar reactions. They all react with water to form a metal hydroxide and hydrogen gas. Metal hydroxides are alkaline. For example:

lithium + water → lithium hydroxide + hydrogen

$2Li(s) + 2H_2O(l) \rightarrow 2LiOH(aq) + H_2(g)$

The equations for the reactions of the other alkali metals are similar, because they all form ions with a charge of +1.

## Reactivity

If a small piece of lithium is dropped into some water, it floats on the surface and fizzes. It gradually disappears as the reaction proceeds. Sodium reacts more vigorously than lithium and sodium also has a lower melting point. The reaction between sodium and water produces enough heat to melt the metal, which forms a molten ball that whizzes around on the surface of the water until the reaction is complete. Sometimes the hydrogen produced catches fire. Potassium reacts even more vigorously and the hydrogen catches fire, producing a lilac flame. The **reactivity** of the alkali metals increases as you go down the group.

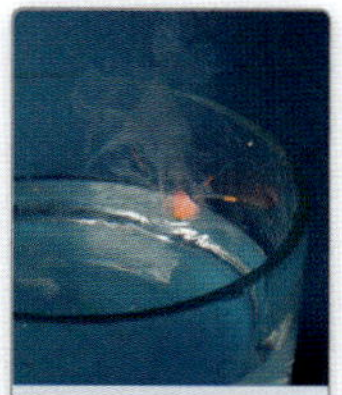

**D** *A ball of molten potassium reacting on water. The hydrogen produced catches fire immediately.*

H The elements at the bottom of group 1 have more electrons, and so more electron shells in their atoms, than the elements at the top of the group. This means that the outer electrons are further from the nucleus. The force between positive and negative charges is greatest when the charges are close together, so the outer electron in a caesium atom is not held as strongly as the outer electron in a lithium atom. These metals react by losing the outer electron, so this explains why caesium is more reactive than lithium.

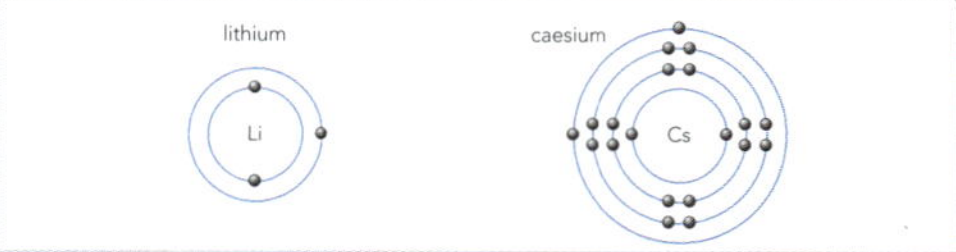


**E** *The outer electron in a caesium atom is much further from the nucleus than the outer electron in a lithium atom.*

3 A piece of potassium is dropped into water. Describe what you will see.

4 Universal indicator is added to a beaker of water before a piece of lithium is dropped into it. Explain what colour the indicator will be:

a before the lithium is added

b after the reaction.

(H) 5 Explain why potassium is more reactive than sodium.

6 Describe the differences between an alkali metal such as sodium and a transition metal such as copper.

**Skills spotlight**

Scientists interpret data to help them to test ideas and develop theories.

**a** Look at the information about the reactions of lithium, sodium and potassium with water. What trends can you see in the reactions?

**b** The next two elements in group 1 of the periodic table are rubidium and caesium. Predict how these two elements will react with water.

**Learning Outcomes**

4.1 Classify elements as alkali metals (group 1) ... based on their position in the periodic table

4.6 Describe alkali metals as: *a* soft metals *b* metals with comparatively low melting points

4.7 Describe the reactions of lithium, sodium and potassium with water to form hydroxides which are alkaline, and hydrogen gas

4.8 Describe the pattern in reactivity of the alkali metals lithium, sodium, and potassium with water and use this pattern to predict the reactivity of other alkali metals (H) and explain the pattern

HSW 2 Describe how data is used by scientists to provide evidence that increases our scientific understanding



What are halogen light bulbs? 

## ActiveTeach

- **AT** *Sodium*
  [video]
  Properties and uses of sodium
- **AT** *Caesium*
  [video]
  Properties and uses of caesium
- **AT** *Potassium*
  [video]
  Properties and uses of potassium
- **AT** *Reactivity of alkali metals*
  [interactive]
  Reactivity: alkali metals – ordering activity
- **AT** *Sentence starters*
  [word document]
  Alkali metals and reactions
- **AT** *Alkali metal trends*
  [spreadsheet]
  Plotting scatter graphs

## Answers | Student Book

1 They are soft metals, and have low melting points compared to other metals. Accept malleability or electrical conductivity.

2 **a** sodium + water → sodium hydroxide + hydrogen

**b** $2Na(s) + 2H_2O(l) \rightarrow 2NaOH(aq) + H_2(g)$

3 The potassium will float and start to move around the water. It will melt and form a ball. There will be a flame as the hydrogen gas burns.

4 **a** Green, because water is neutral

**b** Blue or purple, because the reaction produces an alkali.

5 (H) Metals react when they lose their outer electrons to form positive ions. The outer electron in a potassium atom is further from the nucleus than the outer electron in a lithium atom, so a potassium atom will lose this electron more easily.

6 A good answer will include the following points:
- an alkali metal is soft
- whereas transition metals are usually hard
- alkali metals have relatively low melting points
- transition metals usually have high melting points
- transition metals form coloured salts
- and alkali metals do not
- alkali metals are more reactive than transition metals.

**Skills spotlight**

**a** The reactions get more vigorous (or similar phrase) as you go down the group.

**b** Rubidium will react faster than potassium, and caesium will react faster than rubidium.

# C2.20 Halogens

This lesson introduces the halogens, describes their physical states and their reactions with metals.

## Specification coverage

**4.1** Classify elements as alkali metals (group 1), *halogens (group 7), noble gases (group 0) and transition metals* based on their position in the periodic table

**4.9** Recall the colours and physical states of the halogens at room temperature

**4.10** Describe the reactions of halogens with metals to form metal halides

**HSW** *13* How and why decisions about science and technology are made, including those that raise ethical issues, and about the social, economic and environmental effects of such decisions

There are also opportunities to cover **HSW** *7*, **HSW** *10* and **HSW** *11*.

## Key terms

halide
halogen

### Halogen quiz

**Starter 1**

Students should have studied chlorine in earlier work on electrolysis, and also used bromine water to test for unsaturated hydrocarbons. Find out how much of this work they recall by asking them to sort the cards on **Worksheet C2.20a**.

### Producing halogens (AT)

**Exploring 1**

The **AT** spreadsheet *Producing halogens* provides data about the abundances of the halogens in the oceans, in the crust and in the human body. Students are asked to plot the data, and then to use it to answer questions.

**Stretch** Students answer the 'extra challenge' question on the spreadsheet.

**Support** Help students to use the Chart Wizard to plot their bar charts.

### Student Book spread C2.20

**Explaining 1**

Show students the formulae of some compounds such as carbonates and sulfates, and the formulae of chlorides, bromides etc. Elicit the idea that the '-ate' ending indicates the presence of oxygen, whereas the '-ide' ending indicates that the non-metal alone forms the compound with a metal.

**Stretch** Ask students how they could use information about the halogens to predict that oxygen should have lower melting and boiling points than sulfur, and why this could be a valid method of prediction.

**Support** Demonstrate how to balance the equations shown.

### Hot seat

**Plenary 1** **AfL**

Ask each student to think up a question using material from this lesson. A selected student answers a range of questions. Check whether the student in the hot seat got the answer correct or not. Allow one minute for this and then count up the score. Ask students to give the correct answers for any that were deemed incorrect and to discuss the wording of any questions that were ambiguous. Then put another student in the hot seat if there is time.

### Halogens

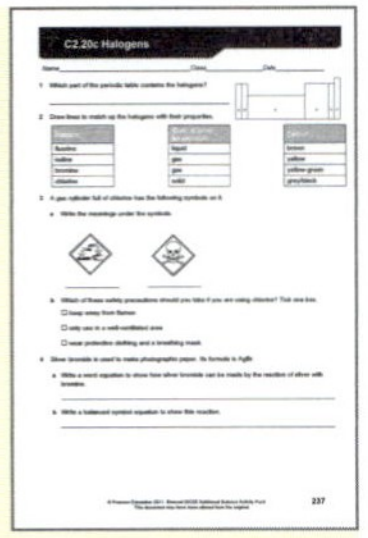

**Homework 1**

**Worksheet C2.20c**, for students needing support, provides questions on this lesson.

**Support** Go through the final question with students before they take the worksheet home.

### Heating bromine

**Starter 2** **Demo**

Show the students what happens as frozen bromine melts and then starts to evaporate. Use this to revise ideas about simple molecular covalent substances. See the Teacher and technician practical sheet C2.20 (1) for full details.

### Photograms

**Exploring 2** **Prac**

See **Worksheet C2.20b** and the Teacher and technician practical sheet C2.20 (2) for full details.

**Stretch** Challenge students to make a picture in shades of grey by making shapes out of cards and removing them at different times during the exposure.

**Support** Explain that removing some objects partway through exposure will give shades of grey.

### Reactions of metals and halogens

**Explaining 2** **Demo**

Demonstrate the reactions of iron or Dutch foil with halogens. See the Teacher and technician practical sheet C2.20 (3) for full details.

**Stretch** Students work out the formulae of the metal halides for themselves, given the fact that iron forms 3+ ions and copper and zinc both form 2+ ions.

**Support** Work through the process of balancing equations with students.

### Making halogen equations (AT)

**Plenary 2** **AfL**

Ask students to write down the formula of a reactant or a product involved when metals react with halogens and then find others who have other formulae that will help them to create a balanced equation. Each group then writes down their balanced equation. Students without matches should work together in a group to complete balanced equations for all their formulae. The **AT** document *Making equations* provides cards that can be used for this activity.

### Halogen reactions

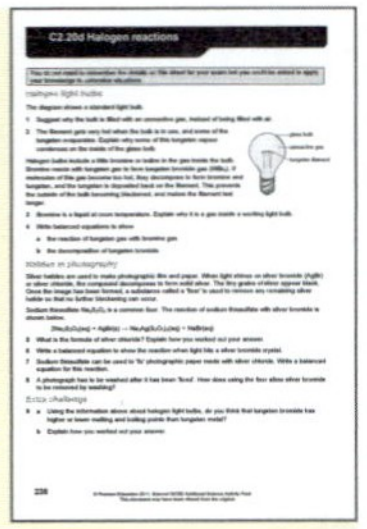

**Homework 2**

**Worksheet C2.20d**, for more able students, provides some questions on the applications of halogens and halides.

**Stretch** Students answer the 'extra challenge' question.

# C2.20 Halogens

What are the properties of the halogens?

Some types of light bulbs with tungsten filaments inside them were banned from sale in Europe in 2009 because they are not very efficient. The filament is very hot when the bulb is working and some of the tungsten evaporates. This vapour condenses and the inside of the bulb gradually becomes coated with a thin layer of metal. This reduces the efficiency of the bulb. Halogen bulbs include a small amount of bromine or iodine inside the bulb. This reacts with the tungsten vapour and prevents the outside of the bulb becoming blackened. This makes these bulbs more efficient and last longer. However, these bulbs are due to be phased out in 2016.

**A** *The inside of the lightbulb on the right has become coated with a thin layer of metal, that will make it less efficient. This does not happen with halogen lamps.*

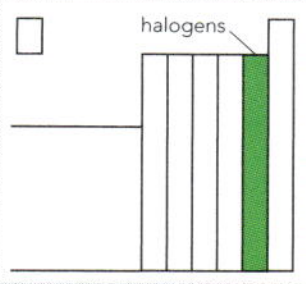


**B** *The position of the halogens in the periodic table*

The **halogens** are the elements in group 7, on the right-hand side of the periodic table. Fluorine and chlorine are gases at room temperature, bromine is a brown liquid and iodine is a grey solid. Fluorine gas is pale yellow and chlorine is yellow-green.

1 What colour is:
a bromine
b iodine?

2 Look at Figure C. What is the state (solid, liquid or gas) of each halogen at room temperature?

3 How do the melting and boiling points of the halogens change as you go down the group? Explain how you worked out your answer.

**C** *The halogens are all coloured elements and they are all corrosive and toxic.*
*Hazard symbols reproduced with the kind permission of the secretariat of the United Nations Commission for Europe.*

## Halogen reactions

The halogens all have similar reactions because they are all in the same group in the periodic table. They react with metals to form metal **halides**. For example, bromine reacts with potassium to form potassium bromide and chlorine reacts with calcium to form calcium chloride. The word 'halide' means that the compound contains only metal ions and ions of one of the halogens.

| | | | | |
|---|---|---|---|---|
| potassium | + | bromine | → | potassium bromide |
| 2K(s) | + | $Br_2$(l) | → | 2KBr(s) |
| calcium | + | chlorine | → | calcium chloride |
| Ca(s) | + | $Cl_2$(g) | → | $CaCl_2$(s) |

Each halogen needs one more electron to complete its outer electron shell, so they all form ions with a charge of –1. Fluorine is the most reactive halogen, and iodine is the least reactive. The reaction between fluorine and a metal happens much faster than reactions between metals and the other halogens.

**D** *Chlorine reacting with iron wool*

**E** *Chlorine reacting with aluminium*

6 a The formula of iron(III) chloride is $FeCl_3$. Write a word equation and a balanced symbol equation for the reaction shown in Figure D.
b Iron loses three electrons when it reacts with a halogen, and so does aluminium. Write a word equation and a balanced symbol equation for the reaction shown in Figure E.

7 Use ideas about electron structures and covalent bonding to explain why all the halogens have low melting and boiling points.

**ResultsPlus Watch Out!**

Be careful in your answers to refer to chloride ions, and not chlorine atoms. Chlorine gas is a molecule made up of two atoms.

4 Name three different compounds that could be described as a 'potassium halide'.

5 Write word and balanced equations for these reactions:
a potassium + chlorine
b calcium + bromine
c sodium + fluorine

**Skills spotlight**

Ethical decisions are based on what people think is right or wrong. Sodium fluoride is usually present at low levels in drinking water. Some scientific studies have shown that there is less tooth decay in people who live in areas with more fluoride in the water. Fluoride is added to products like toothpaste, and in some areas it is also added to drinking water.
**a** Why do you think that adding fluoride to water is an ethical issue?
**b** Write down some of the things you need to think about before deciding whether or not fluoride should be added to drinking water.

**Learning Outcomes**

4.1 Classify elements as … halogens (group 7)… based on their position in the periodic table
4.9 Recall the colours and physical states of the halogens at room temperature
4.10 Describe the reactions of halogens with metals to form metal halides
HSW 13 Explain how and why decisions that raise ethical issues about uses of science and technology are made

156

Which halogens are the most dangerous? 157

## ActiveTeach

- AT *Iodine*
[video]
Properties and uses of iodine
- AT *Fluorine*
[video]
Properties and uses of fluorine
- AT *Bromine*
[video]
Properties and uses of bromine
- AT *Producing halogens*
[spreadsheet]
Plotting data and questions
- AT *Making equations*
[word document]
Reactant and product cards

## Answers | Student Book

1 **a** Brown **b** Grey/black
2 Fluorine and chlorine are gases, bromine is a liquid and iodine is a solid
3 They get higher. Fluorine and chlorine are gases, so they must have low melting and boiling points. Iodine is a solid at room temperature, so it must have a higher melting point.
4 Any three from: potassium fluoride, potassium chloride, potassium bromide, potassium iodide
5 **a** potassium + chlorine → potassium chloride
2K(s) + $Cl_2$(g) → 2KCl(s)
**b** calcium + bromine → calcium bromide
Ca(s) + $Br_2$(l) → $CaBr_2$(s)
**c** sodium + fluorine → sodium fluoride
2Na(s) + $F_2$(g) → 2NaF(s)
6 **a** iron + chlorine → iron chloride
2Fe(s) + $3Cl_2$(g) → $2FeCl_3$(s)
**b** aluminium + chlorine → aluminium chloride
2Al(s) + $3Cl_2$(g) → $2AlCl_3$(s)
7 A good answer will include the following points: the halogens are non-metals; they form simple molecules held together by covalent bonds; the bonds between the atoms in the molecules are very strong; the forces between the molecules are weak; it does not take much energy to pull the molecules away from each other; the melting and boiling points are low.

**Skills spotlight**
**a** By putting fluoride in water, people are not being given a choice whether or not to take in the fluoride.
**b** Suggestions could include: How much tooth decay would adding fluoride prevent; The risks from the long term use of fluoride; Other ways of giving fluoride to people ; Other methods of delivering fluoride as effectively.

# C2.21 Displacement reactions of the halogens

This lesson challenges students to investigate the reactivity of the halogens using displacement reactions. The activity may be run as a practice controlled assessment or as a straight-forward class practical. The initial practical work can be completed within 30 minutes.

## Specification coverage

***4.12*** Investigate displacement reactions of halogens reacting with halide ions in solution

This lesson provides opportunities to cover HSW *1*, HSW *2*, HSW *5*, HSW *6*, HSW *7*, HSW *8*, HSW *10* and HSW *11*.

## Key terms

displacement reaction

### Before the lesson

If you intend to use this activity as a practice controlled assessment task, you should ensure that students are familiar with any equipment they may be expected to use so that they can plan their own investigation. In the week or two before the task show them this equipment and, if appropriate, allow them to practice using it. Students should be familiarised with the fact that reactions involving the halogen elements can be conducted using the element dissolved in water (chlorine water, etc). It may be good preparation to show students one or more of Skills sheets 19 to 26 to show what is expected of them in their actual controlled assessment task.

### Starter

**Displacement reactions of metals**

Show students a beaker of copper sulfate solution and an iron nail. Ask them what will happen if the nail is put into the solution. Remind them about the reactivity series of metals that they looked at in connection with the extraction of metals from their ores in C1. Then show them another beaker of copper sulfate in which an iron nail has been standing for some time and ask them why the nail is coated in a brown substance and what would happen if a piece of copper wire was put into a beaker of iron sulphate solution. Ask them how these two situations can be used to determine the relative reactivities of iron and copper.

Read the additional information below the opening of the section of page 158 of the Student Book.

They may then read the brief description of the activity provided by the 'Your task' box.

### Option 1: Straight-forward class practical

Students follow the instructions on **Worksheet C2.21b** explains how to carry out the reactions. Students decide on the different combinations of halide and halogen to test. The worksheet suggests that students gather data about the reactivity of the halogens by adding the halogen waters to red litmus paper and timing how long it takes them to bleach the paper. This gives students more information to draw a conclusion from. The range of data that students need to collect is given on **Worksheet C2.21c**. This helps students to record, consider their results and evaluate their investigations.

### Plenary

On page 159 of the Student Book you will find two examples of the sort of work that students may produce for this task. The examples focus on identifying and managing risks. You could share these with students after they have completed their own work. This will help them to understand the assessment criteria and so make it easier for them to evaluate their work and to see how they can improve it. Moderator comments on each of the Student Book extracts can be found at the end of the assessment guidance for this investigation on the CD-ROM. The examples can also be found on the **AT** document *Student examples*.

### Option 2: Running the activity as a practice controlled assessment task (PCA)

We have provided a full range of support resources to allow the running of this practical as a practice controlled assessment task. A recommended structure is outlined below (to be used over a number of sessions). Marking guidance for all three parts of the practice task can be found on the CD-ROM that accompanies the TTPP. To save time when using these practice controlled assessment tasks, you may wish to focus on a particular aspect or skill rather than working through all three parts of the task.

#### Part A Planning

1. Students should be given the Student brief on **Worksheet C2.21a**. They can use Part A of the Workbook that is provided to help pupils with their practice controlled assessments. They should be given about 1 hour to do this planning.
2. Show students bottles of chlorine water, bromine water and iodine water, and explain that these can be used instead of trying to use the elements themselves.

#### Part B Observations

3. So long as it is safe and viable, students should be asked to carry out the practical task to collect evidence using the method they have planned in Part A. They should refer to the Student brief on **Worksheet C2.21a.** They can use Part B of the Workbook that is provided to help pupils with their practice controlled assessments. They should be given about 30 minutes to an hour to collect their primary evidence.
4. If there is a problem with their own planned method, students may be asked to follow the method set out on **Worksheet C2.21b**. This will still enable students to access the full range of marks for Part B and Part C of the practice controlled assessment task.
5. Students add the halogen waters to red litmus paper and time how long it takes them to bleach the paper.
6. In Part B, students are required to gather some secondary evidence. This can be quantitative or qualitative. It can be from a variety of sources but students must note where they found their evidence and evaluate the quality of the source as part of this task. Skills sheet 22 helps students with further guidance on researching for and evaluating secondary evidence. This part of the task could be done outside of the lesson but must be supervised.

#### Part C Conclusions

7. Students follow the instructions set out on the Part C section of the Student brief on **Worksheet C2.21a.** They should use their data from Part B and the secondary evidence they have collected when doing this. They can use Part C of the Workbook that is provided to help pupils with their practice controlled assessments. They should be given about 1 hour to work on their conclusions.

The **AT** includes video clips showing a group of students working through elements of this investigation with teacher support.

Practice Controlled Assessment

# C2.21 Displacement reactions of the halogens

How can you work out which halogens are the most reative?

The first cameras often used glass plates coated with silver halides. Many photographers used to make their own plates. Making the plates and developing them required knowing about the reactions of halogen compounds.

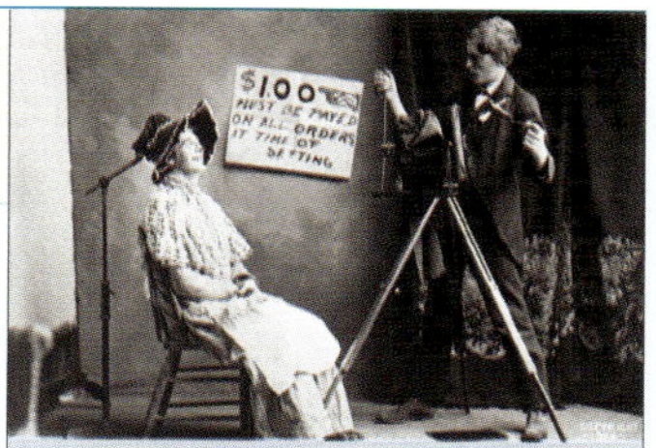


**A** *The exposure times for early photographs were so long that metal frames were used to make sure people kept still!*

Some elements are more reactive than others. A reactive metal will displace (take the place of) a less reactive one from a compound. For example, if you put an iron nail in a solution of copper sulfate, the nail will gradually become coated with copper. Iron is more reactive than copper and has displaced the copper in the compound. The following **displacement reaction** has taken place:

iron + copper sulfate → iron sulfate + copper

This reaction shows that iron is more reactive than copper.

**B** *It is easier and safer to use chlorine water (chlorine dissolved in water) than chlorine gas in this investigation. Bromine water and iodine water can also be used.*

You can use displacement reactions to work out the order of reactivity of the halogens. The word equations below show two reactions you could use to help you to work out which halogens are the most reactive:

potassium bromide + chlorine → ?

potassium chloride + bromine → ?

**Your task**

You are going to plan an investigation that will allow you to find out which halogens are the most reactive. Your teacher will provide you with some materials to help you organise this task.

**Learning Outcomes**

*4.12 Investigate displacement reactions of halogens reacting with halide ions in solution*

## ResultsPlus Build Better Answers

When planning an investigation like this, one of the skills you will be assessed on is your ability to identify and manage any *risks*. There are 4 marks available for this skill. Here are two extracts focusing on this skill. Other skills that you need for the assessment are dealt with in other lessons.

**Student extract 1** — A basic response for this skill

*Chlorine is dangerous, so I shouldn't breathe it in.*

- It would be better to use the correct words for the hazards, for example, chlorine is toxic and corrosive.
- This investigation uses chlorine water, not chlorine gas, so this comment is not relevant.

**Student extract 2** — A good response for this skill

*All the substances used are harmful, and chlorine water and bromine water are also toxic and corrosive. I should wear eye protection, and wash my hands straight away if I spill any of the substances on them.*

- This student has given the correct terms for the hazards of the different substances.
- Eye protection should be worn whenever corrosive substances are used.
- The student has suggested more than one thing that must be done to manage the risks.

**ResultsPlus**

**To access 2 marks**

- Identify a relevant risk which is specific to the investigation
- Suggest how to deal with that risk

**To access 4 marks**

- Identify most of the relevant risks which are specific to the investigation
- Describe how to manage all the risks involved

158 | How can bromine help to prevent deaths in fires? | 159

## ActiveTeach

- **AT** *C2.21 Displacement reactions* [video]
  Students work through the investigation
- **AT** *C2.21 Moderator comments* [word document]
  Moderator comments on the video
- **AT** *C2.21 Assessment criteria* [presentation]
  Understanding the CA marking criteria
- **AT** *C2.21 Student task sheet* [word document]
  CA video checklist
- **AT** *C2.21 Specification points* [word document]
  Edexcel specification points
- **AT** *C2.21 Student examples* [word document]
  Examples for students to assess

## Assessment criteria

### Risks

**0** No relevant detail given.

**1-2** **a)** Identifies one of the following risks, e.g. chlorine and bromine are toxic and corrosive, iodine and halide salts are harmful.
**b)** One of the following suggestions needed, e.g. wear eye protection, wear gloves, handle substances with care so they are not spilled, clear up any spills straight away.

**3-4** **a)** Identifies most of the relevant risks that are specific to the task, e.g. from the list above.
**b)** Measures are suggested to manage the risks, e.g. from the list above.

# C2.22 More halogen reactions

This lesson looks at the formation of hydrogen halides, then reinforces learning from the previous lesson by explaining displacement reactions and how they can be used to work out the relative reactivities of the halogens.

## Specification coverage

***4.11*** Recall that halogens react with hydrogen to produce hydrogen halides, which dissolve in water to form acidic solutions

***4.13*** Describe the relative reactivity of the halogens as shown by their displacement reactions with halide ions in aqueous solution

HSW *7* Working accurately and safely, individually and with others, when collecting first-hand data

There are also opportunities to cover HSW *2*, HSW *3* and HSW *10*.

### Sure, unsure, know more

**Starter 1** AfL

Ask students to individually write down one thing about the halogens and their reactions that they are sure about, one thing that they are unsure about and one thing that they want to know more about. Revise the things that students are having difficulty with.

### Predicting the properties of astatine (AT)

**Exploring 1**

**Worksheet C2.22a** provides some information about the properties of the halogens and asks students to use this to predict the properties of astatine.

Stretch Ask students to find out why astatine is extremely rare.

Support The data is also provided on the **AT** spreadsheet *Predicting the properties of astatine* so students can plot scatter graphs using a computer.

### Student Book spread C2.22 (AT)

**Explaining 1**

The Student Book follows up the Practice Controlled Assessment in C2.21 by explaining displacement reactions.

Stretch Ask students to explain the type of bonding in a metal halide and in a hydrogen halide. Follow this up by asking what is unusual about covalent compounds such as hydrogen chloride.

Support Use the **AT** presentation *Reactivities* to help students to see how the pattern of displacement reactions can be used to work out an order of reactivity.

### Halogen reactions re-visited

**Plenary 1** AfL

Re-visit *Starter 2* by asking students to re-examine the list of halogens in order of reactivity and correct them with reasons, if necessary. Students can also add other information to produce a summary of the lesson.

### Halogen reactions

**Homework 1**

**Worksheet C2.22b**, for students needing support, provides questions on the content of this lesson.

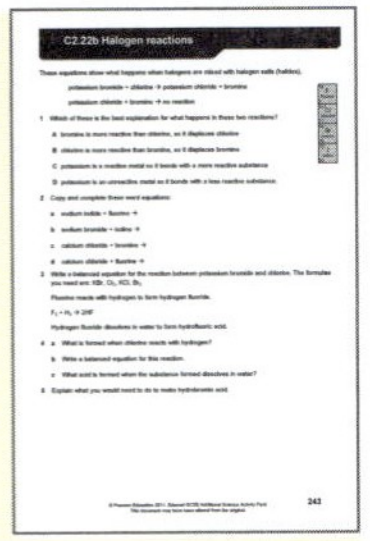

Support Read through the sheet and discuss the questions with students before they take the sheet home.

### Halogen reactivities

**Starter 2**

Ask students to write the names of the halogens in order of reactivity and to state why they have put them in this order. Students should keep their lists for use in *Plenary 1*.

### More halogen reactions (AT)

**Exploring 2** Prac

The **AT** document *More halogen reactions* provides a set of questions about the reactivity of the halogens and some of their reactions. The questions can be answered by watching the videos linked to on the document.

Stretch Students answer questions **5** and **11**.

Support Students watch and answer the questions for the first video only.

### Hydrogen chloride fountain

**Explaining 2** Demo

Demonstrate that hydrogen chloride dissolves in water to form an acid by carrying out a variation of the fountain experiment. See the Teacher and technician practical sheet C2.22 for full details

Stretch Ask students to explain what is happening.

Support Show students the colour change when hydrochloric acid is added to water before asking them to explain the colour change in the demonstration.

### Halogens exam question

**Plenary 2** AfL Lit

Ask students to make up an exam question on any part of the work on halogens, worth 5 marks. They should also write a mark scheme for their question. This can be done individually or in groups, and students could share questions to use for revision later.

### Iodised salt

**Homework 2**

**Worksheet C2.22c**, for more able students, provides questions on the content of this lesson set in the context of providing iodised table salt.

Stretch Students answer the 'extra challenge' question.

# C2.22 More halogen reactions

How reactive are the halogens?

Many deaths from fires in homes are caused by burning sofas and chairs. Furniture now has to be treated with 'fire retardant' compounds. These substances do not prevent fires but they give people in the house more time to escape. Many of these compounds are made using bromine.

A Both these sofas were set alight in the same way and have been burning for the same amount of time. The sofa on the left is from the UK and has been treated with a good fire retardant.

1 Write word and balanced equations for the reactions of hydrogen with:
a chlorine
b bromine.

2 Which acid is formed when hydrogen chloride dissolves in water?

## Halogens and hydrogen

The halogens react with hydrogen gas to form hydrogen halides. Hydrogen halides form acids when they dissolve in water. For example, fluorine reacts with hydrogen to form hydrogen fluoride. When this is dissolved in water it forms hydrofluoric acid, HF(aq).

hydrogen + fluorine → hydrogen fluoride

$H_2(g) + F_2(g) \rightarrow 2HF(g)$

### Skills spotlight

Hydrofluoric acid is used in etching glass. Containers of hydrofluoric acid have the hazard symbols shown in Figure C.
a What do these symbols mean?
b Why is it essential to follow the safety precautions described on the container when using hydrofluoric acid?

C Hazard symbols
Reproduced with the kind permission of the secretariat of the United Nations Commission for Europe.

B Hydrofluoric acid reacts with glass – it can be used to etch patterns in glass.

## Displacement reactions

Seawater contains small amounts of bromide salts. Bromine can be displaced from a solution of bromide salts by reacting them with chlorine. For example:

sodium bromide + chlorine → sodium chloride + bromine

$2NaBr(aq) + Cl_2(g) \rightarrow 2NaCl(aq) + Br_2(aq)$

This is called a displacement reaction because the chlorine has 'displaced' the bromine in the salt. The solution is initially colourless but will turn an orange-brown colour as bromine is formed.



Other halogens can also take part in similar displacement reactions. For example, chlorine will displace iodide ions and the solution will turn brown-black as iodine is formed.

potassium iodide + chlorine → potassium chloride + iodine

However, if you add chlorine to a compound of fluorine, there will be no reaction. We need to look at the reactivity of all the halogens to find out why.

## Reactivity of the halogens

Displacement reactions can be used to work out how reactive the different halogens are. A more reactive halogen will displace a less reactive halogen from its compounds. In the examples above, chlorine is more reactive than bromine, so chlorine displaces bromine from a bromide. Chlorine is more reactive than iodine, so it displaces iodine from an iodide.
You can carry out a series of reactions to investigate the reactivity of the halogens. Figure E shows the results of a series of reactions.

D Chlorine water being added to potassium bromide solution (clear, colourless liquid). The orange-yellow colour in the test tube is bromine, which has been displaced by the chlorine.

| | | Salt | | | |
|---|---|---|---|---|---|
| | | sodium fluoride | sodium chloride | sodium bromide | sodium iodide |
| Halogen | fluorine | | reaction | reaction | reaction |
| | chlorine | no reaction | | reaction | reaction |
| | bromine | no reaction | no reaction | | reaction |
| | iodine | no reaction | no reaction | no reaction | |

E Results of halogen displacement reactions

3 Write a balanced equation for the reaction between potassium iodide (KI) and chlorine.

4 a Which halogens will fluorine displace in a reaction?
b Which halogens will iodine displace?

5 Look carefully at Figure E and write down the halogens in order of their reactivity, starting with the most reactive element.

6 Explain how you can use a series of reactions between halogens and metal halides to work out the reactivity of the different halogen elements.

**ResultsPlus Watch Out!**

Remember the halogens in order fluorine, chlorine, bromine, iodine then you will always know which displaces which in a reaction.

### Learning Outcomes

4.11 Recall that halogens react with hydrogen to produce hydrogen halides, which dissolve in water to form acidic solutions

4.13 Describe the relative reactivity of the halogens as shown by their displacement reactions with halide ions in aqueous solution

HSW 7 Work safely, individually and with others, when collecting first-hand data



## ActiveTeach

- **AT** *Reactivity of the halogens* [interactive]
  Reactivity: the halogens – ordering activity
- **AT** *Halogen displacement reactions* [interactive]
  What colour? – sorting activity
- **AT** *Astatine* [spreadsheet]
  Predicting properties
- **AT** *Reactivities* [presentation]
  Working out reactivities
- **AT** *More halogen reactions* [word document]
  Answering questions

## Answers | Student Book

1 **a** hydrogen + chlorine → hydrogen chloride
$H_2(g) + Cl_2(g) \rightarrow 2HCl(g)$
b hydrogen + bromine → hydrogen bromide
$H_2(g) + Br_2(g) \rightarrow 2HBr(g)$

2 Hydrochloric acid

3 $2KI(s) + Cl_2(g) \rightarrow 2KCl(s) + I_2(s)$

4 **a** All of them
**b** None of them. Alternatively, students could say astatine although it is not one of the halogens studied.

5 Fluorine, chlorine, bromine, iodine

6 A good answer will include the following points:
- mix halogen X with a metal compound of halogen Y
- if there is a reaction, then halogen X is more reactive than halogen Y
- if there is no reaction, then Y is more reactive than X
- repeat this using different halogens for X and Y
- until all combinations have been tested.
- the pattern of results will allow the halogens to be put into an order of reactivity.

**Skills spotlight**

**a** Toxic and corrosive

**b** The substance can kill you (toxic) or damage your skin. The safety precautions will be devised to stop you coming into contact with the substance (e.g. by telling you to wear gloves) so you can avoid possible harm.

# C2.23 Noble gases

This lesson introduces the noble gases and outlines how they were first discovered.

## Specification coverage

**4.1** Classify elements as alkali metals (group 1), *halogens (group 7), noble gases (group 0) and transition metals* based on their position in the periodic table

**4.14** Describe the noble gases as chemically inert, compared with the other elements, and demonstrate an understanding that this lack of reactivity can be explained by the electronic arrangements in their atoms

**4.15** Demonstrate an understanding that the discovery of the noble gases was due to chemists: a) noticing that the density of nitrogen made in a reaction differed from that of nitrogen obtained from air b) developing a hypothesis about the composition of the air c) performing experiments to test this hypothesis and show the presence of the noble gases

**4.16** Relate the uses of the noble gases to their properties, including: a) inertness (including providing an inert atmosphere for welding and in filament lamps) b) low density (including filling balloons) c) non-flammability

**4.17** Use the pattern of a physical property of the noble gases, such as boiling point or density, to estimate an unknown value for another member of the group

**HSW** *2* The interpretation of data, using creative thought, to provide evidence for testing ideas and developing theories

There are also opportunities to cover **HSW** *1*, **HSW** *3*, **HSW** *10*, **HSW** *12* and **HSW** *14*.

### Spot the mistake

**Starter 1** **AfL**

Students work in pairs. Ask them to invent an element. Tell them that it must not react with anything, and it must be a gas. Ask them to design a card for the element with its name, the periodic table group it is in and a use for it. Then introduce the idea that there are elements like this.

### Predicting properties (AT)

**Exploring 1**

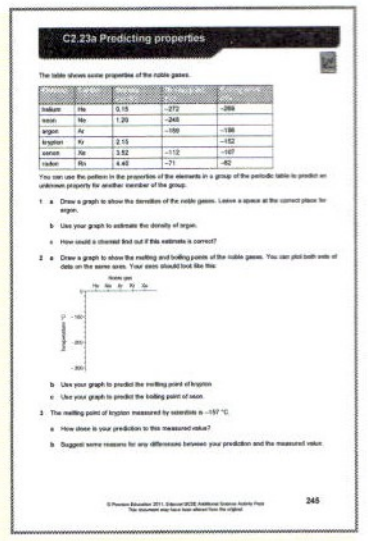

**Worksheet C2.23a** provides information about the physical properties of the noble gases. Data is provided on the **AT** spreadsheet *Predicting properties*.

**Stretch** Ask students to find out what 'cryogenics' means, and why the physical properties of helium are important for its use in cryogenics.

**Support** Help students to prepare the axes for their graphs, or give them graph paper with axes already drawn for them.

### Fire suppression systems

**Exploring 3**

**Worksheet C2.23b** outlines different gases used in fire suppression systems.

**Stretch** Ask students to find out what kind of fire extinguishers are used to put out fires in electrical equipment if fire suppressions systems such as those described are not fitted.

**Support** Discuss the advantages and disadvantages of each system as you read about it.

### Question loop (AT)

**Plenary 1** **Lit**

The **AT** document *Question loop* provides a set of 'follow me' or 'loop' cards with questions and answers on the topic as a whole. These can be used in a question loop game where students stand and read out the answer if they have the correct card, and then read out their question.

### Gases and uses

**Homework 1**

**Worksheet C2.23c**, for students working at a lower level, provides questions helping them to revise the content of this lesson.

**Support** Remind students how the electron structure of an element determines how it reacts.

### Five key facts

**Starter 2**

Ask students to work in small groups to write down five key facts from the topic so far. Combine these to make an agreed class list of 10 facts. This can be added to at the end of the lesson to add a couple of key facts about the noble gases.

### Discovering the noble gases (AT)

**Exploring 2** **Prac**

The **AT** document *Noble gases* provides more detail about how the noble gases were discovered, and provides questions to get students to think about the way science works.

**Stretch** Ask students to find out how fractional distillation is used to produce argon.

**Support** Read through the sheet with students and use the questions as the basis for a class discussion.

### Student Book spread C2.23 (AT)

**Explaining 1**

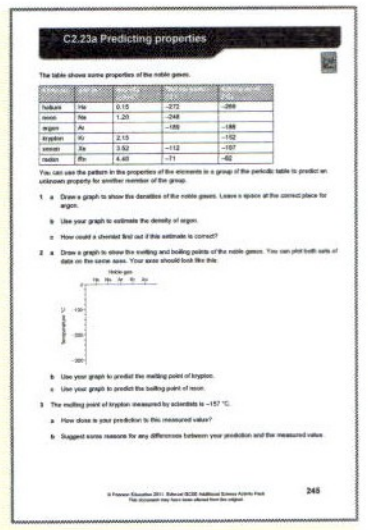

Students will need graph paper to carry out the suggested activity in the Skills spotlight box. Note that the same data is repeated on **Worksheet C2.23a** *(Exploring 1)*.

**Stretch** Ask students to explain why the noble gases are monatomic.

**Support** Provide graph paper with axes already labelled for the skills box.

### Periodic table poster (AT)

**Plenary 2** **Lit**

The **AT** document *Periodic table poster* provides a small outline of the periodic table. Ask students to annotate this with notes about the properties of the different groups they have studied, to act as a summary and revision aid for the topic.

### The noble gases

**Homework 2**

**Worksheet C2.23d**, for students working at a higher level, provides questions helping them to revise the content of this lesson.

**Stretch** Students answer the 'extra challenge' question.

# C2.23 Noble gases

What are the properties and uses of the noble gases?

Many illuminated signs, like those in Figure A, are made using tubes filled with different noble gases. The gases glow when a high voltage is applied across the ends of the tubes.

A City lights

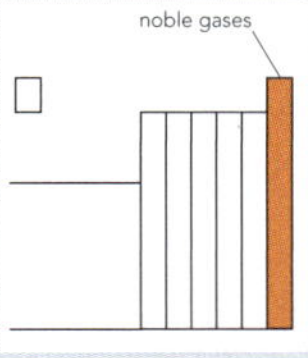


B The position of the noble gases in the periodic table

The **noble gases** are in group 0 of the periodic table. They are **inert** compared with the other elements, which means that it is very difficult to make them react with anything.

C The noble gases are unreactive

All the elements in group 0 have full outer electron shells. Elements in other groups gain full outer shells by forming ions or by forming covalent bonds. Because noble gas atoms already have full shells, it is very difficult to make them react at all.

1 Do you think that the noble gases have high or low boiling points compared with other elements? Explain how you worked out your answer.

2 a Draw the electronic structure of a neon atom (atomic number 10).
b In what way will this drawing be similar to the electronic structures of the other noble gases?
c Use your diagram to help you to explain why the noble gases are very unreactive.

## Discovery of the noble gases

Lord Rayleigh (1842–1919) was measuring the densities of different gases when he noticed that the density of pure nitrogen made in chemical reactions was less than the density of nitrogen made from the air by removing all the other gases. Sir William Ramsay (1852–1916) heard about these results, and hypothesised that the nitrogen made from air also contained a denser gas. They carried out some careful experiments to test this hypothesis and discovered a new gas, which they called argon. During this investigation, Ramsay also discovered helium. He later found neon, krypton and xenon.

| Element | Density (g/cm$^3$) |
|---|---|
| helium | 0.15 |
| neon | 1.20 |
| argon | |
| krypton | 2.15 |
| xenon | 3.52 |
| radon | 4.40 |

D Densities of the noble gases

## Uses of the noble gases

The noble gases are useful because they are unreactive.

- Xenon and argon were formerly used inside filament lamps, instead of air, to stop the hot filament reacting with oxygen and burning away.
- Argon and helium are used in welding, to form a blanket over the hot metal to stop it reacting with oxygen in the air.
- Argon is used in fire-extinguishing systems because it is non-flammable. Spaces such as a computer server room can be filled with argon if a fire breaks out.
- Helium has a low density and so is used for filling balloons and airships.
- Neon is often used in fluorescent lamps and advertising displays as it produces a red coloured light when electric current is passed through the tube under low pressure.

E Welding uses an inert gas to stop the hot metal reacting.

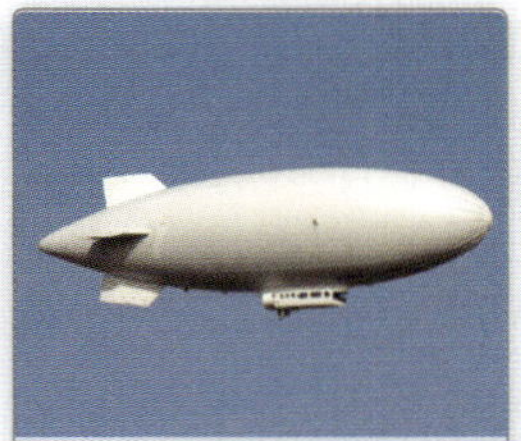

F Helium is used for filling airships.

3 Explain why the noble gases are non-flammable.

4 Hydrogen is the only gas with a lower density than helium. Suggest why helium is used in balloons rather than hydrogen.

5 Suggest why it was easier for early chemists to discover elements such as oxygen, rather than elements such as argon.

6 Explain why the ability to make very accurate measurements was important in the discovery of the noble gases.

### Skills spotlight

Patterns in data can be used to find missing values by **interpolation**. Figure D shows the densities of some noble gases.
**a** Draw a graph to show the densities of the noble gases. Leave a space at the correct place for argon.
**b** Use your graph to estimate the density of argon.
**c** How could a chemist find out if this estimate is correct?

### Maths skills

A line of best fit on a scatter graph can be used to estimate unknown values.

Estimating an unknown value within the range of known values is called **interpolation**.
Estimating an unknown value outside the range of known values is called extrapolation.

### ResultsPlus Watch Out!

You could think of the noble gases as being like noble lords and ladies of old not having anything to do with the other common elements. They are unreactive.

### Learning Outcomes

4.1 Classify elements as … noble gases (group 0) … based on their position in the periodic table

4.14 Describe the noble gases as chemically inert, compared with the other elements and demonstrate an understanding that this lack of reactivity can be explained by the electronic arrangements in their atoms

4.15 Demonstrate an understanding that the discovery of the noble gases was due to chemists: a noticing that the density of nitrogen made in a reaction differed from that of nitrogen obtained from air b developing a hypothesis about the composition of the air c performing experiments to test this hypothesis and show the presence of the noble gases

4.16 Relate the uses of the noble gases to their properties, including: a inertness … b low density … c non-flammability

4.17 Use the pattern in a physical property of the noble gases, such as boiling point or density, to estimate an unknown value for another member of the group

HSW 2 Describe how data is used by scientists to provide evidence that increases our scientific understanding





## ActiveTeach

- AT *Argon* [video]
- AT *Helium* [video]
- AT *Krypton* [video]
- AT *Neon* [video]
- AT *Xenon* [video]
- AT *Why that gas?* [interactive]
  Uses of noble gases – matching activity
- AT *All about noble gases* [interactive]
  Noble gases – quiz
- AT *Predicting properties* [spreadsheet]
  Plotting graphs
- AT *Question loop* [word document]
- AT *Periodic table poster* [word document]
- AT *Noble gases* [word document]
  Discovering the noble gases

## Key terms

inert
noble gases

## Answers | Student Book

1 Low. They are all gases at room temperature.

2 a Atom drawn with 2 electrons in the inner shell and 8 in the outer.
b They will all have full outer shells.
c As they already have full outer shells, they do not need to lose or gain electrons, or to share electrons, to get a full outer shell.

3 They are unreactive, so they will not react with oxygen to burn.

4 Hydrogen is flammable and helium is not. Balloons filled with helium are therefore safer if there is an accident that might start a fire.

5 Elements were often discovered by making compounds containing them decompose. As elements like argon are very unreactive, they are not found in compounds. Alternatively, students may point out that elements such as oxygen are more abundant than argon, and so are likely to be easier to discover.

6 A good answer will include the following points:
- argon forms a very small proportion of the air
- it was detected by Lord Rayleigh because he found a difference between the densities of nitrogen from different sources.
- if his measurements had been less accurate and precise
- he may not have noticed the difference
- or may have assumed that the difference was just due to an error in measurement.

**Skills spotlight**
**a** Graph with densities correctly plotted
**b** The density of argon is 1.4 g/cm$^3$. But as graph is non linear, if students have drawn a line of best fit they may estimate a value around 1.8 g/cm$^3$.
**c** Obtain a sample of gas and measure its density.

# C2.24 Temperature change



This lesson challenges students to investigate how changing the mass of zinc affects the temperature rise in the displacement reaction between copper sulfate solution and zinc powder. The activity may be run as a practice controlled assessment task or as a straight-forward class practical. The practical work can be completed in a one hour lesson.

## Specification coverage

***5.1*** Measure temperature changes accompanying some of the following types of change: a) salts dissolving in water b) neutralisation reactions c) displacement reactions d) precipitation reactions

This lesson provides opportunities to cover HSW *1*, HSW *5*, HSW *6*, HSW *7*, HSW *8*, HSW *10* and HSW *11*.

### Before the lesson

If you intend to use this activity as a practice controlled assessment task, you should ensure that students are familiar with any equipment they may be expected to use so that they can plan their own investigation. In the week or two before the task show them this equipment and, if appropriate, allow them to practice using it. It may be good preparation to show students one or more of Skills sheets 19 to 26 to show what is expected of them in their actual controlled assessment task.

### Starter

An ice pack from a first aid kit could be used and passed round the class. Students should be told that when scrunched, ammonium nitrate mixes and dissolves in water in an endothermic change. Follow this by reading the additional information below the opening section of page 164 of the Student Book. They may then read the brief description of the activity provided by the 'Your task' box.

### Option 1: Straight-forward class practical

Students follow the instructions on **Worksheet C2.24b**. The range of data that students need to collect is given on **Worksheet C2.24**c which students will also need. This sheet guides students through recording, considering their results, and evaluating their investigation. As an extension, students could be asked to hypothesise and test whether the relationship continues as more and more zinc is added.

### Plenary

On page 165 of the Student Book you will find three examples of the sort of work that students may produce for this task. The examples focus on recording primary evidence. You could share these with students after they have completed their own work. This will help them to understand the assessment criteria and so make it easier for them to evaluate their work and to see how they can improve it. Moderator comments on each of the Student Book extracts can be found at the end of the assessment guidance for this investigation on the CD-ROM. The examples can also be found on the **AT** document *Student examples*.

### Option 2: Running the activity as a practice controlled assessment task (PCA)

We have provided a full range of support resources to allow the running of this practical as a practice controlled assessment task. A recommended structure is outlined below (to be used over a number of sessions). Marking guidance for all three parts of the practice task can be found on the CD-ROM that accompanies the TTPP. To save time when using these practice controlled assessment tasks, you may wish to focus on a particular aspect or skill rather than working through all three parts of the task.

#### Part A Planning

1. Students should be given the Student brief on **Worksheet C2.24a**. They can use Part A of the Workbook that is provided to help pupils with their practice controlled assessments. They should be given about 1 hour to do this planning.
2. Students look at the reaction between copper sulfate and zinc. A sample reaction could be done in a boiling tube and students could feel the warmth. You could ask students about factors that could affect the temperature rise and then ways in which an accurate experiment could be done.

#### Part B Observations

3. So long as it is safe and viable, students should be asked to carry out the practical task to collect evidence using the method they have planned in Part A. They should refer to the Student brief on **Worksheet C2.24a**. They can use Part B of the Workbook that is provided to help pupils with their practice controlled assessments. They should be given about 1 hour to collect their primary evidence.
4. If there is a problem with their own planned method, students may be asked to follow the method set out on **Worksheet C2.24b**. This will still enable students to access the full range of marks for Part B and Part C of the practice controlled assessment task.
5. In Part B, students are required to gather some secondary evidence. The evidence can be quantitative or qualitative. It can be from a variety of sources but students must note where they found their evidence and evaluate the quality of the source as part of this task. Skills sheet 22 provides students with further guidance on researching for and evaluating secondary evidence. This part of the task could be done outside of the lesson but must be supervised.

#### Part C Conclusions

6. Students follow the instructions set out on the Part C section of the Student brief on **Worksheet C2.24a**. They should use their data from Part B and the secondary evidence they have collected when doing this. They can use Part C of the Workbook that is provided to help pupils with their practice controlled assessments. They should be given about 1 hour to work on their conclusions.

The **AT** includes an interactive simulation that students can work through to help with elements of this investigation.

Practice Controlled Assessment

# C2.24 Temperature change

How does sherbet work?

When you put sherbet in your mouth, you feel fizzing and your tongue feels cold. Sherbet contains a mixture of an acid and a base. The acid is citric acid and the base is sodium hydrogencarbonate. When they come into contact with moisture in your mouth, they react together. The reaction makes carbon dioxide, which explains the fizzing. The reaction absorbs heat energy from your mouth and so your mouth feels cold as the heat energy is taken away.

A Sherbet fizzes and feels cold on your tongue.

Many chemical and physical changes involve temperature changes. Sometimes, the mixture gets hotter and in some reactions the mixture gets colder.

Many types of chemical and physical changes are accompanied by a temperature change. Some of these include:

- dissolving – when a solid dissolves in a liquid
- neutralisation – when an acid reacts with a base
- displacement – when a metal displaces a less reactive metal from a compound
- precipitation – when two solutions are mixed and a solid is formed.

**Your task**

You are going to plan an investigation that will allow you to find out what happens to the temperature of a solution of copper sulfate when different masses of zinc are added and a displacement reaction takes place. Your teacher will provide you with some materials to help you organise your task.

**Learning outcomes**

*5.1 Measure temperature changes accompanying some of the following types of change:*
*a salts dissolving in water*
*b neutralisation reactions*
*c displacement reactions*
*d precipitation reactions*

## ResultsPlus Build Better Answers

When planning an investigation like this, one of the skills you will be assessed on is your ability to record *primary evidence*. There are 4 marks available for this skill. Here are three extracts focusing on this skill. Other skills are dealt with in other lessons.

**Student extract 1** A basic response for this skill

Starting temperature 21°C. Finishing temperatures 0 = 21°C, 0.5 g = 33°C, 1.0 g = 44°C, 1.5 g = 55°C, 2.0 = 57°C, 2.5 g = 58°C.

A list like this is acceptable but it is quite hard to spot any patterns like this.

This is good because it is a full list of results.

Don't forget units!

**Student extract 2** A better response for this skill

| Mass of zinc (g) | 0.0 | 0.5 | 1.0 | 1.5 | 2.0 | 2.5 |
|---|---|---|---|---|---|---|
| Start temperature (°C) | 20 | 21 | 21 | 20 | 20 | 21 |
| Final temperature (°C) | 20 | 33 | 44 | 55 | 57 | 58 |

Including all the units and headings gives you access to higher marks.

A table makes it easier to spot the patterns in the data.

**Student extract 3** A good response for this skill

| Mass of zinc (g) | 0.0 | 0.5 | 1.0 | 1.5 | 2.0 | 2.5 |
|---|---|---|---|---|---|---|
| Expt 1 Start temperature (°C) | 20 | 21 | 21 | 20 | 20 | 21 |
| Expt 1 Final temperature (°C) | 20 | 33 | 44 | 55 | 57 | 58 |
| Expt 2 Start temperature (°C) | 20 | 21 | 21 | 20 | 20 | 21 |
| Expt 2 Final temperature (°C) | 20 | 33 | 44 | 55 | 45 | 58 |

Carrying out repeat experiments gives you much more data to work with.

You can use your table to spot any results that do not fit the pattern. You can highlight these in your Part C work.

**ResultsPlus**

**To access 2 marks**

- Collect a suitable range of data or observations
- Record some of these appropriately

**To access 4 marks**

- Collect a suitable range of data or observations
- Record all your evidence appropriately
- Record repeat data or further relevant data

164

How can you heat soup without a flame? 165

## ActiveTeach

- **AT** *C2.24 Temperature change* [interactive] Investigating temperature change
- **AT** *C2.24 Assessment criteria* [presentation] Understanding the CA marking criteria
- **AT** *C2.24 Specification points* [word document] Edexcel specification points
- **AT** *C2.24 Student examples* [word document] Examples for students to assess

## Assessment criteria

### Primary evidence and recording

0 No primary data collected.

1 Some data/observations are recorded that are appropriate for the topic, e.g. records end temperatures for each mass of zinc or records both start and end temperatures for some of the masses of zinc.

2 A suitable range of data/observations collected and some recorded appropriately, e.g. records start and end temperatures for all masses of zinc in a simple table or list.

3 A suitable range of data/observations collected and all recorded appropriately, e.g. data is recorded appropriately in a table with clear headings and correct units.

4 A suitable range of data/observations collected and all recorded appropriately, e.g. data is recorded appropriately in a table with clear headings and correct units. Further/repeat data also recorded.

# C2.25 Temperature changes



This lesson focuses on the difference between exothermic and endothermic reactions and explains the difference in terms of bond breaking and making.

## Specification coverage

**5.2** Define an exothermic change or reaction as one in which heat energy is given out, including combustion reactions or explosions

**5.3** Define an endothermic change or reaction as one in which heat energy is taken in, including photosynthesis or dissolving ammonium nitrate in water

**5.4** Describe the breaking of bonds as endothermic and the making of bonds as exothermic

**5.5** Demonstrate an understanding that the overall heat energy change for a reaction is: a) exothermic if more heat energy is released making bonds in the products than is required to break bonds in the reactants b) endothermic if less heat energy is released making bonds in the products than is required to break bonds in the reactants

**5.6** H Draw and interpret simple graphical representations of energy changes occurring in chemical reactions (no knowledge of activation energy is required)

HSW 3 Many phenomena can be explained by developing and using scientific theories, models and ideas

There are also opportunities to cover HSW 11, HSW 12.

## Key terms

endothermic
exothermic

### Heat energy

**Starter 1** AfL

Ask students to write down everything that they know about heat energy. This could be single words or more descriptive. Then ask students to work together in small groups to agree a sentence that describes the relationship between heat energy and temperature.

### Exothermic and endothermic reactions

**Exploring 1** Prac

Instructions are on **Worksheet C2.25a**. See the Teacher and technician practical sheet C2.25 for more information.

Stretch Higher Tier students draw a simple energy change graph for the reactants and products.

Support Give students the names of the individual reactants and products in the reactions, and ask them to write them out in the correct sequence as word equations.

### Student Book spread C2.25 (AT)

**Explaining 1**

Explain that the words 'exothermic' and 'endothermic' have come from 'exo' = outside, 'endo' = inside, and 'thermos' = heat (all Greek). Ask students to complete the table in the **AT** document *Energy changes*.

Stretch Ask students to sketch two energy change diagrams (Higher Tier) to complete their tables.

Support As a model, show he breaking of a breadstick and discuss the idea that energy is needed to break this 'bond'.

### Exothermic or endothermic? (AT)

**Plenary 1** AfL

There is a series of images in the **AT** presentation *Exothermic or endothermic?* Students must decide whether each one represents an exothermic or endothermic reaction. Energy change diagrams are also included for Higher Tier students.

### Everyday examples of exothermic and endothermic reactions

**Homework 1**

Ask students to find more examples of reactions with useful heat energy changes and to classify these as exothermic or endothermic processes.

Support Students could be given a list of common reactions and asked to find if they are exothermic or endothermic.

### Glowsticks

**Starter 2**

Pass a glow stick around the room and discuss the idea that some reactions give out energy. Ask students to suggest other reactions that give out energy.

### Temperature changes in reactions

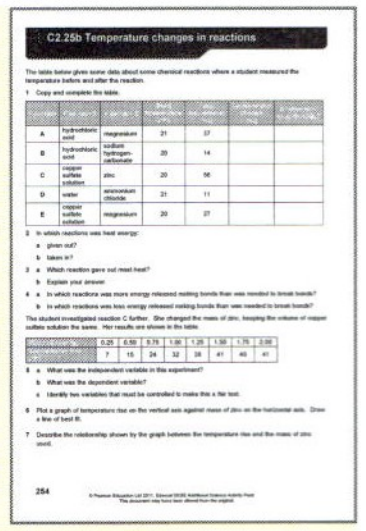

**Exploring 2**

Students work through **Worksheet C2.25b** which examines the temperature changes in some reactions.

Stretch Ask students to suggest some factors that affect the temperature change in a reaction and link this to the idea that there is a 'limiting factor' for the amount of heat energy released.

Support Provide a graph grid with scales and axes already marked.

### H Drawing energy diagrams

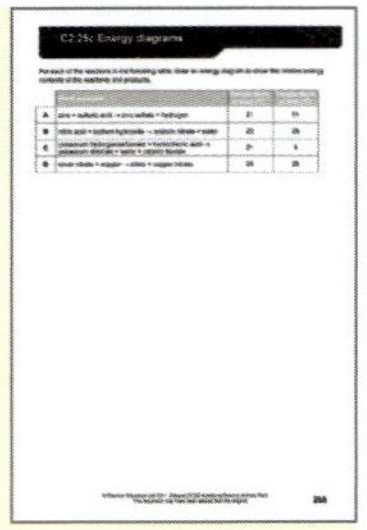

**Explaining 2**

Ask students to draw a series of energy diagrams for the exothermic and endothermic reactions described on **Worksheet C2.25c.**

Stretch Explain that individual bond energies can be measured (in joules). If the sum of the energy involved in forming bonds > sum of energy involved in breaking bonds, the reaction is exothermic.

### Energy change sentence starters

**Plenary 2** AfL Lit

Give students the start of some sentences that they must complete using what they have learned during the lesson. Examples are: 'Exothermic (endothermic) reactions are reactions that …'; 'In terms of bond breaking and making, in exothermic (in endothermic) reactions …'; 'Some uses of exothermic (endothermic) reactions include …'

### Useful heat changes

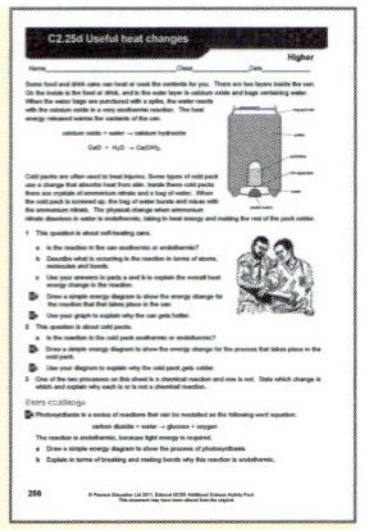

**Homework 2**

**Worksheet C2.25d**, for more able students looks at some examples of reactions with useful heat energy changes. It includes Higher Tier questions about diagrams showing energy changes.

Stretch Students answer the 'extra challenge' question.

# C2.25 Temperature changes

Why do some reactions heat things up and others cool things down?

Some foods and drinks come in self-heating cans. A chemical reaction started in one part of the can gives out lots of heat energy, heating up the food or drink in another part of the can.

**A**

**B** *Combustion reactions are exothermic.*

When a chemical reaction takes place there is often an energy transfer between the reactants and the surroundings. If the energy transfer is in the form of heat energy then there is a change in temperature.

**Exothermic** changes give out heat energy. Most chemical reactions are exothermic. The heat energy given out causes the temperature of the reaction mixture and its surroundings to increase.

All combustion reactions are exothermic reactions.

methane + oxygen → carbon dioxide + water

$CH_4 + 2O_2 \rightarrow CO_2 + 2H_2O$

Explosions are exothermic reactions that release a lot of heat energy and gases very quickly.

1 Give two examples each of reactions that:
a give out heat energy
b take in heat energy.

2 What is an exothermic reaction?

3 What is an endothermic reaction?

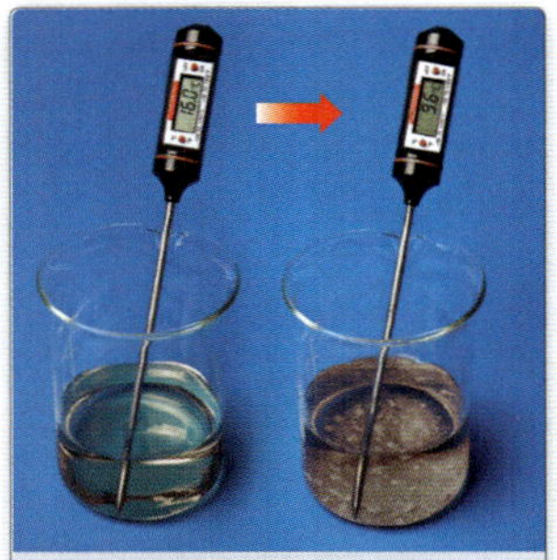

**C** *Endothermic reactions absorb heat energy from the surroundings so the temperature decreases.*

**Endothermic** changes take in heat energy from the surroundings, so the temperature of the surroundings decreases. Not many chemical reactions are endothermic. For example, if you react sodium hydrogencarbonate with hydrochloric acid in a test tube, the test tube feels cold because heat energy is taken from your hand.

Dissolving ammonium nitrate in water is an endothermic change. The process takes in heat energy and so the reaction mixture cools down whatever it is placed against. Photosynthesis is also an endothermic reaction.

## Making and breaking bonds

In chemical reactions, bonds in the reactants are broken and new bonds are formed in the products. It takes energy to break bonds, so breaking bonds is an endothermic process. Energy is released when bonds are made, so making bonds is an exothermic process.

In an exothermic reaction, less energy is needed to break the bonds in the reactants than is released in making bonds in the products. So heat energy is released.

In an endothermic reaction, more energy is needed to break the bonds in the reactants than is released in making bonds in the products. Heat energy is absorbed.

4 a Explain why breaking bonds is an endothermic change.
b Explain why making bonds is an exothermic change.

## Energy diagrams

We can show the energy changes during reactions using diagrams.

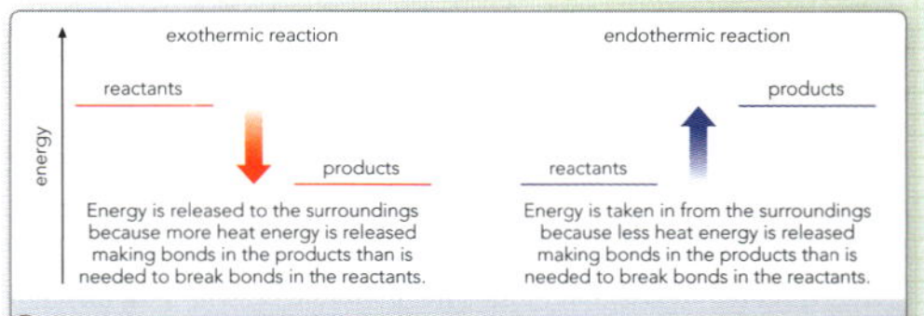


**D** *Graphical representations of energy changes in reactions*

**ResultsPlus Watch Out!**

Many students lose marks in exams by stating that energy is released when bonds are broken. When bonds are broken in the reactants, energy is *needed*. Remember *breakin' bonds means takin' energy.*

5 State whether each of these is exothermic or endothermic:
a copper sulfate reacts with zinc (the temperature rises) b dynamite is detonated to blast rocks c a leaf photosynthesises d coal burns e baking powder is mixed with vinegar (the temperature falls).

H 6 Draw a diagram to show the energy change for these reactions: a sodium hydrogencarbonate with hydrochloric acid b combustion of methane.

7 Explain the difference between endothermic and exothermic reactions by discussing the making and breaking of bonds.

**Skills spotlight**

Scientific theories can help scientists to explain and predict phenomena. In order to burn alkanes such as methane ($CH_4$) and ethane ($C_2H_6$), the bonds in these molecules must be broken. What prediction can you make about the energy needed to break all the bonds in methane compared to ethane?

### Learning Outcomes

5.2 Define an exothermic change or reaction as one in which heat energy is given out
5.3 Define an endothermic change or reaction as one in which heat energy is taken in
5.4 Describe the breaking of bonds as endothermic and the making of bonds as exothermic
5.5 Demonstrate an understanding that the overall heat energy change for a reaction is: a exothermic if more heat energy is released making bonds in the products than is required to break bonds in the reactants b endothermic if less heat energy is released making bonds in the products than is required to break bonds in the reactants
H 5.6 Draw and interpret simple graphical representations of energy changes occurring in chemical reactions
HSW 3 Describe how phenomena are explained using scientific models



What affects how fast limestone rocks weather? 

## ActiveTeach

- **AT** *Energy changes* [word document] Exothermic and endothermic reactions
- **AT** *Exothermic or endothermic* [presentation] Type of reaction

## Answers | Student Book

1 **a** Two examples of exothermic reactions (e.g. any combustion reactions, explosions, magnesium + hydrochloric acid)
**b** Two examples of endothermic reactions or processes (e.g. photosynthesis, dissolving ammonium nitrate in water, reaction of acids with hydrogencarbonates)

2 Reaction that releases/gives out heat energy

3 Reaction that absorbs/takes in heat energy

4 **a** Breaking bonds requires an energy
**b** Making bonds releases energy as heat energy

5 **a** Exothermic
**b** Exothermic
**c** Endothermic
**d** Exothermic
**e** Endothermic

6 H **a**

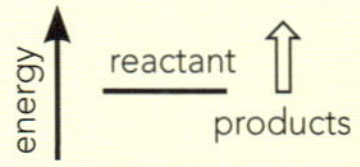


H **b**

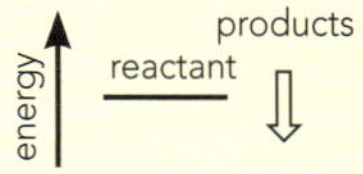


7 A good answer will contain the following points: energy is needed to break bonds; energy is released when bonds form; exothermic: more energy released making bonds than breaking bonds; temperature of reaction mixture and surroundings increases; endothermic: less energy released making bonds than breaking bonds; temperature of reaction mixture and surroundings decreases.

**Skills spotlight**

A good answer would show the structures of methane and ethane, showing the bonds. Methane has 4 C-H bonds while ethane has 6 C-H bonds and 1 C-C bond. As ethane has more bonds to break, it will take more energy to break the bonds.

# C2.26 Rates of reaction

This lesson challenges students to investigate how changing the concentration of hydrochloric acid affects its rate of reaction with calcium carbonate.
The activity may be run as a practice controlled assessment task or as a straight-forward class practical. The practical work can be completed in a one hour lesson.

## Specification coverage

***5.7*** Investigate the effect of temperature, concentration and surface area of a solid on the rate of a reaction such as hydrochloric acid and marble chips

This lesson provides opportunities to cover HSW *1*, HSW *2*, HSW *5*, HSW *6*, HSW *7*, HSW *8*, HSW *10* and HSW *11*.

### Before the lesson

If you intend to use this activity as a practice controlled assessment task, you should ensure that students are familiar with any equipment they may be expected to use so that they can plan their own investigation. In the week or two before the task show them this equipment and, if appropriate, allow them to practice using it. Pupils should be familiar with the use of gas syringes and how to set them up to collect gas from a conical flask. It may be good preparation to show students one or more of Skills sheets 19 to 26 to show what is expected of them in their actual controlled assessment task.

### Starter

**Calcium carbonate and hydrochloric acid**

Demonstrate the reaction of calcium carbonate with hydrochloric acid in a conical flask to show that carbon dioxide gas is produced. This could be followed by a discussion of the factors that might affect the rate of the reaction.

Follow this by reading the additional information below the opening section of page 168 of the Student Book. They may then read the brief description of the activity provided by the 'Your task' box.

### Option 1: Straight-forward class practical

Students follow the instructions on **Worksheet C2.26b**. The range of data that students need to collect is given on **Worksheet C2.26c**, which students will also need. This sheet guides students through recording, considering their results, and evaluating their investigation.

### Plenary

On page 169 of the Student Book you will find three examples of the sort of work that students may produce for this task. The examples focus on drawing a conclusion based on evidence. You could share these with students after they have completed their own work. This will help them to understand the assessment criteria and so make it easier for them to evaluate their work and to see how they can improve it. Moderator comments on each of the Student Book extracts can be found at the end of the assessment guidance for this investigation on the CD-ROM. The examples can also be found on the **AT** document *Student examples*.

### Option 2: Running the activity as a practice controlled assessment task (PCA)

We have provided a full range of support resources to allow the running of this practical as a practice controlled assessment task. A recommended structure is outlined below (to be used over a number of sessions). Marking guidance for all three parts of the practice task can be found on the CD-ROM that accompanies the TTPP. To save time when using these practice controlled assessment tasks, you may wish to focus on a particular aspect or skill rather than working through all three parts of the task.

#### Part A Planning

1 Students should be given the Student brief on **Worksheet C2.26a**. They can use Part A of the Workbook that is provided to help pupils with their practice controlled assessments. They should be given about 1 hour to do this planning.

#### Part B Observations

2. Students should be asked to carry out the practical task to collect evidence using the method they have planned in Part A. They should refer to the Student brief on **Worksheet C2.26a**. They can use Part B of the Workbook that is provided to help pupils with their practice controlled assessments. They should be given about 1 hour to collect their primary evidence.
3. If there is a problem with their own planned method, students may be asked to follow the method set out on **Worksheet C2.26b**. This will still enable students to access the full range of marks for Part B and Part C of the practice controlled assessment task.
4. In Part B, students are required to gather some secondary evidence. The evidence can be quantitative or qualitative. It can be from a variety of sources but students must note where they found their evidence and evaluate the quality of the source as part of this task. Skills sheet 22 provides students with further guidance on researching for and evaluating secondary evidence. This part of the task could be done outside of the lesson but must be supervised.

#### Part C Conclusions

5. Students follow the instructions set out on the Part C section of the Student brief on **Worksheet C2.26a**. They should use their data from Part B and the secondary evidence they have collected when doing this. They can use Part C of the Workbook that is provided to help pupils with their practice controlled assessments. They should be given about 1 hour to work on their conclusions.

The **AT** includes video clips showing a group of students working through elements of this investigation with teacher support.

Practice Controlled Assessment

# C2.26 Rates of reaction

What affects the rate of chemical reactions?

Rain is naturally acidic. Limestone is a rock made from calcium carbonate that weathers when it reacts with the acid in rainwater. In some areas limestone weathers faster than others. There are many factors that affect how fast limestone weathers. We can investigate several of these factors that affect how fast limestone reacts with acid.

**A** *These limestone rock formations in El Torcal Park, Spain, have been formed by weathering*

Chemical reactions take place at different rates. Some reactions are slow and some reactions are fast. There are several factors that affect the rate of chemical reactions, including the temperature, the surface area of the solid and the concentration of solutions.

Calcium carbonate reacts with hydrochloric acid as shown below.

calcium carbonate (s) + hydrochloric acid (aq) → calcium chloride (aq) + carbon dioxide (g) + water (l)

$CaCO_3(s) + 2HCl(aq) \rightarrow CaCl_2(aq) + CO_2(g) + H_2O(l)$

**Your task**

You are going to plan an investigation that will allow you to find out how changing the concentration of the hydrochloric acid changes the rate of reaction with limestone. Your teacher will provide you with some materials to help you organise this task.

**ResultsPlus**

**To access 4 marks**

- Provide a conclusion based on all your collected evidence
- Explain your conclusion
- Describe any relevant mathematical relationships in your conclusion

**To access 6 marks**

You also need to:

- Refer to the original hypothesis in your conclusion
- Refer to other scientific ideas in your conclusion

**Learning Outcomes**

5.7 *Investigate the effect of temperature, concentration and surface area of a solid on the rate of a reaction such as hydrochloric acid and marble chips*

## ResultsPlus Build Better Answers

When planning an investigation like this, one of the skills you will be assessed on is your ability to draw a *conclusion based on evidence*. There are 6 marks available for this skill. Here are three extracts focusing on this skill. Other skills are dealt with in other lessons.

**Student extract 1** A basic response for this skill

*When the concentration of the acid changes, the amount of carbon dioxide changes. I can see this from my graph because there is a change in the amount of carbon dioxide which is produced when different concentrations of acid are used. There is a straight line on my graph which means that when one factor changes another factor changes by the same amount.*

- It would be better here to say that the amount of carbon dioxide produced in 30 seconds changes.
- It is a good idea to use examples from your results or from your secondary evidence.
- The student has given a mathematical relationship.

**Student extract 2** A better response for this skill

*Increasing the concentration of the acid makes the reaction go faster. This supports my hypothesis. I can see this from the graph of my results because there is more carbon dioxide produced in 30 seconds when the concentration of the acid is higher. The increase in the concentration of acid and in the amount of carbon dioxide produced is directly proportional.*

- This is a clear conclusion and explains what has happened during the investigation.
- It is a good idea to explain if your conclusion supports your hypothesis or not.
- This is good use of the evidence from the practical results.

**Student extract 3** A good response for this skill

*Increasing the concentration of the acid makes the reaction go faster. This supports my hypothesis and is what I would expect from my scientific ideas about reactions. I think that for a reaction to take place the reaction molecules need to bump into each other with enough energy to react. If you increase the number of molecules in the reaction there are more of them to bump into each other and reactions are more likely to happen. I can see this from the graph of my results because there is more carbon dioxide produced in 30 seconds when the concentration of the acid is higher. I can also see this from the graph I found in the textbook on rates of reaction. As the concentration of the acid increases, the amount of carbon dioxide produced in the time increases. The amount of carbon dioxide formed in the time is proportional to the concentration of acid.*

- To access higher marks you should refer to scientific ideas.
- You should also explain what the scientific ideas are and use them to explain what is happening in your investigation.
- As well as using your results you can also use secondary evidence.





## ActiveTeach

- **AT** *C2.26 Rates of reaction* [video]
  Students work through the investigation
- **AT** *C2.26 Moderator comments* [word document]
  Moderator comments on the video
- **AT** *C2.26 Assessment criteria* [presentation]
  Understanding the CA marking criteria
- **AT** *C2.26 Student task sheet* [word document]
  CA video checklist
- **AT** *C2.26 Specification points* [word document]
  Edexcel specification points
- **AT** *C2.26 Student examples* [word document]
  Examples for students to assess

## Assessment criteria

### Conclusions based on evidence

**0** No relevant conclusions are made.

**1-2 a)** Makes a relevant conclusion based on all collected evidence but no link is made to the hypothesis.

**b)** An attempt is made to explain the conclusion using all collected evidence including mathematical relationships.

**3-4 a)** A conclusion is made that links to the hypothesis and is based on all the collected evidence, e.g. 'Increasing the concentration of the acid increases the volume of carbon dioxide produced in 30 seconds. This supports my hypothesis.'

**b)** The conclusion is explained using all collected evidence and mathematical relationships, e.g. uses evidence from own graph to show how volume of gas produced increases as concentration increases. Explains that the graph shows the relationship is directly proportional.

**5-6 a)** A conclusion is made that is linked to the hypothesis and based on the primary data and secondary evidence as well as scientific ideas, e.g. explains that the increasing concentration increases the volume of gas produced and that this matches both the hypothesis and scientific ideas.

**b)** The conclusions are explained using relevant scientific ideas, all collected evidence and relevant mathematical relationships, e.g. explains that increasing concentration of acid means that there are more ions available to react with the calcium carbonate and so collisions are more frequent. As the number of ions increases, the number of collisions increases by the same factor.

# C2.27 Rates of reaction



This lesson looks at three factors that can affect the rate of a reaction – temperature, concentration of solutions and surface area of solids. The lesson focuses on what effect they have rather than why they have that effect. The explanation follows in lesson C2.28.

## Specification coverage

**5.8** Recall that the rates of chemical reactions vary from very fast, explosive reactions to very slow reactions

**5.9** Describe the effect of changes in temperature, concentration and surface area of a solid on the rate of reaction

HSW *11* Presenting information, developing an argument and drawing a conclusion, and using scientific, technical and mathematical language, conventions and symbols and ICT tools

There are also opportunities to cover HSW *6*, HSW *7*, HSW *8* and HSW *10*.

## Key terms

concentration
rate of a chemical reaction
surface area

### Factors affecting rates

**Starter 1**

Show students the reaction between magnesium and hydrochloric acid which will be used in *Exploring 1*. Then ask them to list all the factors that they think will affect how fast the reaction takes place.

### The effect of concentration on reaction rate

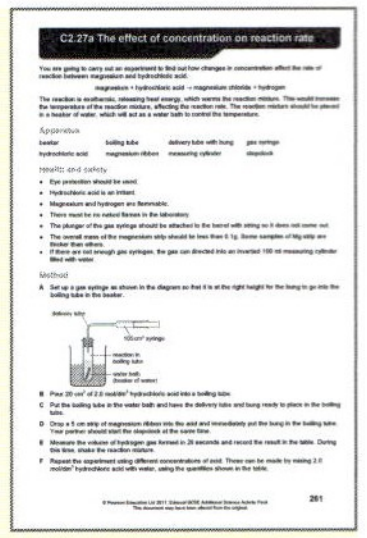

**Exploring 1** Prac

See **Worksheet C2.27a** and the Teacher and technician practical sheet C2.27 for full details.

Stretch Ask students to write a balanced equation, with state symbols, for the reaction.

Support Give students ready-prepared solutions of different concentrations rather than preparing these themselves.

### Explaining surface area and concentration

**Explaining 1**

Students measure the surface area of a block of Plasticine® and the total surface area of the two halves when the block is cut into two. They are then shown three solutions of copper sulfate and three solutions of hydrochloric acid with different concentrations and asked to rank them in order of concentration from their colour.

Stretch Ask students to calculate the surface area-to-volume ratio of the Plasticine® in each case.

Support Provide the equation for calculating the surface area of a rectangular block.

### Making a reaction safer

**Plenary 1**

Like magnesium, calcium also reacts with acid but the reaction can be dangerous. Ask students to suggest safe ways to react calcium with an acid to slow the reaction down.

### Rates top 10

**Homework 1**

Ask students to list 10 chemical reactions, either from school experiments or from everyday reactions, and list them in order of rate of reaction.

Support Provide some examples and ask them to come up with 3–5 more, and list them in order of rate of reaction.

### Fast and slow reactions

**Starter 2**

Ask students to think of three very fast, everyday reactions and three very slow, everyday reactions.

### Rates and data analysis 1

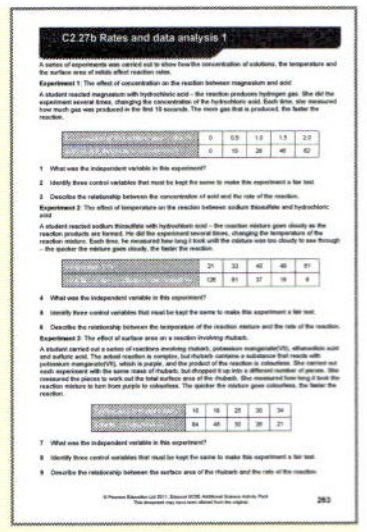

**Exploring 2**

Students work through **Worksheet C2.27b**, which presents data about rates of reaction for analysis.

Stretch Ask students to sketch a graph showing how the rate of reaction varies with the concentration, temperature or surface area in each case.

Support In order to help with questions 2, 5 and 8 ask students to produce a set of cards with variables that could affect rate, and to pick out those cards showing variables that were changed.

### Student Book spread C2.27 (AT)

**Explaining 2**

Students use the information in the Student Book to sketch graphs of how different temperatures, concentrations or surface areas affect the rate of a reaction in which a gas is formed.

Stretch Students could consider and suggest which factor has the greatest effect on rate.

Support Suitable graphs are available in the **AT** document *Rates of reaction.*

### Reaction rates true or false (AT)

**Plenary 2** AfL Lit

The **AT** presentation *Reaction rates* has a series of statements about reaction rates. Students must decide whether each one is true or false, and where false write a correct statement.

### Rates and data analysis 2

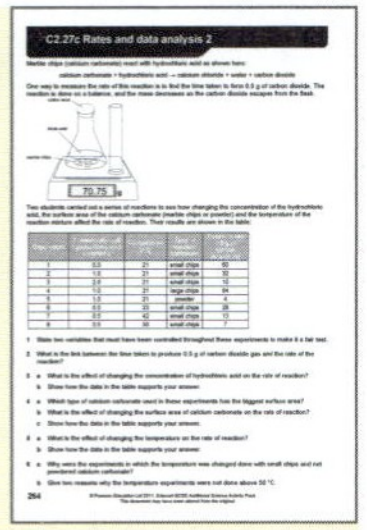

**Homework 2**

**Worksheet C2.27c**, for more able students, presents data about reaction rates for analysis.

Stretch Students could write a balanced equation for the reaction.

# C2.27 Rates of reaction

What affects the speed of a chemical reaction?

Industrial chemists have to find ways of controlling the speed of chemical reactions. Some reactions need to be speeded up and some must be slowed down. Ammonia is needed to make fertilisers and chemical engineers have to find ways to speed up the slow reaction that makes ammonia.

**A** *Chemical engineers find ways to control the speed of chemical reactions.*

The **rate of a chemical reaction** is the speed at which it takes place. It tells us how fast products are made and reactants are used up.

Explosions are very fast chemical reactions that release a large amount of heat energy and gas in a very short time. The burning of fuels such as methane and petrol are also fast exothermic reactions. The rusting of iron and the browning of freshly peeled apples are everyday examples of slow chemical reactions.

**B** *Rusting is a slow chemical reaction between iron with oxygen and water in the air.*

## The effect of temperature

The higher the temperature of the reactants, the faster the reaction. For example, eggs cook faster in boiling water than in warm water. Sometimes we cool reactions to slow them down. Food is put in a fridge to slow down the chemical reactions that make food go off.

## The effect of concentration

Many reactions involve solutions. The **concentration** of a solution is a measure of how much solute is dissolved in a solvent. The more solute dissolved in a fixed volume of solvent, the higher the concentration of the solution. The higher the concentration of a reactant in a solution, the faster the reaction.

**C** *Concentrated acid (far right) reacts faster with marble chips than dilute acid (far left).*

1 Give one example of a chemical reaction that at room temperature: a is very fast b is very slow.

2 Put the following chemical reactions in order of rate, from fastest to slowest: bananas ripening, oil burning, dynamite exploding, iron rusting.

3 Parts of Brazil and the UK often have the same amount of rain, but the climate is warmer in Brazil. In which of these locations will a piece of iron rust faster? Explain your answer.

## The effect of surface area on the rate of a reaction

Some reactions involve solids. If a solid is broken up into smaller pieces, more of the solid is at the surface. This means that the solid has a bigger **surface area**. The greater the surface area of a solid, the faster the reaction. For example, coal is ground up into a fine powder before burning in the furnaces in a power station to help it burn faster.

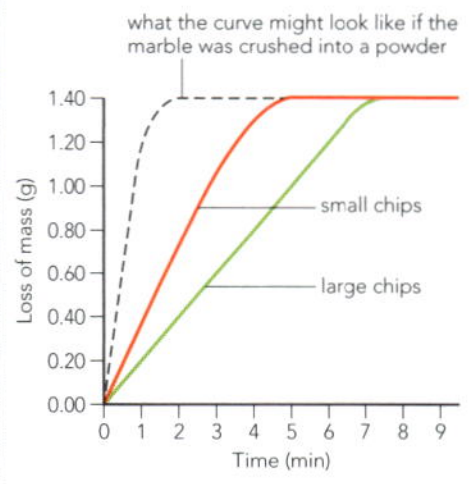


**D** *For small pieces of marble chip, more mass is lost as gas in the same time – the reaction is faster.*

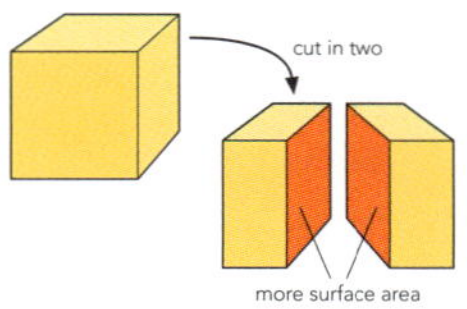


**E** *Breaking up a solid into more pieces increases it's surface area.*

**Skills spotlight**

Graphs can be useful for comparing sets of data. In reactions that produce gases, the volume of gas formed can be plotted against time. The gradient (steepness) of the line shows the rate. Which of the reactions in Figure D is fastest at the start? Explain your answer.

**ResultsPlus Watch Out!**

Many students get confused about the link between the sizes of pieces of a solid and the surface area. Remember – when a cube is cut into two there are two new surfaces and the surface area is increased. There are more surfaces to react.

4 Explain each of the following:
a Butter goes off faster if it is left out of the fridge.
b Iron filings react faster than an iron nail with an acid.
c Concentrated cleaning solution works faster than dilute cleaning solution.

5 The reaction between a metal and hydrochloric acid is slow at room temperature. Discuss three ways this reaction could be made to go faster.

**Learning Outcomes**

5.8 Recall that the rates of chemical reactions vary from very fast, explosive reactions to very slow reactions

5.9 Describe the effect of changes in temperature, concentration and surface area of a solid on the rate of reaction

HSW 11 Present information using scientific conventions and symbols



Why do reactions go faster at higher temperatures? 

## ActiveTeach

- **AT** *Rates of reaction* [word document] Labelling graphs
- **AT** *Reaction rates* [presentation] True or false statements

## Answers | Student Book

1 a Explosion/combustion reaction
b Rusting

2 Dynamite exploding, oil burning, bananas ripening, iron rusting

3 Faster in Brazil, temperature is higher

4 a Higher temperature speeds up reaction
b Bigger surface area speeds up reaction
c Higher concentration speeds up reaction

5 A good answer will contain the following points:
- increase the temperature
- use smaller pieces of the metal
- which have bigger surface area compared to same mass of a solid lump
- use higher concentration of hydrochloric acid.

**Skills spotlight**

The reaction with the small chips is the fastest as the gradient (at the start) is the steepest, i.e. the gas is produced at a faster rate. The reaction with the large chips is the slowest as the gradient is the least steep, i.e. the gas is produced at the slowest rate.

# C2.28 Collision theory

This lesson looks at why temperature, concentration of solutions and surface area of solids affect the rate of reactions by a consideration of collision theory.

## Specification coverage

**5.10** Describe how reactions can occur when particles collide (H) and explain how rates of reaction are increased by increasing the frequency and/or energy of collisions

**5.11** (H) Demonstrate an understanding that not all collisions lead to a reaction, especially if particles collide with low energy

HSW **3** Many phenomena can be explained by developing and using scientific theories, models and ideas.

## Key terms

collision theory

### Basic particle theory

**Starter 1** AfL

Use marbles in a tray to remind students about the movement of particles in a solid, liquid or gas and ask students to look at collisions between particles and to think what would affect how often particles collide.

### Collision theory model

**Exploring 1** Demo

**Worksheet C2.28a** and Teacher and technician practical sheet C2.28 link to this activity.

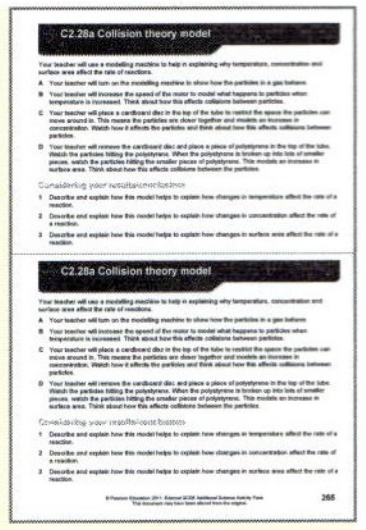

Stretch Students could predict how and why changes in pressure would affect reactions between gases.

Support Foundation tier work should focus on the fact that particles must collide to react.

### (H) Student Book spread C2.28

**Explaining 1**

Students use the information in the Student Book, plus **Worksheet C2.28b**, to make notes on the diagrams about why each factor affects the rate of a reaction.

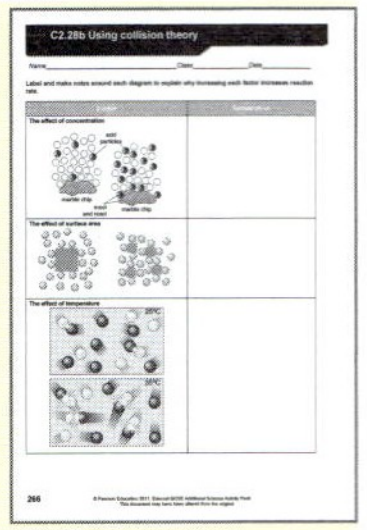

Stretch Ask students to describe the limitations of two dimensional, static diagrams to explain how these factors affect rates.

### Calcium carbonate and acid

**Plenary 1** AfL Lit

Ask students to list three ways of speeding up the reaction between calcium carbonate and hydrochloric acid. They work in pairs to produce an explanation for each factor in terms of collision theory, using no more than 20 words for each one. Foundation tier student could try to explain why two solids do not react together, whereas solutions of the same substances do react.

### Collisions

**Homework 1**

Ask students to list examples of everyday situations where things cannot happen unless things come into contact with each other.

Support Give students a couple of examples to start off e.g. cannot write on paper without pen coming into contact with paper, cannot tie a shoe lace without hands coming into contact with it.

### Speeding up a reaction

**Starter 2**

The key ingredient in iron tablets is the salt, iron(II) sulfate, which is often made by the reaction of iron with sulfuric acid. This reaction could be demonstrated by adding an iron nail to some sulfuric acid. Ask students to suggest ways that a company manufacturing the tablets could speed up the reaction.

### (H) Role play

**Exploring 2**

Students could work in groups to plan and then act out why one or all of concentration of solutions, surface area of solids and temperature affect reaction rates.

Stretch More able students could be used as a judging panel on the performances, which would also prevent them dominating the planning of the performances.

### Collision theory cartoon strip

**Explaining 2**

Use Figure B in the Student Book page 172 or *Exploring 1*. For Higher Tier students explain that increased frequency of collisions and increased energy of collisions both increase the rate of a reaction. Students draw a cartoon strip to show that reactions can occur when particles of the reactants collide.

Stretch Students write a set of criteria for assessing the cartoon strips.

Support Students focus on the need for collisions between particles for a reaction to take place.

### (H) Correct explanations? (AT)

**Plenary 2** AfL Lit

There are a series of explanations in the **AT** document *Correct explanations?* about factors affecting rates. Students should work in pairs to comment on the accuracy of each statement. Where there are issues with the statements, students should note what they are and then rewrite the statement.

### (H) Collision theory diagrams

**Homework 2**

**Worksheet C2.28c**, for more able students, gives a diagram showing particles colliding in a reaction. Students redraw the diagram to show how changes in concentration and surface area affect rates.

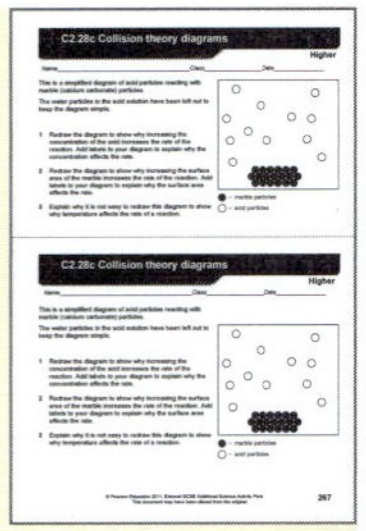

Stretch Students could try to find out how particles that are too low in energy to react do eventually react.

# C2.28 Collision theory

How can we explain the factors that affect reaction rates?

Commercial explosives need energy to start the very fast, explosive reaction. The energy is provided by a small amount of a second explosive in a detonator inside the main explosive. The detonator is set off by a burning fuse or an electric current.

A Energy is needed to start this explosive reaction.

1 Give three ways of speeding up a chemical reaction.

2 What must happen for particles to react with each other?

For a reaction to occur, particles of the reacting substances must collide with each other.

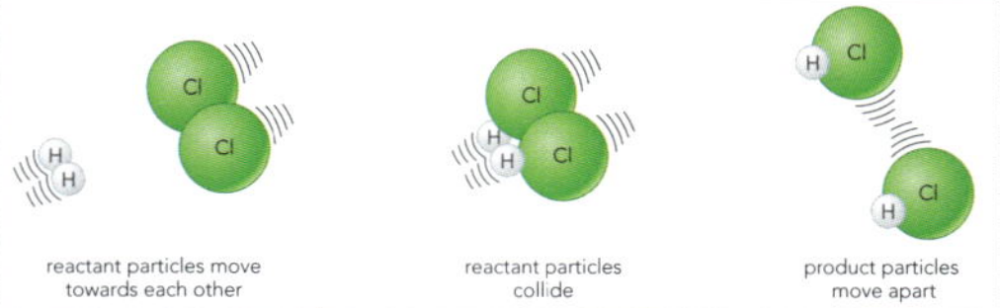


B Collision and reaction of hydrogen and chlorine molecules

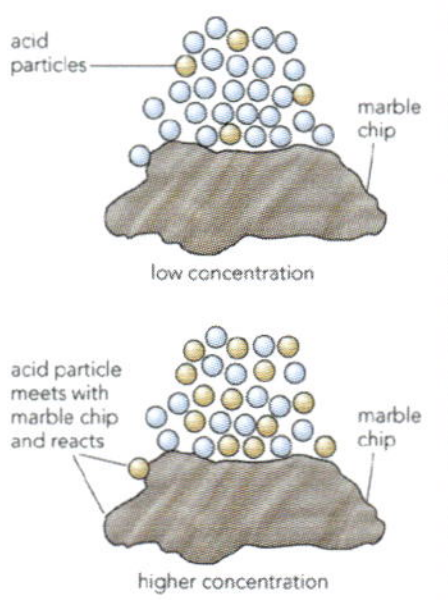


C Collisions between reactant particles are more frequent at higher concentrations.

The rate of any reaction will increase if the particles collide more frequently. Particles can only react with other particles when they collide, so the more often particles collide, the faster the reaction.

The collision must also have enough energy to break the bonds in the reactants. Many collisions do not have enough energy to get the reaction started. The rate of reaction will be increased if there are more high-energy collisions because the particles are more likely to react when they collide.

## The effect of concentration

The more concentrated a solution, the more solute particles there are in a given volume. This means that it is more likely that reactant particles will collide with one another – and the more collisions there are between reactant particles, the faster the rate of reaction will be.

## The effect of temperature

The higher the temperature, the faster the particles move. This means they collide with more energy and so are more likely to react. They also move faster at higher temperatures and so collide more frequently. This means that increasing the temperature increases the rate of reaction.

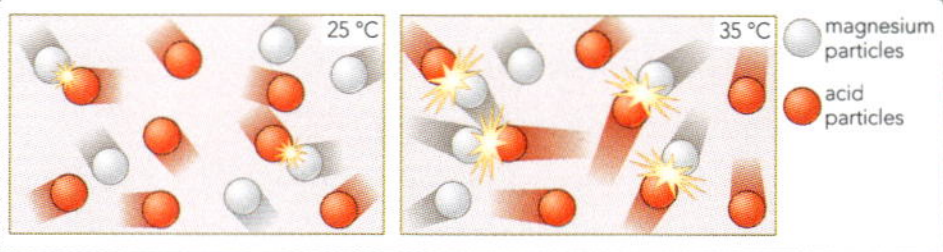


D Collisions have more energy and are more frequent at higher temperatures.

## The effect of surface area

In a solid, only the particles on the surface can be involved in collisions. Those under the surface cannot react until those at the surface have reacted and left the solid. The greater the surface area of a solid, the more particles there are at the surface. This means that there will be more frequent collisions between reactants and so a higher rate of reaction.

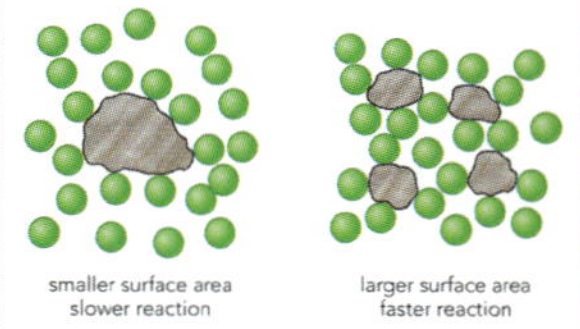


E The greater the surface area, the more frequent the collisions

**ResultsPlus Watch Out!**

When asked about collisions and rates of reaction, students often forget about the time of the reaction. The rate only increases if there are more collisions in one minute. The increased *frequency* of collisions increases the rate.

**Skills spotlight**

Models can help us to understand how complex processes happen, especially processes that we cannot see.

- Describe the main features of the collision theory model.
- Describe how these features help to explain why increasing the temperature increases the rate of a reaction.

(H) 3 Why do particles need energy to react when they collide?

(H) 4 Explain why some collisions between particles do not result in a reaction.

(H) 5 Concentrated bleach solutions remove stains faster than dilute solutions of bleach. Use the collision theory to explain why.

(H) 6 Powdered calcium carbonate reacts faster than lumps of calcium carbonate with an acid. Explain why using the collision theory.

(H) 7 Iron rusts faster if it is left in a warm place. Explain why using the collision theory.

(H) 8 Explain fully, using the collision theory, why powdered magnesium reacts faster with a warm acid than magnesium ribbon does with an acid at room temperature.

**Learning Outcomes**

5.10 Describe how reactions can occur when particles collide (H) and explain how rates of reaction are increased by increasing the frequency and/or energy of collisions

(H) 5.11 Demonstrate an understanding that not all collisions lead to a reaction, especially if particles collide with low energy

HSW 3 Describe how phenomena are explained using scientific models



Platinum is one of the most expensive metals. Why is it used in cars?



## ActiveTeach

- **AT** *What affects rate of reaction?* [interactive] Understanding kinetic theory – quiz
- **AT** *Correct explanations* [word document] Statement accuracy

## Answers | Student Book

1 Any three from increase temperature, increase concentration (of solutions), increase surface area (of solids), use a suitable catalyst (catalysts not covered until Lesson C2.29).

2 Must collide ((H) with enough energy)

3 (H) Energy is needed to break bonds

4 (H) Particles do not have enough energy

5 (H) Particles closer together (more bleach particles in a given volume of liquid), so more frequent collisions between the bleach and particles in the stain

6 (H) Powdered calcium carbonate has a bigger surface area than the same mass of solid, so more particles at surface / exposed, so more frequent collisions between the acid and calcium carbonate, so rate of reaction increased.

7 (H) At higher temperatures, both iron and oxygen particles move faster, collide more frequently, so rate of reaction increased; also particles have more energy, so more likely to react on collision

8 (H) A good answer with include: At higher temperatures: particles of acid and magnesium both move faster; collide more often; particles have more energy; particles more likely to react on collision; powder has greater surface area than the same mass of solid; more particles exposed; more chance of collisions; so rate of reaction increased.

**Skills spotlight**

In the collision theory model, particles must collide and have enough energy in order to react. An increase in temperature increases reaction rate because (i) particles have more energy and so collisions are more likely to result in a reaction and (ii) particles move faster and so collide more often.

# C2.29 Catalysts



This lesson looks at the effect of catalysts on chemical reactions. The main focus is their use in catalytic converters.

## Specification coverage

***5.12*** Recall the effect of a catalyst on the rate of reaction

***5.13*** Demonstrate an understanding that catalytic converters in cars: a) have a high surface area to increase the rate of reaction of carbon monoxide and unburnt fuel from exhaust gases with oxygen from the air to produce carbon dioxide and water b) work best at high temperatures

HSW ***13*** How and why decisions about science and technology are made, including those that raise ethical issues, and about the social, economic and environmental effects of such decisions

There are also opportunities to cover HSW *1*, HSW *6*, HSW *7*, HSW *8* and HSW *12*.

## Key terms

catalyst
catalytic converter

### Speeding up the decomposition of hydrogen peroxide

**Starter 1** Demo

Show students some hydrogen peroxide solution. Ask them to suggest ways of speeding up this reaction. Now add a spatula measure of manganese(IV) oxide and they will see a rapid reaction. The manganese(IV) oxide is a catalyst and this simple demonstration introduces catalysts very well. See the Teacher and technician practical sheet C2.29 (1) for full details.

### Investigating catalysts

**Exploring 1** Prac

**Worksheet C2.29a** gives instructions and asks questions. See the Teacher and technician practical sheet C2.29 (2) for full details.

Stretch Students could plan a way to produce quantitative comparisons for this experiment.

Support Students could answer questions 1 and 2 only.

### Pros and cons of catalytic converters

**Exploring 3**

Students look at the Skills spotlight box, which gives reasons why catalytic converters were introduced. They should prepare a brief presentation that some groups will give to the class.

Stretch Students could look for pros and cons of all three factors – namely social, economic and environmental.

Support Students could just look at environmental factors.

### Catalysts true/false (AT)

**Plenary 1** AfL Lit

There are a series of statements on the **AT** document *Catalysts* – students have to decide whether they are true or false. For false statements they should write correct statements.

### Catalysts

**Homework 1**

**Worksheet C2.29c**, for students needing support, looks at uses of catalytic converters and at rates of reaction.

Support Students can omit question **5**.

### Factors affecting reaction rates

**Starter 2** AfL Lit

Ask students to draw a concept map about the reaction rates work so far, including what factors affect reaction rates and (for Higher Tier) explanations using collision theory.

### Car emissions data

**Exploring 2**

**Worksheet C2.29b** gives data about emissions from car exhausts and asks questions using it.

Stretch Students could write a balanced equation for the reactions that remove carbon monoxide and unburned hydrocarbons/petrol and explain why the catalyst does not appear in the equation.

Support Students could be provided with a grid for drawing their bar charts.

### Student Book spread C2.29 (AT)

**Explaining 1**

Students use the information in the Student Book, plus the car exhaust system diagram from the **AT** document *Car exhaust system*, to make suitable notes about what catalysts are and key features about catalytic converters in cars.

Stretch Students include ideas from collision theory about why the elements of catalytic converters have a large surface area.

Support Students may need some key words such as 'reaction rate', 'surface area', 'hot'.

### Factors affecting reaction rates

**Plenary 2** AfL Lit

Students create (or complete if started in *Starter 2*) a concept map covering all the factors affecting reaction rates, to include catalysts and information they have learned in this lesson.

### Hydrogen peroxide data analysis

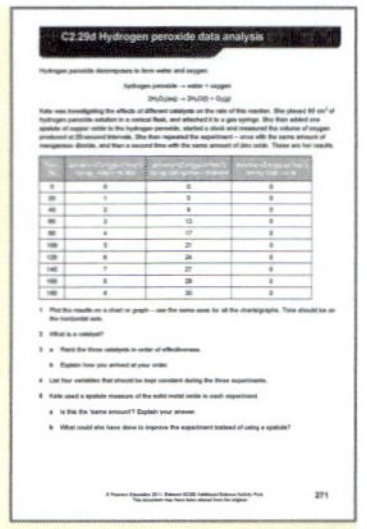

**Homework 2**

**Worksheet C2.29d**, looks at the effect of catalysts on the rate of reaction for the decomposition of hydrogen peroxide. Students will need graph paper.

Stretch Students could sketch three lines on the graph to predict the results for 50 $cm^3$ of hydrogen peroxide with manganese dioxide as catalyst at 30 °C rather than at room temperature.

# C2.29 Catalysts

What do catalysts do to reactions?

Fireworks used in stage effects must have very carefully controlled explosions otherwise they would be very dangerous. These fireworks contain many substances – some are added to control the rate of the reactions.

A

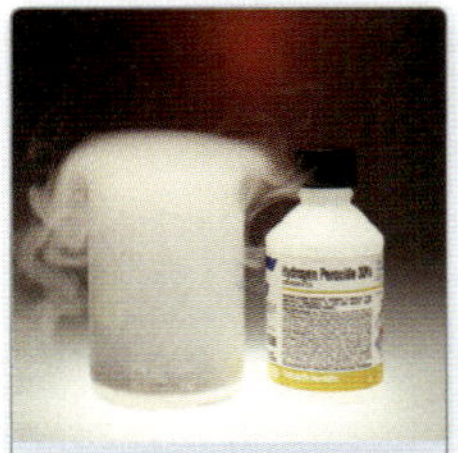


**B** *Hydrogen peroxide breaks down to form water and bubbles of oxygen gas much faster if the catalyst manganese dioxide is added.*

**Catalysts** are substances that speed up chemical reactions without being used up in the reactions. Many chemical processes use catalysts to increase the rate of production of products.

**C**

| Name of catalyst | Process |
|---|---|
| iron | making ammonia from nitrogen and hydrogen |
| nickel | making margarine from liquid vegetable oils |
| aluminium oxide | for cracking alkanes |

1 What is a catalyst?

2 Why are catalysts important in industrial processes?

3 Suggest why catalysts save money in industrial processes.

Using a catalyst often means that reactions can be done at lower temperatures and pressures than they would otherwise. This means that less energy is used, which saves money and energy resources.

## Catalytic converters

The combustion of petrol in car engines produces toxic carbon monoxide and unburned hydrocarbons. Since 1993, new petrol-engine cars in the EU have been built with **catalytic converters** to reduce these pollutants in exhaust gases. Catalytic converters help to combine carbon monoxide and unburned petrol with oxygen from the air to form carbon dioxide and water vapour.

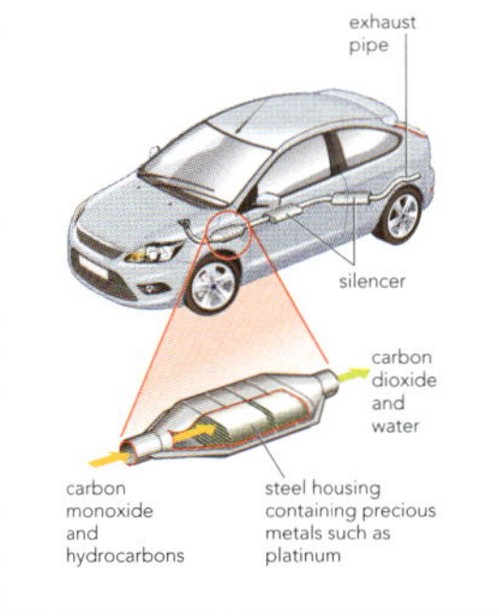


**D** *The location of a catalytic converter in a car*

Catalytic converters contain the transition metals platinum, rhodium or palladium. These all speed up reactions that remove the pollutants in exhaust gases. The metals used as catalysts are very expensive. To make a catalytic converter as efficient as possible while using as little of the metals as possible, scientists have refined the designs of converters to give the catalyst a high surface area. The converter is about the size of a shoe box but has a total internal surface area of about three football pitches due to a honeycomb structure. A very thin surface coat of the catalyst is used on this structure to minimise the amount of catalyst used.

Reactions are faster at higher temperatures, and catalytic converters work best at high temperatures. When an engine is first started, a catalytic converter is cool and does not work as well. However, the hot gases from the engine quickly heat it up.

**E** *Inside a catalytic converter*

**Skills spotlight**

There are many factors that affect how laws are made about the use of science and technology. Describe some of the social, economic and environmental factors in the decision to pass the law that all new cars should be fitted with catalytic converters.

**ResultsPlus Watch Out!**

Students sometimes make mistakes when writing catalysts in a word equation. The catalyst must *never* be written with the reactants or the products. It should be written above the arrow.

4 a Why are cars fitted with catalytic converters?
b Which metals are used as catalysts in catalytic converters?
c What pollutants do they remove?
d What do they convert these pollutants into?

5 a Explain why catalysts are usually made with a high surface area.
b (H) Explain why a high surface area has the effect it has.
c How is a high surface area achieved in a catalytic converter?
d Why do catalytic converters work best at high temperature?

6 Suggest two reasons why we should not throw away old catalytic converters but recycle the metal catalysts.

7 A company wants to speed up the reaction it uses to make an important product. It plans to either increase the temperature or use a catalyst. Explain how each method works and suggest why using a catalyst may be the cheaper way to do it.

**Learning Outcomes**

*5.12* Recall the effect of a catalyst on the rate of reaction

*5.13* Demonstrate an understanding that catalytic converters in cars: *a* have a high surface area to increase the rate of reaction of carbon monoxide and unburnt fuel from exhaust gases with oxygen from the air to produce carbon dioxide and water *b* work best at high temperatures

HSW *13* Explain how and why decisions about uses of science and technology are made





## ActiveTeach

- **AT** *How to increase the rate of reaction* [interactive] Rate of chemical reaction – matching activity
- **AT** *Catalysts* [word document] True or false statements
- **AT** *Car exhaust system* [word document] Unlabelled image
- **AT** *Location of a catalytic converter in a motor vehicle* [diagram] Figure C – diagram labelling activity

## Answers | Student Book

1 A substance that increases rate of reaction, does not get used up

2 Speed up processes; time can be an economic factor

3 Allow lower temperature/pressure, saves energy and money

4 **a** To reduce harmful emissions
**b** Platinum / rhodium / palladium
**c** Carbon monoxide, unburned hydrocarbons in the petrol
**d** Carbon dioxide, water vapour

5 **a** Increases reaction rate, requires less catalyst (which is a valuable metal)
**b** More particles at surface, higher collision frequency
**c** Spread metal in thin layer, onto a honeycomb support with lots of tubes/pipes
**d** Reaction rate faster at high temperature

6 Economic: catalysts are expensive metals; environmental: these metals may be toxic (harm people or the environment); conserve metal resources and energy used in manufacture

7 A good answer will contain the following points: increased temperature; particles of the reactants have more energy; more likely to react when they collide; more frequent collisions at higher speeds; catalyst also speeds up the reaction; catalyst cheaper as although initial cost may be high; the energy savings are greater.

Skills spotlight

- **Social**: air is less polluted, particularly in places where there is a lot of traffic.
- **Economic**: cars with catalytic converters cost; need to be sure that devices will not affect performance/running of the engine or increase servicing/maintenance costs.
- **Environmental**: less pollutants are put into the atmosphere (although the heavy metals used may be toxic.
- **Ethical**: use of catalytic converters does less harm to our world (for the greater good).

# C2.30 Relative masses

This lesson follows on from the idea of relative atomic mass in Topic 1 and involves calculating the relative formula mass and finding the empirical formula of a compound.

## Specification coverage

***6.1*** Calculate relative formula mass given relative atomic masses

***6.2*** Calculate the formulae of simple compounds from reacting masses and understand that these are empirical formulae

HSW ***11*** Presenting information, developing an argument and drawing a conclusion, using scientific, technical and mathematical language, conventions and symbols and ICT tools

There are also opportunities to cover HSW ***6*** and HSW ***10***.

## Key terms

empirical formula
molecular formula
relative atomic mass
relative formula mass

### Firework video

**Starter 1**

Show a video clip of fireworks. Tell the students that the fireworks contain different metal compounds that give them their different colours. For example, strontium and lithium salts give red, calcium salts give orange, sodium salts yellow, barium salts green and copper salts blue. In this lesson they will be learning how to work out the formulae for some of these salts.

### Relative masses

**Exploring 1**

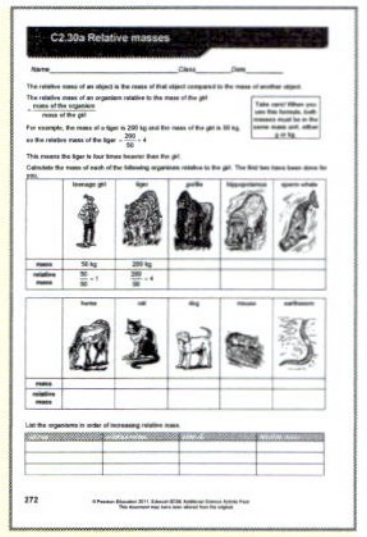

Students complete **Worksheet C2.30a** to calculate the masses of various animals relative to a girl.

Stretch Ask the students to choose one of the animals – for example, the gorilla – and work out the mass of all the others relative to that.

Support Help students in working out the relative masses. Also provide the first two or three in the list of increasing relative mass.

### Student Book spread C2.30 (AT)

**Explaining 2**

Explain that an empirical formula is the simplest whole number ratio of atoms in a formula and that it may be different from the molecular formula. Show how to determine the empirical formula of a compound from reacting masses.

Stretch Explain that the empirical formula can also be calculated from percentage mass composition. Tell students not to round the ratios in empirical formulae too soon.

Support The **AT** document *Empirical formula* provides tables with the working already printed to guide students through the calculation.

### Quiz

**Plenary 1** AfL

Provide a short quiz with questions on names, formulae and relative formula masses. Students can work in pairs to answer the questions. They then swap their answers with another pair for marking and correct any wrong answers.

### Relative masses and formulae

**Homework 1**

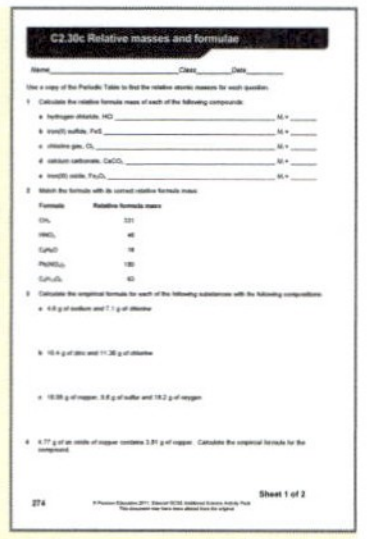

**Worksheet C2.30c**, for students needing support, tests all the material covered in this lesson.

Support Photocopy the worksheet with the worked examples of how to calculate an empirical formula from masses of elements, and how to determine an empirical formula from a molecular formula.

### Where do formulae come from?

**Starter 2**

Write several formulae on the board, for example, $H_2O$, $CO_2$, NaCl, $K_2SO_4$, $Mg(NO_3)_2$. Ask the students the names of each of these compounds and remind them of the difference between sulfate and sulfide or nitrate and nitride from Topic 2. Tell the students they will be finding out how to work out these formulae from the masses of each element in the compound.

### Relative formula mass

**Explaining 1**

Show students how to calculate relative formula mass. Start with simple binary compounds then move on to slightly more complex formulae then formulae with brackets. Warn students not to write units with their numerical values of relative atomic and formula masses.

Stretch Work out the relative formula mass of salts containing water of crystallisation.

Support Use models of molecules or draw diagrams of the molecules so that students can see how many atoms of each type are present.

### Molecular formulae

**Explaining 3**

Show a model of a molecule such as glucose ($C_6H_{12}O_6$) then break it up and count the atoms of each element. This gives the formula for an actual molecule of glucose – tell students it is called the 'molecular formula'.

Stretch Draw other structures – such as $C_6H_{14}$, $C_2H_2Br_2$ and $C_3H_8O$ – on the board and ask the students to determine the empirical formulae.

Support Use simple binary compounds such as $H_2O_2$, $C_2H_6$ and $N_2H_4$.

### Matching definitions

**Plenary 2** Lit

Students work in pairs to match the key words with the correct definitions on **Worksheet C2.30b**. The phrases can be printed onto a sheet of card which is then cut up.

### Find the formula

**Homework 2**

**Worksheet C2.30d**, is for more able students. They research the formulae for eight compounds, show how to calculate the relative formula mass and find a use for the compound.

Stretch Students answer the 'extra challenge' question.

# C2.30 Relative masses

How do you calculate the relative mass and formula for a compound?

Some metal ions produce colours when burned – this is why they can be added to fireworks. For example, calcium ions in calcium chloride give fireworks an orange colour and lithium ions in lithium carbonate give red colours. Chemists need to know the formulae for these compounds.

A

| Element | Relative atomic mass |
|---|---|
| hydrogen | 1 |
| lithium | 7 |
| carbon | 12 |
| nitrogen | 14 |
| oxygen | 16 |
| magnesium | 24 |
| aluminium | 27 |
| sulfur | 32 |
| chlorine | 35.5 |
| calcium | 40 |
| iron | 56 |

**B** *Relative atomic masses*

The **relative atomic mass**, $A_r$, of an element compares the mass of an atom to the mass of a $^{12}C$ atom. Carbon-12 atoms have a relative atomic mass of 12. $^{1}H$ atoms are twelve times lighter than $^{12}C$ atoms so they have a relative atomic mass of 1. Figure B lists some of the common relative atomic masses.

The **relative formula mass**, $M_r$, of a substance is the sum of the relative atomic masses of all the atoms or ions in its formula. For example, carbon dioxide has the formula $CO_2$ because each molecule contains one carbon atom and two oxygen atoms:

$$M_r = A_r(C) + 2 \times A_r(O)$$
$$= 12 + (2 \times 16) = 44$$

For magnesium sulfate, $MgSO_4$,

$$M_r = A_r(Mg) + A_r(S) + 4 \times A_r(O)$$
$$= 24 + 32 + (4 \times 16) = 120$$

The brackets in the formula $Ca(NO_3)_2$ show that for each calcium ion there are two nitrate ions. This means that each unit of calcium nitrate contains one calcium, two nitrogen and six oxygen atoms:

$$M_r = A_r(Ca) + 2 \times A_r(N) + 6 \times A_r(O)$$
$$= 40 + (2 \times 14) + (6 \times 16) = 164$$

1 Calculate the relative formula masses of:
a oxygen, $O_2$
b water, $H_2O$
c ammonia, $NH_3$

2 Work out the number of atoms of each element present in:
a copper sulfate, $CuSO_4$ b iron(III) hydroxide, $Fe(OH)_3$

3 Calculate the relative formula mass for:
a magnesium hydroxide, $Mg(OH)_2$ b aluminium nitrate, $Al(NO_3)_3$

**ResultsPlus Watch Out!**
Relative formula masses are measured *relative* to $^{12}C$ and have *no* units.

## Empirical formulae

A substance can be represented by an **empirical formula**. This shows the simplest whole number ratio of atoms or ions of each element in the substance. The empirical formula of water is $H_2O$ because there are twice as many hydrogen atoms as oxygen in one molecule.

A sample of a compound can be analysed to find the mass of each element present in the compound. You can then calculate the empirical formula. Figure C shows how to work out an empirical formula, using calcium chloride (made by reacting 10.0 g of calcium and 17.8 g of chlorine) as an example.

| Symbol for element | Ca | Cl |
|---|---|---|
| Mass in g | 10.0 | 17.8 |
| Relative atomic mass | 40 | 35.5 |
| Divide the mass of each element by its relative atomic mass | $\frac{10.0}{40} = 0.25$ | $\frac{17.8}{35.5} = 0.5$ |
| Divide the answers by the smallest number to find the simplest ratio | $\frac{0.25}{0.25} = 1$ | $\frac{0.5}{0.25} = 2$ |
| Empirical formula | $CaCl_2$ | |

**C** *How to calculate an empirical formula. If there are three elements in the compound add an extra column for the additional element.*

The true formula for a simple molecular compound is called the **molecular formula**. This shows the actual number of atoms of each element in a molecule. Ethene has the molecular formula $C_2H_4$ and propene is $C_3H_6$ – but both have the empirical formula $CH_2$.

4 Calculate the empirical formula of the following substances:
a water, if a sample contains 0.6 g of hydrogen and 4.8 g of oxygen
b lithium carbonate, if a sample contains 2.8 g of lithium, 2.4 g of carbon and 9.6 g of oxygen
c potassium nitrate, if a sample contains 5.85 g of potassium, 2.1 g of nitrogen and 7.2 g of oxygen.

5 Write a short paragraph to show how the following are connected:
- relative atomic mass
- relative formula mass
- empirical formula
- molecular formula.

**ResultsPlus Watch Out!**
Some students round the simplest ratios too much. For example, a ratio of 1 : 1.5 should be multiplied by 2 to give 2 : 3, not rounded to 1 : 2.

**Skills spotlight**
Scientific information can be presented concisely using symbols and formulae. Explain to a friend what is meant by the formula $Fe(OH)_2$ and how to calculate the relative formula mass.

**Maths skills**
Finding the empirical formula of a compound from its molecular formula is the same as **simplifying ratios**.
For example:
The molecular formula of glucose is $C_6H_{12}O_6$, which means the ratio of carbon to hydrogen to oxygen atoms is 6 : 12 : 6.
To simplify this ratio we divide by a common multiple, in this case 6, to get 1 : 2 : 1.
The empirical formula of glucose is therefore $CH_2O$.

**Learning Outcomes**
6.1 Calculate relative formula mass given relative atomic masses
6.2 Calculate the formulae of simple compounds from reacting masses and understand that these are empirical formulae
HSW 11 Present information using scientific conventions and symbols

176 | How can you find a formula? 177

**ActiveTeach**

- **AT** *Empirical formula* [word document] Template for calculations

## Answers | Student Book

1 a 32
b 18
c 17
2 a 1 copper, 1 sulfur, 4 oxygen
b 1 iron, 3 oxygen, 3 hydrogen
3 a 58
b 213
4 a $H_2O$
b $Li_2CO_3$
c $KNO_3$
5 A good answer will contain the following points.
- relative atomic mass – average mass of an atom compared to the mass of 1/12 of a $^{12}C$ atom.
- relative formula mass – sum of the relative atomic masses of all the atoms in a formula.
- empirical formula – formula showing the simplest whole number ratio of atoms of each element in the compound.
- molecular formula – formula showing the actual number of atoms of each element in a molecule.

**Skills spotlight**
$Fe(OH)_2$ is iron hydroxide, some students may realise it is iron(II) hydroxide. The brackets in the formula show that there are two hydroxide ions for each iron ion. Each molecule of the compound contains one iron atom, two oxygen atoms and two hydrogen atoms. The relative formula mass is
$A_r(Fe) + 2 \times A_r(O) + 2 \times A_r(H) = 56 + 32 + 2 = 90$

# C2.31 To determine the empirical formula for magnesium oxide

130

This lesson challenges students to investigate the relationship between the masses of magnesium and oxygen then to calculate the empirical formula for magnesium oxide. The activity may be run as a practice controlled assessment task or as a straight-forward class practical. The practical work can be completed in 1 hour.

## Specification coverage

***6.3*** Determine the empirical formula of a simple compound, such as magnesium oxide

This lesson provides opportunities to cover **HSW** *1*, **HSW** *2*, **HSW** *5*, **HSW** *6*, **HSW** *7*, **HSW** *8*, **HSW** *10* and **HSW** *11*.

### Before the lesson

If you intend to use this activity as a practice controlled assessment task, you should ensure that students are familiar with any equipment they may be expected to use so that they can plan their own investigation. In the week or two before the task show them this equipment and, if appropriate, allow them to practice using it. Students should be familiar with heating a crucible on a pipe clay triangle and using a pair of tongs. It may be good preparation to show students one or more of Skills sheets 19 to 26 to show what is expected of them in their actual controlled assessment task.

### Starter

**What makes a good flare?**

Show a short video clip of a flare such as the AC 130 Spectre Firing Flares or SOLAS Approved Parachute Flares clips on *YouTube*.

Ask the students what they would need to make a good flare. Use this discussion to remind pupils that magnesium burns with a very bright flame and then go on to talk about the reaction between magnesium and air.

Follow this by reading the additional information below the opening section of page 178 of the Student book. They may then read the brief description of the activity provided by the 'Your task' box.

### Option 1: Straight-forward class practical

Students follow the instructions on **Worksheet C2.31b**. The range of data that students need to collect is given on **Worksheet C2.31c**, which students will also need. This sheet guides students through recording, considering their results, and evaluating their investigation.

### Plenary

On page 179 of the Student Book you will find three examples of the sort of work that students may produce for this task. The examples focus on evaluating the method. You could share these with students after they have completed their own work. This will help them to understand the assessment criteria and so make it easier for them to evaluate their work and to see how they can improve it. Moderator comments on each of the Student Book extracts can be found at the end of the assessment guidance for this investigation on the CD-ROM. The examples can also be found on the **AT** document *Student examples*.

### Option 2: Running the activity as a practice controlled assessment task (PCA)

We have provided a full range of support resources to allow the running of this practical as a practice controlled assessment task. A recommended structure is outlined below (to be used over a number of sessions). Marking guidance for all three parts of the practice task can be found on the CD-ROM that accompanies the TTPP. To save time when using these practice controlled assessment tasks, you may wish to focus on a particular aspect or skill rather than working through all three parts of the task.

#### Part A Planning

1 Students should be given the Student brief on **Worksheet C2.31a**. They can use Part A of the Workbook that is provided to help pupils with their practice controlled assessments. They should be given about 1 hour to do this planning.

#### Part B Observations

2. Students should be asked to carry out the practical task to collect evidence using the method they have planned in Part A. They should refer to the Student brief on **Worksheet C2.31a**. They can use Part B of the Workbook that is provided to help pupils with their practice controlled assessments. They should be given about 1 hour to collect their primary evidence.
3. If there is a problem with their own planned method, students may be asked to follow the method set out on **Worksheet C2.31b**. This will still enable students to access the full range of marks for Part B and Part C of the practice controlled assessment task.
4. In Part B, students are required to gather some secondary evidence. The evidence can be quantitative or qualitative. It can be from a variety of sources but students must note where they found their evidence and evaluate the quality of the source as part of this task. Skills sheet 22 provides students with further guidance on researching for and evaluating secondary evidence. This part of the task could be done outside of the lesson but must be supervised.

#### Part C Conclusions

5. Students follow the instructions set out on the Part C section of the Student brief on **Worksheet C2.31a**. They should use their data from Part B and the secondary evidence they have when doing this. They can use Part C of the Workbook that is provided to help pupils with their practice controlled assessments. They should be given about 1 hour to work on their conclusions.

The **AT** includes video clips showing a group of students working through elements of this investigation with teacher support.

Practice Controlled Assessment

# C2.31 To determine the empirical formula for magnesium oxide

How do you work out the formula for magnesium oxide from an experiment?

Magnesium burns in air or oxygen with a bright white flame. This reaction is used in fireworks and also in flares to protect military aircraft from missiles. Infra red missiles are guided towards the heat from an aircraft's engines. Decoy flares contain magnesium that burns producing a temperature higher than the aircraft's engine so the missile hits the flare and not the aircraft.

**A** *Decoy flares used to protect aircraft from attack.*

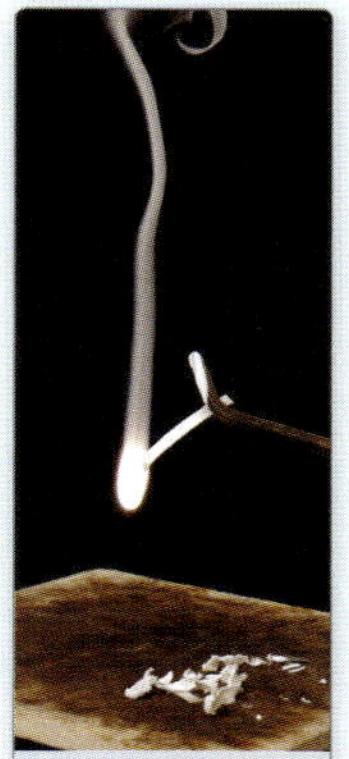

**B** *Magnesium burning in a Bunsen flame*

Magnesium reacts with oxygen from the air to produce magnesium oxide.

magnesium + oxygen → magnesium oxide

If you carry out this experiment in a crucible you can find the mass of oxygen that reacts from the initial mass of magnesium and the mass of magnesium oxide produced.

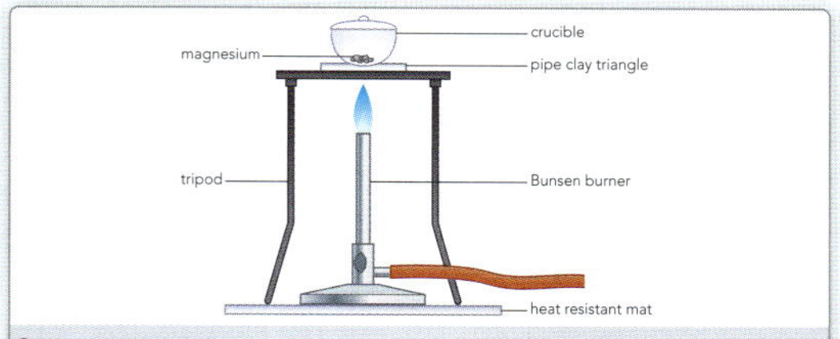


**C** *Apparatus used to burn magnesium*

**Your task**

You are going to plan an investigation that will allow you to find out the empirical formula for magnesium oxide. Your teacher will provide you with some materials to help you organise this task.

**Learning Outcomes**

*6.3 Determine the empirical formula of a simple compound, such as magnesium oxide.*

## ResultsPlus Build Better Answers

When planning an investigation like this, one of the skills you will be assessed on is your ability to *evaluate your method*. There are 6 marks available for this skill. Here are three extracts focusing on this skill.

**Student extract 1** — **A basic response for this skill**

*The method was difficult to do because I dropped the crucible lid. It would be easier to leave the lid off.*

You need to suggest at least one strength or weakness in the method

Although this would make the method easier it would also reduce the quality of your results because you need to keep as much magnesium oxide in the crucible as you can.

**Student extract 2** — **A better response for this skill**

This is a better answer because the student has identified both a strength and a weakness.

*The method was quite good as all of the magnesium burnt but it was hard to lift the lid without letting the fumes out. We should have tried lifting the lid just a little before we lit the Bunsen.*

Suggesting an improvement is good but you should explain why this would improve the method and relate this back to the hypothesis.

**Student extract 3** — **A good response for this skill**

This is a good explanation of how the weakness in the method affects the mass of oxygen.

*We measured the mass of magnesium carefully on a balance but some of the magnesium oxide escaped when we lifted the crucible lid. This made the mass of magnesium oxide lower than it should be so the mass of oxygen was lower as well. We could practice lifting the lid just a little to let less fumes out but do it more often. If we used bigger pieces of magnesium we would get more magnesium oxide so it would be easier to measure the masses so the mass of oxygen would be more accurate.*

These are good suggestions that would improve the method and give better quality data.

**ResultsPlus**

**To access 4 marks**

- Describe strengths or weaknesses in your method
- Provide reasons for any anomalies
- Suggest how to improve your method and explain how this will improve the quality of the evidence you could collect

**To access 6 marks**

You also need to:

- Relate your comments back to the original hypothesis of the investigation





## ActiveTeach

- **AT** *C2.31 Magnesium oxide* [interactive]
  Working out the formula
- **AT** *C2.31 Assessment criteria* [presentation]
  Understanding the CA marking criteria
- **AT** *C2.31 Specification points* [word document]
  Edexcel specification points
- **AT** *C2.31 Student examples* [word document]
  Examples for students to assess

## Assessment criteria

### Evaluation of method

**0** No relevant evaluation is made.

**1-2** **a)** A strength or weakness in the method is identified, e.g. 'It was difficult to lift the lid of the crucible while it was being heated'.
**b)** Makes a sensible suggestion about how the method could be improved, e.g. 'It would be better to leave the lid slightly to one side so air could get in all the time'.

**3-4** **a)** Strengths or weaknesses in the method are identified, e.g. it was difficult to lift the lid of the crucible while it was being heated, the masses were very small, it was difficult to tell when all the magnesium had burned.
**b)** Suggests how to improve method and justifies comments made by relating to hypothesis.

**5-6** **a)** Strengths or weaknesses in the method are described and are related to the quality of the data collected, e.g. 'Some magnesium oxide escaped as the lid was lifted so the mass of magnesium oxide was too low and the mass of oxygen was lower than expected'.
**b)** Suggests how to improve method, justifies comments made by relating to the hypothesis and explains how better quality data/observations would be produced, e.g. 'Use a bigger range of masses of magnesium and a larger mass of magnesium so it is easier to measure the change in mass'

# C2.32 Percentage composition



This lesson involves calculating the percentage by mass of elements in compounds – and for Higher Tier students, using balanced equations to calculate reacting masses.

## Specification coverage

**6.4** Calculate the percentage composition by mass of a compound from its formula and the relative masses of its constituent elements

**6.5** H Use balanced equations to calculate masses of reactants and products

HSW *10* Using both qualitative and quantitative approaches

There are also opportunities to cover HSW *6*, HSW *7*, HSW *8* and HSW *11*.

## Key terms

percentage by mass

### Percentages

**Starter 1**

Revise percentage calculations by asking students, for example, to calculate the percentage of the class who have a dog at home.

### Finding percentage compositions

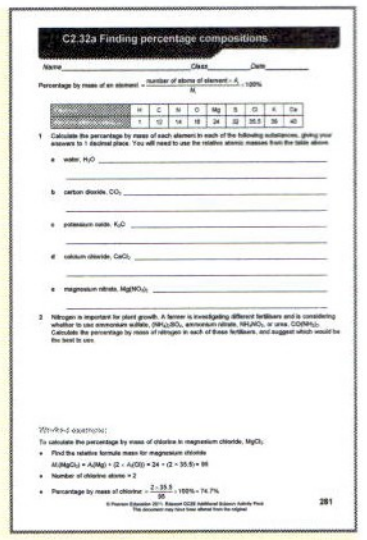

**Exploring 1**

Students complete **Worksheet C2.32a**.

Stretch Photocopy the worksheet without the formula and worked example and use more complex formulae, for example $Al_2(SO_4)_3$.

Support Photocopy the worksheet with the formula and worked example.

### Percentage composition (AT)

**Explaining 1**

Use the **AT** presentation *Percentage by mass*.

Stretch Give the students a formula, for example CO, and ask them to work out a way of calculating the percentage by mass of oxygen in this compound.

Support Use simple binary compounds – such as NaCl, KBr, MgO. Remind students that they must use relative atomic masses and not atomic numbers for these calculations.

### Percentage composition

**Plenary 1** AfL

Provide four formulae – for example MgO, $Na_2CO_3$, $K_2SO_4$ and $Ca(OH)_2$ – and ask students to work out the relative formula mass of each and the percentage of oxygen in each. The students can work in pairs to answer the questions and then check their answers with another pair.

### Using percentages by mass

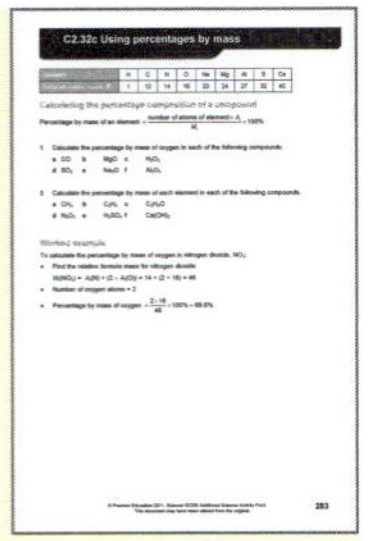

**Homework 1**

**Worksheet C2.32c**, for students needing support, involves calculating the percentage by mass of elements in compounds.

Support Photocopy the worksheet with the worked example at the bottom.

### H Equations and masses

**Starter 2**

Write a balanced equation on the board, for example, $Mg + H_2SO_4 \rightarrow MgSO_4 + H_2$. Ask the students how much magnesium sulfate is likely to be made from 24 g, 48 g or 12 g of magnesium. Explain that we can use relative masses to find the answer.

### H Heating zinc carbonate

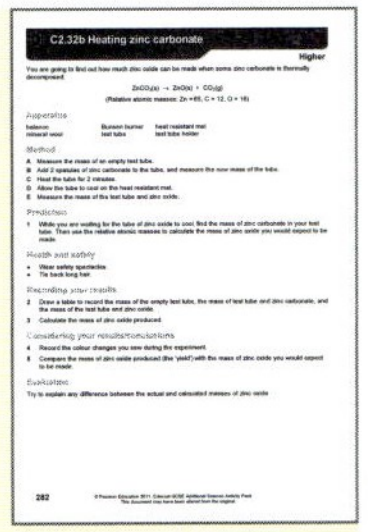

**Exploring 2** Prac

See **Worksheet C2.32b** and the Teacher and technician practical sheet C2.32 for full details. This practical leads naturally to a discussion of percentage yield.

Stretch Discuss heating to constant mass to ensure that complete decomposition has taken place.

Support Students could calculate the percentage loss in mass instead of predicting the mass of zinc oxide that should be produced.

### Student Book spread C2.32

**Explaining 2**

Show the students how to use balanced equations and relative masses to calculate the mass of a reactant or product in a reaction. See the example in *Starter 2* and examples and questions in the Student Book.

Stretch Use examples in which, after scaling, the numbers are not whole integers and explain that students should give their answers to the number of significant figures of the data in the question.

### H Snowball – reacting masses problem

**Plenary 2** Lit

Set a more complex problem to answer. For example, 10.0 g of separate samples of zinc carbonate, magnesium carbonate and copper(II) carbonate were heated to constant mass – which solid should lose the most mass?

### H Equations and masses

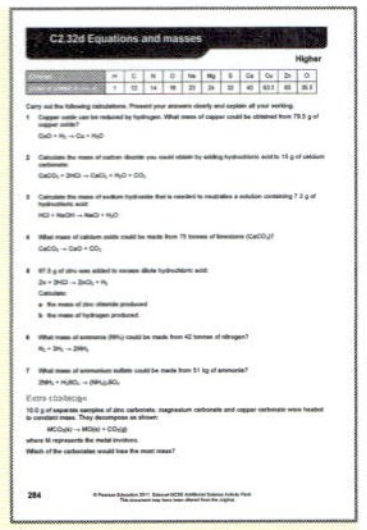

**Homework 2**

**Worksheet C2.32d**, is aimed at more able pupils and includes Higher Tier content.

Stretch Students answer the 'extra challenge' question.

# C2.32 Percentage composition

How do you find the percentage of each element in a compound?

Fireworks contain compounds called oxidising agents, which supply oxygen so that other compounds can combust. When making a firework, it is very important to know how much oxygen there is in the oxidising agent and how much oxidising agent should be added to each firework.

**A** *Making fireworks*

| Element | Relative atomic mass |
|---|---|
| hydrogen | 1 |
| carbon | 12 |
| nitrogen | 14 |
| oxygen | 16 |
| sodium | 23 |
| magnesium | 24 |
| chlorine | 35.5 |
| potassium | 39 |
| calcium | 40 |
| zinc | 65 |

**B** *Some relative atomic masses*

You can use relative masses to calculate the **percentage by mass** of each element in a compound.

$$\text{percentage by mass of an element in a compound} = \text{number of atoms of element} \times \frac{A_r}{M_r} \times 100$$

Figure C shows how to calculate the percentage by mass of oxygen in potassium nitrate, $KNO_3$, which is used as the oxidising agent in fireworks.

| | |
|---|---|
| Relative formula mass of potassium nitrate, $KNO_3$ | $A_r(K) + A_r(N) + 3 \times A_r(O)$<br>$= 39 + 14 + (3 \times 16)$<br>$= 101$ |
| Number of atoms of oxygen in $KNO_3$ | 3 |
| Relative atomic mass of oxygen | 16 |
| % of oxygen in $KNO_3$ | $3 \times \frac{16}{101} \times 100 = 47.5\%$ |

**C** *Steps to calculate percentage by mass*

**ResultsPlus Watch Out!**

Remember when looking up relative atomic masses in a periodic table that the one you need is the mass number is the one at the top and is the bigger number.

1 Calculate the percentage by mass of oxygen in a molecule of:
a carbon monoxide, CO b carbon dioxide, $CO_2$

2 Calculate the percentage by mass of nitrogen in each of the following:
a ammonia, $NH_3$ b ammonium chloride, $NH_4Cl$ c ammonium sulfate, $(NH_4)_2SO_4$

## Calculating the masses of reactants or products (H)

During a chemical reaction, no atoms are lost or made, they are just rearranged to make new substances. You can use relative masses and the balanced equation for a reaction to calculate the mass of a reactant or a product.

In a firework, potassium nitrate ($KNO_3$) is decomposed to potassium nitrite ($KNO_2$) and oxygen ($O_2$). What mass of potassium nitrate is needed in a firework to make 1.6 g of oxygen?

| | |
|---|---|
| Write the balanced equation. | $2KNO_3 \rightarrow 2KNO_2 + O_2$ |
| Work out the relative masses of the substances needed in the calculation. Notice that we need to multiply the relative mass of $KNO_3$ by 2 because there are two particles of $KNO_3$ in the balanced equation. | 2 x 101 → 32<br>202 → 32 |
| Convert the relative masses into the units in the question. You don't really need this step, but it's useful as a reminder of the units to use. | 202 g → 32 g |
| Divide the answers by the smallest number to find the ratio. | $\frac{202}{32} \rightarrow \frac{32}{32}$<br>6.3 → 1 |
| Find the mass of potassium nitrate needed to make 1.6 g of oxygen. | 6.3 x 1.6 → 1 x 1.6<br>10.1 → 1.6 |
| Answer | 10.1 g of potassium nitrate are needed to make 1.6 g of oxygen |

**D** *Steps to calculate a reacting mass*

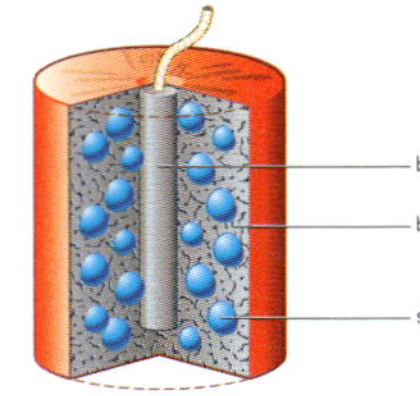


**E** *When this firework is blasted into the air, the fuse lights. The fuse then ignites the bursting charge and the firework explodes. Both the bursting charge and the 'black powder' contain an oxidiser (for example potassium nitrate).*

(H) 3 What mass of water is formed when 4 g of hydrogen is burnt?
$2H_2 + O_2 \rightarrow 2H_2O$

(H) 4 What is the mass of carbon dioxide formed when 36 g of carbon is burnt?
$C + O_2 \rightarrow CO_2$

(H) 5 What mass of sodium chloride is formed when 10 g of sodium hydroxide reacts with hydrochloric acid?
$NaOH + HCl \rightarrow NaCl + H_2O$

**Skills spotlight**

Scientific ideas can be described using words and numbers. Explain, using words and relative atomic masses, how you would calculate the percentage of nitrogen in ammonium nitrate, $NH_4NO_3$.

6 Make notes to explain how to calculate the percentage composition by mass for a friend who has missed the lesson. Use one or more of the compounds in the following equation as an example.
$MgCO_3 + H_2SO_4 \rightarrow MgSO_4 + H_2O + CO_2$

**Learning Outcomes**

6.4 Calculate the percentage composition by mass of a compound from its formula and the relative atomic masses of its constituent elements

(H) 6.5 Use balanced equations to calculate masses of reactants and products

HSW 10 Use qualitative and quantitative approaches when presenting scientific ideas and arguments, and recording observations





## ActiveTeach

- **AT** *What is the % composition by mass?* [interactive] Percentage composition calculations – quiz
- **AT** *Percentage by mass* [presentation] Exemplar calculation

## Answers | Student Book

1 a 57.1%
b 72.7%

2 a 82.4%
b 26.2 %
c 21.2%

3 (H) 36 g

4 (H) 132 g

5 (H) 14.625 g

6 Answer to include:

- Calculate the relative formula mass of magnesium carbonate, $MgCO_3$
  $M_r = A_r(Mg) + A_r(C) + 3 \times A_r(O)$
  $= 24 + 12 + (3 \times 16) = 80$
- Calculate the relative formula mass of magnesium sulfate, $MgSO_4$
  $M_r = A_r(Mg) + A_r(S) + 4 \times A_r(O)$
  $= 24 + 32 + (4 \times 16) = 120$
- 84 g of magnesium carbonate will make 120 g of magnesium sulfate
- so, 1 g of magnesium carbonate will make 120/84 g of magnesium sulfate and 4.2 g of magnesium carbonate will make

$\frac{120}{84} \times 4.2$ g of magnesium sulfate = 6 g

**Skills spotlight**

First calculate the relative formula mass for ammonium nitrate, $NH_4NO_3$

$M_r = 2 \times A_r(N) + 4 \times A_r(H) + 3 \times A_r(O)$
$= (2 \times 14) + (4 \times 1) + (3 \times 16)$
$= 80$

Number of nitrogen atoms = 2

Percentage by mass of nitrogen
$= \frac{\text{number of nitrogen atoms} \times A_r(N)}{M_r(NH_4NO_3)} \times 100$
$= \frac{2 \times 14}{80} \times 100$
$= 35\%$

# C2.33 Yields

This lesson involves calculating percentage yields for reactions and some reasons why yields are less than expected.

## Specification coverage

**6.6** Recall that the yield of a reaction is the mass of product obtained in the reaction

**6.7** Demonstrate an understanding that the actual yield of a reaction is usually less than the yield calculated using the chemical equation (theoretical yield)

**6.8** Calculate the percentage yield of a reaction from the actual yield and the theoretical yield

**6.9** Demonstrate an understanding of the reasons why reactions do not give the theoretical yield due to factors including: a) incomplete reactions b) practical losses during the preparation c) competing, unwanted reactions

HSW *12* The use of contemporary science and technological developments and their benefits, drawbacks and risks

There are also opportunities to cover HSW *10*, HSW *11*.

## Key terms

actual yield
percentage yield
theoretical yield
yield

### Percentage yield of zinc carbonate

**Starter 1**

Use the results of the experiment in C2.32 *Exploring 2* to calculate the percentage yield of the reaction. Ask students to suggest reasons why it is less than 100%. If they have not carried out this practical, describe the experiment to them and tell them that starting from 2.50 g of zinc carbonate, the theoretical yield of carbon dioxide is 0.88 g and the actual yield is 0.66 g. Explain how the percentage yield is 75%.

### Finding a percentage yield

**Exploring 1** Prac

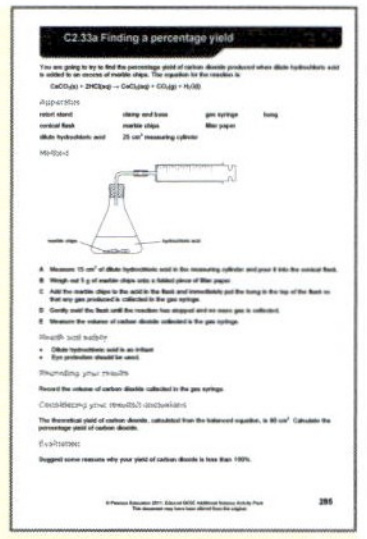

See **Worksheet C2.33a** and the Teacher and technician practical sheet C2.33 for full details.

Stretch Students should have time to repeat the experiment a few times so they can spot any anomalous results to ignore and take an average.

Support Give the students the formula to calculate percentage yield from actual and theoretical yields.

### Student Book spread C2.33 (AT)

**Explaining 1**

Use the examples in the Student Book and the **AT** presentation *Percentage yield.*

Stretch Explain that the reacting masses they calculated in the Student Book are the theoretical yields.

Support Write the formula to calculate the percentage yield on the board and just use simple numbers for the actual and percentage yields where they have the same unit and the answer is a whole number.

### What's the question?

**Plenary 1** AfL

Give the students words as 'answers' and ask them to suggest questions that match. For example:

'Waste product' – What is a product of a reaction that is not required or has no uses called?

'Actual yield' – What do we call the amount of product actually formed during a reaction?

'Incomplete reaction' – What do we call a reaction where not all of the products react?

### Using percentage yields

**Homework 1**

Students complete **Worksheet C2.33d.**

Support Photocopy the worksheet with the formulae and the worked example.

### Why don't all reactions work perfectly?

**Starter 2**

Ask students to work in pairs to discuss why reactions don't work perfectly. For example, explain that if they burn 0.24 g of magnesium in air, they should make 0.40 g of magnesium oxide. You could demonstrate burning a small piece of magnesium in air. Ask the students to think of any reasons why they would get less than 0.40 g. They feedback their ideas to the rest of the class.

### Calculating percentage yields

**Exploring 2**

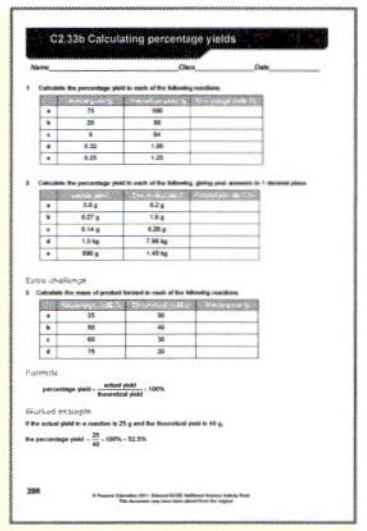

Students complete questions **1** and **2** on **Worksheet C2.33b**.

Stretch Students also answer question 3. This tests their ability to rearrange the formula. They will not be asked to do this in examination questions.

Support Students answer just question 1 on the worksheet. Photocopy the worksheet with the formula and the worked example.

### Why is the yield less than 100%?

**Explaining 2**

Use the results of *Starter 1* or *Exploring 1* to discuss some of the reasons why yields are less than 100%.

Stretch Explain that some manufacturing processes take place in many steps, for example drug manufacture. Each step has its own percentage yield, so the final yield is a percentage of a percentage

Support Emphasise that not all the reactants are used up to form products. There will always be losses during an experiment.

### Matching activity

**Plenary 2** Lit

Use **Worksheet C2.33c** and cut up the sheet into nine cards. Ask the students to work in groups of three and give each student a set containing different question, working and answer cards. The students have to work together to match up each question with the correct working and answer.

### Explaining percentage yields

**Homework 2**

**Worksheet C2.33e**, is for more able students.

Stretch Ask the students to answer the 'extra challenge' question.

# C2.33 Yields

How do we calculate the yield of a reaction?

Ammonia is an important chemical used to make fertilisers and nitric acid. It is made by reacting nitrogen and hydrogen, but only about 25% of the gases are converted to ammonia in the reaction.

A The ammonia produced at Terra Nitrogen, Billingham, is used to make fertilisers.

1 Calculate the percentage yields for these reactions:
a actual yield = 2.0 g; theoretical yield = 5.0 g
b actual yield = 3.2 g; theoretical yield = 4.0 g
c actual yield = 19.5 g; theoretical yield = 25.0 g

A factory making a certain compound needs to produce the compound as cheaply as possible. So, chemists need to make sure that the reaction converts as much of the reactants into products as possible. The amount of useful product obtained from a reaction is called the **yield**.

You can calculate the yield of reactions. For example, if you react 4 g of hydrogen with 32 g of oxygen, you expect to get 4 + 32 = 36 g of water. However, this is a **theoretical yield** and in practice you often do not get this much. The theoretical yield can be calculated from the balanced equation.

**ResultsPlus Watch Out!**

Students often get muddled when calculating percentage yield. Remember it is actual ÷ theoretical and the answer should always be less than 100%.

**e.g.**

Reaction between hydrogen and oxygen to form water

| | | | | | |
|---|---|---|---|---|---|
| | $2H_2$ | + | $O_2$ | → | $2H_2O$ |
| Calculate formula masses | 2 × (1 + 1) | + | (16 + 16) | → | 2 × (1 + 1 + 16) |
| | 2 × 2 | + | 32 | | 2 × 18 |
| Multiply according to the balanced equation | 4 | | 32 | | 36 |
| Put in units | 4 g | | 32 g | → | 36 g |

So, 36 g of water should theoretically be produced when 4 g of hydrogen reacts with 32 g of oxygen.

**Maths skills**

To find the **percentage** of one number out of another you divide the first number by the second number and multiply by 100.

Percentage yield is the percentage of the actual yield out of the theoretical yield.

The amount of product obtained is known as the **actual yield** of the reaction. The **percentage yield** compares the actual yield to the theoretical yield.

$$\text{percentage yield} = \frac{\text{actual yield}}{\text{theoretical yield}} \times 100$$

**e.g.**

For example, in the reaction above between hydrogen and oxygen the actual yield was 30 g. So:

$$\text{percentage yield} = \frac{30}{36} \times 100 = 83.3\%$$

## Why is the yield less than expected?

The theoretical yield of a reaction assumes that all the reactants are turned into products, and that the products are successfully separated from the reaction mixture. There are three main reasons why reactions do not give 100% yields:

- the reaction may be incomplete – this means that not all of the reactants are used up and some are left at the end
- some of the product is lost during the practical preparation – for example, when a liquid is transferred from one container to another, some of it will be left behind
- there may be other unwanted reactions taking place – for example, some of the reactants may react in different ways to make a different product.

B Calcium oxide is produced by heating calcium carbonate in a lime kiln. Modern lime kilns are much better at converting all the calcium carbonate than older ones.

(H) 2 When limestone is heated, the calcium carbonate decomposes to form calcium oxide:
$CaCO_3 \rightarrow CaO + CO_2$
a Calculate the theoretical yield of calcium oxide that could be made from 125 tonnes of limestone. Use the periodic table in Appendix A to find the relative atomic masses.
b The actual yield of calcium oxide made is 45.5 tonnes. Calculate the percentage yield.

(H) 3 One of the steps in the production of sulfuric acid is:
$2SO_2 + O_2 \rightarrow 2SO_3$
a Calculate the theoretical yield of sulfur trioxide that could be obtained from 256 tonnes of sulfur dioxide.
b The actual yield of sulfur trioxide produced is 202 tonnes. Calculate the percentage yield.

(H) 4 Iron is extracted from iron oxide by reducing with carbon:
$Fe_2O_3 + 3CO \rightarrow 2Fe + 3CO_2$
a Calculate the theoretical yield of iron that could be obtained from 320 tonnes of iron oxide.
b The actual yield of iron produced is 89.6 tonnes. Calculate the percentage yield.

5 Explain the reasons why the actual yield of a reaction may be less than the theoretical yield.

**Skills spotlight**

There are benefits and drawbacks with using technology. Suggest some benefits and drawbacks of increasing the pressure in a reaction between nitrogen and hydrogen gases to increase the yield of ammonia to 50%.

**Learning outcomes**

6.6 Recall that the yield of a reaction is the mass of product obtained in the reaction
6.7 Demonstrate an understanding that the actual yield of a reaction is usually less than the yield calculated using the chemical equation (theoretical yield)
6.8 Calculate the percentage yield of a reaction from the actual yield and the theoretical yield
6.9 Demonstrate an understanding of the reasons why reactions do not give the theoretical yield due to factors, including: a incomplete reactions b practical losses due to the preparation c competing, unwanted reactions
HSW 12 Describe the benefits, drawbacks and risks of using new scientific and technological developments

182

How do chemists increase the profit in manufacturing? 183

## ActiveTeach

- **AT** *Brine electrolysis: yield* [video]
  Yield of chemical reactions
- **AT** *How much can you make* [interactive]
  Factors in chemical yields – ideas mapping
- **AT** *Percentage yield* [presentation]
  Exemplar calculations

## Answers | Student Book

1 a 40%
b 80%
c 78%

2 (H) a 100 tonnes of $CaCO_3$ gives 56 tonnes CaO
125 tonnes $CaCO_3$ will give 70 tonnes CaO
b 65%

3 (H) a 320 tonnes
b 63%

4 (H) a 224 tonnes
b 40%

5 Answer to include: explanations of incomplete reaction, practical losses during the preparation, competing, unwanted reactions. Students may also say (this is not required) that the starting material is not pure.

**Skills spotlight**

**Benefits** could include – higher yield, faster rate

**Drawbacks** could include – increased cost of energy for the pump, increased cost of thicker pipes

# C2.34 Waste and profit in the chemical industry



This lesson covers the problems in disposal of waste products from the chemical industry and, for Higher Tier, the demands to find economically favourable reactions.

## Specification coverage

***6.10*** Demonstrate an understanding that many reactions produce waste products which: a) are not commercially useful b) can present economic, environmental and social problems for disposal

***6.11*** (H) Demonstrate an understanding that chemists in industry work to find the economically most favourable reactions where: a) the percentage yield is high b) all the products of the reaction are commercially useful c) the reaction occurs at a suitable speed

HSW *13* How and why decisions about science and technology are made, including those that raise ethical issues, and about the social, economic and environmental effects of such decisions

There are also opportunities to cover HSW *12*.

## Key terms

by-product
waste product

### Useful substances in the chemical industry

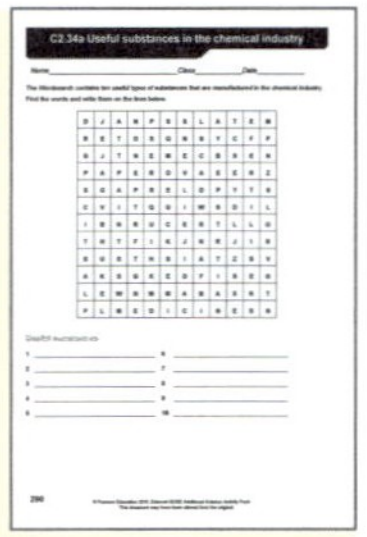

**Starter 1** Lit

Ask students to think of useful substances that are made in the chemical industry. Students then join in pairs to agree a list, and then pairs join to form fours to pool their lists and feedback to the rest of the class. Alternatively use the word search on **Worksheet C2.34a**.

### Extracting copper

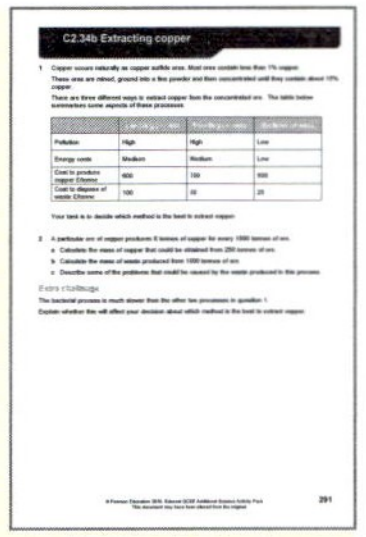

**Exploring 1**

**Worksheet C2.34b** has information about extracting copper from its ore by three different processes.

Stretch Tell students that the bacterial process is much slower than the other two processes. Ask them to explain whether or not this will affect their decision.

Support Guide groups to prepare an argument for one method.

### Student Book spread C2.34 (AT)

**Explaining 1**

Explain the meaning of 'by-product'. If substances had no uses they would be waste products and would need to be disposed of.

Stretch Tell the students that hydrogen can be made from methane and steam, with carbon monoxide as a by-product.

Support The **AT** *Products and by-products* provides some word equations.

### Beg of my neighbour

**Plenary 1** AfL

Ask each student to write down three things that they think the student sitting next to them should have learnt from this topic. Then ask the students to ask each other, in pairs, whether they agree on the things they should have learnt. Ask them to agree a final list of the three most important points.

### Problems in aluminium extraction

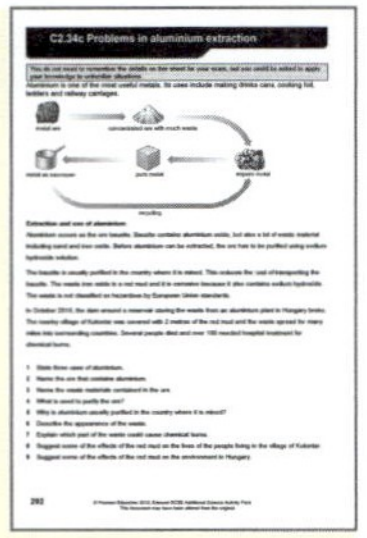

**Homework 1**

Students needing support do **Worksheet C2.34c**.

Support Describe the aluminium waste disaster in Hungary in October 2010 before setting this homework – this will help show the effect on people's lives and on the environment.

### Problems with disposal of waste products

**Starter 2**

Tell the students that the chemical industry produces many useful products and ask them to suggest some examples. Explain that some reactions also produce waste products and that disposal of these can cause problems.

### (H) Increasing the profit

**Exploring 2**

Students research the production of 'slag' in iron production and problems of slag heaps on brownfield sites, and ways in which chemists in industry try to increase profits by finding uses for the slag produced in iron and steel making. They then produce a short presentation or report.

Stretch Ask students to write the equations for the production of slag in making iron. Tell them first that limestone is added and that it thermally decomposes, then reacts with silicates in the ore impurities.

### (H) Increasing the profit

**Explaining 2**

Use the examples in the Student Book to discuss the need for a high percentage yield, making all products useful and increasing the rate to save time.

Stretch Discuss one of the disasters that have occurred, such as the Bhopal disaster in India in 1984, itai-itai disease from cadmium poisoning from 1912 in Japan or the disposal of toxic waste by the Hooker Chemical Company in Love Canal, USA in 1976.

### Questions for an industrial chemist

**Plenary 2**

Ask students to prepare questions they would like to ask a chemist in industry about their work. Pick out the top four to put to an industrial chemist. You could submit the questions to a chemical company or a website such as *WikiAnswers* or *Yahoo!Answers* and compare the answers you get back.

### (H) Making ibuprofen

**Homework 2**

**Worksheet C2.34d**, for more able students compares the two processes for making ibuprofen in terms of the mass of waste products and advantages of the new process.

Stretch Students answer the 'extra challenge' question.

# C2.34 Waste and profit

How does the chemical industry minimise waste and make a profit?

Aluminium is extracted from its ore in a smelter. This process creates solid and gaseous fluoride waste, which destroyed the farmland near to this smelter. In older designs in the 1940s, 12 kg of fluoride waste was produced for each tonne of aluminium. Chemists have worked to reduce this waste to about 0.5 kg per tonne and the farmland has recovered.

**A** *An aluminium smelter*

1 Name three products made in the chemical industry.

## Disposal of waste products

The chemical industry manufactures many useful substances such as pesticides, fertilisers, cement, metals, plastics and medicines.

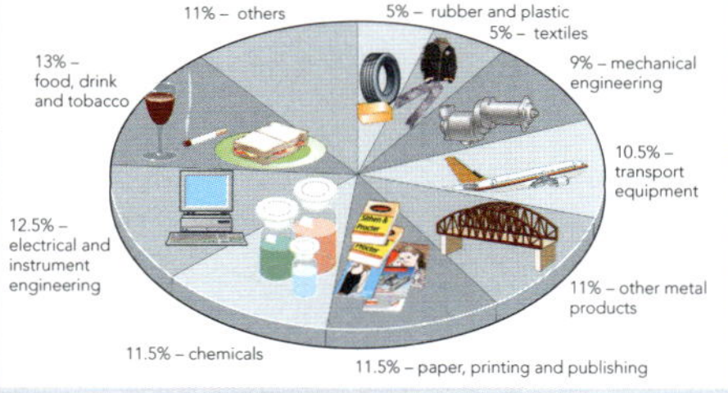


**B** *Some products formed in the chemical industry*

**C** *Metal ions in factory waste – such as copper, chromium, cadmium or mercury – may be toxic and damage the environment.*

2 Ethanol can be produced by the fermentation of glucose:

glucose → ethanol + carbon dioxide

What is the by-product in this reaction?

3 Suggest why it is expensive to dispose of waste chemicals.

However, many chemical reactions produce substances other than the substance that is wanted. The additional substances are called **by-products**. For example, when chlorine is produced during the electrolysis of sodium chloride solution, sodium hydroxide and hydrogen are also produced and are by-products. Some by-products, such as sodium hydroxide and hydrogen, are useful and can be sold, but many are useless. These useless products are called **waste products** and have to be disposed of. Today, strict laws apply to the disposal of substances that could cause pollution. Disposal can:

- be expensive – the waste may have to be transported to a landfill site or it may have to be treated with another substance to make it safe
- cause environmental problems
- cause social problems, for example, house prices could drop if a chemical plant is built near to them or there may be unpleasant smells emitted.



## Finding the most cost effective process

H

In the UK, the law says that all chemical factories must consider the environmental impact of their production methods, including the disposal of any waste. Chemical companies also want to use reactions that will make the most profit. To do this, they try to use reactions in which:

- the percentage yield is high – low yields increase costs
- all the products of the reaction are useful so there are no waste products
- the reaction takes place quickly – the longer it takes the more expensive it becomes.

For example, when ammonia is made there are no waste products:

$N_2 + 3H_2 \rightarrow 2NH_3$

When iron is extracted from iron oxide there is always waste carbon dioxide:

$Fe_2O_3 + 3CO \rightarrow 2Fe + 3CO_2$

However, if a use can be found for waste products then a reaction becomes more economically viable.

**D** *Iron ore contains many substances apart from iron oxide. During iron extraction, these substances form a waste called slag. This used to be piled up in to huge hills. Today, it is used to make roads.*

### Skills spotlight

Decisions made by chemists working in industry about the processes they use can have economic, environmental and social consequences.

Aspirin can be synthesised from salicylic acid:

salicylic acid + ethanoic anhydride → aspirin + ethanoic acid

Suggest why there is a waste problem for this process, and how chemists could try to reduce these problems.

H 4 Explain, in terms of atoms, why there is no waste product when ammonia is made.

H 5 Suggest some possible uses for the carbon dioxide produced when iron is extracted from iron oxide.

H 6 State four ways of increasing the rate of a reaction.

7 Using ideas about waste products, suggest why people object when there is a proposal to build a new chemical plant to manufacture plastics near to their homes.

**ResultsPlus Watch Out!**

Some students think that all waste products are harmful – but even water can be a waste product!

### Learning Outcomes

6.10 Demonstrate an understanding that many reactions produce waste products which: a are not commercially useful b can present economic, environmental and social problems for disposal

H 6.11 demonstrate an understanding that chemists in industry work to find the economically most favourable reactions where: a the percentage yield is high b all the products of the reaction are commercially useful c the reaction occurs at a suitable speed

HSW 13 Describe the social, economic and environmental effects of decisions about the uses of science and technology



## ActiveTeach

- **AT** *Products and by-products* [presentation] By-product waste and disposal
- **AT** *Products formed in the chemical industry* [diagram] Interactive Figure B – diagram labelling activity

## Answers | Student Book

1 Any three, for example, metals, plastics, medicines, fertilisers, paints, dyes

2 carbon dioxide

3 It is expensive to dispose of waste products because they may need to be transported to a suitable landfill site or they may need to be treated to make them safe.

4 H All of the atoms in the reactants/nitrogen and hydrogen are made into ammonia molecules.

5 H For example, in making fizzy drinks, making fire extinguishers, controlling the pH in swimming pools, as a refrigerant

6 H Increasing the temperature, increasing the concentration of a solution or pressure of a gas, increasing the surface area of a solid, adding a catalyst

7 Answer to include:

- risk of gases released causing smog or unpleasant smells
- risk of pollution in water supply
- house prices may fall
- there may be waste products stored on site and these may be unsightly or hazardous
- increase in traffic and noise.

**Skills spotlight**

Answer to include:

- ethanoic acid is a waste or by-product
- it is expensive to dispose of it
- reduce this problem by finding a use for it
- suggested use, for example in vinegar

Higher Tier students could also include:

- chemists could research a process that produces aspirin with no waste products or if there are waste products, find uses for them.
- this contributes to sustainability by not being wasteful of resources.

# P2.1 Static electricity



This lesson introduces the structure of the atom and how insulating materials can be given a charge of static electricity.

## Specification coverage

***1.1*** Describe the structure of the atom, limited to the position, mass and charge of protons, neutrons and electrons

***1.2*** Explain how an insulator can be charged by friction, through the transfer of electrons

***1.3*** Explain that the material gaining electrons becomes negatively charged and the material losing electrons is left with an equal positive charge

***1.4*** Recall that like charges repel and unlike charges attract

***1.5*** Demonstrate an understanding of common electrostatic phenomena in terms of movement of electrons, including: *a) shocks from everyday objects b) lightning* c) attraction by induction such as a charged balloon attracted to a wall and a charged comb picking up small pieces of paper

**HSW** ***3*** Many phenomena can be explained by developing and using scientific theories, models and ideas.

### Van de Graaff generator

**Starter 1** **Demo**

Use a Van de Graaff generator to demonstrate some effects of static electricity. Ask students to bear these in mind during the lesson, and then revisit the demonstrations as a plenary so they can explain the effects. See the Teacher and technician practical sheet P2.1 (1) for full details.

### Attracting and repelling

**Exploring 1** **Prac**

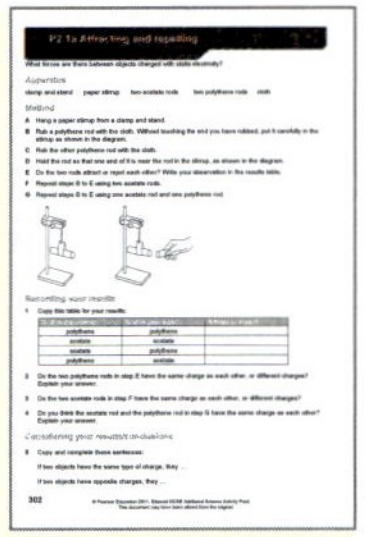

Students use rods of different materials to investigate when static charges attract or repel each other. See **Worksheet P2.1a** and the Teacher and technician practical sheet P2.1 (2) for full details.

**Stretch** Students plan and carry out their own method to demonstrate the 'rules' for attraction and repulsion using only the information in the Student Book.

**Support** Help students with the explanations asked for in questions **2** and **4** on the worksheet.

### Student Book spread P2.1

**Explaining 1**

Note that 'static' electricity involves the same charged particles as current electricity – the term is used to describe the effects of charges on insulating materials.

**Stretch** Ask students to write an explanation similar to that in Figure F to explain how a positively charged balloon can stick to a wall.

**Support** Ensure students recall that the electrons are the only particles that can be transferred away from atoms, so it is always the electrons that move when something is given an electrostatic charge.

### Van de Graaff revisited

**Plenary 1** **Demo**

Show students the Van de Graaff demonstrations again (or show different ones) and ask them to use their knowledge of electrostatic charges to explain them. See the Teacher and technician practical sheet P2.1 (1) for full details.

### Static electricity questions

**Homework 1**

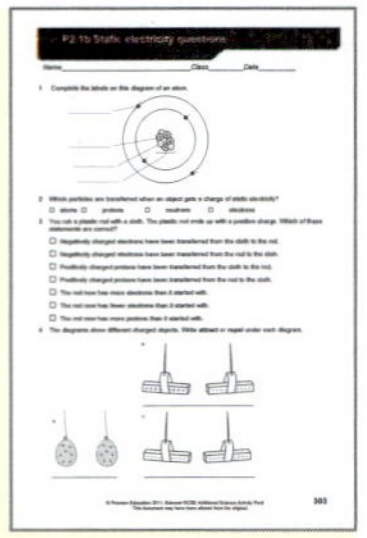

**Worksheet P2.1b**, for students needing support, provides questions on the content of this lesson.

**Support** A completed copy of the cloze summary exercise can be found on the **AT** presentation *Summary exercise answers* and will help students to complete the worksheet.

### Powers of Ten

**Starter 2**

Show students part of the Powers of Ten video or the animation from the *Molecular Expressions* website. This will give them an idea of the scale of an atom and its nucleus relative to their own bodies. The animation allows you to control the progress through the different size scales.

### Static effects

**Exploring 2** **Prac**

Students produce various effects using static electricity and attempt to explain them. See the Teacher and technician practical sheet P2.1 (3) for full details and the **AT** document *Static effects*.

**Stretch** Ask students to suggest how static electricity could be used to remove smoke from the waste gases going through a chimney.

**Support** Go through the explanation of the effects with students, prompting them to look at the explanation in the Student Book (or in *Explaining 2*).

### Induced charges

**Explaining 2**

The **AT** presentation *Induced charges* provides a more detailed explanation of how charges can be induced, and some questions to help students to apply the explanation to different examples.

**Stretch** Ask students to explain why rubbing a mirror hard to clean it may not be a good idea.

**Support** Use the questions for class discussion.

### Sentence starters

**Plenary 2** **AfL** **Lit**

Ask students to complete a set of sentence starters, including a connecting word (and, because, but, however, is, so, such as, therefore, to, which). Possible starters are: 'An atom is made of smaller particles such as…', 'Electrons are found outside the nuclei of atoms and…', 'Negative charges repel each other therefore…'

### Static charges

**Homework 2**

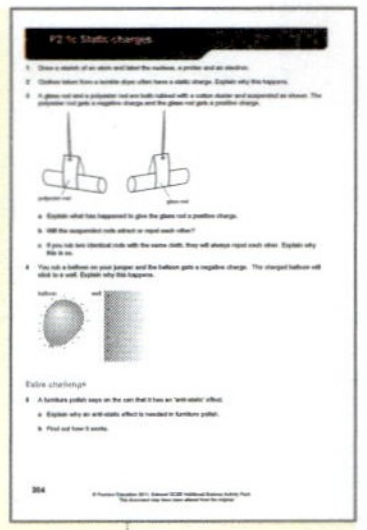

**Worksheet P2.1c**, for students working at a higher level, provides questions on the content of this lesson.

**Stretch** Students answer the 'extra challenge' question.

# P2.1 Static electricity

What causes static electricity and what can it do?

The machine in the photo is producing static electricity. The sparks it creates are similar to lightning. The man in the cage is safe because the electricity is conducted around him in the metal wires.

A

If you have ever had a shock when getting out of a car or heard clothing crackle as you take it off, you have experienced an effect of **static electricity**. This is caused by an electrical charge (often called an **electrostatic charge**) building up on insulating materials – including you.

All atoms contain electrically charged particles called **protons** and **electrons**. Protons have a positive charge and are found in the **nucleus** of atoms. Electrons move around the nucleus of the atom. An atom normally has no overall charge because the positive charges on the protons are balanced by the negative charges on the electrons. The nucleus also contains **neutrons**, which have no charge.

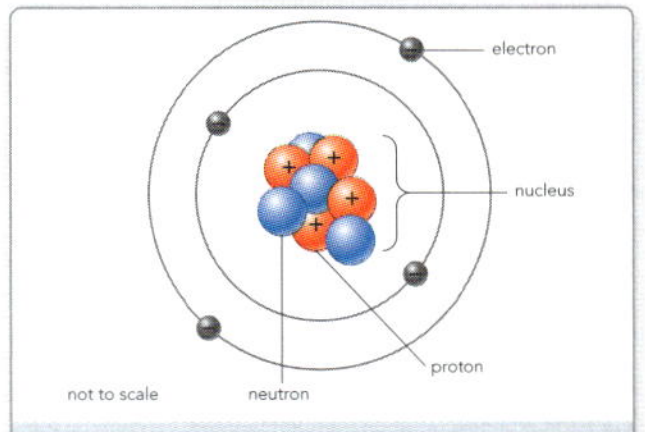

**B** A model of an atom

**Skills spotlight**

Scientists often use models to help them to explain why things happen, such as the model shown in Figure B. Suggest some of the differences between Figure B and a real atom.

| Property | Particle | | |
|---|---|---|---|
| | proton | neutron | electron |
| relative charge | +1 | 0 (neutral) | –1 |
| relative mass | 1 | 1 | 0.0005 (negligible) |

**C** Particles in an atom

1 What kind of materials can be given a charge?

2 Where are the following particles found in an atom:
a proton
b electron?

3 An atom has five protons. Explain how many electrons it normally has.

If you rub two insulating materials together, electrons may be transferred from one material to the other. Protons cannot be transferred because they are fixed in the nuclei of atoms. The combination of the two materials determines which material gains electrons and which loses them.

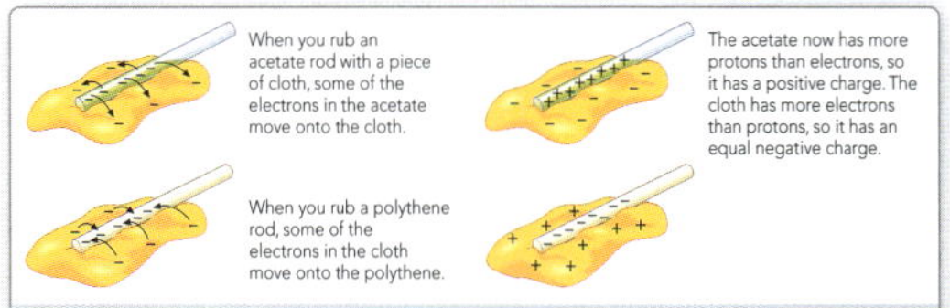

**D** The effect of rubbing two insulating materials together

4 In Figure D, the bottom right drawing has no caption next to it. Write a caption for this drawing.

**E** This person has a charge of static electricity.

Objects charged with static electricity can attract or repel each other. If the charges are the same as each other (both positive or both negative) the objects will repel. If the charges on the two objects are different, they will attract each other.

You may have tried making a balloon stick to a wall by rubbing it on your jumper. Figure F explains how this works. This process is called charging by **induction** and the charge is an **induced charge**.

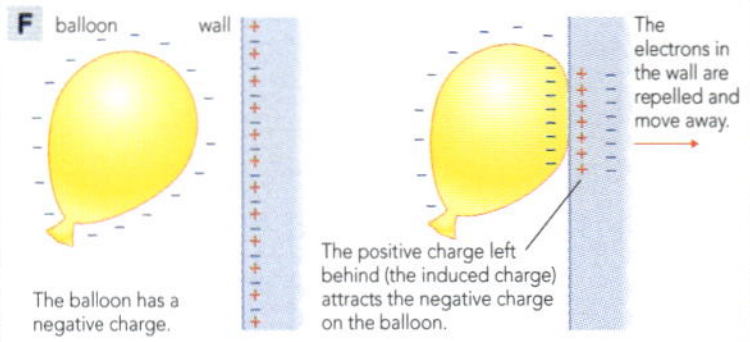

**F**

5 Explain why only negatively charged particles can be transferred when you rub an insulating material.

6 Look at Figure E. Explain why the girl's hair is standing up.

7 You rub two balloons on your jumper. Explain why the balloons will then repel each other.

8 You rub a plastic comb with a cloth and then hold it near some small pieces of paper. Explain why the comb will pick up the pieces of paper.

**ResultsPlus Watch Out!**

Students often lose marks in static electricity questions by not giving a full answer. Make sure you refer to *electrons* moving to create an overall charge, not just charged particles moving.

**Learning Outcomes**

1.1 Describe the structure of the atom, limited to the position, mass and charge of protons, neutrons and electrons

1.2 Explain how an insulator can be charged by friction, through the transfer of electrons

1.3 Explain how the material gaining electrons becomes negatively charged and the material losing electrons is left with an equal positive charge

1.4 Recall that like charges repel and unlike charges attract

1.5 Demonstrate an understanding of common electrostatic phenomena in terms of movement of electrons, including:
c attraction by induction such as a charged balloon attracted to a wall and a charged comb picking up small pieces of paper

HSW 3 Describe how phenomena are explained using scientific models



## ActiveTeach

- **AT** *Induced charges* [presentation] Explanation and questions
- **AT** *Static effects* [word document] Practical instructions
- **AT** *Model of an atom* [diagram] Figure B – diagram labelling activity

## Key terms

electron
electrostatic charge
induced charge
induction
neutron
nucleus
proton
static electricity

## Answers | Student Book

1 Insulating materials

2 a Nucleus
b Around the nucleus

3 5, as the positive and negative charges normally balance

4 The polythene now has more electrons than protons, so it has a negative charge. The cloth has more protons than electrons, so it has a positive charge.

5 They are on the outside of the atom. Positive charges are fixed inside the nucleus of the atom and cannot move.

6 All the strands of her hair have the same charge, so they are all repelling each other.

7 If the balloons are both made of the same material, they will both get the same type of charge when they are rubbed on the jumper (this could be positive or negative). As both balloons have the same charge, they will repel each other.

8 A good answer will contain the following points: Rubbing the comb gives it a static charge; if this is a negative charge, it repels electrons in the pieces of paper, leaving the sides nearest the comb with a positive charge; the negative charge on the comb and the positive charge on the pieces of paper attract each other. (Accept similar answer written assuming a positive charge on the comb.)

**Skills spotlight**

A real atom is much smaller than the atom shown. A real atom is three dimensional. Other differences include: the relative sizes of the nucleus and the overall atom – the nucleus is much smaller than the atom; the particles are not coloured spheres, as drawn here, and they do not have + and – signs on them!

# P2.2 Uses and dangers

This lesson looks at how you can get shocks from everyday objects and at some of the dangers and uses of static electricity.

## Specification coverage

**1.5** Demonstrate an understanding of common electrostatic phenomena in terms of movement of electrons, including: a) shocks from everyday objects b) lightning c) *attraction by induction such as a charged balloon attracted to a wall and a charged comb picking up small pieces of paper*

**1.6** Explain how earthing removes excess charge by movement of electrons

**1.7** Explain some of the uses of electrostatic charges in everyday situations, including paint and insecticide sprayers

**1.8** Demonstrate an understanding of some of the dangers of electrostatic charges in everyday situations, including fuelling aircraft and tankers together with the use of earthing to prevent the build-up of charge and danger arising

HSW *12* Use of contemporary scientific and technological developments and their benefits, drawbacks and risks

There are also opportunities to cover HSW *3* and HSW *13*.

### Van de Graaff sparks

**Starter 1** Demo

Use a Van de Graaff generator to demonstrate that sparks can jump through the air. See the Teacher and technician practical sheet on P2.2 (1) for full details.

### Static and helicopters

**Exploring 1** Lit

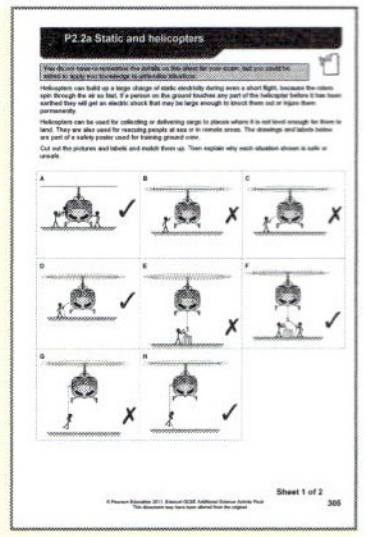

**Worksheet P2.2a** shows a series of drawings illustrating some of the safety precautions needed to deal with static electricity when helicopters are used for rescue operations or for picking up cargo.

Stretch Ask students to explain why similar safety precautions are not needed for aeroplanes.

Support Students are also given the cards with explanations rather than having to write their own explanations.

### Earthing demonstrations

**Explaining 2** Demo

Demonstrate how a static charge can be earthed, using a Van de Graaff generator or gold leaf electroscope. See the Teacher and technician practical sheet P2.2 (3) for full details.

Stretch Ask students to explain why the Earth is sometimes described as a 'source or sink' of electrons.

Support Remind students of the explanation for the charged 'hair' standing up.

### Writing question

**Plenary 1** Lit

Ask students to work in small groups to write a list of five words or phrases based on the content of this lesson. Each group swaps lists with another group and has to write a set of questions to which the phrases are the answers. More able students should be able to write more than one question for each answer.

### Using static electricity

**Homework 1**

**Worksheet P2.2b**, for students needing support, provides questions on the content of this lesson.

Support Talk through Figure B in the Student Book before students take the worksheet home.

### Attracting and repelling

**Starter 2** AfL Demo

Demonstrate attraction and repulsion using a comb and dry breakfast cereal and ask students to use what they learned about static electricity in lesson P2.1 to explain what they see. See the Teacher and technician practical sheet P2.2 (2) for full details.

### Student Book spread P2.2

**Explaining 1**

Remind students that similar charges repel each other, and explain the sparks caused by lightning or contact with door handles etc. as charge spreading out as much as it can.

Stretch Ask students to find out why the chance of sparks from static electricity is less on a humid day.

Support Talk through the example of refuelling an aircraft to explain why the bonding line prevents sparks occurring.

### Spray paint demonstration

**Explaining 3** Demo

Demonstrate the amount of paint that can be wasted when spraying small objects. This is best done before *Explaining 1*. See the Teacher and technician practical sheet P2.2 (4) for full details.

Stretch Ask students to explain what would happen if the object to be painted were given the same charge as the paint.

Support Remind students that similar charges repel and opposite charges attract.

### Sorting explanations

**Plenary 2** AfL Lit

The **AT** document *Static electricity* provides sets of cards explaining shocks from static electricity, paint spraying and using bonding lines for refuelling. Students sort the cards into sets and then sort the sets into order to give explanations.

### Static problems

**Homework 2**

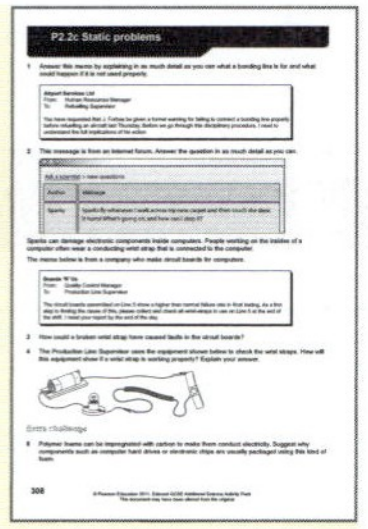

**Worksheet P2.2c**, for students working at a higher level, provides questions on some of the problems that can be caused by static electricity.

Stretch Students answer the 'extra challenge' question.

# P2.2 Uses and dangers of static electricity

What are the uses and dangers of static electricity?

Helicopters build up a large charge of electricity in flight. The ground crew for this helicopter are earthing the static charge by holding up a wand that is connected to the ground with a wire. Once the helicopter has been discharged they can safely touch it.

A

1 You have a negative charge because your shoes have been rubbing on a carpet. Explain what happens to the charge when you touch a doorknob.

You can sometimes build up an electrostatic charge by walking on a carpet or just sitting on a chair. You only find out that you have become charged when you touch a metal object such as a doorknob. You feel a small electric shock when the electrons flow between you and the object. Electrons move from you to earth through the object or the other way around. This process is called **earthing**. You have been **discharged** (you no longer have a charge).

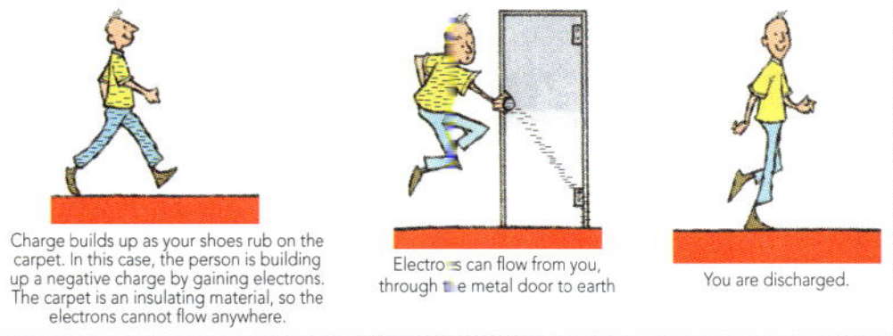


**B** *Earthing through a door handle*

Static electricity can build up on clouds and can cause a huge spark to form between the cloud and the ground. The lightning we see is caused by charged particles flowing through the atmosphere. The lightning also makes sound waves that we hear as thunder. Lightning strikes can kill or injure people and damage buildings.

**C** *Refuelling an aircraft*

The charge of static electricity that builds up on most everyday objects is usually much smaller than the charge that causes lightning. Static electricity on everyday objects is usually only dangerous when it is likely to cause a spark. If a conducting path can be provided to discharge the static electricity then there will be no spark.

Static electricity can build up as fuel flows through a refuelling pipe, and aircraft can also build up a static charge as they move through the air. A bonding line (a metal wire) is used to connect the aircraft to earth before it is refuelled. This discharges the aircraft so there will be no sparks.

A similar problem can occur when tankers deliver fuel to filling stations. In this case, the hose used to fill the underground fuel tanks is made of a conducting material so there will be no sparks.

## Using static electricity

Static electricity can also be useful. It can be used in insecticide sprayers to make the spray spread out and is also used in electrostatic spray painting.

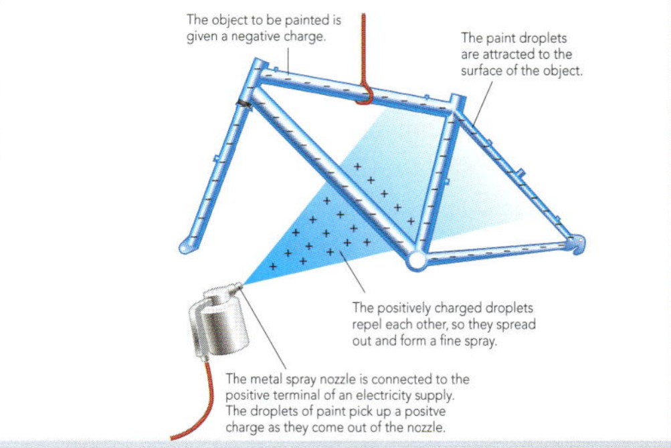


**D** *Electrostatic paint spraying*

**Skills spotlight**

Suggest one advantage and one disadvantage of using static electricity:
**a** when spraying insecticides onto crops
**b** when spraying paint (*Hint:* many paints are flammable).

2 a How could a spark cause an accident when an aircraft is being refuelled?
b How does a bonding line prevent this?
c Why is it important that a bonding line is connected before the fuel nozzle touches the aircraft?

3 Look at Figure D.
a Why do the drops of paint spread out when they leave the nozzle?
b Why does the object have to be given a negative charge?

4 a Explain how using static electricity affects the spraying of insecticides.
b What are the economic effects of using static electricity?
c Suggest some possible environmental effects.

5 Describe some of the dangers of static electricity and explain how electrostatic charges can be discharged safely.

**ResultsPlus Watch Out!**

A common mistake is to say that when an object is earthed, electrons always flow towards the ground. The direction in which the electrons flow depends on the charge on the object. For a positively charged object, electrons will flow from the earth to the object.

**Learning Outcomes**

1.5 Demonstrate an understanding of common electrostatic phenomena in terms of movement of electrons, including: *a* shocks from everyday objects *b* lightning

1.6 Explain how earthing removes excess charge by movement of electrons

1.7 Explain some of the uses of electrostatic charges in everyday situations, including paint and insecticide sprayers

1.8 Demonstrate an understanding of some of the dangers of electrostatic charges in everyday situations, including fuelling aircraft and tankers together with the use of earthing to prevent the build-up of charge and danger arising

HSW 12 Describe the benefits, drawbacks and risks of using new scientific and technological developments




## ActiveTeach

- **AT** *What's the charge?* [interactive]
  All about static electricity – quiz
- **AT** *How a paint sprayer works* [interactive]
  Electrostatic paint sprayer – scene investigation
- **AT** *Static electricity* [word document]
  Card sort on shocks

## Key terms

discharge
earth

## Answers | Student Book

1 The charge flows through the door to earth.

2 **a** The spark could ignite fuel vapour in the air.
**b** Any charge built up would be discharged through the bonding line, so there will be no charge to make a spark.
**c** The static charge needs to be discharged before the fuel nozzle gets close enough to the aircraft for a spark to jump across the gap.

3 **a** They all have the same charge, and like/similar charges repel each other.
**b** The object must have the opposite charge to the paint drops, so that they will be attracted to the object.

4 **a** The drops of insecticide all have the same charge, so they spread out to provide a more even coverage.
**b** It means there is less wasted insecticide, so costs of spraying are cheaper. It might also mean that it is quicker to spray a given area of crops, so again costs will be less.
**c** If it reduces the amount of wasted insecticide, it means that the insecticide is only going where it is needed and is less likely to harm other wildlife.

5 A good answer will contain the following points:

- static electricity can be dangerous if it causes sparks
- this is particularly so in places where the spark might cause a fire or an explosion
- this danger is avoided by making sure that any static charge is discharged before the spark can occur
- this can be done by earthing the charged object.

**Skills spotlight**

**a Advantage**: the spray spreads out more, so the insecticide can cover the crop more evenly.
**Disadvantage**: the spray may spread out so much that it gets onto crops/hedges that it is not intended for, or it might be easier for the spread-out spray to be breathed in by people.
**b Advantage**: paint spreads out if it is charged, so it gives a more even coverage, or charged drops of paint are attracted to the object being painted, so less paint is wasted.
**Disadvantage**: a fine mist of paint produced by charging it might be more flammable/easier to ignite than a paint spray that is less spread out.

# P2.3 Electric currents

This lesson introduces the idea of current as a flow of electrons and the equation that links charge, current and time.

## Specification coverage

***1.9*** Recall that an electric current is the rate of flow of charge

***1.10*** Recall that the current in metals is a flow of electrons

***1.11*** Use the equation: charge (coulomb, C) = current (ampere, A) × time (second, s), $Q = I \times t$

***1.12*** Recall that cells and batteries supply direct current (d.c.)

***1.13*** Demonstrate an understanding that direct current (d.c.) is movement of charge in one direction only

HSW ***11*** Presenting information, *developing an argument and drawing a conclusion*, using scientific, technical and mathematical language, conventions and symbols and *ICT tools*

There are also opportunities to cover HSW ***3*** and HSW ***10***.

## Key terms

alternating current (a.c)
ampere (A)
coulomb (C)
current (I)
direct current (d.c)

### Sorting materials

**Starter 1**

Give students a list of different materials to sort into groups of their choosing and ask them to explain their reasoning. If necessary, follow this up by reminding them that they are studying electricity and ask them to sort the materials again into conductors and insulators.

### Revising circuits and circuit symbols

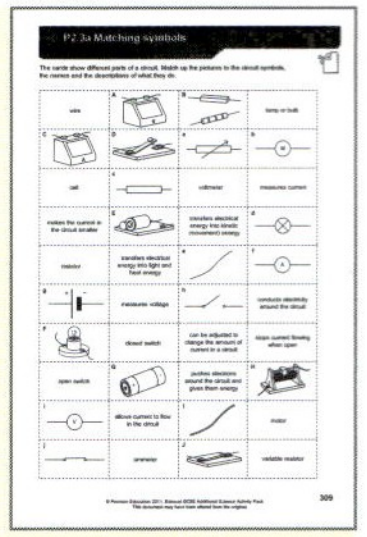

**Exploring 1**

Help students revise their knowledge of electricity and circuits using **Worksheet P2.3a**. This provides a set of cards showing components, their symbols and what they do for students to match up.

**Stretch** Give students only the symbols and ask them to explain what the components are and what they do.

**Support** Students work in mixed ability groups for peer support.

### Student Book spread P2.3

**Explaining 1**

Students contrast the two forms of current.

**Stretch** Ask students to look at Figure B on page 212 and at Figure A on page 210 and then to explain why a helicopter, made mostly of metal, can build up a static charge. Students could also be asked to find out why I is the symbol for current.

**Support** The symbols Q for charge and I for current may cause some confusion – students will be given the equations in word form in an examination, so they do not need to remember the symbols.

### Exam questions

**Plenary 1** AfL Lit

Ask students to work in pairs to write an exam question worth 5 marks involving the use of the formula relating charge, current and time. They should also provide a mark scheme for their question. Encourage Higher Tier students to include changing the subject of the equation as part of their question.

### Currents and calculations

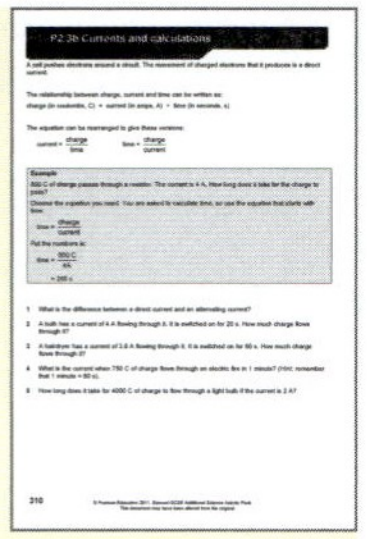

**Homework 1**

**Worksheet P2.3b**, for students needing support, provides questions on the material covered in the lesson.

**Support** Help students to note down which form of the equation they need for each question.

### Electricity concept map

**Starter 2** AfL Lit

Ask students to draw concept maps showing what they know about electricity and circuits. They should be able to recall some work on electricity from Key Stage 3. You might need to use word or diagram prompts.

### Models for electricity (AT)

**Exploring 2**

The **AT** document *Hearts and cells* provides some cards showing how the circulatory system can be used as a model for a circuit. The **AT** document *Other models* provides other models that can be used to explain various phenomena. There is a further model introduced on **Worksheet P2.3c**.

**Stretch** Students answer the 'extra challenge' section of the worksheet.

**Support** Students only use the model in the **AT** document *Hearts and cells*.

### Lighting fluorescent tubes

**Explaining 2** Demo

See the Teacher and technician practical sheet P2.3(1) for full details.

**Stretch** Ask students to evaluate whether this demonstration really does show that static charges and current electricity are the same thing.

**Support** Explain that electrons from the dome are jumping to the bulb and running to earth through you, and that this has the same effect as plugging the bulb into an electricity supply.

### Sure, unsure, know more

**Plenary 2** AfL Lit

Ask students write down one thing from this lesson that they are sure about, one thing they are unsure about and one thing that they want to know more about. Revise the things that students are having difficulty with.

### Charges and currents

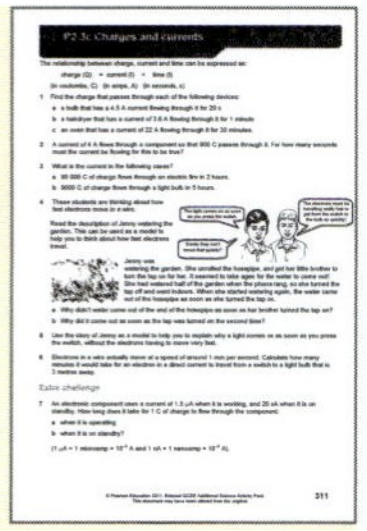

**Homework 2**

**Worksheet P2.3c**, for students working at a higher level, provides questions using the equation for charge, current and time and questions on using models to explain phenomena.

**Stretch** Students answer the 'extra challenge' question.

# P2.3 Electric currents

What is an electric current?

The ULTra system is used at Heathrow Airport to carry some passengers to Terminal 5. Batteries in the vehicle supply an electric current which drives a motor. The batteries are recharged when the vehicle stops at a station.

A *The ULTra system has no driver. A computer controls all the vehicles in the system.*

An insulating material can be given a charge of static electricity because any charge transferred to the material is not conducted away.

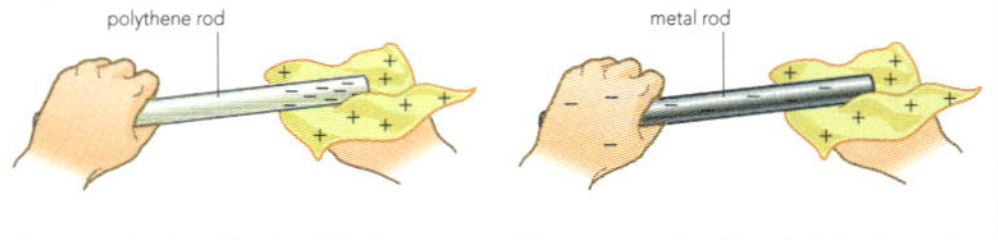


B *Why it is difficult to charge a conducting material with static electricity*

1 What is an electric current?

2 What is the difference between conductors and insulators? Use the word 'electrons' in your answer.

All materials contain electrons. The electrons in insulating materials cannot move around but in metals some of the electrons from each atom are free to move about. If the electrons in a metal flow, there is an electric **current**.

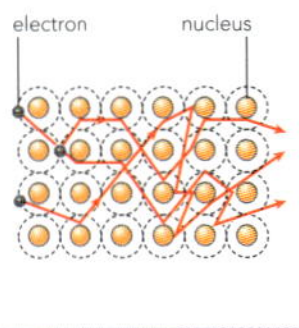


C *Current flowing through a wire*

In a piece of metal the free electrons are moving around all the time in different directions. When we put a metal wire in an electrical circuit, the cell pushes the free electrons in one direction around the circuit. There must be a complete circuit for this to happen and for the current to flow.

Cells and batteries supply **direct current**, in which the current flows only in one direction. Generators produce **alternating current**, in which the electrons change direction many times each second.

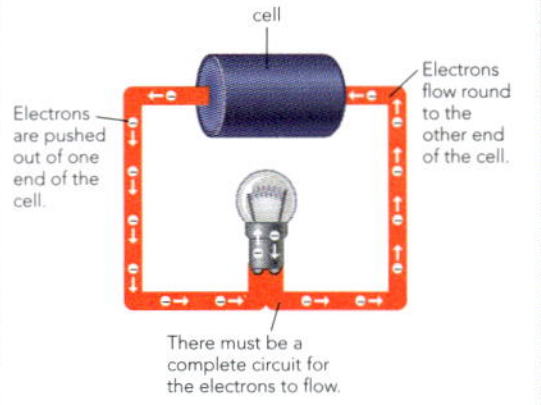


D *Cells supply direct current.*

## Charge and current

A current is a rate of flow of charged particles. The size of the current depends on how much charge is passing a point in a circuit each second. The units for charge are **coulombs** (**C**) and the units for current are **amperes** (or amps, **A**). 1 ampere is a flow of 1 coulomb of charge per second.

charge (coulombs, C) = current (amperes, A) × time (seconds, s)

This can also be written in symbols:

$$Q = I \times t$$

**e.g.** A current of 5 A flows for 10 seconds. How much charge has flowed through the circuit?

charge = current × time

= 5 A × 10 s = 50 C

**ResultsPlus Watch Out!**

Students are often confused by the symbols used for the quantities and units in the charge equation. Remember that the *units* have sensible abbreviations (coulombs = C, amps = A) but that charge is represented in equations using *Q*, and current is represented with *I*.

**H** This equation can be rearranged to work out the size of the current from the charge and the time.

$$\text{current (amperes, A)} = \frac{\text{charge (coulombs, C)}}{\text{time (seconds, s)}}$$

$$I = \frac{Q}{t}$$

**H**

E *A formula triangle can help you to rearrange equations. Cover up the quantity you need to calculate and the symbols you can see give you the rest of the equation.*

3 a What is the difference between direct and alternating current?
b What component provides direct current?

4 What are the units for measuring: a charge b current?

5 A current of 3 A flows for 30 seconds. How much charge has flowed through the circuit?

**H** 6 A current of 20 A flows in a circuit. How long does it take for 5000 C of charge to flow?

7 Explain how to make a current flow in a piece of wire and why this will not work if you use an insulating material.

**Skills spotlight**

A German scientist might write the equation relating charge, current and time like this:

Ladung = Strom × Zeit

Explain why scientists usually replace words in equations with symbols.

**Learning Outcomes**

1.9 Recall that an electric current is the rate of flow of charge
1.10 Recall that the current in metals is a flow of electrons
1.11 Use the equation:
charge (coulomb, C) = current (ampere, A) × time (second, s) $Q = I \times t$
1.12 Recall that cells and batteries supply direct current (d.c.)
1.13 Demonstrate an understanding that direct current (d.c.) is movement of charge in one direction only
HSW 11 Present information using scientific conventions and symbols



How can you count electrons? 213

## ActiveTeach

- **AT** *Electric cars 1* [BBC video] Report on Chevrolet Volt 1
- **AT** *Electric cars 2* [BBC video] Report on Chevrolet Volt 2
- **AT** *Hearts and cells* [word document] Model similarities and differences
- **AT** *Other models* [word document] Further models to explain

## Answers | Student Book

1 A flow of charge – in a metal these moving charges are electrons.

2 Conducting materials have electrons that are free to move around between the atoms. Insulating materials do not.

3 a A direct current always flows in the same direction. In an alternating current, the electrons change direction many times each second.
b Cells and batteries (students may also answer power supplies)

4 a Coulombs
b Amperes

5 3 A × 30 s = 90 C

6 (H) Time = charge/current = 5000 C / 20 A = 250 s

7 A good answer will contain the following points:
- make a circuit using the wire and a cell
- the cell will cause some of the electrons from the metal atoms to move along the wire
- this is a current
- this will not work with an insulating material
- this is because there are no electrons that are free to move around.

**Skills spotlight**

The words for different quantities are often different in different languages, which could cause problems if scientists in different countries are communicating with each other. Symbols are quicker to write, and an agreed set of symbols can be used internationally.

# P2.4 Current and voltage



This lesson looks at how ammeters and voltmeters are used to measure current and potential difference and (for Higher Tier students) defines potential difference in terms of energy.

## Specification coverage

***2.1*** Describe how an ammeter is placed in series with a component to measure the current, in amps, in the component

***2.2*** Explain how current is conserved at a junction

***2.3*** Explain how the current in a circuit depends on the potential difference of the source

***2.4*** Describe how a voltmeter is placed in parallel with a component to measure the potential difference (voltage), in volts, across it

H ***2.5*** Demonstrate an understanding that potential difference (voltage) is the energy transferred per unit charge passed and hence that the volt is a joule per coulomb

HSW *3* Many phenomena can be explained by developing and using scientific theories, models and ideas

There are also opportunities to cover HSW *11*.

### Key facts

**Starter 1** AfL

Ask each student to write down three facts that he/she has learned during the topic and share these within a group. Select a spokesperson for one group at random to share their ideas with the class. Then ask whether other groups had the same 'most common fact'.

### Measuring current and voltage

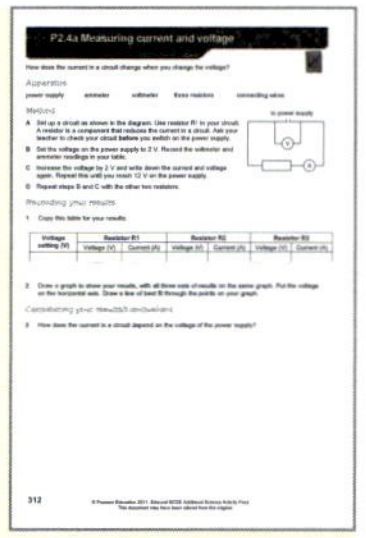

**Exploring 1** Prac

See **Worksheet P2.4a** and the Teacher and technician practical sheet P2.4 (1) for full details.

Stretch Ask students to repeat the measurements for one resistor, with the connections to the power supply reversed.

Support Students may need help drawing graph axes and scales.

### Student Book spread P2.4

**Explaining 1**

Stretch Tell students that the voltage across each branch of a parallel circuit is the same, and ask them to explain why this is so.

Support Use the analogy of a TV series (one episode after another) to explain the idea of a series circuit, where the current goes through one component after another. Drawing parallel lines on the board and a simple parallel circuit should help to get across the idea of a parallel circuit.

### Spot the mistakes

**Plenary 1** AfL

Ask students to work in small groups to draw three circuit diagrams, each of which contains at least one mistake. These can include things such as the readings on different ammeters in a circuit. Groups swap drawings and try to identify the mistakes. Check selected samples to make sure that there are no misconceptions being reinforced.

### Measuring in circuits

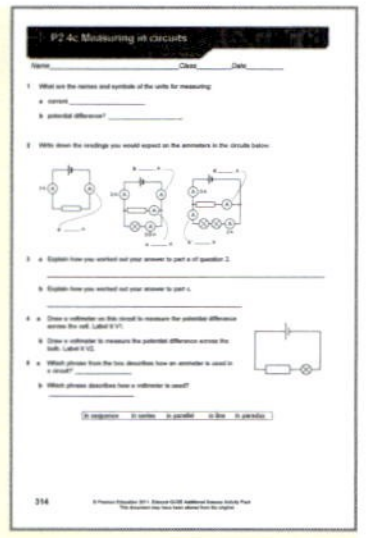

**Homework 1**

**Worksheet P2.4c**, for students needing support, provides questions on the content of this lesson.

Support Remind students that the current is the same everywhere in a series circuit, and that the current in a parallel circuit is the sum of the currents in the branches.

### Yo! Sushi

**Starter 2**

Explain to students how the Yo! Sushi restaurants work (a conveyor belt winds through the restaurant and diners take dishes from it as they pass, then pay at the end depending on how many and which kinds of dishes they have eaten).

Ask students to compare how the restaurants work to an electric circuit, listing similarities and differences.

### Modelling circuits

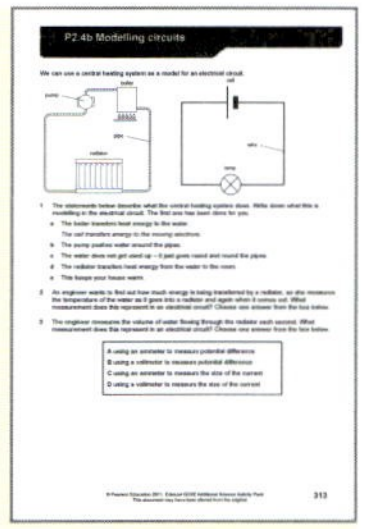

**Exploring 2**

**Worksheet P2.4b** and the **AT** presentation *Central heating model* provide the same model as the Skills spotlight box.

The **AT** presentation *Conveyor belt model* show different models to help students to think about electricity and circuits.

Stretch Ask students to compare the various models and to develop some criteria to help them explain which they think is the most helpful.

Support Students look only at the central heating model.

### Conservation of current

**Explaining 2** Demo

See the Teacher and technician practical sheet P2.4 (2) for full details.

Stretch Ask students to predict what will happen to the current readings if a third bulb is added to the same branch.

Support Students could act out a circuit, with each student being a unit of charge.

### Jumbled sentences

**Plenary 2** AfL Lit

Ask students to make sentences using groups of three given words. Possible lists include: ammeter, current, series; voltmeter, energy, parallel; series, parallel, current.

Ask various students to read out their sentences and ask the rest of the class to say whether or not the sentences are correct.

### Current and circuits

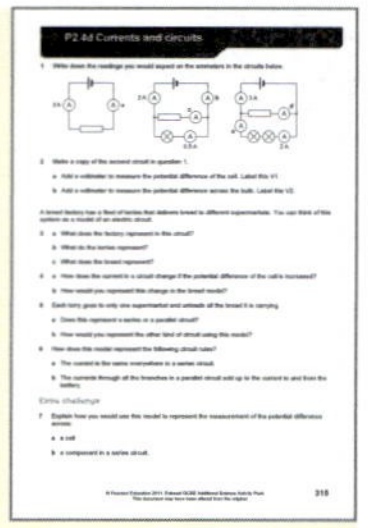

**Homework 2**

**Worksheet P2.4d**, is designed for students working at a higher level.

Stretch Students answer the 'extra challenge' question.

# P2.4 Current and voltage

How do we measure current and voltage?

Electric cars usually have an ammeter mounted in the instrument panel so the driver can check how much current the engine is using. This can help them to select the best gear.

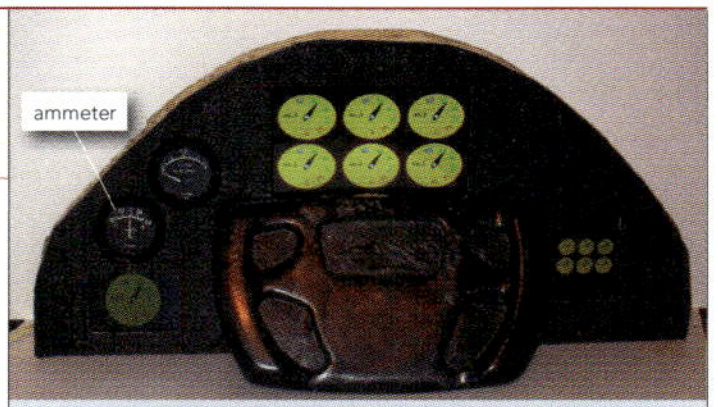


**A** *An ammeter is important in solar cars. Here is a dashboard from a solar car built by a team at Glyndwr University in Wales to compete in races.*

The size of a current is measured using an **ammeter**, placed **in series** with other components in the circuit. The electrons are not 'used up' and the current leaving the cell is the same as the current that flows back into the cell, so an ammeter can be placed anywhere in a **series circuit**.

1 a Draw a series circuit with two bulbs in it.
b Draw a parallel circuit with two bulbs in it.

2 Look at Figure B. Ammeter $A_1$ reads 2 A. What does ammeter $A_2$ read?

3 Look at Figure C. Ammeter $A_2$ reads 1 A and ammeter $A_3$ reads 3 A. What is the reading on:
a ammeter $A_1$
b ammeter $A_4$?

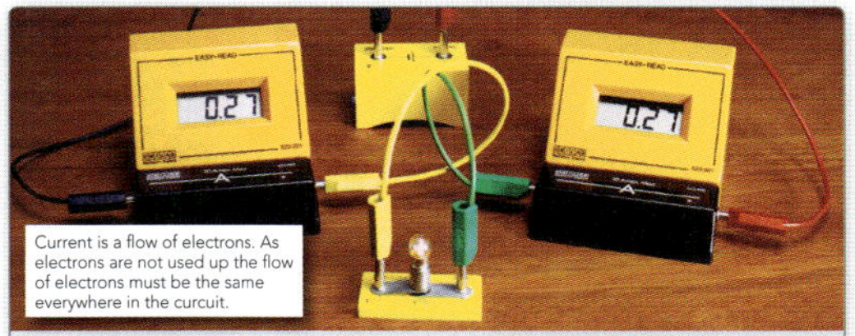


**B** *The two ammeters in this series circuit all show the same reading.*

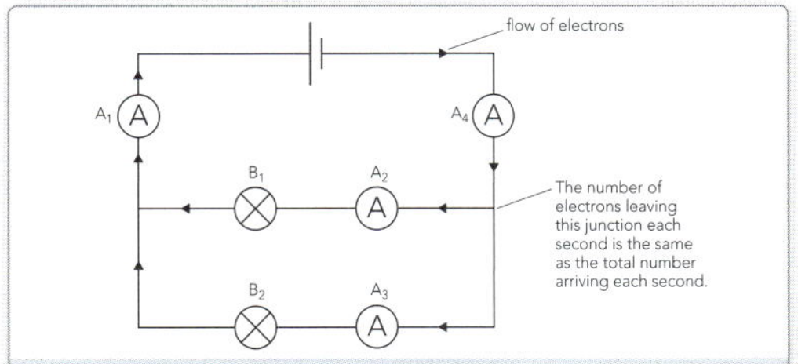


**C** *In a parallel circuit, the current flowing into a junction is the same as the total current flowing out of it. The current is said to be 'conserved' at the junction.*

In a **parallel circuit** the current splits up when it reaches a junction. In Figure C, the reading on ammeter $A_1$ will be the total of the readings on ammeters $A_2$ and $A_3$.

One way to change the size of the current in a circuit is by changing the **potential difference (voltage)** of the cell or power supply. The higher the potential difference, the bigger the current.



## Measuring voltage

The potential difference is a way of measuring the amount of energy transferred to a component by a current. Potential difference is measured using a **voltmeter**. The voltmeter is placed **in parallel** with the component. It measures the difference in energy between the electrons going into the component and those coming out.

H The potential difference measures the energy transferred to a component for each unit of charge that passes through that component. As energy is measured in joules and charge is measured in coulombs, 1 volt = 1 joule per coulomb.

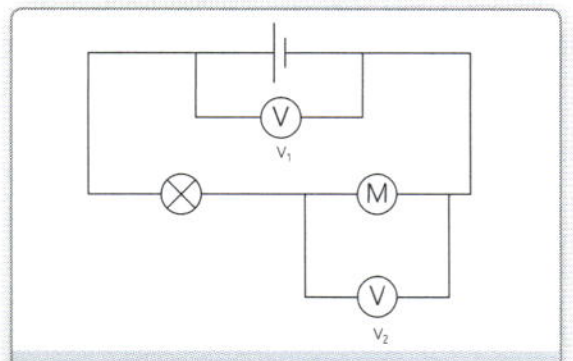


**D** *Voltmeter $V_1$ is measuring the potential difference of the cell. Voltmeter $V_2$ is measuring the potential difference across the motor.*

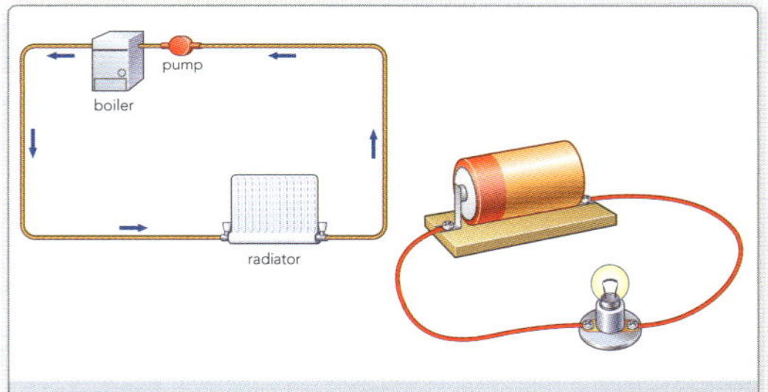


**E** *A central heating system can help you think about what happens in a circuit.*

**Skills spotlight**

Scientists often use models to help them to think about how things work. Figure E shows how a central heating system can be used as a model for a circuit. Explain which parts of the model represent each part of the circuit. What measurements in the central heating system would represent the measurements made by an ammeter and a voltmeter?

4 Look at Figure D. Draw a version of the circuit with just one voltmeter in the correct position to measure the potential difference across the bulb.

H 5 How much energy is transferred when 20 C of charge flows through a bulb if the potential difference across the bulb is 5 V?

6 Look at Figure C. Describe how you can use ammeters $A_1$ and $A_2$ to find out the current flowing through bulb $B_2$ and why this method will work.

**ResultsPlus Watch Out!**

Potential difference is just another name for voltage. You can use either term in an examination.

**Learning Outcomes**

2.1 Describe how an ammeter is placed in series with a component to measure the current, in amps, in the component
2.2 Explain how current is conserved at a junction
2.3 Explain how the current in a circuit depends on the potential difference of the source
2.4 Describe how a voltmeter is placed in parallel with a component to measure the potential difference (voltage), in volts, across it
H 2.5 Demonstrate an understanding that potential difference (voltage) is the energy transferred per unit charge passed and hence that the volt is a joule per coulomb
HSW 3 Describe how phenomena are explained using scientific models

How can sand conduct electricity?


## ActiveTeach

- **AT** *Series and parallel circuits* [interactive]
  Calculations in circuits – labelling activity
- **AT** *Central heating model* [presentation]
  Current model
- **AT** *Getting better data* [word document]
  Calculate resistance and means
- **AT** *Conveyor belt model* [presentation]
  Three conveyor belt models

## Key terms

ammeter
in parallel
in series
parallel circuit
potential difference
series circuit
voltage
voltmeter

## Answers | Student Book

1 a

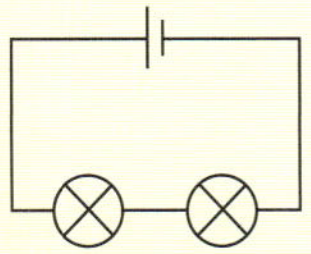

b

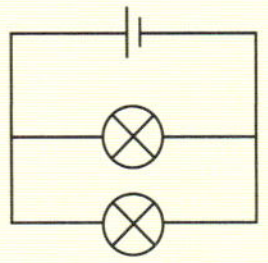

2 2 A

3 a 4 A
b 4 A

4

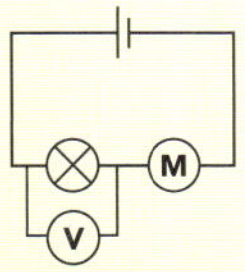


5 H 1 V is 1 J per coulomb, so 20 C at 5 V is 20 × 5 = 100 J

6 A good answer will contain the following points:
- subtract the reading on $A_2$ from the reading on $A_1$ to get the current flowing through $B_2$
- this works because the current flowing through the main part of the circuit splits up at the junction
- therefore the sum of the currents through $B_1$ and $B_2$ is the same as the current in the main part of the circuit.

**Skills spotlight**

The boiler and pump represent the cell, the pipes represent the wires, the water in the pipes represents the moving electrons, the heat energy in the water represents the energy transferred by the electrons, and the radiator represents the bulb.

An 'ammeter' in the central heating system would measure the volume of water passing a point in the circuit each second. A voltmeter would measure the temperature of the water going into and out of the radiator (or into and out of the boiler).

# P2.5 Investigating voltage, current and resistance



This lesson challenges students to investigate the relationship between current, voltage and resistance. The activity may be run as a practice controlled assessment or as a straight-forward class practical. The practical work can be completed within an hour.

## Specification coverage

***2.6*** Investigate the relationship between potential difference (voltage), current and resistance

This activity provides opportunities to cover HSW *1*, HSW *2*, HSW *3*, HSW *5*, HSW *6*, HSW *7*, HSW *8*, HSW *10* and HSW *11*.

## Key terms

resistance
ohm (Ω)

### Before the lesson

In the week or two before the task show students the equipment and, if appropriate, allow them to practice using it. Students who have done *Exploring 1* in P2.4 will have had experience of setting up a suitable circuit and taking measurements of current and voltage. Students may find Skills Sheet 18 useful because it deals with mathematical relationships. In addition perhaps show students one or more of Skills Sheets 19 to 26 to show what is expected of them in their actual controlled assessment task.

### Starter

**Blowing bulbs**

Use a low voltage bulb in a circuit where the voltage produces too high a current for it, and show students that the bulb 'blows'. Set up the circuit again with a new bulb, but this time with a resistor in the circuit as well. Show students that the bulb survives this time, and ask them to suggest why this is.

Follow this by reading the additional information below the opening section of page 216 of the Student Book. They may then read the brief description of the activity provided by the 'Your task' box.

### Option 1: Straight-forward class practical

Students follow the instructions on **Worksheet P2.5b**. This prompts students to take current and voltage readings at several different power pack voltage settings for each of five resistors. The range of data that students need to collect is given on **Worksheet P2.5c** which students will also need.

You could ask students to come up with one or two further hypotheses, based on their observations in this practical.

### Plenary

On page 217 of the Student Book you will find two examples of the sort of work that students may produce for this task. The examples focus on quality of evidence. You could share these with students after they have completed their own work. This will help them to understand the assessment criteria and so make it easier for them to evaluate their work and to see how they can improve it. Moderator comments on each of the Student Book extracts can be found at the end of the assessment guidance for this investigation on the CD-ROM. The examples can also be found on the **AT** document *Student examples*.

### Option 2: Running the activity as a practice controlled assessment task (PCAT)

We have provided a full range of support resources to allow the running of this practical as a practice controlled assessment task. A recommended structure is outlined below (to be used over a number of sessions). Marking guidance for all three parts of the practice task can be found on the CD-ROM that accompanies the TTPP. To save time when using these practice controlled assessment tasks, you may wish to focus on a particular aspect or skill rather than working through all three parts of the task.

#### Part A Planning

1. Students should be given the Student Brief on **Worksheet P2.5a**. They can use Part A of the Workbook that is provided to help with their practice controlled assessments. They should be given about 1 hour to do this planning.
2. If students have not carried out *Exploring 1* in P2.4, show them how to set up a circuit with a voltmeter and ammeter, as shown on the Worksheet P2.5b. Explain that the voltmeter is needed because the power pack does not always deliver exactly the voltage set on it.

#### Part B Observations

3. Students should be asked to carry out the practical task to collect evidence using the method they have planned in Part A. Once again, they should refer to the Student Brief on **Worksheet P2.5a**. They can use Part B of the Workbook that is provided to help pupils with their practice controlled assessments. They should be given about 1 hour to collect their primary evidence.
4. If there is a problem with their own planned method, students may be asked to follow the method set out on **Worksheet P2.5b**. This will still enable students to access the full range of marks for Part B and Part C of the practice controlled assessment task.
5. In Part B, students are required to gather some secondary evidence. The evidence can be quantitative or qualitative. It can be from a variety of sources but students must note where they found their evidence and evaluate the quality of the source as part of this task. Skills Sheet 22 provides students with further guidance on researching for and evaluating secondary evidence. This part of the task could be done outside of the lesson but must be supervised.

#### Part C Conclusions

6. Students follow the instructions set out on the Part C section of the Student Brief on **Worksheet P2.5a**. They should use their data from Part B and the secondary evidence they have collected when doing this. They can use Part C of the Workbook that is provided to help pupils with their practice controlled assessments. They should be given about 1 hour to work on their conclusions.

The **AT** includes video clips showing a group of students working through elements of this investigation with teacher support.

# P2.5 Investigating voltage, current and resistance

What is the relationship between voltage, current and resistance?

The photo shows a fulgurite, sometimes called 'petrified lightning'. It was made when lightning struck sand. The voltage of the lightning was high enough to make a current flow for a short distance through the sand, and the heat from this current melted the sand to form this glassy structure.

The current that can flow in a circuit depends on the potential difference (voltage) and the **resistance** of the circuit. The resistance is a measure of how easy or difficult it is for electricity to flow. Resistance is measured in **ohms** (Ω).

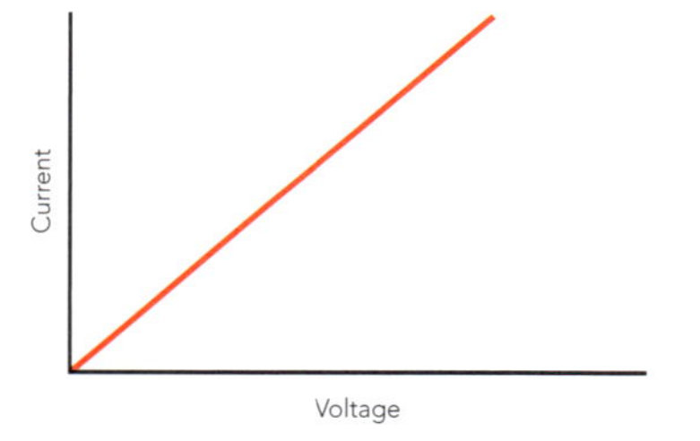


**B** *A manufacturer would obtain this kind of graph when testing a resistor.*

**A** *This fulgurite was found in Arizona.*

Resistors are used in many different types of electronic equipment to control the size of the currents. Manufacturers checking their resistors therefore need to test them at different voltages.

**Your task**

You are going to plan an investigation that will allow you to find out the relationship between voltage, current and resistance. You will be given resistors with different resistances. Your teacher will provide you with some materials to help you organise this task.

**Learning Outcomes**

*2.6 Investigate the relationship between potential difference (voltage), current and resistance*

## ResultsPlus Build Better Answers

When planning an investigation like this, one of the skills you will be assessed on is your ability to consider the *quality of the evidence*. There are 4 marks available for this skill. Here are two extracts focusing on this skill. Other skills are dealt with in other lessons.

**Student extract 1 — A basic response for this skill**

*I ignored the measurement at 4 V when I drew the line on my graph for the 50 Ω resistor because it did not fit the pattern made by the other measurements. There were no measurements that seemed to be wrong in the secondary evidence.*

The student has correctly dealt with the anomaly (the point that did not fit the pattern) by excluding the point when drawing the graph.

Commenting on the secondary evidence is also important.

If there are no anomalies in your evidence it is important to say so.

**Student extract 2 — A good response for this skill**

*I excluded the reading for 4 V for the 50 Ω resistor when I drew my graph because it did not seem to fit the pattern made by the other readings. The reading was probably a mistake, and if I included it when considering my conclusion, my conclusion could be wrong. I used two points from the lines of best fit when I worked out the gradients of each line, because the line of best fit evens out any errors there may have been in the ammeter or voltmeter reading.*

The student has *explained* why it was necessary to exclude the anomalous point.

They have shown that they have taken any possibly incorrect points into account when processing their results.

### ResultsPlus

**To access 2 marks**

- Comment on the quality of your primary and secondary evidence
- Deal with any anomalies appropriately
- Say if you do not think there are any anomalies in your evidence

**To access 4 marks**

- Take account of any anomalies in your primary and secondary evidence
- Explain any adjustments you need to make to your evidence
- If you do not think there are anomalies, explain this and say that you are using all your evidence





## ActiveTeach

- **AT** *P2.5 Voltage, current, resistance* [interactive]
  Investigating volts, amps and ohms
- **AT** *P2.5 Assessment criteria* [presentation]
  Understanding the CA marking criteria
- **AT** *Investigating LDRs* [word document]
  Changes of resistance
- **AT** *P2.5 Specification points* [word document]
  Edexcel specification points
- **AT** *P2.5 Student examples* [word document]
  Examples for students to assess

## Assessment criteria

### Quality of evidence

**0** No comments made on the quality of the data/observations.

**1-2 a)** Comments on the quality of the primary evidence, dealing with anomalies appropriately (if no anomalies in evidence, candidates need to state this). For example, draws line of best fit ignoring any obvious outliers.

**b)** Comments on the quality of the secondary evidence, dealing with anomalies appropriately (if no anomalies in evidence, candidates need to state this). For example, does not include anomalous values in any comparisons with their primary data.

**3-4 a)** Explains any adjustments to the evidence needed, or decision not to exclude evidence, e.g. explains that point X has been ignored when drawing the graph as it is a long way from the line formed by the other points. Explains that including the anomalous point would distort the true shape of the graph.

**b)** Takes account of anomalies in primary and secondary evidence when processing evidence (using all evidence if no anomalies). For example, uses line of best fit (ignoring anomalous data) if working out gradient, rather than using values from measured data.

# P2.6 Changing resistances



This lesson looks at how devices with changing resistances can be used to control the current in a circuit.

## Specification coverage

**2.7** Explain how changing the resistance in a circuit changes the current and how this can be achieved using a variable resistor

**2.8** Use the equation: potential difference (volt, V) = current (ampere, A) × resistance (ohm, Ω), $V = I \times R$

**2.9** Demonstrate an understanding of how current varies with potential difference for the following devices: a) filament lamps b) diodes c) fixed resistors

**2.10** Demonstrate an understanding of how the resistance of a light-dependent resistor (LDR) changes with light intensity

**2.11** Demonstrate an understanding of how the resistance of a thermistor changes with change of temperature (negative temperature coefficient thermistors only)

HSW **11** Presenting information, *developing an argument* and drawing a conclusion, using scientific, technical and mathematical language, conventions and symbols and ICT tools

There are also opportunities to cover HSW **3** and HSW **10**.

### Pressure switches

**Starter 1** Demo

Demonstrate that circuits can be controlled by pressure switches and then introduce the idea that other components can be controlled by environmental conditions such as light and temperature. See the Teacher and technician practical sheet P2.6 (1) for full details.

### Varying the potential difference

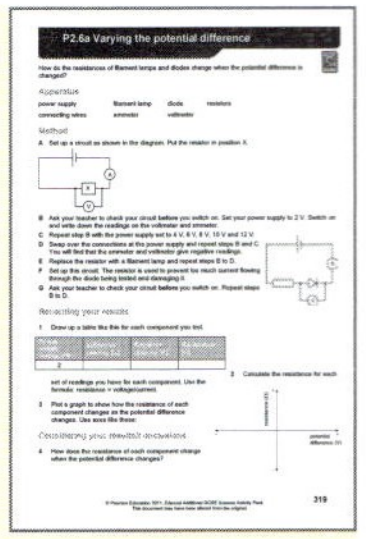

**Exploring 1** Prac

See **Worksheet P2.6a** and the Teacher and technician practical sheet P2.6 (2) for full details.

Stretch Do not give students the part of the worksheet showing them how to tabulate and present their results.

Support Help students to draw a table for their results and help them to work out the resistances for each set of current and voltage readings.

### Student Book spread P2.6

**Explaining 1**

The resistance of some thermistors goes up when they are heated; students are not required to know about these.

Stretch Ask students to suggest why an ammeter should have a very low resistance and a voltmeter should have a very high resistance.

Support It may help students to remember how the resistances of LDRs and thermistors vary if they are told that the more energy there is the lower the resistance.

### Components and graphs

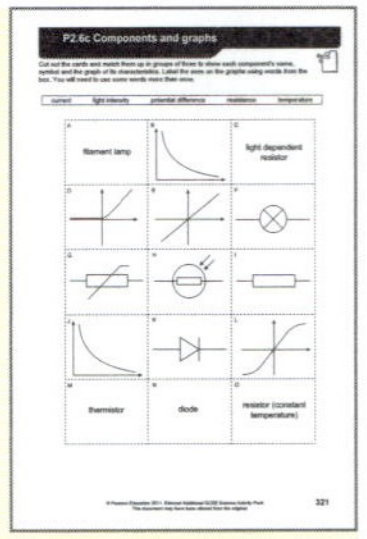

**Plenary 1**

Using the set of cards provided in **Worksheet P2.6c**, ask students to match up the cards and label the axes on the graphs.

### Components and resistances

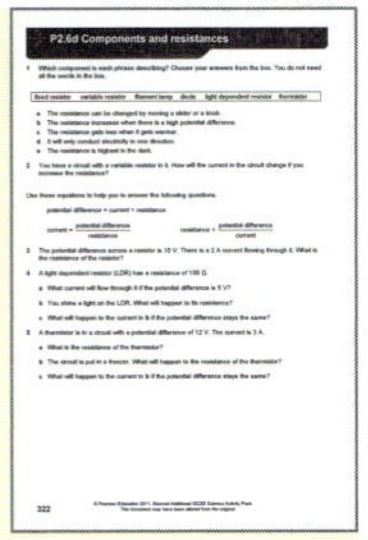

**Homework 1**

**Worksheet P2.6d**, for students needing support, provides questions on the content of this lesson.

Support A completed copy of the cloze summary will help students with the worksheet.

### Design a circuit

**Starter 2**

Ask students to design an automatic control circuit for car lights that go on when it gets dark (or any other simple task they may come up with themselves). Keep students' ideas and revisit later in the lesson so they can amend their ideas if necessary.

### Investigating LDRs and thermistors

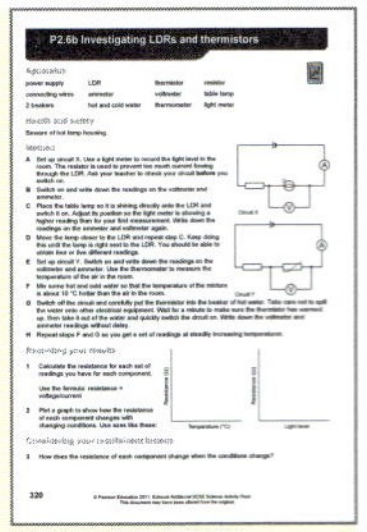

**Exploring 2** Prac

See **Worksheet P2.6b** and the Teacher and technician practical sheet P2.6 (3) for full details.

The **AT** document *Investigating LDRs* could be used if there is insufficient time for the practical work.

Stretch Students plan and carry out their own method for investigation.

Support Help students to draw a table and to work out the resistances for each set of current and voltage readings.

### Demonstrate V = I × R

**Explaining 2** Demo

See the Teacher and technician practical sheet P2.6 (4) for full details.

Stretch Demonstrate to students that the gradient of the graph can be used to work out the resistance and discuss why this may be a more accurate method of calculating resistance than using a mean of resistances calculated from separate pairs of readings.

Support Do the graph plotting via a spreadsheet and computer projector.

### Word meanings

**Plenary 2** AfL Lit

Give students a set of cards with the key words from this lesson and another set of cards with their meanings. Ask students to match the correct word with the correct meaning. More able students could be asked to write their own glossary entries for the words.

### Changing resistances

**Homework 2**

**Worksheet P2.6e**, for students working at a higher level, provides questions about the components studied in this lesson. Students will also need a sheet of graph paper.

Stretch Students answer the 'extra challenge' question.

# P2.6 Changing resistances

How can the resistance of a circuit be changed?

We are used to modern cars having many automatic systems, such as headlights that come on when it gets dark, windscreen wipers that start when it rains and brakes that are applied if an obstacle is detected. Some scientists predict that automatic systems will allow driverless cars to be on the road by 2018.

**A** *The car is competing in a 132-mile driving competition through the desert. All the cars in the competition are driverless!*

## Resistors and lamps

The size of a current flowing in a circuit depends on the potential difference of the supply and on the **resistance** of the circuit. Resistance is a way of measuring how hard it is for electricity to flow. Resistance is measured in **ohms** (Ω).

The resistance of a whole circuit depends on the resistances of the different components in the circuit. The higher the total resistance, the smaller the current.

If a resistor remains at a constant temperature, the potential difference, current and resistance are related by the equation:

potential difference (volts, V) = current (amperes, A) × resistance (ohms, Ω)

$$V = I \times R$$

**e.g.**

What potential difference is needed to make a 2 A current flow through a 10 Ω resistor?

potential difference = current × resistance

= 2 A × 10 Ω

= 20 V

The current flowing in a circuit can be changed by changing the resistance. This can be done by putting a different resistor into the circuit or by using a **variable resistor**.

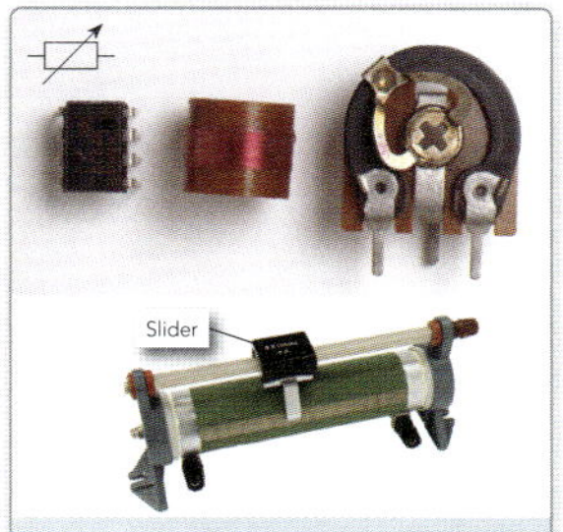


**B** *The resistance of a variable resistor can be changed by turning the knob or moving the slider.*

1 If you increase the potential difference of the power supply in a circuit, what happens to the current?

2 A circuit has a resistance of 50 Ω and the current is 5 A. What is the voltage of the supply?

3 Resistance is not measured directly. What two measurements would you need to make to work out the resistance of a component?

H 4 A 4.5 V cell produces a current of 0.5 A in a circuit. What is the resistance of the circuit?



## Other components

Some electrical components change their resistance depending on the potential difference or on the conditions surrounding them.

**Filament lamps** heat up when they are used. A higher potential difference makes them hotter, and as they get hotter the resistance increases.

**Diodes** conduct electricity in one direction only. If a potential difference is applied in the other direction no current will flow. The resistance of a **light-dependent resistor** (**LDR**) is large in the dark and gets less when light is shone on it. **Thermistors** have a high resistance when they are cold and their resistance gets less if they are heated up.

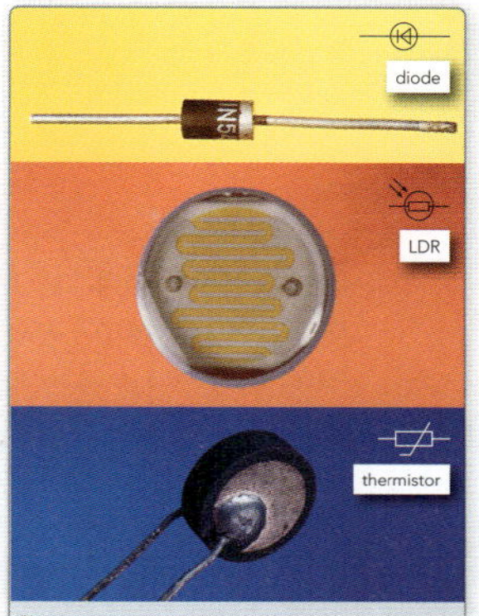


**C** *Components with changing resistances*

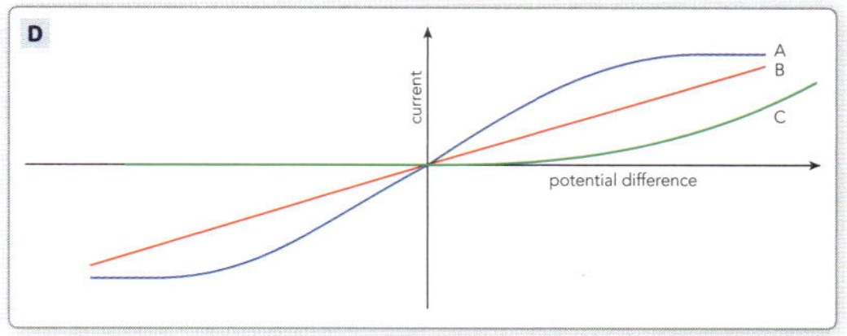


6 A fan is driven by an electric motor. Explain how adding a thermistor to the circuit would make the fan move faster when the room is warmer.

**ResultsPlus Watch Out!**

Students sometimes get mixed up about how resistance in a circuit changes the current. Remember that for a given voltage, the current goes *down* if the resistance goes *up*.

5 You are designing an electrical system for a new car. Which of the components on this page would you need to:

a automatically switch the lights on when it gets dark

b switch the air conditioning on when it gets too hot

c adjust the volume of the radio?

**Skills spotlight**

Sometimes a graph can be a more effective and scientific way of describing something than using words. Figure D shows the graphs of potential difference and current for a normal resistor, a diode and a filament lamp. Which one is which?

**Learning Outcomes**

2.7 Explain how changing the resistance in a circuit changes the current and how this can be achieved using a variable resistor

2.8 Use the equation: potential difference (volt, V) = current (ampere, A) × resistance (ohm, Ω)
$V = I \times R$

2.9 Demonstrate an understanding of how current varies with potential difference for the following devices:
a filament lamps b diodes c fixed resistors

2.10 Demonstrate an understanding of how the resistance of a light-dependent resistor (LDR) changes with light intensity

2.11 Demonstrate an understanding of how the resistance of a thermistor changes with change of temperature (negative temperature coefficient thermistors only)

HSW 11 Present information using scientific conventions and symbols



## ActiveTeach

- **AT** *Do you know your symbols?* [interactive] Electric circuit symbols – matching activity
- **AT** *Electrical resistance characteristics* [interactive] Characteristics graphs – scene investigation

## Key terms

diode
filament lamp
light-dependent resistor (LDR)
resistance
thermistor
variable resistor

## Answers | Student Book

**1** It increases

**2** 5 A × 50 Ω = 250 V

**3** Current and potential difference (or voltage)

**4** H R = V/I = 4.5 V / 0.5 A = 9 Ω

**5** **a** LDR
**b** Thermistor
**c** Variable resistor

**6** A good answer will contain the following points:

- the resistance of the thermistor will control the current flowing through the circuit
- if the temperature rises the resistance of the thermistor will decrease
- therefore more current can flow in the circuit
- if the current is higher, the motor driving the fan can turn faster.

**Skills spotlight**

A is the filament lamp, B is the normal resistor and C is the diode.

The diagrams show complex mathematical relationships but students should be able to describe the general shape of the graph and use this evidence to draw a conclusion about which component it represents.

# P2.7 Transferring energy



This lesson introduces the heating effect of a current and explains how power and energy transferred can be calculated.

## Specification coverage

***2.12*** Explain why, when there is an electric current in a resistor, there is an energy transfer that heats the resistor

H ***2.13*** Explain the energy transfer (in ***2.12*** above) as the result of collisions between electrons and the ions in the lattice

***2.14*** Distinguish between the advantages and disadvantages of the heating effect of an electric current

***2.15*** Use the equation: electrical power (watt, W) = current (ampere, A) × potential difference (volt, V), $P = I \times V$

***2.16*** Use the equation: energy transferred (joule, J) = current (ampere, A) × potential difference (volt, V) × time (second, s), $E = I \times V \times t$

HSW ***12*** The use of contemporary science and technological developments and their benefits, drawbacks and risks

There are also opportunities to cover HSW ***3***, HSW ***10*** and HSW ***11***.

### Heating wire wool
**Starter 1** Demo

Demonstrate the heating effect of a current using wire wool. If students are to do Exploring 1, you may also wish to demonstrate the action of a fuse. See the Teacher and technician practical sheet P2.7 for full details.

### Power and fuses (AT)
**Exploring 1**

The **AT** spreadsheet *Power and fuses 1* provides students with practice using the power equation, in the context of choosing the correct fuses for various appliances.

Stretch The **AT** spreadsheet *Power and fuses 2* provides the same data but without guidance.

Support Help students to set up the formulae in the spreadsheet and show them how to use the 'Fill Down' function.

### Student Book spread P2.7
**Explaining 1**

Students have already met the equation for calculating power from current and potential difference, in P1 Topic 5. Lesson P1.29 included a practical to measure the power of various low voltage devices. This could be repeated here.

Stretch Ask students to explain why the heating effect of a current increases with a higher current.

Support Work through the examples in the Student Book with the students.

### Power questions
**Plenary 1** AfL

Write some typical power ratings on the board (e.g. electric drill 1500 W) and ask students to work in pairs to create three power or energy calculation questions each using this data. They should also write mark schemes for their answers. Higher Tier students should be encouraged to include questions that involve changing the subject of the equation.

### Electrical heating
**Homework 1**

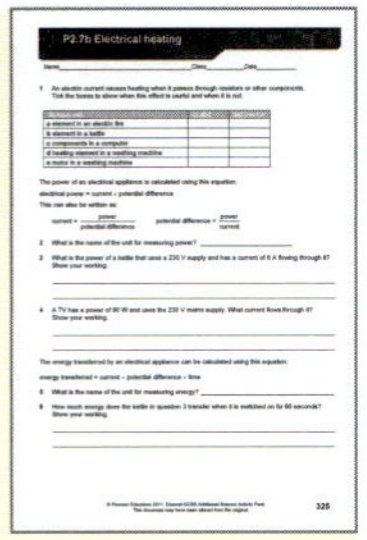

**Worksheet P2.7b**, for students needing support, provides questions on the content of this lesson.

Support Remind students of the useful and wasteful results of the heating effect.

### Sorting appliances
**Starter 2**

Write a list of electrical appliances on the board and ask students to sort them into two groups of their own choosing. The list should include items designed for heating (such as kettles, cookers, etc.) and those where heat is a wasted form of energy transfer (such as TVs, computers, motors, etc.).

### Choosing the wiring
**Exploring 2**

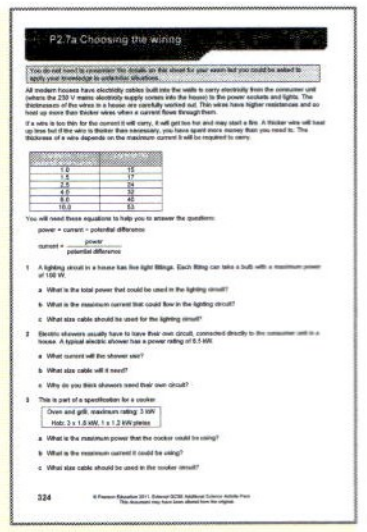

**Worksheet P2.7a** provides some information about the currents that can safely be carried by various thicknesses of house wiring.

Stretch Give students lengths of fuse wire of different ratings and ask them to rank in order of the current they can carry. If time permits, students could test their predictions.

Support Use the worksheet as the basis for a class discussion.

### H Modelling electron flow (AT)
**Explaining 2**

The **AT** presentation *Modelling electron flow* shows a simple model that can be used to represent the flow of electrons through a wire. It also provides questions helping students to carry out a 'thought experiment' into various aspects of electron flow.

Stretch Ask students to devise criteria by which to judge the validity of the model.

### Revision notes
**Plenary 2** AfL Lit

The **AT** document *Electricity revision notes* summarises the work in this topic but contains errors. Ask students to identify the errors and correct them. They can do this by marking up a printout of the sheet or by amending and saving the document on a computer.

### Heating and power
**Homework 2**

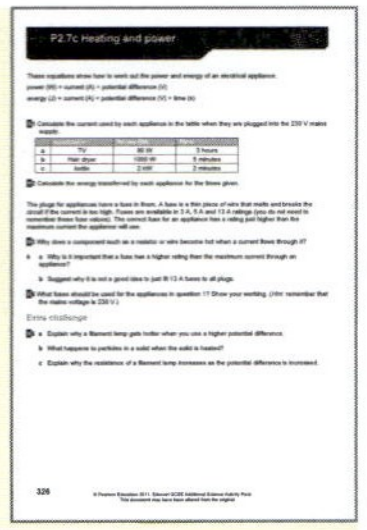

**Worksheet P2.7c**, for students working at a higher level, provides questions on the content of this lesson.

Stretch Students answer the 'extra challenge' question.

## Key terms

power
watt

# P2.7 Transferring energy

How much energy is transferred by electric currents?

People working or playing outdoors in cold weather can wear electrically heated clothing to make sure they stay warm.

When current flows through a resistor, energy is transferred to the resistor and it becomes warm. This heating effect is useful in appliances such as electric fires and kettles. These appliances are effectively large resistors.

A similar thing happens with all components – even components such as motors where the main energy transfer is from electrical energy to kinetic (movement) energy. In the case of a motor, the heat produced is wasted energy. Some electrical appliances may produce so much waste heat energy that they become too hot to touch and could cause burns.

A *An electrically heated jacket*

**Skills spotlight**

Scientists consider the benefits, drawbacks and risks of using new scientific and technological developments. Describe what these might be when comparing an electric heater with an open log fire.

B

C *Wires can catch fire if too much current flows. Plugs are fitted with fuses, which melt and break the circuit if the current is too high. This plug had the wrong type of fuse fitted.*

1 Why do computers need cooling fans inside them?

2 Give two examples of appliances where the heating effect of a current is:
a useful energy.
b wasted energy.

(H) A current in a wire is a flow of electrons. As the electrons move in a metal, they collide with the **ions** in the lattice and transfer some energy to them.

## Calculating power and energy

**Power** is the energy transferred every second. For electrical appliances the power can be worked out from the current and the potential difference. The unit of power is joules per second or **watts** (W) (1 watt = 1 joule/second).

electrical power (watts, W) = current (amperes, A) × potential difference (volts, V)

$$P = I \times V$$

**e.g.** A kettle uses the mains electricity supply at 230V. The current is 13A. What is the power of the kettle?

power = current × potential difference
= 13A × 230V
= 2990W

The total energy transferred by an appliance depends on its power and for how long it is switched on. The energy transferred can be calculated using the following equation:

energy transferred (joules, J) = current (amperes, A) × potential difference (volts, V) × time (seconds, s)

$$E = I \times V \times t$$

**e.g.** The kettle in the example above takes 2 minutes to boil some water. How much energy does it transfer?

energy = current × potential difference × time
2 minutes = 120 seconds
energy = 13A × 230V × 120s
= 358 800 J (or 358.8 kJ)

6 Explain why a travel kettle using a 12V supply takes much longer to boil water than a kettle that uses the mains supply.

3 An electric travel blanket uses a car's 12V supply. The current through it is 3A.
a What is the power of the blanket?
b How much energy does it transfer if it is switched on for 10 minutes?

(H) 4 A soldering iron has a power of 25W. It uses the 230V mains supply. What is the current when it is switched on?

(H) 5 A travel kettle has a power of 0.5kW. How long would it take to boil the same amount of water as in the example on the left?

**ResultsPlus Watch Out!**

Students often lose marks by being careless with units. Make sure the time is converted to seconds before you put numbers into the equation. In written tests always show your working.

**Learning Outcomes**

2.12 Explain why, when there is an electric current in a resistor, there is an energy transfer which heats the resistor
(H) 2.13 Explain the energy transfer (in 2.12 above) as the result of collisions between electrons and the ions in the lattice
2.14 Distinguish between the advantages and disadvantages of the heating effect of an electric current
2.15 Use the equation:
electrical power (watt, W) = current (ampere, A) × potential difference (volt, V)
$P = I \times V$
2.16 Use the equation: energy transferred (joule, J) = current (ampere, A) × potential difference (volt, V) × time (second, s)
$E = I \times V \times t$
HSW 12 Describe the benefits, drawbacks and risks of using new scientific and technological developments



How is it possible to run with a velocity of 0 m/s?



## ActiveTeach

- **AT** *Key electrical definitions* [interactive]
  Quantities & definitions – matching activity
- **AT** *Power and fuses 1* [spreadsheet]
  Support choosing fuses
- **AT** *Power and fuses 2* [spreadsheet]
  Choosing fuses
- **AT** *Revision notes* [word document]
  Identify and correct errors
- **AT** *Modelling electron flow* [presentation]
  Thought experiment

## Answers | Student Book

1 Components heat up when electric current flows through them, and they do not work properly if they get too hot.

2 **a** Any two useful effects, such as in kettles, electric fires, cookers, electric blankets, tumble dryers, etc.
**b** Any two examples of wasted heat energy, such as TVs, radios, computers.

3 **a** 12 V × 3 A = 36 W
**b** 10 minutes = 600 s
Energy = 12 V × 3 A × 600 s = 21 600 J (or energy = 36 W × 600 s)

4 (H) Current = power/potential difference = 25 W/230 V = 0.11 A

5 Energy transferred = 358 800 J
Energy = power × time
Time = energy/power = 358 800 J/500 W = 718 seconds (to the nearest second)

6 A good answer will contain the following points: electricity passing through a resistor (such as the element of a kettle) causes a heating effect; the power of an electrical appliance can be calculated using the potential difference and current; for the same kettle, a lower potential difference will mean that a lower current flows; the power will be much less than with a higher potential difference; it takes a certain amount of energy to boil a fixed volume of water; the power is the energy transferred per second; if the power is lower it will take longer for the same amount of energy to be transferred.

**Skills spotlight**

NB requires knowledge from Units C1 and P1 to answer this fully.

**Advantages**: electric heaters are efficient; do not produce waste gases that can be toxic; easier to start than a wood fire; can be used sustainably if the electricity comes from renewable resources.

**Drawbacks**: overall efficiency depends on the efficiency of the power station that produced the electricity, so they may not be as efficient; many people prefer the appearance of flames from a 'real' fire; a wood fire is a sustainable means of heating, as long as the wood is harvested sustainably.

**Risks**: risks of electric shocks as well as burns if the heater is not installed and maintained correctly.

# P2.8 Vectors and velocity



This lesson introduces the idea of displacement, velocity and force as vector quantities. Speed is calculated from the equation speed = distance/time and by interpreting distance–time graphs.

## Specification coverage

***3.1*** Demonstrate an understanding of the following as vector quantities: a) displacement b) velocity *c) acceleration* d) force

***3.2*** Interpret distance–time graphs including determination of speed from the gradient

***3.3*** Recall that velocity is speed in a stated direction

***3.4*** Use the equation: speed (m/s) = distance (m) / time (s)

HSW *11* Presenting information, *developing an argument and drawing a conclusion,* using scientific, *technical and mathematical language,* conventions and symbols *and ICT tools*

There are also opportunities to cover HSW *1*, HSW *6*, HSW *7*, HSW *8* and HSW *10*.

## Key terms

displacement
distance–time graph
gradient
speed
velocity
vector

### Runners in motion

**Starter 1** Demo

Runner A starts at one end of a 100 m track and Runner B starts at the opposite end. They run towards each other. Runner A covers 50 m in 10 seconds. Runner B covers 50 m in 7 seconds. Discuss students' answers about the motion of the two runners and explain that movement has a direction as well as a speed and that quantities with a direction as well as a size are called vectors.

### Measuring speed (AT)

**Exploring 1**

See the TTPP for full details. Calculate speed and draw a distance–time graph for each runner. Instructions can be found on the **AT** document *Measuring speed.*

Stretch Plot two runners on the same graph and describe the similarities and differences in their motion. Measure the gradients of their graphs and compare with the speeds calculated.

Support Round times to the nearest second and provide scales for the graph.

### Using distance–time graphs

**Exploring 3**

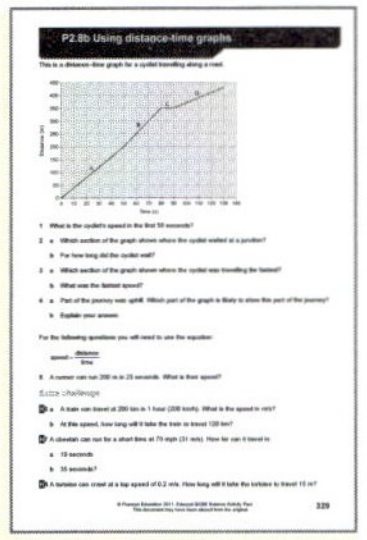

**Worksheet P2.8b** provides a distance–time graph for students to interpret and calculate the gradient. They also use the equation for speed.

Stretch Ask students to work in pairs. Each sketches a distance–time graph and writes a short scenario to describe the motion. They give their partner the words only, and both sketch the graph from the story. They then compare their graphs.

Support Students only work on questions **1** to **5**.

### Graph sketching

**Plenary 1** AfL

Describe different scenarios and ask students to sketch the distance–time graphs. Start with simple examples, such as someone walking at a steady speed who travels 400 m in 100 s. Ask for the speed (in this case 4 m/s), which they can calculate from the equation. Compare graphs.

### Country walk

**Homework 1**

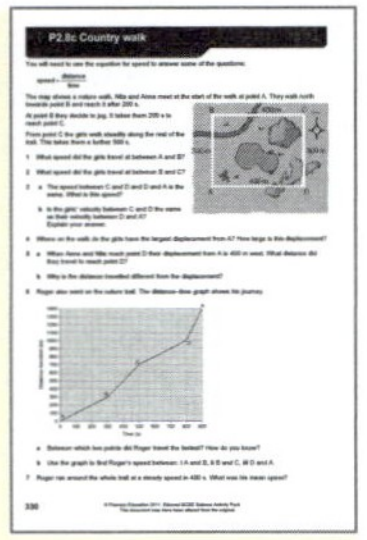

**Worksheet P2.8c**, for students needing support, gives students a map of a rectangular walk. They answer questions about speed, distance, displacement and velocity.

Support Convert all times to seconds.

### Crazy car control

**Starter 2**

Show a short video of synchronised driving (there are a number of good examples on *YouTube*). Ask students to think about how they would plan some of the manoeuvres. Elicit that the drivers need to know both the speed and the direction in which they are travelling (their velocity), so that they are at exactly the right position at the right time (displacement).

### Marble run

**Exploring 2** Prac

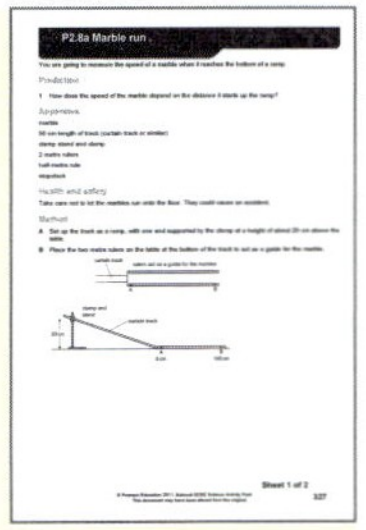

See **Worksheet P2.8a** and Teacher and technician practical sheet P2.8 for details.

Stretch Ask students to do two-step distance–time graphs by recording the time taken for the marble to shoot down the curtain track and the distance travelled on the track.

Support Help students to work with their data to calculate speed and plot their graphs. Encourage visual comparison of gradients.

### Student Book spread P2.8

**Explaining 1**

Use the text and illustrations in the Student Book to get across the idea of displacement as a vector quantity.

Stretch Ask how they could draw a distance–time graph if they knew the speed and time, but not the distance.

Support Emphasise the need to use the correct units when calculating speed. Question **3** has the time in minutes, so they need to convert the time to seconds.

### High Street (AT)

**Plenary 2** Lit

The **AT** document *High Street* has a story about Harry shopping on the High Street. He moves back and forth, travelling different distances in different times. Give different groups different tasks to focus on such as working out the greatest speed, working out how far Harry has travelled and working out his final position.

### Lane swimming

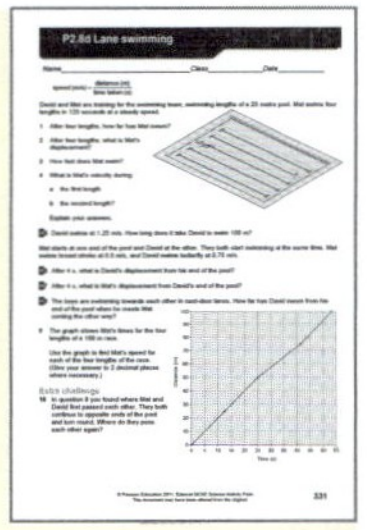

Using **Worksheet P2.8d**, students work out speed, distance and time from the equation, interpret distance–time graphs, and will be aware of the difference between displacement and distance, velocity and speed.

Stretch Ask students to complete the 'extra challenge' question.

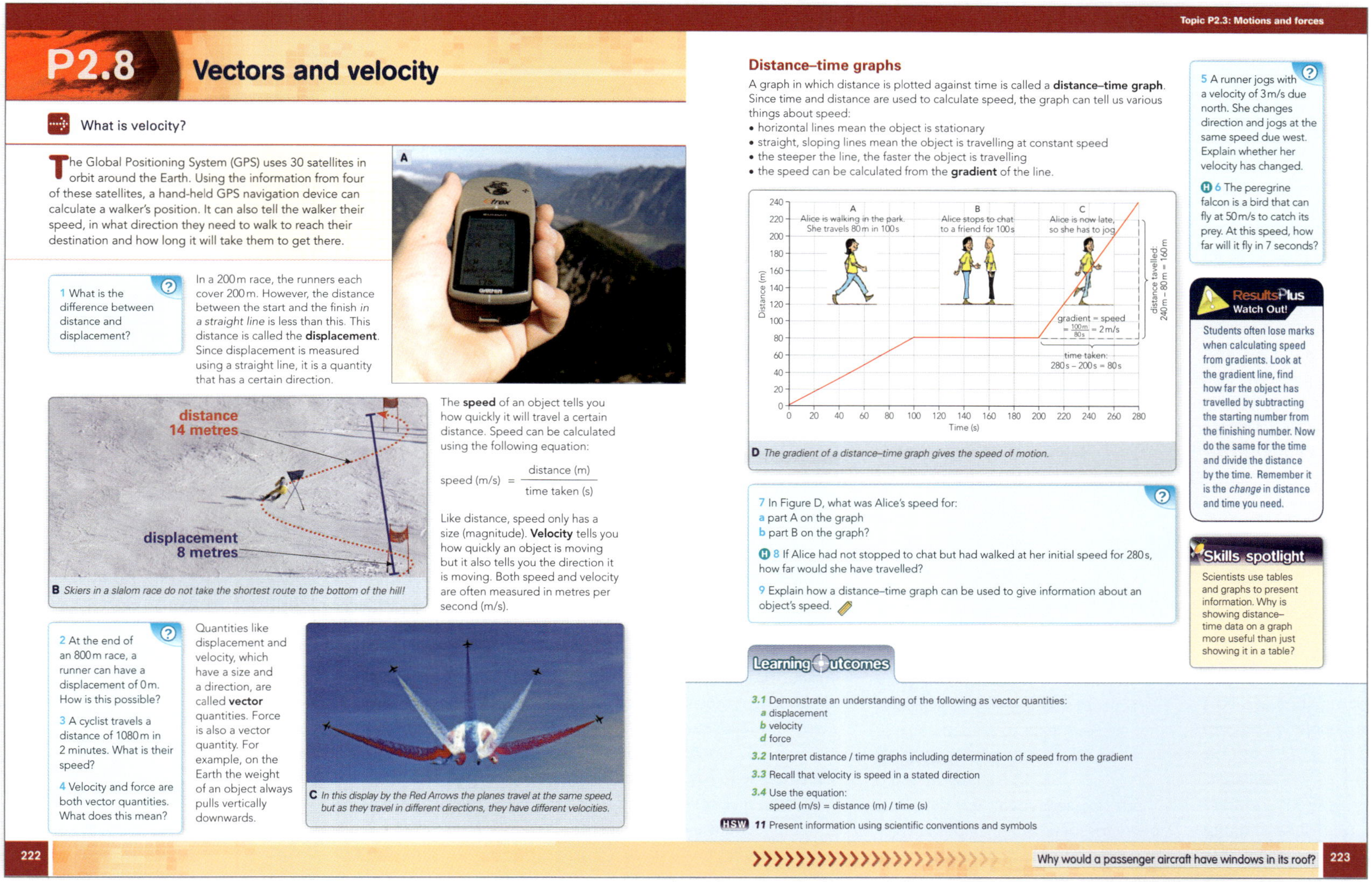
Topic P2.3: Motions and forces

# P2.8 Vectors and velocity

What is velocity?

The Global Positioning System (GPS) uses 30 satellites in orbit around the Earth. Using the information from four of these satellites, a hand-held GPS navigation device can calculate a walker's position. It can also tell the walker their speed, in what direction they need to walk to reach their destination and how long it will take them to get there.

A

1 What is the difference between distance and displacement?

In a 200 m race, the runners each cover 200 m. However, the distance between the start and the finish *in a straight line* is less than this. This distance is called the **displacement**. Since displacement is measured using a straight line, it is a quantity that has a certain direction.



**B** *Skiers in a slalom race do not take the shortest route to the bottom of the hill!*

The **speed** of an object tells you how quickly it will travel a certain distance. Speed can be calculated using the following equation:

$$\text{speed (m/s)} = \frac{\text{distance (m)}}{\text{time taken (s)}}$$

Like distance, speed only has a size (magnitude). **Velocity** tells you how quickly an object is moving but it also tells you the direction it is moving. Both speed and velocity are often measured in metres per second (m/s).

2 At the end of an 800 m race, a runner can have a displacement of 0 m. How is this possible?

3 A cyclist travels a distance of 1080 m in 2 minutes. What is their speed?

4 Velocity and force are both vector quantities. What does this mean?

Quantities like displacement and velocity, which have a size and a direction, are called **vector** quantities. Force is also a vector quantity. For example, on the Earth the weight of an object always pulls vertically downwards.

**C** *In this display by the Red Arrows the planes travel at the same speed, but as they travel in different directions, they have different velocities.*

## Distance–time graphs

A graph in which distance is plotted against time is called a **distance–time graph**. Since time and distance are used to calculate speed, the graph can tell us various things about speed:

- horizontal lines mean the object is stationary
- straight, sloping lines mean the object is travelling at constant speed
- the steeper the line, the faster the object is travelling
- the speed can be calculated from the **gradient** of the line.



**D** *The gradient of a distance–time graph gives the speed of motion.*

7 In Figure D, what was Alice's speed for:

a part A on the graph

b part B on the graph?

(H) 8 If Alice had not stopped to chat but had walked at her initial speed for 280 s, how far would she have travelled?

9 Explain how a distance–time graph can be used to give information about an object's speed.

5 A runner jogs with a velocity of 3 m/s due north. She changes direction and jogs at the same speed due west. Explain whether her velocity has changed.

(H) 6 The peregrine falcon is a bird that can fly at 50 m/s to catch its prey. At this speed, how far will it fly in 7 seconds?

**ResultsPlus Watch Out!**

Students often lose marks when calculating speed from gradients. Look at the gradient line, find how far the object has travelled by subtracting the starting number from the finishing number. Now do the same for the time and divide the distance by the time. Remember it is the *change* in distance and time you need.

**Skills spotlight**

Scientists use tables and graphs to present information. Why is showing distance–time data on a graph more useful than just showing it in a table?

**Learning Outcomes**

3.1 Demonstrate an understanding of the following as vector quantities:
a displacement
b velocity
d force

3.2 Interpret distance / time graphs including determination of speed from the gradient

3.3 Recall that velocity is speed in a stated direction

3.4 Use the equation:
speed (m/s) = distance (m) / time (s)

HSW 11 Present information using scientific conventions and symbols

222 Why would a passenger aircraft have windows in its roof? 223

## ActiveTeach

- **AT** *How far, how fast, how long?* [interactive] Distance-time graph – quiz
- **AT** *High Street* [word document] Distances and times
- **AT** *Measuring speed* [word document] Plot distance-time graphs
- **AT** *Yacht navigation* [video] Inertial yacht navigation

## Answers | Student Book

**1** Displacement is the straight-line distance moved in a particular direction; distance is how far an object has moved.

**2** The runner has arrived back exactly where they started.

**3** 9 m/s

**4** Vector quantities, such as force and velocity, have both a size and a direction.

**5** The velocity has changed because the direction is different.

**6** (H) 350 m

**7** **a** 0.8 m/s

**b** 0 m/s

**8** (H) 224 m

**9** A good answer will include the following points:

- a distance-time graph shows distance travelled plotted against time
- the gradient of a distance-time graph gives the speed because speed is distance/time
- a horizontal line shows an object is stationary
- a straight sloping line shows an object with a constant speed
- the steeper the line, the greater the speed.

**Skills spotlight**

Suggestions such as: it is easier to see the change in an object's motion from a graph, shown as a change in the slope of the line, than just by comparing values in a table.

# P2.9 Acceleration

This lesson introduces acceleration as a vector quantity and uses the equation for acceleration.

## Specification coverage

***3.1*** Demonstrate an understanding of the following as vector quantities: *a) displacement b) velocity* c) acceleration *d) force*

***3.5*** Use the equation: acceleration (metre per second squared, m/s²) = change in velocity (metre per second, m/s) / time taken (second, s), a = (v – u) / t

HSW ***11*** Presenting information, *developing an argument and drawing a conclusion,* using scientific, *technical and mathematical language,* conventions and symbols *and ICT tools*

There are also opportunities to cover HSW *1*, HSW *2*, HSW *6*, HSW *7*, HSW *8* and HSW *10*.

## Key terms

acceleration

### Feeling acceleration

**Starter 1**

Ask the class what they understand by the word 'acceleration' and write examples on the board. Elicit that on take-off in an airplane you feel as if you are being pushed back in your seat – explain that this is due to acceleration. Compare this with how you feel once in steady flight. Lead the discussion to agree that the greater the change in velocity and the shorter the time, the greater the acceleration.

### Using a spreadsheet to calculate acceleration

**Exploring 1**

Using the data on the **AT** spreadsheet *Velocity* data, students create a spreadsheet that will automatically calculate the acceleration for the different parts of the motion from the velocity and time data.

**Stretch** Ask students to look up some data on cars and use the 0–60 mph data to calculate accelerations, making use of the spreadsheet to convert mph to m/s.

**Support** Help them to input the equation for acceleration into their spreadsheet, and work through it with them.

### Student Book spread P2.9

**Explaining 1**

Work through the questions in the Student Book

**Stretch** Ask students to consider velocity and acceleration for someone swimming at a steady speed up and down a swimming pool.

**Support** Give several examples of different pairs of initial and final velocities, to give students practice in using the equation.

### Acceleration sentences

**Plenary 1** **Lit**

**Worksheet P2.9b** gives parts of sentences in three columns. Students have to trace a path through the columns to make true statements. Students then work in pairs to check each other's work and agree a set of sentences that are all true.

### Acceleration

**Homework 1**

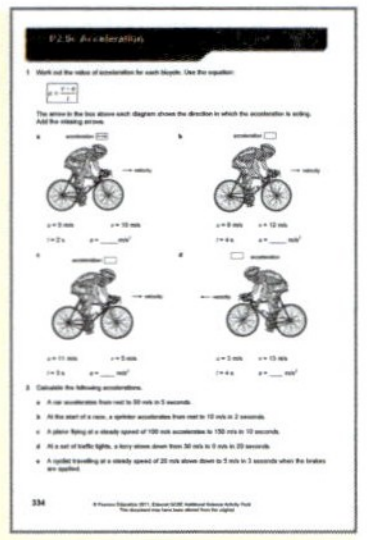

**Worksheet P2.9c**, for students needing support, provides practice in calculating acceleration using the equation.

**Support** Students colour in the initial velocity in one colour and the final velocity in another colour.

### Racing acceleration

**Starter 2**

Show students a video clip of a race (search for 'Olympic Sprint' on *YouTube* and the distance, e.g. 100 m, 200 m) and ask them to point out the parts that are showing changes in speed/ velocity. Tell students that this is acceleration. Explain that at the end of the race, where the athletes slow down, they are also accelerating, but in the opposite direction.

### Theme park

**Exploring 2**

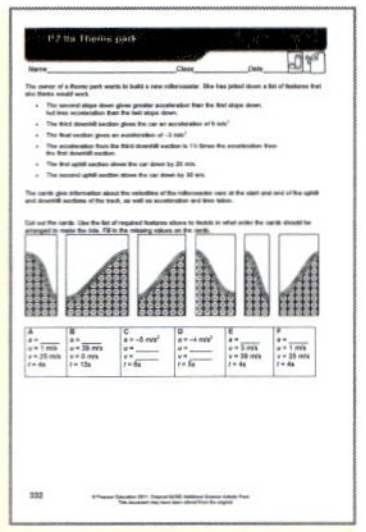

Students have to design their own rollercoaster using cut-out sections from **Worksheet P2.9a**.

**Stretch** Ask students to design the initial section of the rollercoaster, which would bring the cars to the top of the first hill.

**Support** Write the missing values u and v on cards B and D (B: *u* = 25 m/s, *v* = 5 m/s; D: *u* = 33 m/s, *v* = 3 m/s).

### Acceleration down a ramp

**Explaining 2** **Demo**

A demonstration of acceleration using a vehicle and a ramp. Full details are provided on the Teacher and technician practical sheet P2.9.

**Stretch** Ask students how you could demonstrate a negative acceleration.

**Support** Work with students to calculate acceleration from data for *u* and *v*.

### Acceleration calculations

**Plenary 2** **AfL**

Give students simple questions with initial and final velocities and times. The data can be added to a table on the board, with headings: Initial velocity *u* (m/s), Final velocity *v* (m/s), Time taken *t* (s) and Acceleration *a* (m/s²). Students work out the result and show their answers.

### Changing velocity

**Homework 2**

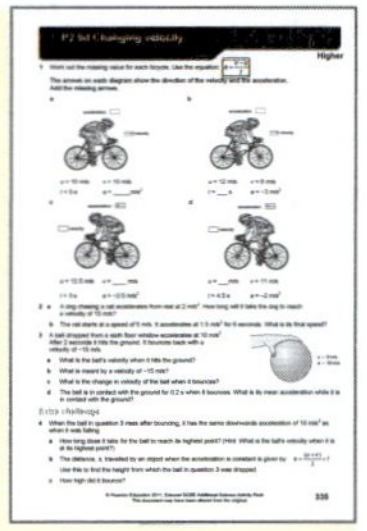

**Worksheet P2.9d**, for students working at a higher level, provides practice in working out accelerations and Higher Tier questions in which the equation is rearranged to find time and velocity.

**Stretch** Students complete the 'extra challenge' question on the sheet.

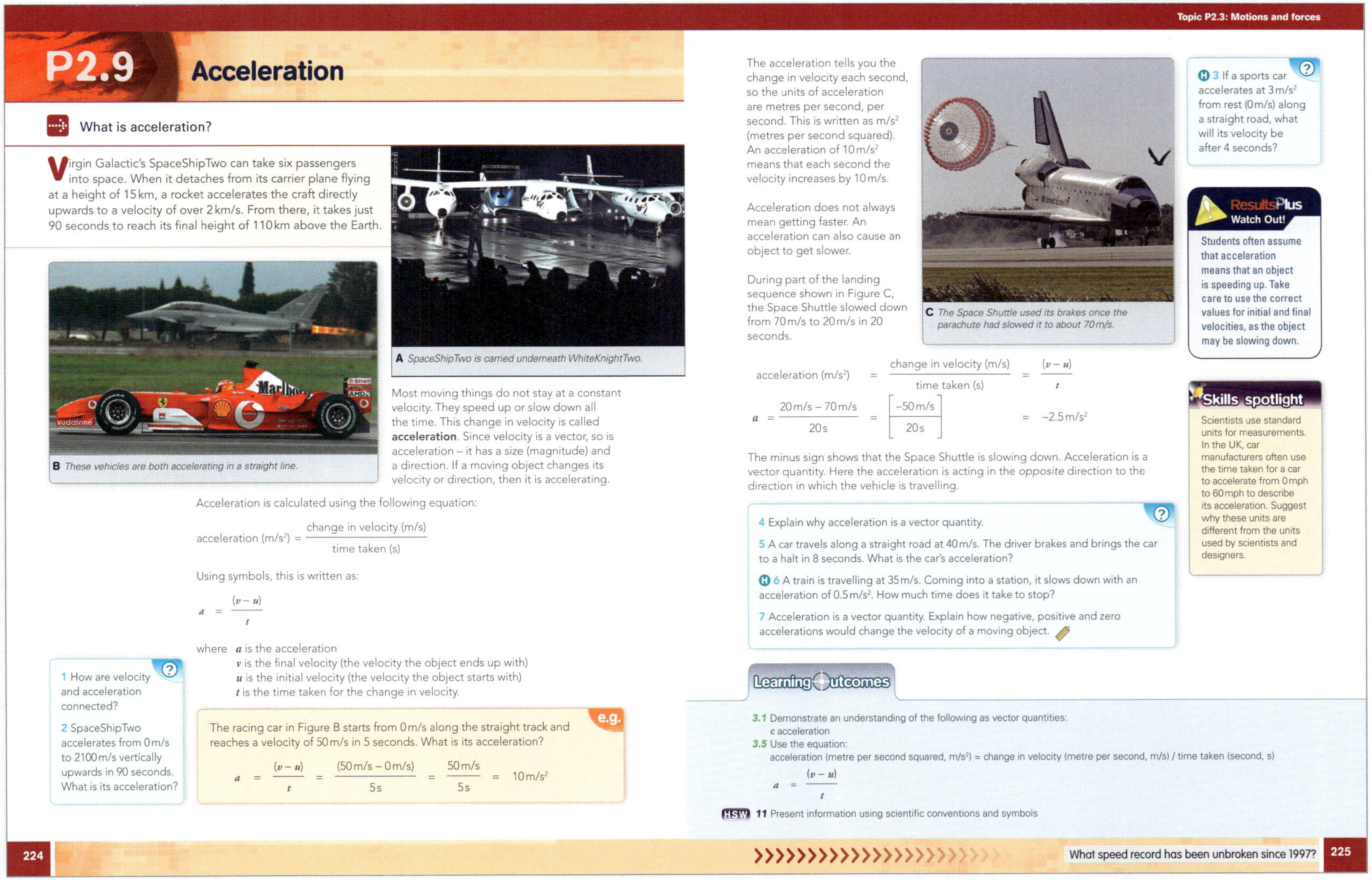


# P2.9 Acceleration

What is acceleration?

Virgin Galactic's SpaceShipTwo can take six passengers into space. When it detaches from its carrier plane flying at a height of 15 km, a rocket accelerates the craft directly upwards to a velocity of over 2 km/s. From there, it takes just 90 seconds to reach its final height of 110 km above the Earth.

A SpaceShipTwo is carried underneath WhiteKnightTwo.

B These vehicles are both accelerating in a straight line.

Most moving things do not stay at a constant velocity. They speed up or slow down all the time. This change in velocity is called **acceleration**. Since velocity is a vector, so is acceleration – it has a size (magnitude) and a direction. If a moving object changes its velocity or direction, then it is accelerating.

Acceleration is calculated using the following equation:

$$\text{acceleration (m/s}^2) = \frac{\text{change in velocity (m/s)}}{\text{time taken (s)}}$$

Using symbols, this is written as:

$$a = \frac{(v - u)}{t}$$

where $a$ is the acceleration
$v$ is the final velocity (the velocity the object ends up with)
$u$ is the initial velocity (the velocity the object starts with)
$t$ is the time taken for the change in velocity.

1 How are velocity and acceleration connected?

2 SpaceShipTwo accelerates from 0 m/s to 2100 m/s vertically upwards in 90 seconds. What is its acceleration?

e.g.
The racing car in Figure B starts from 0 m/s along the straight track and reaches a velocity of 50 m/s in 5 seconds. What is its acceleration?

$$a = \frac{(v - u)}{t} = \frac{(50\,\text{m/s} - 0\,\text{m/s})}{5\,\text{s}} = \frac{50\,\text{m/s}}{5\,\text{s}} = 10\,\text{m/s}^2$$

The acceleration tells you the change in velocity each second, so the units of acceleration are metres per second, per second. This is written as m/s² (metres per second squared). An acceleration of 10 m/s² means that each second the velocity increases by 10 m/s.

Acceleration does not always mean getting faster. An acceleration can also cause an object to get slower.

During part of the landing sequence shown in Figure C, the Space Shuttle slowed down from 70 m/s to 20 m/s in 20 seconds.

C The Space Shuttle used its brakes once the parachute had slowed it to about 70 m/s.

$$\text{acceleration (m/s}^2) = \frac{\text{change in velocity (m/s)}}{\text{time taken (s)}} = \frac{(v - u)}{t}$$

$$a = \frac{20\,\text{m/s} - 70\,\text{m/s}}{20\,\text{s}} = \frac{-50\,\text{m/s}}{20\,\text{s}} = -2.5\,\text{m/s}^2$$

The minus sign shows that the Space Shuttle is slowing down. Acceleration is a vector quantity. Here the acceleration is acting in the *opposite* direction to the direction in which the vehicle is travelling.

H 3 If a sports car accelerates at 3 m/s² from rest (0 m/s) along a straight road, what will its velocity be after 4 seconds?

**ResultsPlus Watch Out!**
Students often assume that acceleration means that an object is speeding up. Take care to use the correct values for initial and final velocities, as the object may be slowing down.

**Skills spotlight**
Scientists use standard units for measurements. In the UK, car manufacturers often use the time taken for a car to accelerate from 0 mph to 60 mph to describe its acceleration. Suggest why these units are different from the units used by scientists and designers.

4 Explain why acceleration is a vector quantity.

5 A car travels along a straight road at 40 m/s. The driver brakes and brings the car to a halt in 8 seconds. What is the car's acceleration?

H 6 A train is travelling at 35 m/s. Coming into a station, it slows down with an acceleration of 0.5 m/s². How much time does it take to stop?

7 Acceleration is a vector quantity. Explain how negative, positive and zero accelerations would change the velocity of a moving object.

**Learning Outcomes**

3.1 Demonstrate an understanding of the following as vector quantities:
c acceleration

3.5 Use the equation:
acceleration (metre per second squared, m/s²) = change in velocity (metre per second, m/s) / time taken (second, s)

$$a = \frac{(v - u)}{t}$$

HSW 11 Present information using scientific conventions and symbols

224

What speed record has been unbroken since 1997?

225

**ActiveTeach**

- **AT** *Speeding up and slowing down* [interactive]
  Velocity–time graph – scene investigation
- **AT** *Velocity data* [spreadsheet]
  Calculating accelaration

## Answers | Student Book

1 Acceleration is the change in velocity per second. It is calculated from the equation acceleration = change in velocity/time taken.
2 23.3 m/s²
3 H 12 m/s
4 Because velocity is a vector quantity/it has a direction as well as a size.
5 –5 m/s²
6 H 70 s
7 A good answer will include the following points:
- negative acceleration means the acceleration is acting in the opposite direction to the object's velocity (provided the initial velocity is taken to be positive) so the object's velocity in the original direction will decrease – it will slow down
- if a negative acceleration continues to act, then eventually the object will stop and then start to get faster in the opposite direction
- positive acceleration acts in the same direction as the object's velocity so the object's velocity will increase (it will get faster)
- an acceleration of zero will not change the object's velocity so it will continue at a constant speed.

**Skills spotlight**
In a car none of the instruments give the speed in m/s and people are unlikely to understand speed in m/s. Acceleration from 0 to 60 mph uses speed values people understand and gives an idea of how quickly a car can pull away from traffic lights, or accelerate when overtaking or merging on a motorway.

# P2.10 Velocity–time graphs



This lesson introduces acceleration as a vector quantity and uses the equation for acceleration.

## Specification coverage

**3.6** Interpret velocity–time graphs to: a) compare acceleration from gradients qualitatively b) calculate the acceleration from the gradient (for uniform acceleration only) H c) determine the distance travelled using the area between the graph line and the time axis (for uniform acceleration only)

HSW *10* Using both qualitative and quantitative approaches

There are also opportunities to cover HSW *1*, HSW *2*, HSW *6*, HSW *7*, HSW *8* and HSW *11*.

## Key terms

gradient
speed
velocity
velocity–time graph

### Sketching motion

**Starter 1**

On the board sketch two distance–time graphs, one with a horizontal line and one with the line sloping upwards. Label the axes of each, and ask the class what these show. Now change the label on the vertical axis to read 'Velocity'. Ask what the horizontal line now shows (moving in a particular direction at a steady speed). Ask what the sloping line now shows (a steadily increasing velocity – acceleration.)

### Shooting script

**Exploring 1**

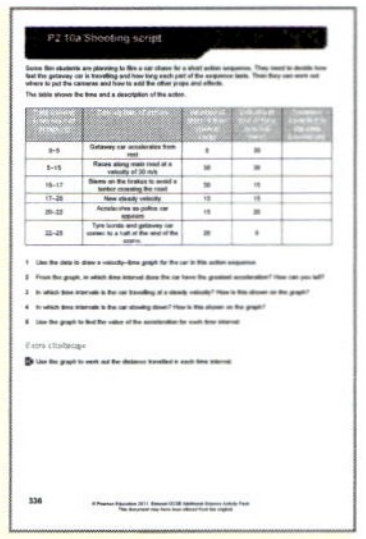

Using **Worksheet P2.10a**, students work out missing information about velocity and time, and use this to draw a velocity–time graph. From this they calculate accelerations and distances travelled.

**Stretch** Students think about how they would ameand the table and the velocity–time graph if the car reversed at some points.

**Support** Students only work on questions **1** to **5**.

### Student Book spread P2.10

**Explaining 1**

Work through the examples in the Student Book.

**Stretch** Students think about what happens if a negative acceleration acts so that the object reverses its direction.

**Support** In Figure C, read off the values of velocity at 0 s, 10 s and 20 s to help students understand that the velocity is increasing by the same amount for each time interval.

### Interpreting graphs (AT)

**Plenary 1** Lit

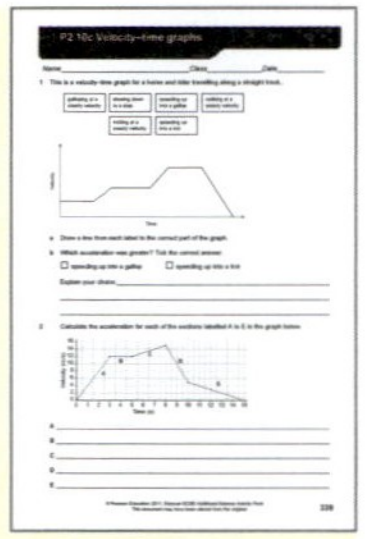

Use the set of graphs supplied on the **AT** presentation *Motion graphs*. Ask students to drag and drop the labels to the appropriate parts of the graphs. If you don't have access to the **AT**, then draw your own graphs on the board, based on those on **Worksheet P2.10c**.

### Velocity–time graphs

**Homework 1**

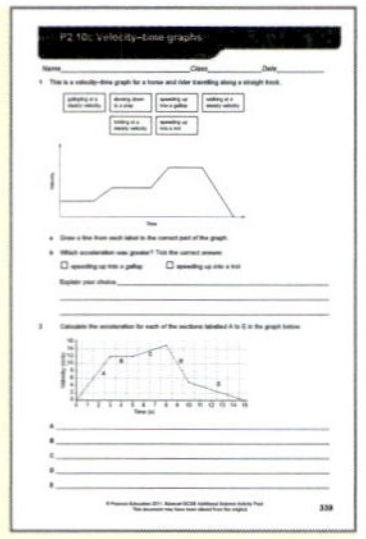

**Worksheet P2.10c**, for students needing support, asks them to interpret the slope of a velocity–time graph in a qualitative way and calculate some acceleration.

**Support** Work through the calculation of the gradient of part D in question 2.

### Long jump

**Starter 2** Lit

Show a clip from *YouTube* of an athlete making a long jump. Ask students to write brief notes to describe the athlete's motion, using the words 'acceleration' and 'velocity'. Using values from the clip, show how to plot the motion as a velocity–time graph. Use students' notes to annotate the graph.

### Bringing graphs to life

**Exploring 2** Prac

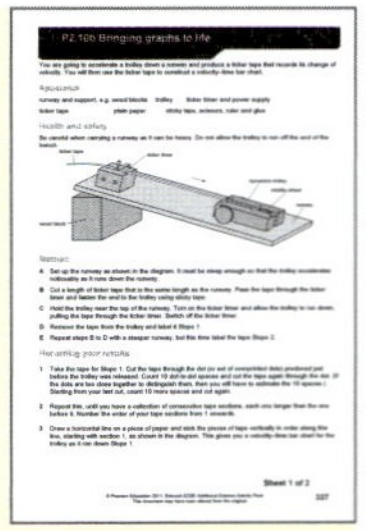

Students use ticker-tape and a trolley on a ramp to produce velocity–time bar charts as described on **Worksheet P2.10b**. Full details are provided on the Teacher and technician practical sheet P2.10.

**Support** Ask students to explain the different slopes of their two graphs.

**Stretch** Ask students to compare the calculated acceleration with the acceleration shown by the slope on the chart.

### Moving man (AT)

**Explaining 2**

Instructions are supplied on the **AT** document *Moving man*.

**Stretch** Pause the animation at suitable points and use the values to calculate the acceleration and the distance travelled.

**Support** Use very small values of acceleration so the motion is slower. Print the screen to get an image to help compare graphs with different values of acceleration.

### Describing motion

**Plenary 2** AfL

Students work in groups to work out different quantities that describe motion and the units they are measured in. Draw up a table with headings 'Quantity', 'Unit', 'How to work it out', and 'Is it a vector?'. Give one of the quantities 'speed', 'velocity', 'acceleration', 'displacement' and 'distance' to each group. Groups then complete the table on the board, explaining their answers.

### Velocities and accelerations on graphs

**Homework 2**

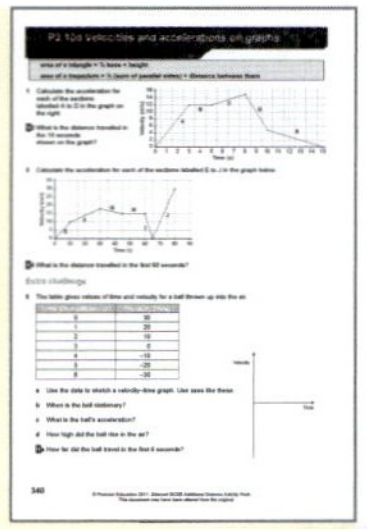

**Worksheet P2.10d** is for more able students. They calculate accelerations and distance travelled from two different velocity–time graphs.

**Stretch** Ask students to complete the 'extra challenge' question.

# P2.10 Velocity-time graphs

How can a graph show changes in an object's velocity?

On 15 October 1997 the *ThrustSSC*, driven by Royal Air Force pilot Andy Green, broke the land speed record. It recorded an average speed of 763.035 mph over a straight stretch of 1 mile in the Black Rock Desert – faster than the speed of sound. This is still the world record.

A

A velocity-time graph shows how the velocity of an object changes with time. Figure B shows velocity-time graphs for cars moving in different ways along a straight road.

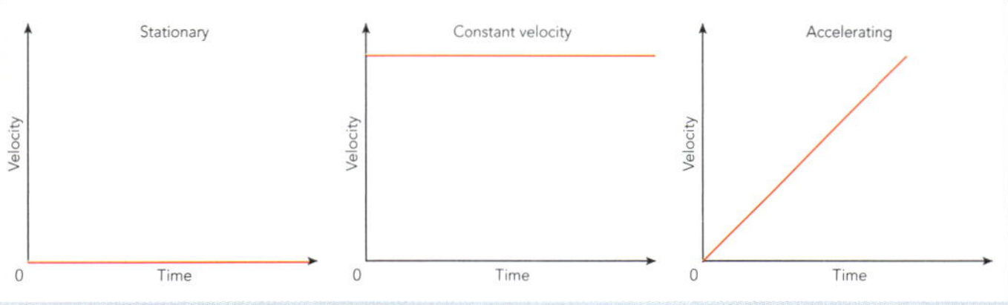


**B** *A sloping line on a velocity-time graph shows that the velocity is changing.*

1 What does a horizontal line on a velocity-time graph tell you about an object's velocity?

2 a In which part of Figure C is the train travelling at a constant velocity?
b In which part of the graph does the train have its greatest acceleration?
c Which part of the graph shows that the train is slowing down?

- A horizontal line means the object is travelling at constant velocity. The higher the line, the higher the velocity.
- A sloping line shows that the object is accelerating. The steeper the line, the greater the acceleration.

Figure C is a velocity-time graph for a train travelling along a straight track.

C

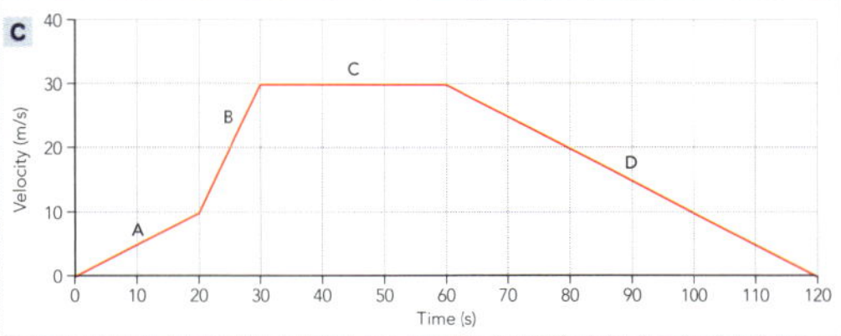


## Calculations using a velocity-time graph

The acceleration of an object can be calculated from a velocity-time graph. From the graph, find the change in velocity and the time taken for that change. Use these to calculate the acceleration.

For the graph in Figure D: acceleration $= \frac{8\,m/s}{4\,s} = 2\,m/s^2$

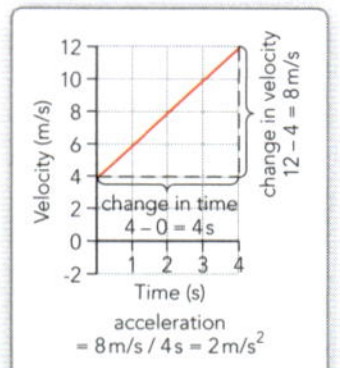


**D** *Calculating acceleration from a velocity-time graph.*

## Calculating distance

H

The area under a velocity-time graph tells us the distance the object has travelled. The distance travelled in the first 5 s is the area of a rectangle. The distance travelled in the next 5 s can be found by splitting the shape into a triangle and a rectangle, and finding their areas separately.

The total distance travelled by the object in Figure E is the sum of the areas.

total distance travelled = 50 m + 50 m + 75 m = 175 m

E

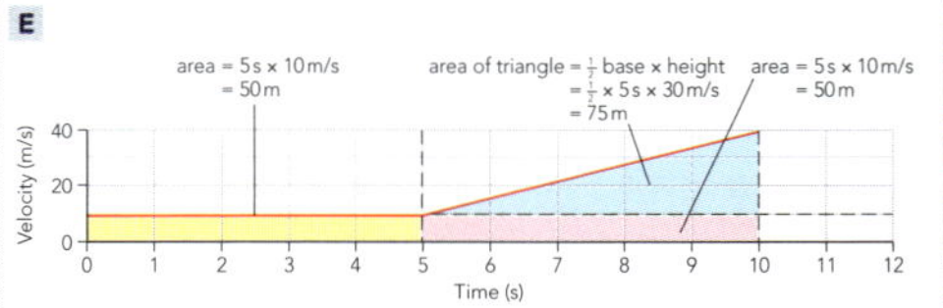


3 Use the graph in Figure C to calculate the acceleration of the train in each of parts A to D.

H 4 a Calculate the distance travelled in each part of the graph (A–D) in Figure C.
H b What is the total distance travelled by the train?

5 Table F gives some data for a run of the *ThrustSSC*. Draw a velocity-time graph from this. Label your graph with all the things you can tell from it.

F

| Time after start of run (s) | Speed (m/s) |
|---|---|
| 0 | 0 |
| 4 | 40 |
| 16 | 280 |
| 30 | 380 |
| 35 | 330 |
| 85 | 0 |

**ResultsPlus Watch Out!**

Students often confuse distance-time graphs and velocity-time graphs. Make sure you read the axes carefully and take note of the units.

**Skills spotlight**

Scientists work with data in different forms. What are the advantages and disadvantages of using numbers rather than graphs to compare accelerations?

**Learning Outcomes**

3.6 Interpret velocity/time graphs to:
a compare acceleration from gradients qualitatively
b calculate the acceleration from the gradient (for uniform acceleration only)
H c determine the distance travelled using the area between the graph line and the time axis (for uniform acceleration only)

HSW 10 Use qualitative and quantitative approaches when presenting scientific ideas and arguments, and recording observations



Why do astronauts spend a lot of time underwater?



## ActiveTeach

- **AT** *Motion graphs* [presentation] Drag and drop labels
- **AT** *Moving man* [word document] Activity instructions

## Answers | Student Book

1 Velocity is constant.

2 **a** C
**b** B
**c** D

3 A 0.5 m/s$^2$,
B 2 m/s$^2$,
C 0 m/s$^2$,
D −0.5 m/s$^2$

4 H **a** A 100 m, B 200 m, C 900 m, D 900 m
**b** 2100 m

5 A good answer will contain the following points:
- suitable graph with time on horizontal axis and speed on the vertical axis
- values of acceleration for the different parts (10 m/s$^2$, 20 m/s$^2$, 7.1 m/s$^2$, −10 m/s$^2$, −6.6 m/s$^2$)
- possible extra information could be: label to show where the greatest acceleration was (from 4 to 16 s); label to show where the thrust started to slow down (peak of graph).

**Skills spotlight**

Advantages: very easy to compare sizes and sign of acceleration in number form; numbers are quicker to use for calculations; would have to find the gradient to put a value on an acceleration from a graph.
Disadvantages: not as visual, so not as easy to compare changes in acceleration over time as on a graph.

# P2.11 Forces



This lesson teaches students how to draw and interpret free-body diagrams showing the forces acting on a single body. It also introduces the idea of action-reaction pairs of forces, where the forces act on different bodies.

## Specification coverage

***3.7*** Draw and interpret a free-body force diagram

***3.8*** Demonstrate an understanding that when two bodies interact, the forces they exert on each other are equal in size and opposite in direction and that these are known as action and reaction forces

HSW ***11*** Presenting information, *developing an argument and drawing a conclusion,* using scientific, *technical and mathematical language,* conventions *and symbols and ICT tools*

There are also opportunities to cover HSW ***2***, and HSW ***10***.

## Key terms

action force
force
free-body diagram
interact
reaction force

### Types of forces

**Starter 1**

Using a ball and beaker of water to demonstrate, discuss the forces acting on the ball and sketch how they can be shown. Ask students if they can think of any other forces that could be demonstrated (e.g. friction, squashing (compression), pulling (tension)).

### Forces at play

**Exploring 1**

**Worksheet P2.11b** shows a clown simultaneously doing a variety of actions where forces are involved. There is also a set of force labels to cut up.

**Stretch** Ask students to identify the forces on the clown without looking at the labels provided on the worksheet.

**Support** Suggest they colour all the labels that have forces on the clown.

### Student Book spread P2.11

**Explaining 1**

Work through the questions in the Student Book.

**Stretch** Ask students how an astronaut floating away from their spaceship in space could propel themselves back to safety using their hammer (throw the hammer in the opposite direction).

**Support** Ask them to explain why there are no action-reaction pairs on a free-body diagram.

### Draw me

**Plenary 1** *AfL*

Describe an object with forces on it, such as an aeroplane flying in the sky. Students sketch a free-body diagram and show the result. Include one, such as a stone in the air, where there is no propelling force, just weight, air resistance and buoyancy (or upthrust).

### Forces and diagrams

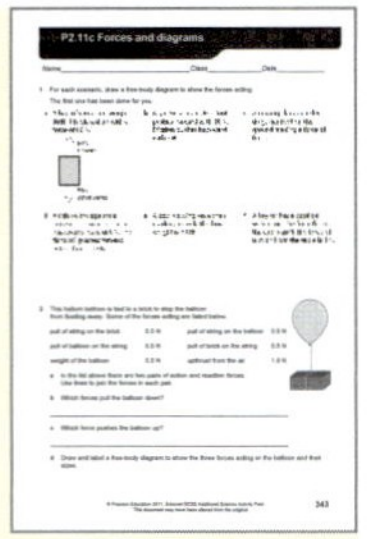

**Homework 1**

**Worksheet P2.11c** is for students needing support. Students draw some free-body diagrams and answer questions about the forces acting on an object.

**Support** Tell students which diagrams show action-reaction pairs.

### Everyday forces

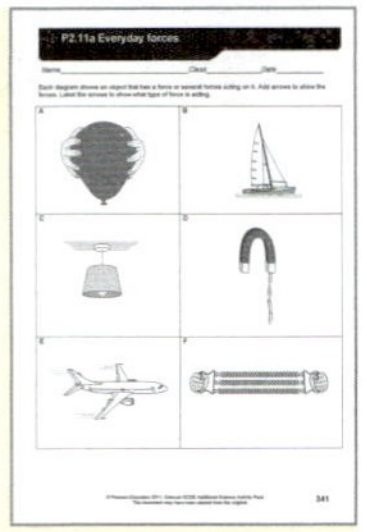

**Starter 2**

*AfL*

A set of objects subjected to different forces is shown on **Worksheet P2.11a**. Discuss what the forces are on the object and how they could be shown by arrows. Students work through the sheet and check their answers, and then draw their own diagram and an answer diagram.

### Action-reaction miming

**Exploring 2**

In groups students develop a mime involving an action–reaction pair. When the students act out the mime, they hold up the signs – 'action' or 'reaction' - in appropriate places. Ask the class what was being mimed, what the action–reaction pair shown was and whether this really is an action–reaction pair.

**Stretch** Ask them to name the type of force in their action–reaction pair, for example friction force, gravitational force.

**Support** Provide some examples of force pairs.

### Moving man (AT)

**Explaining 2** Demo

Full details are provided on the Teacher and technician practical sheet P2.11.

**Stretch** Discuss whether the newtonmeters could register different values – would this be an impossible situation?

**Support** Model part of the chain using students in place of the string, with instructions to keep the reading the same. They will feel that they are pulling with equal force with both hands, as registered by the newtonmeters.

### Rapid free-body diagrams

**Plenary 2**

Use the sheet of forces and diagrams provided for *Starter 2* (**Worksheet P2.11a**). Ask students to draw each of these as a free-body diagram.

### Moving in space

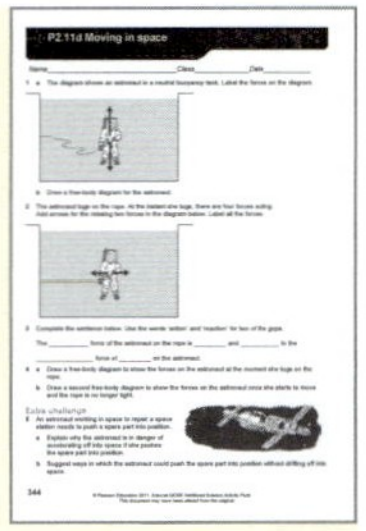

**Homework 2**

**Worksheet P2.11d**, for students working at a higher level, asks students to analyse forces on an astronaut in a neutral buoyancy pool, as well as to consider action–reaction forces in space.

**Stretch** Ask students to complete the 'extra challenge' question.

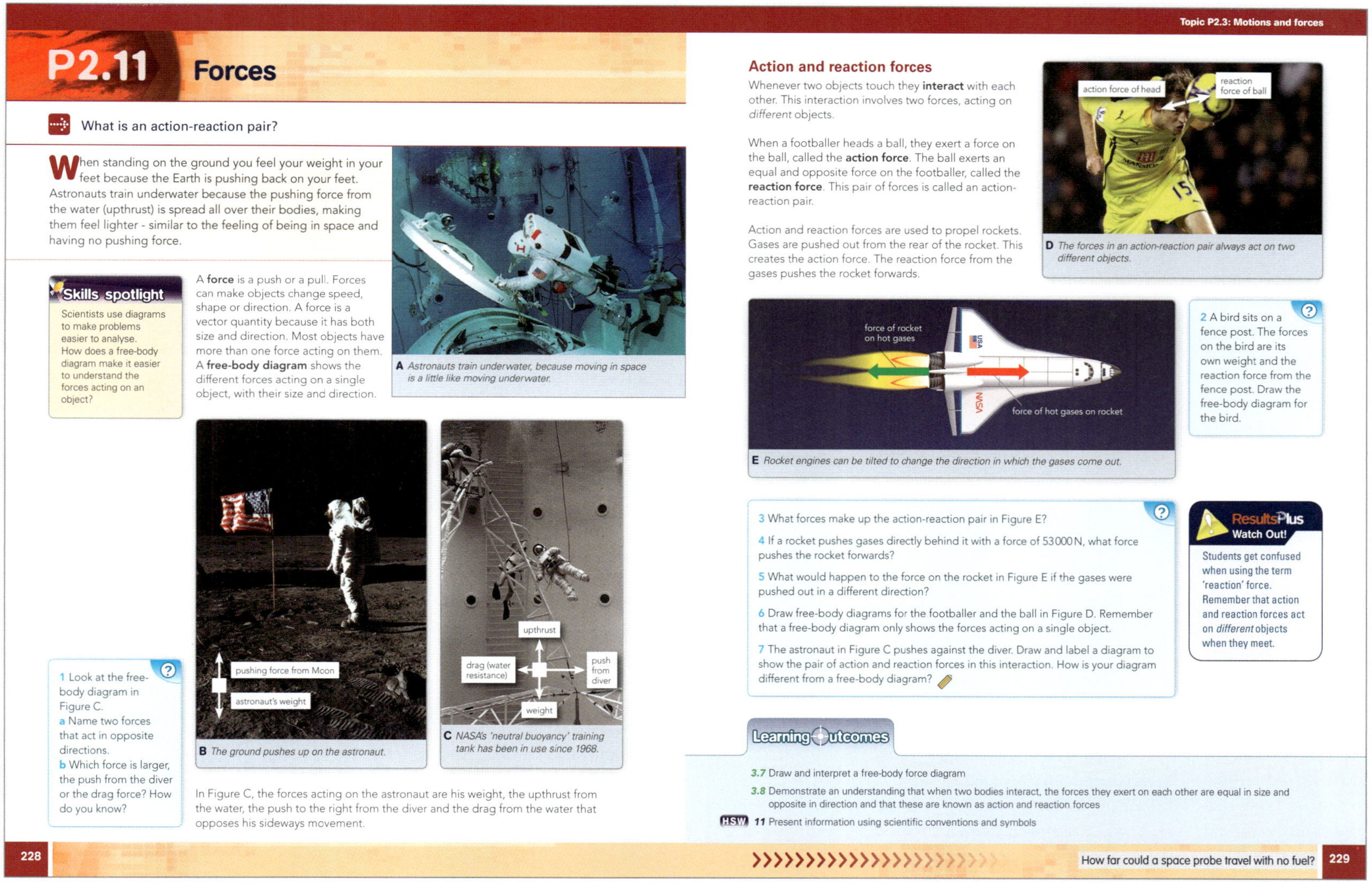


# P2.11 Forces

What is an action-reaction pair?

When standing on the ground you feel your weight in your feet because the Earth is pushing back on your feet. Astronauts train underwater because the pushing force from the water (upthrust) is spread all over their bodies, making them feel lighter - similar to the feeling of being in space and having no pushing force.

**Skills spotlight**

Scientists use diagrams to make problems easier to analyse. How does a free-body diagram make it easier to understand the forces acting on an object?

A **force** is a push or a pull. Forces can make objects change speed, shape or direction. A force is a vector quantity because it has both size and direction. Most objects have more than one force acting on them. A **free-body diagram** shows the different forces acting on a single object, with their size and direction.

A *Astronauts train underwater, because moving in space is a little like moving underwater.*



B *The ground pushes up on the astronaut.*



C *NASA's 'neutral buoyancy' training tank has been in use since 1968.*

1 Look at the free-body diagram in Figure C.
a Name two forces that act in opposite directions.
b Which force is larger, the push from the diver or the drag force? How do you know?

In Figure C, the forces acting on the astronaut are his weight, the upthrust from the water, the push to the right from the diver and the drag from the water that opposes his sideways movement.

## Action and reaction forces

Whenever two objects touch they **interact** with each other. This interaction involves two forces, acting on *different* objects.

When a footballer heads a ball, they exert a force on the ball, called the **action force**. The ball exerts an equal and opposite force on the footballer, called the **reaction force**. This pair of forces is called an action-reaction pair.

Action and reaction forces are used to propel rockets. Gases are pushed out from the rear of the rocket. This creates the action force. The reaction force from the gases pushes the rocket forwards.



D *The forces in an action-reaction pair always act on two different objects.*



E *Rocket engines can be tilted to change the direction in which the gases come out.*

2 A bird sits on a fence post. The forces on the bird are its own weight and the reaction force from the fence post. Draw the free-body diagram for the bird.

3 What forces make up the action-reaction pair in Figure E?
4 If a rocket pushes gases directly behind it with a force of 53 000 N, what force pushes the rocket forwards?
5 What would happen to the force on the rocket in Figure E if the gases were pushed out in a different direction?
6 Draw free-body diagrams for the footballer and the ball in Figure D. Remember that a free-body diagram only shows the forces acting on a single object.
7 The astronaut in Figure C pushes against the diver. Draw and label a diagram to show the pair of action and reaction forces in this interaction. How is your diagram different from a free-body diagram?

**ResultsPlus Watch Out!**

Students get confused when using the term 'reaction' force. Remember that action and reaction forces act on *different* objects when they meet.

**Learning Outcomes**

3.7 Draw and interpret a free-body force diagram
3.8 Demonstrate an understanding that when two bodies interact, the forces they exert on each other are equal in size and opposite in direction and that these are known as action and reaction forces
HSW 11 Present information using scientific conventions and symbols




## ActiveTeach

- **AT** *Balanced and unbalanced forces* [interactive] Labelling forces – matching activity

## Answers | Student Book

1 **a** Upthrust and weight; or drag and push from diver
**b** Push from diver, because the arrow is larger

2 Simple free-body diagram showing downward force arrow from bird labelled 'weight' and upward force arrow for reaction labelled 'reaction from fence post'. The fence post should not be shown.

3 Force of rocket on hot gases and force of hot gases on rocket

4 53 000 N

5 The force on the rocket would be in a different direction too, so it would change its direction of motion.

6 Suitable free-body diagrams – each should only show one object and the forces acting on it.

7 A good answer will contain the following points:
- clear diagram showing push of astronaut on diver and push of diver on astronaut
- the two forces should be shown as arrows in opposite directions
- the two arrows should be equal in size
- diagram shows forces on two objects, whereas free-body diagrams just show forces on a single object

**Skills spotlight**

A free-body diagram shows just the forces acting on a single object, so they are not confused with the forces acting on other objects.

# P2.12 Resultant forces

In this lesson students learn how to calculate the resultant of a number of forces acting on an object and describe the effect of both zero and non-zero resultant forces on the motion of an object.

## Specification coverage

***3.9*** Calculate a resultant force using a range of forces (limited to the resultant of forces acting along a line) including resistive forces

***3.10*** Demonstrate an understanding that if the resultant force acting on a body is zero, it will remain at rest or continue to move at the same velocity

***3.11*** Demonstrate an understanding that if the resultant force acting on a body is not zero, it will accelerate in the direction of the resultant force

**HSW** ***10*** Use both qualitative and quantitative approaches

There are also opportunities to cover **HSW** ***1***, **HSW** ***2***, **HSW** ***3*** and **HSW** ***14***.

## Key terms

air resistance
drag
resultant

### Balloon forces

**Starter 1**

Use a balloon to demonstrate different forces. At each stage ask students about the forces involved, where they come from and what will happen as a result of these forces when you release the balloon.

### Why do things move?

**Exploring 1** **Lit**

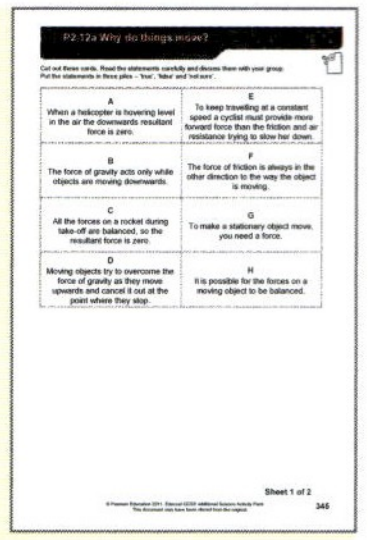

Students cut out the statements from **Worksheet P2.12a** and separate them into piles: true, false, not sure. They then take the 'extra information' cards and see if they want to move any of the 'statement' cards to a different pile.

**Stretch** Ask students to develop some more cards of their own for others to work from.

**Support** Remove some of the statement cards.

### Student Book spread P2.12

**Explaining 1**

Work through the text and questions in the Student Book.

**Stretch** Ask students to draw free-body diagrams with forces of 10 N, 6 N, 5 N, 4 N, 3 N and 2 N, which can act in vertical and horizontal directions only.

**Support** Remind students that a change in velocity means there is an acceleration, so no change in velocity is no acceleration, and hence no force.

### Rules of forces and motion

**Plenary 1** **AfL**

Students write a list of rules that connect the forces on an object and what it might do. Provide the stems and key words. For example:

If the forces on an object are ***balanced*** and the object is ***moving*** then …

If the forces on an object are ***unbalanced*** and the object is ***stationary*** then …

### Forces and motion

**Homework 1**

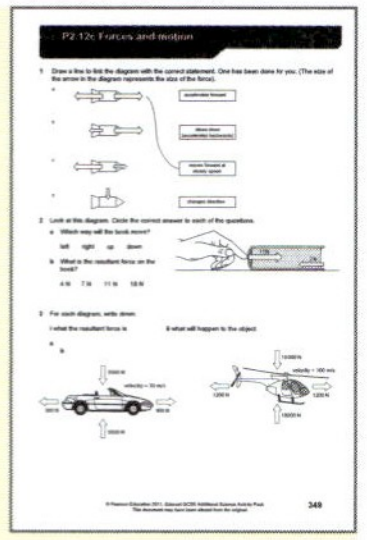

**Worksheet P2.12c**, for students needing support, asks students to interpret simple force diagrams to say what will happen to the object shown, and also provides practice in calculating resultant forces.

**Support** Students only attempt questions 1 and 2.

### Sliding on ice

**Starter 2**

Ask students to imagine that there was no friction. Would objects then be able to carry on moving forever? The aim is to introduce the idea that a force is needed to change velocity, but if there is no resultant force, then there is no change in velocity, i.e. no change in an object's speed or direction of motion.

### Theories of motion

**Exploring 2**

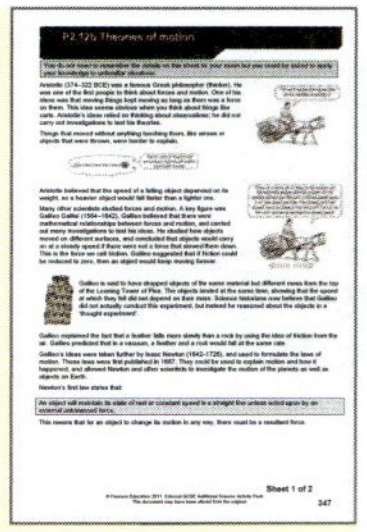

Students use **Worksheet P2.12b** to look at the development of ideas of motion.

**Stretch** Ask students to explain how the equation F = ma comes from the formal definition of Newton's second law given on the worksheet.

**Support** Ask students to work in pairs.

### Tug of war

**Explaining 2** **Demo**

Tell students that they are to work together to balance forces. Full details are provided on the Teacher and technician practical sheet P2.12.

**Stretch** Give students three forces for one side and one for the other. Students work out possible values and try them out.

**Support** Have two students on each side rather than three, so there is less mathematics.

### What will happen?

**Plenary 2**

Draw free-body diagrams labelled with forces acting in opposite directions. Ask students to say what the resultant force is and what will happen to the object.

### Resultant forces

**Homework 2**

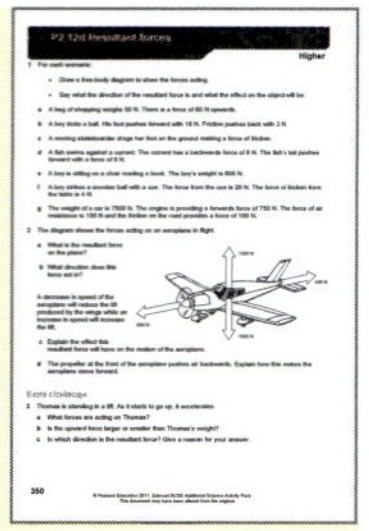

Using **Worksheet P2.12d**, students draw free-body diagrams and work out resultant force and motion for different situations described in words.

**Stretch** Ask students to complete the 'extra challenge' question.

# P2.12 Resultant forces

What is a resultant force?

This is a hypersonic aeroplane that could travel at up to 4000 mph. The plane would carry 300 passengers and fly very high in the Earth's atmosphere (25 km) where the air is very thin.

A *A flight to Australia would take about five hours on this plane. However, there are no windows!*

Aeroplane designers think a lot about forces. Figure B shows some forces on the aeroplane. The force of gravity (the plane's weight) pulls it towards Earth. A force called 'lift' is produced by the wings and pushes the plane up. Forces that are equal but act in opposite directions are 'balanced'. In Figure B, lift and weight are balanced.

1 In Figure B, how can you tell that drag and thrust are unbalanced?

2 Draw a free-body diagram for the aeroplane in Figure B.

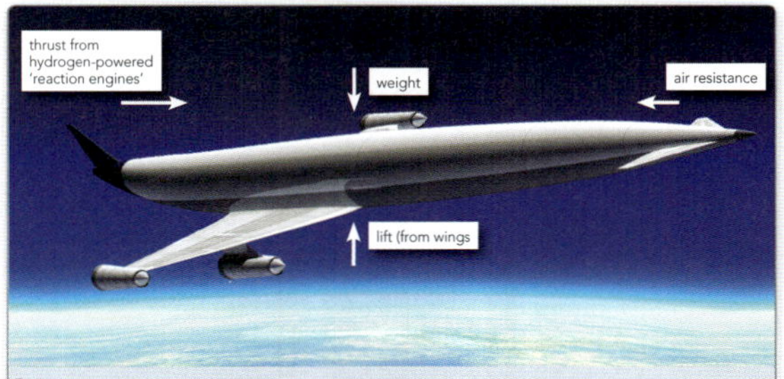


B *The hypersonic aeroplane is designed to fly very high, where there is less air resistance.*

'Thrust' is a force produced by the engines to push the aeroplane forwards. As it flies, air molecules push against it producing an opposite force called **air resistance** (a type of **drag**). In Figure B, the thrust is greater than the air resistance. The forces are unbalanced.

## Resultant force

When more than one force acts on an object, the effect is the same as if they were combined into a single force – the **resultant** force. If the forces act in the same direction, we add them together. If they act in opposite directions we subtract them.

e.g.

For Figure B:
total thrust force to right = 100 000 N
total drag force to left = 25 000 N

resultant force = 100 000 – 25 000 = 75 000 N of force to the right.

3 A boat has 1000 N of thrust. It is slowed by air resistance (300 N) and friction between the boat and the water (700 N). What is the resultant force?

## Resultant force and acceleration

If the resultant force on an object is zero then the movement of the object does not *change*. If it is stationary, it will remain stationary. If it is moving, it will carry on moving at a constant velocity (in a straight line).

If the resultant force on an object is not zero, the object will accelerate in the direction of the resultant force.

C *Voyager 1 doesn't need engines to keep it moving and has travelled over 10 billion miles so far. There is no air in space to slow it down.*

D *With no thrust from the engines, Virgin Galactic's SpaceShipTwo has a negative acceleration (slows down) as it comes in to land.*

7 Look at Figure D. Explain, using the idea of resultant forces, why SpaceShip Two is losing forward speed and height.

**ResultsPlus Watch Out!**

In exams, you will only be asked to work out the resultant of forces acting along a straight line.

4 Jane, Sameer and Kent are pushing a car. Jane pushes with 50 N, Sameer with 45 N and Kent with 60 N. Friction between the tyres and the road is 50 N and air resistance is 2 N. What is the resultant force?

5 Look at Figure B.
a Why will the aeroplane remain at a constant height?
b Why is the aeroplane accelerating?

6 Why does Voyager 1 not need engines on its journey through space?

**Skills spotlight**

Scientists look at things both quantitatively (using numbers) and qualitatively (not using numbers). Identify an example of each approach on this page.

**Learning Outcomes**

*3.9* Calculate a resultant force using a range of forces (limited to the resultant of forces acting along a line) including resistive forces

*3.10* Demonstrate an understanding that if the resultant force acting on a body is zero, it will remain at rest or continue to move at the same velocity

*3.11* Demonstrate an understanding that if the resultant force acting on a body is not zero, it will accelerate in the direction of the resultant force

HSW *10* Use qualitative and quantitative approaches when presenting scientific ideas and arguments, and recording observations

230 Why does an ice hockey puck go faster than a curling stone? 231

## ActiveTeach

- **AT** *Resultant forces* [spreadsheet] Calculating resultant forces

## Answers | Student Book

1 The arrow for thrust is bigger than the arrow for air resistance (drag).

2 Simple free-body diagram with labelled forces lift (upwards), weight (downwards), thrust (to the right) and drag or air resistance (to the left). Sizes of arrows same relative size as in Student Book.

3 0 N

4 103 N

5 **a** Because the lift is equal to the weight.
**b** Because the thrust is greater than the air resistance.

6 There is no air resistance in space.

7 A good answer will contain the following points:
- no thrust means that there is no forward force
- there is still drag because the craft is moving
- there is a resultant force in the opposite direction to the craft's motion
- this gives a negative acceleration that slows the craft down in the forward direction
- the lift must be less than the weight
- the resultant force is therefore downwards
- this gives an acceleration downwards, which means the craft loses height.

**Skills spotlight**

Qualitative: The diagram in Figure B uses arrows with different sizes to compare forces.
Quantitative: Worked example uses numerical values to show the resultant force.

# P2.13 Investigating force, mass and acceleration

This lesson challenges students to investigate the relationship between force, mass and acceleration. The activity may be run as a practice controlled assessment task or as a straight-forward class practical. The practical work should take about an hour.

## Specification coverage

***3.15*** Investigate the relationship between force, mass and acceleration

This activity provides opportunities to cover HSW *1*, HSW *5*, HSW *6*, HSW *7*, HSW *8* and HSW *10*.

### Before the lesson

In the week or two before the task show students the equipment and, if appropriate, allow them to practice using it. Suitable equipment for the investigation includes dynamics trolleys, ramps, and light gates used as velocity sensors. For this investigation Skills Sheet 18 may be particularly useful because it helps students to interpret line graphs. In addition, show students one or more of Skills Sheets 19 to 26 to show what is expected of them in their controlled assessment task.

### Starter

**Sporting speeds**

Ask students to look at the introductory paragraph in the book and suggest why a cricket ball moves much faster than a bowling ball. A cricket ball has a mass of around 160 g, and bowling balls can have masses up to 7.2 kg. Ask students to comment on these relative speeds and suggest reasons for the differences. Elicit that the way the items are hit or thrown will affect the force used to accelerate them, as well as discussing the obvious differences in mass. Follow this by reading the additional information below the opening section of page 232 of the Student Book. They may then read the brief description of the activity provided by the 'Your task' box.

### Option 1: Straight-forward class practical

Students follow the instructions on **Worksheet P2.13b**. This explains how to set up a friction-compensated ramp and how to use light gates to measure speeds. Students are left to make their own decisions about the masses to investigate and the number of repeat measurements needed. The range of data that students could collect is given on **Worksheet P2.13c** which students will also need.

As students' initial hypothesis is likely to have predicted the effect of changing of mass on acceleration, they could be asked to suggest a further hypothesis involving changing force and the effect on acceleration.

### Plenary

On page 233 of the Student Book you will find two examples of the sort of work that students may produce for this task. The examples focus on choosing equipment. You could share these with students after they have completed their own work. This will help them to understand the assessment criteria and so make it easier for them to evaluate their work and to see how they can improve it. Moderator comments on each of the Student Book extracts can be found at the end of the assessment guidance for this investigation on the CD-ROM. The examples can also be found on the **AT** document *Student examples*.

### Option 2: Running the activity as a practice controlled assessment task (PCAT)

We have provided a full range of support resources to allow the running of this practical as a practice controlled assessment task. A recommended structure is outlined below (to be used over a number of sessions). Marking guidance for all three parts of the practice task can be found on the CD-ROM that accompanies the TTPP. To save time when using these practice controlled assessment tasks, you may wish to focus on a particular aspect or skill rather than working through all three parts of the task.

#### Part A Planning

1. Students should be given the Student Brief on **Worksheet P2.13a**. They can use Part A of the Workbook that is provided to help with their practice controlled assessments. They should be given about 1 hour to do this planning.
2. Show students how a light gate and data logger can be used to measure speed by measuring the time a card of known length attached to a trolley takes to go through the gate.
3. Also discuss the idea of a friction-compensated ramp.
4. Students could choose to plan an investigation into the effect of force on acceleration. See the TTPP for points to note.

#### Part B Observations

5. Students should be asked to carry out the practical task to collect evidence using the method they have planned in Part A. Once again, they should refer to the Student Brief on **Worksheet P2.13a**. They can use Part B of the Workbook that is provided to help pupils with their practice controlled assessments. They should be given about 1 hour to collect their primary evidence.
6. If there is a problem with their own planned method, students may be asked to follow the method set out on **Worksheet P2.13b**. This will still enable students to access the full range of marks for Part B and Part C of the practice controlled assessment task.
7. In Part B, students are required to gather some secondary evidence. The evidence can be quantitative or qualitative. It can be from a variety of sources but students must note where they found their evidence and evaluate the quality of the source as part of this task. Skills Sheet 22 provides students with further guidance on researching for and evaluating secondary evidence. This part of the task could be done outside of the lesson but must be supervised.

#### Part C Conclusions

8. Students follow the instructions set out on the Part C section of the Student Brief on **Worksheet P2.13a**. They should use their data from Part B and the secondary evidence they have collected when doing this. They can use Part C of the Workbook that is provided to help pupils with their practice controlled assessments. They should be given about 1 hour to work on their conclusions.

The **AT** includes an interactive simulation that students can work through to help with elements of this investigation.

Practice Controlled Assessment

# P2.13 Investigating force, mass and acceleration

What is the relationship between force, mass and acceleration?

If you go ten pin bowling, you may be able to throw the ball with a speed of around 8 m/s. A top cricketer can throw a cricket ball with a speed of up to 45 m/s. Why are the two top speeds so different?

The way you throw a ball depends on its size and mass. The top speed of a ball depends on the acceleration you give it while it is in contact with your hand.

Once a cricket ball leaves your hand the only forces on it are air resistance, gravity and friction. Gravity pulls the cricket ball downwards as it flies through the air, so it accelerates the ball downwards. Gravity does not affect its forward speed.

Gravity does not affect the path of a bowling ball because it runs along the lane. If the bowling alley were long enough, the ball would eventually come to a stop because of friction and air resistance. The effects of friction could be compensated for by having the bowling alley on a slight slope. If the angle of the slope is just right, gravity pulling the ball down the slope will just cancel out the forces of friction trying to make the ball slow down.

**A** *A bowling ball moves at speeds of up to 8 m/s.*

You can use trolleys and ramps to investigate force, mass and acceleration. The angle of the ramp can be adjusted to cancel out the effects of friction.

**Your task**

You are going to plan an investigation that will allow you to find out how the mass of an object affects its acceleration. Your teacher will provide you with some materials to help you organise this task.

**Learning Outcomes**

**3.15** *Investigate the relationship between force, mass and acceleration*

## ResultsPlus Build Better Answers

When planning an investigation like this, one of the skills you will be assessed on is your ability to *choose suitable equipment*. There are 2 marks available for this skill. Here are two extracts focusing on this skill. Other skills are dealt with in other lessons.

**Student extract 1** **A basic response for this skill**

I will use a trolley running down a ramp. I need the weights to pull on the trolley.

The student describes one piece of apparatus but explains why they need something else.

This is describing some apparatus that the student will use. However, it would be better to also explain why the trolly will be needed.

**Student extract 2** **A good response for this skill**

I will use a trolley on a ramp, as the wheels will help to reduce the effects of friction. I will pull the trolley using masses on a string going over the pulley, as this will allow me to apply a constant force to the trolley. I will use light gates to measure the speed at two points and the time taken to go between the two points, as I can use this information to calculate the acceleration. Light gates and a computer will provide better quality data than I could obtain using a stopclock.

Explain why each piece of equipment is needed as you list it.

This is a good response as the student has described each piece of equipment needed *and* explained why it is needed.

**ResultsPlus**

**To access 2 marks**

- Choose the most relevant equipment and resources
- Explain the reasons for your choices and why they are relevant to your method

232 233 What makes a winning race bike?

## ActiveTeach

- **AT** *P2.13 F = ma* [interactive]
  Force, mass and acceleration
- **AT** *P2.13 Assessment criteria* [presentation]
  Understanding the CA marking criteria
- **AT** *P2.13 Specification points* [word document]
  Edexcel specification points
- **AT** *P2.13 Student examples* [word document]
  Examples for students to assess

## Assessment criteria

### Choosing equipment

**0** No relevant detail given.

**1-2 a)** Specifies most or all of required equipment, e.g. trolley, ramp, string and pulley, light gates and data logger (or stopclock and ruler), masses.

**b)** Explains why the equipment/materials above have been chosen, e.g. the trolley is the object to be accelerated and the wheels will help to reduce friction, the ramp is needed for the trolley to run along so that the acceleration can be calculated, the string and pulley give a constant force on the trolley to allow us to compare the effect of changing the mass, the light gates (or stopclock) will be used to measure the speed so that acceleration can be calculated, the masses can be used to change the mass of the trolley to allow us to compare the acceleration of the trolley with different masses.

# P2.14 Forces and acceleration



This lesson follows on from the previous one, showing that the acceleration produced by a resultant force depends on the size of the force and the mass of the object (F = ma). The equation is used to calculate forces.

## Specification coverage

***3.12*** Demonstrate an understanding that a resultant force acting on an object produces an acceleration which depends on a) the size of the resultant force b) the mass of the object

***3.13*** Use the equation: force (newton, N) = mass (kilogram, kg) × acceleration (metre per second squared m/s2), $F = m \times a$

HSW ***11*** Presenting information, *developing an argument and drawing a conclusion,* using scientific, *technical and mathematical language,* conventions and symbols *and ICT tools*

There are also opportunities to cover HSW *1*, HSW *6*, HSW *7*, HSW *8* and HSW *10*.

### Just a minute

**Starter 1** AfL Lit

Whisper a word or term relating to the work they have done on motion to a student, who then has to talk about it for 15 seconds without saying the word. Other students guess the word. Include words/terms such as velocity, acceleration, vector, speed, displacement, free-body diagram, resultant, force.

### Investigating force, mass and acceleration (AT)

**Exploring 1**

The **AT** spreadsheet *Investigating force, mass and acceleration 1* illustrates an investigation similar to the one described in P2.13.

**Stretch** Students use **AT** spreadsheet *Investigating force, mass and acceleration 2*, which is a more open-ended task.

**Support** Students look at the effect of changing the mass only.

### Student Book spread P2.12

**Explaining 1**

Use the text and questions in the Student Book to explain how force, mass and acceleration are related, and to introduce and use the equation $F = ma$.

**Stretch** Discuss how the equation can be rearranged to give acceleration as force/mass.

**Support** Give several examples of forces acting on objects of the same mass to give different accelerations, asking which force is larger, without actually calculating the force.

### Skateboard motion

**Plenary 1**

A demonstration with two skateboards, some rope and some volunteers. Volunteers stand on the skateboards several metres apart and one student pulls continuously on the rope, trying to keep it taut as they pull it towards them. This provides the 'constant' force acting on both volunteers, as an action-reaction pair. Ask what students think will happen in each case before the rope is pulled.

### Force, mass and acceleration

**Homework 1**

**Worksheet P2.14b**, for students needing support, gives students practice in calculating the force from mass and acceleration data. They complete statements relating acceleration to the size of the force and to the mass.

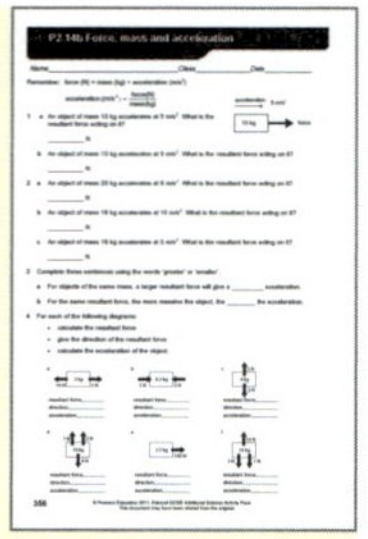

**Support** Work through the first question with students.

### Kicking objects

**Starter 2**

After a short discussion about the 'standard teacher kick' being approximately the same force, kick a number of different sized objects along the floor (e.g. football, tennis ball, medicine ball etc). It is important to include an object with a very large mass to help reinforce the key ideas here. The aim is to get across a sense of how fast the balls are moving away.

### Accelerating vehicles

**Exploring 2**

**Worksheet P2.14a** provides cards giving mass, engine force and acceleration data for different vehicles. Students match up cards to give vehicles with the required specification. To do this they must calculate force from $F = ma$.

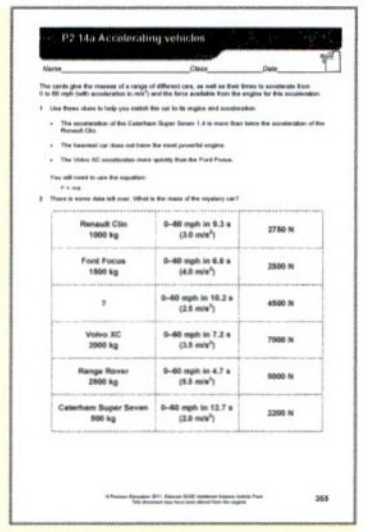

**Stretch** Ask them to suggest values for the missing data.

**Support** Suggest that students miss out question **2**.

### Repelling gliders

**Explaining 2** Demo

Full details of the demonstration are given on the Teacher and technician practical sheet P2.14.

**Stretch** Ask students to predict what would happen if the heavier glider had three times the mass of the lighter one.

**Support** Give students pairs of disc magnets so they can feel the repelling force as they bring like poles together.

### Motion loop cards (AT)

**Plenary 2** AfL Lit

Use the loop cards provided on the **AT** document *Motion loop cards* to review the lesson content and also to review previous work in the topic. Some cards require very simple calculations, so be prepared to write up the numbers on the board if necessary.

### Resultant forces

**Homework 2**

**Worksheet P2.14c** is designed for students working at a higher level. Students practise calculations of force, mass and acceleration.

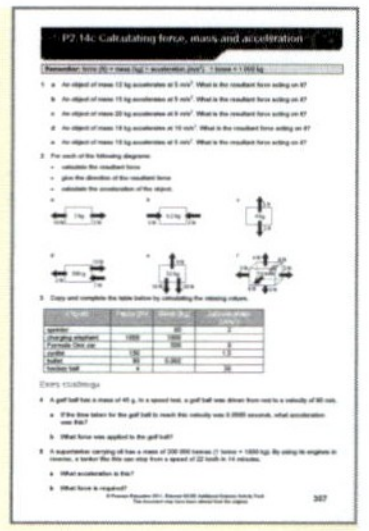

**Stretch** Ask students to complete the 'extra challenge' question.

Topic P2.3: Motions and forces

# P2.14 Forces and acceleration

How is acceleration related to the size of a force?

Rockets and racing bikes both need to be strong and as light as possible. Racing cyclists need to get as much acceleration as they can from the force they apply to the pedals. Research into strong, light materials for use in space can give us new materials that we can put to other uses, including making faster bikes for the future.

**A** *Nicole Cooke winning Gold for the road race at the Beijing Olympics in 2008. Her bike had a mass of just 6.8 kg.*

1 The resultant force on an object is not zero. What will happen to the object?

2 The same force is used to throw a tennis ball and a cricket ball. What will be different about their motions? Explain your answer.

3 If you wanted to make a small car and a large lorry accelerate at the same rate, what can you say about the forces needed to do this? Explain your answer.

When there is a resultant force acting on an object, the object will accelerate in the direction of the resultant force. The size of that acceleration will depend upon two things:

- the size of the force (for the same mass, the bigger the force the bigger the acceleration)
- the mass of the object (for the same force, the more massive the object the smaller the acceleration).

If the same force is applied to two objects, the one with the smaller mass will accelerate more. If two objects of different mass are to have the same acceleration, then a larger force must be applied to the object with the greater mass.

**B** *Two very different catapults*

4 The catapults in Figure B both fire a rock of the same mass. Which will fire it faster and why?

## Calculating forces

The force needed to accelerate a particular object can be calculated using the equation:

force (N) = mass (kg) × acceleration (m/s²)

This is often written as $F = m \times a$

A newton is the force needed to accelerate a mass of 1 kg by 1 m/s².

The shorter the time it takes a car to reach 60 mph from rest, the larger the acceleration. The small car in Figure C accelerates three times as quickly as the larger car.

**C** *Both cars have the same engine.*

**e.g.** The larger car in Figure C has an acceleration of 3.0 m/s². What is the force provided by the engine?

$F = m \times a$

$F = 1500\,\text{kg} \times 3\,\text{m/s}^2$

$F = 4500\,\text{N}$

5 The smaller car in Figure C has an acceleration of 9.0 m/s². What is the force provided by its engine?

(H) 6 A cheetah of mass 40 kg can produce a force of 360 N to push itself forwards. What acceleration does this give the animal?

7 Explain in terms of mass, force and acceleration why racing cyclists and their bikes need to be as light as possible to achieve the greatest possible acceleration at the start of a race.

**Maths skills**

**Rearranging simple equations** like $F = ma$ can be done using a formula triangle, as shown in Figure E in P2.3.

$F = m \times a$

$a = \frac{F}{m}$

$m = \frac{F}{a}$

F / m × a

**ResultsPlus Watch Out!**

Students can lose marks by using the wrong units. To find the force in newtons, the mass must be in kg and the acceleration in m/s².

**Skills spotlight**

Scientists use symbols to represent things. Write down the symbols that are used in the equation that relates force, mass and acceleration and what they stand for.

**Learning Outcomes**

**3.12** Demonstrate an understanding that a resultant force acting on an object produces an acceleration which depends on:
*a* the size of the resultant force
*b* the mass of the object

**3.13** Use the equation:
force (newton, N) = mass (kilogram, kg) × acceleration (metre per second squared, m/s²)
$F = m \times a$

**HSW 11** Present information using scientific conventions and symbols

234 When would a hammer and a feather both fall in the same way? 235

## ActiveTeach

- **AT** *Plotting graphs 1* [spreadsheet] Force, mass and accelaration
- **AT** *Plotting graphs 2* [spreadsheet] Force, mass and accelaration
- **AT** *Motion loop cards* [word document] Questions and answers

## Answers | Student Book

1 It will accelerate in the direction of the resultant force.

2 A cricket ball has more mass than a tennis ball so the same force will give the tennis ball a greater acceleration.

3 You would need a much larger force for the lorry, because it has much more mass.

4 The larger catapult will fire the rock faster because it can produce more force, and so more acceleration.

5 4500 N

6 (H) 9 m/s²

7 A good answer will contain the following points:

- force = mass × acceleration
- to achieve the fastest speed at the start the cyclist needs the most acceleration
- a more massive bike will need more force to give the same acceleration
- a cyclist with more mass needs to produce more force to give the same acceleration on the same bike
- a cyclist can only produce a certain amount of force
- so the lowest mass of bike/rider combined will give the greatest acceleration for the same force.

**Skills spotlight**

*F* – stands for force, measured in N

*m* – stands for mass, measured in kg

*a* – stands for acceleration, measured in m/s²

# P2.15 Terminal velocity

This lesson looks at objects falling through the air and how gravity, air resistance and terminal velocity are connected.

## Specification coverage

**3.14** Use the equation: weight (newton, N) = mass (kilogram, kg) × gravitational field strength (newton per kilogram, N/kg), W = m × g

**3.16** Recall that in a vacuum all falling bodies accelerate at the same rate

**3.17** Demonstrate an understanding that: a) when an object falls through an atmosphere air resistance increases with increasing speed b) air resistance increases until it is equal in size to the weight of the falling object c) when the two forces are balanced, acceleration is zero and terminal velocity is reached

HSW **5** Planning to test a scientific idea, *answer a scientific question or solve a scientific problem*

There are also opportunities to cover HSW *1*, HSW *2*, HSW *6*, HSW *7*, HSW *8*, HSW *10* and HSW *11*.

## Key terms

gravitational field strength
mass
terminal velocity
weight

### How does it feel?
**Starter 1**

Ask the question, 'Does it feel the same if you are bungee jumping, free fall parachuting or diving off a high diving board?' Encourage discussion of forces, acceleration and gravity. Explain that you are going to look more closely at the forces on falling objects in the lesson.

### Terminal velocity
**Exploring 1**

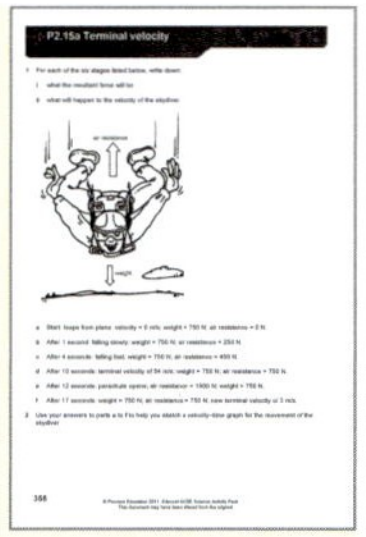

**Worksheet P2.15a** takes students through the stages in a parachute jump. They then plot a velocity-time graph of the journey.

**Stretch** Ask students to comment on the shape of their graph. Would the lines be straight or curved?

**Support** Ask them to colour the velocities in one colour, the weight in another, and air resistance in a third colour.

### Student Book spread P2.15
**Explaining 1**

Show the famous video of the feather and hammer drop on the Moon, available on *YouTube*. Connect the weight of an object, (mg), with the force on it due to gravity, (ma). Work through the text and questions in the Student Book.

**Stretch** Ask how a skydiver in freefall could change their terminal velocity.

**Support** Guide students through simple calculations of the weight of objects.

### Parachute misconception
**Plenary 1**

Why does the skydiver not go up when they open their parachute? Either as a follow on if the class did *Starter 2*, or as a new activity, revisit this common misconception.

### Weight and terminal velocity
**Homework 1**

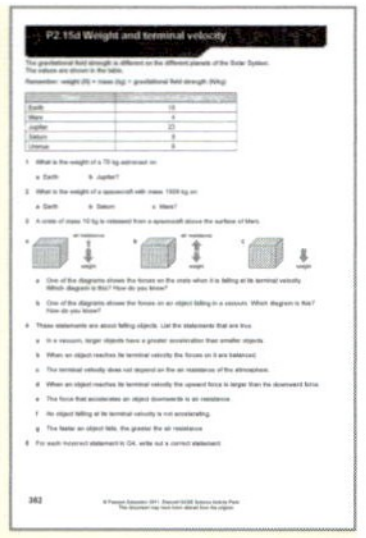

Using **Worksheet P2.15d**, students calculate the weight for different values of gravitational field strength on different planets. Then they answer a set of true/false questions about terminal velocity and interpret force diagrams.

**Support** Students do not do question **5**.

### Free fall
**Starter 2**

Show a video clip of a parachutist falling and then opening the parachute. Ask students to try and note down what is happening and why. Draw out that we are seeing the relative velocity of the camera and the skydiver and the skydiver does not actually go upwards.

### Terminal velocity of baking cases
**Exploring 2** Prac

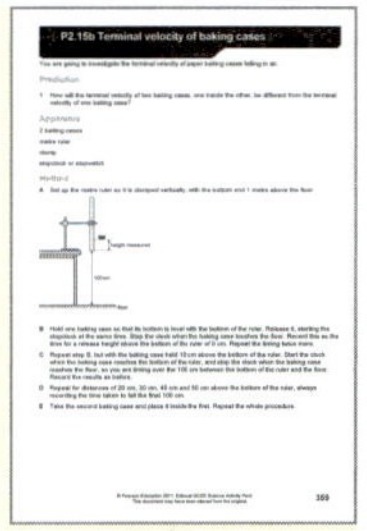

Full instructions for students are given on **Worksheet P2.15b**. Details of equipment and how to set up the practical are provided on the Teacher and technician practical sheet P2.15.

**Stretch** Would the terminal velocity continue to increase as the number of baking cases increased? How could they test this?

**Support** Provide a scale for the graph to make plotting easier.

### Falling cans
**Explaining 2**

Drop two identical food cans, both appearing to be full. They appear exactly the same and fall at the same rate but have significantly different masses. The heavier object has a larger mass and so needs a larger force to accelerate at the same rate.

**Stretch** Students use the masses of the objects in the demonstration to calculate the forces involved.

**Support** Attach the cans to newtonmeters and jerk them horizontally across the bench.

### Free fall labels
**Plenary 2**

AfL Lit

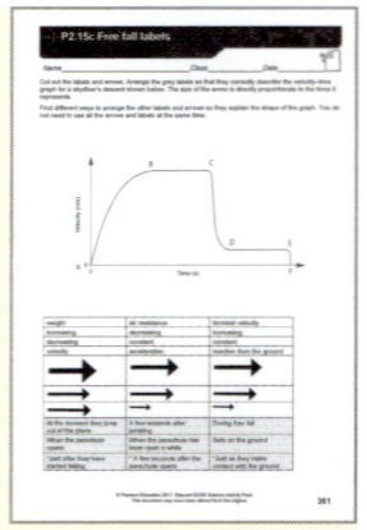

Give the velocity–time graph for a skydiver and the labels and arrows from **Worksheet P2.15c** to groups of students. Ask the groups to work through the journey, labelling their diagram with descriptions in the correct sequence. Compare results and reinforce the concept of terminal velocity.

### Safe landing
**Homework 2**

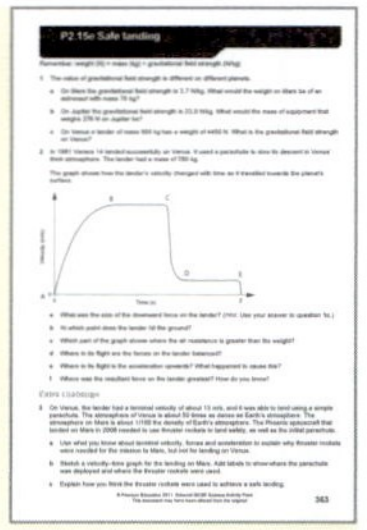

Using **Worksheet P2.15e**, students calculate mass, weight and gravitational field strength for objects on different planets. They interpret a more complex graph for a lander on Venus and answer questions about forces and accelerations.

**Stretch** Students do the 'extra challenge' question.

# P2.15 Terminal velocity

What is terminal velocity?

In 1960, Joseph Kittinger jumped from the gondola of a balloon at a height of 31 333 m. It took him 13 minutes and 45 seconds to reach the ground, accelerating to a maximum speed of 988 km/h (614 mph) when he was in 'free fall'.

**A** *Joseph Kittinger jumping in 1960. A sign by the door of the gondola read 'This is the highest step in the world'.*

**Mass** is the quantity of matter there is in an object and does not change, but **weight** is a measure of the pull of gravity on an object and can change. To describe how strong gravity is we talk about **gravitational field strength**, measured in newtons per kilogram (N/kg). On Earth this has a value of 10 N/kg. This means that each kilogram is pulled down with a force of 10 N. The weight of any object on Earth can be calculated using the following equation.

weight (N) = mass (kg) × gravitational field strength (N/kg)

This is often written as: $W = m \times g$

1 What is the difference between mass and weight?

2 A landing craft of mass 300 kg goes to Jupiter, where the gravitational field strength is 25 N/kg.
a What would its mass be?
b What would its weight be?

**e.g.**
What is the weight of a 300 kg planetary landing craft on the surface of the Earth?

$W = m \times g$

$W = 300\,kg \times 10\,N/kg = 3000\,N$

**ResultsPlus Watch Out!**
Students can confuse force and acceleration when answering questions about falling objects. In a vacuum, all falling objects accelerate at the same rate but that does not mean that the forces are the same.

Larger masses need more force to get them to accelerate than smaller masses. As mass increases, so does the force from gravity (weight). This means that gravity accelerates all objects down towards the Earth by the *same* amount. So a feather and a hammer dropped together should accelerate by the same amount and so hit the ground at the same time. They do not do this on Earth because there is more air resistance on the feather, which slows it down.

**B** *In a vacuum, all falling objects accelerate at the same rate.*

3 Why did the hammer and feather hit the ground together when dropped on the Moon?

On the Moon in 1971, astronaut David Scott tried this experiment. The feather and the hammer both hit the ground at the same time because they were both dropped in a vacuum.

## Terminal velocity

When an object just starts to fall from above the Earth, the only force acting on it is its own weight, which accelerates it towards the Earth. As it gains speed, air resistance begins to act in the opposite direction, reducing the resultant force.

Figure C shows how the resultant force on a falling skydiver changes as their velocity increases. As with all objects, eventually the weight and air resistance forces are balanced. The resultant force on the skydiver is then zero, so they will stop accelerating. They will travel at a constant velocity, called the **terminal velocity**.

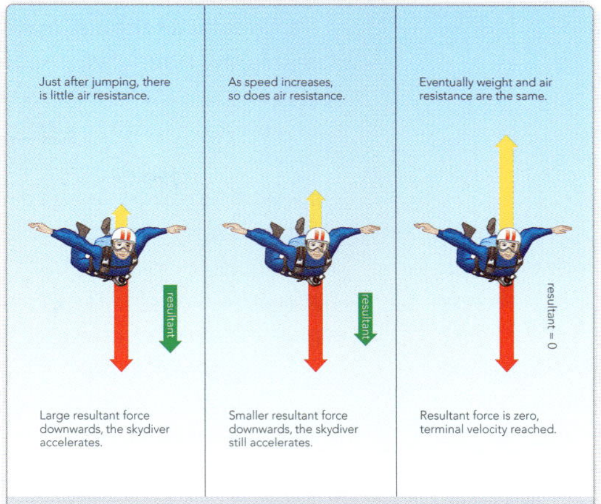


**C** *Eventually a skydiver reaches a terminal velocity.*

4 What is the name for the maximum velocity any object falling in air can reach?

5 What happens to the size of the air resistance force on an object as its speed increases?

6 a What is the weight of a skydiver of mass 60 kg?
b In what direction does this force act?
c What is the force of air resistance when this skydiver is at their terminal velocity?
d In what direction does this force act?

7 Two identical crates are dropped from an aircraft. One is empty and the other is full. Which crate will reach the ground first? Explain your answer.

**Skills spotlight**
Scientists plan how to test ideas. How could you use a stopclock and a ruler to find whether paper cupcake cases reach a terminal velocity when dropped?

**Learning Outcomes**

3.14 Use the equation:
weight (newton, N) = mass (kilogram, kg) × gravitational field strength (newton per kilogram, N/kg)
$W = m \times g$

3.16 Recall that in a vacuum all falling bodies accelerate at the same rate

3.17 Demonstrate an understanding that:
a when an object falls through an atmosphere air resistance increases with increasing speed
b air resistance increases until it is equal in size to the weight of the falling object
c when the two forces are balanced acceleration is zero and terminal velocity is reached

HSW 5 Plan to test a scientific idea by controlling relevant variables



How did astronauts drive on the Moon?



## ActiveTeach

- **AT** *Falling bodies* [BBC video]
  Galileo's experiments with falling objects
- **AT** *Forces and acceleration* [interactive]
  Mass, weight, gravity – noughts and crosses
- **AT** *Terminal velocity* [diagram]
  Figure B – diagram labelling activity

## Answers | Student Book

1 Mass is the amount of matter in an object; weight is the gravitational force on the object, which depends on the gravitational field strength.

2 **a** 300 kg
**b** 7500 N

3 The hammer and feather had the same acceleration, and there was no air resistance.

4 Terminal velocity

5 Air resistance increases with speed.

6 **a** 600 N
**b** Acts towards the Earth (downwards)
**c** 600 N
**d** Acts upwards

7 A good answer will contain the following points:
- both crates travel the same distance to reach the ground
- the full crate has greater mass and so greater weight
- the full crate will need a larger air resistance to balance its greater weight
- the full crate will have a larger terminal velocity
- a larger terminal velocity means the full crate will travel the same distance as the empty crate in a shorter time
- so the full crate will reach the ground first.

**Skills spotlight**
Look for suggestions where students time cupcake cases over consecutive distances, say 0–10 cm, 10–20 cm, and so on. They find the velocity for each distance and see how the velocity changes as the cupcake case falls. A constant value would show that the falling cupcake cases did reach a terminal velocity.

# P2.16 Stopping distances

This section explains how to calculate the stopping distance for a vehicle and discusses the factors that affect both thinking distance and braking distance.

## Specification coverage

***4.1*** Recall that the stopping distance of a vehicle is made up of the sum of the thinking distance and the braking distance

***4.2*** Demonstrate an understanding of the factors affecting the stopping distance of a vehicle, including: a) the mass of the vehicle b) the speed of the vehicle c) the driver's reaction time d) the state of the vehicle's brakes e) the state of the road f) the amount of friction between the tyre and the road surface

HSW ***13*** How and why decisions about science and technology are made, including those that raise ethical issues, and about the social, *economic and environmental* effects of such decisions

There are also opportunities to cover HSW ***5***, HSW ***6***, HSW ***7*** and HSW ***8***.

## Key terms

braking distance
friction
reaction time
stopping distance
thinking distance

### The Highway Code stopping distances

**Starter 1**

Display the Highway Code's chart of increasing stopping distances with speed. Ask students to write down what they think braking distance and thinking distance might be and how each changes with the speed. Students discuss their ideas in pairs and then feed back a joint agreed answer to a class discussion.

### Stopping distances spreadsheet (AT)

**Exploring 1**

The **AT** spreadsheet *Stopping distances* can be used to input thinking distance and braking distance and it calculates overall stopping distance.

**Stretch** Students formulate the spreadsheet themselves.

**Support** Suggest that students use a calculator to check the calculations.

### Road speed safety

**Explaining 1** Lit

Discuss carefully with students how increasing speed affects the thinking and braking distances, and hence why reducing speed limits improves safety.

**Stretch** Give students the stopping distances chart from *Starter 1* and ask them to work out the relationship between 'velocity squared' and 'braking distance'.

**Support** Ask students to make a campaign poster version of the answer to the Skills spotlight, reducing the explanatory detail demanded.

### Stopping distances pyramid

**Plenary 1**

Students should attempt to draw a pyramid-style diagram with 'stopping distance' at the top and the things that affect it spreading beneath. Each tier includes the things that affect those in the tier above.

### Stopping distances summary

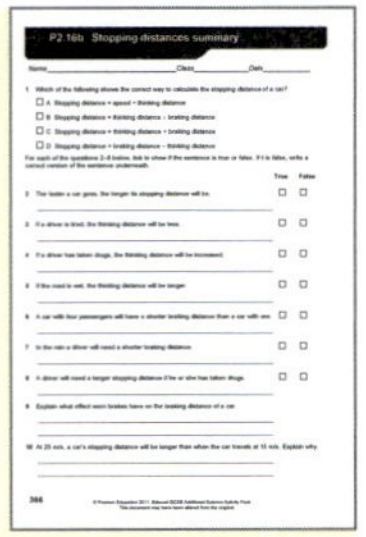

**Homework 1**

Using **Worksheet P2.16b**, students decide whether statements about how different factors affect thinking, braking and stopping distances are true or false, and re-write any statements that are false to make them true.

**Support** Provide some starter text for the sentences they have to re-write.

### Stop running!

**Starter 2**

Have eight or ten students run parallel in a mock race, but at your shout they must stop as quickly as possible. Follow this up with a discussion of the ideas of thinking distance and braking distance, and what might make either shorter or longer. Finally, relate to vehicle emergency stopping.

### Emergency sand traps

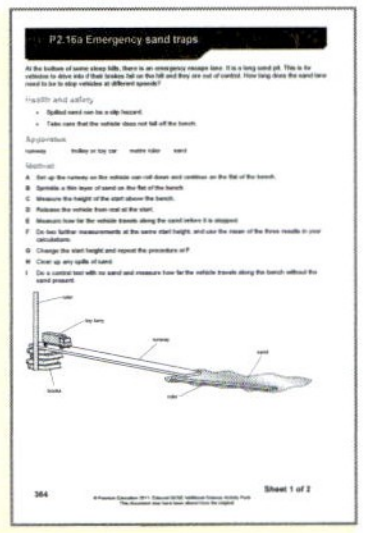

**Exploring 2** Prac

This experiment is detailed on **Worksheet P2.16a**. Refer to the Teacher and technician practical sheet P2.16 for further guidance.

**Stretch** Students write a plan for adapting this experiment to find out how the mass of a lorry will affect its stopping distance.

**Support** Help students draw the graph axes so they only have to plot their points.

### Student Book spread P2.16

**Explaining 2**

Explain the sum of thinking and braking distance, plus what affects each, and hence the overall stopping distance.

**Stretch** Students write out an idea for how NASA could have experimented on Earth to find out what the Moon buggy's stopping distances would be on the Moon where the gravity is much lower.

**Support** Students copy out Figure C onto graph paper and make the length of each arrow exactly match the number of metres it represents.

### Making the sums add up

**Plenary 2**

The **AT** presentation *Making the sums add up* has a drag and drop activity with values for thinking distance, braking distance and overall stopping distance. These have to be ordered in appropriate groups of three, so that the sum is correct.

### Stopping distances graphs

**Homework 2**

**Worksheet P2.16c** is designed for more able students. They will need graph paper in order to complete the worksheet.

**Stretch** Students undertake the 'extra challenge' on the worksheet.

# P2.16 Stopping distances

What affects the distance covered when a vehicle tries to stop?

In 1971, Dave Scott of the Apollo 15 Moon mission said that driving the Moon buggy was 'quite good… the steering is responsive… and we average eight kilometres per hour'. NASA called them Lunar Rover Vehicles but because it was like driving a sand kart known as a dune buggy, these vehicles were nicknamed Moon buggies.

**A** *Driving a Moon buggy was like driving a go-kart with very bouncy suspension.*

1 Why is it important for a driver to know their stopping distance?

2 A go-kart driver has a thinking distance of 5 m and a braking distance of 12 m. What is the overall stopping distance?

## Stopping safely

Go-kart drivers need to know what affects the distance it takes for a kart to stop safely in an emergency.

When a driver sees a problem ahead, the go-kart will travel some distance whilst the driver reacts to seeing the problem. This is called the **thinking distance**. The kart will then go some distance further whilst the brakes are working to bring it to a halt. This is called the **braking distance**. The overall **stopping distance** for any road vehicle will be the sum of the thinking and braking distances.

**B** *If there is a crash on a go-karting circuit, the next kart along has nowhere to go – it must stop.*

stopping distance = thinking distance + braking distance

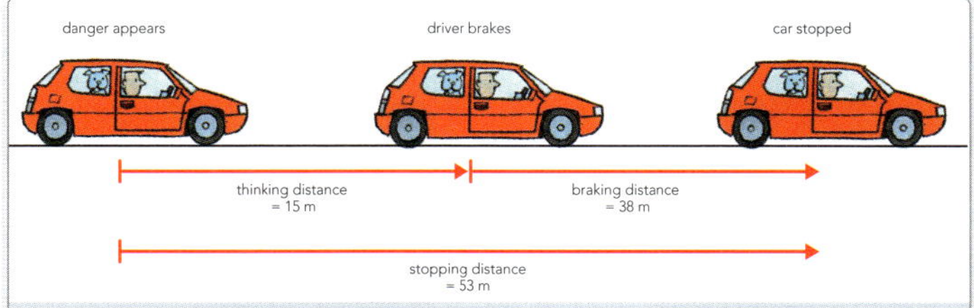


**C** *Stopping a car or kart travelling at 50mph requires thinking and then braking.*

## Changing stopping distances

A driver's thinking distance will be longer if their **reaction time** is greater – for example, if they are tired, or ill, or have taken drugs or alcohol.

If a vehicle is moving at a greater speed, then both the thinking distance and the braking distance are increased.

The force of **friction** slows vehicles down. Brakes create a lot of friction. If the brakes are worn, they create less friction and do not slow the vehicle so well. Friction between the tyres and road is also important. If the road is wet or has loose gravel on it, there is less friction and the braking distance is increased.

If a vehicle has more mass, more force is needed to decelerate it. So, if the same amount of friction is used to stop a vehicle, a heavier vehicle will travel further than a lighter one (it has a greater braking distance).

**Skills spotlight**

Science provides evidence that is used in making decisions about social issues. Write a scientific explanation as to why there are now many 20 mph zones in residential areas.

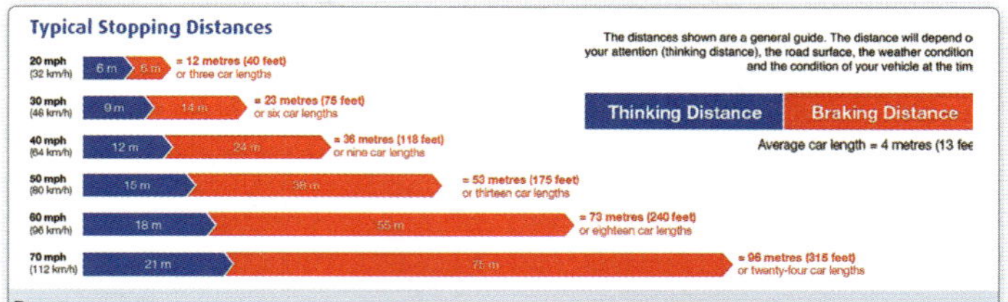


**D** *At faster speeds, the braking distance is much greater.*

3 Lorry drivers have the same thinking distance as car drivers but their braking distance is greater. Why are the overall stopping distances for cars less than for lorries?

4 How would ice on the road affect thinking distance and braking distance?

5 Why is drinking-and-driving illegal?

6 The *Highway Code* is a government book about driving. Prepare a summary for a new version of the *Highway Code* explaining what things increase and decrease the stopping distance and why.

**ResultsPlus Watch Out!**

Students often confuse reactions and reaction time. Faster reactions means shorter reaction time.

**Learning Outcomes**

*4.1* Recall that the stopping distance of a vehicle is made up of the sum of the thinking distance and the braking distance

*4.2* Demonstrate an understanding of the factors affecting the stopping distance of a vehicle, including
*a* the mass of the vehicle
*b* the speed of the vehicle
*c* the driver's reaction time
*d* the state of the vehicle's brakes
*e* the state of the road
*f* the amount of friction between the tyre and the road surface

HSW *13* Explain how and why decisions about uses of science and technology are made



What would cycling on ice be like?



**ActiveTeach**

- **AT** *Stopping distances*
  [BBC video]
  How tyres affect stopping distances
- **AT** *Thinking distance or braking distance?*
  [interactive]
  Stopping distance – sorting activity
- **AT** *Stopping distances*
  [spreadsheet]
  Calculating stopping distance
- **AT** *Making the sums add up*
  [presentation]
  Drag and drop
- **AT** *Distance required to stop a car*
  [diagram]
  Figure C – diagram labelling activity

## Answers | Student Book

**1** In order to leave a safe distance so they do not crash when a hazard appears.

**2** 17 m

**3** Braking distance plus thinking distance = stopping distance, so if braking distance is shorter but thinking distance is the same then stopping distance will be less.

**4** Thinking distance – no change; braking distance – longer

**5** Drinking alcohol increases reaction time, therefore increasing thinking distance. This increases stopping distance, leading to more crashes.

**6** A good answer will contain the following points:
- thinking distance is increased by: alcohol; drugs; tiredness; faster speed
- braking distance is increased by: faster speed; extra weight; worn brakes; lower friction road surface, e.g. mud, gravel, wet, ice.

**Skills spotlight**

Faster speed increases both thinking distance and braking distance (the latter significantly). Reducing vehicle speeds reduces the number of accidents, making the roads safer.

Also, faster speeds significantly increase kinetic energy, so accidents at reduced speeds are significantly less dangerous.

# P2.17 Friction with different surfaces

This lesson challenges students to investigate the friction force in sliding a weighted wooden block across various different surfaces. The activity may be run as a practice controlled assessment task or as a straight-forward class practical. The practical work should easily be completed in 30–40 minutes.

## Specification coverage

***4.3*** Investigate the forces required to slide blocks along different surfaces, with differing amounts of friction

This activity provides opportunities to cover HSW *1*, HSW *2*, HSW *3*, HSW *5*, HSW *6*, HSW *7*, HSW *8*, HSW *10* and HSW *11*.

### Before the lesson

In the week or two before the task show students the equipment and, if appropriate, allow them to practice using it. The use of a spring balance, including reading it whilst it is moving, is particularly recommended. It may be good preparation to show students one or more of Skills Sheets 19 to 26 to show what is expected of them in their actual controlled assessment task.

### Starter AfL

**Playground designers**

Students should write a list of 6-8 solid materials. Then ask them to choose from their list those they would use for the surface of a children's playground slide, and those they would choose for the surface of a playground 'wobble board'. Ask students to pair up and discuss their materials and choices. They choose the best material for each job and justify each choice. Follow with a class discussion. The concepts of static and sliding friction, along with surface roughness, should all come up.

Read the additional information below the opening section of page 240 of the Student Book and the brief description of the activity provided by the 'Your task' box.

### Option 1: Straight-forward class practical

Students follow the instructions on **Worksheet P2.17b**. Students measure the sliding friction for a wooden block with fixed weight and contact area. The surface type, and hence its roughness, is changed as the independent variable. The tests are repeated three times for each surface, plus extra repeats for tests in which the block stops or jumps. The range of data that students need to collect is given on **Worksheet P2.17c** which students will also need.

You could ask students to come up with one or two further hypotheses, based on their observations in this practical, and the control variables.

### Plenary

On page 241 of the Student Book you will find two examples of the sort of work that students may produce for this task. The examples focus on writing a hypothesis. You could share these with students after they have completed their own work. This will help them to understand the assessment criteria and so make it easier for them to evaluate their work and to see how they can improve it. Moderator comments on each of the Student Book extracts can be found at the end of the assessment guidance for this investigation on the CD-ROM. The examples can also be found on the **AT** document *Student examples*.

### Option 2: Running the activity as a practice controlled assessment task (PCAT)

We have provided a full range of support resources to allow the running of this practical as a practice controlled assessment task. A recommended structure is outlined below (to be used over a number of sessions). Marking guidance for all three parts of the practice task can be found on the CD-ROM that accompanies the TTPP. To save time when using these practice controlled assessment tasks, you may wish to focus on a particular aspect or skill rather than working through all three parts of the task.

#### Part A Planning

1. Students should be given the Student Brief on **Worksheet P2.17a**. They can use Part A of the Workbook that is provided to help with their practice controlled assessments. They should be given about 1 hour to do this planning.
2. You will need to highlight to the students what materials are available to be used as surfaces.

#### Part B Observations

3. Students should be asked to carry out the practical task to collect evidence using the method they have planned in Part A. Once again, they should refer to the Student Brief on **Worksheet P2.17a**. They can use Part B of the Workbook that is provided to help pupils with their practice controlled assessments. They should be given about 30–40 minutes to collect their primary evidence.
4. If there is a problem with their own planned method, students may be asked to follow the method set out on **Worksheet P2.17b**. This will still enable students to access the full range of marks for Part B and Part C of the practice controlled assessment task.
4. In Part B, students are required to gather some secondary evidence. The evidence can be quantitative or qualitative. It can be from a variety of sources but students must note where they found their evidence and evaluate the quality of the source as part of this task. Skills Sheet 22 provides students with further guidance on researching for and evaluating secondary evidence. This part of the task could be done outside of the lesson but must be supervised.

#### Part C Conclusions

8. Students follow the instructions set out on the Part C section of the Student Brief on **Worksheet P2.17a**. They should use their data from Part B and the secondary evidence they have collected when doing this. They can use Part C of the Workbook that is provided to help pupils with their practice controlled assessments. They should be given about 1 hour to work on their conclusions.

The **AT** includes video clips showing a group of students working through elements of this investigation with teacher support.

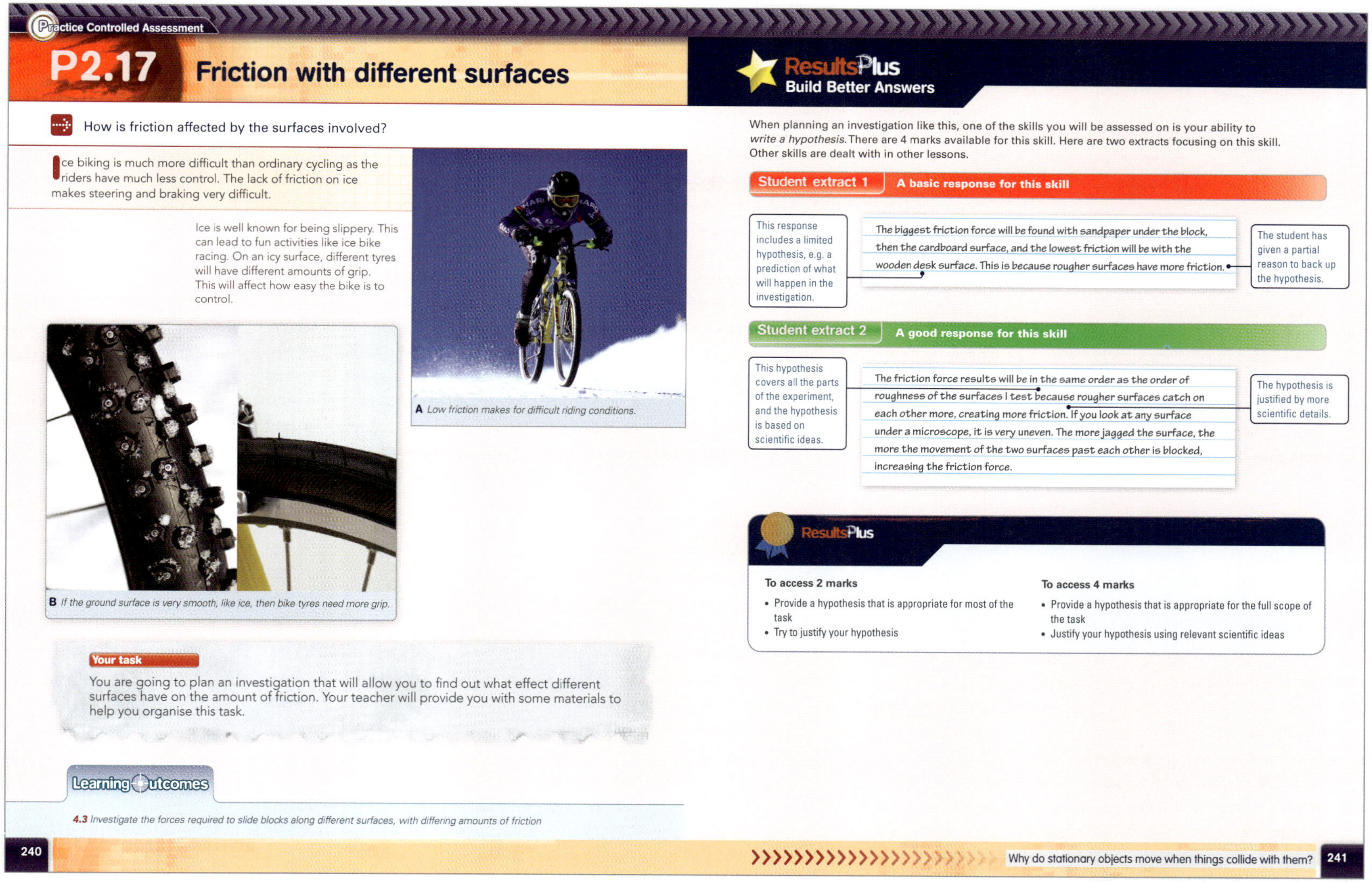

Practice Controlled Assessment

# P2.17 Friction with different surfaces

How is friction affected by the surfaces involved?

Ice biking is much more difficult than ordinary cycling as the riders have much less control. The lack of friction on ice makes steering and braking very difficult.

Ice is well known for being slippery. This can lead to fun activities like ice bike racing. On an icy surface, different tyres will have different amounts of grip. This will affect how easy the bike is to control.

**A** *Low friction makes for difficult riding conditions.*

**B** *If the ground surface is very smooth, like ice, then bike tyres need more grip.*

**Your task**

You are going to plan an investigation that will allow you to find out what effect different surfaces have on the amount of friction. Your teacher will provide you with some materials to help you organise this task.

**Learning Outcomes**

*4.3 Investigate the forces required to slide blocks along different surfaces, with differing amounts of friction*

**ResultsPlus Build Better Answers**

When planning an investigation like this, one of the skills you will be assessed on is your ability to *write a hypothesis.* There are 4 marks available for this skill. Here are two extracts focusing on this skill. Other skills are dealt with in other lessons.

**Student extract 1 — A basic response for this skill**

*The biggest friction force will be found with sandpaper under the block, then the cardboard surface, and the lowest friction will be with the wooden desk surface. This is because rougher surfaces have more friction.*

This response includes a limited hypothesis, e.g. a prediction of what will happen in the investigation.

The student has given a partial reason to back up the hypothesis.

**Student extract 2 — A good response for this skill**

*The friction force results will be in the same order as the order of roughness of the surfaces I test because rougher surfaces catch on each other more, creating more friction. If you look at any surface under a microscope, it is very uneven. The more jagged the surface, the more the movement of the two surfaces past each other is blocked, increasing the friction force.*

This hypothesis covers all the parts of the experiment, and the hypothesis is based on scientific ideas.

The hypothesis is justified by more scientific details.

**ResultsPlus**

**To access 2 marks**

- Provide a hypothesis that is appropriate for most of the task
- Try to justify your hypothesis

**To access 4 marks**

- Provide a hypothesis that is appropriate for the full scope of the task
- Justify your hypothesis using relevant scientific ideas

240 — Why do stationary objects move when things collide with them? — 241

**ActiveTeach**

- **AT** *P2.17 Friction* [video] Students work through the investigation
- **AT** *P2.17 Moderator comments* [word document] Moderator comments on the video
- **AT** *P2.17 Assessment criteria* [presentation] Understanding the CA marking criteria
- **AT** *P2.17 Student task sheet* [word document] CA video checklist
- **AT** *P2.17 Specification points* [word document] Edexcel specification points
- **AT** *P2.17 Student examples* [word document] Examples for students to assess

## Assessment criteria

**Hypothesis**

**0** No relevant hypothesis provided.

**1-2** **a)** Hypothesis provided is appropriate for most of the task, e.g. 'The biggest friction force will be found with sandpaper under the block, and then the cardboard surface. The lowest friction will be with the wooden desk surface.'

**b)** Partially justifies the hypothesis, e.g. 'This is because rougher surfaces create more friction'.

**3-4** **a)** Provides a hypothesis that is appropriate for the full scope of the task based on relevant scientific ideas, e.g. 'Rougher textures will have a larger friction force, because rougher surfaces catch on each other more, creating more friction'.

**b)** Justifies the hypothesis fully using relevant scientific ideas, e.g. 'Friction is caused by bumps on surfaces colliding. Rougher surfaces have more surface bumps and so more friction.'

# P2.18 Momentum



This lesson introduces momentum as a vector quantity to be calculated and covers the qualitative conservation of linear momentum in one dimension. Students practise and investigate these things in a variety of ways, and in the context of road safety can refer back to P2.16 and forwards to P2.20 and to the Practice Controlled Assessment of P2.19.

## Specification coverage

**4.4** Use the equation: momentum (kilogram metre per second, kg m/s) = mass (kilogram, kg) × velocity (metre per second, m/s) to calculate the momentum of a moving object

**4.5** Demonstrate an understanding of momentum as a vector quantity

**4.6** Demonstrate an understanding of the idea of linear momentum conservation

HSW *10* Using both qualitative and quantitative approaches

There are also opportunities to cover HSW *6*, HSW *7* and HSW *11*.

## Key terms

conservation of momentum
vector quantity

### Knocking down the house

**Starter 1** AfL

In pairs, ask students to decide which would cause more damage if it crashed into a house; an empty truck or the same truck, moving at the same speed, filled with bricks. They should also work out an explanation to justify their answer. Add a selection of answers on the board, which can be referred to later if using *Plenary 1*.

### Investigating momentum experiment

**Exploring 1** Prac

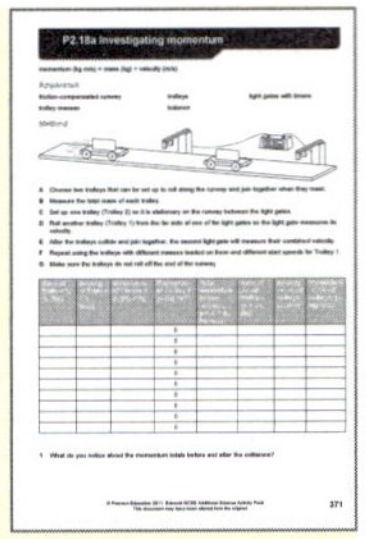
P2.18a Investigating momentum

This experiment is detailed on **Worksheet P2.18a**. Refer to the Teacher and technician practical sheet P2.18 for further guidance.

Stretch Ask more able students to justify a prediction regarding a similar but different type of collision.

Support Students work in pairs and could each focus on only one half of the table.

### Student Book spread P2.18

**Explaining 1**

Work through pages 242 and 243 with the class. Discuss the ideas of calculating momentum and what happens to it in collisions.

Stretch Challenge students to explain why crash test dummies are made very carefully to mimic human masses and joints very closely.

Support Students should be encouraged to write out the calculations step by step..

### How the lorry knocked down the house

**Plenary 1** AfL

Refer back to Starter 1. Students look at all the suggestions and decide which is the best scientific explanation, or come up with a new explanation if none of the original ones satisfy them. Encourage students to use the new vocabulary they have learned in their explanations.

### Momentum calculations

**Homework 1**

P2.18c Momentum calculations

Using **Worksheet P2.18c**, students practise using the equation for calculating momentum.

Support Take students through the sheet and let them colour/highlight all masses and all velocities, and m and v in the equation.

### Movement measurements

**Starter 2** AfL

Have eight or ten students run parallel in a mock race, but at your shout they must stop as quickly as possible. Follow this up with a discussion of the ideas of thinking distance and braking distance, and what might make either shorter or longer. Finally, relate to vehicle emergency stopping.

### Momentum conservation spreadsheet

**Exploring 2**

The **AT** spreadsheet *Momentum conservation* calculates momentum.

Stretch This can be extended to find speeds after collisions based on momentum being conserved.

Support Less able students could be given pairs of significantly disparate examples in which they simply have to estimate which has the larger momentum.

### Momentum conservation

**Explaining 2** Lit

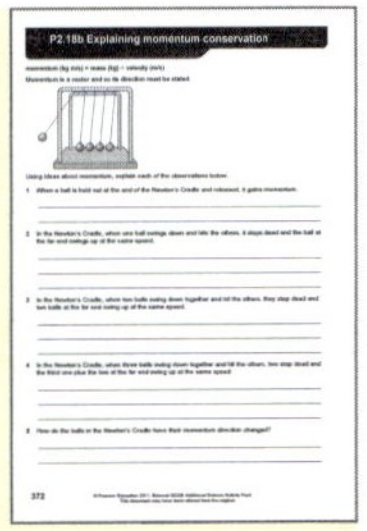
P2.18b Explaining momentum conservation

Demonstrate a Newton's Cradle. Discuss how to calculate the momentum. Lead the students through the questions on **Worksheet P2.18b**.

Stretch Students could invent figures for the situations in questions **1**, **2** and **3** and calculate the momentum for each object.

Support The perfect answers could be written out for them with blank words to be completed.

### Crash test video explanations

**Plenary 2**

Show a video of car crash tests. Pause after each one and discuss with the class how you can see momentum being conserved. The class could also make estimates of masses and velocities and practise calculating momentum for each vehicle seen.

### H Penguin collisions

**Homework 2**

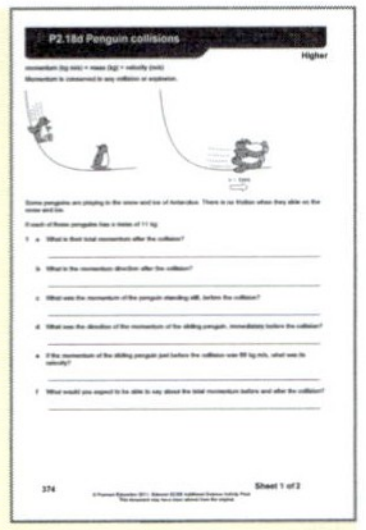
P2.18d Penguin collisions

Using **Worksheet P2.18d**, students calculate momentums, and discuss momentum as a vector quantity and the conservation of momentum.

Stretch Ask students to show by calculation that the total momentum is conserved in each case.

# P2.18 Momentum

What is momentum?

To create a monster truck, a normal vehicle is fitted with a powerful engine, strong suspension and huge oversized wheels. Apart from being a very bouncy ride, drivers find them difficult to control, as all the truck's movements are oversized too.

1 Calculate the momentum of:
a a 730 kg Smart car moving north at 20 m/s
b a 2500 kg monster truck moving at a velocity of 8 m/s south.

In a race, if a vehicle goes out of control and hits a barrier, the barrier moves. If two vehicles are going at the same speed and hit a barrier, the barrier moves more when hit by a monster truck than by a small car. The reason for this is because the larger vehicle has more **momentum**.

A *A small car can become a monster.*

**Skills spotlight**

Scientists use knowledge of physics laws to analyse real situations and develop solutions to problems. Look at Figure B and explain how car designers could monitor the changes in momentum of the crashing car. How could they make quantitative measurements, how could they make qualitative measurements and what is an advantage of each?

B *Much more damage would have been caused to the crash barrier if it had been hit by a heavier vehicle, such as a truck.*

Momentum is a measure of how strongly something is moving. It is calculated by multiplying mass by velocity.

| momentum | = | mass | × | velocity |
|---|---|---|---|---|
| (kilogram metre per second, kg m/s) | = | (kilogram, kg) | × | (metre per second, m/s) |

e.g. The momentum of the monster truck in Figure A (mass = 4500 kg) when it is travelling at 12 m/s east would be:

momentum = mass × velocity = 4500 × 12 = 54 000 kg m/s east

2 Why would a stationary monster truck have no momentum?

H 3 A meteorite flies through space at 250 m/s towards Earth. It has a momentum of 30 000 kg m/s towards Earth. What is its mass?

Notice that since velocity is a **vector quantity** (it has a size *and* direction), so is momentum. So we should always state the amount of momentum an object has and the direction of that momentum, which will be the same direction as its velocity.

## Conservation of linear momentum

When a moving object collides with another object, the *total* momentum of both objects is the same before the collision as it is after the collision. This is known as conservation of linear momentum. A crash barrier isn't moving and so has zero momentum. If a vehicle hits it, the barrier will start to move. The velocity of the barrier and the vehicle together is less than the vehicle on its own (because the combined mass is greater). However, the total momentum remains the same.

If you find the total momentum before a collision and then the total momentum after the collision, they will be the same. Remember, momentum is a vector so you need to consider direction when you 'add' the quantities together.

C *Some of the car's momentum is transferred to the ball.*

4 a Calculate the momentum of each penguin before they collide.
b Calculate the total momentum before the penguins collide.
c Say which direction the total momentum is in before the collision.
d Calculate the total momentum after the collision and say in which direction it is.
e Has the momentum been conserved?



**ResultsPlus Watch Out!**

Students often forget that a stationary object has mass and zero momentum. When a moving object collides with it the two masses are added together so the combined speed will be slower but the momentum will be the same as at the start.

5 Put the following things in order of increasing momentum and explain how you worked out the order: a monster truck in a race; a running dog; a sleeping cat; the meteorite from question 3.

6 Think about a car crashing. Write an explanation of how to work out its momentum and explain what is meant by conservation of linear momentum.

**Learning Outcomes**

4.4 Use the equation: momentum (kilogram metre per second, kg m/s) = mass (kilogram, kg) × velocity (metre per second, m/s) to calculate the momentum of a moving object

4.5 Demonstrate an understanding of momentum as a vector quantity

4.6 Demonstrate an understanding of the idea of linear momentum conservation

HSW 10 Use qualitative and quantitative approaches when presenting scientific ideas and arguments, and recording observations



How do crash test dummies tell us when they are hurt?



## ActiveTeach

- **AT** *How much momentum?* [interactive]
  Momentum, mass and velocity – quiz
- **AT** *Momentum conservation* [spreadsheet]
  Calculating momentum
- **AT** *Momentum calculations* [word document]
  Drag and drop

## Answers | Student Book

1 a 14 600 kg m/s north
  b 20 000 kg m/s south
2 Velocity is zero, so mass × velocity is zero.
3 H 120 kg
4 a 120 kg m/s and zero
  b 120 kg m/s
  c To the right
  d 120 kg m/s to the right
  e Yes
5 A sleeping cat – not moving so zero momentum. A running dog – moving but it is slower and has less mass than both the others. The meteorite from question **3**. A monster truck in a race – in the worked example the monster truck has more momentum than the meteorite and is not going at race speed.
6 A good answer will contain the following points: need to know the mass and velocity; multiply these to calculate momentum; conservation of linear momentum means same total momentum before and after a collision; it will be conserved in a crash; able to work out the velocity of vehicles after crashing if you know their mass.

**Skills spotlight**

- Video recording of crash allows qualitative by just looking and describing what happens to each car.
- Could use markers painted on road and car to actually measure movements in video, also know time for each video frame.
- Could use datalog speedometers from cars, plus additional sensors like accelerometers or forcemeters.
- Qualitative advantage: can produce general conclusion for all crashes (such as head-on crashes are more dangerous than glancing impacts).
- Quantitative advantage: can use results to inform design specifically

# P2.19 Crumple Zones

This lesson challenges students to investigate the effectiveness of home-made crumple zones on model vehicles. The activity may be run as a practice controlled assessment task or as a straight-forward class practical. The practical work could be relatively brief (one lesson) but is likely to be far more engaging and instructive if it is taken over several lessons and includes an R & D element, with the pupils working in teams.

## Specification coverage

***4.8*** Investigate how crumple zones can be used to reduce the forces in collisions

This activity provides opportunities to cover HSW *1*, HSW *2*, HSW *3*, HSW *5*, HSW *6*, HSW *7*, HSW *8*, HSW *10* and HSW *11*.

## Key terms

crumple zone

### Before the lesson

In this investigation students should be familiar with dynamics trolleys and ramps, along with datalogging equipment and sensors, such as light gates and force sensors. Also, video analysis of crash testing is very important. If students are to use video analysis, they should practise with the video capture and editing equipment. This will allow them to concentrate on the experimental work.

It may be good preparation to show students one or more of Skills Sheets 19 to 26 to show what is expected of them in their actual controlled assessment task.

### Starter

**Crash Test Game**

Ask students to critique the game *Crash Test Launcher* at www.maxgames.com/play/crash-test-launcher.html. In particular, students should be asked to identify how the various scoring attributes could be measured if the events happened in real crash tests. Variables like speed, distance, and damage to the dummy are scored, so students should make suggestions for equipment and variables to be measured. Alternatives can also be found at: www.crashtestdummyolympics.co.uk/

Follow this by reading the additional information below the opening section of page 244 of the Student Book. They may then read the brief description of the activity provided by the 'Your task' box.

### Option 1: Straight-forward class practical

Students follow the instructions on **Worksheet P2.19b**. Using thin card and the head of a 15 cm nail as an impact post, along with 1–2 cm depth of Blu-tack will give small dents up to 10 mm in depth for a shallow angle ramp run of about 30–50 cm. Video analysis will be very engaging for the students, although it is likely to only produce qualitative results unless you spend considerable time setting up the tests to mimic those of the professional government crash testing agencies. The range of data that students need to collect is given on **Worksheet P2.19c** which students will also need.

You could ask students to come up with one or two further hypotheses, based on their observations in this practical.

### Plenary

On page 245 of the Student Book you will find three examples of the sort of work that students may produce for this task. The examples focus on controlling variables. You could share these with students after they have completed their own work. This will help them to understand the assessment criteria and so make it easier for them to evaluate their work and to see how they can improve it. Moderator comments on each of the Student Book extracts can be found at the end of the assessment guidance for this investigation on the CD-ROM. The examples can also be found on the **AT** document *Student examples*.

### Option 2: Running the activity as a practice controlled assessment task (PCAT)

We have provided a full range of support resources to allow the running of this practical as a practice controlled assessment task. A recommended structure is outlined below (to be used over a number of sessions). Marking guidance for all three parts of the practice task can be found on the CD-ROM that accompanies the TTPP. To save time when using these practice controlled assessment tasks, you may wish to focus on a particular aspect or skill rather than working through all three parts of the task.

#### Part A Planning

1. Students should be given the Student Brief on **Worksheet P2.19a.** They can use Part A of the Workbook that is provided to help with their practice controlled assessments. They should be given about 1 hour to do this planning.

#### Part B Observations

2. Students should be asked to carry out the practical task to collect evidence using the method they have planned in Part A. Once again, they should refer to the Student Brief on **Worksheet P2.19a**. They can use Part B of the Workbook that is provided to help pupils with their practice controlled assessments. They should be given about 1 hour to collect their primary evidence.
3. If there is a problem with their own planned method, students may be asked to follow the method set out on **Worksheet P2.19b**. This will still enable students to access the full range of marks for Part B and Part C of the practice controlled assessment task.
4. In Part B, students are required to gather some secondary evidence. The evidence can be quantitative or qualitative. It can be from a variety of sources but students must note where they found their evidence and evaluate the quality of the source as part of this task. Skills Sheet 22 provides students with further guidance on researching for and evaluating secondary evidence. This part of the task could be done outside of the lesson but must be supervised.

#### Part C Conclusions

5. Students follow the instructions set out on the Part C section of the Student Brief on **Worksheet P2.19a**. They should use their data from Part B and the secondary evidence they have collected when doing this. They can use Part C of the Workbook that is provided to help pupils with their practice controlled assessments. They should be given about 1 hour to work on their conclusions.

The **AT** includes video clips showing a group of students working through elements of this investigation with teacher support.

Practice Controlled Assessment

# P2.19 Crumple zones

How can we reduce the forces on a crashing car?

New cars are tested to see how safe they are in a crash, and are given a score. Crash test dummies are used to model the people. The dummies sometimes have different coloured paints applied to different areas to show which parts of a person's body will hit which part of the inside of the car.

A *Crash test dummies have force sensors which are linked to data logging computers.*

Cars contain many safety features, like air bags and **crumple zones**. If you look at the car in Figure A you will see that the front of the car has crumpled. The car was designed to do this. The crumpling of the metal means that the deceleration of the people in the car is less, and so there is less force on them. This means they are less likely to be injured.

B *This trolley has been set up to model crashes.*

In school, we could model crash testing. This can be filmed for analysis afterwards, or you can use sensors attached to a computer for data logging measurements like speed and force. Like the real scientists though, we could also think low-tech. Soft materials like plasticine will deform when hit, and so looking at the dents in the plasticine can show how hard it was hit.

**Your task**

You are going to plan an investigation that will allow you to find out how crumple zones can be used to reduce the forces in collisions. Your teacher will provide you with some materials to help you organise this task.

**Learning Outcomes**

**4.8** *Investigate how crumple zones can be used to reduce the forces in collisions*

## ResultsPlus Build Better Answers

When planning an investigation like this, one of the skills you will be assessed on is your ability to *control variables.* There are 6 marks available for this skill. Here are three extracts focusing on this skill. Other skills are dealt with in other lessons.

**Student extract 1 — A basic response for this skill**

I will make it a fair test. I am going to make sure the impact is at the same speed every time, using a light gate, just before it hits the block.

- The phrase 'fair test' is too general, you must 'control variables'.
- You must identify a control *variable* – something that can be measured.
- You need to say how to control this variable.

**Student extract 2 — A better response for this skill**

The total mass of the vehicle and attached crumple zone, and the collision speed must both be kept the same each time. If I start with the heaviest design of crumple zone, then for each other design, I can add a Blu-Tack weight to make it up to the same as the first one. I will check the weight is always the same using a digital balance. The slide distance for each test run will be kept constant by releasing from a marked point on the ramp each time.

- Identify as many variables as you can.
- You must explain what will be measured to control the variables, and how it will be measured. You should not just say 'use the same equipment' or similar statements.

**Student extract 3 — A good response for this skill**

The total mass of the vehicle and attached crumple zone are weighed using a balance and must be kept the same each time. If I start with the heaviest design of crumple zone, then for each other design, I can add a Blu-Tack weight to make it up to the same as the first one. The slide distance for each test run will be kept constant by releasing from a marked point on the ramp each time, so the speed is always the same at impact. Mass and velocity will affect the momentum in the collision so must be kept constant. The front end surface area of crumple zone will be kept constant, by using a ruler when building it, so that the design shape is not a factor in the crumpling force involved. The ramp angle will be maintained by keeping the top and bottom ends at the same heights each time. This will also keep the speed the same every time.

- Each variable must be identified, and then you must explain how to control it.
- You must explain *why* it is important to control the variables you suggest, as well as *how* to control them.



## ActiveTeach

- **AT** *P2.19 Crumple zones* [video]
  Students work through the investigation
- **AT** *P2.19 Moderator comments* [word document]
  Moderator comments on the video
- **AT** *P2.19 Assessment criteria* [presentation]
  Understanding the CA marking criteria
- **AT** *P2.19 Student task sheet* [word document]
  CA video checklist
- **AT** *P2.19 Specification points* [word document]
  Edexcel specification points
- **AT** *P2.19 Student examples* [word document]
  Examples for students to assess

## Assessment criteria

**Controls**

**0** No relevant controls given.

**1-2 a)** Identifies one appropriate variable that needs to be controlled.

**b)** Describes how this variable is controlled, e.g. total mass of vehicle and attached crumple zone weighed using balance and Blu-Tack™ added if necessary to ensure the same mass each time; slide distance for each test run will be kept constant by releasing from a marked point on the ramp each time; front-end surface area of crumple zone will be kept constant by cutting the crumple zone to the same dimensions on the front each time; ramp angle will be maintained by keeping the top and bottom ends of the ramp at the same heights each time.

**3-4 a)** Identifies at least 2 relevant variables.

**b)** Describes how these variables are controlled.

**5-6 a)** Identifies a range of variables appropriate to control, e.g. all of the above.

**b)** An appropriate explanation is given of why these variables are controlled, e.g. total mass of vehicle and attached crumple zone weighed using balance and Blu-Tack™ added if necessary to ensure the same mass each time, because mass will affect the momentum in the collision etc

# P2.20 Momentum and safety



This lesson explains the idea that decreasing rate of change of momentum reduces forces and the application of this to road safety. Higher Tier students are also expected to make calculations to demonstrate this.

## Specification coverage

**4.7** Demonstrate an understanding of the idea of rate of change of momentum to explain protective features including bubble wraps, seat belts, crumple zones and air bags

H **4.9** Use the equation:
force (newton, N) = change in momentum (kilogram metre per second, kg m/s) / time (second, s),
F = (*mv* – *mu*) / t, to calculate the change in momentum of a system

HSW **5** Planning to test a scientific idea, *answer a scientific question* or solve a scientific problem

There are also opportunities to cover HSW **6**, HSW **7**, HSW **8**, HSW **10**, HSW **11**, HSW **13** and HSW **14**.

## Key terms

air bag
bubble wrap
crumple zone
seat belt

### Accidents hurt

**Starter 1**

Students create a list of accidents in which people could hurt themselves. They then select those in which somebody moving at speed came to a sudden stop and attempt to order the list by increasing severity of injury. Highlight that the worst injuries come from situations with the greatest momentum being removed in the briefest times.

### Egg air bags

**Exploring 1** Prac

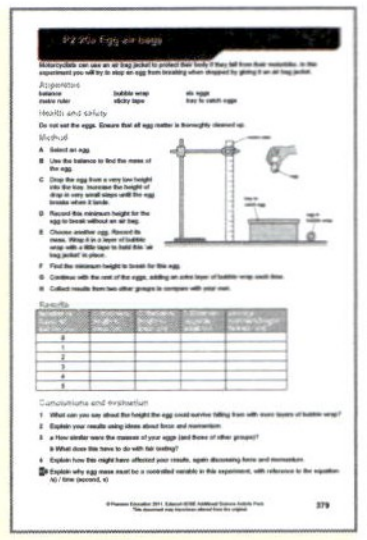

Students can use **Worksheet P2.20a**, and the experiment is also explained in the Teacher and technician practical sheet P2.20

Stretch Students plan an adapted version of the experiment in which it is possible to measure the egg's speed, and the time of collision, in order to use the equation to find the force acting on the egg.

Support Pair students for support.

### Student Book spread P2.20

**Explaining 1**

Use the Student Book to explain how air bags, seat belts and crumple zones work to reduce injuries in crashes.

Stretch Students write a list of bullet points to explain the potential problem of reckless driving caused by driver sense of security in well-protected vehicles.

Support Ask students to make a note of the safety devices shown in each image in the Student Book and how they help.

### Safety features listening cloze

**Plenary 1** AfL Lit

Pairs of students write a cloze paragraph explaining how one vehicle safety feature works. Missing words should come from a list given by the teacher. Then two pairs join together and take turns to read each other their paragraph. The listening pair decides which words fill in the blanks.

### Momentum and car safety

**Homework 1**

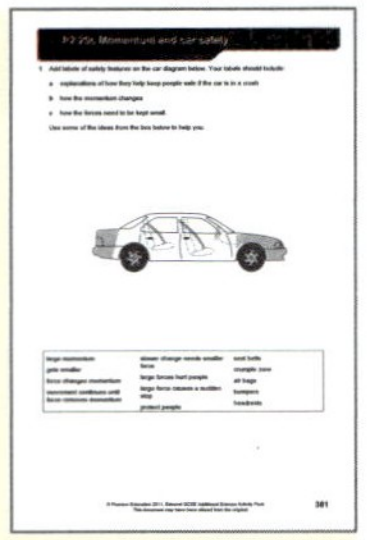

Students undertake **Worksheet P2.20c**, in which they have to identify how car safety devices reduce the forces upon passengers in an accident.

Support Give the sentence parts already connected.

### Road safety devices

**Starter 2** AfL

Ask students to sketch ideas for keeping a motorcyclist safe in a crash. This is extended by asking students to list other safety devices found in vehicles and then compare their answers with a partner. They should discuss whose sketches are likely to provide the better protection.

### Momentum changes and road safety

**Exploring 2** Prac

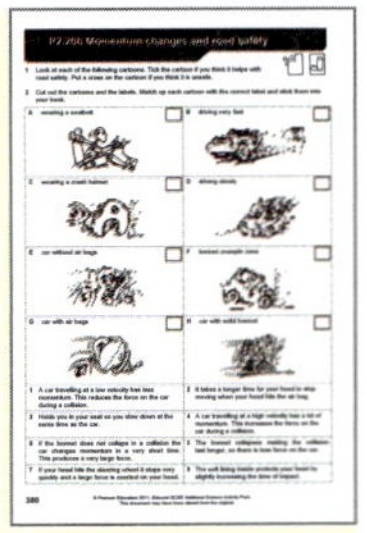

Using **Worksheet P2.20b**, students cut and stick pictures of road safety with the corresponding written explanations.

Stretch Students add an explanation of how the equation F = (mv – mu) / t could be related to each case.

Support Tell students which are the safe pictures and the safe explanations. This will make the options easier to link together.

### H Rate of change of momentum

**Explaining 2**

The **AT** spreadsheet *Rate of change of momentum* covers the equation *F* = (*mv* – *mu*) / *t*. Higher Tier students can understand this as an inverse relationship between force and time for the same momentum change.

Stretch More able students could try to work out how this links with the equation F = ma.

Support Give an example, such as a car colliding with a wall and identify what is represented by *F*, *mv*, *mu* and *t*.

### Road safety devices revisited

**Plenary 2** AfL

Recap the ideas students sketched in *Starter 2*. The student pairs should discuss which of their ideas would be most effective. They should try to provide an explanation of how (or if) each safety device does its job in terms of reducing forces by reducing rate of change of momentum.

### Forces change momentum

**Homework 2**

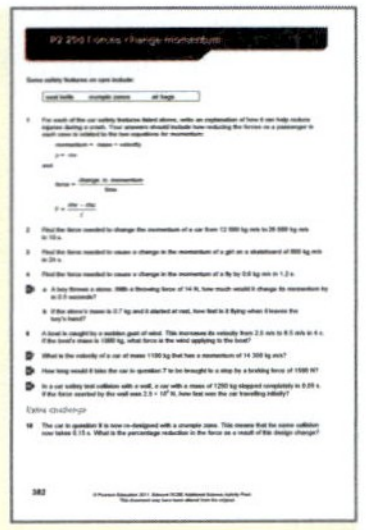

Students complete **Worksheet P2.20d**, in which they have to explain road safety features and also use the equation linking force with the rate of change in momentum.

Stretch The 'extra challenge' question pushes students to a harder mathematical level.

# P2.20 Momentum and safety

How is momentum used in the design of vehicle safety devices?

Figure A shows an internal air bag jacket for motorcyclists. It contains compressed gas. If the rider comes off the bike in an accident, a trigger releases the gas to fill the bag, protecting the rider.

A Air bags reduce the forces acting on people in collisions.

When you are travelling in a car, your body is going at the same speed as the car. If the car stops suddenly, your momentum continues to carry you forward. If your body is stopped very suddenly, by hitting the dashboard for example, the huge forces can cause very serious injury.

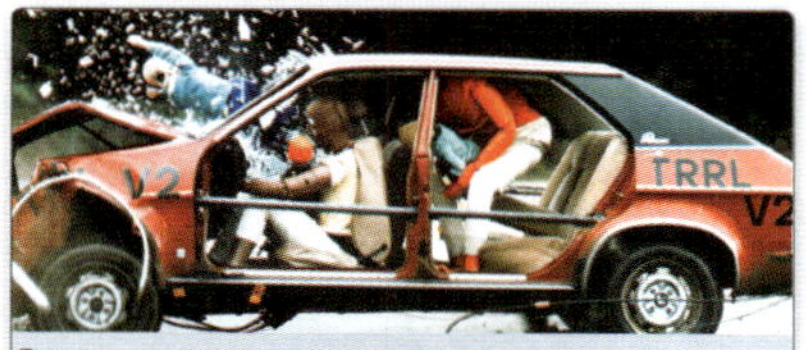


B Your momentum carries you forward in a car accident.

The faster the momentum of an object changes, the greater the force on the object. So vehicle safety measures try to reduce the rate of change of momentum to reduce the forces.

In an accident, a **seat belt** stretches. This reduces the rate of change of momentum and so reduces the force on the passenger. However, in high-speed accidents the force is so great that the seat belt itself may cause injury.

1 Why do vehicle safety measures try to reduce momentum over a long period of time?

2 Why is it more dangerous for your head to hit the car dashboard than for it to hit an air bag?

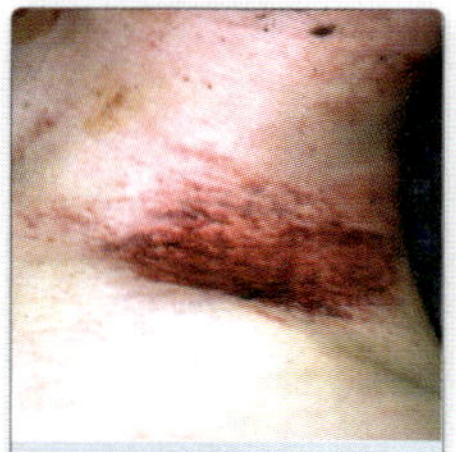

C A car seat belt injury.

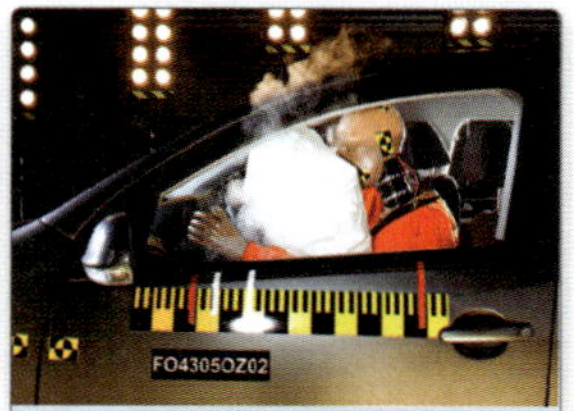

D Air bags spread the change in momentum over a longer period of time.

Cars are now fitted with **air bags**, which reduce momentum to zero more slowly and help prevent seat belt injuries. However, they only inflate at speeds of more than 10–15 mph and so do not replace seat belts.

Cars also have **crumple zones**. In an accident, the material in these crumple zones squashes and folds in a specific way to reduce the momentum of the car over a longer period of time.

E Crumple zones increase the time taken to stop a car.

3 'Bubble wrap' is plastic covering with many air bubbles. How do you think bubble wrap protects fragile items?

4 Think about an empty egg carton. How is a car crumple zone:
a similar to an egg carton
b different from an egg carton?

## Changing momentum

H

A force is needed to change the momentum of an object. The rate of change of the momentum is equal to the force applied. The force can be worked out using this equation:

force (newton, N) = rate of change of momentum = $\frac{\text{change in momentum (kilogram metre per second, kg m/s)}}{\text{time taken for the change (second, s)}}$

$$F = \frac{mv - mu}{t}$$

Here, $u$ is the initial velocity and $v$ is the final velocity, so $mv - mu$ is the change in momentum.

**e.g.** What is the force needed to change a cyclist's momentum by 24 kg m/s in 4 seconds?

$$F = \frac{\text{change in momentum}}{\text{time}} = \frac{24}{4} = 6\text{ N}$$

H 5 Calculate the following:
a What is the force needed to change a car's momentum by 3000 kg m/s in 5 seconds?
b The momentum of a boat changes from 120 kg m/s to 320 kg m/s in 5 seconds. What is the rate of change of momentum? What is the force needed?

H 6 A 75 kg man starts a sprint race. He increases his velocity from rest to 6 m/s using a force of 200 N. How long did it take him to reach 6 m/s?

7 List three vehicle safety devices. For each one write a brief explanation of how it can reduce injuries in a traffic accident.

### Skills spotlight

Scientists need to be able to plan tests for new devices to show how they will perform. Write a plan for an experiment to find out how many layers of bubble wrap are needed to protect an egg when dropped from a fixed height.

### Maths skills

H **To change the subject of a formula**, carry out the same operations on both sides of the equals sign until the subject is on it's own on one side of the equals sign.

E.g. To make $v$ the subject of $F = \frac{mv - mu}{t}$ you can:

1. multiply both sides by $t$ so $Ft = mv - mu$
2. add $mu$ to both sides so $Ft + mu = mv$
3. divide both sides by $m$ so

$$v = \frac{Ft + mu}{m} \text{ or } v = \frac{Ft}{m} + u$$

### Learning Outcomes

4.7 Demonstrate an understanding of the idea of rate of change of momentum to explain protective features including bubble wraps, seat belts, crumple zones and air bags

H 4.9 Use the equation:
force (newton, N) = change in momentum (kilogram metre per second, kg m/s) / time (second, s)
$F = (mv - mu) / t$
to calculate the change in momentum of a system, as in 4.6

HSW 5 Plan to test a scientific idea, answer a scientific question, or solve a scientific problem by controlling relevant variables





## ActiveTeach

- **AT** *Crash tests*
  [BBC video]
  News report on crash testing
- **AT** *Air bags*
  [BBC video]
  News report on car external air bags
- **AT** *Features that provide protection*
  [interactive]
  Safety, protection, survival – quiz
- **AT** *Car safety*
  [spreadsheet]
  Drag and drop
- **AT** *Momentum*
  [word document]
  Rate of change calculations

## Answers | Student Book

1 This reduces the forces involved. Lower force means lesser injury.

2 On impact, the air bag squashes, reducing the rate of change of momentum and so reducing the force on your head. If your head hits the dashboard it will stop suddenly, reducing the momentum very quickly and so causing your head to connect with great force.

3 On impact, the bubbles squash slowly, reducing the rate of change of momentum, and so reducing the force on the object being protected.

4 **a** They both squash to reduce the rate of change of momentum, protecting the contents.
**b** The car has designed failure points so it crushes in a designed way.

5 H **a** 600 N
**b** 40 kg m/s/s; 40 N

6 H 2.25 s

7 A good answer will contain the following points: crumple zone reduces a car's momentum more slowly; this means less force; Air bag reduces a passenger's momentum more slowly; this means less force; Seat belt reduces a passenger's momentum more slowly; this means less force; Less force means lesser injuries.

**Skills spotlight**

Variables to be measured: **Independent**: number of layers of bubble wrap; **Dependent**: damage suffered by egg; **Control variables**: drop height, egg mass, uniformity of wrapping, landing surface. Students use method similar to **Worksheet P2.20a** as in *Exploring 1*.

# P2.21 Work and power



This lesson explains the mathematics of calculating work and power. It also takes Higher Tier students through the idea that braking distance for a vehicle is proportional to the square of the vehicle's initial velocity.

## Specification coverage

***4.10*** Use the equation: work done (joule, J) = force (newton, N) × distance moved in the direction of the force (metre, m); *E* = *F* × *d*

***4.11*** Demonstrate an understanding that energy transferred (joule, J) is equal to work done (joule, J)

***4.12*** Recall that power is the rate of doing work and is measured in watts, W

***4.13*** Use the equation: power (watt, W) = work done (joule, J) / time taken (second, s); *P* = *E* / *t*

***4.14*** Recall that one watt is equal to one joule per second, J/s

H ***4.18*** Carry out calculations on work done to show the dependence of braking distance for a vehicle on initial velocity squared (work done to bring a vehicle to rest equals its initial kinetic energy)

HSW ***10*** Using both qualitative and quantitative approaches

There are also opportunities to cover HSW ***11***.

### Do we know anything already?

**Starter 1** AfL

In small groups, students should write down any equations or definitions they already know about forces and/or energy and their units. The group should classify their ideas into two lists: 'definitely correct' and 'hopefully correct but we're not 100% certain'. Save these lists of ideas for review in Plenary 2.

### Human work and power

**Exploring 1** Prac

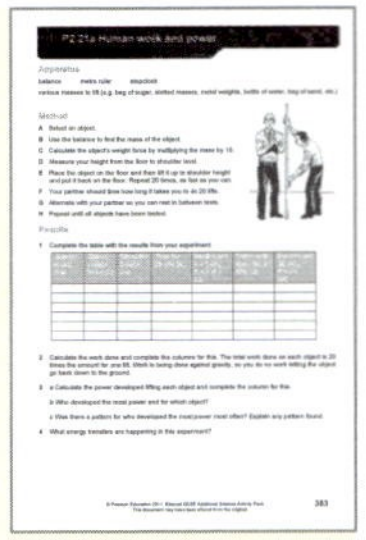

Students can use **Worksheet P2.21a**, and the experiment is also explained on the Teacher and technician planning sheet P2.21.

**Stretch** Ask students to explain areas in which the energy used by the body has not been accounted for in the measurements taken.

**Support** Take students through the calculations one by one.

### Student Book spread P2.21

**Explaining 1**

Explain the idea of work done being a technical phrase for energy transferred. Then extend this to cover the mathematics of calculating work.

**Stretch** Students should try to show how the equations for work and power could be combined into one equation that gives the power to overcome a constant force if something travels at constant velocity.

**Support** Students needing more support could write out the question and the equation for that section.

### Calculations cut up

**Plenary 1** AfL

Each student makes up a complete numerical example calculation for work and another for power. The numbers should be written large and separately on a piece of rough paper, with their quantity, symbol and units. Each quantity is then cut out separately and they are mixed up. Then one group's cut-up equations are given to another group to reassemble and to comment on any mistakes.

### So much work

**Homework 1**

Students undertake **Worksheet P2.21c** in which they practise calculations on work and power.

**Support** Students could go through the sheet and colour/highlight each question to match parts of the equations with numbers in the questions.

### Everyday 'work' and 'power'

**Starter 2** Lit

Ask students to write two sentences in which they use the word 'work', two sentences in which they use the word 'power', and a final sentence including both words. Discuss the definitions of the words in the contexts used. Proceed to offer the scientific definitions of each, especially emphasising the idea that 'work done = energy transferred'.

### Warehouse work

**Exploring 2** Prac

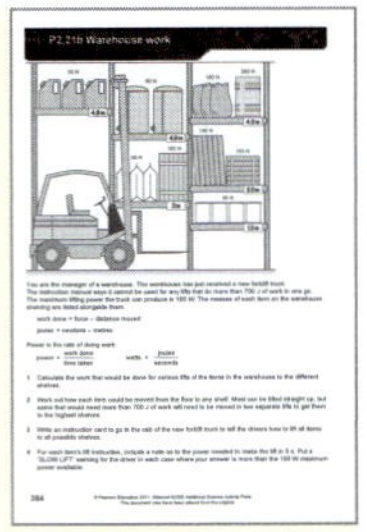

Students undertake **Worksheet P2.21b** in which they have to calculate values of work and power in the context of a forklift truck lifting weights.

**Stretch** Students calculate what lifting power the forklift truck would need to produce, to avoid having any 'SLOW LIFT' warnings.

**Support** Take students through some example calculations until they can continue alone.

### Work and power

**Explaining 2**

The **AT** spreadsheet *Work and power* covers the equations for work and power. H The spreadsheet has a Higher Tier extension that includes calculations of braking distances from speeds (and kinetic energies).

**Stretch** More able students could work out the spreadsheet cell formulae for each column.

**Support** Students needing more support could be taken through the calculations step by step with a calculator and then shown that this concurs with the spreadsheet outcome. Highlight that this result is because both used the same equations.

### Do we know anything now?

**Plenary 2** AfL

Revisit the ideas generated in Starter 1. The groups should now be able to confirm the accuracy of the equations and definitions they first came up with, and correct those that were wrong. They should also now add any ideas that they have learned from this section.

### Work and power and work to stop cars

**Homework 2**

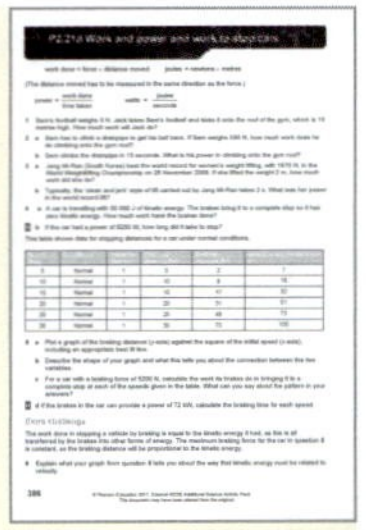

Students complete **Worksheet P2.21d** to practise calculations on work and power. They then plot graphs of stopping distance against speed squared to see the relationship.

**Stretch** The 'extra challenge' question leads on to allow students to establish that kinetic energy is proportional to velocity squared.

# P2.21 Work and power

What do we mean by power?

Motorbike licences have different categories depending on the power the engine can produce.

A Motorbikes have different power outputs.

1 Give the scientific meaning for 'work done'.

2 How much work is done when:
a motorbike brakes change 2000 joules of kinetic energy into thermal energy.
b a car crumple zone in a crash changes 5000 J of kinetic energy into 4500 J of thermal energy and 500 J of sound energy?

3 Calculate the work done when:
a a weightlifter lifts a 280 N barbell weight 1.5 m straight up
b a boy cycles 760 m against friction forces of 140 N
c a crane raises a box with a weight of 1200 N upwards 4 m.

**ResultsPlus Watch Out!**

Students sometimes use the wrong distance in work calculations. Remember, you must measure the distance moved *in the direction of the force.*

## The physics meaning of 'work'

**Work** is done when energy is transferred from one form to another.

Work is an amount of **energy transferred** so it is measured in **joules (J)**. The amount of work done is equal to the amount of energy transferred.

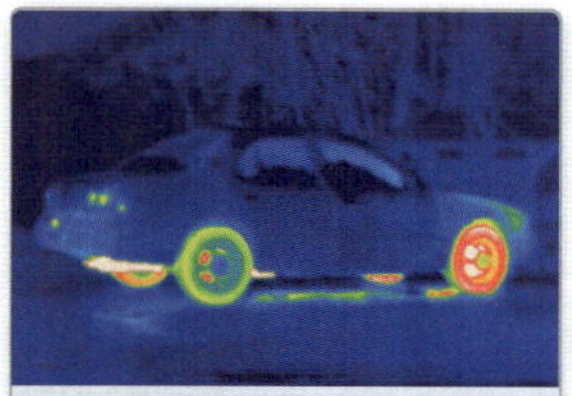

B Car brakes 'do work' by transferring kinetic energy to thermal energy (heat). Work can be done in many different ways.

C Work done in sailing

## Calculating work

work done = force × distance moved (in the direction of the force)

$E = F \times d$

(joules, J) = (newtons, N) × (metres, m)

**e.g.** A sailor lifts a 300 N sail from the deck to a height 4 m up. How much work does the sailor do?

work done = force × distance moved (in the direction of the force)

$E = F \times d$

$E = 300 \times 4$

$E = 1200$ joules

## Power

**Power** is the rate of doing work. It is measured in **watts (W)**. 1 watt means 1 joule of work done per second.

$$\text{power (watt, W)} = \frac{\text{work done (joule, J)}}{\text{time taken (second, s)}}$$

$$P = \frac{E}{t}$$

**e.g.** A motorbike engine increases the bike's **kinetic energy** over 40 m, using a force of 6000 N. It takes 5 seconds to do this. What power did the engine provide?

$E = F \times d = 6000 \times 40 = 240\,000\text{ J}$

$P = \frac{\text{work done}}{\text{time taken}} = \frac{E}{t} = \frac{240\,000}{5} = 48\,000\text{ W}$

4 From question 3, calculate the power in each case if the times taken were:
a 2 seconds
b 400 s
c 8 s.

5 Explain why the breaking distance is greater for a greater speed.

## Braking distances and work (H)

The work done stopping a vehicle is the braking force multiplied by the braking distance. When stopped, all of the vehicle's kinetic energy has been removed. So, the work done is equal to the initial kinetic energy.

(H) 6 In each of four braking tests, a car brakes with a force of 5000 N. In the first test the car has an initial velocity of 5 m/s, and initial kinetic energy of 12 500 J. It brakes in 2.5 m. In the next test, the car goes twice as fast and initially has 50 000 J of kinetic energy. In the next test, the car has an initial velocity of 15 m/s and an initial kinetic energy of 112 500 J. In the last test, the car has an initial velocity of 20 m/s and braking distance of 40 m. Present the data for the tests as a table, clearly showing the initial velocity and kinetic energy, the work done, the braking force and the braking distance for each test.

7 Brakes that overheat can fail. Write a short leaflet for a company that makes brake parts, to tell people why brakes get hot and why braking more suddenly might make them get even hotter.

**Skills spotlight**

Power outputs are sometimes compared using figures (quantitatively) and sometimes just ranked in order (qualitatively). Suggest one situation in which each type of comparison would be more appropriate than the other.

**Learning Outcomes**

4.10 Use the equation:
work done (joule, J) = force (newton, N) × distance moved in the direction of the force (metre, m) $E = F \times d$

4.11 Demonstrate an understanding that energy transferred (joule, J) = work done (joule, J)

4.12 Recall that power is the rate of doing work and is measured in watts, W

4.13 Use the equation:
power (watt, W) = work done (joule, J) / time taken (second, s) $P = E / t$

4.14 Recall that one watt is equal to one joule per second, J/s

(H) 4.18 Carry out calculations on work done to show the dependence of braking distance for a vehicle on initial velocity squared (work done to bring a vehicle to rest equals its initial kinetic energy)

HSW 10 Use qualitative and quantitative approaches when presenting scientific ideas and arguments, and recording observations





**ActiveTeach**

- **AT** *Watts the power* [interactive]
  Power, work and energy – quiz
- **AT** *Is that what you call work?* [interactive]
  Work and energy – true-or-false quiz
- **AT** *Work and power* [spreadsheet]
  Calculating work and power

## Key terms

energy transfered
kinetic energy
joule (J)
watt (W)
work

## Answers | Student Book

1 Amount of energy transferred

2 **a** 2000 joules **b** 5000 J

3 **a** 420 J **b** 106 400 J **c** 4800 J

4 **a** 210 W **b** 266 W **c** 600 W

5 At higher speeds a car has more kinetic energy. The brakes have to do more work to remove all of this kinetic energy. The maximum braking force is constant, so the time taken must be greater if the work done is greater.

6 (H)

| Initial velocity (m/s) | Initial kinetic energy (J) | Work done to stop (J) | Braking force (N) | Braking distance (m) |
|---|---|---|---|---|
| 5 | 12 500 | 12 500 | 5000 | 2.5 |
| 10 | 50 000 | 50 000 | 5000 | 10 |
| 15 | 112 500 | 112 500 | 5000 | 22.5 |
| 20 | 200 000 | 200 000 | 5000 | 40 |

7 A good answer will contain the following points:
- Braking changes kinetic energy into heat; if you brake hard, so that this heat is generated faster than the brakes can cool, they will get hot; heat can damage the brakes; so if they overheat the brakes may fail; braking more suddenly uses more force; braking more suddenly generates heat more quickly; so brakes are less likely to cool quickly enough; this makes them more likely to overheat and fail.

**Skills spotlight**

Example answers: If the amount of energy used was an important cost factor, then the appropriate power could be chosen using the quantitative information. If only certain machines are available, then knowing which are more or less powerful will allow an appropriate change of machine when one is found to be lacking.

# P2.22 Potential and kinetic energy



This section explains the mathematics of calculating gravitational potential energy and kinetic energy. It also reinforces the P1 concept of the conservation of energy during transfers.

## Specification coverage

**4.15** Use the equation: gravitational potential energy (joule, J) = mass (kilogram, kg) × gravitational field strength (newton per kilogram, N/kg) × vertical height (metre, m); GPE = $m \times g \times h$

**4.16** Use the equation: kinetic energy (joule, J) = ½ × mass (kilogram, kg) × velocity² (metre/second)², (m/s)²); $KE = ½ \times m \times v^2$

**4.17** Demonstrate an understanding of the idea of conservation of energy in various energy transfers

**HSW** *11* Presenting information, developing an argument and drawing a conclusion, using scientific, technical and mathematical language, conventions and symbols, and ICT tools

There are also opportunities to cover **HSW** *10*.

## Key terms

gravitational potential energy
kinetic energy

### Energy of falling

**Starter 1**

Show students something falling and ask what sort of energy it has as it falls. Then ask where did this energy come from? Lead on to the idea of gravitational potential energy (GPE) as a store of energy by virtue of height above the ground. Recap the idea of conservation of energy and how it might apply here.

### The car catapult (AT)

**Exploring 1** **Prac**

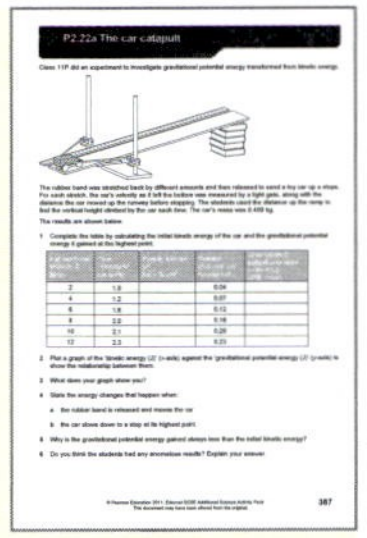

**Worksheet P2.22a** provides results from an experiment in which a toy car was launched up a ramp at varying speeds.

**Stretch** More able students could be asked to explain why the gradient of the graph is less than 1.

**Support** The **AT** spreadsheet *Calculating GPE and KE* could be used to help students needing more support.

### Student Book spread P2.21

**Explaining 1**

Use the text and diagrams in the Student Book to explain the transfers of GPE into KE and vice versa.

**Stretch** Students could be challenged to work out a formula for finding the velocity, v, of an object as it lands from a fall from a height, h.

**Support** In answering questions, students needing more support should lay out the calculations in a step by step manner.

### GPE and KE calculations all mixed up (AT)

**Plenary 1** **Lit**

The **AT** presentation *Mixed up equations* has the bits of the equations for KE and GPE mixed up. Clicking through the presentation sorts them out into the two equations, with units shown. There is then a drag and drop version of the same thing, which can be used to test the students.

### Sports day energy transfers

**Homework 1**

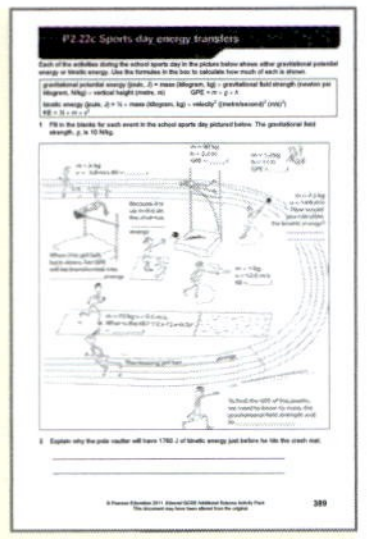

Students undertake **Worksheet P2.22c** in which they explain energy transfers and conservation, and practise calculations of GPE and KE.

**Support** Students could go through the sheet and colour/highlight each calculation to match parts of the equations with numbers in the questions.

### Energy transfers recap

**Starter 2** **AfL**

Ask students to write a list of the nine forms of energy. Then show students a variety of everyday objects (e.g. computer, radio, kettle) and ask them to write down the energy transfers that happen for each. Recap the idea of conservation of energy and how it might apply to each device.

### Mars Rover energy transfers

**Exploring 2**

Students work through the cut and paste **Worksheet P2.22b**.

**Stretch** Students extend their energy transfers to identify useful and wasted forms of energy.

**Support** Tell students which energy forms are needed for each technology and they then simply order them.

### GPE converting to KE (AT)

**Explaining 2** **Demo**

Demonstrate an object falling and measure the speed on landing for different heights of drop. Then lead the class through calculations of GPE before and KE afterwards and see that the two are equivalent.

**Stretch** More able students could set up a spreadsheet to undertake the calculations for them.

**Support** Students needing more support could use the **AT** spreadsheet *Calculating GPE and KE*.

### Equation nonsensequences

**Plenary 2** **Lit**

This exercise reinforces the structure of the equations for GPE and KE. See the TTPP for further information. The process can be made more entertaining if at the very start, a student writes a situation, such as 'cat in a tree', and folds over and passes on to the energy value writer.

### Sports day energy calculations

**Homework 2**

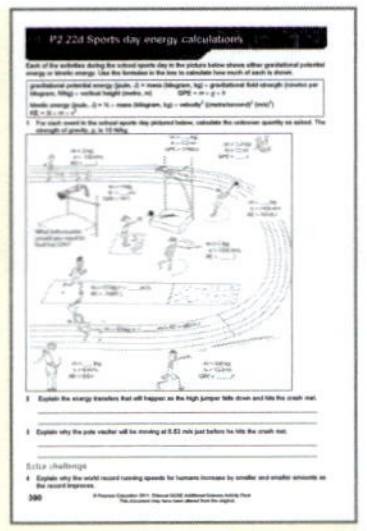

Students undertake **Worksheet P2.22d** in which they practise *calculations of GPE and KE*, including re-arrangement of the equations and the idea of energy conservation.

**Stretch** Students answer the 'extra challenge' question on the worksheet.

# P2.22 Potential and kinetic energy

How are kinetic and gravitational potential energies calculated?

When NASA deliberately crash landed the Rover Exploration Missions on Mars, they were travelling very fast. The delicate instruments were protected using air bags.

A The Mars Exploration Rover's gravitational potential energy was transferred into kinetic energy so it landed at high speed.

B Testing the Mars Rover air bag system involved giving it gravitational potential energy by lifting it with a crane.

## Gravitational potential energy

**Gravitational potential energy** is energy that is stored because of an object's position in a gravitational field. Essentially, on Earth if something can fall it has gravitational potential energy. It can be calculated using this equation:

gravitational potential energy (joule, J) = mass (kilogram, kg) × gravitational field strength (newton per kilogram, N/kg) × vertical height (metre, m)

$GPE = m \times g \times h$

On Earth, the strength of the gravitational field is 10 N/kg.

**e.g.** What is the gravitational potential energy gained by a 500 kg Mars Rover when it is lifted 15 m by a test crane on Earth?

$GPE = m \times g \times h$

$= 500 \times 10 \times 15 = 75000\text{ J}$

1 Calculate the gravitational potential energy of the following:
a A 2 kg toy robot dog jumps up 1 metre.
b A lift has a mass of 400 kg and rises 24 m.
c The Mars Exploration Rover, 15 m above the surface of Mars, where the gravitational field strength is 4 N/kg.

## Kinetic energy

**Kinetic energy** is the scientific name for movement energy. We can calculate the kinetic energy an object has using the equation:

Kinetic energy (joule, J) = ½ × mass (kilogram, kg) × (velocity)² (metre/second)², (m/s)²

$KE = \frac{1}{2} \times m \times v^2$

**e.g.** What is the kinetic energy of a 65 kg girl running at 6 m/s?

$KE = \frac{1}{2} \times m \times v^2$

$= \frac{1}{2} \times 65 \times 6^2 = \frac{1}{2} \times 65 \times 36$

$= 1170\text{ J}$

**ResultsPlus Watch Out!**

Students often forget to square the velocity in kinetic energy calculations.

## Conservation of energy

When energy is transferred, the total amount always remains the same. So when an object with gravitational potential energy falls down, the amount of kinetic energy it has at the instant of hitting the ground is equal to its initial gravitational potential energy.

For example, when the Mars Exploration Rover was dropped in the test shown in Figure B, the 75 000 joules of gravitational potential energy were all transferred to kinetic energy by the time it hit the ground.

**e.g.** How fast did the Mars Exploration Rover land in its air bag test?

$KE = 75000\text{ J} = \frac{1}{2} \times m \times v^2$

$= \frac{1}{2} \times 500 \times v^2$

$v^2 = \frac{75000}{(\frac{1}{2} \times 500)} = \frac{75000}{250} = 300$

$v = \sqrt{300} = 17.3\text{ m/s}$

### Braking distances (H)

We have seen that the braking distance for a car is much greater if its speed is faster. This is because the maximum braking force is constant for any given vehicle, but the amount of kinetic energy to be removed goes up with the square of the speed, since $KE = \frac{1}{2}mv^2$.

C This car's kinetic energy was changed suddenly into other forms of energy.

5 Why do brakes get hot when a car slows down?

6 How can a landing spacecraft's gravitational potential energy be calculated? How would its kinetic energy be calculated? Explain the energy transfers that happen.

2 Calculate the kinetic energy of the following:
a A 2 kg toy robot dog walks at 2 m/s.
b A boy on a bike rides at 8 m/s. The mass of the boy and his bike is 70 kg.
c A whale swims at 7 m/s. The whale's mass is 4000 kg.

(H) 3 The whale squirts 25 kg of water into the air with 1250 J of kinetic energy. How fast is the water moving initially?

(H) 4 A 55 kg girl jumps upwards at 2 m/s. If all her kinetic energy is transferred to gravitational potential energy, how high did she jump?

**Skills spotlight**

To store gravitational potential energy, we have to do work. Note down the equations for work done and for gravitational potential energy and write an explanation of why equations are useful to scientists.

**Learning Outcomes**

4.15 Use the equation:
gravitational potential energy (joule, J) = mass (kilogram, kg) × gravitational field strength (newton per kilogram, N/kg) × vertical height (metre, m)
$GPE = m \times g \times h$

4.16 Use the equation:
kinetic energy (joule, J) = ½ × mass (kilogram, kg) × velocity² ((metre/second)², (m/s)²)
$KE = \frac{1}{2} \times m \times v^2$

4.17 Demonstrate an understanding of the idea of conservation of energy in various energy transfers

(H) 4.18 Carry out calculations on work done to show the dependence of braking distance for a vehicle on initial velocity squared (work done to bring a vehicle to rest equals its initial kinetic energy)

HSW 11 Present information using scientific conventions and symbols





## ActiveTeach

- **AT** *Energy roller coaster* [video]
  Energy transfers: roller-coaster
- **AT** *Riding the water chute: transfer* [video]
  Energy transfers: water chute
- **AT** *Energy calculations* [interactive]
  Potential and kinetic energy – quiz
- **AT** *Calculating GPE and KE* [spreadsheet]
  Using equations
- **AT** *Mixed up equations* [presentation]
  GPE and KE equations

## Answers | Student Book

1 a 20 J
b 96 000 J
c 30 000 J

2 a 4 J
b 2240 J
c 98 000 J

3 (H) 10 m/s

4 (H) 0.2 m

5 The kinetic energy is converted into heat.

6 A good answer will contain the following points:
- GPE = mass × height × gravitational field strength
- so need to know m, g and h
- this is transferred into KE as it falls
- because h (and hence GPE) is reducing
- KE = ½ × mass × (velocity)²
- so need to know m and v.

**Skills spotlight**
- Work = force × distance
- GPE = mass × gravitational field strength × height
- Equations allow scientists to make quantitative statements.
- This allows design to be informed by a need to use specific numerical values.
- For example, lifting against gravity is doing work, so F × d = m × g × h
- So F = m × g
- So a crane would need to be designed to provide a force equal to the weight of anything it needs to be able to lift.

# P2.23 Isotopes

This lesson introduces the shorthand notation $^{14}_{6}C$ for representing elements and then goes on to discuss isotopes.

## Specification coverage

**5.1** Describe the structure of nuclei of isotopes using the terms atomic (proton) number and mass (nucleon) number and using symbols in the format

**HSW 11** Presenting information, *developing an argument and drawing a conclusion*, using scientific, *technical and mathematical language*, conventions and symbols, and *ICT tools*

There are also opportunities to cover **HSW 3** and **9**.

## Key terms

atomic number
isotope
mass number
nucleon
nucleon number
proton number
sub-atomic particle

### Parts of the atom

**Starter 1** Lit

Write the words 'protons', 'neutrons' and 'mass number' on the board. Ask students to work in pairs to write a sentence connecting all three words. Then ask students to put up their hands to show how confident they are that their sentence is correct (sure, unsure, don't know).

### Find the isotopes

**Exploring 1** Prac

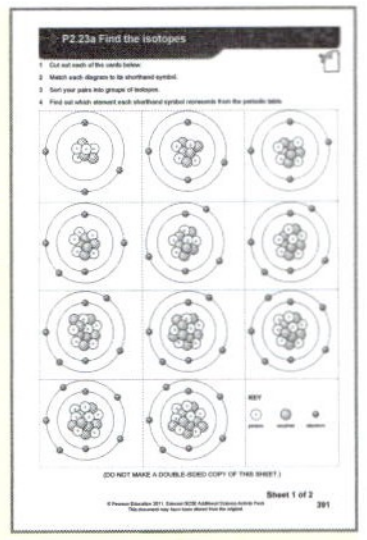

Students use the cards on **Worksheet P2.23a**.

**Stretch** Only give students the first page of **Worksheet 2.23a** and ask them to write the shorthand for each isotope shown in the diagrams. Students should ignore instruction 2 on the sheet.

**Support** Change the X to Be, B, C and N as appropriate.

### Atomic nuclei

**Exploring 3**

Ask students to make models of atomic nuclei. As a class activity students could produce a diorama.

**Stretch** Ask students to make models of at least two nuclei, which should be isotopes of the same element.

**Support** Tell students that they will be making models of simple atoms such as lithium-6 or lithium-7 and tell them how many protons and neutrons they need for each nucleus.

### Isotope display

**Plenary 1** AfL

Ask students to plan a design for an open-day display to show what an isotope is, using a model. They can use whatever equipment they like in their models.

### Isotopes

**Homework 1**

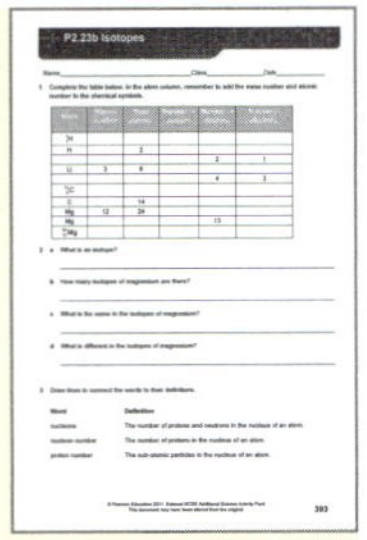

**Worksheet P2.23b** gives students practice in writing elements using the shorthand form and reinforces the similarities and differences between isotopes.

**Support** Fill in at least one more cell in each row of the table before giving the worksheet to students.

### Model of an atom

**Starter 2**

Ask students to use themselves to make a model of an atom. Ask students what the various parts are and ask them for a fact about each of them.

### Are they isotopes? (AT)

**Exploring 2**

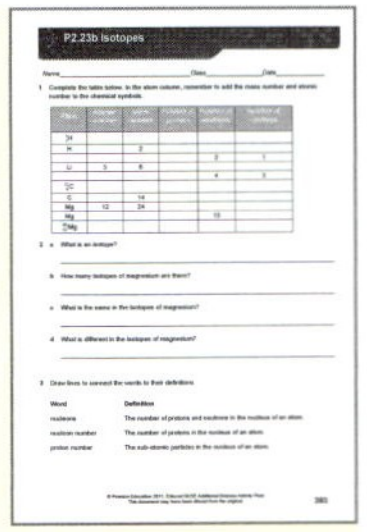

Using **AT** document *Are they isotopes?* students match isotopes in the format $^{14}_{6}C$ with diagrams showing the protons and neutrons in different nuclei. Students could also use the **AT** spreadsheet *Atomic masses and numbers*, which contains data on the mass numbers and atomic numbers of different atoms.

**Stretch** Increase the number of nuclei you show to students and include at least two isotopes.

**Support** Remove the unmatched nuclei.

### Student Book spread P2.23

**Explaining 1**

It is assumed that students will already have covered atomic structure. Students can do the Skills spotlight activity in the Student Book.

**Stretch** Give students examples of an object to represent a nucleus and ask them what could represent the atom and vice versa.

**Support** Explain that there are conventions to show what's in the nuclei of atoms.

### Isotopes true/false

**Plenary 2** AfL Lit

Students work in small groups to write a set of five statements about what they have learned in the lesson about isotopes. Three of the statements are to contain errors. They then swap statements with another group to identify the incorrect statements and write correct versions.

### Are they isotopes?

**Homework 2**

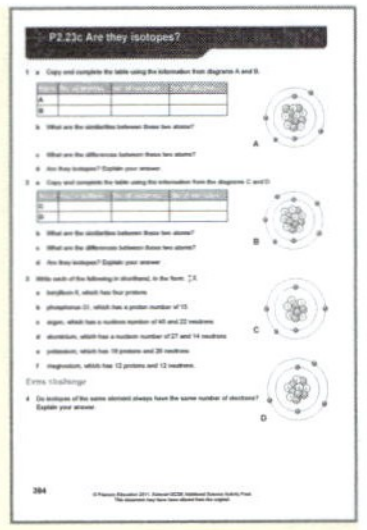

**Worksheet P2.23c** contains questions that require students to demonstrate their understanding of the terms isotope, nucleon number and proton number.

**Stretch** Ask students to do the 'extra challenge' question.

# P2.23 Isotopes

What is an isotope?

During missions to the Moon in the 1960s and 1970s, 381 kg of Moon rocks and soil were brought back to Earth. Scientists can find the ages of these rocks by comparing different types of atoms (called isotopes) in the rocks.

A *This piece of moon rock is 3.9 billion years old.*

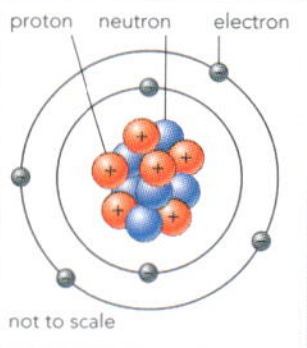


B *The structure of an atom*

Atoms contain electrons, protons and neutrons, which are called **sub-atomic particles**. Protons and neutrons are in the nucleus and electrons surround the nucleus. The particles found in the nucleus are called **nucleons**.

All atoms of a particular element have the same number of protons. This number is called the **atomic number** or **proton number** of the element. Atoms of different elements have different numbers of protons and so have different atomic numbers.

The number of neutrons in an atom can vary. The **mass number** or **nucleon number** is the total number of protons and neutrons in the nucleus.

We can represent the atomic number and mass number of an element in symbol form, as shown in Figure C.

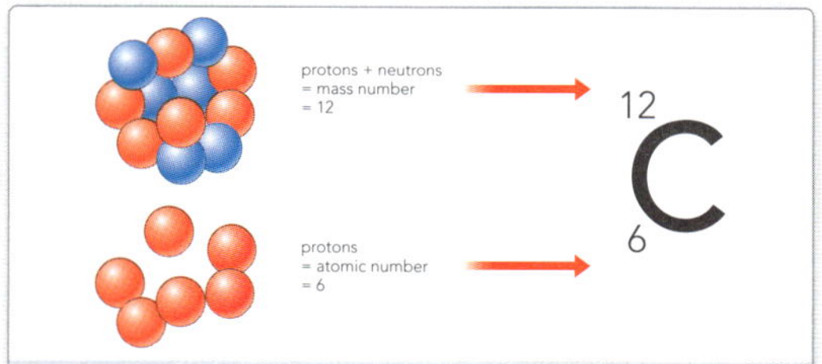


C *The symbol for carbon-12*

1 What does the atomic number of an element tell you?

2 What does the mass number of an element tell you?

3 A helium nucleus has 2 protons and 2 neutrons. Write down the symbol for the helium nucleus, showing the atomic number and mass number.

4 The symbol for a beryllium nucleus is $^{9}_{4}Be$. How many of the following particles does it contain?
a protons
b neutrons

e.g. For example, an atom of sodium (Na) has 11 protons and 12 neutrons. Its mass number is 11 + 12 = 23. We can show its nucleus as $^{23}_{11}Na$.

## Isotopes

Two atoms of the same element will always have the same atomic number. However, they can have different mass numbers if they contain different numbers of neutrons. Atoms of a single element that have different numbers of neutrons are called **isotopes**.

For example, atoms of lithium can exist as both lithium-6 and lithium-7. A number attached to an element's name shows we are referring to a particular isotope. The number is the mass number of the isotope. The nucleus of an atom of lithium-6 has three protons and three neutrons, so its mass number is 3 + 3 = 6. The nucleus of an atom of lithium-7 has three protons and four neutrons, so its mass number is 3 + 4 = 7.

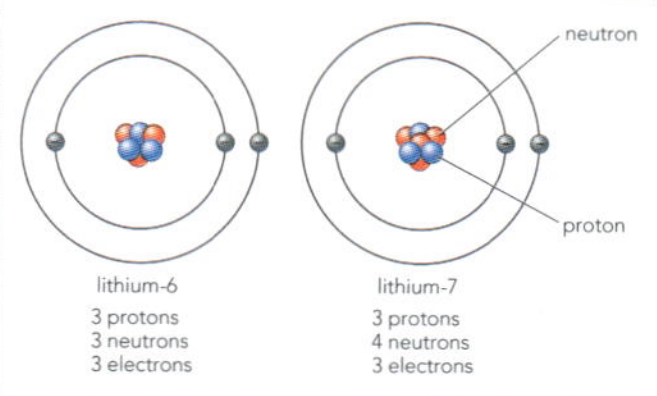


D *Isotopes of lithium. Atoms have the same number of electrons as protons, so these isotopes both have 3 electrons.*

5 For each of the nuclei shown in Figure E:
a work out its atomic number b look up its name using the periodic table in Appendix A. (The periodic table does not show the information in the same form as is used on this page, so take care when identifying the atomic number in the table.)
c write out its symbol (in the form show in Figure C).

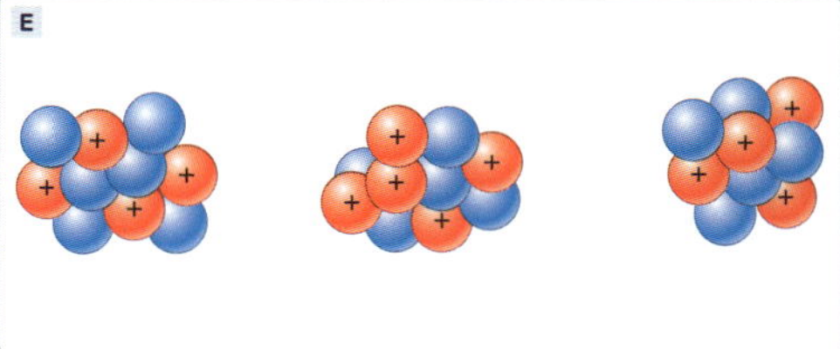

E

6 An atom of fluorine has 9 protons and 10 neutrons. Write down the symbol for a fluorine nucleus, showing the atomic number and nucleon number.

7 Sam says that as two different atoms have the same mass number, they must be isotopes. Is Sam correct? Explain your answer.

8 Hydrogen has three isotopes, hydrogen-1, hydrogen-2 and hydrogen-3. Explain what an isotope is and the similarities and differences between these three isotopes.

**Skills spotlight**

Scientists often use shortened ways of writing things down. Suggest why it is important that all scientists agree on the same symbols and conventions.

**ResultsPlus Watch Out!**

Students often get the mass numbers and atomic numbers muddled in exams. Remember that the *mass* number is *more* than the atomic number.

**Learning Outcomes**

5.1 Describe the structure of nuclei of isotopes using the terms atomic (proton) number and mass (nucleon) number and using symbols in the format $^{14}_{6}C$

HSW 11 Present information using scientific conventions and symbols





## ActiveTeach

- **AT** *What's in an atom?* [interactive]
  Atomic structure – quiz
- **AT** *Understanding isotopes* [interactive]
  Isotope structures – matching activity
- **AT** *Are they isotopes?* [word document]
  Matching isotope pairs
- **AT** *Atomic masses and numbers* [spreadsheet]
  Calculating neutron numbers
- **AT** *Carbon-12* [diagram]
  Figure C – diagram labelling activity
- **AT** *Isotopes of lithium* [diagram]
  Figure D – diagram labelling activity

## Answers | Student Book

1 The number of protons in the nucleus

2 The total number of protons and neutrons

3 $^{4}_{2}He$

4 **a** 4 protons
**b** 5 neutrons

5 **a** 4, 5 and 4
**b** Beryllium and boron
**c** $^{10}_{4}Be$, $^{10}_{5}Be$ and $^{9}_{4}Be$

6 $^{19}_{9}F$

7 No, isotopes have the same number of protons but different numbers of neutrons so they actually have different mass numbers.

8 A good answer will contain the following points:
- isotopes contain the same number of protons but different numbers of neutrons – they have the same atomic number
- all three isotopes of hydrogen contain one proton
- hydrogen-1 does not contain any neutrons
- hydrogen-2 contains one neutron
- hydrogen-3 contains two neutrons.

**Skills spotlight**

Sensible suggestions such as: so that these do not depened on the language spoken by the scientist: so that any scientist will understand the shortened way.

# P2.24 Ionising radiation

This lesson introduces ionisation and the three types of ionising radiation.

## Specification coverage

***5.2*** Explain how atoms may gain or lose electrons to form ions

***5.3*** Recall that alpha and beta particles and gamma rays are ionising radiations emitted from unstable nuclei in a random process

***5.4*** Recall that an alpha particle is equivalent to a helium nucleus, a beta particle is an electron emitted from the nucleus and a gamma ray is electromagnetic radiation

***5.5*** Compare alpha, beta and gamma radiations in terms of their abilities to penetrate and ionise

HSW *3* Many phenomena can be explained by *developing and* using scientific theories, *models and* ideas

There are also opportunities to cover HSW *1, 2, 6, 7, 10* and *11*.

## Key terms

alpha particle
beta particle
decay
electron
gamma ray
ion
ionising radiation
penetration distance
radiation
radioactive
radioactivity
random
unstable

### Radiation

**Starter 1**

Write the word 'radiation' on the board. Give students, working in groups, a few minutes to write down as many things as possible that they know about radiation. Draw up a class summary on the board.

### Ionising radiation

**Exploring 1**

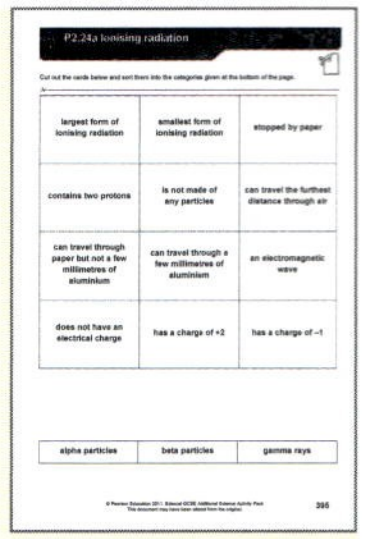

Using **Worksheet P2.24a** students sort statements about radiation into different categories.

**Stretch** Remove the three headings from the bottom of the worksheet and ask students to come up with ideas as to how they will sort the statements.

**Support** Remove the bottom three statements about charge.

### Blocking radiation

**Explaining 2** Demo

See the Teacher and technician practical sheet P2.24 (1) for full details. You can also explain how a GM tube works by recording ionisation.

**Stretch** Ask students why the clicks they can hear from the count rate are not 'smooth'.

**Support** Ask students to identify the material that is the 'most useful' for stopping radiation and to justify their answer using evidence from the demonstration.

### Types of radiation

**Plenary 1**

Students answer the questions on **Worksheet P2.24b**, which has statements about ionising radiation, all with the answers alpha, beta or gamma.

### Radiation penetration

**Homework 1**

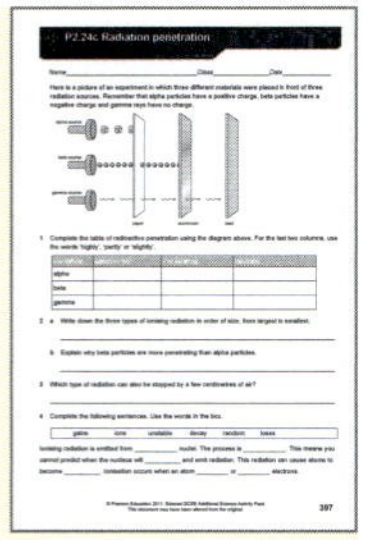

**Worksheet P2.24c** reinforces the penetrating properties of the three types of radiation.

**Support** Discuss with students how the most ionising type of radiation is the one that travels the shortest distance because it loses its energy by ionising atoms when it collides with them.

### Ions

**Starter 2**

Show students a diagram or molecular model of two atoms of lithium-6, one of which has the outer electron missing. Ask students what the differences are between the two atoms.

### Student Book spread P2.24

**Explaining 1**

Students may think that alpha and beta particles and gamma rays are the only forms of ionising radiation. See the TTPP for further details.

**Stretch** Ask students what happens to an atom of an element when it emits an alpha particle.

**Support** Focus students' attention on Figure F, which summarises the properties of alpha and beta particles and gamma rays.

### Cloud chamber

**Explaining 3** Demo

See the Teacher and technician practical sheet P2.24 (2) for full details.

**Stretch** Ask students why the tracks stop before they get to the edge of the chamber.

**Support** Draw attention to the fact that the length of the track depends on how much energy the alpha particle has.

### Radiation sentences

**Plenary 2** Lit

Write some terms on the board: radiation, alpha, beta, gamma, charge, ionising, radioactive, helium nucleus, electron, electromagnetic. Ask students, working in groups, to write a couple of sentences.

### Alpha, beta and gamma radiation

**Homework 2**

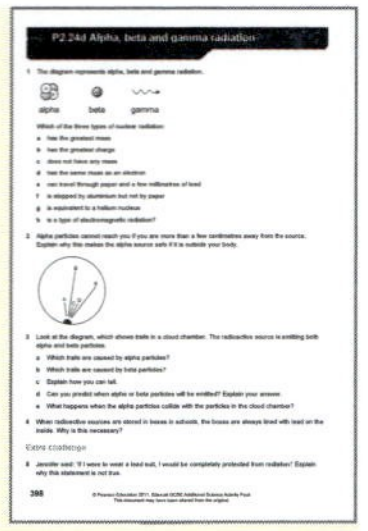

**Worksheet P2.24d** contains questions covering the learning objectives for this lesson, and asks students to apply their knowledge to interpret traces in a cloud chamber.

**Stretch** Ask students to do the 'extra challenge' question on the worksheet.

# P2.24 Ionising radiation

What makes some isotopes radioactive?

The spectacular glow of the aurora borealis is caused by charged particles or 'cosmic rays' being funnelled towards the north pole by the Earth's magnetic field. Scientists have recently found this happens on other planets too.

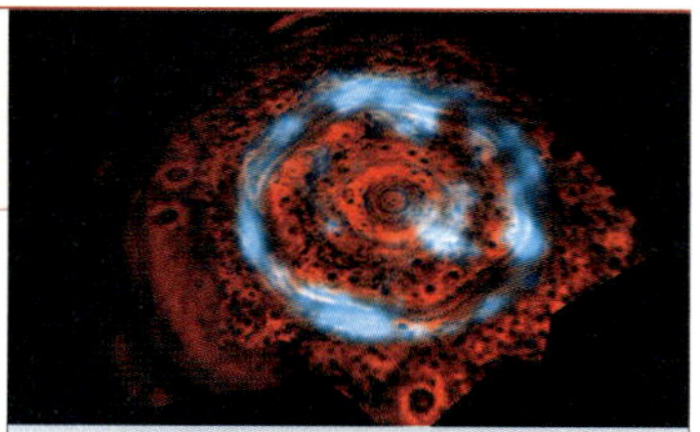

**A** *The aurora (in blue) over the north pole of Saturn, taken by the Cassini orbiter*

1 What is an ion?

2 A fluorine atom has seven electrons. It gains an electron when it becomes an ion. What charge does a fluoride ion have?

Protons carry a charge of +1. Neutrons have no charge and electrons carry a charge of -1. Since the number of electrons in an atom matches the number of protons, an atom has no overall charge. If an atom loses (or gains) an electron, it gains a charge and becomes an **ion**.

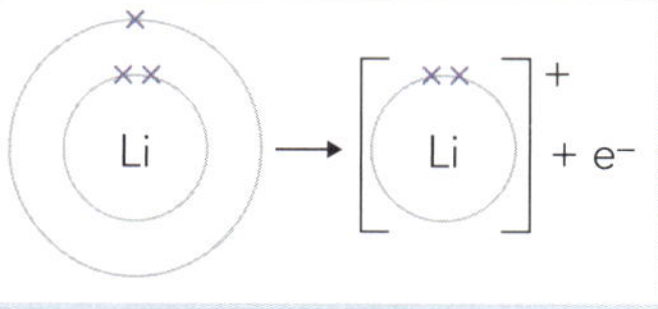


**B** *A lithium atom can lose one electron to become an ion. The brackets show that the whole ion is positively charged.*

## Ionising radiation

**Ionising radiation** is radiation that has enough energy to cause atoms to lose electrons and become ions.

A **radioactive** substance has an **unstable** nucleus. The unstable nucleus **decays** to become more stable by losing energy when certain types of ionising radiation are emitted from the nucleus. These types are alpha particles, beta particles and gamma rays. You cannot predict when a nucleus will decay – it is a **random** process.

**ResultsPlus Watch Out!**

Alpha, beta and gamma are not the only types of ionising radiation, but they are the commonest types of ionising radiation produced by unstable nuclei.

3 What is the mass number of an alpha particle?

**Alpha particles** contain two protons and two neutrons, just like the nucleus of a helium atom. They have no electrons and so have a charge of +2.

Alpha particles are emitted from the nucleus at high speeds. However, each time they ionise an atom they lose some energy. Since they produce many ions in a short distance, they lose energy quickly and have a short **penetration distance**. They are stopped by a few centimetres of air or a few millimetres of paper.

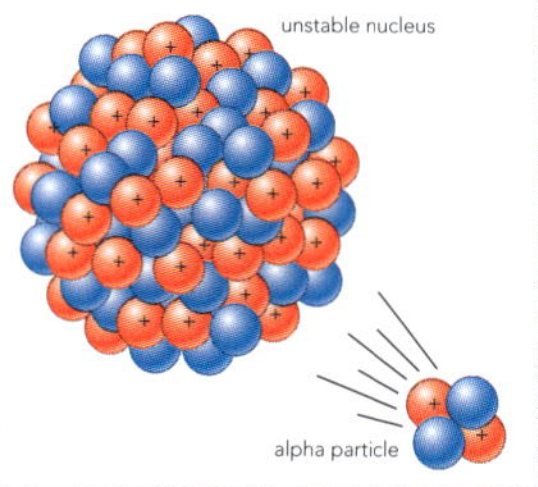


**C** *An unstable nucleus emitting an alpha particle*

**Beta particles** are electrons that are emitted from an unstable nucleus. They are much less ionising than alpha particles and so can penetrate much further into matter than alpha particles can. They can be stopped by a few millimetres of aluminium or by an even smaller thickness of lead.

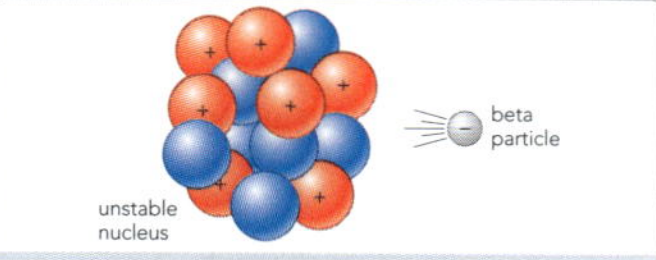


**D** *An unstable nucleus emitting a beta particle*

**Gamma rays** are high-frequency electromagnetic waves emitted by some unstable nuclei and so travel at the speed of light. They do not have an electric charge.

Gamma rays are about ten times less ionising than beta particles and can penetrate matter very easily. They can be partly stopped by a few centimetres of lead and absorbed by many metres of concrete.

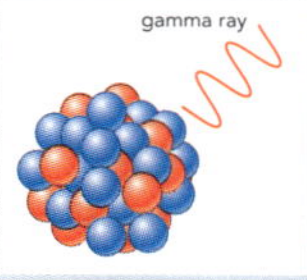


**E** *An unstable nucleus emitting a gamma ray*

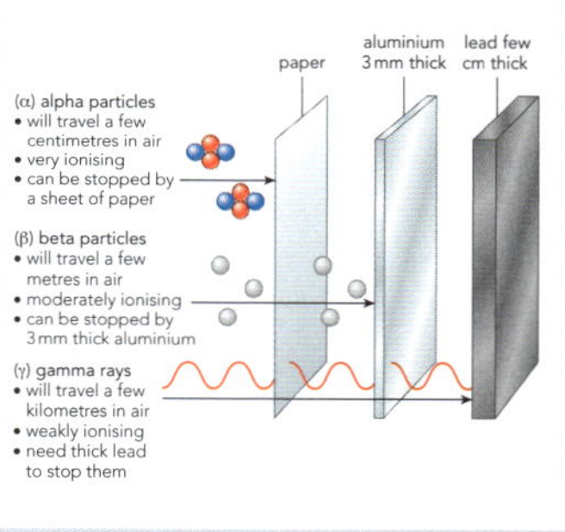


**F** *The penetration properties of three types of ionising radiation*

4 What materials will absorb and stop beta particles?

5 The reactor in a nuclear power station is surrounded by large amounts of concrete. Why is this necessary?

**Skills spotlight**

Scientific ideas can explain how things work. A 'Geiger counter' counts the number of ions produced by ionising radiation inside its tube. Explain how this instrument can be used to identify the type of radiation emitted by a radioactive source.

6 Draw up a table to summarise the form, charge, penetration and ionisation properties of the three types of radiation.

7 What changes take place in a nucleus when it emits an alpha particle?

8 Explain how an oxygen molecule in the air might become an ion by being near a radioactive source.

**Learning Outcomes**

5.2 Explain how atoms may gain or lose electrons to form ions

5.3 Recall that alpha and beta particles and gamma rays are ionising radiations emitted from unstable nuclei in a random process

5.4 Recall that an alpha particle is equivalent to a helium nucleus, a beta particle is an electron emitted from the nucleus and a gamma ray is electromagnetic radiation

5.5 Compare alpha, beta and gamma radiations in terms of their abilities to penetrate and ionise

HSW 3 Describe how phenomena are explained using scientific theories and ideas





**ActiveTeach**

- **AT** *Penetration properties of ionising radiation* [diagram] Figure F – diagram labelling activity

## Answers | Student Book

1 An atom with an electrical charge

2 –1

3 4

4 A few millimetres of aluminium or a smaller thickness of lead

5 To stop gamma rays

6

| | form | charge | penetration | ionisation |
|---|---|---|---|---|
| Alpha particle | equivalent to the nucleus of a helium atom – contains 2 protons and 2 neutrons | charge of +2 | stopped by a few cm of air or a few sheets of paper | most ionising type of radiation |
| Beta particle | electron emitted from nucleus | charge of –1 | stopped by a few mm of aluminium | moderately ionising |
| Gamma ray | electromagnetic wave | not charged | stopped by a few cm of lead or many metres of concrete | least ionising form of radiation |

7 Its mass number goes down by 4 and its atomic number goes down by 2 – it becomes a different element.

8 A good answer will contain the following points: radioactive source emits ionising radiation (e.g. alpha particles, beta particles or gamma rays); Ionising radiation collides with oxygen atom; collision knocks an electron out of the oxygen atom; charge in the nucleus is now not balanced by the charge on the electrons; the atom has a net charge and so is an ion.

**Skills spotlight**

Use the GM tube to measure the activity of a source. Put a sheet of paper between the source and GM tube. If the count rate drops to almost zero, it is an alpha source. If not, replace the paper with an aluminium sheet a few mm thick. If the count rate drops to almost zero, it is a beta source. If not, it is a gamma source.

# P2.25 Nuclear reactions



This lesson introduces fission using the fission reaction of uranium-235 and describes the principle of a chain reactions.

## Specification coverage

**5.6** Demonstrate an understanding that nuclear reactions can be a source of energy, including fission, fusion and radioactive decay

**5.7** Explain that the fission of U-235 produces two daughter nuclei and two or more neutrons, accompanied by a release of energy

**5.8** Explain the principle of a controlled nuclear chain reaction

**5.13** Explain the difference between nuclear fusion and fission

HSW **10** Using both qualitative and quantitative approaches

There are also opportunities to cover HSW **1**, **2**, **3**, **6**, and **11**.

## Key terms

chain reaction
daughter nuclei
nuclear fission
nuclear fusion

### Chain reaction sentences

**Starter 1**

Do a little demonstration with some items to form a simple chain reaction. Elicit the idea that a chain reaction is a reaction in which the 'output' is the 'input' for the next step. Don't use the terms reactant and product to describe nuclear fission reactions.

### Chain reaction models

**Exploring 1** Prac

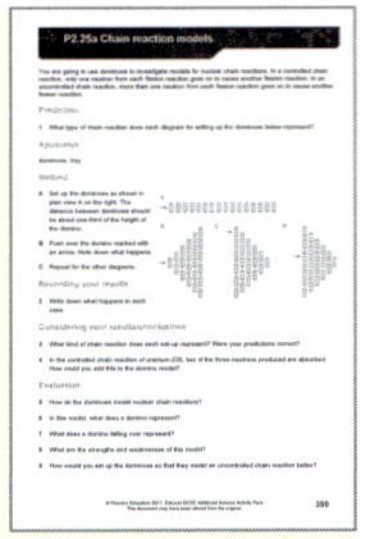

See **Worksheet P2.25a** and the Teacher and technician practical sheet P2.25 (1).

Stretch Give students some other models. Ask them what each part represents in a nuclear chain reaction. How good a model is each of these?

Support Students work in groups and only do setups A and B on the worksheet.

### Student Book spread P2.25 (AT)

**Explaining 1**

The **AT** presentation *Nuclear reactions* is a sequence of slides showing what happens in nuclear fusion, but in the wrong order.

Stretch Ask students to compare what will happen if for every 100 fissions, 99 or 101 neutrons go on to cause further fissions.

Support Focus students' attention on Figure D.

### Fission red/amber/green

**Plenary 1** AfL

Students hold up red (the statement is wrong), amber (I'm not sure) or green (the statement is correct) cards as appropriate. Suggested statements are:

fission is the joining of two nuclei (wrong)

a daughter nucleus is a product of fission (correct)

fission is the same as radioactive decay (wrong)

a nucleus of uranium-235 becomes more stable when it absorbs a neutron (wrong).

### Nuclear chain reactions

**Homework 1**

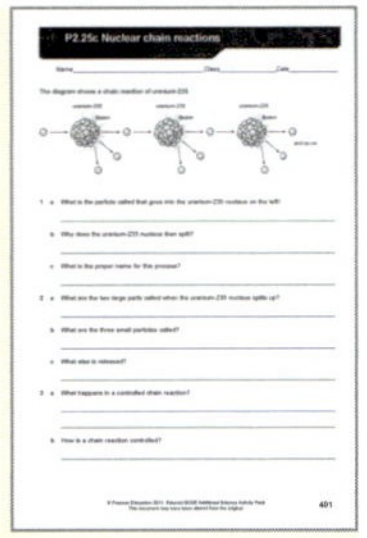

**Worksheet P2.25c** provides questions to test the key points that students should have learned in the lesson.

Support Give students a list of key words from the Student Book that they can choose some of the answers from.

### Nuclear countdown

**Starter 2** Lit

Choose one of the 'Key terms' from the first two lessons of this topic (Lesson P2.23 and P2.24) and play 'hangman' with three students. Challenge the 'winning' student to say what the word means and ask the other two students whether they agree or disagree.

### Nuclear fission jigsaw

**Exploring 2**

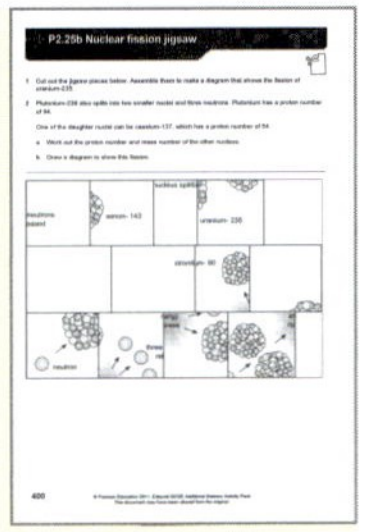

**Worksheet P2.25b** is a jigsaw puzzle on uranium-235 fission, with some additional questions on the fission of plutonium-239.

Stretch Ask students to draw up a table comparing the two fission processes.

Support Students just complete the jigsaw.

### Mousetrap chain reaction

**Explaining 2** Demo

See the Teacher and technician practical sheet P2.25 (2).

Stretch Ask students what the limitations of this model are.

Support Tell students what the ping pong balls and mousetraps represent.

### Chain reactions

**Plenary 2**

Ask students to write a plan for a teaching activity to explain the different types of chain reaction, in which students are used to do the modelling.

### Nuclear reactions

**Homework 2**

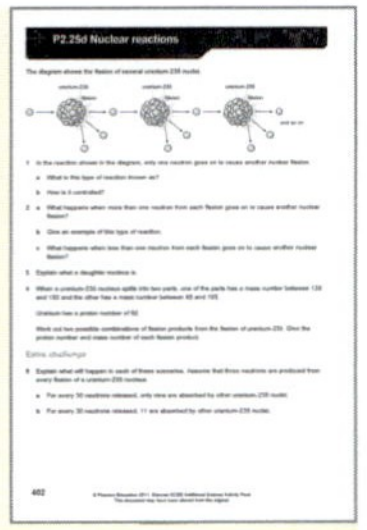

**Worksheet P2.25d** includes a question where students work out possible products from the fission of uranium-235.

Stretch Students answer the 'extra challenge' question.

# P2.25 Nuclear reactions

How do nuclear reactions provide an energy source?

The Cassini-Huygens space probe, launched in 1997, is now orbiting Saturn. The electrical power needed for its scientific instruments and communications equipment is generated from the thermal energy produced by radioactive plutonium as it decays.

**A** *The Cassini orbiter uses radioactivity as a power source.*

**ResultsPlus Watch Out!**

Students often get nuclear reactions and chemical reactions mixed up in exams – they are not the same thing. In a chemical reaction, the atoms themselves do not change. In a nuclear reaction such as fission, the nuclei of the atoms change.

1 What particle triggers nuclear fission in uranium-235?

2 What are the products of the fission of uranium-235 in the example in Figure B?

## Radioactive decay

The process of radioactive decay releases energy. Alpha and beta particles are emitted at high speed and so have kinetic energy. Gamma rays have energy in the form of electromagnetic radiation.

## Other nuclear reactions

Other types of nuclear reaction can also release energy. In some large unstable nuclei, the nucleus can split into two smaller nuclei called **daughter nuclei**. This process is called **nuclear fission**. For example, when a uranium-235 nucleus absorbs a neutron it immediately splits into two smaller daughter nuclei. Two or more neutrons are also released. This is not the same as radioactive decay, when an alpha or beta particle or gamma radiation is emitted from the nucleus.

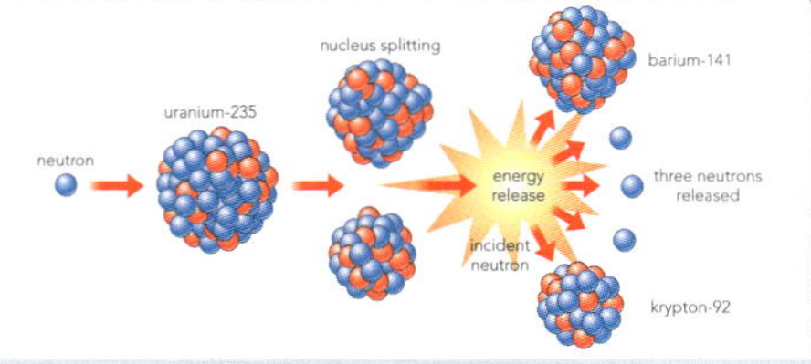


**B** *Example of the fission of uranium-235. Other daughter nuclei could be formed.*

Nuclear fission releases a huge amount of energy – 1 g of uranium releases 10 000 times more energy than burning 1 g of oil.

Most of the energy is in the form of kinetic energy. Both daughter nuclei and the neutrons have a lot of kinetic energy because they are moving at high speeds. Thermal energy is also released.

If the neutrons released are absorbed by other uranium-235 nuclei, each of these nuclei will become unstable and release more neutrons when their nucleus splits. These neutrons can then be absorbed by yet more uranium nuclei, which in turn split up, releasing more neutrons. This is an uncontrolled nuclear **chain reaction**, such as occurs in an atomic bomb.

The chain reaction can be controlled if other materials absorb some of the neutrons. A chain reaction can be created in which only one of the neutrons produced by fission is absorbed by another uranium-235 nucleus. This regulates the amount of energy produced and is the type of chain reaction that occurs in a nuclear reactor.

**C** *Enormous amounts of energy are released in a nuclear explosion.*

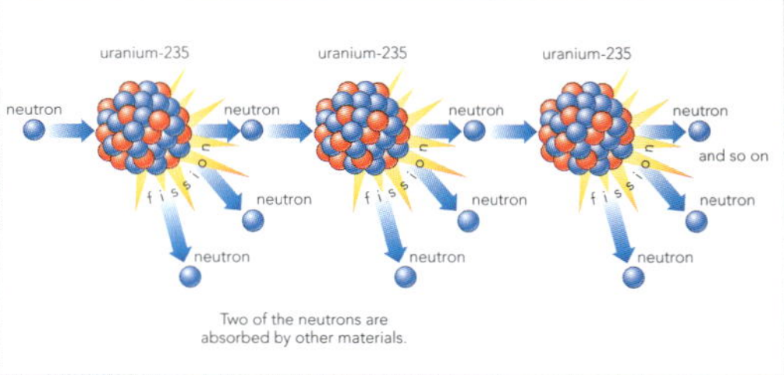


**D** *A controlled nuclear chain reaction. Only one neutron from each fission is absorbed by a uranium-235 nucleus.*

3 What form of energy is released?

4 How can a chain reaction be controlled?

## Nuclear fusion

Instead of splitting large nuclei, small nuclei can be combined to form larger ones. The process is called **nuclear fusion** and it also releases lots of energy.

5 Why does an atomic bomb release a large amount of energy in a short time?

6 Match each of these sentences to one of the following: no chain reaction, controlled chain reaction, uncontrolled chain reaction.

a An average of more than one neutron per fission causes another fission.

b An average of less than one neutron per fission causes another fission.

c Exactly one neutron per fission causes another fission.

7 Explain the principle of a controlled nuclear chain reaction.

**Skills spotlight**

The number of fissions differs in controlled and uncontrolled chain reactions. Work out the number of atoms of uranium-235 that have split up after 10 cycles when one, two and three neutrons go on to trigger new fissions.

**Learning Outcomes**

5.6 Demonstrate an understanding that nuclear reactions can be a source of energy, including fission, fusion and radioactive decay

5.7 Explain how the fission of U-235 produces two daughter nuclei and two or more neutrons, accompanied by a release of energy

5.8 Explain the principle of a controlled nuclear chain reaction

5.13 Explain the difference between nuclear fusion and nuclear fission

HSW 10 Use qualitative and quantitative approaches when presenting scientific ideas and arguments, and recording observations

256 | How did Russian radioactive material get spread over Canada in 1978? | 257

**ActiveTeach**

- **AT** *Uranium*
  [video]
  Properties and uses of uranium
- **AT** *Chain reactions*
  [video]
  How chain reactions keep going
- **AT** *What triggers a chain reaction?*
  [interactive]
  Fission chain reaction – ordering activity
- **AT** *Nuclear reactions*
  [presentation]
  Nuclear fission reactions
- **AT** *Nuclear fission*
  [diagram]
  Figure B – diagram labelling activity
- **AT** *Controlled nuclear chain reaction*
  [diagram]
  Figure D – diagram labelling activity

## Answers | Student Book

1 Neutron

2 Two daughter nuclei (barium-141 and krypton-92) and three neutrons

3 Mostly kinetic energy and some thermal energy.

4 By other materials absorbing neutrons so that only one from each fission goes on to cause another fission.

5 Because there are many fissions in an uncontrolled chain reaction.

6 **a** Uncontrolled chain reaction
**b** No chain reaction
**c** Controlled chain reaction

7 A good answer will contain the following points:
- two or three neutrons are produced in each fission
- each of these neutrons can be absorbed by other uranium-235 nuclei
- the uranium-235 nuclei then become unstable and split up
- some of these neutrons need to be absorbed by other materials
- only one neutron should go on to cause another fission
- the reaction will then continue at a steady rate.

**Skills spotlight**

One neutron: 10 atoms; two neutrons: 1024 atoms; three neutrons: 59 049 atoms

# P2.26 Nuclear power

This lesson covers how the chain reaction is controlled in a nuclear power station and how thermal energy is converted into electrical energy.

## Specification coverage

**5.9** Explain how the chain reaction is controlled in a nuclear reactor including the action of moderators and control rods

**5.10** Describe how thermal (heat) energy from the chain reaction is converted into electrical energy in a nuclear power station

**5.11** Recall that the products of nuclear fission are radioactive

HSW **13** How and why decisions about science and technology are made, including those that raise ethical issues, and about the social, economic and environmental effects of such decisions

There are also opportunities to cover HSW **3**, **11** and **12**.

## Key terms

control rod
core
moderator
nuclear reactor
radioactive waste
shielding

### Generating electrical energy

**Starter 1**

Set up a model power station, consisting of a steam engine connected to a generator and light bulb. Tell the students that this is a model for how most nuclear and fossil fuel power stations work.

### Nuclear power station model

**Exploring 1**

Ask students to build a model of a nuclear power station using materials such as oasis, nails or pipe cleaners, etc. You could ask students to construct this for use in a diorama about generating electricity using nuclear resources.

**Stretch** Students could show a cut through or a cross-section.

**Support** Provide at least some of the shapes already cut out for students to assemble.

### Control rod feedback loop

**Exploring 3**

Using Worksheet P2.26a students construct a flow chart for using control rods to regulate the reaction in a nuclear reactor.

**Stretch** Do not give students the boxes at the bottom of the worksheet.

**Support** Give students the words that they need to use to label the lines leading out from the decision box in the control rods flow chart.

### Nuclear connecting words

**Plenary 1** Lit

Ask students to do a connecting words exercise for the statement 'Nuclear power stations produce electrical energy…'. They should try to complete the sentence in at least three different ways.

### Nuclear power station

**Homework 1**

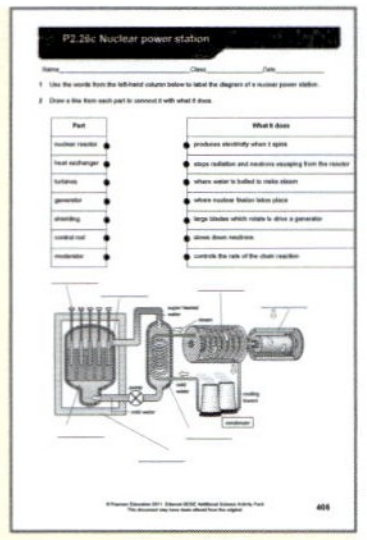

Using **Worksheet P2.26c**, students label a diagram of a nuclear power station and match each part to its function.

**Support** Write the first letter of some of the parts on the labelling lines on the diagram.

### Power generation sentences

**Starter 2** Lit

Tell students the story of the Chernobyl disaster briefly. Ask them to suggest how the reactor became overheated (eliciting the idea that the chain reaction became uncontrolled, which led to the explosion).

### Local nuclear power

**Exploring 2** Lit

Students find out where their nearest nuclear power station is, what type it is, when it was built, what they do with the waste, etc and write a newspaper article.

**Stretch** Ask some students to put a positive 'spin' and others to put a negative 'spin' on the article.

**Support** Give students some specific questions to answer. You could also provide sentence starters or writing frames.

### Student Book spread P2.26

**Explaining 1**

Explain to students how the chain reaction is controlled in a nuclear power station. Students often confuse the functions of the control rods and moderator.

**Stretch** Ask students what they think would happen to the chain reaction if there was not a moderator in a reactor core.

**Support** Concentrate students' attention on Figure D.

### Nuclear reactor core

**Plenary 2**

AfL

Using **Worksheet P2.26b**, students label a drawing of a reactor core.

### Parts of a nuclear power station

**Homework 2**

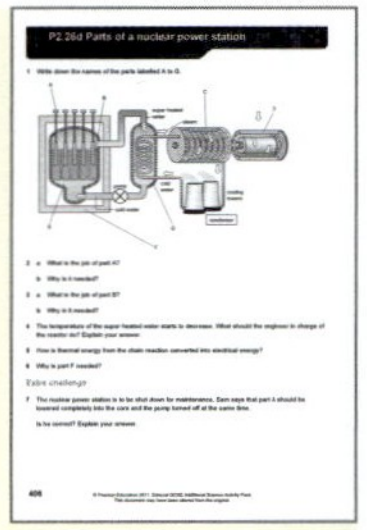

Using **Worksheet P2.26d** students answer questions about the functions of the various parts of a nuclear power station.

**Stretch** Students answer the 'extra challenge' question.

# P2.26 Nuclear power

How does a nuclear reactor work?

In 1978 radioactive material was spread over a large area of Canada. The Russian satellite Kosmos 954, which was powered by a nuclear reactor, re-entered the Earth's atmosphere and broke up. Nuclear power plants are still used in spacecraft today but some people think this should be banned.

A Radioactive debris from Kosmos 954

1 What energy transfer takes place in a nuclear reactor?

B An array of fuel rods

**Nuclear reactors** in nuclear power stations transform energy contained in the nuclei of uranium and plutonium atoms (nuclear energy) into thermal energy using nuclear fission. The mainly uranium fuel is made into pellets, which are inserted into hollow fuel rods several metres long. The rods are placed inside the reactor **core**.

The rate at which nuclear energy is transferred to thermal energy is kept constant by controlling the chain reaction. If just one of the neutrons released by decay of a uranium nucleus is absorbed by another uranium nucleus (causing it to decay), then the chain reaction continues at a constant rate. The number of free neutrons will not increase or decrease.

To control the fission chain reaction, the extra neutrons released by the decay of each nucleus have to be absorbed. The **control rods** contain elements that absorb neutrons. These rods are placed between the fuel rods in the reactor core.

If the rate of fission needs to be increased, the control rods are moved out of the core so that fewer neutrons are absorbed, and vice versa. When the control rods are fully lowered into the core, the chain reaction stops and the reactor shuts down.

2 Why must the chain reaction in a nuclear reactor be controlled?

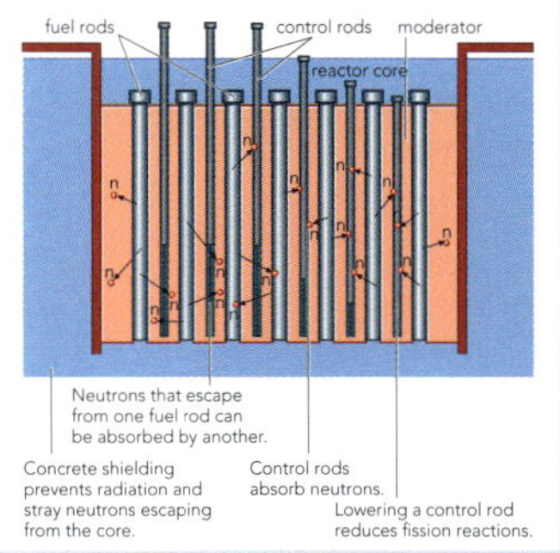


C A nuclear reactor core

## Moderators

The neutrons emitted from the fission of a uranium-235 nucleus are moving very fast. They need to be slowed down so that it is more likely that they will be absorbed by another uranium-235 nucleus. Another material in the core, called a **moderator**, slows down the neutrons.

3 In a nuclear reactor, what are the functions of:
a the control rods
b a moderator?

## Generating electricity

Thermal energy from the core is transferred to a coolant, which is pumped through the reactor. The coolant is usually water at high pressure. This super-heated water is pumped to a 'heat exchanger' where it is used to produce steam. The steam drives a turbine, which turns a generator. The generator transfers kinetic energy to electrical energy.

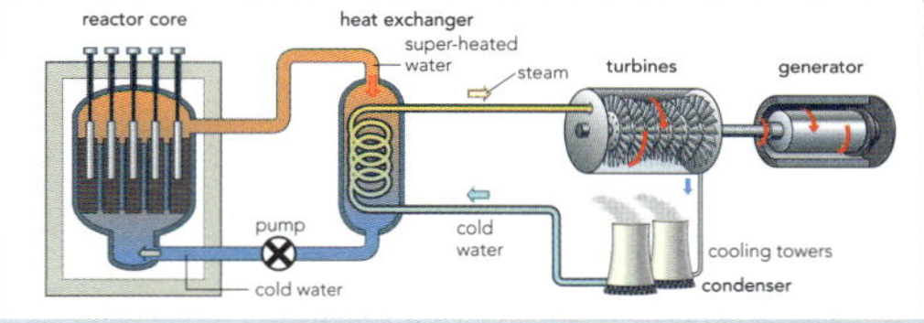


D The main parts of a nuclear power station

**Skills spotlight**

There are social, environmental and economic factors involved in the decision to build a nuclear power station. What issues need to be considered when deciding if and where a nuclear power station should be built?

## Radioactive waste

After a period of time, **radioactive waste** builds up in the reactor core. This waste is made up of radioactive daughter nuclei and radioactive isotopes formed when the materials in the core absorb neutrons.

4 What precautions would you need to take when storing fuel rods?

5 Draw a flow diagram to show how nuclear energy is transformed into electrical energy in a nuclear power station.

6 Explain what is done to increase the temperature of the core of a nuclear reactor.

7 What materials in a reactor core can affect the speed of the neutrons emitted in nuclear fission?

8 Describe how control rods are used to control the rate of the chain reaction in a reactor core.

**ResultsPlus Watch Out!**

In exams students often lose marks by stating that the rate of a nuclear reaction can be changed by changing the moderator. The control rods can be lowered to absorb more neutrons and act as the moderator, to slow down the reaction.

**Learning Outcomes**

5.9 Explain how the chain reaction is controlled in a nuclear reactor including the action of moderators and control rods

5.10 Describe how thermal (heat) energy from the chain reaction is converted into electrical energy in a nuclear power station

5.11 Recall that the products of nuclear fission are radioactive

HSW 13 Understand how and why decisions about science and technology are made, including those that raise ethical issues, and about the social, economic and environmental effects of such decisions



Has a nuclear-powered car ever been made?



## ActiveTeach

- **AT** *Making nuclear fuel* [video]
  How nuclear fuel is made
- **AT** *What's inside a nuclear reactor?* [interactive]
  Reactor components – matching activity
- **AT** *Nuclear reactor core* [diagram]
  Figure C – diagram labelling activity
- **AT** *Nuclear power station* [diagram]
  Figure D – diagram labelling activity

## Answers | Student Book

1 Nuclear energy to thermal energy

2 To maintain a steady rate of fission – if this does not happen, the reactor could explode like a nuclear bomb.

3 **a** To absorb neutrons
**b** To slow down neutrons

4 Do not store too many of them together and keep them a reasonable distance apart.

5 Flow diagram should include the following stages:
nuclear energy → kinetic energy → thermal energy → kinetic energy → electrical energy

6 Raise the control rods to increase the rate of the chain reaction.

7 The moderator

8 A good answer will contain the following points:
- the rate of reaction needs to be maintained at only one neutron from each fission going on to cause another fission
- if the reactor core is cooling down, the rate of reaction needs to be increased
- control rods are raised to increase the reaction rate and hence the temperature
- if the reactor is heating up too much, the rate of reaction needs to be decreased
- control rods are lowered to reduce the reaction rate and hence the temperature.

**Skills spotlight**

Sensible suggestions including; effect on jobs; site needs to be outside major population centres; local population may have worries about having a nuclear power station nearby; potential hazards in areas that are prone to earthquakes.

# P2.27 Fusion – our future?

This lesson introduces the idea that fusion is the source of energy in stars.
Higher Tier material then looks at the practicalities of fusion reactors and what the problems are.

## Specification coverage

***5.12*** Describe nuclear fusion as the creation of larger nuclei from smaller nuclei, accompanied by a release of energy and recognise fusion as the energy source for stars

***5.13*** Explain the difference between nuclear fusion and nuclear fission

H ***5.14*** Explain that nuclear fusion does not happen at low temperatures and pressures, due to electrostatic repulsion of protons

H ***5.15*** Relate the conditions for fusion to the difficulty of making a practical and economic form of power

***5.16*** Demonstrate an understanding that new scientific theories, such as 'cold fusion', are not accepted until they have been validated by the scientific community

HSW *14* How uncertainties in scientific knowledge and scientific ideas change over time and the role of the scientific community in validating these changes

There are also opportunities to cover HSW *2*, *3*, *10*, *11*, *12* and *13*.

## Key terms

electrostatic repulsion
peer review
validate

### Fission revision

**Starter 1**

Use Blu-Tack® to show a ball splitting into two. Ask students what nuclear process this represents. Then do the opposite and ask students what they think is going on. What do they think this process is called?

### Accepting new theories

**Exploring 1**

**Worksheet P2.27a** provides a card sort activity on what a scientist needs to do to get a new discovery accepted. Use the results of this to evaluate the publicising of the Fleischmann and Pons results on cold fusion.

**Stretch** Students could research the claims made by Fleischmann and Pons.

**Support** Outline the process that scientists go through to get a new discovery accepted.

### H Fusion costs (AT)

**Exploring 3**

Using Worksheet **P2.27b**, students prepare arguments for or against continued research into nuclear fusion reactors.

The **AT** spreadsheet *Fission and fusion* contains additional data to allow further comparison of the costs of fusion with fission and other methods of generating electricity.

**Stretch** Give students a person or organisation and ask them to prepare an argument from this person or organisation's point of view.

### Fission, fusion or both?

**Plenary 1** AfL

Give students **Worksheet P2.27c**. They cut out and assemble the boxes to make two diagrams, one showing fusion and the other showing fission.

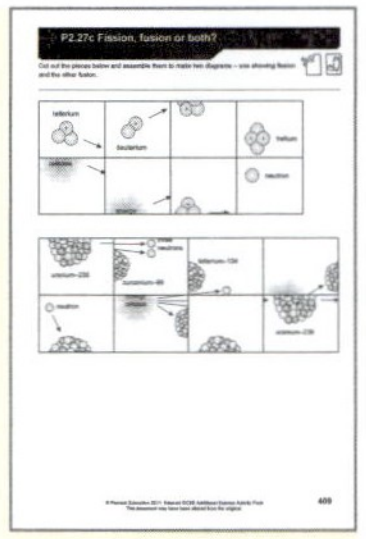

### Fission and fusion

**Homework 1**

**Worksheet P2.27d** consolidates students knowledge of the differences and similarities between fission and fusion.

**Support** Tell students which statements in question 1 are false.

### H Fusion

**Starter 2**

Write the word 'fusion' on the board. Ask students what it means. Repeat this with 'nuclear fusion', 'nuclear fusion reactor' and 'economic nuclear fusion reactor'. Finally, you could ask students to think up a newspaper heading using the words 'economic nuclear fusion reactor'.

### Fusion animation

**Exploring 2**

Demonstrate the fusion reaction of two deuterium nuclei using molecular models or modelling clay. Also show the reaction of tritium and deuterium. Then set students the challenge of writing a shooting brief for a stop-animation film about nuclear fusion.

**Stretch** Ask students what happens when all of the hydrogen in the Sun's core has been fused into helium.

**Support** Demonstrate with the Blu-tack® models.

### Student Book spread P2.27

**Explaining 1**

Students often confuse fission and fusion. It is important to emphasise that these are two different processes and make sure students are clear on which is which. One way to help them remember is that in fusion nuclei fuse or join together.

**Stretch** Students could add information to the table based on the Higher material.

**Support** Provide students with the headings for the table.

### Nuclear sentences

**Plenary 2** Lit AfL

Students to work in pairs to write a sentence using at least two of these words: nucleus, fission, fusion, energy, neutron. They compare their sentence with another pair's sentence and all four work together to come up with two sentences that use all five words.

### H Fusion reactions

**Homework 2**

**Worksheet P2.27e** is designed for more able students. It looks in more detail at fusion reactions in stars.

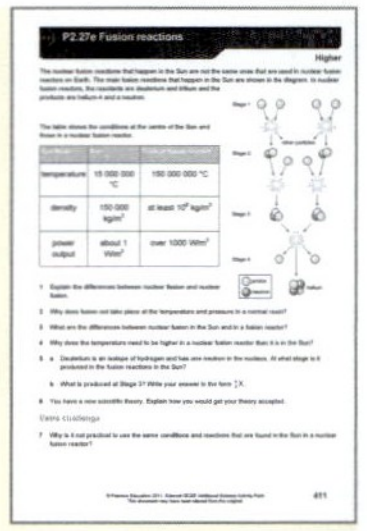

**Stretch** Students answer the 'extra challenge' question.

# P2.27 Fusion – our future?

What is nuclear fusion?

In 1958, Ford developed a concept car called the nucleon, which was to be powered by a small nuclear reactor. However, safety concerns mean that such a car will only ever exist in films.

**A** *The Ford nucleon*

Nuclear fusion occurs when small nuclei combine to form larger ones. A fusion reaction in which hydrogen nuclei combine to form helium is the energy source for stars, including our Sun. Scientists are investigating using a similar fusion reaction here on Earth to generate electricity. This reaction fuses two isotopes of hydrogen, hydrogen-2 (deuterium) and hydrogen-3 (tritium), to form helium. The reaction frees a neutron from the nucleus and releases an enormous amount of energy.

The helium produced in nuclear fusion is not radioactive but any materials used to contain fusion do become radioactive.

1 What is the source of energy in the Sun?

2 What are the products of the fusion of hydrogen?

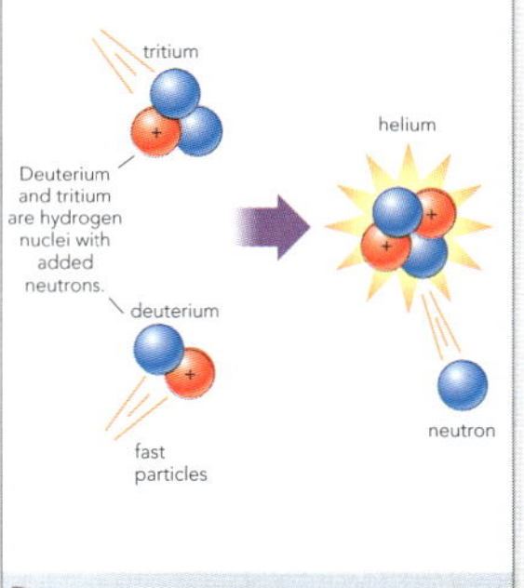


**B** *This fusion reaction could be used to generate electricity from the energy carried by the neutrons.*

## Getting new ideas accepted

New scientific theories have to be **validated** by the scientific community before they are accepted. A report of the method and results is **peer-reviewed** – different scientists working in the same field check it. Other scientists must be able to carry out the experiment and get the same results.

### Skills spotlight

In 1989, Martin Fleischmann and Stanley Pons claimed to have achieved nuclear fusion at 50 °C, raising hopes of a cheap and carbon-free source of energy. However, their results have not been accepted. Suggest what criteria scientists used to reject their claim.

## Fusion and temperature

H

In nuclear fusion research, a deuterium nucleus and a tritium nucleus have to be forced together. The nuclei are positively charged and like charges repel. This is called **electrostatic repulsion**.

For the nuclei to fuse, they need to get within a million millionth of a millimetre of each other. The Sun has a very strong gravitational field, which creates very high densities of nuclei at its centre. Nuclei are much more likely to collide if their density is higher. We can't create these conditions on Earth but fusion reactors try to produce very high pressures.

If the nuclei are travelling fast enough, some can overcome their electrostatic repulsion and collide. The higher the temperature, the faster the nuclei move, and the more likely they are to collide. This means that the temperature inside a fusion reactor must be very high – about 150 000 000 °C (ten times hotter than the Sun).

It is very difficult to sustain the very high temperature and pressure required for fusion. So far none of the experimental reactors have produced more energy than has been put in, so fusion power is a long way off.

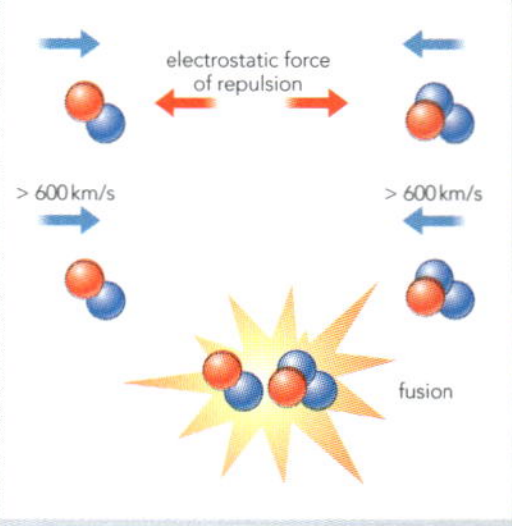


**D** *High speeds are needed to fuse deuterium and tritium nuclei in order to overcome the electrostatic force of repulsion.*

**C** *This fusion reactor uses 192 lasers, all pointed at a 2 mm wide target containing tritium and deuterium gases at its centre.*

**ResultsPlus Watch Out!**

Students often confuse fission and fusion. These are two different processes. One way to remember the difference is that in fusion nuclei fuse, or join together.

H 3 Why does fusion not happen at room temperature?

H 4 Why does fusion happen at a lower temperature in the Sun than in a fusion reactor on Earth?

H 5 Explain the differences between nuclear fission and nuclear fusion.

H 6 Use scientific ideas to suggest why the idea of 'cold fusion' from Pons and Fleischmann's results was not accepted.

7 Describe the difficulties of building a commercial fusion power station.

### Learning Outcomes

5.12 Describe nuclear fusion as the creation of larger nuclei from smaller nuclei, accompanied by a release of energy and recognise fusion as the energy source for stars

5.13 Explain the difference between nuclear fusion and nuclear fission

H 5.14 Explain why nuclear fusion does not happen at low temperatures and pressures, due to electrostatic repulsion of protons

H 5.15 Relate the conditions for fusion to the difficulty of making a practical and economic form of power station

5.16 Demonstrate an understanding that new scientific theories, such as 'cold fusion', are not accepted until they have been validated by the scientific community

HSW 14 Describe how scientists share data and discuss new ideas, and how over time this process helps to reduce uncertainties and revise scientific theories

260

What substance can burn skin, even if it is completely sealed in a tube? 261

## ActiveTeach

- AT *Hydrogen* [video] Properties and uses of hydrogen
- AT *Fission now or fusion for the future?* [interactive] Fission or fusion? – evidence weighing activity
- AT *Fission and fusion* [spreadsheet] Comparing electricity costs
- AT *Nuclear fusion* [diagram] Figure B – diagram labelling activity
- AT *Forces in nuclear fusion* [diagram] Figure D – diagram labelling activity

## Answers | Student Book

1 Nuclear fusion of hydrogen

2 Helium and neutrons

3 H Hydrogen nuclei do not have enough energy to overcome the electrostatic force of repulsion.

4 H The pressure is much greater in the Sun (so nuclei are closer together).

5 H Nuclei split up in fission but join together in fusion; fission can take place at normal temperatures and pressures but fusion needs high temperatures and pressures; fission creates radioactive waste from fuel while fusion does not (but in both processes containment vessels become radioactive).

6 H Other scientists could not get the same results when they repeated the experiment.

7 A good answer will contain the following points:

- very high temperatures and pressures are needed to overcome electrostatic forces of repulsion
- very difficult to sustain the high temperatures and pressures
- so far none of the experimental reactors have produced more energy than was put in to heat up the hydrogen nuclei and contain them.

**Skills spotlight**

Sensible suggestions including: Fleischmann and Pons did not go through the validation process; other scientists were not able to carry out the experiment and get the same results; they did not produce a paper that was subjected to peer review.

# P2.28 Changing ideas



This lesson looks at how scientific ideas about radioactivity have changed over time. It also looks at the dangers of ionising radiation.

## Specification coverage

***6.9*** Demonstrate an understanding of the dangers of ionising radiation in terms of tissue damage and possible mutations and relate this to the precautions needed

***6.10*** Describe how scientists have changed their ideas of radioactivity over time, including a) the awareness of hazards associated with radioactive sources b) why the scientific ideas change over time

HSW *14* How uncertainties in scientific knowledge and scientific ideas change over time and the role of the scientific community in validating these changes

There are also opportunities to cover HSW *12*.

## Key terms

mutation

### Radioactivity knowledge

**Starter 1** AfL

Ask students to apply their learning from Topic 5 by asking questions such as: 'What would happen if you swallowed an alpha source?; What if there was an alpha source a metre away from you?; Would gamma radiation be dangerous inside/outside your body?; Is background radiation dangerous?'

### Handling radioactive sources

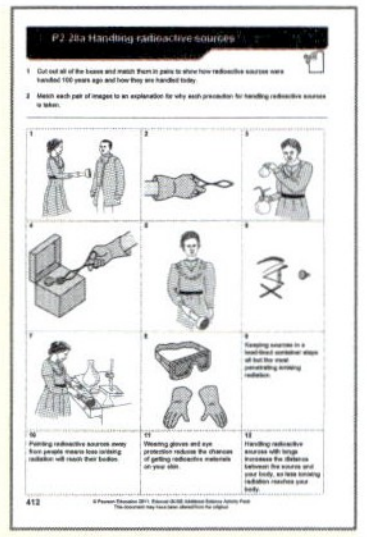

**Exploring 1** AfL

Using **Worksheet P2.28a** students match boxes showing 'bad' and 'good' practice.

**Stretch** Ask students to write a paragraph about how our knowledge of radioactivity has led to the changes in procedure shown in the drawings.

**Support** Give students the whole worksheet including the explanations from the start.

### Student Book spread P2.28

**Explaining 1**

Bring all of the students' previous knowledge about nuclear decay together to show how ideas about radioactivity and its dangers have changed since its discovery. Students then answer the Skills spotlight on page 263.

**Stretch** Ask students to find out more about the discoveries and explain how each discovery changed our understanding of radioactivity.

**Support** Pick out some of the key phrases for students and ask them to build new sentences.

### Sentence completion

**Plenary 1** Lit

Give students the first part of a sentence and ask them to complete it. Suggested sentence starters are:

- You should always hold a radioactive source with tongs....
- You should not point radioactive sources at people...
- Radioactive sources should be placed in a lead-lined box when they are not being used...

### Safe use of radioactive sources

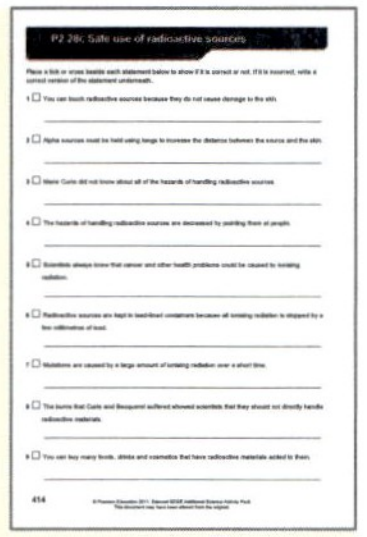

**Homework 1**

**Worksheet P2.28c** consolidates students knowledge of the risks of handling radioactive sources and how ideas have changed over time.

**Support** Give students some hints about the questions.

### Radioactivity precautions

**Starter 2**

Tell students that some people have to work with radioactive sources (for instance in chemical and biological research). Ask half the class to write down one safety precaution that a research scientist should take to avoid being exposed to ionising radiation. Ask the other half of the class to write down one way of stopping ionising radiation reaching someone.

### Radioactive discoveries timeline

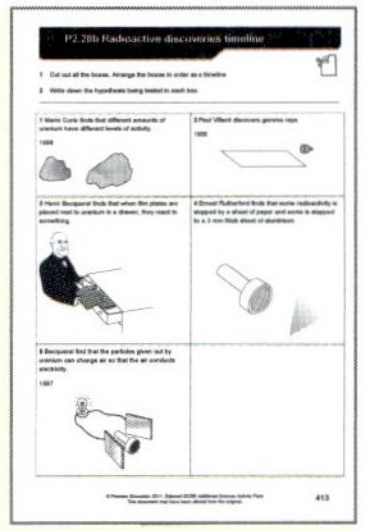

**Exploring 2**

Using **Worksheet P2.28b** students order the boxes into a timeline on radioactivity discoveries. Students identify the hypothesis being tested in each box.

**Stretch** Students write a paragraph that explains how hypotheses are converted into theories using the example of nuclear decay shown on their timeline.

**Support** Help students to arrange the boxes without dates into the correct places on the timeline.

### Incorrect handling

**Explaining 2**

Explain to students that you are handling a 'dummy' radioactive source and tell them what sort of ionising radiation it is producing. Deliberately mishandle it, breaking one or more of the following safe handling rules. Ask students to spot how the source was not handled safely and how you should have handled it.

**Stretch** Go through a whole routine and ask students what you did wrong at the end.

**Support** Only break one rule at a time.

### Radioactivity timeline

**Plenary 2** Lit

Ask students to draw a timeline showing how our knowledge of radioactivity has changed over time. Students could work on their timelines in pairs or small groups.

### Marie Curie in the laboratory

**Homework 2**

Students read the passage in **Worksheet P2.28d** and pick out the ways in which we handle radioactive sources has changed.

**Stretch** Students research, and draw a concept map, of how precautions with radioactive sources has changed over time.

# P2.28 Changing ideas

How have ideas about radioactivity changed?

Marie Curie (1867–1934) worked extensively with radioactive materials. Her laboratory notebooks are now considered too dangerous to handle because of the radioactive fingerprints. Even her cookbook is highly radioactive. These papers are now kept in lead-lined boxes – if researchers want to view them, they have to wear protective clothing.

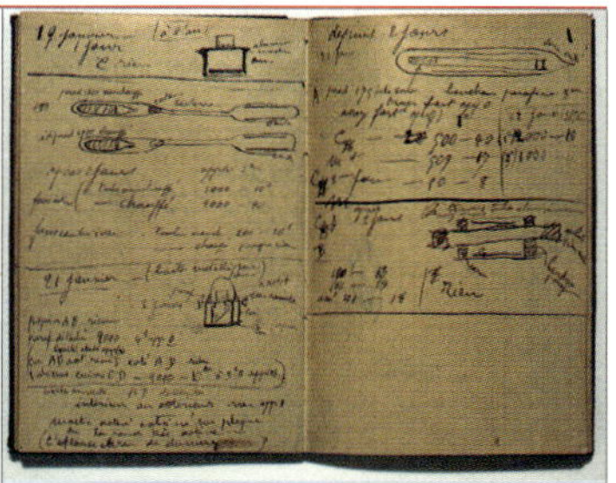

A One of Marie Curie's notebooks

Henri Becquerel (1852–1908) investigated how uranium phosphoresces (emits light) after being exposed to sunlight. He observed that 'invisible rays' also emitted by uranium could expose (darken) photographic plates. In 1896 during some cloudy weather, he put some uranium away in a drawer with a photographic plate. The plate unexpectedly became exposed. Becquerel had discovered that the radiation emitted by uranium did not need an external energy source. He had discovered radioactivity.

Becquerel then showed that this radiation could ionise gases. He noticed his skin was burned after accidentally leaving a container of radium in his pocket but he did not realise that ionisation could occur in cells and was the cause of the damage.

Marie Curie and her husband Pierre (1859–1906) also burned their hands by handling radioactive materials such as radium. The Curies discovered that some materials emitted much more radiation than others.

1 a What did Becquerel discover?
b What did the Curies discover about radioactivity?

B After Marie Curie discovered radium, this element became so popular it was soon put in food and even water. This face cream, advertised in 1933, contained radioactive thorium and radium.

## Changing ideas about safety

In the 1920s scientists began to link cancer and other health problems to the effects of ionising radiation. Marie Curie and her daughter Irene both died from leukaemia, which was probably caused by the radioactive materials they worked with.

We now know that a large amount of ionising radiation can cause tissue damage such as reddened skin (radiation burns) and also other effects that cannot be seen. Much smaller amounts of ionising radiation over long periods of time can damage the DNA inside a cell. This damage is called a **mutation**. DNA contains the instructions controlling a cell, so some mutations can cause the cell to malfunction and may cause cancer.

2 a What does ionising radiation do to cells?
b What can this lead to?

3 Suggest why experts in the early 20th century thought that working with small amounts of radioactive materials was safe.

## Handling radioactive sources

We now know about the **hazards** of radioactive sources and how to protect people who work with radioactivity. The **risk** of harm decreases with distance from the source, so sources are always handled with tongs. The risk can also be reduced by not pointing sources at people. We also know that all but the most penetrating radiation is stopped by a few millimetres of lead, so sources are kept in a lead-lined container.

C Protective clothing worn by a radiation worker

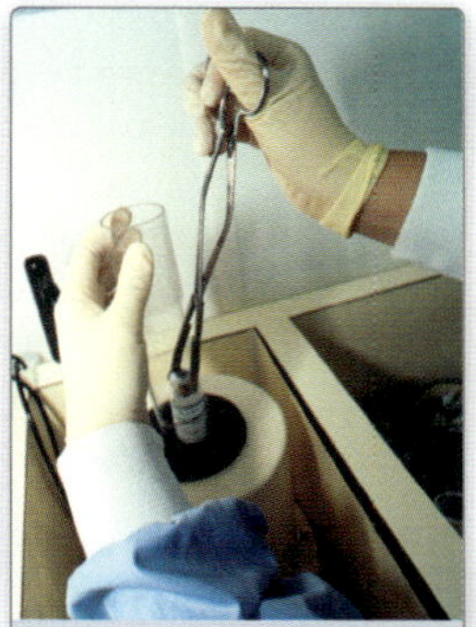

D Handling a radioactive source with tongs

4 What caused ideas about the safety of ionising radiation to change in the 1920s?
5 a List four precautions that someone working with radioactivity today needs to take to reduce the risks from radiation.
b Explain why each precaution should be taken.

**Skills spotlight**
Scientific knowledge changes over time as more observations and data are collected. Which observations about the effects of radioactivity did Marie and Pierre Curie know about? What effects did they not know about?

**ResultsPlus Watch Out!**
Not all forms of radiation are ionising. Light and microwaves are not ionising radiation as they have low frequency and low energy. They do not have enough energy to ionise atoms.

**Learning Outcomes**
6.9 Demonstrate an understanding of the dangers of ionising radiation in terms of tissue damage and possible mutations and relate this to the precautions needed
6.10 Describe how scientists have changed their ideas of radioactivity over time, including:
a the awareness of the hazards associated with radioactive sources
b why the scientific ideas change over time
HSW 14 Describe how scientists share data and discuss new ideas, and how over time this process helps to reduce uncertainties and revise scientific theories


What made parts of the UK more radioactive in 1986?


## Answers | Student Book

1 **a** Radioactivity – the emission of 'invisible' rays that came from uranium, which penetrated through solid materials. He also discovered that these rays exposed photographic plates.
**b** Some materials emit more (ionising) radiation than others.

2 **a** Ionises atoms in cells
**b** Causes tissue damage, such as skin burns, and damages DNA, leading to mutations. Some mutations can lead to cancer. (And if mutations are formed in a gamete-producing cell, the resulting child may have a deformity.)

3 They did not know about the long-term effects.

4 Longer-term effects such as mutations that lead to cancer (and other effects such as sterility and blood disorders) became more obvious as time went by.

5 A good answer will contain the following points:
- handle sources with tongs, which increases the distance between the source and your body, so less ionising radiation reaches your body
- do not point sources at people, which means less ionising radiation will reach their body
- keep sources in a lead-lined container, as all but the most penetrating ionising radiation is stopped by a few millimetres of lead
- wear gloves and eye protection to reduce the chances of getting radioactive materials on your skin.

**Skills spotlight**
They knew that it could burn the skin and, from Becquerel's earlier work, that it could ionise gases.
They did not know that it can also cause ionisation in cells that can lead to mutations and cancer.

# P2.29 Nuclear waste



This lesson briefly looks at the different types of nuclear waste and then discusses the options for disposing of it. The advantages and disadvantages of nuclear power are also discussed.

## Specification coverage

***6.11*** Discuss the long-term possibilities for storage and disposal of nuclear waste

***6.12*** Evaluate the advantages and disadvantages of nuclear power for generating electricity, including the lack of carbon dioxide emissions, risks, public perception, waste disposal and safety issues

**HSW** *11* Presenting information, developing an argument and drawing a conclusion, using scientific, technical and mathematical language, *conventions and symbols and ICT tools*

There are also opportunities to cover **HSW** *12*, *13* and *14*.

## Key terms

high-level waste (HLW)
intermediate-level waste (ILW)
low-level waste (LLW)
radioactive

### Nuclear power PMI

**Starter 1**

Ask students to conduct a PMI exercise (where students think of three statements, one plus, one minus and one interesting) on the following statement: 'We should build more nuclear power stations'.

### Advantages and disadvantages of nuclear power

**Exploring 1**

Students sort the cards on **Worksheet P2.29a** into advantages and disadvantages of nuclear power.

**Stretch** Students rank the cards in order of which issues they think are the most important. They should justify the order they have given.

**Support** Students could either work in pairs or in small groups to do the sorting.

### Public perception

**Exploring 3**

Ask students to design a questionnaire to find out about the public's perception of the nuclear industry. You could also ask students to say how they plan to analyse and process the data that they obtain.

**Stretch** Students consider whether their method of conducting the survey will produce a representative view. Is it biased? If so, how.

**Support** Provide some ideas on what sort of questions students should be asking.

### Nuclear power charades (AT)

**Plenary 1**

Students mime a sentence on an advantage or disadvantage of nuclear power. The audience has to guess what is being acted out and state whether it is an advantage or a disadvantage. There are some further suggestions in the **AT** presentation *Nuclear power charades*.

### Nuclear power and nuclear waste

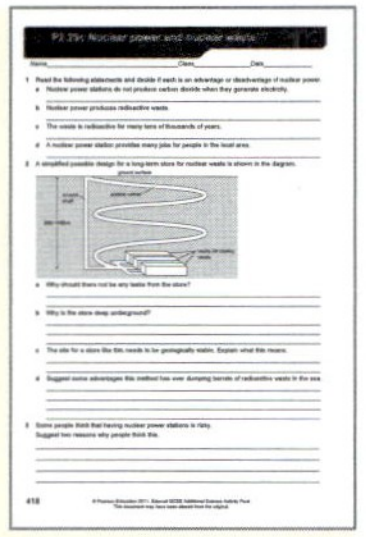

**Homework 1**

**Worksheet P2.29c** provides questions on long-term storage of nuclear waste and the advantages, disadvantages and risks of nuclear power.

**Support** Talk through the diagram before students take the worksheet home.

### Nuclear power true/false (AT)

**Starter 2** Lit

Give students a set of statements, some true and some false. Ask them to say whether they are true or false and to provide corrected versions of false ones.

There are some more statements in the **AT** document *Nuclear power*.

### Storage and disposal of nuclear waste

**Exploring 2** Lit

Students write a letter in favour of one method of storage or disposal of nuclear waste, using information on **Worksheet P2.29b**.

**Stretch** Students could compare approaches taken by different countries and evaluate their advantages and disadvantages.

**Support** Provide students with phrases as a writing frame for their argument.

### Student Book spread P2.29 (AT)

**Explaining 1**

Ask students to sort the statements in the **AT** document *Different types of waste* into columns headed HLW, ILW and LLW.

**Stretch** Ask students to write statements about each type of waste and its storage options and to evaluate the risks of each storage option.

**Support** Put some of the statements into the correct column in the table for students.

### Nuclear sentence completion

**Plenary 2** Lit

Provide a set of sentences for students to complete in their own words. Examples: High-level waste is much more radioactive than intermediate-level waste...; Radioactive waste can be disposed of at sea...; A nuclear power station does not produce carbon dioxide... .

### Storing and disposing of nuclear waste

**Homework 2**

Using **Worksheet P2.29d**, students consider in more detail the issues of storing and disposing of nuclear waste.

**Stretch** Students answer the 'extra challenge' question.

# P2.29 Nuclear waste

What happens to nuclear waste?

From 1953 until the late 1980s, British nuclear waste was dumped at sea. Over 28 000 barrels of waste were dumped off the Channel Islands. These barrels are now corroding and breaking up and could be releasing radioactive materials into the sea.

**A** *A corroding barrel of waste on the sea bed near the Channel Islands*

1 Where does HLW come from?

## Types of waste

The fission products from the uranium fuel used in nuclear power stations are very **radioactive**. This is **high level waste** (**HLW**) and it produces large amounts of ionising radiation for about 50 years.

After about 50 years HLW is much less radioactive but it remains moderately radioactive for many tens of thousands of years. It is now **intermediate level waste** (**ILW**). ILW also includes the metal cylinders that contained the uranium fuel. These were changed by radiation from the fuel and became radioactive themselves.

**Low level waste** (**LLW**) is only slightly radioactive but will remain so for tens of thousands of years, like ILW. It includes clothing and cleaning materials from nuclear power stations. Hospitals are also a source of LLW because of the radioactive isotopes used in radiotherapy treatment for cancer.

2 What are the similarities between ILW and LLW?

3 What are the differences between HLW and ILW?

4 How is HLW stored?

**ResultsPlus Watch Out!**

Many students lose marks by saying that nuclear power stations make the local area more radioactive. Remember that radioactive waste is only released into the environment if there is an accident.

## Storage and disposal of nuclear waste

HLW is transported inside thick concrete and steel containers, which absorb the radiation. It is then sealed in glass to stop the radioactive material escaping, and stored in canisters until the waste is less radioactive (and has become ILW).

ILW is currently stored in concrete and steel containers, but none has been disposed of yet.

LLW is compacted and buried in special landfill sites because of the possibility of radioactive material leaking into soil or water.

**B** *HLW from all UK nuclear power stations is transported by train to Sellafield in Cumbria.*

| Method of disposal | Problems |
|---|---|
| Firing into space | Launch vehicle could fall back to Earth, spreading radioactive material over a wide area. |
| Dumping in barrels at sea | Barrels can corrode and release radioactive materials which could enter the food chain. |
| Storage underground | Site needs to be geologically stable, i.e. very low risk of earthquakes. |

**C** *Some of the options for disposing of nuclear waste*

5 The UK government has decided that ILW should be buried deep underground. Suggest some factors that could affect the choice of a long-term deep disposal site.

## Advantages and disadvantages of nuclear power

A nuclear power station itself does not produce carbon dioxide (which contributes to global warming). However, the processes used to make the fuel rods require energy and generating this energy may produce carbon dioxide.

Nuclear waste has to be stored for tens of thousands of years, until the radioactivity has decreased to safer levels. During this time, nothing should leak from the waste into the environment.

In 1986, the reactor at the Chernobyl nuclear power station in the Ukraine exploded. Radioactive material was spread by wind over a very wide area before falling out with the rain, including over the UK. Some people think that nuclear power is unsafe because of the risk of accidents like the one at Chernobyl.

**D** *Anatoly Rasskazov flew over Chernobyl the day after the accident to take official photos. The radiation burn on his forehead is still there.*

**Skills spotlight**

In a scientific discussion, evidence is presented for and against an idea and then used to reach a decision for or against. Write an argument in support of one method of disposing of nuclear waste.

6 a Describe the advantages of nuclear power.
b Explain why some people think that nuclear power is unsafe.

7 Explain why it is difficult to dispose of radioactive waste safely.

**Learning Outcomes**

**6.11** Discuss the long-term possibilities for storage and disposal of nuclear waste

**6.12** Evaluate the advantages and disadvantages of nuclear power for generating electricity, including the lack of carbon dioxide emissions, risks, public perception, waste disposal and safety issues

HSW **11** Present information, develop an argument and draw a conclusion, using scientific, technical and mathematical language



What happens in a 'half-life'? 265

## ActiveTeach

- **AT** *Nuclear waste 1* [BBC video] Sellafield & nuclear waste storage 1
- **AT** *Nuclear waste 2* [BBC video] Sellafield & nuclear waste storage 2
- **AT** *Radioactive waste* [video] Disposal and reprocessing
- **AT** *Should we build more nuclear fission power plants?* [interactive] Nuclear power – evidence weighing activity
- **AT** *Different types of waste* [word document] Properties of waste
- **AT** *Nuclear power* [presentation] True or false statements
- **AT** *Nuclear power charades* [presentation] Advantages and disadvantages

## Answers | Student Book

**1** Fission products, i.e. used nuclear fuel

**2** They both remain radioactive for tens of thousands of years.

**3** HLW produces large amounts of ionising radiation while ILW produces a smaller amount.

**4** Inside thick concrete and steel for temporary storage and transport, and then sealed in glass.

**5** Geological stability of site, number of people living near the site, access for transporting waste to the site.

**6** **a** Does not produce carbon dioxide when it is generating electricity. Does not use up fossil fuels.
**b** Because of the risk of accidents like Chernobyl, where radioactive material was spread over a large area.

**7** A good answer will contain the following points: it needs to be stored safely for many tens of thousands of years; it takes many tens of thousands of years for the levels of radioactivity to decrease to safer levels; the materials it is stored in have to last all this time; the building structure also has to last for many tens of thousands of years; any materials that leak have to be contained so they do not get into groundwater etc.

**Skills spotlight**

Answers could include the following points.

- Firing into space: in space waste cannot contaminate the Earth if it leaks; already lots of radiation in space from the Sun so not increasing the danger.
- Dumping at sea: the oceans contain a huge amount of water, so waste that leaks will be diluted and not likely to cause harm to people.
- Storage underground: any radiation leaking from containers will not be able to get through rock to harm people; the earth naturally contains radioactive elements, so putting waste here will not increase the danger.

# P2.30 Half-life

This lesson introduces the becquerel as the unit of activity and the concept of half-life. Students work out half-lives from some graphs of count rate against time.

## Specification coverage

**6.4** Describe how the activity of a radioactive source decreases over a period of time

**6.5** Recall that the unit of activity of a radioactive isotope is the Becquerel, Bq

**6.6** Recall that the half-life of a radioactive isotope is the time taken for half the undecayed nuclei to decay

**6.7** Use the concept of half-life to carry out simple calculations on the decay of a radioactive isotope, including graphical representations

**HSW** ***10*** Using both qualitative and quantitative approaches

There are also opportunities to cover **HSW** ***11***.

## Key terms

activity
becquerel (Bq)
count rate
Geiger-Müller (GM) tube
half-life
radioactive decay

### Knock-out competition (AT)

**Starter 1**

Ask students what happens to the number of players or teams in a knock-out competition. Relate this to the idea of radioactive half-lives. Plot this as a graph on the board. There is also an **AT** presentation *Knock-out competition* to show this.

### Half-life graph (AT)

**Exploring 1** **Prac**

Students label the diagram of count against time on the **AT** document *Half-life graph* by dragging the boxes.

**Stretch** Ask students why the unit for becquerels is $s^{-1}$ and why a graph of count rate against time shows inverse proportion.

**Support** Put the axis labels in place before students start the activity.

### Decay of protactinium-234 (AT)

**Explaining 1** **Demo**

See the Teacher and technician practical sheet P2.30 for full details. Students can also use the sample data in the **AT** spreadsheet *Half-life graph* and use Excel® to plot a graph and find the half-life.

**Stretch** Students consider why the graph produced by a datalogger is not a smooth curve.

**Support** Ask students to describe the main features of the decay curve produced.

### Half-life true or false

**Plenary 1** **Lit**

Give students some statements and ask them to say if they are true or false. Suggested statements: 'Half-life depends on the amount of radioactive material there is' [F]; 'After two half-lives, three-quarters of the unstable nuclei will have decayed' [T]; 'One becquerel is one nuclear decay each second' [T]; 'As radioactive decay is a random process, you can predict when a stable nucleus will decay' [F].

### Half-life of carbon-14

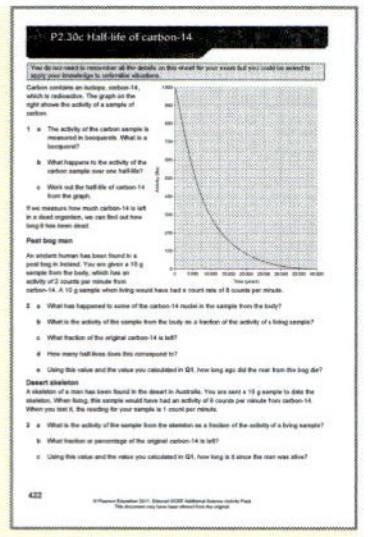

**Homework 1**

Using **Worksheet P2.30c** students calculate the half-life of carbon-14 from a graph and look at the application of half-lives to radiocarbon dating.

**Support** Mark points on the graph where students can read off values to calculate the half-life.

### Questions, questions

**Starter 2**

Ask all students to stand up. Then ask a series of questions that is likely to apply to only half those standing. At each round only the students who the question applies to remain standing. Explain to students that this is a model for radioactive decay.

### Half-lives from graphs

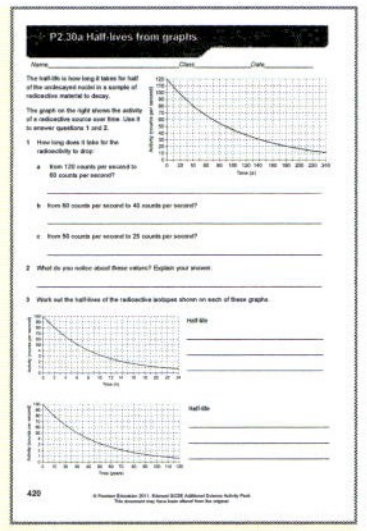

**Exploring 2**

Using **Worksheet P2.30a**, students calculate a half-life from graphs.

**Stretch** **Worksheet P2.30b** provides further graph examples and asks students to plot a graph from data provided.

**Support** Work through a couple of examples with students.

### Student Book spread P2.30 (AT)

**Explaining 2**

Explain that the activity depends on the number of radioactive particles that are undecayed at any one time. You could also show the **AT** presentation *Uranium-235 fission products*.

**Stretch** Ask students to work out how long it would take for the activity of a sample containing an isotope with a particular half-life to decrease by 90%.

**Support** Go through an example to show how half-life does not depend on the number of atoms present.

### Counting atoms remaining

**Plenary 2**

Challenge students to draw a graph of the number of atoms remaining in a sample against time, with some arbitrary initial conditions. For example, start with 1000 atoms and a half-life of 4 minutes.

### Radioactive dating

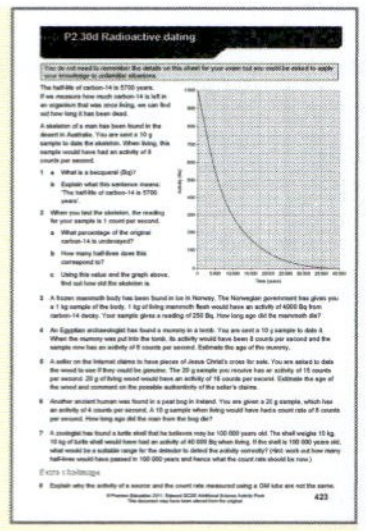

**Homework 2**

**Worksheet P2.30d** includes additional, more complex calculations. Students do not need to be able to recall details of radioactive dating techniques.

**Stretch** Students answer the 'extra challenge' question.

# P2.30 Half-life

What is the half-life of a radioactive material?

After Chernobyl, Arctic lichens absorbed large amounts of radioactive caesium-137. The lichens are eaten by reindeer, which are eaten by humans. Some reindeer herders in the Arctic have caesium-137 levels that are 300 times higher than normal. This situation will continue for hundreds of years because caesium-137 decays slowly.

A

1 How many nuclei decay each second in a sample of uranium-235 that has an activity of 2 Bq?

2 What is the half-life of an isotope?

3 A 10 kg sample of caesium-137 has a half-life of 30 years. What will the half-life of a 5 kg sample be?

4 Strontium-90 has a half-life of 29 years. How many strontium-90 half-lives is:
a 29 years
b 58 years
c 116 years
d 14.5 years?

5 There are 10 million atoms in a sample of radon-222. How many undecayed nuclei are left after:
a 3.8 days
b 7.6 days
c 11.4 days
d 1.9 days?

When an unstable nucleus undergoes **radioactive decay** its nucleus changes to become more stable. The **activity** of any radioactive substance is the number of nuclear decays per second and is measured in **becquerel** (**Bq**). 1 Bq is one nuclear decay each second.

Radioactive decay is a random process – we cannot predict when it will happen. When you throw a die, sometimes you get a six and sometimes you don't. In a similar way, at any given moment there is a certain probability that a particular unstable nucleus will decay.

The **half-life** is the time taken for half the unstable nuclei in a sample of a radioactive isotope to decay. Some isotopes have half-lives of fractions of a second but others have half-lives of millions of years. The half-life is the same for however much of an isotope there is.

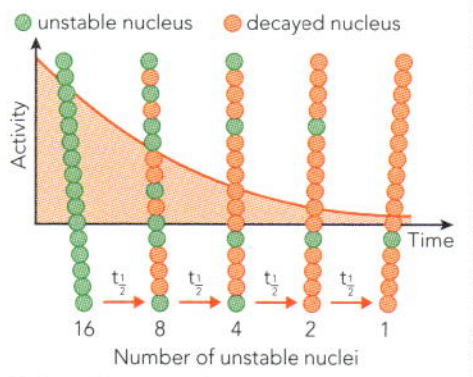


**B** *After each half-life, the number of unstable nuclei halves.*

| Isotope | Half-life | Ionising radiation emitted |
|---|---|---|
| uranium-235 | 700 million years | alpha particle |
| technetium-99 | 211 000 years | beta particle |
| carbon-14 | 5730 years | beta particle |
| strontium-90 | 29 years | beta particle |
| caesium-137 | 30 years | beta particle |
| radon-222 | 3.8 days | alpha particle |
| thallium-208 | 3.1 minutes | beta particle |
| polonium-216 | 0.15 seconds | alpha particle |

**C** *Half-lives of some radioactive isotopes*

After decaying, a nucleus may become stable. The more stable nuclei a sample of a substance contains, the lower its activity. The half-life of an isotope is found by recording the activity of a sample over a period of time.

The radioactivity of a source is measured using a **Geiger-Müller (GM) tube**. A GM tube can be connected to a counter or alternatively it may give a click each time ionising radiation is detected in the GM tube. The **count rate** is the number of clicks per second or minute. You can work out how long it takes the count rate to halve from a graph.

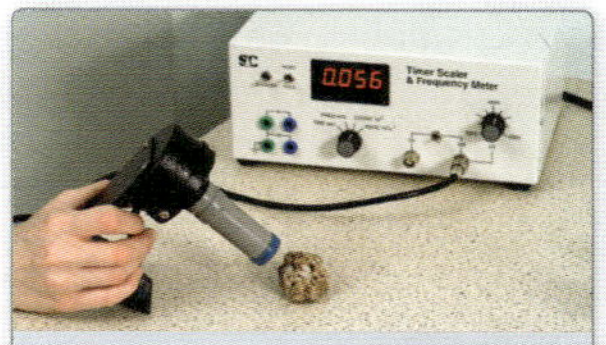

**D** *Using a GM tube to measure radioactivity.*

**ResultsPlus Watch Out!**

Many students lose marks because they are not careful enough with the definition of half-life. Don't make the mistake of saying it is the time for an *atom* to decay by half – it is the time for the activity to decrease by half.

In Figure E, the count rate at 5 minutes is 600 counts per second. After one half-life the count rate will have decreased to 300 counts per second. This occurs at 12 minutes. So the half-life is 12 minutes – 5 minutes = 7 minutes.

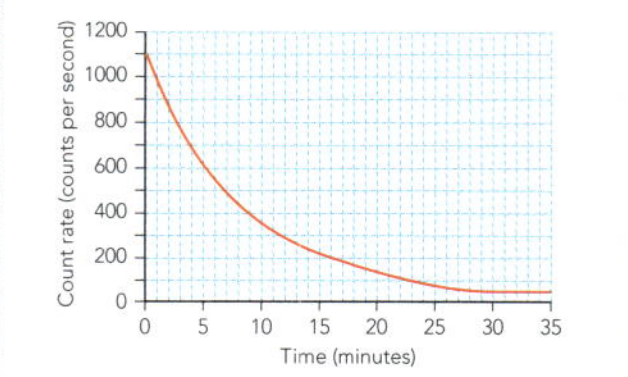


**E** *Graph of count rate against time for a radioactive source.*

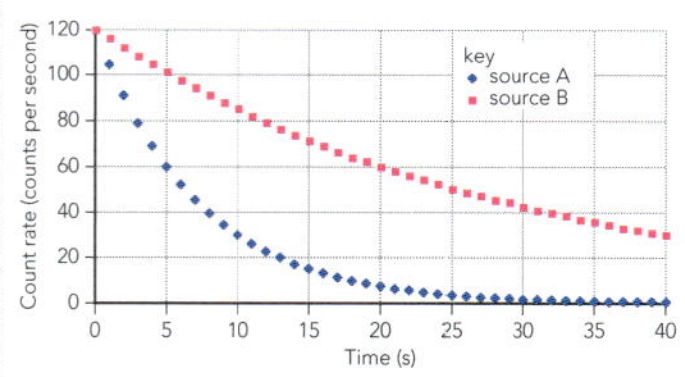


**F** *Graph showing the decay of two different radioactive sources.*

6 Work out the half-lives of the two sources shown in Figure F.

7 Explain how the activity of a radioactive sample relates to the number of unstable nuclei.

**Skills spotlight**

Scientists often collect quantitative data to answer a question. Describe how you could find the half-life of a newly discovered radioactive substance.

**Learning Outcomes**

6.4 Describe how the activity of a radioactive source decreases over a period of time

6.5 Recall that the unit of activity of a radioactive isotope is the becquerel, Bq

6.6 Recall that the half-life of a radioactive isotope is the time taken for half the undecayed nuclei to decay

6.7 Use the concept of half-life to carry out simple calculations on the decay of a radioactive isotope, including graphical representations

HSW 10 Use qualitative and quantitative approaches when presenting scientific ideas and arguments, and recording observations



Is the landing of dropped buttered toast a random process?



## ActiveTeach

- **AT** *Half-life* [video] Explanation of half-life
- **AT** *Isotopes: half-life, activity and decay* [interactive] All about half-life and radioactivity – quiz
- **AT** *Half-life of protactinium* [spreadsheet] Plotting graphs
- **AT** *Half-life graph* [word document] Labelling graphs
- **AT** *Uranium-235 fission* [presentation] Product activity
- **AT** *Knock-out competition* [presentation] Relating to half-life

## Answers | Student Book

1 Two nuclei

2 The time taken for the activity to decrease by half.

3 30 years

4 a One half-life b Two half-lives c Four half-lives d 0.5 half-lives

5 a 5 million b 2.5 million c 1.25 million d 7.5 million

6 Source A: about 5 seconds; source B: about 20 seconds

7 A good answer will contain the following points: activity of a source is given in becquerels; one becquerel is one nuclear decay per second; an unstable nucleus is one that will undergo radioactive decay; when an unstable nucleus decays it may become stable; the more stable nuclei a substance contains, the lower its activity.

**Skills spotlight**

Measure the activity (for example using a Geiger counter to measure the count rate in counts per second) of the material, for a period such as 1 minute. Then measure the activity again over further time periods. The half-life is how long it takes for the activity to decrease by half. Students may comment on how frequently you should measure the activity, based on preliminary results and the rate at which the activity is decreasing. Students may also comment that you should plot a graph of the activity against time and take several pairs of readings from the graph in order to get a mean value for the half-life, to show that the half-life is constant.

# P2.31 Investigating radioactive decay models

This lesson challenges students to investigate a model for radioactive decay using cubes with a dot on one face. The activity may be run as a practice controlled assessment task or as a straight-forward class practical. The practical work should take between one and two hours to complete

## Specification coverage

***6.8*** Investigate models which simulate radioactive decay

This activity provides opportunities to cover HSW *1*, HSW *5*, HSW *6*, HSW *7*, HSW *8*, HSW *9* and HSW *10*.

### Before the lesson

In the week or two before the task show students required equipment and, if appropriate, allow them to practice using it. It may be good preparation to show students one or more of Skills Sheets 19 to 26 to show what is expected of them in their actual controlled assessment task.

### Starter

**Modelling**

Tell students that scientists use models to help them understand what happens in the world around us, from very simple to very complex things. Models are used them to help them explain science that they cannot study in a laboratory. Discuss with students how scientists produce a model to help explain a phenomenon: 'What do they need to produce a model?; Where do they get their data from?; How do they test their models?; What happens if the model produces unexpected results?'

Follow this by reading the additional information below the opening section of page 268 of the Student Book. They may then read the brief description of the activity provided by the 'Your task' box.

### Option 1: Straight-forward class practical

Students follow the instructions on **Worksheet P2.31b**. Students roll 50 cubes repeatedly, each time removing ones with the marked face uppermost, until they have no cubes left. Students repeat this, and then repeat it with 1000 cubes.

The range of data that students need to collect is given on **Worksheet P2.31c** which students will also need.

### Plenary

On page 269 of the Student Book you will find 2 examples of the sort of work that students may produce for this task. The examples focus on evaluating the conclusion. You could share these with students after they have completed their own work. This will help them to understand the assessment criteria and so make it easier for them to evaluate their work and to see how they can improve it. Moderator comments on each of the Student Book extracts can be found at the end of the assessment guidance for this investigation on the CD-ROM. The examples can also be found on the **AT** document *Student examples*.

### Option 2: Running the activity as a practice controlled assessment task (PCA)

We have provided a full range of support resources to allow the running of this practical as a practice controlled assessment task. A recommended structure is outlined below (to be used over a number of sessions). Marking guidance for all three parts of the practice task can be found on the CD-ROM that accompanies the TTPP. To save time when using these practice controlled assessment tasks, you may wish to focus on a particular aspect or skill rather than working through all three parts of the task.

#### Part A Planning

1. Students should be given the Student Brief on **Worksheet P2.31a**. They can use Part A of the Workbook that is provided to help pupils with their practice controlled assessments. They should be given about 1 hour to do this planning.
2. Students could be shown the cubes that they will be using in their model for radioactive decay.

#### Part B Observations

3. Students carry out the practical task to collect evidence using the method they have planned in Part A. Once again, they should refer to the Student Brief on **Worksheet P2.31a**. They can use Part B of the Workbook that is provided to help pupils with their practice controlled assessments. They should be given between 1 and 2 hours to collect their primary evidence.
4. If there is a problem with their own planned method, students may be asked to follow the method set out on **Worksheet P2.31b**. This will still enable students to access the full range of marks for Part B and Part C of the practice controlled assessment task.
5. In Part B, students are required to gather some secondary evidence. The evidence can be quantitative or qualitative. It can be from a variety of sources but students must note where they found their evidence and evaluate the quality of the source as part of this task. Skills Sheet 22 provides students with further guidance on researching for and evaluating secondary evidence. This part of the task could be done outside of the lesson but must be supervised.

#### Part C Conclusions

6. Students follow the instructions set out on the Part C section of the Student Brief on **Worksheet P2.31a**. They should use their data from Part B and the secondary evidence they have collected when doing this. They can use Part C of the Workbook that is provided to help pupils with their practice controlled assessments. They should be given about 1 hour to work on their conclusions.

The **AT** includes video clips showing a group of students working through elements of this investigation with teacher support.

Practice Controlled Assessment

# P2.31 Investigating radioactive decay models

How can you model radioactive decay?

In Sweden each December Nobel Prizes are awarded to scientists who have made big contributions to science. In the USA each October, 'Ig® Nobel Prizes' are given to scientists whose research makes people laugh and then makes them think. The Ig® Nobel physics prize for 2009 was won by Prof. Robert Matthews from Aston University, Birmingham, for his research showing that the falling of buttered toast is not a random process – and that toast does land buttered side down more often than not.

**A** *The Ig® Nobel Awards are given out by a real Nobel Prize winner.*

Radioactive decay is a random process. So a model for radioactive decay needs to be based on something that is also random. Flipping a coin is a random process, so you can use it to model radioactive decay.

You can think of an unstable nucleus as having two states – undecayed and decayed. A coin also has two states when you flip it – heads and tails.

If you flip a large number of coins once, you would expect that about half of them would land showing heads and the other half tails. This can be used as a model of a half-life – half of the coins are in each 'state'. Rolling dice is also a random process and can be used to model radioactive decay.

**B** *Using coins to model radioactive decay.*

**Your task**

You are going to plan an investigation that will allow you to find out about a model that simulates radioactive decay. Your teacher will provide you with some materials to help you organise this task.

**Learning Outcomes**

*6.8 Investigate models which simulate radioactive decay*

## ResultsPlus Build Better Answers

When planning an investigation like this, one of the skills you will be assessed on is your ability to *evaluate your conclusion*. There are 4 marks available for this skill. Here are two extracts focusing on this skill. Other skills are dealt with in other lessons.

**Student extract 1 — A basic response for this skill**

*The pattern I obtained matches that of radioactive decay. My conclusion would have been supported more if I had used even more cubes to start off with.*

- The student has not explained *how* it matches.
- The student does suggest how to strengthen the conclusion.
- This is correct but it is not linked to the theory and does not say if the conclusion is a good one or not.

**Student extract 2 — A good response for this skill**

*My conclusion is strong, but the number of cubes you start off with could be increased to provide stronger evidence. My conclusion supports my hypothesis and matches my scientific knowledge. As radioactive decay is a random process and there are large numbers of nuclei in even a small sample, larger numbers of cubes are needed to model radioactive decay more effectively. This is backed up by the simulation I found on the internet.*

- The hypothesis has been linked in with scientific ideas.
- The secondary evidence has also been linked to the conclusion.
- An explanation is given of how the investigation could be improved. The student has also included ways that the investigation could be extended.

**ResultsPlus**

**To access 2 marks**

- Evaluate how well all your evidence supports your conclusion
- Suggest how your evidence can be improved to strengthen your conclusion

**To access 4 marks**

You also need to:

- Evaluate how well other scientific ideas support your conclusion
- Suggest how the investigation could be extended to support your conclusion



## ActiveTeach

- **AT** *P2.31 Radioactive decay models* [interactive]
  Investigating decay models
- **AT** *P2.31 Assessment criteria* [presentation]
  Understanding the CA marking criteria
- **AT** *P2.31 Specification points* [word document]
  Edexcel specification points
- **AT** *P2.31 Student examples* [word document]
  Examples for students to assess

## Answers | Student Book

**Evaluation of conclusion**

**0** No relevant evaluation is made.

**1-2 a)** Notes strengths or weaknesses in the conclusion based on both the primary data and secondary evidence, e.g. 'My conclusion is good because the pattern I obtained matches that of radioactive decay'.

**b)** Makes suggestions about how the conclusion could be supported more by the primary data and secondary evidence, e.g. 'My conclusion would have been supported more if I had used even more cubes to start off with'.

**3-4 a)** Conclusion is evaluated based on all collected evidence and relevant scientific ideas, e.g. 'I think that my conclusion is good because radioactive decay is a random process and there are large numbers of nuclei in even a small sample. Larger numbers of cubes are therefore needed to model random radioactive decay more effectively. This is backed up by the simulation I found on the internet.'

**b)** Suggests how all collected evidence can be improved and extended to provide stronger support for the conclusion, e.g. 'Flipping coins could provide a better model as there are only two possible outcomes instead of the six that there are with the cubes'.

# P2.32 Background radiation



This lesson introduces background radiation and its sources. Students also look at how the background radiation due to radon gas varies over the UK.

## Specification coverage

***6.1*** Explain what is meant by background radiation, including how regional variations within the UK are caused in particular by radon gas

***6.2*** Recall the origins of background radiation from Earth and space

**HSW** *1* The collection and analysis of scientific data

There are also opportunities to cover **HSW** *6*, *10* and *12*.

## Key terms

background count
background radiation
cosmic ray
radon

### Background noise

**Starter 1**

If you search for 'background noise Prelinger Archives' in *YouTube*, you should find some examples of films that have been treated to remove background noise. Play students the before and after versions and ask them what differences there are.

### Interpreting background radiation

**Exploring 1**

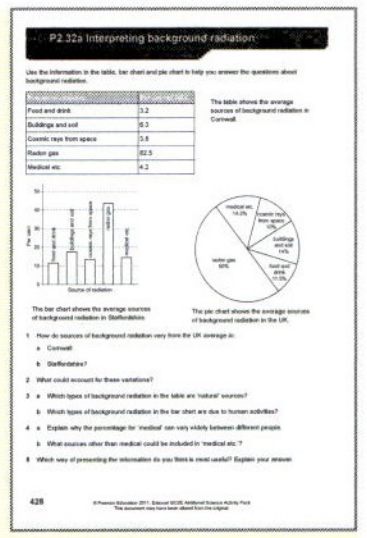

Students answer the questions on **Worksheet P2.32a**.

**Stretch** Show students the **AT** document *Radon levels in the UK* and ask them to estimate how the percentages of background radiation from different sources in your area will differ from the average for the UK given on the worksheet.

**Support** Give students the approximate values for the bars on the bar chart.

### Demonstrating background radiation

**Explaining 1** **Demo**

Demonstrate background radiation using a Geiger-Müller tube. See the Teacher and technician practical sheet P2.32

**Stretch** Ask students why the count rate for any particular object varies.

**Support** Remind students of the units and emphasise that even with an 'object' there is still a background count.

### Background radiation sentences

**Plenary 1** **Lit**

Students write a couple of sentences, each of which should contain at least two of the following terms: background radiation, radioactivity, background count, corrected count, cosmic rays, radon. Write a selection of students' sentences on the board.

### Background radiation

**Homework 1**

**Worksheet P2.32c**

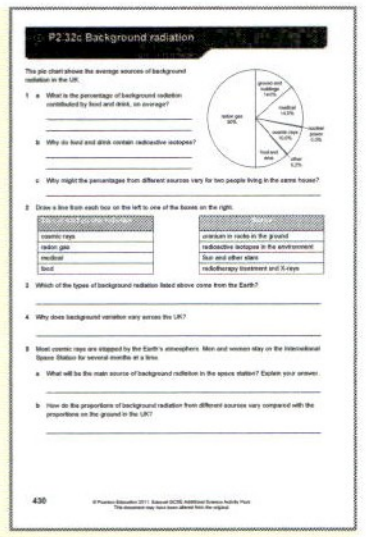

reinforces what students learned about background radiation in the lesson.

**Support** Students answer only questions 1–4.

### Sure, unsure, know more

**Starter 2** **AfL**

Pupils write down one thing about radioactivity in the environment that they are sure about, one thing they are unsure about and one thing that they want to know more about. Focus on the things that they want to know more about.

### Monitoring radon levels

**Exploring 2**

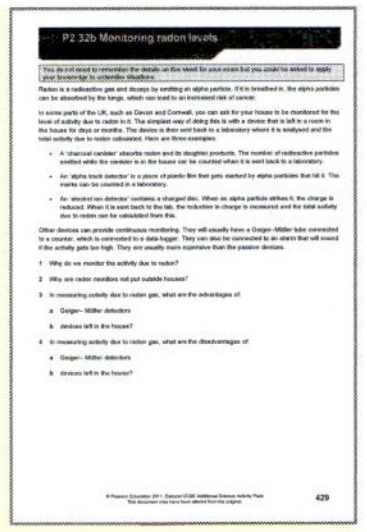

**Worksheet P2.32b** provides more information on testing radon levels.

**Stretch** Ask students why radon test kits are used and why radon gas levels may vary between different places.

**Support** Discuss with students why home owners might wish to buy a radon test kit.

### Student Book spread P2.32

**Explaining 2**

Discuss with students the pie chart (Figure B) in the Student Book. Show students the map in the **AT** document *Radon levels in the UK*. Students then do the Skills spotlight task.

**Stretch** Ask students to plan how they would show whether the map is accurate for their area.

**Support** Students use the key to read off what the background radiation level is in their area by reading from the key.

### Website claims

**Plenary 2**

Tell students that a website claims that nuclear weapons testing has increased the radiation that people are exposed to all over the world and so should be stopped. Ask students to comment on whether they think the evidence used in this sentence is enough to justify the conclusion, and why they think that.

### Sources of background radiation

**Homework 2**

**Worksheet P2.32d**

reinforces what students learned about background radiation in the lesson.

**Stretch** Students answer the 'extra challenge' question.

# P2.32 Background radiation

What is background radiation?

The nuclear facility at Sellafield in Cumbria is permitted to release a certain amount of radioactive material into the air or sea. It is allowed to do this because the activity of this material is so low that it does not contribute significantly to natural levels of radioactivity.

**A** *Part of the nuclear facility in Sellafield, Cumbria*

1 What is background radiation?

2 Tom records background counts of 15, 22 and 17 counts per minute. He then records a count rate of 186 counts per minute from a sample of granite. What is the corrected count for the sample's activity?

We are constantly being exposed to ionising radiation at a low level, from space and from naturally radioactive substances in the environment. This is called **background radiation**.

When scientists measure the activity of a source, they need to measure the **background count** first by taking several readings and averaging them. This background count is then subtracted from measurements to give a corrected reading of the source's activity.

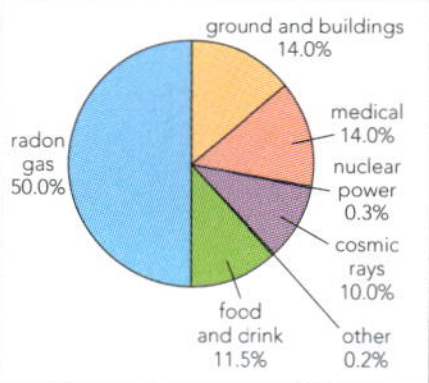


**B** *Sources of background radiation in the UK*

## Sources of background radiation

Figure B shows the sources of background radiation averaged over the UK. The main source is **radon** gas. When uranium in rocks decays, it produces other radioactive isotopes that also decay. One of these is a gas called radon.

3 Where does radon gas come from?

4 Why do you think radon gas could be dangerous?

Radon diffuses into the air from rocks and soil and can build up in houses, especially where there is poor ventilation. Radon has a half-life of 3.8 days and decays by giving out an alpha particle. The amount of radon in the air depends on the type of rock and its uranium content. Rock type and building stone vary around the country and so does the amount of radon.

**C** *This radon outlet pipe sucks air containing radon from beneath a solid concrete floor, stopping it from entering the house.*

The contribution from medical sources results from having X-rays and gamma ray scans, and from treatments for cancer. Some foods naturally contain small amounts of radioactive substances.

High-energy charged particles stream out of the Sun and other stars, as well as supernovae, neutron stars and black holes. They are known as **cosmic rays** and are a form of ionising radiation. Many cosmic rays are stopped by the upper atmosphere but some still reach the Earth's surface.

5 How do you think your food and drink becomes naturally radioactive?

6 During a 'solar storm' the Sun's output of high-energy charged particles increases dramatically. Explain why some scientists suggest that aeroplanes should fly at lower altitudes during a solar storm.

**D** *A cosmic ray detector has been put beneath the Pyramid of the Sun in Teotihuacan, Mexico. By detecting whether cosmic rays are stopped more by some parts of the pyramid than others, scientists hope to find hidden chambers.*

**Skills spotlight**

Scientists collect and analyse data on background radiation. What data would you need to find to compare how people's exposure to background radiation varies in the UK?

**ResultsPlus Watch Out!**

Many students lose marks in cosmic ray questions because they do not state that cosmic rays are high energy particles that can ionise atoms. Another type of ionising radiation.

7 Explain why background radiation varies in different parts of the UK.

8 The following was found on a blog: 'Natural radiation won't hurt you but human-made radiation will.' Write a response to this blogger.

**Learning Outcomes**

6.1 Explain what is meant by background radiation, including how regional variations within the UK are caused in particular by radon gas

6.2 Recall the origins of background radiation from Earth and space

HSW 1 Explain how scientific data is collected and analysed





## ActiveTeach

- **AT** *Radon in Cornwall* [BBC video] High levels of radon in Cornwall
- **AT** *Radon* [video] Properties and uses of radon
- **AT** *Where does background radiation come from?* [interactive] Background radiation – scene investigation
- **AT** *Staying safe with radioactivity* [interactive] Radioactivity and safety – true-or-false quiz
- **AT** *Radon levels* [word document] UK radon levels

## Answers | Student Book

1 The low level of ionising radiation that is around us all the time

2 168 counts per minute

3 From rocks in the ground

4 If radon is breathed in, alpha particles emitted from the radon gas can damage the lungs.

5 Plants and animals take in radioactive isotopes from their environments.

6 People in aeroplanes receive more cosmic rays than people on the ground because the atmosphere has absorbed fewer cosmic rays at that height. As there are more high-energy particles during a solar storm, there are more cosmic rays reaching the Earth, so aeroplanes should fly lower to reduce the amount of cosmic rays received by people in them.

7 A major part of background radiation comes from radon gas, which comes from the decay of uranium isotopes in rocks. Different rocks and building stones contain different amounts of uranium in different parts of the country.

8 A good answer will contain the following points: recognition of difference between ionising and non-ionising radiation; majority of background radiation comes from natural sources; human-made ionising radiation mainly comes from medical sources such as X-rays and radiotherapy treatment; only a very small proportion of background radiation comes from nuclear power stations/nuclear waste. the biggest part of natural sources is radon gas; radon gas can be dangerous if levels build up and it is breathed in; so it is more likely that natural radiation will hurt you but human-made radiation won't.

**Skills spotlight**

Need to measure the background count in many different places and over a long period of time to account for regional variation in radon levels and time variation in differences in cosmic rays. Would also need to collect data on the food people eat, the number of X-ray scans they have had and their occupations.

# P2.33 Uses of radiation



This lesson looks at the uses of ionising radiation for irradiating food, sterilising equipment and the diagnosis and treatment of cancer.

## Specification coverage

**6.3** Describe uses of radioactivity, including: a) household fire (smoke) alarms b) irradiating food c) sterilisation of equipment d) tracing and gauging thicknesses e) diagnosis and treatment of cancer

HSW *13* How and why decisions about science and technology are made, including those that raise ethical issues, and about the social, economic and environmental effects of such decisions

There are also opportunities to cover HSW *12*.

## Key terms

irradiate
radiotherapy
sterilise
tracer

### Alpha, beta and gamma quickfire revision

**Starter 1** AfL

Each student has scraps of paper with the words 'alpha', 'beta' and 'gamma' on separate pieces. Ask questions related to the properties of the three types of radiation and ask students to hold up the scrap(s) of paper with the correct answer(s) on it.

### Food irradiation opinions and facts

**Exploring 1**

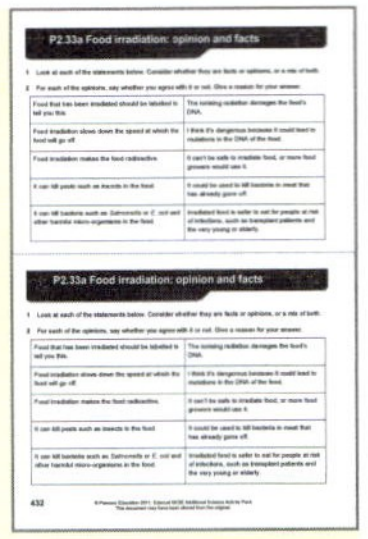

Students consider the opinions and facts on **Worksheet P2.33a**. If you wish to extend this into a debate, students can each take the position of one of the opinions given on the worksheet.

Stretch Ask students to explain in their own words why irradiating food does not make it radioactive.

Support Go through the facts and opinions as a whole-class activity.

### Radiotherapy

**Exploring 3**

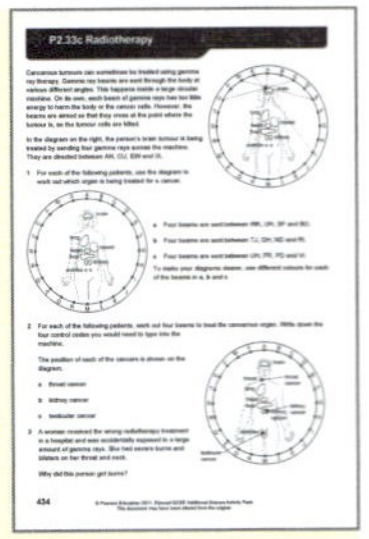

Using **Worksheet P2.33c** students answer questions on how gamma rays are aimed at a tumour from several different angles to help minimise overdoses and radiation burns.

Stretch Ask students to suggest some factors that affect the 'dose'.

Support Students only do the first two questions on the worksheet.

### Using radioactive materials – the facts

**Plenary 1** AfL

In groups, students share three facts that they have learned during this lesson. The group then compiles a master list including the most common fact learned and the least common fact and shares these with the class.

### Ionising radiation wordsearch

**Homework 1**

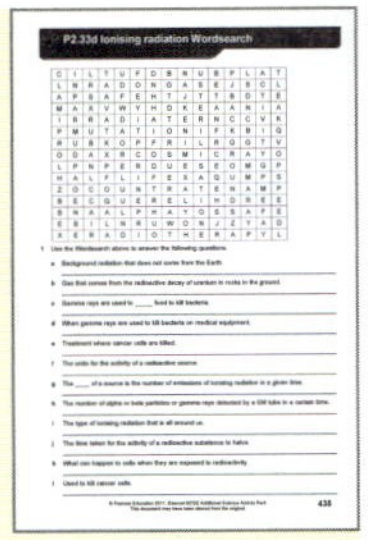

**Worksheet P2.33d**, is for students needing support. Students answer questions on radioactivity and then find the words in a wordsearch.

Support Give students one or more letters from each of the answers.

### Effects of ionising radiation

**Starter 2**

Ask students to look at the photo of Anatoly Rasskazov on page 265 of the Student's Book. Then ask students to write a sentence to explain how he got the mark on his forehead. Share students' sentences with the rest of the class.

### Ionising radiation webquest

**Exploring 2**

**Worksheet P2.33b** is a webquest where students find the answers to questions on the applications of ionising radiation covered in the Student Book.

Stretch Ask students to research applications of ionising radiation which are no longer used and why they are no longer used.

Support Give students the weblinks for the pages they need to look at.

### Student Book spread P2.33

**Explaining 1**

Explain to students the applications of ionising radiation given in the Student Book. Students can also do the Skills spotlight exercise.

Stretch Ask students to consider the half-lives of the sources used for each application and why this is important.

Support Students should work in pairs or small groups to answer the questions on the Student Book pages.

### Uses of ionising radiation concept map

**Plenary 2**

Ask students to make a concept map about what ionising radiation from radioactive sources can be used for and why it is used. They should then keep these maps and add to them at the end of the next lesson.

### Other uses of gamma rays

**Homework 2**

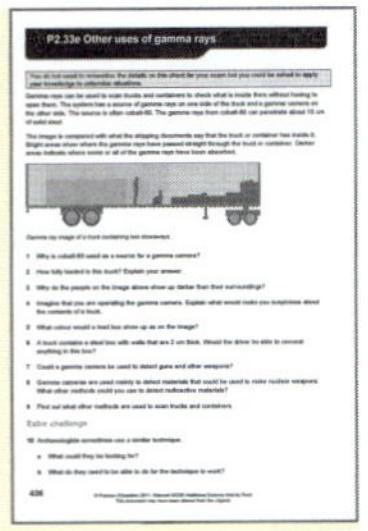

**Worksheet P2.33e**, designed for more able students, covers other uses of gamma rays such as vehicle imaging to detect weapons and stowaways.

Stretch Students do the 'extra challenge' question.

# P2.33 Uses of radiation

How is ionising radiation used in medicine and in food preparation?

Marie Curie worked with doctors to develop a treatment using radium that could reduce or even cure cancer tumours. She collected radon gas and sealed it in thin glass tubes about 1 cm long. These tubes were then covered in platinum and placed in a person's body. Cervical cancer was first treated in this way in 1905.

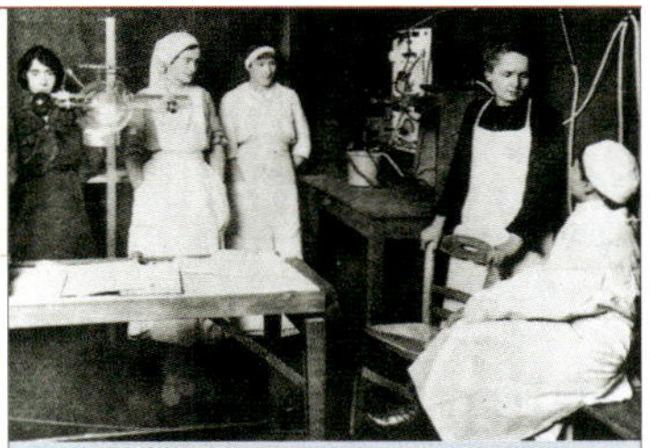

*A Marie Curie explains the potential benefits of radium treatment to nurses.*

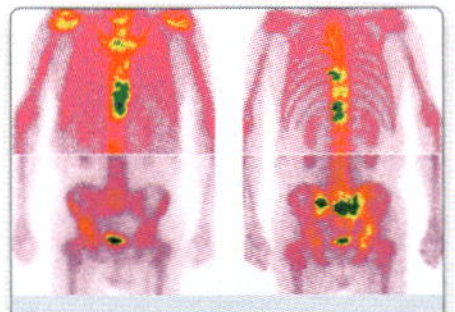

*B A radioactive tracer shows bone tumours in this gamma ray scan. The areas of bone cancer are coloured green.*

## Diagnosis of cancer

Gamma rays can be used to help diagnose cancer. A **tracer** solution containing a source of gamma rays is injected into the body. The tracer collects where there are areas of abnormal activity, e.g. cancers. The gamma rays are then detected using a 'gamma camera'.

Gamma sources are used because they pass straight through the body, allowing them to be detected.

1 Why are alpha and beta sources not used in radioactive tracers to diagnose cancer?

2 What is radiotherapy?

## Treatment of cancer

Ionising radiation can also be used to treat diseases such as cancer. This is known as **radiotherapy**. Some ways of doing this involve radioactive substances that produce gamma rays. For example, gamma rays can be used as beams of radiation to target and kill cancer cells. Radioactive sources can also be put inside a person for a limited amount of time at the place where the cancer is.

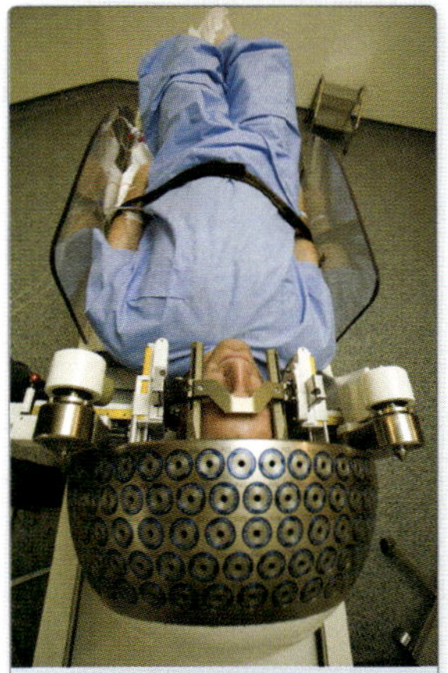

*C This patient is about to have treatment with a 'gamma knife'. The patient's head is held in place so that it cannot move while the gamma rays are aimed.*



## Sterilisation of equipment

Before they can be used on patients, surgical instruments need to be **sterilised** to kill microorganisms. The usual method is to heat them. Some instruments such as plastic syringes cannot be sterilised using heat, so they are **irradiated** with gamma rays.

3 a Why does surgical equipment need to be sterilised?
b Why is some of the equipment sterilised by irradiation?

## Irradiating food

All food contains bacteria in varying amounts. The bacteria eventually cause the food to decompose. Some types of bacteria also cause food poisoning.

Food can be irradiated with gamma rays to kill bacteria. This makes it safer to eat and also means that it can be stored for longer before going off. Irradiating the food also kills any pests such as insects that may be in it. It does not make the food more radioactive, although some foods are naturally radioactive.

Types of foods that are allowed to be irradiated in the UK are fruit, vegetables, cereals, bulbs (e.g. onions) and tubers (e.g. potatoes), herbs and spices, fish, shellfish and poultry.

*D These containers are full of medical equipment and are being positioned over the source of gamma radiation.*

**ResultsPlus Watch Out!**

Don't get irradiated and radioactive mixed up. Irradiated things are not radioactive – they have just been exposed to ionising radiation.

**Skills spotlight**

In the UK, irradiated food must be labelled with the words 'irradiated' or 'treated with ionising radiation'. Discuss the advantages and disadvantages of labelling food that has been irradiated. Try to include any ethical issues about using these technologies.

4 What are the benefits and drawbacks of irradiating food?

5 Explain what happens when food is irradiated.

6 Explain what the properties of a radioactive tracer used to diagnose medical problems should be.

**Learning Outcomes**

6.3 Describe uses of radioactivity, including:
b irradiating food
c sterilisation of equipment
e diagnosis and treatment of cancer

HSW 13a Explain how and why decisions about uses of science and technology are made

Where can you find a source of radioactive americium in a house?



## ActiveTeach

- **AT** *Uses of radioactivity* [BBC video]
  Radioactive tracers check function of a transplanted kidney

**Skills spotlight**

Students' answers should include the following.

**Benefits**: public l know if food has been irradiated and can make their own choice.

**Disadvantages**: people may avoid safer food because they don't want to consume irradiated food.

**Ethical issues**: it might be unethical not to irradiate food since it makes it safer to eat; alternatively it may be unethical to distribute irradiated food because not enough is known about the effects, e.g. on vitamin content, or because the motive behind it is for profit, not for health reasons. The ethical treatment of the environment might also be considered.

## Answers | Student Book

1 Radiation from alpha and beta sources inside the body would be stopped by the body so could not be detected outside it. Also, alpha particles emitted inside the body would cause a lot of harm to cells and tissue, whereas gamma rays tend to pass through the flesh without being absorbed.

2 The use of ionising radiation to treat diseases like cancer by targeting and killing the cancer cells.

3 a To reduce the risk of infection by microorganisms
b Some heat-sensitive instruments (e.g. plastic) cannot be sterilised using heat.

4 Benefits: kills bacteria in food; food can be stored for longer before going off; kills pests such as insects that may be in the food. Drawbacks: public acceptance; perceived risks.

5 The food is exposed to gamma rays.

6 A good answer will include the following points: should not all be absorbed by the body – should have some penetrating power; some tracers should be absorbed by certain parts of the body but not by others; should have a short half-life, of the order of hours, so that the body is not exposed to too much radiation; should have a low activity level – as above; the radioactive isotope, or the decay product, should not have toxic side effects unconnected with the ionising radiation.

# P2.34 More uses of radiation



This lesson looks at three uses of radioactivity: in a smoke alarm, to check thicknesses and as tracers in the environment.

## Specification coverage

**6.3** Describe uses of radioactivity, including: a) household fire (smoke) alarms b) irradiating food c) sterilisation of equipment d) tracing and gauging thicknesses e) diagnosis and treatment of cancer

HSW *12* The use of contemporary science and technological developments and their benefits, drawbacks and risks

There are also opportunities to cover HSW *1*, *6*, *7*, and *13*.

### Moving charges

**Starter 1** Demo

Explain to students how charged particles that are free to move allow a current to flow in a circuit using a simple circuit with a gap and a simple demonstration of electrolysis.

See the Teacher and technician practical sheet P2.34 (1).

### Diagram labelling

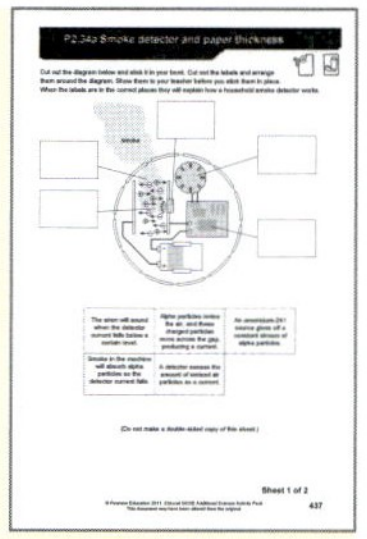

**Exploring 1**

**Worksheet P2.34a** provides diagrams of a smoke detector and how paper thickness can be controlled that can be cut out and labelled.

Stretch Delete the labels and ask students to write their own labels.

Support Do this as a class activity, or ask students to work in small groups.

### Checking thickness

**Explaining 2** Demo

See the Teacher and technician practical sheet P2.34 (3).

Stretch Ask how this could be applied to other processes (e.g. making aluminium foil or clingfilm). You could also ask students about the activity of the source needed for checking thickness.

Support Ask why thallium-208 would not be used.

### Sure, unsure, know more

**Plenary 1** AfL

Students write down one thing about the uses of radioactivity that they are sure about, one thing that they are unsure about and one thing that they want to know more about. Revise the things that students are having difficulty with.

### Choosing radioactive sources

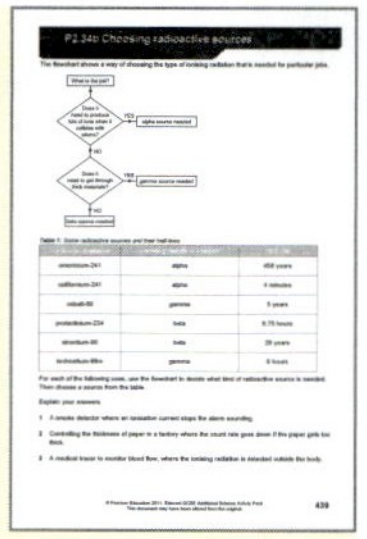

**Homework 1**

**Worksheet P2.34b** helps to reinforce why different sources are used for different purposes, based on the properties of each type of radiation.

Support Students also need to think about how long the application lasts or is used for.

### Word connections

**Starter 2** Lit

Ask students to make sentences using these groups of three words: alpha, air, paper; beta, paper, aluminium; gamma, aluminium, lead. If students do not spot the connections between the words in terms of the ability of different types of radiation to penetrate materials, this starter is usefully repeated as a plenary.

### Smoke alarm

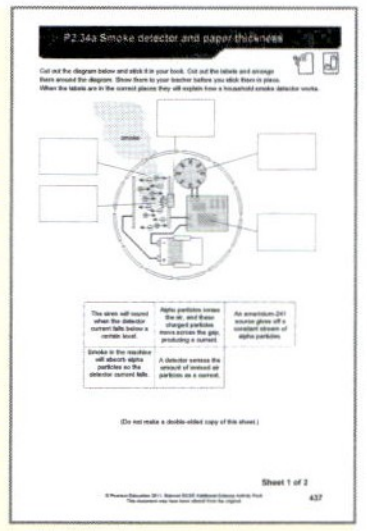

**Explaining 1** Demo

Show students an open smoke detector and explain what causes it to work. See the Teacher and technician practical sheet P2.34 (2).

Stretch Ask why alpha particles are used rather than beta particles or gamma rays. You could also ask why the half-life needs to be of the order of hundreds of years.

Support Give students **Worksheet P2.34a** and ask them to label the diagram after the explanation.

### Student Book spread P2.34

**Explaining 3**

Go through the Student Book pages and consider how ionising radiation is used in each of the applications.

Stretch Students should also consider the half-lives of the sources used for each application and why this is important.

Support Students should work in pairs or small groups.

### Uses of ionising radiation concept map

**Plenary 2** Lit

Ask students to complete the concept map they started in the previous lesson on the uses of ionising radiation to summarise what they have learned.

### Choosing the correct radioactive sources

**Homework 2**

**Worksheet P2.34c** helps to reinforce why different sources are used for different purposes based on their properties, including their half-lives.

Stretch Students answer the 'extra challenge' question.

# P2.34 More uses of radiation

What are some of the other uses of ionising radiation?

In 1994, a 17-year-old boy called David Hahn tried to build a nuclear reactor in a garden shed using over 100 smoke detectors. His Geiger counter detected increased levels of radioactivity from down the street so he tried to dispose of his project.

A David Hahn was arrested and his 'project' was placed into 39 barrels like these ones, sealed and buried at a radioactive disposal site.

## Smoke alarms

A smoke alarm contains a source of alpha particles, usually a radioisotope called americium-241. There is an electrical circuit with an air gap between two electrically charged plates. The americium-241 source releases alpha particles, which ionise the air to give electrons (knocked out of the air molecules) and ions. These charged particles are attracted to opposite charged plates and so allow a small electrical current to flow.

1 What type of radiation is produced by americium-241?

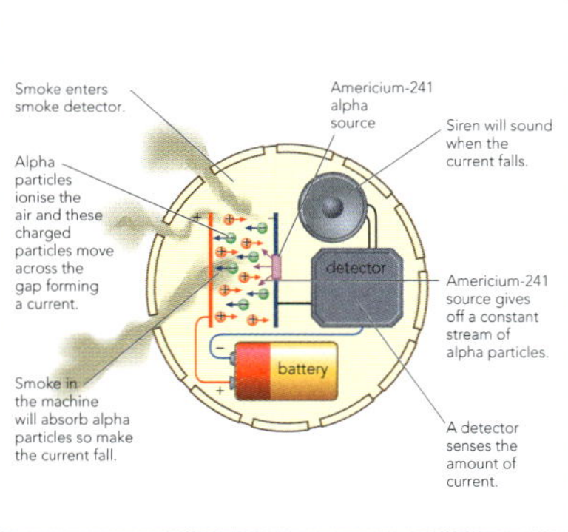


B How a smoke detector works

The air is constantly being ionised by the americium-241 source. This means that there is a constant electric current. As long as this current is flowing, the alarm will not sound.

When smoke gets into the air gap, the smoke particles absorb the alpha particles. This means that the current flowing across the gap decreases. The alarm sounds when the current drops below a certain level.

## Checking thicknesses

Paper is made by squeezing wood pulp between rollers. Paper can be made in different thicknesses and the rollers need to squeeze the wood pulp with a force that produces the correct thickness of paper.

The detector in Figure C counts the rate at which beta particles get through the paper from a source on one side.

When the paper is too thin, more beta particles penetrate the paper and the detector records a higher count rate. A computer senses that the count rate has risen and reduces the pressure applied to the rollers to make the paper thicker. When the paper is too thick, the opposite happens.

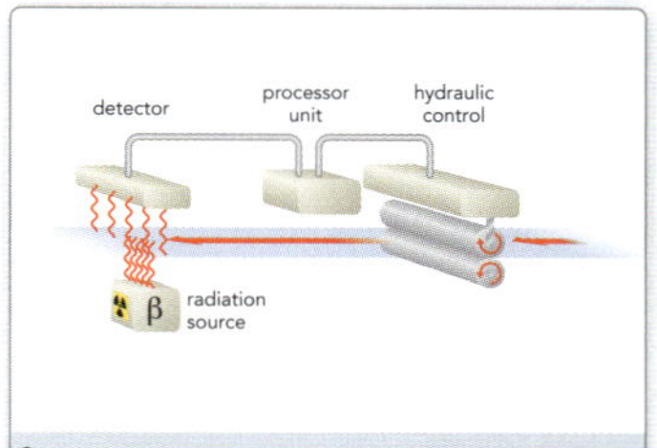


C A beta particle detector being used to control the thickness of paper

2 Look at Figure C. What happens when the paper is too thick?

3 Why would you not use an alpha source to monitor paper thickness?

## Tracers in the environment

Radioactive isotopes can also be added to water and used as tracers, for example to monitor pollution. A gamma source added to water is used to detect leaks in pipes buried underground, such as water pipes. Where there is a leak, water leaks into the surrounding earth. A GM tube following the path of the pipe will detect higher levels of radiation where there is a leak.

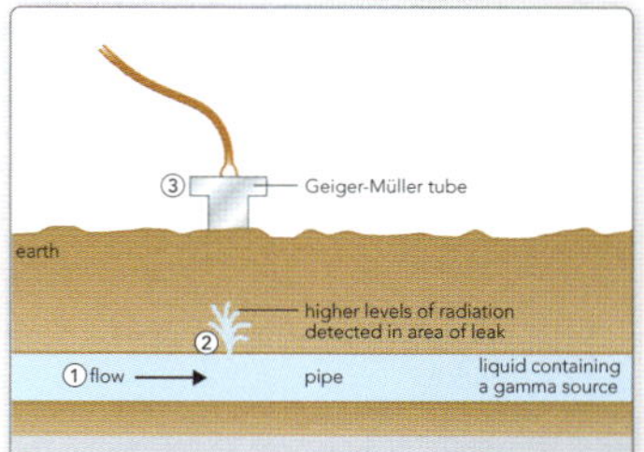


D Using radioactivity to detect leaks in pipelines

**Skills spotlight**

There are always benefits, drawbacks and risks involved in using radioactive materials. How would you decide whether the benefits of smoke detectors outweigh the drawbacks and risks?

**ResultsPlus Watch Out!**

Be careful to match examples of the uses of radioactivity correctly to the types of radiation. Many students lose marks because they get the properties of alpha and beta particles and gamma rays mixed up.

4 The half-life of americium-241 is 432 years. Why does this make it suitable as a source of alpha particles in a smoke alarm?

5 How could you use radioactivity to monitor the thickness of aluminium foil as it is being made?

6 Draw a flow chart to show how the thickness of paper is controlled.

7 Explain what properties a tracer used to detect leaks should have and what the drawbacks of using a tracer might be.

**Learning Outcomes**

6.3 Describe uses of radioactivity, including:
a household fire (smoke) alarms
d tracing and gauging thicknesses

HSW 12 Describe the benefits, drawbacks and risks of using new scientific and technological developments




## ActiveTeach

- AT *Uses of radioactivity* [interactive]
  Radiation types and uses – sorting activity
- AT *Radiation has its uses* [interactive]
  Uses of radiation – scene investigation
- AT *How a smoke detector works* [diagram]
  Figure B – diagram labelling activity

## Answers | Student Book

1 Alpha particles
2 Count detected by monitor decreases, so computer increases pressure applied to the rollers.
3 Paper would stop alpha particles.
4 The half-life is much greater than the life of the product, so the radioactivity of the americium will remain approximately the same while the smoke alarm is in use.
5 Use same method as for paper, as described in Student Book.
6 Flow chart should have three feedback loops showing what happens when: the paper is too thin; the paper is too thick; the paper is the right thickness.
7 A good answer should include the following points: long half-life; gamma emitter so that it can get to the detector through the ground; low activity level so that it does not damage any living things; not poisonous to organisms; increases the background count.

**Skills spotlight**

Need data on the number of people whose lives have been saved in a fire because a smoke detector warned them and allowed them to get out of the house in time. Also need information about the risks of smoke detectors. For example, has radiation emitted by them caused illness. This is not likely as alpha particles do not travel far through air. However they may cause harm if they are not disposed of properly, or if people take them apart. If more people have been helped by smoke detectors than have been harmed by them, then the benefits outweigh the risks.

## Part A – Planning

| Element | Marks | | Criteria |
|---|---|---|---|
| **Equipment** | 2 | **0 marks** | Gives no relevant detail |
| | | **1–2 marks** | a) Chooses most relevant resources/equipment<br>b) Explains reasons for choices and choices are fully relevant to method |
| **Controls**<br>(If variables are to be controlled, criteria a1 and b1 will be used.<br>If there are no variables to control, criteria a2 and b2 will be used. The specific criteria needed will be in the controlled assessment task.) | 6 | **0 marks** | Gives no relevant controls |
| | | **1–2 marks** | a1) Identifies one appropriate variable to control<br>b1) Describes how this variable can be controlled<br>OR<br>a2) Identifies one appropriate way to control the task<br>b2) Describes this way of controlling the task |
| | | **3–4 marks** | a1) Identifies some relevant variables to control<br>b1) Gives an appropriate description of how to control these variables<br>OR<br>a2) Identifies some relevant ways to control the task to produce meaningful results<br>b2) Describes how these ways control the task |
| | | **5–6 marks** | a1) Identifies a range of variables appropriate to control<br>b1) Gives an appropriate explanation of how to control these variables<br>OR<br>a2) Provides a comprehensive list of relevant ways to control the task to produce meaningful results<br>b2) Explains how these ways control the task |

| Element | Marks | | Criteria |
|---|---|---|---|
| **Hypothesis** | 4 | **0 marks** | Provides no relevant hypothesis |
| | | **1–2 marks** | a) Provides a hypothesis that is appropriate for most of the task<br>b) Partially justifies the hypothesis |
| | | **3–4 marks** | a) Provides a hypothesis that is appropriate for the full scope of the task, based on relevant scientific ideas<br>b) Justifies the hypothesis fully using relevant scientific ideas |
| **Risks** | 4 | **0 marks** | No relevant detail given |
| | | **1–2 marks** | a) Identifies a relevant risk which is specific to the task<br>b) Suggests measure(s) to manage the risk |
| | | **3–4 marks** | a) Identifies most of the relevant risks which are specific to the task<br>b) Method reflects how risks need to be managed |
| **Overall plan** | 4 | **0 marks** | Gives no relevant controls |
| | | **1–2 marks** | a) Method is logically ordered to produce results<br>b) Chooses range of data/observations that would test the hypothesis |
| | | **3–4 marks** | a) Method is logically ordered to produce results and includes an explanation of why it would test the hypothesis<br>b) Chooses range of data/observations that would test the hypothesis and explains why the range was chosen |
| **Total marks** | 20 | | |

## Part B – Observations

| Element | Marks | | Criteria |
|---|---|---|---|
| **Primary evidence and recording** | 4 | 0 marks | Collects no primary evidence |
| | | 1 mark | Records some data/observations that are appropriate for the topic |
| | | 2 marks | Collects a suitable range of data/observations and records some appropriately (depends on the practical) |
| | | 3 marks | Collects a suitable range of data/observations and records all appropriately (depends on the practical) |
| | | 4 marks | Collects a suitable range of data/observations and records all appropriately (depends on the practical) and records further/repeat data |
| **Element** | **Marks** | | **Criteria** |
| **Secondary evidence** | 2 | 0 marks | Gives no relevant controls |
| | | 1 mark | Collects and records secondary evidence relevant to the hypothesis in a way appropriate for the topic |
| | | 2 marks | Collects and records secondary evidence relevant to the hypothesis in a way appropriate for the topic<br>Comments on the quality of the sources of secondary evidence |
| **Total marks** | 6 | | |

| Element | Marks | | Criteria |
|---|---|---|---|
| **Processing evidence** | 4 | **0 marks** | Evidence is not processed |
| | | **1–2 marks** | a) Attempts to process all collected evidence, using appropriate mathematical skills<br>b) Attempts to present the processed evidence in a way appropriate for the topic |
| | | **3–4 marks** | a) Processes all collected evidence in a way that is appropriate to the task, using appropriate mathematical skills<br>b) Presents processed evidence in a way that allows conclusions to be drawn |
| **Quality of evidence** | 4 | **0 marks** | Makes no comments on the quality of the evidence |
| | | **1–2 marks** | a) Comments on the quality of the primary evidence, dealing with anomalies appropriately (if no anomalies in evidence candidates need to state this)<br>b) Comments on the quality of the secondary evidence, dealing with anomalies appropriately (if no anomalies in evidence candidates need to state this) |
| | | **3–4 marks** | a) Explains any adjustments to the evidence needed, or decision not to exclude evidence<br>b) Takes account of anomalies in primary and secondary evidence when processing evidence (using all evidence if no anomalies) |
| **Conclusions based on evidence** | 6 | **0 marks** | Makes no relevant conclusions |
| | | **1–2 marks** | a) Provides a conclusion based on all collected evidence, but does not link it to the hypothesis<br>b) Attempts to explain the conclusion using all collected evidence, including appropriate mathematical relationships |
| | | **3–4 marks** | a) Provides a conclusion which refers to the hypothesis based on all collected evidence<br>b) Explains the conclusion using the evidence, including appropriate mathematical relationships |
| | | **5–6 marks** | a) Provides a conclusion which refers to the hypothesis based on all collected evidence and relevant scientific ideas<br>b) Explains the conclusion using relevant scientific ideas and all collected evidence, including appropriate mathematical relationships |

Part C – Conclusions (continued)

| Element | Marks | | Criteria |
|---|---|---|---|
| Evaluation of conclusion | 4 | 0 marks | Makes no relevant evaluation |
| | | 1–2 marks | a) Evaluates conclusion based on all collected evidence<br>b) Suggests how all collected evidence can be improved to provide stronger support for the conclusion |
| | | 3–4 marks | a) Evaluates conclusion based on all collected evidence and relevant scientific ideas<br>b) Suggests how all collected evidence can be improved and extended to provide stronger support for the conclusion |
| Evaluation of method | 6 | 0 marks | Makes no relevant evaluation |
| | | 1–2 marks | a) Identifies a strength or weakness in the method<br>b) Suggests how to improve method and justifies comments made |
| | | 3–4 marks | a) Describes strengths or weaknesses in the method and reasons for any anomalies<br>b) Suggests how to improve method and justifies comments made relating to the quality of the evidence collected (including reasons for anomalies) |
| | | 5–6 marks | a) Describes strengths and weaknesses in the method and relates them to the hypothesis, and reasons for any anomalies<br>b) Suggests how to improve method, justifying comments made relating to the hypothesis and how better quality evidence could be produced (including reasons for anomalies) |
| Total marks | 24 | | |